SECOND EDITION

SOCIOLOGY FOR CANADIANS

A READER

ALEXANDER HIMELFARB • C. JAMES RICHARDSON

SECOND EDITION

SOCIOLOGY FOR CANADIANS
A READER

ALEXANDER HIMELFARB • C. JAMES RICHARDSON

ALEXANDER HIMELFARB
National Parole Board of Canada
Ottawa

C. JAMES RICHARDSON
Department of Sociology
University of New Brunswick

McGRAW-HILL RYERSON LIMITED
Toronto   Montreal   New York   Auckland   Bogotá   Caracas   Lisbon   London
Madrid   Mexico   Milan   New Delhi   Paris   San Juan   Singapore   Sydney   Tokyo

SOCIOLOGY FOR CANADIANS: A READER 2/E

Copyright © McGraw-Hill Ryerson Limited, 1992.
All rights reserved. No part of this publication may be reproduced or transmitted in any form or by any means, or stored in a data base or retrieval system, without the prior written permission of McGraw-Hill Ryerson Limited.

ISBN: 0-07-551283-1

1 2 3 4 5 6 7 8 9 10   D   10 9 8 7 6 5 4 3 2

Printed and bound in Canada

Sponsoring Editor: Catherine A. O'Toole
Supervising Editor: Margaret Henderson
Permissions Editor: Norma Christensen
Cover & Text Design: Hania Fil
Technical Artist: Hania Fil
Typesetting: Computer Composition of Canada, Inc.
Printing & Binding: John Deyell Company
Text set in: Cheltenham Book

CANADIAN CATALOGUING IN PUBLICATION DATA

Main entry under title:

Sociology for Canadians

2nd ed.
Includes bibliographical references.
ISBN 0-07-551283-1

1. Sociology. 2. Canada – Social conditions.
I. Himelfarb, Alexander, 1947-   . II. Richardson,
C. James, 1941-   .

HM51.S63 1992   301   C92-093346-7

CONTENTS

PREFACE

The first edition of this Reader, under the title *People, Power and Process: A Reader*, was published in 1980. It was followed in 1984 by a revised collection of sociological readings for first-year students but was renamed *Sociology for Canadians: A Reader*. This is, then, our third attempt to put together a collection of readings but, from a publishing point of view, this is the second edition of the 1984 book.

From the outset, we viewed these edited collections as a supplement to, not a substitute for, the texts on which they have been based. This remains true for this present edition. As in the previous editions, this Reader is intended to parallel, illustrate and extend the discussion of the main Text, *Sociology for Canadians* (2nd ed.). Still, the two previous editions of the Reader have often been used on their own. We assume that this is partly because, as well as the readings, there is sufficient textual material for students to have a context in which to view what has been selected. This is not to suggest that the articles we have chosen share one perspective, one ideological position or one methodological stance. Indeed we have, in previous editions as well as in this one, worked to ensure that we are including selections that reflect both the richness and the diversity of recent Canadian sociology.

As we have described in the previous edition, what integrates this text is not the readings *per se* but the organization of chapters, our introductions to each Part and our comments regarding not only what is important but also what may be lacking in the selections we have included. Our aim remains as it was at the beginning of the 1980s: we want to convey to students of sociology a sense of how social structure and everyday life are interrelated and act back upon one another. We are still drawing upon the insights of Peter Berger and Thomas Luckmann, who articulated the human paradox that we are simultaneously the producers and products of society, and C. Wright Mills, who viewed the sociological imagination as the ability to link *private troubles* and *public issues.* While many things have occurred in the discipline since the works of these authors were first published, we are not convinced anyone has expressed the sociological enterprise better.

While we will have more to say about what this perspective is and means in the first Part and throughout the book, for now it is enough to say that our emphasis is on power and inequality on the one hand, and people's common sense perceptions and everyday behaviour on the other. Furthermore we shall, again, argue that sociologists cannot avoid having (and living) a commitment to human values which guide their work. As we indicated, not all of the authors in this collection express the values that underpin our own sociological perspective. To represent only one ideological position would be undesirable, as we feel that explicating and arguing about value commitments — admitting to them and worrying about them — is a crucial aspect of the sociological enterprise.

Those who have been users of our first two efforts to put together text and readings for introductory students have sometimes pointed out the flaws in our selections. Some readers have noted that the classical readings in Chapter 1 were simply too intimidating for first-year students. While we tend to agree, there are others who want these available to students and we have, therefore compromised by leaving these in but also including in the first chapter the thoughts of two more contemporary sociologists as to the direction of and enduring issues in the discipline. It will, therefore, be up to individual instructors whether you are to be exposed at this point to the classical writings of Marx, Weber and Durkheim.

Another criticism is that we have not adequately conveyed the symbolic interactionist tradition in Canadian sociology. This is a criticism that, from time to time, has also been directed at our major Canadian sociological journals. Both of your authors have, at one time or another, served as reviewers and/or associate editors of both of these journals and have also viewed ourselves as highly sympathetic to the symbolic interaction perspective. Our sense is that this has not been a decade in which very many Canadian sociologists have been working in and publishing in this tradition, or that what is being produced in Canada is not being submitted to Canadian journals. We have scanned what is available and have tried to include works which, in our view, are understandable to beginning students but the pickings have been slim.

In selecting material for this third set of readings, we have, perhaps more so than was true for the earlier editions, been frustrated by our failure to find sociological material which addresses the remarkable changes occurring in Canada and the world at large. We are putting this book "to bed" at a time of unprecedented change nationally and internationally. Over the past year or so, Canadians have been involved in the events at Oka; the development of splinter parties such as the Bloc Quebois, the COR Party and the Reform Party; the Senate-driven crisis over the GST and the general national malaise that came to be known as the National Unity Debate. Internationally, we have seen the demise of the Berlin Wall; the unification of Germany; the apparent demise of the Soviet Union, particularly as the Ukraine moves towards becoming a sovereign state; the scaling down — some believe the end — of the Cold War; and Middle East talks emerging out of the aftermath of the Gulf War. We are, in other words, presenting this book to you in the midst of a "firestorm of change" but, because sociology must, perhaps, by definition, proceed more slowly and differently than journalism, sociologists, at least in the academic journals and books, have as yet been largely silent on these momentous and largely unanticipated events.

Nevertheless, while one might complain about sociology's relevance compared to what was available to us a decade ago, we have been faced with an "embarrassment of riches" in many areas of Canadian sociology, notably in feminist theory and scholarship. But, of course, not all of the writing that is informing the field is very understandable to students facing their first encounter with sociology and some of the debates within feminism and political economy over the 1980s are subtle and require considerable background. As in previous editions, we have avoided as much as possible articles filled with unnecessary jargon or those which take an overly polemical stand on just how sociology is to be done. The first will, of course, simply (and rightly) lose most introductory students and the second will simply be confusing when students are just learning about the variety of questions within the sociological perspective and the variety of research methods available to answer them. While we did not believe it possible or desirable to exclude articles containing sophisticated statistical analysis, we have abridged some of these and, in choosing articles in the positivist tradition, selected those which deal with questions and data more readily accessible to the beginning student.

The major changes between this edition and the previous one are the selection of readings, a much greater emphasis on feminist-based research and some restructuring of chapters and Parts to make the Reader parallel with changes made in the Text. Of the fifty-two selections included, only ten have been retained from the previous edition (of which four are the classic works by Marx, Durkheim, Weber and Mills) and with one or two exceptions have been published since 1984.

However, as with the Text, the revision is, for at least three reasons, more than merely an updating of readings and face-lifting of the textual material. First, some of the issues and debates that informed our first book are now history, and some of what seemed like great breakthroughs at the time have not come to fruition or have not had all that much impact on how sociologists go about their business. Thus our Text and this collection of readings are written and assembled from a different vantage point than was the case in 1978 or even in 1982 when the ideologies of the 1960s were so present in the sociological literature.

The second reason is that, in recent years, we have seen considerable rethinking among Canadian sociologists about a whole lot of issues that seemed almost universal truths a decade ago. We have had to rethink much of what we "knew" about ethnic inequality. We have had to revise many of the earlier pronouncements about the nature of power and inequality in Canada and the way in which capitalism developed in this country. While dependency theory has not been abandoned completely, some of what we described in the earlier editions now seems overly simplistic, based on incomplete evidence or dubious assumptions and parochial. We have sought, then, to include selections that reflect something of the dynamic nature of the sociological enterprise. But in certain areas, notably the sociology of education and ethnic relations, our readings perhaps best reflect what seems a lack of direction in terms of both theory and research during the 1980s: simply, the promise of new directions in our thinking about education and ethnicity that developed in the late 1970s have not fully materialized during the 1980s.

Third, sociology in Canada, as elsewhere, is in the process of being transformed by feminist scholarship and perspectives. Superficially, this means a change in language. Our textual material and introductions, this reader conforms to recent guidelines about sexist language and suggestions for how to avoid the more subtle manifestations of sexism in what one writes and says. At a more crucial level, feminist critiques have made all social scientists more sensitive to the fact that men and women have often inhabited different but equally important social worlds, something that did not emerge very clearly, if at all, in earlier theory and research. And, with that sensitivity, has come recognition that much of our sociology while purporting to be about people, has really been about men, their lives, their work, their social mobility and so on. In so far as women have been studied, they were so from a male perspective. We do not claim this edition of the Reader fully incorporates a feminist perspective, partly because the Text which it parallels remains the product of two men and partly because the penetration of feminism has not occurred evenly into all the areas of sociology we have chosen to include in this introductory collection. But it has been informed by that perspective and, in both our writing and the articles we have selected, this is a different book than we wrote in the early 1980s. Nevertheless, as the selections we have included should suggest, there is quite a distance to go before we can present and introductory collection of readings which is truly non-sexist in nature.

For those familiar with the earlier editions of the Text and Reader, we should note that there has been some modification of the order and placement of the material. First, we have bowed to pressure from previous users and moved the chapter on the sociology of family and marriage from the end of the book to Part 2. It now follows Chapter 5, "Socialization and Interaction." Second, there is now a separate chapter on the development and state of Canadian sociology, what in earlier editions had been subsumed within a more general discussion of political culture and ideology. Some of the latter material has been incorporated into Chapter 3, "Culture", and some has made its way into the final part and chapter on "Collective Behaviour and Social Change."

Finally, we have benefitted from and wish to thank our colleagues who have used and have commented on our earlier efforts to put together a collection of readings. These include but are not limited to Frum Himelfarb, Jennie Hornosty, Larry Wisniewski, Cheryl and Dan Albas, Tom Murphy, Sandra Lonergan, Lori Forbes-Petrovich and, in particular, Pat Baker of Mount Saint Vincent University who provided such a detailed and thoughtful review of our proposed revision: as she will recognize, in the end, we incorporated most of her suggestions. Despite our failings with respect to meeting deadlines, Catherine O'Toole of McGraw-Hill Ryerson has retained her sense of humour and is everything we could ask in a Sponsoring Editor and for this we thank her. In the actual editing of this Reader and the Text we have benefitted from and learned much from both Rodney Rawlings, also of McGraw-Hill Ryerson, and from Dick Hemingway who chooses to retain his independence by working as a free-lance editor. As in previous editions, we remain, finally, indebted to UNB secretaries Susan Doherty and Dianne Bawn, both of whom do their best to keep at least one of us more or less insane.

Alexander Himelfarb   C. James Richardson
Ottawa, 1991   Fredericton, 1991

SECOND EDITION

SOCIOLOGY FOR CANADIANS

A READER

ALEXANDER HIMELFARB • C. JAMES RICHARDSON

PART

1

PERSPECTIVES and METHODS

For more than two decades your authors have, at least in part, described themselves as sociologists. We are frequently asked what it means to be a sociologist and what is sociology anyway? We have found that in the usual casual encounters in which they are asked, these are not easy questions to answer unless we feel prepared to dominate the conversation at the dinner or cocktail party. Our inclination is to mumble clichés about sociology being the study of people in groups, or the study of society and so forth and quickly to change the topic.

Chances are that you are, right now, wanting to ask the same question. Probably you will be more able to answer the question as you read through our brief summaries of the field and the many illustrations of the sociological perspective. However, even then you will not likely have an answer that will satisfy you once and for all or that will be comfortably condensed into a few sentences for the benefit of those who are simply making polite enquiry or engaging in small talk and are not expecting a lecture.

WHY SOCIOLOGY?

For now, let us define sociology as the study of relationships among people, the study of society and its change and how various kinds of societies and social structures and our position within these shape our behaviour and our thinking. Like any definition, this will become clearer as you read the examples of sociologists doing their work.

The selections in Part 1 are intended to introduce you to the development of sociology and to the theoretical, ideological and methodological controversies that sociologists themselves must resolve in coming to grips with the field. In the process of working your way through these selections, you will come to learn how ambiguous any definition of sociology is and must be. Notwithstanding this, you will learn something of the boundaries of sociology — how it differs from, say, psychology or philosophy.

Many of our students seem to enter the discipline with one of two preconceptions. Some expect that sociology will offer little more than a common sense understanding of their social *milieu*. And, when this is what is offered, they wonder, why we need sociology at all? Certainly, much of what you do know will be confirmed in these selections. Indeed, this is perhaps what makes sociology unique: we are always tapping our own experiential base. Why should it be otherwise? Much of our physical and natural sciences are simply attempts to systematize what we have always "known."

Ideally, however, you will learn to ask the right questions so that you can distinguish between "answerable" and "unanswerable" issues and learn the kinds of evidence necessary to support different kinds of answers. At the very least, even a descriptive awareness of your own country should enable you to begin to sort out "fact" and "fancy."

However, for those students who are disappointed in the common sense base of much of social science, we can only point out the tired cliché that common sense is not so very common. Certainly people have very different, often competing, common sense theories about how society and its institutions operate. But, we expect that you will find that what you "know" about the social world will often be challenged; as Peter Berger (1963) maintains, sociologists are in the business of upsetting apple carts, of *debunking* much of what passes as conventional wisdom about everyday life. Do the poor commit the bulk of crimes? Are the disenfranchised and powerless the leaders of new social movements? Are the high divorce rates an indication of the disintegration of the family as an institution? Is the gap between rich and poor in Canada narrowing? Are women's earnings becoming more equal to men's earnings? It may be interesting for you to contrast what you know about such issues now with what you believe at the end of the book.

In short, much of our common sense theorizing has come to us prepackaged. Parents, church leaders, politicians, the variety of specialized experts in contemporary society, the media, all represent our *authorities* for knowledge. But sociology will ask you to be skeptical, to question what you know and what you are told by these authorities and by sociologists as well.

Others of our students come in with a rather different preconception of what they may learn. For them, sociology will offer professional training, the skills and techniques to answer particular questions: how to run a business more efficiently, how to be a more effective teacher or social worker, how to reduce crime, or, perhaps, how to make theirs a better society. Often they will complain about all of the "abstract theorizing" and "pointless" ideological debates, when what they want to do is get down to cases and solve problems.

In some ways we are sympathetic to their lament; we, too, like to think of sociology as useful in making society better. Indeed, these "pointless" ideological debates exist because there is controversy about how sociology ought to be used, the role of the sociologists' values in determining what they study and how they use their knowledge and, most fundamentally, what constitutes a better society.

Furthermore, it is important that sociologists, and perhaps all of us, make our answers to these questions clear because our assumptions about human nature, society and the direction of history underpin our theories — both common sense and sociological. And these theories directly guide our work. "Theory" has a great "practical" utility for understanding social life: it organizes our knowledge; it allows us to ask questions that we can test against empirical facts; and it permits us to link a particular phenomenon to a more general understanding of society.

THE ROOTS OF SOCIOLOGY

It is such a conception of the sociological enterprise that encourages us to trace its origins to the intellectual revolution of the eighteenth century, to the *Enlightenment*. It was in this period, prior to the chaos and unrest of the French Revolution (1789), that a new optimism about human nature and the future of society was born. Those thinkers we now call *philosophers* began to appreciate that the *scientific method*, which had developed to examine the physical world, could also be used to understand, criticize and improve the social world.

The central message of the Enlightenment was that reason and observation could be united, that traditional authority and superstition must give way to theories which could be tested through observation. So the scientific method asked that knowledge be systematized. One way was to look for the *pattern* in observations: this pattern would constitute a theory, and the theory would be tested with further observations. And, just as the physicial world seemed to be governed by certain laws, so too, it was assumed, the social world must be.

Coupled with this was a radical change in assumptions about "humankind." Whereas the Judeo-Christian view was that we are fallen creatures, the eighteenth-century thinkers viewed people as essentially good. People, by nature good, had been corrupted by society. This view encouraged the belief in the *idea of progress*; if society were perfected, so, too, would be the people in it. The scientific method was seen as the tool for discovering how society could be improved.

The experience of the French Revolution forced social thinkers to recognize that the eighteenth-century optimism was in some ways naive and that a desire for progress meant coming to grips with questions of values and ideology. For example, August Comte (1893), who in fact coined the term "sociology," came to the conclusion that "order" and "progress" must go hand in hand, that the "excesses" and social upheaval of the French Revolution must, at all costs, be avoided. In other words, for moral reasons many sociologists are what Robert Nisbet (1967) calls part of the "conservative tradition."

Karl Marx, on the other hand, had available to him not only the experience of the French Revolution, but also the actual misery for ordinary working people of the more protracted period of change brought about by the rise of *industrial capitalism*, what you may know as the *industrial revolution*. His concerns about the economic, social and psychological costs of living in the capitalist societies he studied led him to believe that a much more radical re-ordering of society was not only necessary but inevitable.

Both Comte and Marx and those who followed them believed in the value of science; their differences can be traced to different assumptions about human nature and our relationship to society. Emile Durkheim (1895; 1897), who in many respects followed in the footsteps of Comte, was perhaps most influential in developing what we now call the *order perspective*: the view that social solidarity is necessary for human development and happiness.

In contrast, at the heart of the work of Karl Marx is the view that existing forms of social organization are repressive and alienating. His emphasis was not on the harmony and integration of society, but rather on the divisive and destructive impact of social inequality. This *conflict perspective* viewed class antagonism and warfare as endemic and the major cause of social change.

ORDER AND CONFLICT

This debate — the order-conflict debate — remains at the centre of many of the contemporary controversies in the field. The "order perspective," as represented particularly in the works of Talcott Parsons and his students, what is called *structural-functionalism*, has placed a great deal of emphasis on the idea of harmony — among people, among groups and among the parts of society.

In other words, most people supposedly share the same values; that is, they have been socialized in more or less the same way. People tend to think alike about what goals to pursue and how to pursue them. These theorists go further and argue that each part of a society — its economic, political, kinship and educational institutions, for example — fit together, are interdependent and have functions that contribute to the coherence and survival of society.

For instance, functionalists have often argued that the extended family had to give way to the more mobile nuclear family because the latter served better the demands of industrial and bureaucratic society. Similarly, they would view contemporary education as a necessary institution for preparing people for the more specialized skills demanded in complex societies.

Conflict theorists challenge this view by focusing on the layers of inequality in society. For them, the central fact of life in all societies to date is that some groups have more of the scarce and desirable resources — particularly wealth but also prestige and other forms of power. This leads to an appreciation of the importance of competing *interests* (as opposed to shared values), which means, at the simplest level, that "people who have" will act to maintain the *status quo* and thereby their position, and "people who have not" will seek to change society in their own interests.

Inequality, in other words, implies conflict. Certainly conflict theorists recognize that often societies *seem* to be ordered and stable, even tied together by value consensus, but they also appreciate the fragility of order and the inevitability of change. If, indeed, societies seem to be stable, this is simply an indication of how successful the dominant group has been in making its values *the* values.

This means that conflict theorists emphasize the role of coercion and manipulation as the means of maintaining order. They are likely to ask not how, say, educational institutions fulfill the functions of providing good citizens and expert technicians necessary in complex societies, but instead how these institutions serve the interests of the "haves" in maintaining the existing system of inequality. They may, for example, examine how our schooling encourages us to believe that things are as they should be, that we live in a "just society," that the existing order is inevitable.

INDIVIDUAL AND SOCIETY

A second fundamental debate in sociology revolves around the relationship between individual and society. The two perspectives can perhaps best be captured by comparing the orientations of Max Weber and Emile Durkheim, both of whom wrote in the early twentieth century. Weber was concerned with human action and meaningful behaviour. He felt it imperative to examine the subjective worlds of people because they use these perceptions and definitions to shape and guide their behaviour.

Durkheim, on the other hand, was not concerned with action, that is, with how people shape their behaviour, but with how society constrains people and, in effect, stands outside of them. He advocated, then, that sociologists study "social facts" (the law, for example, or religious doctrine), and not people's individual subjective worlds. By emphasizing those aspects of the social world that we can "get our hands on" and measure, Durkheim was attempting to make sociology a *positivistic* discipline. Weber gave more room to intuitive understanding, *verstehen*, to get at the subjective and to move from observation to theory.

We should point out that we have simplified and exaggerated. Durkheim came increasingly to appreciate the importance of the subjective and Weber was concerned throughout his work with rules of scientific method. Nevertheless, this debate is still very much with us. It takes place on two levels. First, do we focus on how society shapes behaviour or on how people shape society? And second, each position demands a different solution as to how to do sociology. Simply, an action approach demands that we somehow gain access to what goes on inside people's heads, however difficult this may be to measure. A focus on society and societal constraint allows sociologists to concentrate on more "objective" data, more easily measurable but more difficult to assess and interpret.

Perhaps these issues can be made clearer by a brief description of a fairly contemporary sociological perspective, *symbolic interactionism*. Herbert Blumer (1969), in systematizing the work of the philosopher George Herbert Mead (1934), has been one of the most forceful voices of criticism against a narrowly conceived positivistic sociology. He has consistently argued that meanings — the definitions people attach to things, especially themselves and other people — must have a central place in sociology. People's actions are based on their definition of the situation; societal behaviour is not some automatic response to internal forces (drives, needs, motives) or external forces (social class, ethnic group, sex gender). In Pirandello's words, "Right you are if you think you are." I believe that education will assure me a good job; I believe I am capable of succeeding at university; I believe that others will respect me more the further I go and I know that this will make me feel good about myself. I therefore go as far as I can in school. It does not matter so much if my beliefs are right in some objective sense; I do not act on the basis of the objective world but on my perceptions of it.

Three concepts are central to the symbolic interactionist perspective: (1) definition of the situation; (2) self; and (3) negotiation. First, definition of the situation simply means that we interpret before we act. We decide what is significant in the situation, what the intentions of other people are, and we act accordingly. This process of making attributions is called the *self process*. But, the self is also reflexive; it can treat itself as an object. So, one of the significant things in any situation is our view of ourselves, how we think and feel about ourselves in relation to others. We establish our own identity as a key element of the situation.

Symbolic interactionists emphasize and study how people create these definitions, particularly on self and other, through interaction and how these definitions are continuously modified through negotiation. In short, they study how people modify their action for one another through a negotiation of meanings. While Durkheim saw the social rules (the norms) as constraining people, symbolic interactionists emphasized how people interpret and modify these rules, even create new rules, in interaction.

Critics of this approach argue that symbolic interactionism leaves out too much. Much of the criticism might be summarized by saying that this perspective gives too little weight to issues of social structure, particularly the realities of power and inequality. It tells us little about whose rules guide human behaviour, about where cultural norms come from and about how the unequal distribution of resources — wealth and other forms of power — determines whose definition of situation prevails. And it fails to tell us very much about what *happens* to people. For example, whatever my definition of the situation, if I am born poor or Indian in a white society, this will have consequences for my life chances, perhaps for my ability to translate this into a good job or even for how long I live. And I may be totally unaware of how these objective factors are affecting me.

CONCLUSION

So, in a sense, we return to the beginning, the paradox of people as producers and products of culture and society. Symbolic interactionism illustrates one side of this paradox — people as innovators, interpreters, producers of the social world. It will become evident that, in our view, the conflict perspective, with its emphasis on power and inequality, illustrates the flip side: how the social world acts back upon people and limits their freedom.

Some combination of symbolic interactionism and conflict theory, we believe, will allow us most successfully to capture the interpenetration of private troubles and public issues in Canadian society. And this will mean that the kinds of evidence we look for, the kinds of research strategies we employ, objective or subjective or some combination, will depend on which questions we are asking.

chapter

1

Sociological Perspectives

We begin this book with a mixture of classical and current selections. It will be up to your instructor whether you are to be exposed immediately to the classical works we have included — the writings of Marx, Weber and Durkheim — or whether she or he will want to save these for a later point in the course when you have become more familiar with the issues and debates in sociology. Whatever the decision of your instructor, we hope that you will begin your exploration into the world of sociology by reading what we view as a sociological classic and deserving of starting off this book, C. Wright Mills', "The Promise." Mills, an American sociologist, wrote during a time of considerable conservatism in American society and American sociology and, in focusing on power and class inequality and in drawing upon Karl Marx's analyses, he

was regarded as something of a pariah in the American academic community of the 1950s. As a student of the 1990s, you may find Mill's constant use of the term "men" archaic, sexist and therefore distracting. However, keep in mind that Mills was writing more than thirty years ago and he was, in this regard, merely following convention. What is important for you to take away from the selection is his emphasis on the meaning of *social structure*, which is perhaps the central concept of sociology. It is in this essay that he introduces the now famous distinction between *private troubles* and *public issues* and demonstrates in vivid terms what is meant by "the sociological imagination": the attempt to link the world of everyday life to the larger and generally invisible structures that constrain us.

The next two selections in this Chapter were written by two contemporary Canadian sociologists. The first of these, by Robert Brym of the University of Toronto, is the opening to his book *From Culture to Power: The Sociology of English Canada* (in collaboration with Bonnie Fox, also of the University of Toronto). This book presents a thorough but also controversial and critical examination of the development of anglophone sociology, particularly since the 1960s. Canadian sociology has of course been heavily influenced by American sociology and its emphasis on structural functionalism. This perspective, in turn, drew heavily from both Max Weber and Emile Durkheim but, with the exception of sociologists like C. Wright Mills, ignored the insights and approaches of Karl Marx. In describing the major debates within sociology as represented by Marx, Weber and Durkheim, Brym sets the stage for his later argument that Canadian sociology, initially a kind of watered-down version of American sociology, was transformed in the late 1960s. Young Canadian sociologists, in rejecting the basic assumptions of structural functionalism, did so through a "rediscovery" of Karl Marx and his emphasis on social structure (the economy) rather than culture as the main determinant of social behaviour. Finally, in this excerpt, Brym introduces you to a central theme of sociology, one you will repeatedly encounter throughout this Reader, the "causes" and "consequences" of social inequality.

The selection by Rosalind Sydie of the University of Alberta, is an abridged version of the last chapter of her book, *Natural Women, Cultured Men*. This book sought to examine the classical sociologists and their respective sociologies from the critical standpoint of feminist theory. In this selection she briefly describes the theoretical and methodological debates generated by the thinking of classical sociologists. But she also shows how these perspectives were based on assumptions about human nature which, for the most part, were assumptions about men's rather than men's and women's natures and ways of experiencing and knowing the world. It will become apparent as you read through this text that sociological theory and research have been under considerable attack because of their male bias and implicit or explicit sexism. Yet, as Sydie makes clear, feminist theorists are not in full agreement about whether the scientific method developed by and advocated by the classical sociologists needs to be modified, transformed or more or less abandoned; and she views this as a healthy sign of renewed vitality within the sociological tradition and the social sciences generally.

The three excerpts from the works of Karl Marx, Emile Durkheim and Max Weber are intentionally brief. They give you a taste and a summary of the often contrasting ways these important sociologists tried to work out what is and what ought to be the nature of the sociological enterprise: what is meant by a sociological perspective, a sociological approach to understanding human behaviour. It is in these works that we see articulated the fundamental debates that Brym and Sydie see as persisting in contemporary sociology; they provide different answers, different perspectives to what are fundamentally similar questions. There is, for example, agreement about the urgency of understanding the social, economic and political consequences of the rapid growth of capitalism and industrialism in their respective societies and times. These theorists share a common desire to develop some version of the scientific method as a way, if not the only way, to develop such an understanding, but they disagree on how this might best be accomplished.

In the first of these classical selections, Karl Marx (1818-1883) summarizes his general theory of historical materialism, what is sometimes referred to as "economic determinism." Perhaps the key notion here is that social being precedes consciousness and not the other way around. For Marx, human nature is not something we are born with but is a product of society. Society, in turn, develops out of and is shaped by the ways people organize to produce their basic needs — food, clothing, shelter and so on. As he points out, "what individuals are, therefore, depends on the material condition of their production." And institutions, laws, religious beliefs, even knowledge and common sense are shaped and constrained by the mode of production dominant at a particular period of history. According to Marx, institutions and beliefs appropriate to hunting and gathering societies, for example, will be inappropriate for a society whose economy is based on agriculture, such as was found in, say, Europe during its feudal period.

In sum, Marx gave explanatory pre-eminence to the social order rather than the individual or "human nature." We are collectively shaped by our mode of production and our relationship within this mode of production. Much could be understood about a person, according to Marx, simply by knowing the kind of production dominant in that person's society (feudalism, capitalism) and by knowing his or her relationship to others within the system (landowner, serf, capitalist, labourer). The Judeo-Christian image of humankind as evil — greedy, selfish, acquisitive — might better be viewed from Marx's perspective as a *product* of competitive, unequal societies, not their cause. And, because this "nature" is a product, it is not truly our inevitable human nature.

The optimism in humankind's potential to reshape (or have reshaped) its nature is not evident in the next selection. Rather, Emile Durkheim (1858-1917) took for granted the Judeo-Christian view of humankind as intrinsically evil and viewed

society — the social order — as not only standing outside and against people but as necessary to social life and individual well-being. Society protected people from themselves. As new modes of production and new modes of social organization seemed to be replacing the old, Durkheim's concern was not with how individuals were diminished by their social place and role, but how they were becoming confused by the lack of certainty about their place and role. Durkheim and Marx agreed that the social order was more powerful than the individual. Marx was concerned about the costs to all who were entrapped in the system of inequality. Durkheim was concerned about the costs to all if the trap — society's hold on the individual — was weakened, which he feared was becoming increasingly so. His methods of understanding the social world reflected Durkheim's belief that it stood outside and apart from, and was greater than, any individual. If such is the social world, then it follows that "social facts" can be studied like "things" with a distinct and separate reality.

In working one's way through these selections, one is forcefully reminded that these were thoughts created in a different century, in different worlds in many ways, and their language and references may be forbidding to many students. At the same time one must at least try to understand those social worlds to understand the work. A modest beginning is reading them in the original. Our final classical selection, by Max Weber (1864-1920), is perhaps the most demanding — in part because his work was so far ranging, in part because of the distinctive, often difficult Germanic sentence constructions. Much of what remains opaque to you after a first reading will become clearer after a second and clearer still as you encounter his work more concretely in discussion of social stratification, religion, bureaucracies and the like. We have selected this particular excerpt largely because it illustrates Weber's rather unique contribution — his emphasis on understanding the social world not only as it exists outside people but also as it is directly experienced by them. His appreciation of the importance of subjective understanding (*Verstehen*) is an important antidote to any sociological perspective that ignores the dialectic of individual and society. Society, its organization and structure, is constraining in two very real ways: as objectively encountered and as subjectively experienced. Weber shared with Marx and Durkheim a conviction in the power of the society over the individual. He insisted, nevertheless, that to understand the nature of the social world and its powers, sociologists must understand people's experience of it.

RELATED READINGS

Robert J. Brym: "The Great Identity Trap: Implications of the Comparative Study of Class and Power" (Chapter 9)
William K. Carroll: "The Thesis of Canadian Dependency" (Chapter 9)
M. Patricia Marchak: "The Uncertainty Principle" (Chapter 14)

THE PROMISE
C. Wright Mills

Nowadays men often feel that their private lives are a series of traps. They sense that within their everyday worlds, they cannot overcome their troubles, and in this feeling, they are often quite correct: What ordinary men are directly aware of and what they try to do are bounded by the private orbits in which they live; their visions and their

From *The Sociological Imagination* by C. Wright Mills. Copyright © 1959 by Oxford University Press, Inc. Reprinted by permission.

powers are limited to the close-up scenes of job, family, neighborhood; in other milieux, they move vicariously and remain spectators. And the more aware they become, however vaguely, of ambitions and of threats which transcend their immediate locales, the more trapped they seem to feel.

Underlying this sense of being trapped are seemingly impersonal changes in the very structure of continent-wide societies. The facts of contemporary history are also facts about the success and the failure of individual men and women. When a society is industrialized, a peasant becomes a worker; a feudal lord is liquidated or becomes a businessman. When classes rise or fall, a man is employed or unemployed; when the rate of investment goes up or down, a man takes new heart or goes broke. When wars happen, an insurance salesman becomes a rocket launcher; a store clerk, a radar man; a wife lives alone, a child grows up without a father. Neither the life of an individual nor the history of a society can be understood without understanding both.

Yet men do not usually define the troubles they endure in terms of historical change and institutional contradiction. The well-being they enjoy, they do not usually impute to the big ups and downs of the societies in which they live. Seldom aware of the intricate connection between the patterns of their own lives and the course of world history, ordinary men do not usually know what this connection means for the kinds of men they are becoming and for the kinds of history-making in which they might take part. They do not possess the quality of mind essential to grasp the interplay of man and society, of biography and history, of self and world. They cannot cope with their personal troubles in such ways as to control the structural transformations that usually lie behind them.

Surely it is no wonder. In what period have so many men been so totally exposed at so fast a pace to such earthquakes of change? That Americans have not known such catastrophic changes as have the men and women of other societies is due to historical facts that are now quickly becoming "merely history." The history that now affects every man is world history. Within this scene and this period, in the course of a single generation, one sixth of mankind is transformed from all that is feudal and backward into all that is modern, advanced, and fearful. Political colonies are freed; new and less visible forms of imperialism installed. Revolutions occur; men feel the intimate grip of new kinds of authority. Totalitarian societies rise, and are smashed to bits — or succeed fabulously. After two centuries of ascendancy, capitalism is shown up as only one way to make society into an industrial apparatus. After two centuries of hope, even formal democracy is restricted to a quite small portion of mankind. Everywhere in the underdeveloped world, ancient ways of life are broken up and vague expectations become urgent demands. Everywhere in the overdeveloped world, the means of authority and of violence become total in scope and bureaucratic in form. Humanity itself now lies before us, the super-nation at either pole concentrating its most co-ordinated and massive efforts upon the preparation of World War Three.

The very shaping of history now outpaces the ability of men to orient themselves in accordance with cherished values. And which values? Even when they do not panic, men often sense that older ways of feeling and thinking have collapsed and that newer beginnings are ambiguous to the point of moral stasis. Is it any wonder that ordinary men feel they cannot cope with the larger worlds with which they are so suddenly confronted? That they cannot understand the meaning of their epoch for their own lives? That — in defense of selfhood — they become morally insensible,

trying to remain altogether private men? Is it any wonder that they come to be possessed by a sense of the trap?

It is not only information that they need — in this Age of Fact, information often dominates their attention and overwhelms their capacities to assimilate it. It is not only the skills of reason that they need — although their struggles to acquire these often exhaust their limited moral energy.

What they need, and what they feel they need, is a quality of mind that will help them to use information and to develop reason in order to achieve lucid summations of what is going on in the world and of what may be happening within themselves. It is this quality, I am going to contend, that journalists and scholars, artists and publics, scientists and editors are coming to expect of what may be called the sociological imagination.

1   The sociological imagination enables its possessor to understand the larger historical scene in terms of its meaning for the inner life and the external career of a variety of individuals. It enables him to take into account how individuals, in the welter of their daily experience, often become falsely conscious of their social positions. Within that welter, the framework of modern society is sought, and within that framework the psychologies of a variety of men and women are formulated. By such means the personal uneasiness of individuals is focused upon explicit troubles and the indifference of publics is transformed into involvement with public issues.

The first fruit of this imagination — and the first lesson of the social science that embodies it — is the idea that the individual can understand his own experience and gauge his own fate only by locating himself within his period, that he can know his own chances in life only by becoming aware of those of all individuals in his circumstances. In many ways it is a terrible lesson; in many ways a magnificent one. We do not know the limits of man's capacities for supreme effort or willing degradation, for agony or glee, for pleasurable brutality or the sweetness of reason. But in our time we have come to know that the limits of "human nature" are frighteningly broad. We have come to know that every individual lives, from one generation to the next, in some society; that he lives out a biography, and that he lives it out within some historical sequence. By the fact of his living he contributes, however minutely, to the shaping of this society and to the course of its history, even as he is made by society and by its historical push and shove.

The sociological imagination enables us to grasp history and biography and the relations between the two within society. That is its task and its promise. To recognize this task and this promise is the mark of the class social analyst. It is characteristic of Herbert Spencer — turgid, polysyllabic, comprehensive; of E. A. Ross — graceful, muckraking, upright; of Auguste Comte and Emile Durkheim; of the intricate and subtle Karl Mannheim. It is the quality of all that is intellectually excellent in Karl Marx; it is the clue to Thorstein Veblen's brilliant and ironic insight, to Joseph Schumpeter's many-sided constructions of reality; it is the basis of the psychological sweep of W. E. H. Lecky no less than of the profundity and clarity of Max Weber. And it is the signal of what is best in contemporary studies of man and society.

No social study that does not come back to the problems of biography, of history and of their intersections within a society has completed its intellectual journey. Whatever the specific problems of the classic social analysts, however limited or however broad the features of social reality they have examined, those who have been imaginatively aware of the promise of their work have consistently asked three sorts of questions:

(1) What is the structure of this particular society as a whole? What are its essential components and how are they related to one another? How does it differ from other varieties of social order? Within it, what is the meaning of any particular feature for its continuance and for its change?

(2) Where does this society stand in human history? What are the mechanics by which it is changing? What is its place within and its meaning for the development of humanity as a whole? How does any particular feature we are examining affect, and how is it affected by, the historical period in which it moves? And this period — what are its essential features? How does it differ from other periods? What are its characteristic ways of history-making?

(3) What varieties of men and women now prevail in this society and in this period? And what varieties are coming to prevail? In what ways are they selected and formed, liberated and repressed, made sensitive and blunted? What kinds of "human nature" are revealed in the conduct and character we observe in this society in this period? And what is the meaning for "human nature" of each and every feature of the society we are examining?

Whether the point of interest is a great power state or a minor literary mood, a family, a prison, a creed — these are the kinds of questions the best social analysts have asked. They are the intellectual pivots of classic studies of man in society — and they are the questions inevitably raised by any mind possessing the sociological imagination. For that imagination is the capacity to shift from one perspective to another — from the political to the psychological; from examination of a single family to comparative assessment of the national budgets of the world, from the theological school to the military establishment; from considerations of an oil industry to studies of contemporary poetry. It is the capacity to range from the most impersonal and remote transformations to the most intimate features of the human self — and to see the relations between the two. Back of its use there is always the urge to know the social and historical meaning of the individual in the society and in the period in which he has his quality and his being.

That, in brief, is why it is by means of the sociological imagination that men now hope to grasp what is going on in the world, and to understand what is happening in themselves as minute points of the intersections of biography and history within society. In large part, contemporary man's self-conscious view of himself as at least an outsider, if not a permanent stranger, rests upon an absorbed realization of social relativity and of the transformative power of history. The sociological imagination is the most fruitful form of this self-consciousness. By its use men whose mentalities have swept only a series of limited orbits often come to feel as if suddenly awakened in a house with which they had only supposed themselves to be familiar. Correctly or incorrectly, they often come to feel that they can now provide themselves with adequate summations, cohesive assessments, comprehensive orientations. Older decisions that once appeared sound now seem to them products of a mind unaccountably dense. Their capacity for astonishment is made lively again. They acquire a new way of thinking, they experience a transvaluation of values: in a word, by their reflection and by their sensibility, they realize the cultural meaning of the social sciences.

2 Perhaps the most fruitful distinction with which the sociological imagination works is between "the personal troubles of milieu" and "the public issues of social structure." This distinction is an essential tool of the sociological imagination and a feature of all classic work in social science.

Troubles occur within the character of the individual and within the range of his immediate relations with others; they have to do with his self and with those limited areas of social life of which he is directly and personally aware. Accordingly, the statement and the resolution of troubles properly lie within the individual as a biographical entity and within the scope of his immediate milieu — the social setting that is directly open to his personal experience and to some extent his willful activity. A trouble is a private matter: values cherished by an individual are felt by him to be threatened.

Issues have to do with matters that transcend these local environments of the individual and the range of his inner life. They have to do with the organization of many such milieux into the institutions of an historical society as a whole, with the ways in which various milieux overlap and interpenetrate to form the larger structure of social and historical life. An issue is a public matter: some value cherished by publics is felt to be threatened. Often there is a debate about what that value really is and about what it is that really threatens it. This debate is often without focus if only because it is the very nature of an issue, unlike even widespread trouble, that it cannot very well be defined in terms of the immediate and everyday environments of ordinary men. An issue, in fact, often involves a crisis in institutional arrangements, and often too it involves what Marxists call "contradictions" or "antagonisms."

In these terms, consider unemployment. When, in a city of 100,000, only one man is unemployed, that is his personal trouble, and for its relief we properly look to the character of the man, his skills, and his immediate opportunities. But when in a nation of 50 million employees, 15 million men are unemployed, that is an issue, and we may not hope to find its solution within the range of opportunities open to any one individual. The very structure of opportunities has collapsed. Both the correct statement of the problem and the range of possible solutions require us to consider the economic and political institutions of the society, and not merely the personal situation and character of a scatter of individuals.

Consider war. The personal problem of war, when it occurs, may be how to survive it or how to die in it with honor; how to make money out of it; how to climb into the higher safety of the military apparatus; or how to contribute to the war's termination. In short, according to one's values, to find a set of milieux and within it to survive the war or make one's death in it meaningful. But the structural issues of war have to do with its causes; with what types of men it throws up into command; with its effects upon economic and political, family and religious institutions, with the unorganized irresponsibility of a world of nation-states.

Consider marriage. Inside a marriage a man and a woman may experience personal troubles, but when the divorce rate during the first four years of marriage is 250 out of every 1,000 attempts, this is an indication of a structural issue having to do with the institutions of marriage and the family and other institutions that bear upon them.

Or consider the metropolis — the horrible, beautiful, ugly, magnificent sprawl of the great city. For many upper-class people, the personal solution to "the problem of the city" is to have an apartment with private garage under it in the heart of the city, and forty miles out, a house by Henry Hill, garden by Garrett Eckbo, on a hundred acres of private land. In these two controlled environments — with a small staff at each end and a private helicopter connection — most people could solve many of the problems of personal milieux caused by the facts of the city. But all this, however splendid, does not solve the public issues that the structural fact of the city poses. What

should be done with this wonderful monstrosity? Break it all up into scattered units, combining residence and work? Refurbish it as it stands? Or, after evacuation, dynamite it and build new cities according to new plans in new places? What should those plans be? And who is to decide and to accomplish whatever choice is made? These are structural issues; to confront them and to solve them requires us to consider political and economic issues that affect innumerable milieux.

In so far as an economy is so arranged that slumps occur, the problem of unemployment becomes incapable of personal solution. In so far as war is inherent in the nation-state system and in the uneven industrialization of the world, the ordinary individual in his restricted milieu will be powerless — with or without psychiatric aid — to solve the troubles this sytem or lack of system imposes upon him. In so far as the family as an institution turns women into darling little slaves and men into their chief providers and unweaned dependents, the problem of a satisfactory marriage remains incapable of purely private solution. In so far as the overdeveloped megalopolis and the over-developed automobile are built-in features of the over-developed society, the issues of urban living will not be solved by personal ingenuity and private wealth.

What we experience in various and specific milieux, I have noted, is often caused by structural changes. Accordingly, to understand the changes of many personal milieux we are required to look beyond them. And the number and variety of such structural changes increase as the institutions within which we live become more embracing and more intricately connected with one another. To be aware of the idea of social structure and to use it with sensibility is to be capable of tracing such linkages among a great variety of milieux. To be able to do that is to possess the sociological imagination.

3   What are the major issues for publics and the key troubles of private individuals in our time? To formulate issues and troubles, we must ask what values are cherished yet threatened, and what values are cherished and supported, by the characterizing trends of our period. In the case both of threat and support we must ask what salient contradictions of structure may be involved.

When people cherish some set of values and do not feel any threat to them, they experience *well-being*. When they cherish values but *do* feel them to be threatened, they experience a crisis — either as a personal trouble or as a public issue. And if all their values seem involved, they feel the total threat of panic.

But suppose people are neither aware of any cherished values nor experience any threat? That is the experience of *indifference*, which, if it seems to involve all their values, becomes apathy. Suppose, finally, they are unaware of any cherished values, but still are very much aware of a threat? That is the experience of *uneasiness*, of anxiety, which, if it is total enough, becomes a deadly unspecified malaise.

Ours is a time of uneasiness and indifference — not yet formulated in such ways as to permit the work of reason and the play of sensibility. Instead of troubles — defined in terms of values and threats — there is often the misery of vague uneasiness; instead of explicit issues there is often merely the beat feeling that all is somehow not right. Neither the values threatened nor whatever threatens them has been stated; in short, they have not been carried to the point of decision. Much less have they been formulated as problems of social science.

In the thirties there was little doubt — except among certain deluded business circles — that there was an economic issue which was also a pack of personal troubles. In these arguments about "the crisis of cap-italism," the formulations of Marx and the many unacknowledged re-formulations of his work probably set the leading terms of the issue, and some men came to understand their personal troubles in these terms. The values threatened were plain to see and cherished by all; the structural contradictions that threatened them also seemed plain. Both were widely and deeply experienced. It was a political age.

But the values threatened in the era after World War Two are often neither widely acknowledged as values nor widely felt to be threatened. Much private uneasiness goes unformulated; much public malaise and many decisions of enormous structural relevance never become public issues. For those who accept such inherited values as reason and freedom, it is the uneasiness itself that is the trouble; it is the indifference itself that is the issue. And it is this condition, of uneasiness and indifference, that is the signal feature of our period.

All this is so striking that it is often interpreted by observers as a shift in the very kinds of problems that need now to be formulated. We are frequently told that the problems of our decade, or even the crises of our period, have shifted from the external realm of economics and now have to do with the quality of individual life — in fact with the question of whether there is soon going to be anything that can properly be called individual life. Not child labor but comic books, not poverty but mass leisure, are at the center of concern. Many great public issues as well as many private troubles are described in terms of "the psychiatric" — often, it seems, in a pathetic attempt to avoid the large issues and problems of modern society. Often this statement seems to rest upon a provincial narrowing of interest to the Western societies, or even to the United States — thus ignoring two-thirds of mankind; often, too, it arbitrarily divorces the individual life from the larger institutions within which that life is enacted, and which on occasion bear upon it more grievously than do the intimate environments of childhood.

Problems of leisure, for example, cannot even be stated without considering problems of work. Family troubles over comic books cannot be formulated as problems without considering the plight of the contemporary family in its new relations with the newer institutions of the social structure. Neither leisure nor its debilitating uses can be understood as problems without recognition of the extent to which malaise and indifference now form the social and personal climate of contemporary American society. In this climate, no problems of "the private life" can be stated and solved without recognition of the crisis of ambition that is part of the very career of men at work in the incorporated economy.

It is true, as psychoanalysts continually point out, that people do often have "the increasing sense of being moved by obscure forces within themselves which they are unable to define." But it is *not* true, as Ernest Jones asserted, that "man's chief enemy and danger is his own unruly nature and the dark forces pent up within him." On the contrary: "Man's chief danger" today lies in the unruly forces of contemporary society itself, with its alienating methods of production, its enveloping techniques of political domination, its international anarchy — in a word, its pervasive transformations of the very "nature" of man and the conditions and aims of his life.

It is now the social scientist's foremost political and intellectual task — for here the two coincide — to make clear the elements of contemporary uneasiness and indifference. It is the central demand made upon him by the other cultural workmen — by physical scientists and artists, by the intellectual community in general. It is because of this task and these demands, I believe, that the social sciences are becoming the common denominator of our cultural period, and the sociological imagination our most needed quality of mind.

THE CLASSIC QUESTIONS OF EUROPEAN SOCIOLOGY
Robert J. Brym

The three most important and enduring debates in the history of sociology concern the nature of the relationship between individual and society; the relative importance of economy versus culture in determining social behaviour; and the social bases of inequality. These issues invigorated social discourse in nineteenth-century Europe and, as we shall see, they continue to engage sociologists in English Canada and elsewhere.

The first debate originated at the time of the French Revolution. The revolutionaries were liberals, and they proclaimed liberty, equality before the law, and fraternity as their goals. They believed that the well-being of the French citizenry could be secured if traditional social constraints were eliminated so that people could be free to develop their natural talents. Implicit in this view was the idea that the social standing of the individual should not be fixed at birth; the revolutionaries argued that the individual should be able to rise (or fall) to a position in the social hierarchy that matched his or her talents.

In contrast, their conservative opponents saw the overthrow of the old government and the old ruling class as a grave threat to the well-being of the citizenry. In their view, if the individual were completely free society could not exist. The conservatives thus emphasized how established secular and religious authority, tra-

From *From Culture to Power: The Sociology of English Canada* by Robert J. Brym with Bonnie Fox, 1989. Reprinted by permission of Oxford University Press Canada.

ditional forms of community, and rigid social hierarchy constrain human aspirations and actions, thereby preventing disorganization and anarchy. They also believed that society is not just an agglomeration of individuals, but a real corporate unit that stands over and above the wills of individuals.

Individual and Society in Durkheim

It was out of this conservative ideological animus that sociology first emerged. Its influence can be clearly seen in the work of Emile Durkheim, who is generally regarded as one of the founding fathers of the discipline. Usually we assume that any act — prayer, marriage, war, revolution — is the outcome of an individual's (or many individuals') motives. Features of society, in turn, are usually viewed as the result of many individual passions and decisions. Durkheim, however, turned this conventioned liberal-individualist wisdom on its head. He argued that individual passions and decisions are the result of certain features of society. And the study of how social forces influence individual behaviour is what sociology is all about (Durkheim, 1895).

Even an act like suicide, which appears to be highly individualistic, anti-social, and wholly determined by one's state of mind, is in fact a socially determined phenomenon, wrote Durkheim. He made his case in part by examining the association betweem rates of suicide and rates of psychological disorder for different groups. The notion that psychological disorder causes suicide is supported, he reasoned, only if suicide rates tend to be high where rates of psychological disorder are high, and low where rates of psychological disorder are low. But his analysis of European government statistics, hospital records,

and other sources revealed nothing of the kind. For example, he discovered that there were slightly more women than men in insane asylums; but there were four male suicides for every female suicide. Jews had the highest rate of psychological disorder among the major religious groups in France; but they also had the lowest suicide rate. Psychological disorders occurred most frequently when a person reached maturity; but suicide rates increased steadily with age.

Clearly, suicide rates and rates of psychological disorder did not vary directly; in fact, they often appeared to vary inversely. Why? Durkheim argued that in modern societies suicide rates vary as a result of differences in the degree of "social solidarity" in different categories of the population. Accordingly, he expected groups whose members interact more frequently and intensely to exhibit lower suicide rates. For example, Durkheim held that married adults are half as likely as unmarried adults to commit suicide because marriage creates social ties that bind the individual to society. Where these ties are absent, suicide is more likely. In general, he wrote, "suicide varies with the degree of integration of the social groups of which the individual forms a part" (Durkheim, 1951: 209). Of course, this generalization tells us nothing about why any particular individual may take his or her life; but it does say something uniquely sociological about why the suicide rate varies from group to group.

The Phenomenological Response

Many contemporary sociologists continue to argue that the proper focus of the discipline is the study of social pressures that constrain or influence individuals. Today, using sophisticated statistical techniques, researchers can measure the independent and combined effects of many social variables on many types of behaviour. For nearly a century, however, detractors from the Durkheimian view have been pointing to an important flaw in the theory. They argue that Durkheim paints an altogether too mechanical and deterministic view of the individual in society, depicting people as if they behaved like billiard balls, knocked about on predetermined trajectories, unable to choose to alter their destinations. But we know from our everyday experience that this is not the case. People do make choices — often difficult ones. Moreover, two people with similar social characteristics may react quite differently to similar social circumstances because, according to Durkheim's critics, they may interpret these circumstances differently. In the opinion of such "phenomenological" sociologists, an adequate explanation of social phenomena requires that we understand the subjective meanings that people attach to social facts and the ways in which they actively create these social facts.

In order better to understand the phenomenological school of thought, let us return to the problem of suicide. If a police officer discovers a dead person at the wheel of a car that has run into a tree, it may be very difficult to establish with certainty whether the death was accidental or suicidal. Interviewing friends and relatives in order to find out the dead person's state of mind immediately before the crash may help to rule out the possibility of suicide. But, as this example illustrates, understanding the intention or motive of the actor is critical to explaining or labelling a social action. Suicide, then, is not just an objective social fact, but an inferred, and therefore subjective, social fact. A state of mind must be interpreted — usually by a coroner — before the dead body becomes a suicide statistic (Douglas, 1967).

Some phenomenological sociologists tend to ignore the impact of objective, outside social forces on the lives of men and women, reducing the study of society to an analysis of subjective interactions in small settings: how person A perceives person B's actions, how person A responds to these actions, how B in turn perceives and responds, and so forth. Just as one-sidedly, strict Durkheimians ignore the subjective side of social life and draw attention only to objective, outside forces. But many modern sociologists endorse neither extreme. They think it makes more sense to combine the Durkheimian and phenomenological approaches and analyze how men and women interpret, create, and change their social existence within the limits imposed on them by powerful social constraints. This synthetic approach is found in the work of Karl Marx and, to an even greater degree, Max Weber, who, along with Durkheim, established the groundwork of modern sociology. Let us now turn to a brief examination of their work.

Structure Versus Culture in Marx

Both Marx and Weber stressed the importance of analyzing subjective social actions and objective social constraints (Marx, 1932: 118; Weber, 1922: 103; Gerth and Mills, 1946: 57–8). They also had compatible (though different) ideas about the nature of these constraints.

Marx, like Weber, recognized that the external determinants of behaviour consist of economic, political, and cultural forces. Marx tended to assign overwhelming causal priority to the economic realm. Weber did not deny the primacy of economic arrangements, but he rounded out Marx's analysis by showing how the political and cultural facts of life can act as important independent causes of many social phenomena.

In the middle of the nineteenth century Marx proposed a sweeping theory of the development of human societies. In this theory the locus of change is economic organization — more precisely, society's class structure and its technological base. He explained the rise and decline of capitalism as follows.

In European feudal society peasants tilled small plots of land that were owned not by the peasants themselves but by landlords. Peasants were legally bound to the land, obliged to give their landlords a set proportion of their harvest and to continue working for them under any circumstances. In turn landlords were expected to protect peasants against marauders and poor economic conditions.

By the late fifteenth century certain processes had been set in motion that eventually transformed feudal society into a modern capitalist system. Most important was the growth of exploration and trade, which increased the demand for many goods and services in commerce, navigation, and industry. By the seventeenth and eighteenth centuries some urban dwellers — successful artisans and merchants — had accumulated sufficient capital to expand their production significantly. In order to maximize their profits, these capitalists required an abundant supply of workers who could be hired in periods of high demand and fired without obligation during slack times. It was necessary to induce and coerce indentured peasants from the soil and transform them into legally free workers who would work for wages (Marx and Engels, 1848).

In Marx's view, the relations between wage labourers and capitalists at first facilitated rapid technological innovation and economic growth. Capitalists were keen to reorganize the labour process and adopt new tools, machines, and production techniques. These changes allowed them to produce more efficiently, earn higher profits, and drive their competitors out of business. Efficiency also required that workers be concentrated in larger and larger industrial establishments, that wages be kept as low as possible, and that as little as possible be invested in improving working conditions. Thus, according to Marx, workers and capitalists would stand face-to-face in factory and mine: a large and growing class of relatively impoverished workers opposing a small and shrinking class of increasingly wealthy owners.

Marx argued that in due course all workers would become aware of belonging to the same exploited class. This sense of "class consciousness" would, he felt, encourge the growth of working-class organizations, such as trade unions and political parties. These organizations would be bent on overthrowing the capitalist system and establishing a classless society. According to Marx, this revolutionary change was bound to occur during one of the recurrent and worsening "crises of overproduction" characteristic of the capitalist era. The productive capacity of the system would, he said, come to far outstrip the ability of the relatively impoverished workers to purchase goods and services. Hence in order to sell goods and services, capitalists would be forced to lower their prices. Profits would then fall, the less efficient capitalists would go bankrupt, and massive unemployment of workers would result — thus deepening the economic crisis still further. The capitalist class system had originally encouraged economic growth, but eventually the crises of overproduction it generated would hinder such growth. At that time the capitalist class system would be destroyed and replaced by socialism.

As this thumbnail sketch shows, beliefs, symbols, and values — in short, culture —

play a quite minor independent causal role in Marx's theory. He analyzed how, under most circumstances, ruling-class ideology forms a legitimizing cement in society and how, in rare circumstances, subordinate class consciousness can become an important force for change. But in his work it is always the material circumstances of existence that ultimately determine the role ideas play.

Weber on Capitalism and the World Religions

Weber, like Marx, was interested in explaining the rise of modern capitalism. And, like Marx, he was prepared to recognize the "fundamental importance of the economic factor" in his explanation (Weber, 1904–5: 26). But he was also bent on demonstrating the one-sidedness of any exclusively economic interpretation. After all, the economic conditions that Marx said were necessary for capitalist development existed in Catholic France during the reign of Louis XIV; yet the wealth generated in France by international trade and commerce tended to be consumed by war and the luxurious lifestyle of the aristocracy rather than invested in the growth of capitalist enterprise. For Weber, what prompted vigorous capitalist development in non-Catholic Europe and North America was a combination of propitious economic conditions such as those discussed by Marx and the spread of certain moral values by the Protestant reformers of the sixteenth century and their followers in the seventeenth.

For specifically religious reasons, followers of the Protestant theologian John Calvin stressed the need to engage in intense worldly activity, to demonstrate industry, punctuality, and frugality in one's everyday life. In the view of men like John Wesley and Benjamin Franklin, religious doubts could be reduced, and a state of grace assured, if one worked diligently and lived ascetically. This idea was taken up by Puritanism, Methodism, and other Protestant denominations; Weber called it the "Protestant work ethic."

According to Weber, this ethic had wholly unexpected economic consequences: where it took root, and where economic conditions were favourable, early capitalist enterprise grew robustly. In other words, two independent developments — the Protestant work ethic (which derived from purely religious considerations) and the material conditions favouring capitalist growth (which derived from specifically economic circumstances) — interacted to invigorate capitalism.

Subsequent research has demonstrated that the association between the Protestant ethic and the strength of capitalist development is weaker than Weber thought. In some places Catholicism has co-existed with vigorous capitalist growth and Protestantism with relative stagnation. Nonetheless, even if Weber was wrong about this particular case, his general view — that religious developments cannot be reduced to economic developments, and that religious ideas have economic consequences — is still widely regarded as a valid insight.

Just as some Marxist sociologists have adopted a strict economic determinism, some Weberians have misinterpreted Weber's ideas in a way that supports a sort of cultural determinism. But the plain fact is that Weber assigned nearly the same relative weight to economic and cultural forces as did Marx; and there is nothing in Marx's work that is incompatible with Weber's insights into the relative autonomy of religious developments. Disputes between orthodox Marxists and orthodox Weberians over the relative weight of economic versus cultural causes of change may thus be as specious as the disagreement between rigid Durkheimians and phenomenologists.

The Bases of Social Inequality

Thus far I have singled out areas of similarity or compatibility in the thought of Marx and Weber. In Weber's "long and intense debate with the ghost of Karl Marx," however, there also emerged some ideas that are incompatible with those of Marx. Such ideas are especially obvious in Weber's work on social inequality.

Marx regarded ownership or non-ownership of property as the fundamental basis of inequality in capitalist society. In his view, there are two main classes under capitalism. Members of the capitalist class, or bourgeoisie, own means of production but they do not work them. Members of the working class, or proletariat, work but do not own means of production. In addition, Marx discussed some minor classes that are vestiges of precapitalist times. Most important, members of the petite bourgeoisie (e.g., farmers, owners of small family businesses) both own and work means of production. Marx also analyzed various divisions within the major classes. These class segments were distinguished from one another by their sources of income (e.g., financial and industrial capitalists) or skill level (e.g., skilled and unskilled manual workers).

In defining classes in this way Marx was not trying to account for gradations of rank in society. Instead, he sought to explain the massive historical change that results from the materially grounded opposition of interests between classes. In his view, the major classes were potentially self-conscious groups engaged in conflict that would eventually result in societal transformation.

Weber agreed that " 'property' and 'lack of property' are . . . the basic categories of all class situations," but his analysis of inequality differed from Marx's in three main ways. First, he was profoundly skeptical about Marx's interpretation of historical development. As a result he stressed that members of classes do not necessarily become class-conscious and act in concert. Second, Weber argued that property relations are just one aspect of a more general "market situation" that determines class position. For example, expertise acquired through formal education is a scarce commodity on the labour market. Such expertise increases one's advantages or "life-chances" and is therefore an important factor structuring the class system. On this basis, and in addition to the capitalist and manual working classes, Weber distinguished large and growing classes of technical/managerial personnel and white-collar workers who perform routine tasks.

Third, Weber was less concerned than Marx with the sources of conflict between discrete classes and more concerned with the structure of complex social hierarchies. For this reason he showed that the bases of social inequality are not exclusively economic. One non-economic source of inequality is the way honour (or esteem or prestige) is distributed in society. Weber referred to groups distinguished from one another in terms of prestige as status groups. For example, line of descent (including ethnic origin) may account for the level of esteem in which a status group is held, and esteem affects the life-chances of status group members. A second non-economic source of inequality is the political party. A party, in Weber's definition, is an association that seeks to gain control over an organization — ranging all the way from, say, a sports club to a state — for purposes of implementing specific policies. Parties may recruit members from specific classes or status groups, or both. In so doing, and to the degree that they achieve organizational control, parties bestow more advantages on their supporters than on non-supporters.

If parties and status groups are independent bases of social inequality, then, according to Weber, they are not wholly independent, especially in capitalist societies. There is an association between status group and party membership, on the one hand, and class position on the other. The structure of class inequality helps to shape status group and party membership; in fact, "today the class situation is by far the predominant factor" (Weber, 1922: 190).

Much of modern sociology has been devoted to exploring the ramifications of Weber's refinement of Marx's stratification model. What are the economic determinants of class that do not derive from ownership versus non-ownership of property? How does the concentration of ethnic and other status groups in particular class locations reinforce status-group cohesion? How do ethnic and other forms of status-group identification serve to reinforce patterns of inequality? To what degree do classes serve as recruitment bases for political parties? To what degree do different types of political parties enact policies that redistribute income? These are among the most popular questions asked by modern sociologists, and they are all indebted to Weber's elaboration of the Marxian schema.

Recent years have also witnessed an important addition to the stratification model sketched above. It is now generally acknowledged that gender is a basis of social inequality quite on a par with status groups, parties, and classes (see Figure 1.1). Thus, in Canada and elsewhere, gender is as important a determinant of annual income as class because women in the paid labour force tend to be segregated in low-pay, low-prestige jobs. Even if one matches a group of Canadian men and a group of Canadian women in terms of education, occupation, amount of time worked each year, and years of job experience, one discovers that the women earn only 63 per cent of what the men earn. Meanwhile, the great bulk of household labour continues to be performed by women, even if both spouses

work; one study conducted in Vancouver found that when their wives entered the paid labour force husbands did on average only one hour more of housework per week (Meissner *et al.*, 1975).

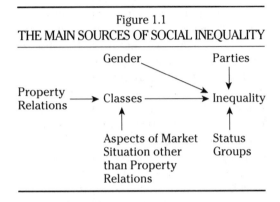

Figure 1.1
THE MAIN SOURCES OF SOCIAL INEQUALITY

Classical theories teach us little about the causes of such gender inequality. That is, while Marx and Weber offered important insights into the reasons for the expansion and contraction of particular locations in the stratification system, they "give no clues about why women are subordinate to men inside and outside the family and why it is not the other way around."

Gender inequality has been explained biologically, culturally, and social-structurally. Accumulated research indicates that while biological factors — especially women's childbearing function — may have encouraged some division of labour between the sexes in primitive societies, there is no biological reason why male and female jobs should have been rewarded differently, let alone why they continue to be rewarded differently today. Cultural theories, which locate the causes of gender inequality in the way people learn established practices, cannot account either for the origins of gender inequality or for the sources of variation in such inequality. Explanations that root gender inequality in social structure appear more promising. While the subordination of women is evident in all but the simplest foraging societies, it takes on different forms and degrees in different times and places. Unravelling the relationship between social structure, on the one hand, and the form and degree of gender inequality, on the other, is a complex task that lies at the cutting edge of contemporary research on social inequality.

The North American Legacy

The three problems isolated above continue to engage lively minds in sociological debates that grow more sophisticated over time. In any given setting, however, some sides of the three debates have tended to dominate. This is certainly evident in the history of sociology in North America. Compared to the European setting in which sociology originated, the U.S. has provided an extraordinarily congenial environment for the entrenchment of presuppositions about the role of individual creativity in producing social structures. Assumptions about the external, coercive power of social facts to shape individual behaviour have fared less well. Moreover, when Americans have analyzed the social determination of economic and political behaviour, they have been inclined to focus on symbolic or cultural determinants above material or political/economic constraints. . . .

FEMINISM AND SOCIOLOGICAL THEORY

Rosalind Sydie

Sociological theory attempts to make sense of the social world. The process of theorizing starts with an idea of the nature of society, and out of this idea a conceptual

From *Natural Women, Cultured Men*, 1987 by Rosalind Sydie. By permission of Nelson Canada, A Division of Thomson Canada Limited.

framework is developed that sets out the terms for what is to count as relevant information for a description and explanation of social reality. Sociological theories can then be said to explain social life through a set of logically connected ideas that can be validated, in some manner, by evidence from social reality. Presumably, if the evidence from the real world conflicts with the theory, then the theory is discarded. On this count, the process of theorizing seems to be a fairly coherent activity and one that contains its own corrective mechanism to guard against the acceptance of extreme flights of theoretical fancy. However, the process for sociology, and for scientific theory in general, is less simple than this description suggests.

First, sociologists do not necessarily agree upon what is to count as the subject matter of investigation. That is, how they define society can vary. For example, Durkheim defined society as a moral, normative order. For Weber, society was the product of meaningful interactions of the participants. Marx and Engels defined society according to the nature of productive relations, and Freud understood it as a product of psychic repression and control.

Second, whatever their definition of the nature of society, theorists disagree on the method of its investigation. For example, both Durkheim and Marx were concerned with providing causal explanations of social processes and structures, whereas Weber and Freud stressed understanding and introspection. Third, although sociologists agree that theory development is a process, so that explanations offered cannot be seen as static, timeless truths, they disagree about how "better" theories can be developed. For example, a better theory for Durkheim might be measured by a theory's greater predictability, in contrast to Weber for whom a greater understanding of the meaning of social action would constitute theoretical progress.

Finally, all theorists seek to abstract common features of social existence that will provide them with a basis for generalizations. Again, however, these common features vary with the theorist. For Durkheim, it was social solidarity that provided the important conceptual key; for Weber it was social action; for Marx and Engels it was the nature and distribution of property; and for Freud, psychological development expressed in the Oedipus conflict.

The distinctions between the theorists outlined above have important consequences for the manner in which sociological theory might proceed. In general, these theorists represent different epistemological positions on the nature of sociological theory. Durkheim is usually taken to represent the positivist approach, Weber the idealist approach and Marx, Engels and Freud the realist approach. The three positions emerge out of an understanding of what constitutes the nature of social reality; that is, they represent an "intellectual milieu" that describes the nature of sociology as a science and the subject matter and the methods appropriate to discovery. In Laudan's (1977) terms, the three positions represent "research traditions." They refer to "a set of general assumptions about the entities and processes in a domain of study, and about the appropriate methods to be used in investigating the problems and constucting the theories in that domain."

The positivist tradition represented by Durkheim (1950) sees society as having structures and processes akin to those in the natural world and therefore as being amenable to discovery by methods similar to those employed in the natural sciences. As he pointed out, sociology simply involves "the principle of causality" applied to social reality. It is on this basis that sociology emancipates itself from philosophy. "Since the law of causality has been verified in the other realms of nature, and

since it has progressively extended its authority from the physico-chemical world to the biological, and from the latter to the psychological, we are justified in claiming that it is equally true of the social world." The sociologist must therefore reject metaphysical speculations and "put himself in the same state of mind as the physicist, chemist, or physiologist when he probes into a still unexplored region of the scientific domain."

Like the natural scientist, the sociologist is concerned with the explanatory and predictive knowledge of the social world. Therefore, the sociologist constructs theories that comprise general statements about the regular relationships existing in society. The regular relationships are discovered through observation and experiment, so that "to explain something is to show that it is an instance of these regularities; and we can make predictions only on the same basis" (Keat and Urry, 1982: 4). In society as in nature, regularities become known only through sensory experience and "represented in the universal laws of scientific theory." Therefore, in Durkheim's view, "Any attempt to go beyond this representation plunges science into the unverifiable claims of metaphysics and religion, which are at best unscientific, and at worst meaningless" (Keat and Urry, 1982: 12).

In contrast to the positivist research tradition, idealism understands the social world as the product of consciousness that can be explained through the analysis of ideas, beliefs and motives. The subject matter is the meaningful nature of social-historical reality, and the discovery of what is meaningful cannot be attained "by means of a "presuppositionless" investigation of empirical data" advanced by positivists. In fact, the meaningfulness of sociological data, according to Weber, "does not coincide with laws as such, and the more general the law the less the coincidence"

(Weber, 1949: 76). The major task for sociology is to understand the meaning of social actions. Although this means that the procedures of the natural sciences are inapplicable to sociology, nevertheless, sociology can establish causal links. The key is that the connections between behaviours and events must have "understandable subjective meaning."

The subject matter of sociology distinguishes it from the natural sciences and therefore demands a different methodology. But Weber maintains that this does not mean that sociology is any less objective than the natural sciences.

The type of social science in which we are interested is an empirical science *of concrete reality . . . Our aim is the understanding of the characteristic uniqueness of the reality in which we move. We wish to understand on the one hand the relationships and the cultural significance of individual events in their contemporary manifestations and on the other the causes of their being historically so and not* otherwise. *(Weber, 1949: 72)*

An indispensable tool in the research process is the ideal type, because the "pure" conduct exemplified by the type can be used to understand the actions of individuals in the real social world. The function of the ideal type is to enable "the comparison with empirical reality in order to establish its divergences or similarities, to describe them with the *most unambiguously intelligible concepts*, and to understand and explain them causally" (Weber, 1949: 43). The ideal type is the means by which the multitude of individual actions and subjective understandings can be given a meaningful, coherent basis for sociological investigation.

The realist research tradition also uses ideal type constructs, but in contrast to Weber's ideal types, assigns them a different epistemological status. As Keat and Urry (1982) demonstrate, the approach differs in two ways. First, Weber's ideal types are those "most useful or appropriate for one's particular scientific purposes at the moment." In contrast, Marx constructed his types in terms of the "essential features" of, for example, capitalism, on the basis that "there is a central structural mechanism within capitalism." Secondly, the development of the type is not the result of the "process of abstraction from, and idealization of, the concrete social relations found within actual societies," because the very structure of relations obscures the "underlying and central mechanisms." Therefore, "any process of concept formation which is based on the way that society presents itself will be inadequate, misleading and ideological." This latter point is central to the realist understanding of social reality.

The realist tradition contends that there are real, but not immediately apprehendable, structures in the social world, and the task of sociology is to uncover these structures. Like the positivist, the realist sees sociology as a science that is "an empirically-based, rational and objective enterprise" that can provide explanatory, predictive knowledge. However, the realist makes a distinction between explanation and prediction, "and it's explanation which must be pursued as the primary objective of science."

To explain phenomena is not merely to show they are instances of well-established regularities. Instead, we must discover the necessary connections between phenomena, by acquiring knowledge of the underlying structures and mechanisms at work. (Keat and Urry, 1982: 31)

The realist, therefore, explains *why* something happens by showing *how* and by *what means* it occurs.

Although the work of Marx and Engels is more representative of sociological realism, Freud's approach is also in line with this research tradition. Consciousness is determined by the invisible unconsciousness; that is, the unconscious represents the underlying structure that has real effects on the apprehendable forms of behaviour and consciousness. Consequently, neuroses are explained as the visible consequence of the repression of instinctual sexual and aggresive desires buried in the unconscious. "Normally, there is nothing of which we are more certain than the feeling of our self, or our own ego. This ego appears to us as something autonomous and unitary, marked off distinctly from everything else." This separation is "deceptive" because the ego is in fact the visible evidence of "an unconscious mental entity which we designate as the id and for which it serves as a kind of facade."

All three research traditions have provided fruitful explanations of society and advanced our understanding of social life, at least for one half of humanity. . . . an examination of the particular theorists within these research traditions carries no presupposition that the theories can be weighed in some epistemological balance and accepted or rejected outright. Rather, the point has been to examine the presuppositions and their implications from the perspective of women as subjects rather than objects of the discourse. It is clear that there are fundamental problems originating with the definition of social reality and the resulting descriptions and explanations. The competing research traditions within which the substantive work of the theorists has been examined unite on the question of sex differences. Women are seen as biologically and, therefore, naturally different and constrained by that difference. It is this basic conception that overrides, in the last analysis, the substantive differences between the various theories in the treatment of sex relations.

Sociologists have disagreed about what society is and what valid sociological knowledge is and how it might be obtained.

But in general there is an unquestioned foundation upon which the classical, as well as more recent, theories build — the organizing principle of sex difference. Thus a partial, limited perspective on the nature of social life results, which, in turn, affects the conceptual frameworks and explanations offered by sociologists within the three research traditions.

The feminist critique of sociology has tended to focus on the positivist and Marxist research traditions. Only recently has the idealist tradition been the subject of significant attention. The positivist tradition has received more critical rejection than the Marxist. In general, feminists have been reluctant to abandon the emancipatory promise of Marxism that has generated the sympathy and maintained the relevance of the tradition. Only in the last decade has the idealist tradition received much attention, partly as a response, or an alternative, to positivism and Marxism. The critique of positivism has, however, provided continued debate, which has been conducted at the more general level of a critique of normal science, of which positivism is taken to be the exemplar. To this critique we now turn, followed by a consideration of suggestions for the direction of feminist theory.

Debunking Science

Science, it would seem, is not sexless; she is a man, a father, and infected too. (Woolf, 1977: 159).

Virginia Woolf's comment was made in regard to the nineteenth-century "proofs" provided by craniologists that the female brain was smaller than the male's, and therefore women "were stupider than men." As we saw earlier, Durkheim used some of this "scientific" research to demonstrate the biological as well as the social effects of the progressive division of labour in society.

For the theorists we have discussed, science was an important progressive force in ordering society. Both Marx and Weber believed that the increasing rationalization of life was an inevitable process for western civilization, and that scientific knowledge was an indispensable part of that process. Marx believed in positive results from the march of scientific and technological change, in that they would contribute to both the overthrow of capitalism and the establishment of a more humane future. Weber was more pessimistic about the humanist consequences but did believe that science could "enhance the technical mastery of life." Freud also believed that the progress of civilization was best accomplished through rationality and the renunciation of instinctual impulses such as those embodied in religious beliefs. "Our best hope for the future is that intellect and scientific spirit, reason — may in the process of time establish a dictatorship in the mental life of man" (Freud, 1964: 171).

Bendix (1971) suggests that Freud, Weber and Durkheim, along with others, were "discernible as a group by their common concern with the subjective presuppositions of thought." At the same time, "men like Freud, Durkheim, and Weber, while making room for this new awareness," still attempted to retain an enlightened, rationalist heritage.

Max Weber's essay, "Science as a Vocation" . . . is a document of this generation. It represents a careful blend of rationalist convictions and romantic sensibility. Like the great rationalists before him, but with none of their optimism, Weber commits himself to the scientist's calling (Bendix, 1971: 92).

The origins of faith in science can be traced to the seventeenth-century rejection of "nature" as having purposes and goals like humans and the celebration of mankind's mastery of nature. Nature then became an object that could be controlled by masterful human beings. The man of science could, in Bacon's terms, "mine" nature's secrets and make nature a "slave" to man's needs and desires. The idea of nature as a living, nurturing, growing force was thus replaced with the idea that nature was mere matter to be shaped, moulded and tamed by man, armed with the techniques of science and technology.

In the transformation, nature was frequently thought of as "female." Bacon remarked, "I am come in very truth leading you nature with all her children to bind her to your service and make her your slave" (Bacon, 1964: 62). The association of women with nature and the hierarchical relations between men and women/nature . . . are to be found in the initial philosophical characterization of scientific knowledge.

It is not simply that nature, "like" women, is to be subject to mastery but also that nature, again like women, is understood as a mysterious, unpredictable and, therefore, dangerous Other. To prevent any harm befalling the intrepid investigator (assumed to be male) confronting such a problematic entity, a clear separation had to be maintained between the scientist and nature.

Having divided the world into two parts the knower (mind) and the knowable (nature) scientific ideology goes on to prescribe a very specific relation between the two. It prescribes the interactions which can consummate this union, that is which can lead to knowledge. Not only are mind and nature assigned gender, but in characterizing scientific and objective thought as masculine, the very activity by which the knower can acquire knowledge is also genderized. The relation specified between knower and known is one of distance and separation. It is that between subject and object radically divided, which is to say no worldly relation (Fox Keller, 1983).

The "chaste and lawful marriage between Mind and Nature" promoted by Bacon is one that is consummated through reason rather than feeling, and observation rather than immediate sensory experience.

When sociology makes its intellectual debut as a science of society it invariably inherits the same system of beliefs that result in a "genderization" of science — that is, a belief that science is male thought and male activity. In addition, sociology makes its debut at precisely the time and place when the dichotomized understanding of sex roles provides the guiding ideal for social and political practice . . . the search for the origins of patriarchy, as well as the concern with the range of sexual behaviours and family structures, were basically motivated by the need to define the most "natural" relations between the sexes. It was generally assumed that the domesticity of women, in contrast to the worldly activities of men, was not only an ideal to be pursued but also the "natural" state of affairs that would make the best, most productive use of the divergent talents of the sexes. Such a dichotomy was also thought to be scientifically established by Darwinian science.

Sociology inherited a sex-dichotomized scientific approach as well as the nineteenth-century cultural ideal of the dichotomized relationship between the sexes as appropriate to their "natural" talents. The sociological concern with uncovering the laws of society and improving it was therefore coloured by this inheritance. In general, the resulting focus was on men in the public world and, when women entered the sociological picture, on the family and socialization tasks of women. This dichotomy was often accompanied, in the nineteenth century, by the idea of the moral superiority of the female because of her exclusion from the public sphere and her closer connection to nature. This doctrine of "separate spheres," however, reinforced the seventeenth-century masculinization of thought that had excluded "feminine modes of knowing, not from culture in general, but from the scientific and philosophical arenas, whose objectivity and

purity needed to be guaranteed" (Bordo 1986: 956). The result was that woman was regarded as the mediating form between nature and culture. Woman was "at times saintly and at times evil, but always she seems necessary as the counterpoint to man's self-definition as a being of pure rationality" (Fee, 1983: 12).

Men's pure rationality, in contrast to women's emotional nature, makes them suitable candidates for the pursuit of science. Therefore, science in the western world is a masculine endeavour and as a result,

the attributes of science are the attributes of males; the objectivity said to be characteristic of the production of scientific knowledge is specifically identified as a male way of relating to the world. Science is cold, hard, impersonal, "objective"; women, by contrast, are warm, soft, emotional, "subjective." (Fee, 1983: 12).

In addition, since science is seen to be a masculine endeavour, then "women in science are perceived as unfeminine," and any discussion of women scientists will usually be accompanied by assurances of their ability to be "graceful and feminine, good housekeepers and mothers."

The association of men with science does not mean that there have not been, or are no, women scientists. On the contrary, but the practice of science and the uses to which its findings have been put have largely been directed at controlling the natural and the social worlds in the interests of men. Ruth Hubbard points out, for example, that the scientific "proof" of women's essential nature was only partially applied to actual women and their work.

The ideology of women's nature that is invoked . . . would have us believe that a woman's capacity to become pregnant leaves her at all times physically disabled by comparison with men. The scientific underpinnings for these ideas were elaborated in the nineteenth century by the white, university-educated, mainly upper class men who made up the bulk of the new professions of obstetrics and gynecology, biology, psychology, sociology and anthropology (Hubbard, 1983: 5).

The idea of physical frailty of women was, however, confined to women of the upper classes, and Hubbard suggests that male professionals used the theory "to disqualify the girls and women of their own race and class who would be in competition with them for education and professional status and might also deprive them of the kinds of personal attention and services they were accustomed to receive from their mothers, wives, and sisters." Poor women as well as black women were noticeably excluded from concern over their possible frailty. In fact, their ability to "work so hard while bearing children was taken as a sign that these women were more animal-like and less highly evolved than upper-class women."

In the comments made above, it should not be assumed that some deliberate Machiavellian process has been involved in restricting science to the male domain. However, science has reinforced racist attitudes on occasion and has always promoted a dichotomized view of the sexes. It is the latter view, as Brown and Jordanov (1981) point out, that results in the "association of each sex with universal biological categories, as if all women and all men were really the same regardless of class or other social differences." Through the indentification of men with science and women with nature, "women were conceptualized as the passive recipients of scientific manipulation." The question therefore arises, "What interests were, and are, served by elaborating a set of biologically based, opposed categories which deliberately ignored (or conveniently obscured) social divisions?"

This question, in conjunction with the previous discussion, challenges the basic understanding of science as an objective body of knowledge pursued by unbiased, rational individuals. The theories and methods of science are supposed to be subject to continual re-examination and testing to ensure the validity of the knowledge obtained. Consequently, the researcher who follows the abstract rules could claim authority on the basis that the knowledge produced was objective knowledge. But in simply concentrating on the abstract rules of the game, the "scientific method" ignores the social context in which that method is developed and used. As indicated above, the development of science as objective and unbiased is compromised by its origins and unexamined assumptions. In addition, science is compromised by the day-to-day practice of science. The choice of research topic, the nature of the research tools, the interpretation of the data and the manner in which the results reach either the scientific community and/or the general public are some of the ways in which the genderization of science as theory and practice is maintained.

Feminist Reconstructions

The creation of knowledge is a central concern to feminism because knowledge creation means power. The issue is not simply the absence of women in knowledge creation or, when they are present, that they participate as marginal members of knowledge creation structure. More to the point, it is that their experiences of the world, and those of other subordinate, disadvantaged groups, have no part in the production of authoritative knowledge of the world. As Smith (1975: 365) remarks, "Women do not appear to men as men do to one another, as persons who might share in the common construction of social reality." In sum, women do not "name the world" (Daly 1978).

One of the tasks of feminist sociology, and feminist scholarship in general, is to assert the validity of women's experience of the world and to find ways of incorporating that experience into the "naming" or the definition of the nature of reality. The act of naming and defining is, as O'Brien points out, a way of organizing reality, and as long as "language and theory . . . are shot through with self-serving masculist assumptions," (O'Brien, 1982: 259) then feminist redefinition, or renaming, must always constitute "critical analysis." The exercise is both theoretical and practical, because the "images, vocabularies, concepts, knowledge of and methods of knowing the world are integral to the practice of power" and it is a ruling class of men who "produce for women, as well as for other members of society, the means to think and image." For example, the substitution of abstractions for human actions is a way of obscuring reality and ensuring control. Forces, factors, structures, constraints, processes and the like are some of the abstractions that can be used to describe and alter the meaning of human behaviour. The concealment of abstractions allows, for example, foot-binding, which crippled women, to be seen as an "erotic custom," and witch burning to become a "process of religious legitimation." The point is that abstractions mean that "no agent is named," and the scientist's invisibility and, by extension, his "objectivity" is maintained.

In looking at how feminism can reconstruct knowledge creation and use, one important challenge has been the insistence on the visibility of interested parties, whose interests be served by the construction and use of knowledge. The challenge asserts that, "The claim that science is value-free, objective and purely rational is ideology and not reality," (Benston, 1982) and that what is required is a reassertion of the humanist tradition that insists upon "the centrality of human interests and the primacy of human worth and development." What this means in immediate

tical terms is, according to Benston, the "investigation of the effect that the male/female split has had on scientific methodology and practice." The result of such investigations will produce "modes of rationality and scientific investigation that take into account both subjectivity and the interactions between the knower and the known in the context of care and responsibility for both natural processes and other creatures."

Miles (1982: 222) proposes an "integrative feminism" as the alternative to androcentric knowledge production. This involves the "affirmation of female-associated values," such as "caring, sharing, co-operation and solidarity," as the central features of a feminist epistemology. Miles acknowledges that "we are playing with fire when we accept our special historical identity with reproduction and caring, sharing, nurturing human values as an essential component of our specific political voice, [because] our specificity as women has in the past been inseparable from our oppression as women." Miles is not advocating a glorification or mystification of gynocentric values and behaviours, but she does suggest that the affirmation is the means to the articulation of "new and more universal truths — truths that will end narrow, single-sex definitions of the world, and in the process, feminize and humanize politics."

Hilde Hein (1981) concurs with Miles's view and suggests that women's contributions to science, on the basis of their specificity, are essential to the development of a "more universal and genderless science." The most important contribution that women can make will result from women's connectedness and contextual living in contrast to men. . . . The result of the contextual placing and experiences of women is that the normal science requirement that the scientist exclude self becomes "misplaced, if not meaningless." As a result, if the normal contextual relatedness of women were "to become universally normative, then the ego-detachment now seen as necessary for the very possibility of science and morality would be regarded as pathological." The celebration of ego, and the problem of alienation that it generates, would then become "deviations from an ideal of integrationism," and "ego-involvement would be a symptom of immaturity or incomplete organic development."

The incorporation of women's values associated with their biological specificity is, to some extent, in the idealist research tradition. For example, Weber insisted that value-relevance was integral to the selection of sociological topics: "as soon as we attempt to reflect about the way in which life confronts us in immediate concrete situations, it presents an infinite multiplicity of successively and coexistently emerging and disappearing events, both 'within' and 'outside' ourselves." This multiplicity means that in the study of "infinite reality" by the "finite human mind," only a part of it is seen to be "worthy of being known," and the selection of what is important or significant is the result of a "value-orientation towards these events." "The concept of culture is a *value-concept*. Empirical reality becomes "culture" to us because and insofar as we relate it to value ideas. . . ."

If it were simply a matter of value-relevance in the Weberian sense then the claims advanced for an integrative feminist approach to science could possibly be incorporated into a multi-paradigmatic conception of sociology. However, the claims go further than this, to encompass not only the "objects" of knowledge, but also the process by which they can be known. The "recognition of one's values, interests, intersubjectivity and status as a historical agent" is what enables feminists to gain a "more accurate view of the world" (Miles 1983: 9). In fact, it is "the recognition that no knowledge is ever separate from its context or is ever absolute" that "enables a fuller

understanding of reality." Integrative feminism is not simply the substitution of a female understanding for the current male viewpoint. Feminism escapes such relativism, according to Miles, by virtue of the fact that it is the viewpoint of outsiders to power, who therefore have a more accurate view of reality because they have no stake in mystifying that reality. In addition, because the "perspective on the world forged by a powerless group in struggle must necessarily be tested in practice for its accuracy and usefulness," then "limiting bias" is avoided.

Despite the strong claims for the non-relativity of an integrative feminism, several feminists have reservations about this position. Fox Keller (1981) maintains, "The essential goal of theory in general I take to be to represent our experience of the world in as comprehensive and inclusive a way as possible." In progressing towards that goal, she suggests that it is necessary to give up the simplistic "objective realist's dream of providing an error-free description of the world "out there." But in doing so it is not necessary to "give up on objectivity as a process." Consequently, changes will depend "less on the introduction of a specifically female culture into science than on a rethinking of sexual polarities and the abandonment of a sexual division of intellectual labor." Fox Keller agrees that feminists are in a privileged position in regard to the epistemological critique of science, but that the result cannot simply be changing the definition of science "to include more of what actually women do."

I would prefer to adhere to the traditional uses of the word science and argue instead that what is at issue is what is called "good" science. In effect I am arguing for changes in both the acculturation of women (and men) and in the definition of "good" science, and I see them as proceeding together. (Fox Keller, 1981).

Elizabeth Fee (1981) has also been cautious about the idea that the incorporation of female values, based on the reproductive specificity of women, into the scientific, theoretical enterprise is a sufficient, or even wise, course for feminism. Such theories, she suggests, are based on an acceptance of the traditional sex dichotomy that associates science with masculinity. The problem becomes "not one of making women more scientific, but of making science less masculine." This general aim becomes problematic to the extent that objectivity, associated with the masculine pursuit of knowledge, tends to get thrown out absolutely. . . . As a result, the feminist critique of science, and theory production in general, should not abandon "the ideal that we can come to an ever more complete understanding of the natural [and social] world through a collective and disciplined process of investigation and discovery."

It is clear that the debates among the feminist community on theory and epistemology do not present a unified, and therefore monolithic, front. Indeed, the vitality of feminism is captured in the diversity of these debates. In addition, the fact that the preceding discussion has taken the comments of a range of non-sociological "specialists" is a further indication of the rejection of traditional boundaries and hence of the stimulating nature of the feminist enterprise. Although the feminist critiques that challenge the mainstream ideas of what constitutes knowledge continue to take place more on the fringes of academic disciplines, increasingly the issues cannot be ignored. But current academic myopia is not crushing because feminism is not constrained by, or confined to, the academy with its specializations and separation of theory from practice. Dorothy Smith's point that feminism demands the construction of "a sociology for women rather than of women" is a central tenet for feminism and has the effect of initiating a discourse among women that transcends the traditional academic and knowledge boundaries. "The discourse of women opposes the development of forms of knowledge which presuppose the isolation of the subject, of knower, from the lived historical process of the everyday world — an isolation which the academy has been created to provide" (Smith, 1984: 10).

In many ways the feminist discourse in sociology continues the traditions of the "founding fathers." Their discourse also transcended the barriers and specialties characteristic of current academic knowledge creation. The works of the sociological fathers . . . represent the tip of the iceberg. There remains a potentially fruitful mine of information in other works by the same authors that is tantalizing in, for example, the manner in which they referred to and used each other's ideas. The dialogues among feminists represent a continuation of this theoretical tradition. What detractors might view as eclecticism seems to be more true of the initial presuppositions of the founding fathers. As such, those fathers, like many of their modern counterparts, would be amazed to find that it is the daughters rather than the sons who represent the most active and vital researchers at the present time. The "mothers" would be less surprised, and very proud.

THE MATERIALIST CONCEPTION OF HISTORY
Karl Marx

I was led by my studies to the conclusion that legal relations as well as forms of State could neither be understood by themselves, nor explained by the so-called general progress of the human mind, but that they are rooted in the material conditions

From *Karl Marx: Selected Writings in Sociology and Social Philosophy* by T. B. Bottomore and M. Rubel (eds.), Pitman Publishing Ltd., London. By permission of T. B. Bottomore.

of life, which are summed up by Hegel after the fashion of the English and French writers of the eighteenth century under the name *civil society*, and that the anatomy of civil society is to be sought in political economy. The study of the latter which I had begun in Paris, I continued in Brussels where I had emigrated on account of an explusion order issued by M. Guizot. The general conclusion at which I arrived and which, once reached, continued to serve as the guiding thread in my studies, may be formulated briefly as follows: In the social production which men carry on they enter into definite relations that are indispensable and independent of their will; these relations of production correspond to a definite stage of development of their material powers of production. The totality of these relations of production constitutes the economic structure of society — the real foundation, on which legal and political superstructures arise and to which definite forms of social consciousness correspond. The mode of production of material life determines the general character of the social, political, and spiritual processes of life. It is not the consciousness of men that determines their being, but, on the contrary, their social being determines their consciousness. At a certain stage of their development, the material forces of production in society come in conflict with the existing relations of production, or — what is but a legal expression for the same thing — with the property relations within which they had been at work before. From forms of development of the forces of production these relations turn into their fetters. Then occurs a period of social revolution. With the change of the economic foundation the entire immense superstructure is more or less rapidly transformed. In considering such transformations, the distinction should always be made between the material transformation of the economic conditions of production which can be determined with the preci-

sion of natural science, and the legal, political, religious, aesthetic or philosophical — in short, ideological — forms in which men become conscious of this conflict and fight it out. Just as our opinion of an individual is not based on what he thinks of himself, so can we not judge of such a period of tranformation by its own consciousness; on the contrary, this consciousness must rather be explained from the contradictions of material life, from the existing conflict between the social forces of production and the relations of production. No social order ever disappears before all the productive forces for which there is room in it have been developed; and new, higher relations of production never appear before the material conditions of their existence have matured in the womb of the old society. Therefore, mankind always sets itself only such problems as it can solve; since, on closer examination, it will always be found that the problem itself arises only when the material conditions necessary for its solution already exist or are at least in the process of formation. In broad outline we can designate the Asiatic, the ancient, the feudal, and the modern bourgeois modes of production as progressive epochs in the economic formation of society. The bourgeois relations of production are the last antagonistic form of the social process of production; not in the sense of individual antagonisms, but of conflict arising from conditions surrounding the life of individuals in society. At the same time the productive forces developing in the womb of bourgeois society create the material conditions for the solution of that antagonism. With this social formation, therefore, the prehistory of human society comes to an end.

The premises from which we begin are not arbitrary ones, not dogmas, but real premises from which abstraction can be made only in the imagination. They are real individuals, their activity and their material conditions of life, including those which they find already in existence and those produced by their activity. These premises can thus be established in a purely empirical way.

The first premise of all human history is, of course, the existence of living human individuals. The first fact to be established, therefore, is the physical constitution of these individuals and their consequent relation to the rest of Nature. Of course we cannot here investigate the actual physical nature of man or the natural conditions in which man finds himself — geological, oro-hydrographical, climatic and so on. All historiography must begin from these natural bases and their modification in the course of history by men's activity.

Men can be distinguished from animals by consciousness, by religion, or by anything one likes. They themselves begin to distinguish themselves from animals as soon as they begin to *produce* their means of subsistence, a step which is determined by their physical constitution. In producing their means of subsistence men indirectly produce their actual material life.

The way in which men produce their means of subsistence depends in the first place on the nature of the existing means which they have to reproduce. This mode of production should not be regarded simply as the reproduction of the physical existence of individuals. It is already a definite form of activity of these individuals, a definite way of expressing their life, a definite *mode of life.* As individuals express their life, so they are. What they are, therefore, coincides with their production, with *what* they produce and with *how* they produce it. What individuals are, therefore, depends on the material conditions of their production.

This conception of history, therefore, rests on the exposition of the real process of production, starting out from the simple material production of life, and on the comprehension of the form of intercourse connected with and created by this mode of production, i.e. of civil society in its various stages as the basis of all history, and also in its action as the State. From this starting point, it explains all the different theoretical productions and forms of consciousness, religion, philosophy, ethics, etc., and traces their origins and growth, by which means the matter can of course be displayed as a whole (and consequently, also the reciprocal action of these various sides on one another). Unlike the idealist view of history, it does not have to look for a category in each period, but remains constantly on the real ground of history; it does not explain practice from the idea but explains the formation of ideas from material practice, and accordingly comes to the conclusion that all the forms of and products of consciousness can be dissolved, not by intellectual criticism, not by resolution into "self-consciousness," or by transformation into "apparitions," "spectres," "fancies," etc., but only by the practical overthrow of the actual social relations which gave rise to this idealist humbug; that no criticism but revolution is the driving force of history, as well as of religion, philosophy, and all other types of theory. It shows that history does not end by being resolved into "self-consciousness," as "spirit of the spirit," but that at each stage of history there is found a material result, a sum of productive forces, a historically created relation of individuals to Nature and to one another, which is handed down to each generation from its predecessors, a mass of productive forces, capital, and circumstances, which is indeed modified by the new generation but which also prescribes for it its conditions of life and gives it a definite development, a special character. It shows that circumstances make men just as much as men make circumstances.

This sum of productive forces, capital,

and social forms of intercourse, which every individual and generation finds in existence as something given, is the real basis of what philosophers have conceived as "substance" and the "essence of man," and which they have deified or attacked. This real basis is not in the least disturbed, in its effect and influence on the development of men, by the fact that these philosophers, as "self-consciousness" and the "unique," revolt against it. These conditions of life, which different generations find in existence, also determine whether or not the periodically recurring revolutionary convulsion will be strong enough to overthrow the basis of the existing order. If the material elements of a total revolution — i.e. on the one hand, the available productive forces, and on the other, the formation of a revolutionary mass, which revolts not only against particular conditions of existing society but against the whole existing "production of life," the "total activity" on which it is based — are not present, then it is quite immaterial, as far as practical development is concerned, whether the *idea* of this revolution has been expressed a hundred times already, as is demonstrated by the history of communism.

The whole previous conception of history has either completely neglected this real basis of history or else has considered it a secondary matter without any connexion with the course of history. Consequently, history has always to be written in accordance with an external standard; the real production of life appears as ahistorical, while what is historical appears as separated from ordinary life, as supraterrestrial. Thus the relation of man to Nature is excluded from history and in this way the antithesis between Nature and history is established. The exponents of this conception of history have consequently only been able to see in history the political actions of princes and States, religious and all sorts of theoretical struggles, and in par-

ticular have been obliged to share in each historical epoch the *illusion of that epoch.* For instance, if an epoch imagines itself to be actuated by purely "political" or "religious" motives, although "religion" and "politics" are only forms of its true motives, the historian accepts this opinion. The "idea," the "conception" of these conditioned men about their real practice, is tranformed into the sole determining, active force, which controls and determines their practice. When the crude form in which the division of labour emerges among the Indians and the Egyptians engenders the caste system in their State and religion, the historian believes that the caste system is the power which has produced this crude social form. While the French and the English at least hold by the political illusion, which is moderately close to reality, the Germans move in the realm of "pure spirit," and make religious illusion the driving force of history.

The Hegelian philosophy of history is the last consequence, brought to its "purest expression," of all this German historiography, which is concerned, not with real, nor even with political, interests, but with pure thoughts, which inevitably appear . . . as a series of "thoughts" which devour one another and are finally swallowed up in "self-consciousness. . . ."

WHAT IS A SOCIAL FACT?
Emile Durkheim

Before inquiring into the method suited to the study of social facts, it is important to know which facts are commonly called "so-

Reprinted with permission of The Free Press, a Division of Macmillan, Inc. from Emile Durkheim, *The Rules of Sociological Method* translated by Sarah A. Solovay and John H. Mueller. Edited by George E. G. Catlin. Copyright 1938 by George E. G. Catlin; copyright renewed 1966 by Sarah A. Solovay, John H. Mueller, and George E. G. Catlin.

cial." This information is all the more necessary since the designation "social" is used with little precision. It is currently employed for practically all phenomena generally diffused within society, however small their social interest. But on that basis, there are, as it were, no human events that may not be called social. Each individual drinks, sleeps, eats, reasons; and it is to society's interest that these functions be exercised in an orderly manner. If, then, all these facts are counted as "social" facts, sociology would have no subject matter exclusively its own, and its domain would be confused with that of biology and psychology.

But in reality there is in every society a certain group of phenomena which may be differentiated from those studied by the other natural sciences. When I fulfill my obligations as brother, husband, or citizen, when I execute my contracts, I perform duties which are defined, externally to myself and my acts, in law and in custom. Even if they conform to my own sentiments and I feel their reality subjectively, such reality is still objective, for I did not create them; I merely inherited them through my education. How many times it happens, moreover, that we are ignorant of the details of the obligations incumbent upon us, and that in order to acquaint ourselves with them we must consult the law and its authorized interpreters! Similarly, the church-member finds the beliefs and practices of his religious life ready-made at birth; their existence prior to his own implies their existence outside of himself. The system of signs I use to express my thought, the system of currency I employ to pay my debts, the instruments of credit I utilize in my commerical relations, the practices followed in my profession, etc., function independently of my own use of them. And these statements can be repeated for each member of society. Here, then, are ways of acting, thinking, and feeling that present the noteworthy property of existing outside the individual consciousness.

These types of conduct or thought are not only external to the individual but are, moreover, endowed with coercive power, by virtue of which they impose themselves upon him, independent of his individual will. Of course, when I fully consent and conform to them, this constraint is felt only slightly, if at all, and is therefore unnecessary. But it is, nontheless, an intrinsic characteristic of these facts, the proof thereof being that it asserts itself as soon as I attempt to resist it. If I attempt to violate the law, it reacts against me so as to prevent my act before its accomplishment, or to nullify my violation by restoring the damage, if it is accomplished and reparable, or to make me expiate it if it cannot be compensated for otherwise.

In the case of purely moral maxims, the public conscience exercises a check on every act which offends it by means of the surveillance it exercises over the conduct of citizens, and the appropriate penalties at its disposal. In many cases the constraint is less violent, but nevertheless it always exists. If I do not submit to the conventions of society, if in my dress I do not conform to the customs observed in my country and in my class, the ridicule I provoke, the social isolation in which I am kept, produce, although in an attenuated form, the same effects as a punishment in the strict sense of the word. The constraint is nonetheless efficacious for being indirect. I am not obliged to speak French with my fellow-countrymen nor to use the legal currency, but I cannot possibly do otherwise. If I tried to escape this necessity, my attempt would fail miserably. As an industrialist, I am free to apply the technical methods of former centuries; but by doing so, I should invite certain ruin. Even when I free myself from these rules and violate them successfully, I am always compelled to struggle with them. When finally overcome, they make their constraining power sufficiently felt by the resistance they offer. The enterprises of all innovators, including successful ones, come up against resistance of this kind.

Here, then, is a category of facts with very distinctive characteristics; it consists of ways of acting, thinking, and feeling external to the individual, and endowed with a power of coercion, by reason of which they control him. These ways of thinking could not be confused with biological phenomena, since they consist of representations and of actions; nor with psychological phenomena, which exist only in the individual consciousness and through it. They constitute, thus, a new variety of phenomena; and it is to them exclusively that the term "social" ought to be applied. And this term fits them quite well, for it is clear that, since their source is not in the individual, their substratum can be no other than society, either the political society as a whole or some one of the partial groups it includes, such as religious denominations, political, literary, and occupational associations, etc. On the other hand, this term "social" applies to them exclusively, for it has a distinct meaning only if it designates exclusively the phenomena which are not included in any of the categories of facts that have already been established and classified. These ways of thinking and acting therefore constitute the proper domain of sociology. It is true that, when we define them with this word "constraint," we risk shocking the zealous partisans of absolute individualism. For those who profess the complete autonomy of the individual, man's dignity is diminished whenever he is made to feel that he is not completely self-determinant. It is generally accepted today, however, that most of our ideas and our tendencies are not developed by ourselves but come to us from without. How can they become a part of us except by imposing themselves upon us? This is the whole meaning of our definition. And it is gener-

ally accepted, moreover, that social constraint is not necessarily incompatible with the individual personality.

Since the examples that we have just cited (legal and moral regulations, religious faiths, financial systems, etc.) all consist of established beliefs and practices, one might be led to believe that social facts exist only where there is some social organization. But there are other facts without such crystallized form which have the same objectivity and the same ascendency over the individual. These are called "social currents." Thus the great movements of enthusiasm, indignation, and pity in a crowd do not originate in any one of the particular individual consciousnesses. They come to each one of us from without and can carry us away in spite of ourselves. Of course, it may happen that, in abandoning myself to them unreservedly, I do not feel the pressure they exert upon me. But it is revealed as soon as I try to resist them. Let an individual attempt to oppose one of these collective manifestations and the emotions that he denies will turn against him. Now, if this power of external coercion asserts itself so clearly in cases of resistance, it must exist also in the first-mentioned cases, although we are unconscious of it. We are then victims of the illusion of having ourselves created that which actually forced itself from without. If the complacency with which we permit ourselves to be carried along conceals the pressure undergone, nevertheless it does not abolish it. Thus, air is no less heavy because we do not detect its weight. So, even if we ourselves have spontaneously contributed to the production of the common emotion, the impression we have received differs markedly from that which we would have experienced if we had been alone. Also, once the crowd has dispersed, that is, once these social influences have ceased to act upon us and we are alone again, the emotions which have passed through the mind appear strange to us, and we no longer recognize them as ours. We realize that these feelings have been impressed upon us to a much greater extent than they were created by us. It may even happen that they horrify us, so much were they contrary to our nature. Thus, a group of individuals, most of whom are perfectly inoffensive, may, when gathered in a crowd, be drawn into acts of atrocity. And what we say of these transitory outbursts applies similarly to those more permanent currents of opinion on religious, political, literary, or artistic matters which are constantly being formed around us, whether in society as a whole or in more limited circles.

To confirm this definition of the social fact by a characteristic illustration from common experience, one need only observe the manner in which children are brought up. Considering the facts as they are and as they have always been, it becomes immediately evident that all education is a continuous effort to impose on the child ways of seeing, feeling, and acting which he could not have arrived at spontaneously. From the very first hours of his life, we compel him to eat, drink, and sleep at regular hours; we constrain him to cleanliness, calmness, and obedience; later we exert pressure upon him in order that he may learn proper consideration for others, respect for customs and conventions, the need for work, etc. If, in time, this constraint ceases to be felt, it is because it gradually gives rise to habits and to internal tendencies that render constraint unnecessary; but nevertheless it is not abolished, for it is still the source from which these habits were derived. It is true that, according to Spencer, a rational education ought to reject such methods, allowing the child to act in complete liberty; but as this pedagogic theory has never been applied by any known people, it must be accepted only as an expression of personal

opinion, not as a fact which can contradict the aforementioned observations. What makes these facts particularly instructive is that the aim of education is, precisely, the socialization of the human being; the process of education, therefore, gives us in a nutshell the historical fashion in which the social being is constituted. This unremitting pressure to which the child is subjected is the very pressure of the social milieu which tends to fashion him in its own image, and of which parents and teachers are merely the representatives and intermediaries.

It follows that sociological phenomena cannot be defined by their universality. A thought which we find in every individual consciousness, a movement repeated by all individuals, is not thereby a social fact. If sociologists have been satisfied with defining them by this characteristic, it is because they confused them with what one might call their reincarnation in the individual. It is, however, the collective aspects of the beliefs, tendencies, and practices of a group that characterize truly social phenomena. As for the forms that the collective states assume when refracted in the individual, these are things of another sort. This duality is clearly demonstrated by the fact that these two orders of phenomena are frequently found dissociated from one another. Indeed, certain of these social manners of acting and thinking acquire, by reason of their repetition, a certain rigidity which on its own account crystallizes them, so to speak, and isolates them from the particular events which reflect them. They thus acquire a body, a tangible form, and constitute a reality in their own right, quite distinct from the individual facts which produce it. Collective habits are inherent not only in the successive acts which they determine but, by a privilege of which we find no example in the biological realm, they are given permanent expression in a formula which is repeated from mouth to mouth, transmitted by education, and fixed even in writing.

Such is the origin and nature of legal and moral rules, popular aphorisms and proverbs, articles of faith wherein religious or political groups condense their beliefs, standards of taste established by literary schools, etc. None of these can be found entirely reproduced in the applications made of them by individuals, since they can exist even without being actually applied. . . .

We thus arrive at the point where we can formulate and delimit in a precise way the domain of sociology. It comprises only a limited group of phenomena. A social fact is to be recognized by the power of external coercion which it exercises or is capable of exercising over individuals, and the presence of this power may be recognized in its turn either by the existence of some specific sanction or by the resistance offered against every individual effort that tends to violate it. One can, however, define it also by its diffusion within the group, provided that, in conformity with our previous remarks, one takes care to add as a second and essential characteristic that its own existence is independent of the individual forms it assumes in its diffusion. This last criterion is perhaps, in certain cases, easier to apply than the preceding one. In fact, the constraint is easy to ascertain when it expresses itself externally by some direct reaction of society, as is the case in law, morals, beliefs, customs, and even fashions. But when it is only indirect, like the constraint which an economic organization exercises, it cannot always be so easily detected. Generality combined with externality may, then, be easier to establish. Moreover, this second definition is but another form of the first; for if a mode of behaviour whose existence is external to individual consciousnesses becomes gen-

eral, this can only be brought about by its being imposed upon them.

But these several phenomena present the same characteristic by which we defined the others. These "ways of existing" are imposed on the individual precisely in the same fashion as the "ways of acting" of which we have spoken. Indeed, when we wish to know how a society is divided politically, of what these divisions themselves are composed, and how complete is the fusion existing between them, we shall not achieve our purpose by physical inspection and by geographical observations; for these phenomena are social, even when they have some basis in physical nature. It is only by a study of public law that a comprehension of this organization is possible, for it is this law that determines the organization, as it equally determines our domestic and civil relations. This political organization is, then, no less obligatory than the social facts mentioned above. If the population crowds into our cities instead of scattering into the country, this is due to a trend of public opinion, a collective drive that imposes this concentration upon the individuals. We can no more choose the style of our houses than of our clothing — at least, both are equally obligatory. The channels of communication prescribe the direction of internal migrations and commerce, etc., and even their extent. Consequently, at the very most, it should be necessary to add to the list of phenomena which we have enumerated as presenting the distinctive criterion of a social fact only one additional category, "ways of existing"; and, as this enumeration was not meant to be rigorously exhaustive, the addition would not be absolutely necessary.

Such an addition is perhaps not necessary, for these "ways of existing" are only crystallized "ways of acting." The political structure of a society is merely the way in which its component segments have become accustomed to live with one another. If their relations are traditionally intimate, the segments tend to fuse with one another, or, in the contrary case, to retain their identity. The type of habitation imposed upon us is merely the way in which our contemporaries and our ancestors have been accustomed to construct their houses. The methods of communication are merely the channels which the regular currents of commerce and migrations have dug, by flowing in the same direction. . . .

Our definition will then include the whole relevant range of facts if we say: *A social fact is every way of acting, fixed or not, capable of exercising on the individual an external constraint; or again, every way of acting which is general throughout a given society, while at the same time existing in its own right independent of its individual manifestations.*

THE FUNDAMENTAL CONCEPTS OF SOCIOLOGY

Max Weber

The Definitions of Sociology and of Social Action

I. Sociology (in the sense in which this highly ambiguous word is used here) is a science which attempts the interpretive understanding of social action in order thereby to arrive at a causal explanation of its course and effects. In "action" is included all human behaviour when and in so far as the acting individual attaches a subjective meaning to it. Action in this sense

Reprinted with permission of The Free Press, a Division of Macmillan, Inc. from Max Weber, *The Theory of Social and Economic Organization* translated by A. M. Henderson and Talcott Parsons. Edited by Talcott Parsons. Copyright 1947, renewed 1975 by Talcott Parsons.

may be either overt or purely inward or subjective; it may consist of positive intervention in a situation, or of deliberately refraining from such intervention or passively acquiescing in the situation. Action is social in so far as, by virtue of the subjective meaning attached to it by the acting individual (or individuals), it takes account of the behaviour of others and is thereby oriented in its course.

(a) The Methodological Foundations of Sociology

1. "Meaning" may be of two kinds. The term may refer first to the actual existing meaning in the given concrete case of a particular actor, or to the average or approximate meaning attributable to a given plurality of actors; or secondly to the theoretically conceived *pure type* of subjective meaning attributed to the hypothetical actor or actors in a given type of action. In no case does it refer to an objectively "correct" meaning or one which is "true" in some metaphysical sense. It is this which distinguishes the empirical sciences of action, such as sociology and history, from the dogmatic disciplines in that area, such as jurisprudence, logic, ethics, and esthetics, which seek to ascertain the "true" and "valid" meanings associated with the objects of their investigation.

2. The line between meaningful action and merely reactive behaviour to which no subjective meaning is attached cannot be sharply drawn empirically. A very considerable part of all sociologically relevant behaviour, especially purely traditional behaviour, is marginal between the two. In the case of many psychophysical processes, meaningful, i.e. subjectively understandable, action is not to be found at all; in others it is discernible only by the expert psychologist. Many mystical experiences which cannot be adequately communi-

cated in words are, for a person who is not susceptible to such experiences, not fully understandable. At the same time the ability to imagine one's self performing a similar action is not a necessary prerequisite to understanding; "one need not have been Caesar in order to understand Caesar." For the verifiable accuracy of interpretation of the meaning of a phenomenon, it is a great help to be able to put one's self imaginatively in the place of the actor and thus sympathetically to participate in his experiences, but this is not an essential condition of meaningful interpretation. Understandable and nonunderstandable components of a process are often intermingled and bound up together.

3. All interpretation of meaning, like all scientific observation, strives for clarity and verifiable accuracy of insight and comprehension (*Evidenz*). The basis for certainty in understanding can be either rational, which can be further subdivided into logical and mathematical, or it can be of an emotionally empathic or artistically appreciative quality. In the sphere of action things are rationally evident chiefly when we attain a completely clear intellectual grasp of the action-elements in their intended context of meaning. Empathic or appreciative accuracy is attained when, through sympathetic participation, we can adequately grasp the emotional context in which the action took place. The highest degree of rational understanding is attained in cases involving the meanings of logically or mathematically related propositions; their meaning may be immediately and unambiguously intelligible. We have a perfectly clear understanding of what it means when somebody employs the proposition $2 \times 2 = 4$ or the Pythagorean theorem in reasoning or argument, or when someone correctly carries out a logical train of reasoning according to our accepted modes of thinking. In the same way we also understand what a person is doing when he tries to achieve certain ends by choosing appropriate means on the basis of the facts of the situation as experience has accustomed us to interpret them. Such an interpretation of this type of rationally purposeful action possesses, for the understanding of the choice of means, the highest degree of verifiable certainty. With a lower degree of certainty, which is, however, adequate for most purposes of explanation, we are able to understand errors, including confusion of problems of the sort that we ourselves are liable to, or the origin of which we can detect by sympathetic self-analysis.

On the other hand, many ultimate ends or values toward which experience shows that human action may be oriented, often cannot be understood completely, though sometimes we are able to grasp them intellectually. The more radically they differ from our own ultimate values, however, the more difficult it is for us to make them understandable by imaginatively participating in them. Depending upon the circumstances of the particular case we must be content either with a purely intellectual understanding of such values or when even that fails, sometimes we must simply accept them as given data. Then we can try to understand the action motivated by them on the basis of whatever opportunities for approximate emotional and intellectual interpretation seem to be available at different points in its course. These difficulties apply, for instance, for people not susceptible to the relevant values, to many unusual acts of religious and charitable zeal; also certain kinds of extreme rationalistic fanaticism of the type involved in some forms of the ideology of the "rights of man" are in a similar position for people who radically repudiate such points of view.

The more we ourselves are susceptible to them the more readily can we imaginatively participate in such emotional reactions as anxiety, anger, ambition, envy, jealousy, love, enthusiasm, pride, vengefulness, loyalty, devotion, and appetites of all sorts, and thereby understand the irrational conduct which grows out of them. Such conduct is "irrational," that is, from the point of view of the rational pursuit of a given end. Even when such emotions are found in a degree of intensity of which the observer himself is completely incapable, he can still have a significant degree of emotional understanding of their meaning and can interpret intellectually their influence on the course of action and the selection of means.

For the purposes of a typological scientific analysis it is convenient to treat all irrational, affectually determined elements of behaviour as factors of deviation from a conceptually pure type of rational action. For example a panic on the stock exchange can be most conveniently analysed by attempting to determine first what the course of action would have been if it had not been influenced by irrational affects; it is then possible to introduce the irrational components as accounting for the observed deviations from this hypothetical course. Similarly, in analysing a political or military campaign it is convenient to determine in the first place what would have been a rational course, given the ends of the participants and adequate knowledge of all the circumstances. Only in this way is it possible to assess the causal significance of irrational factors as accounting for the deviations from this type. The construction of a purely rational course of action in such cases serves the sociologist as a type ("ideal type") which has the merit of clear understandability and lack of ambiguity. By comparison with this it is possible to understand the ways in which actual action is influenced by irrational factors of all sorts, such as effects and errors, in that they account for the deviation from the line of conduct which would be expected on the hypothesis that the action were purely rational.

Only in this respect and for these reasons of methodological convenience, is the method of sociology "rationalistic." It is naturally not legitimate to interpret this procedure as involving a "rationalistic bias" of sociology, but only as a methodological device. It certainly does not involve a belief in the actual predominance of rational elements in human life, for on the question of how far this predominance does or does not exist, nothing whatever has been said. That there is, however, a danger of rationalistic interpretations where they are out of place naturally cannot be denied. All experience unfortunately confirms the existence of this danger. . . .

5. Understanding may be of two kinds: the first is the direct observational understanding of the subjective meaning of a given act as such, including verbal utterances. We thus understand by direct observation, in this sense, the meaning of the proposition $2 \times 2 = 4$ when we hear or read it. This is a case of the direct rational understanding of ideas. We also understand an outbreak of anger as manifested by facial expression, exclamations or irrational movements. This is direct observational understanding of irrational emotional reactions. We can understand in a similar observational way the action of a woodcutter or of somebody who reaches for the knob to shut a door or who aims a gun at an animal. This is rational observational understanding of actions.

Understanding may, however, be of another sort, namely explanatory understanding. Thus we understand in terms of *motive* the meaning an actor attaches to the proposition twice two equals four, when he states it or writes it down, in that we understand what makes him do this at precisely this moment and in these circumstances. Understanding in this sense is attained if we know that he is engaged in balancing a ledger or in making a scientific demonstration, or is engaged in some other task of which this particular act would be an appropriate part. This is rational understanding of motivation, which consists in placing the act in an intelligible and more inclusive context of meaning. Thus we understand the chopping of wood or aiming of a gun in terms of motive in addition to direct observation if we know that the woodchopper is working for a wage or is chopping a supply of firewood for his own use or possibly is doing it for recreation. But he might also be "working off" a fit of rage, an irrational case. Similarly we understand the movtive of a person aiming a gun if we know that he has been commanded to shoot as a member of a firing squad, that he is fighting against an enemy, or that he is doing it for revenge. The last is affectually determined and thus in a certain sense irrational. Finally we have a motivational understanding of the outburst of anger if we know that it has been provoked by jealousy, injured pride, or an insult. The last examples are all affectually determined and hence derived from irrational motives. In all the above cases the particular act has been placed in an understandable sequence of motivation, the understanding of which can be treated as an explanation of the actual course of behaviour. Thus for a science which is concerned with the subjective meaning of action, explanation requires a grasp of the complex of meaning in which an actual course of understandable action thus interpreted belongs. In all such cases, even where the processes are largely affectual, the subjective meaning of the action, including that also of the relevant meaning complexes, will be called the "intended" meaning. This involves a departure from ordinary usage, which speaks of intention in this sense only in the case of rationally purposive action. . . .

10. It is customary to designate various sociological generalizations, as for example "Gresham's Law," as scientific "laws." These are in fact typical probabilities confirmed by observation to the effect that under certain given conditions an expected course of social action will occur, which is understandable in terms of the typical motives and typical subjective intentions of the actors. These generalizations are both understandable and definite in the highest degree in so far as the typically observed course of action can be understood in terms of the purely rational pursuit of an end, or where for reasons of methodological convenience such a theoretical type can be heuristically employed. In such cases the relations of means and end will be clearly understandable on grounds of experience, particularly where the choice of means was "inevitable." In such cases it is legitimate to assert that in so far as the action was rigorously rational it could not have taken any other course because for technical reasons, given their clearly defined ends, no other means were available to the actors. This very case demonstrates how erroneous it is to regard any kind of "psychology" as the ultimate foundation of the sociological interpretation of action. The term "psychology," to be sure, is today understood in a wide variety of senses. For certain quite specific methodological purposes the type of treatment which attempts to follow the procedures of the natural sciences employs a distinction between "physical" and "psychic" phenomena which is entirely foreign to the disciplines concerned with human action, at least in the present sense. The results of a type of psychological investigation which employs the methods of the natural sciences in any one of various possible ways may naturally, like the results of any other science, have, in specific contexts, outstanding significance for sociological problems; indeed this has often happened. But this use of the results of psychology is something quite different from the investigation of human behaviour in terms of its subjective meaning. Hence sociology has no closer logical relationship

on a general analytical level to this type of psychology than to any other science. The source of error lies in the concept of the "psychic." It is held that everything which is not physical is *ipso facto* psychic, but that the *meaning* of a train of mathematical reasoning which a person carries out is not in the relevant sense "psychic." Similarly the rational deliberation of an actor as to whether the results of a given proposed course of action will or will not promote certain specific interests, and the corresponding decision, do not become one bit more understandable by taking "psychological" considerations into account. But it is precisely on the basis of such rational assumptions that most of the laws of sociology, including those of economics, are built up. On the other hand, in explaining the irrationalities of action sociologically, that form of psychology which employs the method of subjective understanding undoubtedly can make decisively important contributions. But this does not alter the fundamental methodological situation.

11. It has continually been assumed as obvious that the science of sociology seeks to formulate type concepts and generalized uniformities of empirical process. This distinguishes it from history, which is oriented to the causal analysis and explanation of individual actions, structures, and personalities possessing cultural significance. The empirical material which underlies the concepts of sociology consists to a very large extent, though by no means exclusively, of the same concrete processes of action which are dealt with by historians. Among the various bases on which its concepts are formulated and its generalizations worked out is an attempt to justify its important claim to be able to make a contribution to the causal explanation of some historically and culturally important phenomenon. As in the case of every generalizing science the abstract character of the concepts of sociology is responsible for the fact that, compared with actual historical reality, they are relatively lacking in fullness of concrete content. To compensate for this disadvantage, sociological analysis can offer a greater precision of concepts. This precision is obtained by striving for the highest possible degree of adequacy on the level of meaning in accordance with the definition of that concept put forward above. It has already been repeatedly stressed that this aim can be realized in a particularly high degree in the case of concepts and generalizations which formulate rational processes. But sociological investigation attempts to include in its scope various irrational phenomena, as well as prophetic, mystic, and affectual modes of action, formulated in terms of theoretical concepts which are adequate on the level of meaning. In *all* cases, rational or irrational, sociological analysis both abstracts from reality and at the same time helps us to understand it, in that it shows with what degree of approximation a concrete historical phenomenon can be subsumed under one or more of these concepts. For example, the same historical phenomenon may be in one aspect "feudal," in another "patrimonial," in another "bureaucratic," and in still another "charismatic." In order to give a precise meaning to these terms, it is necessary for the sociologist to formulate pure ideal types of the corresponding forms of action which in each case involve the highest possible degree of logical integration by virtue of their complete adequacy on the level of meaning. But precisely because this is true, it is probably seldom if ever that a real phenomenon can be found which corresponds exactly to one of these ideally constructed pure types. The case is similar to a physical reaction which has been calculated on the assumption of an absolute vacuum. Theoretical analysis in the field of sociology is possible only in terms of such pure types. It goes without saying that in addition it is conven-

ient for the sociologist from time to time to employ average types of an empirical statistical character. These are concepts which do not require methodological discussion at this point. But when reference is made to "typical" cases, the term should always be understood, unless otherwise stated, as meaning *ideal* types, which may in turn be rational or irrational as the case may be (thus in economic theory they are always rational), but in any case are always constructed with a view to adequacy on the level of meaning.

It is important to realize that in the sociological field as elsewhere, averages, and hence average types, can be formulated with a relative degree of precision only where they are concerned with differences of degree in respect to action which remains qualitatively the same. Such cases do occur, but in the majority of cases of action important to history or sociology the motives which determine it are qualitatively heterogeneous. Then it is quite impossible to speak of an "average" in the true sense. The ideal types of social action which for instance are used in economic theory are thus "unrealistic" or abstract in that they always ask what course of action would take place if it were purely rational and oriented to economic ends alone. But this construction can be used to aid in the understanding of action not purely economically determined but which involve deviations arising from traditional restraints, affects, errors, and the intrusion of other than economic purposes or considerations. This can take place in two ways. First, in analysing the extent to which in the concrete case, or on the average for a class of cases, the action was in part economically determined along with the other factors. Secondly, by throwing the discrepancy between the actual course of events and the ideal type into relief the analysis of the non-economic motives actually involved is facilitated. The procedure would

be very similar in employing an ideal type of mystical orientation with its appropriate attitude of indifference to worldly things, as a tool for analysing its consequences for the actor's relation to ordinary life; for instance, to political or economic affairs. The more sharply and precisely the ideal type has been constructed, thus the more abstract and unrealistic in this sense it is, the better it is able to perform its methodological functions in formulating the clarification of terminology, and in the formulation of classifications, and of hypotheses. In working out a concrete causal explanation of individual events, the procedure of the historian is essentially the same. Thus in attempting to explain the campaign of 1866, it is indispensable both in the case of Moltke and of Benedek to attempt to construct imaginatively how each, given fully adequate knowledge both of his own situation and of that of his opponent, would have acted. Then it is possible to compare with this the actual course of action and to arrive at a causal explanation of the observed deviations, which will be attributed to such factors as misinformation, strategical errors, logical fallacies, personal temperament, or considerations outside the realm of strategy. Here, too, an ideal-typical construction of rational action is actually employed even though it is not made explicit.

The theoretical concepts of sociology are ideal types not only from the objective point of view, but also in their application to subjective processes. In the great majority of cases actual action goes on in a state of inarticulate half-consciousness or actual unconsciousness of its subjective meaning. The actor is more likely to "be aware" of it in a vague sense than he is to "know" what he is doing or be explicitly self-conscious about it. In most cases his action is governed by impulse or habit. Only occasionally and, in the uniform action of large numbers often only in the case of a few individuals, is the subjective meaning of the action, whether rational or irrational brought clearly into consciousness. The ideal type of meaningful action where the meaning is fully conscious and explicit is a marginal case. Every sociological or historical investigation, in applying its analysis to the empirical facts, must take this fact into account. But the difficulty need not prevent the sociologist from systematizing his concepts by the classification of possible types of subjective meaning. That is, he may reason as if action actually proceeded on the basis of clearly self-conscious meaning. The resulting deviation from the concrete facts must continually be kept in mind whenever it is a question of this level of concreteness, and must be carefully studied with reference both to degree and kind. It is often necessary to choose between terms which are either clear or unclear. Those which are clear will, to be sure, have the abstractness of ideal types, but they are none the less preferable for scientific purposes.

(b) The Concept of Social Action

1. Social action, which includes both failure to act and passive acquiescence, may be oriented to the past, present, or expected future behaviour of others. Thus it may be motivated by revenge for a past attack, defence against present, or measures of defence against future aggression. The "others" may be individual persons, and may be known to the actor as such, or may constitute an indefinite plurality and may be entirely unknown as individuals. Thus "money" is a means of exchange which the actor accepts in payment because he orients his action to the expectation that a large but unknown number of individuals he is personally unacquainted with will be ready to accept it in exchange on some future occasion.

2. Not every kind of action, even of overt action, is "social" in the sense of the present discussion. Overt action is non-social if it is oriented solely to the behaviour of inanimate objects. Subjective attitudes constitute social action only so far as they are oriented to the behaviour of others. For example, religious behaviour is not social if it is simply a matter of contemplation or of solitary prayer. The economic activity of an individual is only social if, and then only in so far as, it takes account of the behaviour of someone else. Thus very generally in formal terms it becomes social in so far as the actor's actual control over economic goods is respected by others. Concretely it is social, for instance, if in relation to the actor's own consumption the future wants of others are taken into account and this becomes one consideration affecting the actor's own saving. Or, in another connexion, production may be oriented to the future wants of other people.

3. Not every type of contact of human beings has a social character; this is rather confined to cases where the actor's behaviour is meaningfully oriented to that of others. For example, a mere collision of two cyclists may be compared to a natural event. On the other hand, their attempt to avoid hitting each other, or whatever insults, blows, or friendly discussion might follow the collision, would constitute "social action."

4. Social action is not identical either with the similar actions of many persons or with action influenced by other persons. Thus, if at the beginning of a shower a number of people on the street put up their umbrellas at the same time, this would not ordinarily be a case of action mutually oriented to that of each other, but rather of all reacting in the same way to the like need of protection from the rain. It is well known that the actions of the individual are strongly influenced by the mere fact that he is a member of a crowd confined within a limited space. Thus, the subject matter of

studies of "crowd psychology," such as those of Le Bon, will be called "action conditioned by crowds." It is also possible for large numbers, though dispersed, to be influenced simultaneously or successively by a source of influence operating similarly on all the individuals, as by means of the press. Here also the behaviour of an individual is influenced by his membership in the crowd and by the fact that he is aware of being a member. Some types of reaction are only made possible by the mere fact that the individual acts as part of a crowd. Others become more difficult under these conditions. Hence it is possible that a particular event or mode of human behaviour can give rise to the most diverse kinds of feeling — gaiety, anger, enthusiasm, despair, and passions of all sorts — in a crowd situation which would not occur at all or not nearly so readily if the individual were alone. But for this to happen there need not, at least in many cases, be any meaningful relation between the behaviour of the individual and the fact that he is a member of a crowd. It is not proposed in the present sense to call action "social" when it is merely a result of the effect on the individual of the existence of a crowd as such and the action is not oriented to that fact on the level of meaning. At the same time the borderline is naturally highly indefinite. In such cases as that of the influence of the demagogue, there may be a wide variation in the extent to which his mass clientele is affected by a meaningful reaction to the fact of its large numbers; and whatever this relation may be, it is open to varying interpretations.

But furthermore, mere "imitation" of the action of others, such as that on which Tarde has rightly laid emphasis, will not be considered a case of specifically social action if it is purely reactive so that there is no meaningful orientation to the actor imitated. The borderline is, however, so indefinite that it is often hardly possible to discriminate. The mere fact that a person is found to employ some apparently useful procedure which he learned from someone else does not, however, constitute, in the present sense, social action. Action such as this is not oriented to the action of the other person, but the actor has, through observing the other, become acquainted with certain objective facts; and it is these to which his action is oriented. His action is then *causally* determined by the action of others, but not meaningfully. On the other hand, if the action of others is imitated because it is "fashionable" or traditional or exemplary, or lends social distinction, or on similar grounds, it is meaningfully oriented either to the behaviour of the source of imitation or of third persons or of both. There are of course all manner of transitional cases between the two types of imitation. Both the phenomena discussed above, the behaviour of crowds and imitation, stand on the indefinite borderline of social action. The same is true, as will often appear, of traditionalism and charisma. The reason for the indefiniteness of the line in these and other cases lies in the fact that both the orientation to the behaviour of others and the meaning which can be imputed to the actor himself are by no means always capable of clear determination and are often altogether unconscious and seldom fully self-conscious. Mere "influence" and meaningful orientation cannot therefore always be clearly differentiated on the empirical level. But conceptually it is essential to distinguish them, even though merely "reactive" imitation may well have a degree of sociological importance at least equal to that of the type which can be called social action in the strict sense. Sociology, it goes without saying, is by no means confined to the study of "social action"; this is only, at least for the kind of sociology being developed here, its central subject matter, that which may be said to be decisive for its status as a science. But this does not imply any judgment on the comparative importance of this and other factors.

chapter

2

Doing Sociology

Whether sociology is or can be a science in the same way as physics or chemistry is a matter of considerable debate. For now it is enough to recognize that sociology is a science in the sense that it conforms to the norms of the scientific method. Whatever the methods they use and the arguments they have about the appropriate methodology to study human behaviour, there are few sociologists who do not think that the sociological enterprise means, as in the natural sciences, combining reason and observation — theory and research — and making public the findings of their research and allowing them to be scrutinized and challenged by other researchers and further research. It is through this process that, ideally, a particular theory is at times strengthened, at times modified and at times rejected.

In this chapter we can only provide you with a few examples of how sociologists go about "doing sociology." In a sense, the whole of this reader can be seen as a variety of illustrations of how sociologists go about their business or think about how they should do so. The list of "Related Readings," below, is illustrative rather than exhaustive. In this chapter we provide you with four selections, all of which are quite different. One is *about* sociological research and two are intended to demonstrate rather different aspects of the sociological enterprise in practice or action. The final selection tells you something of the limits of survey research as a tool for formulating social policy.

The first selection is a much-abridged article written for the "State of the Art" issue of *The Canadian Review of Sociology and Anthropology* in 1985. In this article Alfred Hunter of McMaster University makes the case for the use of quantitative methods in sociology but does so through consideration of the debate you have just encountered in Chapter 1: whether sociological research should be qualitative or quantitative in its approach. The part of his article we have left out describes and assesses a number of statistical techniques currently in use by sociologists. These go far beyond the scope of an introductory, perhaps any undergraduate, course. In the excerpts we have included, Hunter makes the case for the use of quantitative approaches, particularly if there is a close and genuine linkage between theory and research. At the same time he notes the limitations of these approaches.

The second selection, by Gary Bowden of the University of New Brunswick, is, we think, a good illustration of the kind of positivist sociology Alfred Hunter is promoting. Bowden was interested in testing empirically one of the assertions made by American sociologist Seymour Martin Lipset in his well-known comparison of Canadian-American cultural and political differences. One of Lipset's more recent statements with respect to this problem is included in Chapter 3, "Culture." In this paper Bowden formulates Lipset's somewhat vague and implicit hypothesis about "union density" into a testable hypothesis and then proceeds to collect and analyze data with which to accept or reject the hypothesis. On the basis of the research, he questions Lipset's theory about the "causes" of Canadian-American differences and suggests an alternative explanation. Lest you think numbers "speak for themselves" or are beyond debate, we should add that Bowden's paper elicited a critical response from Lipset and, in turn, a rejoinder from Bowden and, as is often the case in science, the debate is probably not over.

The third selection, by Charlene Gannage of the University of Toronto, is a chapter of her study of immigrant women garment workers in Toronto. Whereas the first two selections in this chapter introduce aspects of quantitative approaches, Gannage here tells us something of the "nuts and bolts" of field work and participant observation or, more generally, qualitative sociological research. By describing her research activities step by step Gannage is able to show not only the advantages but also the difficulties and limitations of what she refers to as "the case study approach."

The final selection, by Alexander Himelfarb of the Department of Justice, Canada, and formerly of The National Parole Board, reflects some of his concerns about how we interpret responses to survey questions. He focuses on public opinion surveys and their usefulness for policy makers; but it is evident that the difficulties he outlines have more general applicability to the most common research method in sociology, the social survey. In forcing us to think about what we are actually doing when asked a question such as "Are you in favour of or opposed to capital punishment?" he is also showing us the major limitation of this research technique.

RELATED READINGS

Stephen Baron:: "The Canadian West-Coast Punk Subculture: A Field Study" (Chapter 3)
Rhonda Lenton:: "Homicide in Canada and the USA: A Critique of the Hagan Thesis" (Chapter 7)
C. James Richardson: "Family Law Research in a Decade of Change" (Chapter 6)

DOING IT WITH NUMBERS

Alfred A. Hunter

". . . new tools of production are often reflected in new ways of intellectual analysis" (Lazarsfeld, 1982: 30).

This paper seeks to chart what some see as a grand divide in sociology between the "qualitative" and the "quantitative," and to identify enlightened applications of quantification in the international enterprise of sociology, as well as in the national one of Anglophone Canadian sociology. To these ends, it assesses the epistemological status of qualitative v. quantitative sociology, traces the historical evolution of quantification in the discipline, and reviews the origins and current state of quantification in Anglophone Canadian sociology.

The Quantitative vs. The Nonquantitative in Sociology

As the pursuit of knowledge of the social, sociology is answerable to philosophy in terms of the epistemology which informs it. At the same time, though, there may be more than one sociology. In this regard, sociologists often contrast the qualitative with the quantitative as a major faultline across their discipline. Where, then, might this line be? Does it mark an epistemological divide?

Perhaps the most common view of the qualitative v. the quantitative is that the former employs descriptions of objects, events and the relationships among them in words, while the latter uses depictions in numerals. This is based on a false dichotomy, however, since every numeral (e.g., "1,000,") can be symbolized in words

("one thousand"), so that every numerical description can be translated mechanically into a verbal one, and many characterizations in words can be given directly in numerals. There is no alchemy in this and, consequently, any logical or mathematical manipulation which can be performed on numerals can also be carried out on their verbal equivalents. Still, most words can not be equated with numerals, although there are techniques, such as the semantic differential, for describing non-numerical aspects of verbal concepts numerically. Finally, classical content analysis enumerates aspects of objects or events verbally described.

Another version of the qualitative and the quantitative is that the qualitative involves statements of the relationships between or among concepts whose constituent categories are unordered, i.e., comprise typologies (e.g., users v. non-users of marijuana), while the quantitative involves propositions in which there is at least one concept which is a set of (at least) ordered categories (e.g., uses marijuana "very often," "often," "sometimes," etc.). This distinction between the qualitative and the quantitative is that between the classical logic of categories and the mathematical logic of ordered relations, which permits several conclusions. First, quantitative concepts and propositions involving them convey more information than do their strictly qualitative counterparts. Specifically, every quantitative concept or proposition containing one implies a qualitative concept or proposition (formed by discarding the information about quantities), but not vice versa. Second, for the same reasons that the calculus of mathematical logic yields stronger conclusions than does that of classical logic (i.e., it takes into account more information about the concepts and their relationships), the statistical and other mathematical procedures for quantitative concepts and propositions

From "Doing It With Numbers" by Alfred E. Hunter in Volume 22:5 December 1984. By permission of *The Canadian Review of Sociology and Anthropology* and the author.

... are more informative than those for qualitative ones. . . . Third, there is no epistemological divide between the qualitative and the quantitative.

There are also a number of conclusions which do not follow from the above. First, nonquantitative research is neither necessary nor useful. For one thing, since qualitative descriptions logically precede quantitative ones, the earliest investigations in a field will necessarily have a qualitative aspect. For another, certain concepts may be best treated as typologies (e.g., gender, Marxian class categories).

Second, sociology is a positivistic science of cause and effect theories. Instead, what is assumed here is that social life is accessible to empirical investigation and scientific generalization, not that it is, say, positivist as opposed to Marxist — cause and effect as over against dialectical. If, however, social life is only an infinitude of situationally and culturally specific events and practices, then we are left to be ethnographers to catalogue them. Given the promises of generalized understanding and potential control which a scientific approach carries, however, it would be a mistake to abandon it a priori.

Third, procedures for measurement and data analysis can be chosen on purely technical grounds. In fact, techniques are theory-laden, in that selecting one over another can be tantamount to choosing one theoretical conception over another. For example, in choosing the classical log-linear model to analyze occupational mobility, one also chooses to conceptualize occupation as a set of unordered categories, which precludes consideration of theories which treat occupations as ordered or arrayed along some continuum (e.g., symbolic or material rewards).

Is there, then, but one sociology? Nothing above should suggest that sociology is a unitary discipline epistemologically — that sociologists are all one big, unhappy family. In particular, there does appear to be an epistemological divide between positivism, realism, naturalism or materialism, as opposed to humanism, idealism, rationalism or hermeneutics. That is, the theory of knowledge carried in an empirical sociology resting on assumptions that knowledge derives ultimately from observations seems incommensurable with that implied in a phenomenological or interpretive sociology grounded in Weberian notions of verstehen. This paper concerns the former.

Finally, how does one assess claims of the inaccessibility to quantitative sociology of certain areas of human experience, including understanding the circumstances of and discovering means for the emancipation of subordinate or oppressed groups? Insofar as such claims assert that a verbal or exploratory sociology is better adapted to the analysis or liberation of such groups than is a numerical or confirmatory one, then they can be rejected on the basis of the above discussion as self-defeating. If, however, they propose that a phenomenological sociology is better suited to these tasks than is an empirical one, then it remains to be shown how a sociology aimed at empathic or intuitive understanding is a superior vehicle for sociological explanation and purposive change than one designed to explicate people's material circumstances and to facilitate human intervention.

The Origins of Quantitative Sociology

Although the systematic gathering of social and economic data can be traced back from the modern census and sample survey to the Domesday Book and the tax rolls of antiquity, it was not until the seventeenth century in Britain and France that the concept of "political arithmetic" was first enunciated. At about the same time, in Germany, a form of cross-tabular analysis, known as "stateistics," was developed. In the late eighteenth century, political arithmetic and stateistics converged as "statistics."

If using empirical observations to inform arguments about society was an early aspect of Enlightenment rationality, a somewhat later one was a "science" of society. But, aside from their common conception, their early lives were lived apart. Comte's inn of the positive science had no room for quantification or statistics, and John Stuart Mill formulated the canons of modern scientific procedure partly in response to Comte's casual use of the comparative method. Quantification and statistics did figure, though, in the work of Le Play, as did the survey and the interview. In this period, too, Quetelet made some of the earliest applications of probability theory to social data. While Le Play and Quetelet had their followers, including the Le Playist Canadien, Leon Gérin, Comte's influence was almost everywhere the greater, and the techniques which they pioneered were subsequently adopted and developed largely outside of sociology. In particular, they found favour in the nineteenth-century British statistical societies and British and French social reform movements, where surveys were often used, and Bowley was the first to use randomization in drawing a sample.

In Britain, Herbert Spencer's ideas on evolution found favour with Francis Galton and Karl Pearson — two of the founders of modern statistics. In fact, however, the association of these men with sociology was essentially accidental, since it was Spencer's biological ideas that interested them, not his sociological ones. It was the British statistician, Yule, who first applied modern statistics to social data when he reanalyzed some results from Booth's surveys using multiple regression. But no no-

tion of theory testing was involved. What is usually regarded as the first authentic attempt to mate a social theory with numbers was Durkheim's (1897) *Suicide*, although Durkheim did not use the (then) modern statistical techniques. Despite this start, however, it was in the United States, that the idea of a quantitative sociology was realized.

THE AMERICAN SCIENCE OF QUANTITATIVE SOCIOLOGY

In 1892, the first department of sociology in the United States was founded at the University of Chicago, followed two years later by one at Columbia. Initially, research was not stressed at Chicago, although "the empirical breakthrough and first transformation of U.S. sociology" (Oberschall, 1972: 239) occurred there. Sociology at Chicago in the 1920s and 1930s was strong on fieldwork, with the community as a "laboratory." It was weak, however, on theory, research design, measurement and statistics. As Thomas expressed it in 1928 in a note to Park, "It is only . . . since we abandoned the search for standardized methods . . . , that we have made the beginnings" (quoted in Oberschall, 1972: 235). Early sociology at Columbia emphasized theory and statistics, but not research. Despite this, "Columbia became the centre for training in the rigorous application of quantitative methods to sociological issues" (Halfpenny, 1982: 40). It was not until the arrival of Paul Lazarsfeld in 1941, however, that the department began to show innovation in research technique.

Lazarsfeld was among the first to see sociological potential in the secondary analysis of market research and public opinion poll data and in the role of an academic survey research unit. With U.S. Army and Office of War Information research contracts, Lazarsfeld and researchers connected with the Bureau for Applied Social

Research led the second tranformation of U.S. sociology. What emerged was an inductivist, empirical sociology with the individual as the unit of analysis and a technology of survey sampling and cross-tabulation.

THE INSTITUTIONALIZATION OF QUANTITATIVE SOCIOLOGY IN ANGLOPHONE CANADA

The European tradition of social reform research came to Canada just before World War I in John MacDougall's Presbyterian Church-sponsored work, *Rural Life in Canada* (1913), and a series of surveys carried out by the Presbyterian and Methodist churches. As in the European tradition, these efforts had no sociological rationale. In 1922, however, Carl A. Dawson arrived at McGill from the University of Chicago to head (what was two years later named) the Department of Social Science — the first such department by many years in Canada.

In 1931, McGill received a five-year, $110,000 Rockefeller Foundation research grant. Recruited from Britain to administer it was a sociologist, Leonard Marsh, who proceeded to participate in or preside over what turned into a decade-long, multidisciplinary research program. Most of the research carried out by sociologists was descriptive and policy-oriented, however, although the best of it was in the Chicago fieldwork tradition. Even though Marsh's name is little known today, he helped set a style for quantitative research in Anglophone Canadian sociology: ambitious empirically, but not especially informed theoretically or advanced methodologically. In 1938, S. D. Clark was hired as the University of Toronto's first (and Canada's first Canadian-trained) sociologist. Clark adopted an historiographic, macrosociological approach which, save for its passing acquaintance with theory and lack of concern with method, was oth-

erwise quite different from that at McGill. He had only limited success, however, in promoting sociology at Toronto in the 1940s and 1950s.

A theoretically infused and technically sophisticated sociology, then, did not develop in Anglophone Canada during the first half of the century. Something close to it, though, can be seen in the work of Enid Charles, who came to Canada from the U.K. around 1940 to work on a Carnegie-sponsored research project and joined the Dominion Bureau of Statistics (DBS) in 1943. Unfortunately, however, her influence was largely confined to demography, and that discipline straddled government and the universities, with closer ties perhaps to economics than to sociology.

In 1956–57, there were only 32 academic sociologists in Canada. There was some survey-based market research in the 1950s, the Canadian Institute of Public Opinion had been polling since the 1940s, the DBS had been conducting the Labour Force Survey since 1946, along with other periodic surveys (e.g., one of student finances in 1956), and the massive Carnegie Study had been carried out in Canadian schools. There were few social scientists interested in survey research, however, and no ready resources for them to do large-scale surveys.

In the 1960s, university enrolments and the complement of university faculty in Canada increased threefold. In sociology, they increased tenfold. As for research, the Canada Council first began to dispense modest grants for sociological research beginning in 1965–66. In this period, too, several national surveys, were carried out, including one of immigrants by Richmond, one of secondary school students by Breton, and one on occupational status by Pineo and Porter. As well, a number of surveys were conducted and research opportunities for sociologists opened up with the royal commissions on Bilingualism and Biculturalism, the Status of Women and the Nonmedical Use of Drugs.

By the mid-1980s, there were over 900 academic sociologists in Canada. The Social Sciences and Humanities Research Council had been carved out of the Canada Council, but social science research funds remained scarce. The (then named) Institute for Behavioural Research had been established at York University, and a number of large-scale surveys had been completed under the direction of sociologists, including the Canadian Mobility Study, the Survey of Ontario Students' Aspirations, a two-wave panel study of twelfth grade students in Ontario, the Marginal Work World study and the three-wave Social Change in Canada project. In addition, long-term projects in the spirit of the Detroit Area Study and directed by sociologists were underway at the universities of Alberta and Manitoba, as well as at York University and the Ontario Institute for Studies in Education. Too, a modest inventory of national, provincial and other major surveys had accumulated, largely through the work of academically-based political scientists and various federal and provincial government agencies. These included a national, post-election survey for every general election since 1965 (save for 1980), a national study on "Canadian Work Values," a longitudinal field experiment in Manitoba on income maintenance programs, a panel study of Ontario men (Long-Term Study on Aging), the Highly Qualified Manpower Survey, the Canada Health Survey, national surveys of 1976 and 1982 post-secondary graduates, a 1984 national survey on post-secondary students' finances, surveys of 1978 and 1982 post-secondary graduates in Ontario, and CIPO polls covering more than forty years.

A generation ago, Anglophone Canadian sociologists were a closely-knit few whose quantitative cadre did small-scale, local surveys and cross-tabulations on counter-

sorters. Today, they are a loosely-linked many whose quantitative practitioners engage in small- and large-scale surveys, secondary analysis and experimental research with statistical packages and electronic digital computers. How well, then, does quantitative sociology in Anglophone Canada serve the discipline at home and away? . . .

Although the theoretically informed use of quantitative data in Anglophone Canadian sociology has probably increased in the recent past, conditions favourable to this are far from fully developed. First, the Chicago-McGill fieldwork style has been continuously and conspicuously represented in sociology in this country since the 1920s. Second, the modern Canadian sociological classic, Porter's (1965) *The Vertical Mosaic*, was conceptually informed, but not theoretically infused, and quantitative data were entertained quite casually. Third, as intellectual descendents of Innis and participants in the larger Toronto tradition, sociologists writing in the political economy genre have often spent their powers on documenting and interpreting the historical development of Canada as a single case (e.g., as in the Laurentian thesis or staples "theory"), rather than on developing or testing explanatory theories which would locate the Canadian experience in relation to those of other societies. Since accounts of and explanations for particular occurrences and singular sequences of events are not tested, but only illustrated, these writers' requirements for quantitative data systematically gathered and analyzed using modern statistical tools are limited.

The U.S.-style sociology which has entered Canada since the 1950s has been largely either empiricist in its main (Lazarsfeldian) themes or abstractly conceptual in its minor (Parsonsian) variations, with later strains of Marx and Mills. What remains elusive, however, is an approach which fuses explanatory theory and quantitative analysis.

Two major barriers to a theoretical, quantitative sociology are the small store of explanatory theory in sociology, along with the ordinary language in which most theory is conveyed. Slow progress has been made in sociological theory since the advances achieved by such pre-twentieth or turn-of-the century theorists as Marx, Durkheim and Weber, although theory in microsociology (especially social psychology) is somewhat better developed . . . than it is in macrosociology. This is, of course, not unique to sociology or, even, to the social sciences generally. In the physical sciences, fluid dynamics, for example, is similarly impoverished theoretically. Too, most sociologists who theorize do so verbally. Few serve up their offerings in precise, formal langauges such as Boolean algebra or linear equations. As long as the vocabulary and grammar of sociological theory remain those of everyday speech, however, the burden is on the tester to formalize it, determine its logical implications, and express its concepts empirically. Again, this is not unique to sociology. Einstein's contributions to physics, for example, were mathematized and their formal implications and concrete manifestations systematically identified by others. . . .

The medium of this paper has been to identify enlightened research practices and technical innovations in quantitative sociology, and to point to how many Anglophone Canadian sociologists have incorporated these into their research and contributed to their development. Its message, however, has not been to celebrate the mystique of quantitative methodology, but rather to indicate how certain practices and techniques represent advances in research procedure and to suggest that they are potentially accessible to working sociologists generally. It means little to be the very model of the modern methodologist; it means a lot to do theoretically informed investigations in which the logic of the research operations matches that of the problem to be solved. With this in mind, I will reiterate the major points of the previous pages and suggest how they might be relevant for future theory and research in Anglophone Canadian sociology.

First, a respectable empirical sociology requires a body of potentially testable, explanatory theory. Such theory is better formalized, e.g., axiomatized, mathematized, etc., than presented in the usual literary forms. Therefore, those concerned to adapt existing or create new theories to account for prominent features of Canadian society (e.g., the vertical mosaic, the Canadian (or regional) hinterland v. the U.S. (or central Canadian) metropole) would serve the discipline well if they formalized their explanations as far as they could. This would not only reduce the difficulties researchers often have in translating others' theories into research operations, but also assist those who offer sociological explanations in laying bare the logic of and locating the ambiguities and inconsistencies in their arguments.

Second, sociologists who acknowledge the distinction between theoretical variables and empirical referents and the requirement for a measurement theory to link these two levels of abstraction together make an important contribution to a quantitative sociology. Theorists alert to the empirical manifestations of their concepts help to avoid the sociological equivalents of ether or phlogiston and to minimize the unproductive labour involved when their constructions are tested with invalid indicators. Researchers who design measurement instruments with highly-discriminating, multiple indicators whose properties are known through pretests or prior research work to advance theory through more convincing confirmatory studies. As for Anglophone Canadian sociology in particular, its quantitative practitioners have as yet made few ambitious or sophisticated attempts to operationalize the central concepts which animate our national version of the discipline (e.g., economic and cultural dependency, uneven economic development and regional dependency, deux nations and linguistic solidarity, social classes and class relations, class consciousness and conflict and so on).

Third, quantitative sociologists have yet fully to appreciate the design limitations of the cross-sectional survey. In general, our theories concern how units change over time; usually, we "test" them with information on how units differ at one point in time. But how to get longitudinal data in a country which, unlike the United States, has never even seen a golden age of the survey? And how to get them where those agencies which gather longitudinal microdata rarely do so with sociologists' needs in mind and seldom release them to social researchers in any case? For one thing, we can exploit those panel studies now in the public domain. For another, we can make more use of existing collections of time-series data and of time-series datasets which we can assemble from government or other documents. Also, given the weaknesses of national surveys and the considerable costs of country-wide panel studies, social researchers should more often consider trading off the representativeness of the national survey for the theory-testing potential of the local panel study. Local studies can also have advantages over national ones in the amount of historical and other background information available at nominal cost. Finally, a worthwhile effort might be for Canadian sociologists to lobby for a general social panel study, perhaps in the model of the Labour Force Survey. There could be an executive committee of sociologists, a common core of questions supplemented by questions purchased by

investigators with research grants, and defrayed costs through sales of the data. . . .

Finally, ". . . new tools of production are often reflected in new ways of intellectual analysis," and it may even be true, as some have argued, that the history of science is the tale of technology. But, while "new tools" can yield more precise or even entirely new observations which advance theory, they can also admit observations which are irrelevant to or which retard theory. For every telescope, there is an orgone energy accumulator. We need theory to help tell us if these "new ways" lead to the promised land, the fiery furnace or somewhere in between.

LABOR UNIONS IN THE PUBLIC MIND: THE CANADIAN CASE

Gary Bowden

Seymour Martin Lipset's theory of Canadian-American differences, although criticized by many, remains the most comprehensive account available. By postulating a small number of fundamental differences in value orientation, Lipset's theory organizes a wide range of seemingly unrelated empirical differences into a coherent framework. However, a fundamental methodological problem emerges from Lipset's extensive reliance upon cross-sectional data. When examined longitudinally, the relationship between theory and data becomes significantly more complex. This paper examines the implications of recasting Lipset's theoretical formulation in order to deal with such complexities.

Specifically, the paper focuses upon Canadian-American differences in union den-

From "Labor Unions in the Public Mind: The Canadian Case" by Gary Bowden in Volume 26:5, November 1989. By permission of *The Canadian Review of Sociology and Anthropology* and the author.

sity. This example was chosen for a variety of reasons. First, the changes in union density exemplify many of the problems encountered in the analysis of longitudinal data. Second, Lipset adduces differences in union density as supporting his theory of Canadian-American differences (Lipset, 1985). Third, Lipset has written extensively on factors affecting union density (Lipset, 1986a; 1986b; Lipset and Schneider, 1983) and has incorporated these insights into a comparison of the Canadian and U.S. cases (Lipset, 1986b). The example, therefore, provides an excellent opportunity to illustrate Lipset's solutions to the complexities of the theory/data relationship when examining longitudinal evidence.

The paper consists of five sections. The first describes historical changes in the level of our dependent variable, union density in Canada and the U.S. The second summarizes Lipset's explanation of the differences in union density. This summary is used to identify a specific body of unexamined empirical findings, Canadian attitudes toward unions, that bear upon the validity of Lipset's theoretical model. The third section summarizes these attitudes. The fourth examines the connection between attitudes toward unions and the level of union density. The final section discusses the implications for Lipset's theory of Canadian-American differences.

Trends in Union Membership in Canada and the United States

Figure 1 graphically compares the changing levels of union density in Canada and the United States for the period 1921–1985. Several significant facts emerge from an examination of these data. First, the level of union density in Canada has been higher than that in the U.S. for most of the last 65 years. The one major exception occurred

during the period from the mid-1930s to the mid-1950s. Second, changes in the level of union density have been more volatile in the U.S. than in Canada (Bain and Price, 1980: 163). Third, the general pattern of rise and fall in union density shows a considerable similarity up until the mid-1960s. The major exception comes in the timing of the major growth spurt; 1933 for the U.S. versus the beginning of World War II for Canada. Fourth, since the mid-1960s the patterns have diverged. Union density in the U.S. has declined dramatically while Canadian union density has increased significantly. By 1986 approximately 40 per cent of the paid non-agricultural workforce in Canada was unionized as compared to roughly 18 per cent in the U.S. In short, it is overly simplistic to speak of *the* difference in union density between Canada and the United States.

Most recent attention has focused upon the mid-1960s divergence in overall pattern. For academics, the many similarities between Canada and the U.S. allow the analyst to "control" certain variables and, hence, eliminate them as potential factors accounting for the emerging differences. For labor organizers, the ability of Canadian unions to prosper at a time of decline in the U.S. suggests the Canadian experience could serve as a model for reviving American unionism (AFL-CIO Committee on the Evolution of Work, 1985: 15).

Two fundamentally different explanations have been provided for the emerging differences in the level of Canadian and American union density. The first, and most common, position focuses upon structural changes in either Canada or the U.S., e.g., changes in occupational distribution, changes in the legal environment, changes in employer practices. In contrast, Lipset takes an idealist approach, emphasizing the role of core values and the impact of public opinion upon union density. This view poses a dramatic challenge to the

Figure 1
UNION DENSITY, 1921 – 1984

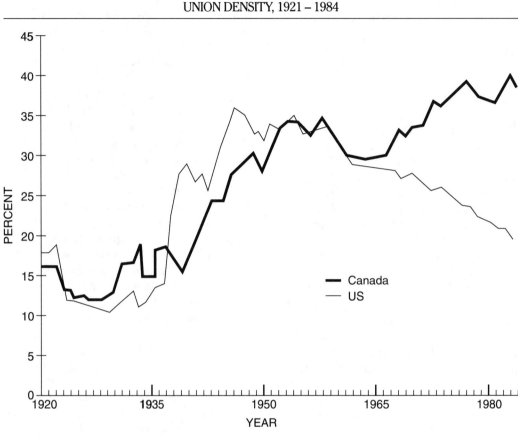

A Summary of Lipset's Analysis

structural accounts in that 1/ it emphasizes a set of previously ignored variables and 2/ it shifts the focus on what needs to be explained.

A Summary of Lipset's Analysis

Lipset's explanation of Canadian-American differences in union density brings together two distinct lines of theoretical reasoning: a theory of Canadian-American differences and a theory of how public opinion impacts upon union growth and

decline. The former theory postulates constant differences in value orientation which Lipset uses to explain cross-sectional differences in the level of union density *between* the two countries. The latter theory postulates a process designed to explicate the longitudinal rise and fall of levels of union density *within* a country. This section examines these theories individually and in combination.

Lipset traces the origin of Canadian-American differences to the influence of certain formative events, specifically the American Revolution and the War of 1812. For the United States, these events marked the birth of a "revolutionary" society; i.e. a society which broke the ties between itself and the mother country. For Canada, these same events resulted in a "counter-revolutionary" society; i.e. the solidification of ties with Britain and a rejection of the revolutionary ethos. Consequently, the value orientations of the two countries differ: Canada is more elitist, ascriptive, particularist and collectivity-oriented, while the U.S. is more egalitarian, achievement-oriented, universalist and self-oriented. In other words, Canadian values tend toward conservatism and the maintenance of tradition, while American values tend toward liberalism and the rejection of traditional authority.

For current purposes, this theory raises two basic questions: How do events roughly 200 years past serve to explain present day differences? And what is the connection between these differences in value orientation and levels of union density? In relation to the former, Lipset argues that the two countries have institutionalized structures which perpetuate the value differences. In relation to the latter, Lipset argues that leftist collectivist and communitarian movements (e.g., labor unions) have emerged in response to the conservative emphasis upon elitism and statism. In countries such as Canada, which have a tradition of state paternalism fostered by national elites, less privileged segments of the society mobilize resources to improve their position through government action. In contrast, the anti-statist ethos of classically liberal societies like the United States has weakened the efforts to mobilize workers and others on behalf of socialist and other collectivist goals. Simply stated, the value orientation of Canadians is more favorably disposed to union movements than that of Americans (Lipset, 1986b: 442–52).

The second relevant strand of Lipset's theoretical thought deals with the relationship between public opinion towards unions and the level of union density. The bulk of Lipset's writing in this area consists of a detailed portrait of American public opinion towards unions, union leaders and union members. Based upon an extensive review of national public opinion poll data dating from 1936 to the present, Lipset reaches the following conclusions. First, Americans lack confidence in unions and their leaders (Lipset, 1986a: 288–99; Lipset and Schneider, 1983: 200–1, 215–20). Second, Americans perceive unions as fulfilling a legitimate social role. They believe unions are essential and do more good than harm, especially for their members (Lipset, 1986a: 299–303; Lipset and Schneider, 1983: 201–5). Third, Americans perceive labor unions as overly powerful, while "workingmen" are seen as having too little influence. In other words, unions are perceived as large organizations which frequently represent their own interests rather than those of their members (Lipset, 1986a: 309–16; Lipset and Schneider, 1983: 206–11). Fourth, Americans have traditionally perceived labor as more responsible for inflation than business (Lipset, 1986a: 316–8; Lipset and Schneider, 1983: 211–5).

Thus, like other studies of U.S. public opinion toward unions, Lipset concludes that American opinion is dominated by two distinct, but by no means mutually exclusive, images: 1) a generally positive image of unions as instrumental organizations that seek to improve the economic and social conditions of their members; and 2) a generally negative image of unions as powerful forces which exert undue influence on the rest of society. Lipset's analysis goes beyond the others, however, in two distinct ways: 1) he generalizes about the longitudinal trend in the data; and 2) he places the descriptive material into a theoretical framework.

Lipset (1986b: 438) claims that "evidence drawn from American opinion polls [indicates] a loss in public support for unions from the mid-1950's to the present." This statement, while substantively and theoretically provocative, is methodologically suspect. Lipset has shifted ground from a discussion of the two-faced nature of public opinion toward unions to a characterization in terms of a single longitudinal trend. While some of the data (e.g., on confidence in union leaders) show the longitudinal slide Lipset describes, other data (e.g., on attitudes about the power of unions) depict a stable or improving perception of unions. More critically, Lipset provides no indication of how these various indicators are weighted in reaching his generalization.

In the light of this methodological quagmire, the strongest evidence that American unions are losing support comes from the changing responses to the question "In general, do you approve or disapprove of unions?" Response to this question displays the longitudinal decline Lipset describes. More importantly, the question measures the respondent's overall opinion toward unions, i.e. it encompasses both the positive and negative dimensions of the respondent's perception. The manner in which Lipset places these descriptive findings into a theoretical model supports this interpretation. Based upon the results of several simple causal models which use the above measure as an independent variable, Lipset concludes that "a major, if not the major, factor affecting union growth or decline and ability to win certification elections is variation in the public estimation of unions" (Lipset, 1986b: 440).

By combining the two lines of argument summarized above, Lipset provides an account designed to explicate both 1) differences in level *between* the two countries and 2) longitudinal changes in level *within* a country. Graphically, this combination of theories can be conceptualized as two lines rising and falling in parallel. A cursory glance at Figure 1 shows that reality is con-siderably more complex than this idealized model. Lipset adduces specific historical circumstances to explain empirical deviation from the idealized model. For example, he claims "[t]he big anomaly in the comparison between the two countries is the growth in union density in the United States from the mid-1930s to the mid-1950s which, as we have seen, temporarily placed the American labor movement ahead of the Canadian" (Lipset, 1986b: 445). The anomaly is then explained away through reference to historical circumstances, i.e. the claim that the poverty of the Depression era temporarily infused Americans with a dose of social democratic values which they promptly dropped when prosperity returned in the postwar years (Lipset, 1986b: 445–8). In other words, temporary historical circumstances affected the values of Americans to an extent that overpowered the continuing differences in fundamental value orientation that flowed from the institutionalization of "revolutionary" and "counter-revolutionary" viewpoints.

In short, Lipset's theoretical model focuses upon two of the characteristics associated with the patterns in Figure 1; relative level between countries and changes in absolute level within a country. The other elements in the pattern (e.g., differences in the timing of periods of growth and decline, and differences in amplification) are treated as transitory deviations from the general process which result from differences in Canadian and U.S. histories.

The main theoretical links in Lipset's model are shown diagrammatically in Figure 2. The independent variables, i.e. the relevant differences in core values drawn from the theory of Canadian-American differences, are shown in Column A. The dependent variable, i.e. the level of union density, is shown in Column C. Public opinion toward unions (Column B) acts as an intervening variable. Stated another way, Lipset's theory of Canadian-American differences is embodied in the vertical dimensions of Column A while the theory of how public opinion impacts upon union density is embodied in the horizontal dimension, i.e. in the theoretical connections between Columns B and C. Displaying Lipset's theory in this manner highlights the fact that his analysis is incomplete. Nowhere does Lipset provide a systematic examination of Canadian public opinion toward unions (the Canadian cell of Column B), despite the fact that the prediction that Canadian attitudes should be relatively more pro-union follows directly from his analysis.

Unions in the Public Mind: Some Canadian Data

Despite the relative lack of Canadian data, there exists empirical evidence pertaining to each of the major areas examined by Lipset. The following subsections summarize data from random national samples of Canadian opinion conducted by the Gallup organization. Where possible, equivalent American data have also been presented.

UNION POWER

Fear of union power constitutes the greatest objection to unions among Canadians. When asked in an open-ended question, to name the "chief argument against labor unions," almost two and a half times as many people (25%) stated that unions have become too powerful and abuse their power as stated the next most frequent response, that unions cause too many strikes and won't work unless they get what they want (11%).

In a series of polls conducted between 1979 and 1984, Gallup found that a large majority of the Canadian population (62–68%) felt that unions are "becoming too powerful" while only 6–7 per cent felt they are "not powerful enough." The most pronounced longitudinal change occurred among those who felt the level of union power is "about right"; increasing from 19 per cent of the population in 1979 to 27 per cent in 1984. Over the period 1971 to 1985 the proportion of Americans who felt that unions are too powerful (46–55%) was significantly lower than in Canada, while the proportion who felt that union power is about right (24–33%) or not powerful

	(A) CORE VALUES→	(B) PUBLIC OPINION→ TOWARDS UNIONS	(C) UNION DENSITY
UNITED STATES	LIBERAL INDIVIDUALIST	Relatively Anti-union	Relatively Low
CANADA	SOCIAL DEMOCRATIC COLLECTIVIST	Relatively Pro-union	Relatively High

Note: Items in upper case represent theoretical terms, items in lower case represent predictions based upon the theoretical terms and their interrelations

Figure 2:

A diagrammatic representation of Lipset's theories

enough (8–20%) was significantly higher than in Canada.

Several other questions provide less direct indicators of the public's opinion of union power. Roughly two thirds of the Canadian population, for example, feel that unions should not engage in political activities (70% in 1959, 58% in 1967, 69% in 1984). The proportion favoring union involvement rose from 13 per cent in 1959 to 20 per cent in 1967 and 1984. Presumably this antipathy reflects the belief that such activities represent an unwarranted intrusion into the political process and, as such, constitute an abuse of union power. Such responses, however, are highly dependent upon question wording. Union participation in the political process is viewed more positively when cast against the backdrop of participation by major corporations. Gallup found that 38 per cent of Canadians felt both unions and corporations should be allowed to donate money to political parties while 37 per cent felt neither group should be able to make such donations. Relatively few people felt that only unions (3%) or only corporations (8%) should be allowed to donate. In contrast, participation is viewed even more negatively when framed as a large organization deciding how to expend the dues of its members. Nearly four out of five Canadians (78%) feel that union members should have voluntary control over whether or not their union dues can be used for non-union purposes (e.g., support of political parties).

Canadian and American perceptions of the "biggest threat to the country" are shown in Table I. Canadians viewed labor as the biggest threat in the late 1960s and 1970s and have considered government the biggest threat in the 1980s. Big business has

Table I

CANADIAN AND AMERICAN PERCEPTIONS OF THE 'BIGGEST THREAT TO THE COUNTRY IN THE FUTURE,' 1959–1987 (PERCENTAGE)

	CANADA			UNITED STATES		
YEAR	BUSINESS	LABOR	GOVT.	BUSINESS	LABOR	GOVT.
1987	15	30	42			
1985	18	24	47	22	19	50
1984	17	34	33			
1983	14	34	45	19	18	51
1982	13	29	46			
1981	16	28	44	22	22	46
1980	20	36	29			
1979	18	34	37	28	17	43
1978	17	37	37	19	19	47
1977	21	38	35	23	26	39
1976	18	43	33			
1975	20	36	29			
1972	27	36	22			
1969	18	34	23			
1968				12	26	46
1967				14	21	49
1959				15	41	14

SOURCES: "Which of the following will be the biggest threat to the country in the future — big business, big labour or big government?" For Canadian data, see *The Gallup Report*: February 16, 1987; January 30, 1986; January 10, 1985; September 5,1983; August 18, 1982; December 2, 1981; February 23, 1980; February 10, 1979; August 16, 1978; December 8, 1976; September 17, 1975; and July 22, 1972. The American data is summarized in *Gallup Poll* (1985: 140–1). For Lipset's comments on these data, see Lipset (1986a: 313).

consistently been viewed as less threatening than the other two. Examining shifts in the attitude toward labor, we find that 1) Canadian opinion about the threat posed by labor has been volatile and 2) the general trend since 1976 has been for fewer Canadians to view labor as the biggest threat.

In 1959 Americans viewed labor as most threatening. A dramatic shift in opinion occurred, however, between 1959 and the period for which we have corresponding Canadian evidence. For the past two decades Americans have viewed government as the biggest threat. Between 1967 and 1977 Americans viewed labor as more threatening than business. Since 1979, however, that opinion has reversed. Compared in either absolute or in relative terms, since 1969 Americans have consistently perceived labor as less threatening than have Canadians.

CONFIDENCE IN THE INSTITUTION AND ITS LEADERS

There exists relatively little information on the confidence of Canadians in unions and their leaders. What evidence exists, however, shows a pattern fairly similar to that in the U.S. In 1974 Gallup asked Canadians how much "respect and confidence" they had in labor unions and large corporations. Neither institution fared well, though labor (25% "a great deal or quite a lot"; 64% "some, very little, nor no") fared marginally less well than large corporations (26% and 61% respectively). Comparing these findings to data from similar questions asked in the U.S. in 1973 and 1975 illustrates two minor, but interesting, differences. First, Americans, unlike Canadians, put more confidence in labor unions (30% in 1973, 38% in 1975) than in big business (26% in 1973, 35% in 1975). Second, a comparison of the absolute level of confidence in labor shows that fewer Canadians

in 1974 had a high level of confidence in labor (25%) than did Americans in either 1973 (30%) or 1975 (38%).

Union leaders, like the institutions they lead, are viewed negatively by the Canadian public. Over the past two decades a majority of Canadians have consistently held that "there are too many troublemakers and agitators among union leaders" (50% in 1966, 67% in 1975, 51% in 1985). In contrast, roughly one in four held that such talk was "only anti-labor propaganda" (22% in 1966, 17% in 1975, 30% in 1985).

Canadians also criticize the personal characteristics of union leaders. Asked to rate the "honesty and ethical standards" of people in different occupations, union leaders ranked lowest among groups considered (see Table II). Only 13 per cent of the population rated union leaders as having high or very high standards, while one in three (36%) considered their standards average, and nearly one half (45%) rated their standards as low or very low. When asked the same question, Americans provided virtually identical ratings. The similarity of these absolute levels, however, could mask differences in the perception of union leaders relative to other groups. If, for example, Americans give generally more positive ratings to other occupations than do Canadians, then the Americans would have a more negative evaluation of union leaders relative to other occupational groups than do Canadians. To test this possibility, the level of response for union leaders was divided by the average level of response for the 11 occupational groups. No significant differences emerged.

UNIONS AND WORKERS

Canadians, like Americans, draw a distinction between union leaders and union members. Between 22 and 28 per cent of Canadians felt that the views of union lead-

Table II

CANADIAN AND AMERICAN ATTITUDES TOWARD THE HONESTY AND ETHICAL
STANDARDS OF INDIVIDUALS IN VARIOUS OCCUPATIONAL GROUPS

	CANADA			UNITED STATES		
	HIGH, VERY HIGH	AVERAGE	LOW, VERY LOW	HIGH, VERY HIGH	AVERAGE	LOW, VERY LOW
Doctors	64%	29%	06%	58%	33%	08%
Police officers	50	39	09	47	41	10
Engineers	48	36	04	53	37	03
University teachers	45	39	05	54	35	05
Lawyers	28	42	26	27	40	30
Journalists	24	49	21	31	47	17
Business executives	21	55	17	23	54	18
Building contractors	20	54	21	20	53	21
Members of Parliament	15	45	35			
Congressmen				20	49	27
Advertising executives	13	51	29	12	42	39
Labor Union leaders	13	36	45	13	35	45
Average	31	43.2	19.8	32.5	42.4	20.3
Labor leaders/average	0.42	0.83	2.27	0.40	0.83	2.22

SOURCES: Canadian data, *The Gallup Report*, November 9, 1987; American data, *The Gallup Poll*, 1985: 191–3

ers represented those of members, while between 52 and 62 per cent felt they did not. Within these ranges, however, opinion has fluctuated considerably over the 1979–1984 period. Hence, one cannot identify a consistent trend in the changes through time.

Similar American data come from two national cross-sectional surveys conducted by the Opinion Research Corporation. In 1985, three fifths of Americans believed that union leaders express their own views rather than those of the membership when they take public stands, up from 54 per cent in 1977 (Lipset, 1986a: 96). Given the volatility of the Canadian responses over much shorter measurement intervals, it would be unsafe to view the U.S. data as reflecting a trend. Moreover, given the differences in response dates and question wording, it would be unsafe to speculate on the significance of the relative minor cross-national differences in level of response.

THE EFFECTS OF UNIONS ON INFLATION

The relationship between wage settlements and inflation provides another problematic area for unions. In an open-ended question asking for the "chief argument against labor unions," 10 per cent of Canadians responded that they raise the cost of living through higher wages, help to cause inflation, or made other statements implying a relationship between union wages and the level of inflation. Unions do even worse in forced choice questions dealing with the person or group of persons most responsible for causing inflation. In 1972, for example, more Canadians blamed labor unions and union leaders (40%) than blamed the federal government (17%), big business (15%), or everybody (33%).

A year later Gallup asked a similar question, without the inclusion of "everybody," in the U.S. More Americans blamed government (39%) than blamed labor (29%) or big business (20%). This result reflects the consistent findings of a series of 10 surveys taken by Gallup and Opinion Research Corporation between 1968 and 1979 (Lipset, 1986a: 316). Despite the inclusion of an additional response category in the Canadian question, a greater proportion of Canadians than Americans expressed the relatively anti-union view that unions are primarily responsible for inflation.

Additional evidence, however, casts doubts upon Lipset's (1986a: 316) implication that fear of inflation accounts for much of the "continued disdain for organized labor." In contrast to the view that wage increases cause inflation is the view that wage increases are driven by inflation. Two polls from the early 1970s suggest that this view carries considerable credence with the Canadian public. In 1970, when asked if the wages of working people had risen enough to keep pace with increases in the cost of living, only 28 per cent replied that they had, while 61 per cent held the view that they had not. Asked to identify the group which was benefiting most from the current

economic prosperity, only 4 per cent identified union members as that group, fewer than identified the middle class (7%) or people on unemployment insurance or welfare (7%).

In sum, Canadian public opinion appears more sophisticated than American opinion as presented by Lipset. Lipset focuses upon the public's desire to fix blame for a problem and implies that unions carry a substantial portion of the burden. In contrast, Canadian opinion seems more consistent with the view that inflation results from a wage and price spiral.

THE FUNCTION OF UNIONS

The preceding sections have documented a variety of negative perceptions about unions held by the Canadian public. But what of their benefits? Do Canadians, like Americans, perceive unions as having an important and legitimiate function within society? The best longitudinal data on this issue come from a forced choice question about the most important thing that unions do for their members (see Table III). These polls show 1) that job security has been

Table III
CANADIAN PUBLIC PERCEPTION OF THE MOST IMPORTANT TASK OF LABOR UNION'S FOR THEIR MEMBERS BY DATE (PERCENTAGE)

	YEAR					
TASK	1958	1971	1976	1981	1983	1985
Security of employment	47	50	45	50	62	52
Better working conditions	11	15	19	19	12	18
Higher wages	9	14	11	10	5	7
Better pensions	12	9	8	8	7	8
Profit sharing	8	6	7	9	6	5
Shorter working hours	4	5	3	1	2	3
Other issues	1	2	2	–	1	1
Can't say	8	6	6	4	6	6

SOURCES: *The Gallup Report*, November 20, 1971; March 24, 1976; April 11, 1981; May 9, 1983; May 13, 1985

viewed as the most important of the listed tasks and 2) that perceptions have been fairly stable over time.

However, the data in Table III suffer from two significant drawbacks. First, the question asks for the relative importance of the tasks and, hence, provides no insight into the absolute importance attached to any of the tasks. Second, the most important task is not included. When asked, in an open-ended format, to identify the chief argument in favor of labor unions, almost twice as many people gave responses indicating that unions are needed to counteract the power of business (e.g., unions protect the workers against exploitation, preserve the rights of workers, help the little man, etc.) than gave the next most common response (i.e. unions keep wages up; insure fair wages; etc.). Significantly, almost five times as many individuals mentioned protection of the workers as mentioned ensuring job security.

The claim that the primary perceived benefit of unions derives from their role in countering the power of big business is consistent with the willingness of Canadians to extend a variety of additional rights to workers. Roughly 70 per cent of Canadians think workers in large companies should be able to elect members to serve on the Board of Directors and nearly two thirds of the population believes workers should have access to information about their companies' financial situation.

Despite the lack of much specific evidence, there exist two factors which strongly suggest that Canadians perceive unions as fulfilling a legitimate role within society. First, in questions asking for overall assessment of unions (to be examined in the next section), more Canadians have rated unions favorably than have rated them unfavorably. This suggests the existence of a conception of unions as beneficial that counters the negative perceptions of unions documented in the previous sub-

sections. Second, studies done in Winnipeg and Edmonton have documented the existence of such perceptions in those cities (Krahn and Lowe, 1984a; 1984b).

SUMMARY

What then can we conclude from our examination of Canadian public opinion toward unions? First, and most importantly, Canadians display the same ambiguity towards unions that characterizes American public opinion. On the one hand Canadians perceive unions as negative forces, while on the other hand they view unions as fulfilling a legitimate and necessary social function. Thus, the differences that exist between Canadian and American public opinion are differences of degree rather than differences of kind. Second, those differences in degree which exist uniformly contradict the directional differences predicted by Lipset's explanation. Lipset's analysis implies Canadian public opinion should be more favorable to unions than American public opinion. The data, however, show the reverse: more Canadians than Americans view unions as too powerful; more Canadians than Americans perceive labor as the greatest threat; fewer Canadians than Americans have confidence in labor as an institution; more Canadians than Americans blame unions for inflation.

Despite the consistency with which the Canadian data have contradicted expectations based on Lipset's analysis, we must be circumspect in our criticism. Up to this point we have examined questions which tap various portions of the public conception of unions and their leaders. We have not, however, examined measures which provide an overall assessment of labor in the public mind. This is an important point since Lipset utilizes such a measure in justifying his claim that a causal connection exists between public attitudes toward unions and union density.

Public Opinion and Union Density: A Causal Connection?

Table IV compares longitudinal changes in Canadian and American overall ratings of unions. Throughout the period 1950 to 1984 more Canadians rated unions favorably (42–69%) than rated them unfavorably (12–42%). The proportion of the Canadian population giving unions a favorable rating rose during the early 1950s, fell for the following two decades and has generally risen since the mid-1970s. The proportion of Canadians expressing overall unfavorable ratings has shown the opposite pattern: falling during the early 1950s, rising from the mid-1950s to the mid-1970s and vacillating up and down since that time. American

approval ratings display this same general pattern. Unfortunately for Lipset, the relative positions of the U.S. and Canadian approval levels are the reverse of those predicted by his theory. The level of union approval in the U.S. (55–76%), has consistently surpassed the Canadian approval rate. Only once during the period 1950–85 (1961) did the level of approval in Canada top that in the United States. Only once since the early 1960s (1980) did fewer Canadians than Americans express an overall unfavorable attitude toward unions.

But what of the causal connection? According to Lipset (1986b: 440) "indicators of union strength move in tandem with variations in public approval of organized labor." This interpretation has undeniable face validity, and it is largely upon the strength of this intuitive appeal that Lipset

Table IV
CANADIAN AND AMERICAN OVERALL RATINGS OF UNIONS, 1947–85 (PERCENTAGE)

YEAR	CANADA		UNITED STATES	
	GOOD	BAD	APPROVE	DISAPPROVE
1985			58	27
1984	51	35		
1982	48	42		
1981			55	35
1980	54	30		
1979	50	35	55	33
1978	46	41	59	31
1976	42	36		
1973			59	26
1970	54	30		
1967			66	23
1965			70	19
1963			67	23
1961	66	23	63	22
1959			68	19
1957			76	14
1956	69	12		
1953			75	18
1950	60	15		
1949			62	22
1947			64	25
1941			61	30
1939			68	24
1936			72	20

SOURCES: See note 16

Table V
CORRELATIONS BETWEEN PUBLIC APPROVAL OF UNIONS AND UNION DENSITY IN
CANADA AND THE UNITED STATES

	U.S.	CANADA
Approval and Union density	$r = .76$	$r = .75$
Net approval and Union density	$r = .81$	$r = .83$

Note: Approval refers to the percent answering "approve" to the questions shown in Table IV. Net approval refers to the percent difference between approve and disapprove. U.S. correlations taken from Lipset, 1986b: 439, Table 4. Canadian correlations based upon union density figures from Labour Canada (1986: xxv; 1976: xvii–xix)

bases his claim that the change in attitudes is the *cause* of the decline in U.S. union density over the past few decades. To test the applicability of this hypothesis to Canada we have replicated Lipset's correlation of approval rates in Gallup Polls with union density using Canadian data. The results, shown in Table V, strikingly contradict Lipset's findings. Where the American data yield a strong positive relationship, the Canadian data yield an equally strong negative relationship. The intuitive appeal of Lipset's claim vis à vis Americans (public approval of unions has declined, therefore the rate at which the public joins unions has decreased) transforms itself into a schizophrenic portrait of the Canadian population (public approval of unions has declined, therefore the rate at which the public joins unions has increased).

Lipset, like most idealists, presumes that attitudes influence behavior. The present analysis calls that presumption into question. Every piece of evidence examined shows Canadian attitudes toward unions are at least as negative as those of Americans. Yet the facts remain: union density is considerably higher in Canada than in the U.S. and has been so for most of this century. If attitudes are influencing behavior in this case, they are doing so in markedly different ways in the two countries.

A more likely explanation for the findings is that 1) roughly similar processes of attitude formation toward unions have taken place in both countries, but 2) these at-

titudes have little, if anything, to do with determining union density. The first element accounts for the basic similarity between the attitudes of Canadians toward unions documented in this paper and those of Americans summarized by Lipset (1986a; Lipset and Schneider, 1983). Such similarity is easily interpretable given the similarities between the Canadian and U.S. situations, the sizable interpenetration of the U.S. communication industry into Canada and the known effects of the mass media on the formulation of public opinion. Evidence of an inverse relationship between the exercise of union power and popular approval of unions also harmonizes with this position (Smith, 1978; Edwards and Bain, 1988). The second element lends credence to the work of Meltz (1985), Rose and Chiason (1985) and others who argue that structural differences between Canada and the U.S. account for the differences in union density. Simply stated, the opportunity for workers to join a union is more important in determining union density than is their attitudes toward unions in general. Differences in legal environment (e.g., regulations affecting ability to organize, the extent to which labor relations boards enforce regulations against anti-union practices), for example, directly affect the number of workers who have the opportunity to join unions. Particularly relevant to the mid-1960s divergence in pattern was the more rapid rise of public sector unionism in Canada (Rose, 1984; Meltz, 1985).

Significantly, public sector unions have been predominantly national unions (i.e. they charter locals only in Canada) and, hence, indicate a transition away from a shared North American environment.

Discussion

The conventional conception of Lipset's theory as an explanation of differences in levels is premised upon a cross-sectional viewpoint. Any attempt to deal with the complexities of longitudinal data *necessitates* an elaboration of the theory beyond mere reference to difference in value orientation. Attitudes and behaviors *within* a country change through time. Since Lipset's hypothesized value orientations remain essentially constant through time, these orientations cannot, by themselves, account for such changes. One cannot explain variation through reference to a constant (Bailey, 1987: 40–1). Thus, Lipset is forced to expand the structure of the explanation through the introduction of an intervening variable, e.g., attitudes toward unions. Basic value orientations become only one of many factors affecting these more proximate causes of the attitudes and behaviors Lipset wishes to explain, e.g., level of union density. In addition, the relative level of an attitude or behavior *between* countries frequently changes through time. In the current case, for example, union density in the U.S. actually exceeded that in Canada between the mid-1930s and the mid-1950s while the reverse situation obtained both before and after. Again, the inclusion of an intervening variable between the value orientation and the phenomenon to be explained provides a method for dealing with such empirical facts. The proximate cause of union density, public attitudes toward unions, is affected not only by fundamental value orientations, but also by a variety of other factors. In this way, Lipset can account for

the apparent empirical contradiction without rejecting the importance of value orientation. When Canadian density is greater than U.S. density, this is a product of differences in value orientation. When U.S. density exceeds Canadian density, this is the result of other factors specific to the historical period overwhelming the still existing effect of differences in value orientation. Simply stated, the complexities of longitudinal data force Lipset to specify a causal channel through which value orientations impact upon attitudes and behaviors.

The specification of such causal channels, however, generates new hypotheses and, hence, provides additional opportunities to test the theory. In this particular case, the data flatly contradict the hypotheses drawn from Lipset's expanded theory. But what is being contradicted? Does our empirical evidence imply 1) that there are no fundamental differences in value orientation between Canada and the U.S., 2) that the causal channel is misspecified, or 3) both 1 and 2? For present purposes let us presume that the causal channel is misspecified. This is a kind and gentle approach to Lipset in that it preserves the general ability to account for cross-national differences while discarding the portion of the theory associated with the explanation of a specific thing, union density. Cast in this manner, the problems posed by the present analysis seem rather trivial. Such an impression, however, misses the point. To explain the complexities of longitudinal trends adequately, an explanation of Canadian-American differences cannot focus solely upon differences in the level of behavioral expression. Thus, minimally, an adequate revision of Lipset's analysis of union density would require the specification of an alternative causal channel. While Lipset should be applauded for confronting the problems of analysing longitudinal trends, the manner in which he has grafted this analysis onto his existing theory of Canadian-American differences is haphazard and incomplete. He seems not to have recognized the fundamental challenge inherent in the project.

THE CASE STUDY APPROACH TO RESEARCH

Charlene Gannagé

Since World War II women's labour force participation in Canada has increased dramatically. Along with this increase, union membership has risen sharply among female workers. The garment industry itself has been unionized since the early 1900s.

The mounting pressure on organized labour to consider the needs of working women is indicated by the growth of women's caucuses at the rank-and-file level. In 1983, the Ontario Federation of Labour elected five female vice-presidents at its annual convention as a result of an affirmative action program designed to increase women's participation at the top levels of union leadership. In 1984, the Canadian Labour Congress followed suit. Despite these developments, however, the number of women actually holding union office at the central leadership levels have been less than representative.

Although more women have joined the ranks of the labour movement and a few have held leadership positions, the majority of working women are not active in their trade unions. One may well ask why this is so. Studies of women's trade-union participation in Canada have either focused on the characteristics of individual officers (e.g., Chaison and Andippan, 1982), thereby ignoring the life experience of the majority of women workers, or they have

From *Double Day, Double Bind* by Charlene Gannagé. Women's Press, 1986. This abridged excerpt reprinted with permission.

been concerned with the attitudes of male trade-unionists toward women workers and women's issues (e.g., Geoffroy and Sainte Marie, 1971; Marchak, 1973; Baker and Robeson, 1981). The major shortcomings of the latter studies is to view trade unions as patriarchal institutions without looking at the political-economic context of the gender division of labour, the nature and operation of the trade union and how both are mediated by an ideological view that defines "women's work" on the job and in the home. It is my contention that the situation facing women workers is far more complex than attitudinal studies indicate.

Women's double day of labour is seen as one major reason for women not being able to participate in union meetings or accumulate years of experience necessary to hold union office. Many socialist and feminist writers have made brief references to the double day of labour and subsequent restriction it places on working women's participation in political activity and in union struggles. Although several historians have recognized the importance of providing a new context for analysing women's union participation by focusing on the interrelationship of work and family life (Baxandall, 1976; Bornat, 1978), few contemporary labour researchers have studied the combined effect of women's work in the home and outside the home on union involvement.

Nor does the feminist literature establish a theoretical framework for understanding working women's collective resistance to their oppression. This study, in addition to explaining the barriers to women's participation in the union, will address questions about gender consciousness: Do women identify as women whose interests are opposed to the interests of men? Do they see linkages between their oppression as women and their exploitation as workers? Do they recognize the necessity of women taking collective action against their oppression? Do they conceive of an alternate society in which women will be free and independent persons? And most importantly, if not, why not?

I will demonstrate that the gender division of labour, both as an integral part of the capitalist labour process (i.e., in the social organization of work) and as an ideological force external to the labour process, has influenced women's participation — or lack of — in their union. I will argue that it is impossible to understand the situation of women workers without taking into account their position within the family. In addition to understanding how the gender division of labour leads to profoundly different experiences for male and female workers, this study will examine how a division of labour along ethnic lines adds to the complexity, not only in obscuring class differences but also in forging alliances between male workers and certain female workers.

Methodology

My research efforts focused on a small garment shop, Edna Manufacture, located in the heart of the Spadina garment district of Toronto. Field research was conducted between January 1980 and January 1982 and centred on the pursuit of interviews with rank-and-file workers. Supplementary information came from the archives of the union. Whenever necessary, I took detailed notes of factories I visited as well as of encounters with workers. In order to assure confidentiality, all names of the respondents have been fictionalized as well as the name of the shop.

Although I was interested specifically in the double day of labour of women workers, I also interviewed male workers who provided me with important background information about the shop's operations and the history of the union. The majority

of the interviews took place in their homes. I also interviewed trade-union officials, management personnel and the owner of the shop. In cases where the wives of male workers were present, I attempted to include them. In the almost-verbatim accounts presented here, the quotations had to be edited for clarity and brevity, since many of the workers were immigrants who spoke English as their second language.

One striking feature of interviewing working-class women was the extent to which their life experiences contradicted the ideology of the gender division of labour. I did not attempt to unravel these contradictions but reported them verbatim. Perhaps an example will clarify what I mean by "contradictions." Ruth Domanski, single mother, took on another job besides the one she had in the factory. I asked what she thought of the commonly held view that the wages in the garment industry were sufficient for a woman but not a man. Her own experience (of needing two jobs) contradicted this perception. In her response, she struggles to accommodate her experience with the ideology of the family wage:

RUTH: Women earn spending money when there are two working ... I wasn't. That's why I took up another job. I had to. I *couldn't make a living, that's true.* A family man considers he have to make a living for a family. It's impossible in needle trade to keep a house or raise a family, pay bills. No. True ...

CHARLENE: *Do you think that the wages are okay for women in the needle trade?*

RUTH: That's what I'm trying to say ... they help out. Almost every woman is married.

The Case for a Case Study Approach

Two issues are relevant in opting for a case-study methodology. The first concerns the importance of developing theory from concrete empirical research. Support for this view comes from the Marxist British historian E. P. Thompson. He also objects to the structuralist influences in Marxism, which tend to be overly theoretical and consequently ignore "contradiction, change or class struggle" (1978: 197). He admonishes socialist feminists "who have a genuine grudge against the 'silences' of Marxism" but reduce their problem to a "pseudo-problem" by attempting to fit their concerns within a framework "designed for (their) exclusion" (p. 358): "But if we return to 'experience' we can move from that point once again into an open exploration of the world and of ourselves." This exploration, he writes, can still be within the Marxist tradition if Marxism is not viewed as a finite conceptual system.

The second issue concerns the choice of empirical inquiry which best suits the questions I asked. In order for me to capture the richly textured lives of trade-union women, especially the complexity of their social relationships in the workplace, in the union and in the family, the case-study methodology seemed more expedient than survey techniques or participant observation, because it facilitates the understanding of the subject from the perspective of the insider. Wax (1971) notes that fieldworkers do not at first share in the understandings of strangers, but once they begin to share meaning they acquire an insider's view. Intricate details about the piece-work system, the way the union operates at the shop level, and the variety of ways that the women of Edna Manufacture handle their domestic labour were best ascertained through this methodology.

The intersection of biography, history and social structure is the cornerstone of classical sociology according to C. Wright Mills (1959). The use of biography has become a popular methodology in other social science disciplines, as well. Recently, historical research has placed an emphasis on oral tradition in exploring dimensions of women's lives that could be obscured or hidden by traditional archival methods (Bornat, 1978). Psychologist Seve (1975) refers to the "science of human biography" in developing a Marxist framework for understanding human personality.

The in-depth interview technique allows the researcher to probe beneath surface appearances to get at meanings that respondents attach to their answers. For example, when I questioned Donna Jakubenaite about the division of labour in her household, she assured me that she and her husband "worked together":

Oh, my husband helps everything. He loves cooking. Sunday mornings I never wake up to go make breakfast or something. He always make me breakfast. Brings me in bed. And Sundays I never go in kitchen for dinner or something. He does everything. I just go clean after . . . We always work together. If we work in the house we work together. If we go outside we work together. We are always doing things together. Never your place in the garden and my place in the house. We are always helping each other.

The fact that Donna and her husband "worked together" stood out as an isolated case among my interviews with other women. I continued to probe Donna about what she meant by "working together." I didn't know if her husband "helped out" in the kitchen, or if she and her husband actually shared all the domestic labour. As the conversation proceeded I found out that, to a certain extent., "working together" meant that Donna did work that other women would have considered "men's work."

Moreover, aside from cooking, Donna's husband did not generally share in "women's work."

DONNA: Vacuuming, washing, ironing I do. But in the kitchen, he doing. Like vacuuming, dusting, washing, ironing I don't let him do, I do.

CHARLENE: *Why don't you let him do it?*

DONNA: Well, I think I know what I'm doing. (She laughs.)

CHARLENE: *What about bringing up the children? Who's responsibility was it, mainly?*

DONNA: Most I was . . . Because I know my husband was busy with the business. The house bills, mortgages . . . everything was my responsibility.

In addition, in-depth interviewing is useful in tracing the historical development of values that change as a result of life experiences. Donna could not attend union meetings because she had to rush home after work to pick up her child from the babysitter. She never had the opportunity to place her son in a daycare centre. When asked if she thought the union should fight for a daycare centre for women workers, she answered:

I think that's just family business. What union got to do with the thing? If mother wants to go to work, then her problem to find [someone].

However, in our second meeting her attitude partially changed because her daughter-in-law had placed Donna's son in a daycare centre:

It's nice to know where your child is when you're working. You are relaxed yourself.

Finally, the use of in-depth interviews allows the respondent to report marital conflicts that could not be easily reported in a questionnaire on, say, family decision-making. Grace Campisi described the struggle between herself and her husband concerning her nine-year-old daughter's right to play with boys:

We don't talk nothing. 'Cause I talk different from my husband. *Maybe sometimes I say to my daughter, "Okay to go . . . to some place but you got to come back here." He no wants.* But I make little bit fight with my husband too . . . *No good to stay all day home . . . He don't want her [to play with] some boys . . . He said she got to find some girls same age. For now I say it's okay [to play with boys]. She's small too [but] when she grows up [it's a] different story. (my emphasis)*

Gaining Access

Few social scientists have documented the preliminary stages of field research, particularly the mistakes made in approaching potential respondents. I have chosen to highlight those that best illuminate some of the methodological challenges I encountered.

Similar to Whyte (*Street Corner Society*) who relied on Doc, a leader of the street-corner gang under study, to play the role of sponsor-guide, I had a valuable guide who eased my entry into the world of the needle trade: he was Matt Kelly, the union business agent. Matt had worked with the union for several years and had come to love some of the "old-timers" who would regale him with stories about the "old days."

One of the important contacts to whom Matt introduced me was Louis Galati, the manager of the union. After I told him about my research and my chosen method — interviewing women workers about their work, the union and their family life — he agreed to cooperate. He introduced his staff, asked them to give their business cards, and told them I was "going to make a paper" on the industry. Louis' referral to "the industry" and not to the "workers" alerted me to the close relationship between the union and the manufacturers. I was also struck by Louis' personal charm and the paternalistic manner with which he treated his staff. After our meeting, Matt suggested that I "flirt" with Louis. At first I was shocked by this suggestion, but I soon realized that my manner was too formal and that I should learn to relax.

Although Louis had assured me of his cooperation, I did not obtain access to all the workers at once. It took many months to compile a list of people whom I could speak with, and rather than wait, I interviewed people in stages as the opportunity arose. Furthermore, my plan to interview all the workers had to be revised as the research proceeded.

In March 1980, I began my field research with a tour of the cloakmakers' shops in the downtown garment district, which I had previously arranged with Matt. Our first stop was Edna Manufacture, where he introduced me to Stephen Bettle, the owner of the shop. By sheer coincidence, it turned out that I purchased a coat made by his company. The owner noticed that I was wearing "his" coat and asked me to show it to a buyer in the showroom, where I pirouetted for him. Perhaps as a result of this coincidence, Mr. Bettle gave me permission to enter his shop with Matt, where I was introduced to a few women at the finishing table who agreed to be interviewed.

While Matt talked about union business with some of the workers, I approached the other women at the finishing table, explaining that I was a student and that I would like to interview them. Several agreed, but several refused on the grounds that they did not speak English. A man named Jacob Cowan gave me my first clue regarding attitudes toward work at Edna when he said "It is very good, what you are doing." He said that he could talk to me about events as far back as 1939 and referred to "the second holocaust on Spadina Avenue." This was a very strong metaphor. When I asked Matt about it, he replied, "no one likes to work here."

Another indication of a conflict brewing presented itself at the next shop where Matt was to meet Louis about some trouble with the lining-makers in this shop. The lining-makers had refused to fill the "special order" of short coats because they were not part of the regular line; however, the rest of the shop had agreed to do so. The former would do so for more money for each piece — 27 cents more. Louis pointed out that the "shorties" involved the same work as the raincoats, which they had already agreed to work on, and that "shorties" would require less time because the seams were not as long. Later, the owner admitted to Matt that the short coats were not his kind of merchandise, but he wanted to provide work. He implored Matt to speak to the lining-makers, "You've got to read them the riot act." This was my first inside view of business unionism. Mr. Galati's charcoal grey pin-stripe matched the owner's grey pin-stripe suit. Except for the cheap black belt encircling Galati's waist, their style of dress was practically indistinguishable. Moreover, although Galati was Italian he spoke in a very heavy Jewish accent. He had been so used to talking to Jewish employers that he took on their speech mannerisms. The union boss and the employer sat together discussing union finances. They were working on a transfer of $250,000 from the union pension fund.

Matt returned and introduced me to the finishers. He explained that I was doing a thesis on the garment business and that I wanted to talk to them "about a long time ago and how things have changed." One finisher said that she was leaving in July after seventeen years. "I hate it," she says, "nervous breakdown." After coaxing from

Matt — he told her it was for the union — she agreed to give me her telephone number. However, she asked if I was Jewish. I told her that I was not, but she persisted and asked me if I came from Israel. I told her that I did not. "You look Jewish" she replied.

In the elevator Matt pointed out that if the matter was not settled, the owner would probably contract out the work. We met Louis in the street. Matt explained the situation. Louis asked, "So what are you going to do?" "I'll go back for another nickel," Matt replied.

Before entering the next shop, the owner complained to Matt that one of the new women operators was "not working out" because she was too slow. It was Matt's job to deal with personnel as well as mediate disputes in the shops. I was introduced to the shop chairperson who made a pun on the word "bundle": "You can make a bundle in this industry" — at which he and Matt roared with laughter. As I gained more of an insider's view, I discovered that a "bundle" referred to the unsewn pieces of merchandise.

The next stop was a shop where sections of the garment were made by individual operators. The coats were of poor quality. Matt called them "garbage." Because this shop was working at full production, my ears were assaulted by incredible noise. The pace of the work appeared to be very fast. There were no windows, the shop was dimly lit and material was strewn everywhere. The owner complained about a presser who had walked off the job. According to the owner, the presser was a $26,000 a year man." The owner's son laughed as his father described the "crazy" presser. I looked around and noticed a presser with sweat pouring from his face and cheeks puffed as he pushed down the lever of his machine. "For some reason, all the pressers go crazy," the owner informed us.

In the business for thirty years, the owner had switched from a *conventional* way of production (in which skilled tailors made the whole garment) to a *sectional* method (in which the garment is made in sections by different operators) because it was difficult to find skilled tailors. He showed us the button hole machine. (In conventional shops, button holes are made by hand.) The operator looked up at me and pointed out, "You just have to make sure you don't lose a finger." The owner announced proudly, "We pay the pressers good money." "Why is that?" I asked, "Because they are more skilled?" "No, anyone can be a presser," he retorted. "It's the job, especially in the summer, it's hard work." "He has lots of trouble with his pressers," interjected Matt. "I don't cause any trouble," the owner defended himself, "I don't care if they go to the union." As we were leaving a woman shouted at Matt to get out of the way because she had to make some money.

When we left this shop, my head was reeling and my ears ringing from the noise. The discussion about the "crazy presser" left me perturbed. Matt sensed that something was wrong and pointed out that at least the people were working — a major accomplishment on "the Avenue," where seasonal layoffs were a characteristic of the needle trade.

The next shop on our tour was one of two factories organized around time work, where workers were paid an hourly rate rather than by the piece. It was cleaner, more spacious, better lit and well organized. "The sanest pressers in the business," Matt told me. The woman operating the fuse machine earned $4.00 an hour. Everyone else earned between $8.00 and $9.00 an hour depending on his/her level of skill.

The last shop was the most marginal according to my guide. Hard-hit by high interest rates, the owner was a good designer but a poor businessman. The shop was practically empty. The winter line was finished and there was very little work.

Once home I collapsed. "Who could go to a union meeting after working all day in the factory?" I wondered.

An Insider's View

When I attended a shop meeting at the union headquarters, I learned about a very important practice concerning piece-work, which provided me with more of an insider's view of the industry. Matt had warned me that the meeting would be unlike my other union meeting that I attended, and asked him why. He did not answer me in terms that made sense to me at the time.

Late for the meeting, the shop chairman rushed into the union hall and took his place on the stage. Only one woman was in attendance. He opened the meeting by giving a brief report, explaining that it had been a bad season. The employer had complained to him that all the workers had withheld their tickets and cashed them at the same time so that he had to meet a huge payroll all at once. "We have to discuss our mistakes so as to learn from the past in order to prepare for the future," he concluded. He asked for discussion. The hall was silent. Realizing that perhaps my note-taking was inhibiting people from speaking, I made an obvious gesture in putting aside my notepad and sitting with my hands in my lap. The silence broke.

There was much discussion about saving tickets. Then an old, frail man stood up and announced, "God has given us piece-work to punish us." The others shouted him down yelling, "God did not give us piece-work." Matt spoke on behalf of Mr. Bettle "who asked that we bend a little" and give into his request. "We bend anymore and we'll be hunchback." "Mr. Bettle is always

crying." "He says the same thing every year," people shouted back.

At the end of the meeting commotion erupted at the back of the hall, with much shouting in Yiddish. Suddenly, Matt turned on his heel, walked over to me and asked to see my notes. I had only written half a sentence but Matt ripped up my notes and informed me in a loud voice that, 'What happened in this meeting was confidential. If you report any of this in your thesis I will have you failed."

This meeting had alerted me to the practice of "saving tickets" and I made certain I had included a question on this topic when I designed my interview schedule. During the interviews, workers were impressed with my "inside" knowledge of the industry.

After the preliminary tour of the "shops," I was able to begin the actual interviewing, the main focus of my field research.

Beginning the Field Research

PREPARING THE INTERVIEW SCHEDULE

Having designed an interview schedule, I conducted a pre-test with three women whom I had met through my activities in the women's movement. The interview consisted of a list of topics covering work history, nature or work, union activity and family relationships. I did not attempt to structure the interview too rigidly, but rather treated it as a conversation. Using a tape recorder allowed me to relax and listen carefully to the conversation. My interviews with the women who agreed to the pre-test helped to build my own self-confidence. After "practising" my questions on them, I decided that it would be easier to follow a chronological order in asking questions, rather than beginning with the present and working back. The recounting of certain aspects of their lives was an obviously painful experience, and their willingness to talk to me honestly assisted in my preparation for the interviews ahead. The pre-test also enabled me to become familiar with the operation of a tape recorder.

Setting up appointments with women workers took a long time because they did not want to commit themselves to a date too far in advance. It was the slow season, and many of the women were home from work; consequently, I could interview them during the day. Some of the women preferred this arrangement because their husbands were not home and they could talk freely. Also, because it took much persuasion to convince the women to be interviewed, I agreed to meet with them whenever it was convenient. At the end of each interview, I asked the respondents to sign an interview release form to grant me permission to use my tapes in my writing and to place a copy in the Public Archives of Canada.

Since my pre-tests went so smoothly, I was surprised when some of my potential respondents were less than eager to be interviewed, even after they had agreed to an interview by telephone. One interview was especially memorable because it illustrated the extent to which it was part of a family affair: throughout my visit, Anna was under a great deal of pressure from her husband and mother not to answer any questions, but she consented to be interviewed in the end.

It took me two hours by bus to reach Anna's house in a suburb of Toronto. Anna answered the door, her hair in rollers. She introduced me to her son, who remained present to translate difficult words from English to Italian. Anna apologized for her inability to speak English, and although I had no difficulty in understanding her, I was careful to speak plainly. We sat on the couch in the family room. Anna was relaxed and cheerful. However, in the middle of the interview her husband phoned. When she got off the phone she told me that her sister-in-law's mother had died and that she couldn't talk anymore. I offered to come back another day, but she couldn't think of another time that I could return.

It did not take me long to suspect that Anna's husband had told her not to talk to me. I asked if I could see her again, explaining that my research was very important to me. She became angry and reminded me that she was helping me with my future at the university. When I said that I was sorry about the death of her sister-in-law's mother, she visibly relaxed. I suggested that she may want to inform her relatives. When she returned from phoning them, she wanted to continue the interview, but she was very uneasy. I assured her of the confidentiality of her answers, and we continued our discussion until the telephone rang again. This time it was her mother calling. Later, by way of explaining family pressures, she said to me that her mother was very strict and would not allow her to go out — not even to take English classes.

Hoping to obtain some insight, I asked Anna, while drinking espresso in her kitchen, how she felt about being interviewed. She replied that she didn't like it because it made her think too much, that she was a simple person and that it would be more interesting to interview people who had travelled. Thus Anna's hesitation about being interviewed had to do with her feelings of inadequacy. She could not understand how her life could be of interest to someone like myself. When she asked me about my family and whether I lived with my parents, I realized that a woman living on her own and writing a Ph.D. thesis seemed to her a strange undertaking.

Fortunately, I did not encounter this hesitance about being interviewed from the rest of the women in the shop. However, I did encounter resistance to questions of a personal nature from union officials.

ENCOUNTERING RESISTANCE TO PERSONAL QUESTIONS

The following account of an interview should illustrate the problems in dealing with resistance to answering questions considered to be personal.

Martha Neumann was not receptive to my research concerns from the beginning. She was one of the few women activists in the Cloakmakers' Union and I was determined to interview her, despite her obvious reluctance. She finally consented. Expecting a long session and being extremely excited about this interview, I brought along six blank one-hour tapes! The stormy session that ensued was certainly not anticipated on my part.

My time with Martha consisted of continual negotiations about the legitimacy of my questions. When I asked her birthplace and birthdate, she argued that this was personal information and that she did not wish to answer personal questions. Whereas she thought I wanted "to know about union history, not about individuals," I was concerned with how she was able to integrate her private life with her union activity.

Several times during the interview I had to negotiate the "meaning" of my research interest. She said that she was suspicious of me when she saw me talking to so many of the workers in the shop. She made it clear that she did not approve of my methodology. "Why do the people at the university want to know this?" I explained I was interested in how work affected life after work. She asked me to repeat this and thought about it. When I added "and vice versa," she became very upset and said families were important to the Italians, but that they didn't know anything (about the history of the union presumably). This comment irritated me because I had spent the summer interviewing women workers,

and I was feeling protective of them. In other words, I was becoming emotionally involved with my research.

Several times Martha got up to make tea, suggested ending the interview and changed her mind. Meanwhile, I was hoping that she would begin to relax and tell me how she managed to be active in the union and be a single parent at the same time. Martha's distinction between "personal" and "non-personal" questions was becoming increasingly blurred. For example, she was willing to talk about her wages but not about her work history. When she could not remember the date of an event, I asked her if the event occurred before or after her daughter was born. She became angry and said "I told you, no personal questions." I explained that some women were able to recall when something happened by the ages of their children.

When she returned from the kitchen to put the kettle on for the second time, I told her that if she didn't want to continue, that was fine. As I was leaving, I made a point of looking her straight in the eye and saying that I thought she was a very special person and that few women would take the time to participate in the union. She misunderstood what I was trying to say and protested. "I didn't neglect my daughter." My patience left me and I said very forcefully, "I did not *accuse* you of neglecting your daughter." As she waved to me from the balcony of her apartment I was feeling very despondent because I desperately wanted this woman's approval of my research and felt that I had failed.

Concerned about the possible repercussions of my session with Martha I contacted my supervisor. As it turned out, I was actually in danger of losing the cooperation of the union leadership over this event. Martha had phoned the union manager to complain about my research. The main objection seemed to be my "social-worker" attitude. I was surprised by this criticism, but I had been a community organizer and youth counsellor years ago and may have unconsciously slipped into a social-worker role. If I was, however, it seemed to work with the other women I had interviewed.

I had declined to drink tea with Martha at the end of the interview, because I was feeling ill. When my supervisor pointed out I had made a mistake, I agreed. It was important for Martha to save face in this situation and so I offered to return the tape of the interview. This gesture smoothed things over with the union leadership. I did not have to return the tape and I was able to continue my research, at least in the formal sense. At the informal level, Martha was doing everything in her power to stop me from getting access to the other workers in the shop.

In retrospect, I should have read the warning signs more carefully and not interviewed Martha. For, the fact that she did not see "personal questions" as political indicated that she was not a good contributor to my research. I had naively expected the men to object to my research but not the women.

I was also discouraged because I had hoped to reach more women workers who had retired from the shop. Instead, given the gender division of labour in the cloak industry, I discovered that I was drawing from a smaller pool of women compared to men. Moreover during the field research I was continuously worried that I was not getting enough information to write a dissertation. I was unaware that these feelings of inadequacy are common among field researchers.

Another unexpected reaction on my part was culture shock.

CULTURE SHOCK

Since I wanted my research to focus primarily on working women, I interviewed the men mainly to obtain background information. My cavalier attitude, however, turned out to be another mistake and revealed to me something about the underlying biased assumptions that I was bringing to the interview situation.

The first man whom I interviewed from Edna Manufacture was Lennie Freedman. I was able to establish rapport with him and his wife easily. An old-timer in the union, Lennie eagerly recounted his experiences during the militant 1930s in the needle trade. When he told me that he was sympathetic to the socialist views of Trotsky I was surprised. Most of the Trotskyists I knew were student intellectuals who radicalized during the antiwar movement of the 1960s. Now I was meeting what Gramsci, a Marxist theorist called an "organic intellectual." Lennie lived during Trotsky's lifetime and took part in political debates as part of his everyday experience in the Toronto garment district of the 1930s. Our interviews made history come alive. The other moving aspect of the interview occurred when Lennie asked me to play back part of the tape. As he listened, tears appeared in his eyes. Inadvertently I erased part of the tape, and Lennie graciously consented to do the interview again.

But it was several months before I was able to come to terms with these two very different interview experiences. I was experiencing what anthropologists in the field call "culture shock": a man who was moved to tears and a woman who was a tough-minded union activist were role reversals that I had hoped to find. And yet when they presented themselves to me, a feeling of inadequacy overwhelmed me. I was aware that culture shock occurred when field-workers went to faraway countries. But I was only down the street! I wasn't sure I could rise to the challenge.

NEGOTIATIONS OVER RESEARCH CONTINUE

My encounters with Sid, the new shop chairman, involved even more negotiations about the meaning of my research. I looked on each of these encounters as a test, for the union leaders wanted to know if I could be trusted.

Sid was not sympathetic to my research. Before assuming his position with the union, he had agreed to an interview; however, once installed his objections were similar to Martha's. He did not understand why I was interviewing "so many workers" and suggested that I should talk to the old-timers who had been in the shop thirty or forty years. In the end, Sid refused to give me an interview on the grounds that he had been working in the shop only ten years. When I explained that I wanted to hear about the work in the workers' own words he retorted, "What does the worker know — go to the union. They trust their union leaders." I also explained that I wanted to understand the different views concerning the history of the union, to which he responded: "There is only one. You can get it from the union."

I decided to try a different tack. I told Sid that I was interested in how piece-work operated in the shop. He acceded on the condition that I would not ask anything personal about individual work history because people in the shop were scared. He warned that destructive criticism should not be discussed and this included how the worker was treated in the shop. The interview should focus only on what was constructive. On the subject of how the trade operated, he pointed out that he could talk about the cycle of the industry, the seasonal nature of the work, stylistic changes in garments, and so on. When I agreed that this would be a useful discussion, Sid told me to go to the union for this information.

Again I tried another approach: I explained that there were few books on the subject. Sid disagreed and said that there were many books. "Not on Canada," I pointed out, but he said that there were many books in the United States on this subject and that the story in Canada was the same because it was an international union

and the work was the same. He agreed to meet me later in the summer during lunch. Then, changing his mind, he said that he was very busy during lunch.

I contacted Matt Kelly, who agreed to talk to Sid but only after I prepared a list of questions for distribution in the shop. Although my list required simplification, Matt was impressed because it demonstrated that on the basis of the interviews conducted thus far I was beginning to grasp some of the fundamental aspects of the trade.

Matt and I visited Edna Manufacture to enlist Sid's help. We sat in the showroom, with Matt strategically placed between Sid and myself. After Matt read the list, Sid stated that the workers did not want to be tape-recorded or to answer personal questions. Showing extreme respect, Matt responded that, as a union staff member, he, Matt, worked for Sid and that he didn't want to pressure him. Several times Matt called on me to speak, but Sid's demeanor toward me was not encouraging. He didn't look at me and appeared to be indifferent to my comments. I wondered if this was because I was a woman. Finally, compelled to break into the debate, I pointed out that I had already interviewed some people in the shop who had not raised any objections. Sid was visibly agitated by my interruption but he was surprised to hear that some workers in the shop had already given an interview. I suggested to him that my research was like a jig-saw puzzle, in that different people remembered different things. "It's not a question of remembering," he corrected me, "they are living it everyday."

Concerning the role of women in the trade, Sid said that women play the same role as men — "they are no different." He concluded that the questions on my list could be answered by the union. Matt explained that my supervisor was a friend of his and that he wanted me to "talk to the workers and not the union bureaucrat." Seemingly placated at last, Sid agreed to call Matt when he could give me an interview. He pointed out that he lived through the war and the holocaust and that he was busy with his family and "the society" (an ethnic organization). I noticed that he had aged considerably in the last year and that he had lost a lot of weight. His new position was taking its toll. (Later in the summer he gave me an interview, but he did not invite me to his home and refused to be tape-recorded.)

BREAK-THROUGH

Although I had encountered many challenges during the interviewing phase of my research, one incident in particular served to highlight the worthwhileness of the research project and gave me the encouragement to complete my work.

On the same day of my negotiations with Sid, Martha, who (as you remember) had refused to cooperate with my research, did not recognize me in the shop and turned on Matt with hostility about "that other girl you brought to me." While Matt talked to Martha, I felt a strange undercurrent in the shop. I looked around, and the people whom I interviewed greeted me with their eyes. Most smiled and a few spoke to me. No longer rivetted to the floor, I became lightheaded, elated and confident — not only did they not bear me any resentment but they were, in fact, glad to see me. The complaints of Martha and Sid could not penetrate the feeling of solidarity that I felt being conveyed to me.

LEARNING TO ACCEPT ADVICE

Following our visit to the factory, Matt advised me that I was too aggressive, too direct in my questions, that I cornered people, that I did not allow them an out, that I was too persistent and academic. He suggested that I be more feminine in my approach. This was not the first time that Matt had offered his advice and I pointed out that he would not say this to a man. He emphasized that I should learn to compliment people in the same way that my supervisor did. I had watched Matt tell the bookkeeper that she did more for the workers than any other bookkeeper, and the cutters were the best group of cutters in the industry, and so on. Matt also criticized me for speaking to the other workers in the shop and not staying where I was, as he had asked me. Feeling buoyed by the greetings I had received, in my own defence I explained that the workers in the shop had recognized me from the previous interviews and I felt that I shouldn't ignore them. "They're people after all, not animals," I said, echoing the words that his workers used in referring to their need to be treated with dignity.

I sensed that it was Matt who needed to be "stroked" and that I had not verbalized my appreciation of his help. I tried not to be so defensive and indicated my acceptance of his advice. When I asked him if we could go into the shop again, he admitted that he felt a moral obligation to help me as much as he could "since I got you into this," but that he could not spend all his time helping me, else his employer would become suspicious. I told him that I appreciated all his help. It was made clear to me that I should rely on him less.

ANOTHER TEST — ETHNIC BACKGROUND

After several attempts, I was able to arrange a visit to the cutting room where I interviewed the workers individually, asking them about their work, their wages and the union. One incident clearly indicated how my ethnic origin complicated the interview situation.

The head cutter was reluctant to talk to me and set the tone for the rest of the cutting room because he had authority over the other workers. He joked about how he suffered, and how when he got off the boat they told him to watch everything and to mind his own business. Making conversation, I asked him where he was from. He asked me to guess. Since I had already interviewed a number of operators who had emigrated from Poland, I surmised correctly that he was from Poland.

When he asked me where I was from, I said that I was born in "the States" but that I had lived in Canada for seventeen years. This was not a satisfactory answer and he demanded to know my ethnic origin. By this time the whole cutting room was listening to our conversation. I suggested that he likewise guess. Italian? French? Greek? and so on he went without guessing correctly. Long ago I had decided to answer questions about my ethnic background honestly, although some had advised me to minimize the risk and tell a white lie. "I am Syrian" I told him. Someone piped up with "What do you think of the Middle East situation?" I said I had no opinion.

The head cutter interjected "What do you think of the Syrian army being on the border of Israel? These questions were catching me off guard. Some of the Jewish workers were Zionists, and I feared that a political discussion could polarize the situation in the rest of the factory and add an unnecessary complication to the already difficult task of establishing rapport with my potential respondents. I repeated, "I have no opinion." "You read the paper?" he asked. At the risk of sounding like a person who did not take an interest in the world around her, I again refused to be taken in. Then the head cutter wanted to know my father's occupation. Hoping to strike a cord of commonality, I told him that my grandmother had been a seamstress and my mother had worked in a garment factory. "I don't care about your mother, what does your father do?" At great risk of

alienating everyone I said, "You are not willing to answer personal questions, so neither will I."

The East Indian sorter buying his lunch was extremely upset. "You shouldn't have told them that you are Syrian — they are all Jews." He added, "I am Moslem." He was obviously sympathetic to my predicament because he told me that he gone through the same line of questioning himself.

THE FINAL STEP: REVISING THE ORIGINAL PLAN

Because of the resistance encountered, I had to revise my original plan to interview all the workers employed in the shop. I next concentrated my efforts on retirees and former workers. The retirees had more time to talk and were less inhibited because they were no longer directly involved with the trade.

I drew up an interim report that provided the basis for second interviews with women. I wanted to understand their double day of labour in more detail. I also conducted interviews with union officials and management personnel of the factory. I was right to leave the owner of the shop to the end of the field research, after I had interviewed the majority of the workers. For, even though he had agreed to let me see the books and to take pictures of the factory, his bookkeeper refused to answer any direct questions about the business. He asked me "to leave us alone" and refused to have anything more to do with me.

In January, 1982, my interviewing came to an end.

The interviewing phase of my research took two years. I was often depressed because I felt that I was inadequate as an interviewer, that I was not getting enough information, or because I feared that I could not rise to the challenge of interviewing people whose life stories, while ordinary were incredibly powerful. During the times when the interviewing was not going well or I did not feel energized enough to continue, I would keep busy by sending out letters requesting interviews, writing thank you notes to my respondents, revising my interview schedule and keeping field notes. Some days were harder than others, but the fact that these women and men had welcomed me into their homes and told me their life story made it all worth the struggle.

PUBLIC OPINION AND PUBLIC POLICY

Alexander Himelfarb

"Surveys show that most Canadians believe" has become a universal phrase in contemporary social analysis and public policy. Opinion surveys are big business and getting bigger. The latest survey findings regularly make the national headlines and in significant ways shape the social policy agenda. Pollsters and survey experts are becoming influential policy advisors. As the use of opinion surveys becomes increasingly pervasive and as their influence grows, we need more than ever to understand their limits and dangers. Some of the most important issues are not empirical, not questions of sampling or accuracy but rather conceptual. That is, we must ask what such a technology can contribute to policy and program development irrespective of technical improvements.

Proponents often point out that public opinion surveys are an example of a uniquely democratic technology. If democracy is to serve "the people," then we must

From "Public Opinion and Public Policy" was reprinted from Vol. 2, No. 1, of *Forum on Corrections Research* with the permission of the Correctional Service of Canada. The opinions expressed in *Forum* do not necessarily reflect the views or policies of the Correctional Service of Canada.

have some way to hear the "people's voice." Surveys, the argument goes, have allowed us to tap public needs and concerns. Without them, we hear only organized interest groups or depend on our best guess of the public mood.

Critics, who have become more adamant over the past few years, argue that our opinion surveys give us at best a partial glimpse and at worst a distortion of the public view. According to this perspective, survey methodology is ill-equipped to get at people's complex, nuanced and shifting perceptions and opinions. Further, they argue, such surveys promote "quick fix" policy solutions, "quick change politics." According to the critics, the proliferation of surveys has resulted in confusion between opinion and judgment informed by experience and research on what works. Some have gone so far as to suggest a moratorium on public opinion surveying and a return to more fundamental research. But these surveys are here to stay and, as practitioners become increasingly sophisticated in their use, they can become a valuable instrument for public policy — if we know their limits and their dangers.

The Problem of Public

Public opinion surveys are limited by the assumption that often underlies them, that there is a singular homogeneous public whose opinions can be recorded. This assumption influences the design of surveys and the analysis of survey data. The very notion of close-ended questions, where the responses are predetermined by the researchers, presumes that the researchers already know, more or less, the range of opinions they are tapping. The set questions and answers, regardless of how often they are pre-tested, constrain the range of responses possible. Surveys may, therefore, altogether miss those answers that do not fit the researchers' preconceived notions of what most people think.

Imagine, for example, that you are asked to rank a list of issues in order of how much they concern you. The list might include issues such as the deficit, inflation, interest rates, unemployment, Canadian unity, violence, crime, aboriginal self-government, sexual equality, cultural sovereignty, and the environment. No doubt you could rank these issues. How different would your answer be if the question were open-ended, if there had been no list? Research shows that there can be significant differences. For example, respondents may rank "crime" relatively high on a list but are far less likely to volunteer it when there is no list.

Generally, it is more expensive to use open-ended questions. They are more difficult to code, quantify, compare and track over time, but they allow respondents to tell it their way. Closed questions inevitably constrain respondents and therefore limit the capacity of surveys to uncover the unexpected. Closed questions have a self-fulfilling effect.

Some critics have gone further to suggest that the way these results are often presented has similar consequences on the opinions of Canadians. Imagine, for example, that you read that most Canadians are concerned about crime and corrections. Might you wonder whether you should rethink your own views? What do they know that you don't know? The bandwagon effect may operate not only in politics but also in public policy. Public opinion surveys, then, can become an instrument for shaping rather than measuring public opinion.

Thus, we read newspaper articles about what "most Canadians" or the "average Canadian" think(s) about crime, corrections, conditional release, or what have you. We read that the average Canadian is concerned about crime and lacks confidence in our system of corrections and conditional release. Sometimes we read that the average Canadian wants a tougher system, or at least one that gives unambiguous emphasis to public protection. All of this is, of course, very important to know for policy and program development, but it represents only some subset of public opinion.

Who is this average Canadian? The average Canadian is a myth. Real people have a particular gender, age, ethnicity, level of education; they also live and work in communities, which shape their views. They draw their views from their experiences and interactions, and as their experiences and interactions vary, so do their views. For policy purposes, it is generally less important to know what most people think than to know how particular groups of people with shared interests and experiences think.

The "quick and dirty" survey cannot capture the views of the many publics that must be taken into account in policy development. While sophisticated sampling techniques may allow us to measure within a few percentage points Canadian opinions on any issue, by surveying fewer than 1,000, they may not give policy makers the information they need, particularly in a country as diverse as ours.

Of course larger surveys may be able to take into account some of the key socio-demographic factors that differentiate publics — gender, age, urban/rural residence, education level, etc. — but even these analyses are limited. First, unless the surveys are very large and therefore expensive, they can only get at a select few of these factors. Selecting the key factors, then, depends on the ingenuity and insight of the researcher in defining the important groupings of opinion. Second, and more important, these techniques are rarely able to tackle the more subtle bases for opinion formation. If we are to understand public opinion, we must know something of how these opinions were formed. Were they a result of direct experience, opinion leaders, the media? In our field, for example, we will want to understand the views of those who have been victimized and those who have not, of those who have had contact with the criminal justice system and those who have not, of the informed and uninformed, etc. It is important for us to know, for example, whether concern about corrections is more common among the uninformed than among those who understand our correctional system. We would imagine a very different policy direction if we found that people became more satisfied with our programs as they learned more about them than if the reverse were the case or if we found that information made no difference at all.

In response, survey researchers are developing more varied, and sometimes more expensive, techniques to allow targeting of particular groups, and to provide some understanding of the various publics — opinion groupings — that may form around any issue. Some may complement their survey findings with more subjective qualitative (open-ended) research, focus groups and the like. In any case, the value of the survey data is not simply a function of the sophistication of the methodology; it is dependent on the skill, knowledge and ingenuity of the researchers and particularly their understanding of the "structure of the Canadian public."

The Problem of Opinion

The second problem resides in the very idea of "opinion." Let's assume we have asked a number of respondents to give us their opinion on whether corrections programs are effective. What have we learned if the answer is "no, corrections is not effective"? Some may be telling us that they are generally cynical or distrustful about government and government institutions. Their answer may reflect their attitudes toward government programs in general.

Some may be saying little more than "I've never thought about this before, but now that you ask, I guess not." Such opinions are not likely strongly held or even very meaningful. Others may be saying that they don't believe anything can work to reform criminals. Their opinion, then, reflects their view of human nature. Yet others, may be saying that their judgment, based on their knowledge, is that we're not as good as we should or could be. The possibilities are virtually limitless. Few surveys help us to know whether the so-called opinions we have tapped reflect enduring attitudes, firmly held beliefs, top-of-the-mind views, judgment based on experience and knowledge, or simply an answer created on the spot in order to fill out the questionnaire.

For policy purposes, we must know whether, for example, some measured public lack of confidence in criminal justice is episodic and transitory, perhaps the result of a particular incident or series of incidents, or enduring and reflective of deeply held concerns. We must know what underlies this apparent lack of confidence. Is it the perception that crime rates are growing, or that we are not doing enough, or that nothing works anyway? Is it the perception that traditional community values are crumbling and the sense of insecurity about what this means? Perhaps most important, we must know whether these views are based on an accurate understanding of crime and corrections or are based on myths and misperceptions.

Pollsters increasingly recognize the limits of one-time snapshots of opinion and argue that only through tracking public opinion over time can we know whether we are getting at views that are enduring and meaningful. In addition, some survey researchers have tried to link people's opinions on specific issues to their general views on the state and future of the nation, the government and their own lives. For policy purposes, it is also crucial to link opinions to level of knowledge and understanding of issues.

But the problems run deeper. You have probably all completed a questionnaire or responded to an interviewer on some issue or other. You were probably not always sure about your answers or your commitment to them. No doubt you sometimes treated the exercise lightly, sometimes seriously. Perhaps you were not always truthful. While researchers have tried to develop technical solutions to these kinds of problems, they can never fully address the difficulty in determining just what we are measuring when we measure opinion. Psychoanalysts, psychologists and sociologists have developed countless techniques to try to get at people's subjective worlds, their views about themselves and others and their concerns and preferences. Social scientists like to argue about which techniques are most suitable but they do tend to agree that no technique allows us to know with confidence people's inner experiences.

Opinion surveys are most useful when they provide information on our various publics; are at least to some extent open-ended; track people's opinions over time; link people's opinions on specific issues to their general views of the world; and link people's opinions to their level of knowledge and understanding of the issues. Even when they are technically sound and methodologically sophisticated, the quality of survey data will always be limited by the researchers' skills and their understanding of the issues.

We often have difficulty in articulating our own views and opinions. We know how difficult it is to penetrate the inner experience of others. The results of the best public opinion surveys can never be more than an approximation.

Closing the gap between these approximations and "reality" generally requires more intensive, often multidisciplinary approaches. Researchers investigating public opinion on capital punishment know how important it can be to close the gap. In poll after poll, the majority of Canadians (between 70% and 80%) appear to support capital punishment in some case or other. When they are given specific case scenarios and asked if they would like to see capital punishment imposed in these cases, we find far less support.

Many Canadians support capital punishment in the abstract but not when confronted with real people in real situations. Similarly, most Canadians support some version of community corrections — but not necessarily in their community.

Nevertheless, opinion surveys can help to ensure that the policy process does not lose touch with the publics the policies aim to serve. They can be useful for getting some sense of public concerns and preferences. They can therefore help to shape public policy objectives and to track the effects of social action (or inaction). They may be less helpful in the really hard decisions. If, for example, public opinion challenges our policies or programs, should we change our thinking and develop new policy directions or should we inform and educate the public about what we do and what is possible? Opinion surveys help us to understand the environment in which policy development must occur — what is demanded or expected, what will be resisted or rejected. The surveys may help us to establish our policy and communications objectives and priorities but they are less useful for developing the specific policies and programs, the means, for achieving our objectives.

BASIC CONCEPTS and PROCESSES

As you read through this part of the text, you may come closer to a definition of sociology. Culture, social structure and interaction are the central concepts of sociology because it is these that define and give unity to the field. At the same time in the first part of this book words such as "culture" and "structure" have been tossed off rather lightly. In many ways this is necessary, as much of the basis of the discipline must be taken for granted if we are to proceed. But when we do stop to define and come to grips with these concepts, we are also likely to find we again unmask the fundamental debates and divisions at the core of sociology.

SOCIETY AND STRUCTURAL FUNCTIONALISM

The organization of the first three chapters in Part 2 is very traditional, as it derives largely from the way structural functionalists have carved up and categorized the social world. As we have seen, their emphasis has been on value consensus — in essence, their answer to *the* question sociology has all along attempted to answer: how is social order possible? Their answer, their emphasis, has dictated that they tell the story in a particular way. From this perspective it makes sense to start with the concept of *culture*: the system of ideas of a group, ideas passed on from generation to generation.

In trying to answer the question of order, structural functionalists have had to face the problem that humans have not relied solely on instincts passed on through the genetic code to provide guides for behaviour. What is passed on, instead, is culture, plans for behaviour, the "recipes" shared by a group. Supposedly people in any group learn to be committed to much the same *values*, and this is the cement of society. The communication and sharing of these values is possible in human society because of our ability to *symbolize*, to develop a language that allows us to store values and ideas for future generations and to draw upon the stock of knowledge of past generations.

It is this aspect of human society — the *symbolic component* — which most clearly distinguishes us from the animal world; it allows us to move beyond the confines of our immediate environment and, at the same time, at least partly confines us to the values and ideas of our own language group.

To simplify, these theorists posit a rather close fit between cultural ideals and behaviour. Those values to which people in a group are most committed become *institutionalized*, that is, become translated into patterned behaviour. In this sense institutions are the human equivalent of instincts. The family and its patterns of rights and obligations is such an institution. So, too, are education, religion, government, the legal system and the economy. *Society*, then, is a system of institutions necessary for the survival of an ordered human community. And all of this implies that the system of institutions is a result of cumulative rationality — generations of people's best attempts to achieve their shared values and goals.

When we say that the structural functionalists posit a close fit between cultural ideals and behaviour, we are saying that they make no sharp distinction between culture and social structure. The cultural ideals, crystallized into institutions, are like narrow corridors through which we all must pass. These corridors have already been built; the institution of the family, for example, prescribes the rights and obligations of father-husband, mother-wife, and so on. The *roles* are set, literally "structured," the script has been written and we learn our lines and act our parts. The script is culture; the actual repetitive patterned performance is structure. And there is little to distinguish the two. Why do we conform? Perhaps because we do not know other scripts are possible or perhaps because we wish to avoid bad reviews — ridicule, rejection or even arrest and incarceration — what sociologists call *mechanisms of social control*.

In fact, structural functionalists go further to suggest that we conform because we learn to want to. In other words, in this view, *child socialization* is the process by which children learn their recipes and "internalize" the values of their group. To put it simply, they come to need to conform. Culture and structure exist outside us and inside us and exert pressure from both directions. For structural functionalists, then, the answer to the "problem of order" is two-fold: it is the result of both institutionalization and socialization, processes backed up by positive and negative *sanctions* — rewards and punishments.

SOCIETY AND CONFLICT THEORY

We find much that is useful in the structural functionalist's position. To use another metaphor, they have, perhaps, described the blueprint of society. It is as though they have managed to stop society and to describe it standing still and with no history.

Perhaps, too, our reliance on metaphors says something about the problems with this approach. Structural functionalism is in itself a metaphor for society. It tells us nothing about how and in whose interests the blueprint was created. And, like all blueprints, it is more harmonious, closer to perfection, than the product ever can be. Conflict theorists address these precise questions when they attack structural functionalists' utopian model of society and its conception of over-socialized people.

These theorists focus not on culture but on social structure, the layers of inequality in society. Some, whom we shall call an elite, have more of what there is to get in society. They are interested in keeping and perhaps in enhancing their privileged position. The "have nots" will, of course, wish to improve their position. Society is, in large part, shaped by the conflict between these two groups. Obviously, the elite have an advantage in this conflict because, almost by definition, they have control of the important societal resources: force, symbols, practices and goods. In other words, according to conflict theorists, the cement of society is not value consensus but coercion and manipulation. Conflict theorists, then, are likely to look at institutions not in terms of how they serve societal functions so much as how they serve the interests of the elite. For example they may examine how the educational institutions, in the process of teaching basic skills, also teach a tolerance of inequality, a respect for authority and perhaps an unreflective conformism. It is in the same sense that religion is said to be the "opiate of the masses." Religion is ideology.

Most sociologists have followed Karl Marx's notion of *ideology* as a world view or belief system which coincides with the interests and concerns of ruling classes and powerful groups in society. For Marx, certain ideas and cultural beliefs are of more consequence because they serve to justify and legitimate the position of the privileged class. For example in Marx's time liberalism, with its emphasis on possessive individualism and freedom from the constraints of society, dovetailed nicely with the desires of nineteenth-century capitalists to develop their enterprises unencumbered by tradition or intervention of the state into their affairs. While capitalists did not "invent" liberalism, they possessed the power and resources to make it a legitimate and dominant system of beliefs. As Marx put it, the ideas of the ruling class are in every age the ruling ideas. Of course at times what is communicated may be more transparently and obviously a rationalization for the existing state of affairs. Religious beliefs, for instance, have often attempted to reconcile people to their low position in society or to imply that inequalities, whether based on sex, class or race, are God-given. But, as Marx was fully aware, the more subtle characteristic of ideology is that its values become so taken for granted as to be a set of limits to consciousness rather than simply a set of justifications. Ideology, then, is a partial world view which prevents us from understanding fully our society and the possibility of changing it.

It is in this latter sense that we can, for example, best appreciate the role of the media in shaping public consciousness. As control of media has become more and more concentrated in the hands of a few, we should not be surprised that they, at times, are going to present views and opinions that deliberately reflect the interests of big business. For example, it is rather predictable and easy to see as "propaganda" that newspapers in New Brunswick, all of which are owned by the Irving family, would be unanimously opposed to policies designed to diversify the ownership of Canadian media. But, what is less easy to see is the more subtle and even unintended results of what is often an implicit commitment to an ideology. Whether intended or not, it is clear that the media ask certain kinds of questions, make selections about what is important and what is not, report events as if they had no history or social context, all within a framework which assumes that if a problem does exist it can be resolved within the existing system. Such perspectives are partial world views because what is presented to us through the media is that only certain kinds of futures can be imagined; essentially their perceptions of "what is" derive from their notions of "what might be." Whether deliberately manipulative or not, this certainly coincides with the ideology, or world view, of the economic elite.

Of course the very fact that we are able to make these statements about ideology indicates that not all Canadians are fully committed to or accept the prevailing or dominant ideology. Indeed one standard that distinguishes a complex from a simple society is that no single ideology prevails. Rather, in describing political culture, we must think in terms of a dominant ideology and a number of competing counter-ideologies. To say, for example, that in Canada the ideology of conservatism has in recent years been replaced by a liberal ideology is to detect some dominant threads, some changes in the conventional wisdom, but not to imply that everyone shares or is equally attached to the dominant ideology. In fact many Canadians will continue to identify themselves in terms of their commitment to conservatism or their rejection of both ideologies in favour of some version of socialist ideology. In sum, describing Canada's political culture requires that we recognize that we hold conflicting images of society and assumptions about human nature, and that these shape what we choose to see, what we ignore, what we celebrate as progress and what we deplore as decline.

It is possible that you may find this kind of discussion of political culture rather abstract and not particulary relevant to how you tend to think about various issues. Like many Canadians you may deny that you are committed to any one ideology. While you may have an intuitive or gut-level belief in certain values — fairness, justice, equality, tradition, order and so on — you prefer to remain pragmatic, to formulate your opinions on an issue-by-issue basis. Like many Canadians, then, you may well believe that no overriding moral or value principle serves as the basis of the stand you take on such issues as abortion, capital punishment, narcotics legislation or Canada's involvement in the recent war in the Persian Gulf.

At one level you would be right, since it is unlikely that many people believe in or are fully committed to the kind of full-blown or all-encompassing world view that, at one level, we mean by an ideology. But the way in which we have been using that term allows us to conclude that Canadians do have an ideology, though for most it is *implicit* or only partially articulated. For example, commitment to a political party probably indicates a belief that the democratic political process works and that social change must proceed through institutionalized means. An issue-by-issue approach probably indicates a rejection of utopian thinking and a taken-for-granted belief that the system itself need not or should not be fundamentally altered.

More specifically, positions people take on such issues as whether pornography should be banned reflect at least their implicit attachment to some of the values contained within a particular ideology. For example, some, who favour banning or censoring it, presumably do so because at some level they share the conservative belief that the role of the state is to protect us, even from ourselves, and to maintain the moral and social order. Others, reflecting perhaps the socialist concern with equality, would ban pornography because it is exploitive of women and, increasingly, children. Finally, some, while possibly feeling uncomfortable that pornography exists and who would like to find ways to protect children, may nevertheless fear the implications of state censorship. They share, at least implicity, the liberal emphasis on the automony and freedom of the individual and our need to be protected *from* and not *by* the state. As you read various selections throughout this book, it is at the level of these taken-for-granted or partially inarticulate assumptions that we ask you to consider ideology.

Perhaps the biggest problem in describing and understanding political culture is that the labels we use to identify the major ideologies — liberalism, conservatism, socialism — have over time changed their meaning. Do liberals, for example, believe in medicare, or is that a socialist cause? Can one be a conservative and still believe in socialized medicine? What these confusions suggest is that we should not assume that ideologies are static belief systems, fixed for all time in what they emphasize. Culture, political or otherwise, is created, recreated and modified through human interaction so that ideologies must always be understood in their socio-historical context. While Canada may have been a conservative society until recently, that conservatism has been modified by the fact that there has been a strong socialist movement in this country. Similarly, though most are agreed that the dominant ideology in Canada is now the liberal ideology, Canadian liberalism does not mean exactly the same thing as American liberalism. It, too, has been influenced by both socialism and conservatism and is, therefore, much more likely than its American counterpart to give room to public enterprise and government intervention in private enterprise and to be committed to the notion of a welfare state.

To the extent that the elite are able to control the symbol-producing institutions, they are able to impose their culture — a culture which justifies their privileged position, in other words, their ideology — on the rest. To the extent that the elite control the rule-making machinery — the practices — they "institutionalize" or "structure" the existing inequalities. To the extent that they control the machinery of production and distribution of goods, they are able to exact compliance through material inducement and sanction. And finally, force, as represented, perhaps, by the army and agencies of law enforcementt (which are never too far below the surface), is the last line of defence.

Order is the result of a history of conflict in which some groups have been more successful than others in imposing their interests. Conflict theorists do not dispute that some degree of value consensus must exist if ordered interaction is to occur. They do not dispute the structural-functionalists' blueprint entirely. They simply ask *whose* values are being used for socialization. Conflict theorists recognize as well that order is always fragile and problematic; that conflict is inevitable and endemic; and that there are always available in complex societies competing ideologies, alternative and conflicting cultures. This perspective is developed much more fully in the second half of this book, which focuses almost exclusively on structured inequality.

Many of you may still be wondering what sociology has to say to you. What about everyday behaviour? You may feel that all of what we have said minimizes how much people create, innovate and act in spontaneous and apparently unpredictable ways. In short, perhaps your experience tells you that "real life" does not run so neatly or smoothly as either the structural functional or conflict approach would have it. The way people perceive, respond to and are constrained by social structure in their everyday lives is the focus of interaction approaches to society.

SOCIETY AND INTERACTION

All interaction approaches share a view of society as built up, maintained and modified by the actions of people. Symbolic interactionism in particular emphasizes the interpretive process. Culture, the ideas and norms of a group, must be interpreted in every situation if it is to be used to guide action. While culture gives us clues about how husbands and wives should behave toward one another, every married couple inevitably works out anew what these cultural prescriptions will mean and look like for them.

From this perspective, social structure is intersubjective, dependent on shared meanings; while we may, for the most part, share the same recipes, these are too general to allow for application in any specific situation. So in each new situation, we must negotiate our definitions of the situation until we arrive at sufficient consensus for practical purposes.

Order, then, is the result of two forces. First, like structural functionalism, the interactionist perspective emphasizes socialization as the mechanism whereby people learn and internalize the general meanings of their group or community. But symbolic interactionists also stress that order is an everyday accomplishment, produced and maintained and modified by people in their everyday interactions. Unlike structural functionalists, who view institutions more or less as fixed structures, symbolic interactionists focus on institutionalization, a process which, like socialization, is never complete. Nevertheless symbolic interactionists realize that people do pattern their interactions and develop fairly regular and predictable *routines* so that at times social structure does *appear* to us as real and objective and something other than a human accomplishment.

Perhaps this becomes clearer if we briefly describe George Herbert Mead's conception of self, which has inspired much of the work on interaction. The *self*, developed in childhood through interaction with other socialized humans, allows us to make indications to ourselves, that is, to assess what is significant in our environment. Selves are dependent on our ability to symbolize because the development of self requires that we be able to see the world through the eyes of others, which can only be achieved if we share with others a set of *significant symbols*: language. As the self develops and the child learns to play a variety of roles, he or she comes to internalize the expectations of others — those whom the child particularly likes or respects (significant others) and, gradually, as well the generalized expectations of the community as a whole (generalized other).

But Mead does not posit a one-to-one relationship between self and society. The internalized expectations we have described capture only one aspect of self, what Mead calls the "Me." He also argues that there is another aspect of self, another mode of interacting: the "I," which contains the impulsive tendencies of the individual. According to Mead, the "I" gives impulse to action and the "Me" gives direction to the impulse. Taken together, the "I" and the "Me" constitute the self process; they are, for Mead, complementary. Certainly, socialization is meant to capture the process whereby the self is increasingly controlled by the "Me" but the "I" does not disappear, and all interaction is the result of the interplay, or internal conversation, between these two aspects of self.

This conception of self gives sociological meaning to our common sense knowledge that people differ substantially in the extent to which they allow expression to their impulse, from the relatively unpredictable to the more rule-bound bureaucratic virtuoso. In this sense, as well, we can appreciate that social situations are never fully structured and that we do not all act like automatons or robots. The "I" allows us to imagine possible futures that we have not simply internalized; the "I" allows us to defy socialization to some extent. It is in the intimate relations of the family that most of us have learned to fear the world or to trust it; it is in the family that we have developed our selves.

FAMILY AND CHANGE

The study of the family is very much the study of change, in the sense that marriage and childbirth create new roles and relationships and, as people grow older, the size and shape of their kinship structure is also transformed. More generally, sociologists have also been interested in the effects of wider changes in society because in their action upon the family they have immediate impact on our everyday lives. And because these kinds of changes are so immediate to us, the focus on the changing family demands that we come to grips with our values about the direction of the change; for instance, few people can remain neutral about rising divorce rates or the increasing numbers of single-parent families. Finally, as we begin to learn more about the family of the past, we also become more sensitive to the possibility that we may often glorify or denigrate the past and falsely assume that almost everything in the present is radically different.

As we do more historical research, then, we grow less certain about what kinds of changes have occurred. For example, the conventional wisdom would have it that the modern family is much smaller than its counterpart in the past. Laslett (1965), however, argues that throughout European society families have remained the same size for at least the last several hundred years. While the *extended family* — several generations under the same roof — may have been the norm for those families who could afford it, few really could. The *nuclear family* — husband, wife and children — is not really a modern phenomenon but probably the most persistent pattern for centuries.

What sort of changes have occurred, then? Undoubtedly one of the most significant changes is that the family has participated in the more general trend toward specialization. Progressively, it has been stripped of its traditional functions: production, education, care for the ill, infirm and perhaps permanently helpless, food preparation and even recreation. These have been parcelled out to other institutions, leaving the family responsible only for primary socialization and, however ineffectively, the social and emotional support of its immediate members.

Also, for most Canadians, marriage and family have progressively become *secular* rather than *sacred* institutions. By this we mean, on the one hand, that few of us believe that our marriage is a pact with God so that the ending of it jeopardizes our souls and, on the other hand, that the family we have experienced or will create in the future is more than a human construction.

Another important change is that while kinship may still be for some an important resource, relationships have for the most part moved from *obligation* to *choice*. Rather than the extended kinship ties and obligations of the past, most people now find themselves members of a *modified extended family*. In a complex society such as ours, not all of our important relationships are likely to be with kin. And, to the extent that we must be mobile to get and keep a job, we may lose contact with kin (and friends) as a normal course of events. To a large extent we assume that our parents will be looked after through their own pensions and savings or by the State, through its various welfare programs. In any event, we do not have the same formal obligations and commitments to kin as was predominantly the case in the past.

Perhaps the change which has produced the most controversy, concern and speculation about the future of the family is what has sometimes been referred to as the *equality revolution*. While this change in family relationships has affected relationships among all members of the family, it is the position of women that has received the most attention and that has, perhaps, the most implications for the future structure of family and marriage. Feminist theory has brought about a fundamental "rethinking" of the family. While feminist research has documented how far we are from having realized equality, it is nevertheless apparent that few marriages are based solely on tradition. Probably most marital relationships are the outcome of a process of negotiation rather than the fixed blueprint of the past.

Demographic factors have also profoundly affected the shape of the family. In the mid 1960s some longer term trends began to reverse themselves. The age at which men and women enter into a first marriage, which had steadily declined since the nineteenth century, began to creep upwards. The marriage rate (the proportion of people ever married), which had reached an all time high by the 1960s, also began to decline somewhat. By the mid-1980s the major reason for family dissolution had shifted from the death of one partner to the separation or divorce of the couple. And, as is now well known, the birthrate fell below "replacement level" in all Western societies. These changes, coupled with the dramatic increase in married women's participation in the labour force, have encouraged and been encouraged by the equality revolution.

What does all this mean? First, the family may seem to many an increasingly problematic institution with fewer functions and therefore fewer ties; people must begin to invent new patterns of "togetherness" or risk seeing the family fall apart. Second, the diminishing importance and availability of kinship probably has both positive and negative implications. It may reduce some of the constraints that come from being engulfed in a kinship structure and may allow us more fully to pursue our individual projects — career, education, and so on. At the same time, it may make us feel that we have been cast adrift, placing an almost unbearable burden on the nuclear family to satisfy the social and emotional needs of its members. Third, the equality revolution has undoubtedly expanded the range of alternatives for women and probably for children, perhaps even for men. But it also has led to a wider possibility of conflict within the family: since negotiation between relatively equal partners may not always lead to an amicable settlement, the eventual dissolution of the relationship may seem the only alternative. And when people cannot negotiate a "happy marriage," the fact that the structure of opportunities for women has opened up means that alternatives to marriage for both husbands and wives now exist.

Many of the fundamental debates about the relationship of the individual and the society come to an explosive head in the sociology of the family. Some have asked whether the family as we know it may be fundamentally inconsistent with sexual and gender equality. Some have asked whether the "weakening" of the family has not been a demonstration of our excessive emphasis on individualism (an emphasis on the "I" at the expense of the "Me," to return to Mead's analysis of the relationship of the individual to his or her society) with obvious consequences for offspring. Some have lamented the weakening of family values and expressed concern about the implications this will have for future rates of crime, deviance and other kinds of social problems; they have called for a return to some perhaps mythical family of the past. Others have lamented the sickness of the modern family and have drawn upon the research that documents the overt and covert family violence and the general oppression of women in this example of a patriarchal structure; and they have expressed the need for alternatives for human relationships. Clearly the changing family is a key indicator of how our society is changing and how we feel about that change.

DEVIANCE AND CONTROL

For structural-functionalists, deviants present something of a problem. If we have all learned to conform, even to need to conform, and basically to the same rules, where do deviants come from? These theorists are forced to put forward a problem to explain the problem. Conservatives in the past explained away deviants and criminals by assuming that they were different types of people, that they were biologically or psychologically different, and not just different but bad. This view has died hard despite the fact that there is no evidence to support it and despite the fact that it makes little sense, given that we have all done something deviant or probably even criminal and that deviants and criminals spend most of their time being normal.

Structural-functionalists have rejected this view for a more sociological emphasis. They define deviance as norm violation, understanding that this will mean different things depending on one's position or status in society. Why do people violate norms? If there is nothing wrong with them then something must be wrong with how they have been socialized, or perhaps there is some "strain" in the social structure. So, for example, juvenile delinquency is often seen as a result of broken homes and the like. The supposedly disproportionately high rates of crime among the poor are seen as a result of *anomie*. Norms no longer control their behaviour because, while the poor have accepted the values and goals of the larger society, they have limited access to the opportunity structures, the institutionalized means of achieving these goals. There is no doubt a good deal of face validity to these "solutions" to deviance. It is hard to argue with the notion that the social structure exerts pressure on the disenfranchised and powerless to commit certain kinds of deviant acts. If young people do not learn the rules, or learn a different set of rules, they are likely to come to be seen as deviant. But a great deal is left out in this approach.

Interactionists are far less likely to find that deviance poses theoretical problems. Rather, they may view deviants as an affirmation of the "I," a confirmation of the creativity of the self, a "predictable" aspect of any interaction. Interaction is, after all, a process of negotiation and manipulation as participants try to discover the appropriate line of action and try to keep themselves and others on it. Interactionists, then, are more concerned with how "deviant," as an identity, is the product of negotiation in everyday life. How is it that some people are so categorized? How does the attribution "deviant" affect one's self-conception and, therefore, behaviour? How does the label influence how others see and treat us? How does one get rid of the label? These have been the central questions of an interactionist approach to deviance — the labelling perspective.

This perspective asks us to examine not the deviant *per se*, but the reactions to the deviant, the labellers. Deviance is a matter of social definition with the result that deviant behaviour is behaviour so labelled. So, labelling theorists ask, who has the power to label particular people as deviant — criminal, sick, crazy — and how do they make their labels stick? They have found, for example, that police are likely to use political criteria to decide which juveniles are "delinquent enough" to arrest. The answer is that there are *master labellers* — the police, the courts, psychiatrists, for example — who will act, in part at least, on their own understanding of the world, on their stereotypes of what Aboriginal peoples, the poor, people in general are like. They have a vested interest in preserving their version of normalcy and they have the resources to make their labels stick. This perspective, then, encourages us to recognize that not all who are designated as deviant are so labelled simply because they have broken a rule and, concurrently, not all who break a rule are labelled as deviant.

The interactionists are interested in what happens to people when they are labelled deviant. Essentially, they conclude that the label has a self-fulfilling effect. The negative label often comes to be a *master status*. One comes to be seen first and foremost as a deviant — a living example of evil. The deviant is transformed through the labelling process so that he or she is seen in a completely new light and is treated unlike other people and generally in unpleasant ways.

Finally deviants may come to accept this designation, to see themselves differently, to internalize the label as part of their self-conception. They may come to restrict their associations to other deviants in part because they feel forced to do so. Here they may learn to justify their deviance, to see the rest of the world as corrupt or square or hypocritical and, eventually, they may find themselves committed to a "deviant way of life." Interactionists study the *process of becoming deviant*.

Conflict theorists too are less concerned with the deviant or criminal than with the ways in which rules are made and enforced. They are most likely to ask *whose* rules dominate, *whose* interests do the rules or laws serve, how do the rules protect the interests of the elite and preserve the structure of inequality. To take one example, most of our laws are designed to protect private property. If conflict theorists look at deviants or criminals at all, they may often conceptualize their actions as inarticulate or primitive "political" protest. Unlike the labelling theory view, this approach does not focus on the role of master labellers; the courts, the police, the psychiatrists are seen as simply part of the machinery of social control — not the villains of the piece but constrained, no less than deviants themselves, by the structures of inequality and the ideologies of justification. It is these structures — power and inequality — that capture their perspective on deviance.

chapter

3

Culture

Culture is one of the most elusive concepts sociologists must deal with. All the readings in this chapter try, in one way or another, to demystify culture and make it accessible and understandable. The first selection, by Marvin Harris, the American anthropologist, tries to demonstrate how even apparently irrational and inexplicable lifestyles, what he refers to as the "riddles of culture," can be made understandable if we link these aspects of culture to material conditions. In this excerpt from his book *Cows, Pigs, Wars and Witches*, he shows us how even the sacred aspects of culture derive from people's solutions to ordinary problems and therefore reflect rationality rather than irrationality.

Similarly, Stephen Baron of the University of Alberta shows us how adolescent subculture is a response to specific histor-

ical conditions. In this selection, Baron links punk subculture to youth unemployment and shows how "style" may become a serious expression of alienation and resistance. Baron's article also provides you with another illustration of the uses of field work in sociological research.

The final selection in this chapter is by the American sociologist Seymour Martin Lipset, who has taught in Canada and offers an important, if somewhat controversial, perspective on Canadian culture. You may, after reading this selection want to return for another look at Gary Bowden's work included in Chapter 2, which provides an empirical test of Lipset's approach. At a time when increasing numbers of Canadians, within and outside of academia, are asking what values Canadians share and how do these differ from American values,

Lipset provides one answer. Just how this answer will hold up over the next decades is an issue addressed in the final chapter of this book, where some of the authors dwell on the implications for a Canada of disunity.

RELATED READINGS

Peter Clark and Anthony Davis: "The Power of Dirt: An Exploration of Secular Defilement in Anglo-Canadian Culture" (Chapter 4)
Esther Greenglass: "Socialization of Girls and Boys: How Roles are Acquired" (Chapter 5)
Michael Asch: "Aboriginal Rights: The View of the Aboriginal Peoples" (Chapter 14)
Reginald Bibby: "Mosaic Madness" (Chapter 14)

MOTHER COW
Marvin Harris

Ours is an age that claims to be the victim of an overdose of intellect. In a vengeful spirit, scholars are busily at work trying to show that science and reason cannot explain variations in human lifestyles. And so it is fashionable to insist that the riddles [of culture] have no solution. The ground for much of this current thinking about lifestyle enigmas was prepared by Ruth Benedict in her book *Patterns of Culture*. To explain striking differences among the cultures of the Kwakiutl, the Dobuans, and the Zuni, Benedict fell back upon a myth which she attributed to the Digger Indians. The myth said: "God gave to every people a cup, a cup of clay, and from this cup they drank their life ... They all dipped in the water but their cups were different." What

this has meant to many people ever since is that only God knows why the Kwakiutl burn their houses. Ditto for why the Hindus refrain from eating beef, or the Jews and Moslems abhor pork, or why some people believe in messiahs while others believe in witches. The long-term practical effect of this suggestion has been to discourage the search for other kinds of explanations. For one thing is clear: If you don't believe that a puzzle has an answer, you'll never find it.

To explain different patterns of culture we have to begin by assuming that human life is not merely random or capricious. Without this assumption, the temptation to give up when confronted with a stubbornly inscrutable custom or institution soon proves irresistible. Over the years I have discovered that lifestyles which others claimed were totally inscrutable actually had definite and readily intelligible causes. The main reason why these causes have been so long overlooked is that everyone is convinced that "only God knows the answer."

Another reason why many customs and institutions seem so mysterious is that we have been taught to value elaborate "spiritualized" explanations of cultural phenomena more than down-to-earth material ones. I contend that the solution to each of the riddles examined in this book lies in a better understanding of practical circumstances. I shall show that even the most bizarre-seeming beliefs and practices turn out on closer inspection to be based on ordinary, banal, one might say "vulgar" conditions, needs, and activities. What I mean by a banal or vulgar solution is that it rests on the ground and that it is built up out of guts, sex, energy, wind, rain, and other palpable and ordinary phenomena.

This does not mean that the solutions to be offered are in any sense simple or obvious. Far from it. To identify the relevant material factors in human events is always a difficult task. Practical life wears many disguises. Each lifestyle comes wrapped in myths and legends that draw attention to impractical or supernatural conditions. These wrappings give people a social identity and a sense of social purpose, but they conceal the naked truths of social life. Deceptions about the mundane causes of culture weigh upon ordinary consciousness like layered sheets of lead. It is never an easy task to circumvent, penetrate, or lift this oppressive burden.

In an age eager to experience altered, nonordinary states of consciousness, we tend to overlook the extent to which our ordinary state of mind is already a profoundly mystified consciousness — a consciousness surprisingly isolated from the practical facts of life. Why should this be?

For one thing, there is ignorance. Most people achieve awareness of only a small portion of the range of lifestyle alternatives. To emerge from myth and legend to mature consciousness we need to compare the full range of past and present cultures. Then there is fear. Against events like growing old and dying, false consciousness may be the only effective defense. And finally, there is conflict. In ordinary social life, some persons invariably control or exploit others. These inequalities are as much disguised, mystified, and lied about as old age and death.

Ignorance, fear, and conflict are the basic elements of everyday consciousness. From these elements, art and politics fashion that collective dreamwork whose function it is to prevent people from understanding what their social life is all about. Everyday consciousness, therefore, cannot explain itself. It owes its very existence to a developed capacity to deny the facts that explain its existence. We don't expect dreamers to explain their dreams; no more should we expect lifestyle participants to explain their lifestyles.

Some anthropologists and historians take the opposite view. They argue that the participants' explanation constitutes an irreducible reality. They warn that human consciousness should never be treated as an "object," and that the scientific framework appropriate to the study of physics or chemistry has no relevance when applied to the study of lifestyles. Various prophets of the modern "counter-culture" even blame the inequities and disasters of recent history on too much "objectification." One of them claims that objective consciousness always leads to a loss of "moral sensitivity," and thereby equates the quest for scientific knowledge with original sin.

Nothing could be more absurd. Hunger, war, sexism, torture, and exploitation have occurred throughout history and prehistory — long before anybody got the idea of trying to "objectify" human events.

Some people who are disillusioned with the side effects of advanced technology think that science is "the commanding lifestyle of our society." This may be accurate with respect to our knowledge of nature, but it is terribly wrong with respect to our knowledge of culture. As far as lifestyles are concerned, knowledge can't be original sin because we are still in our original state of ignorance. . . .

Whenever I get into discussions about the influence of practical and mundane factors on lifestyles, someone is sure to say, "But what about all those cows the hungry peasants in India refuse to eat?" The picture of a ragged farmer starving to death alongside a big fat cow conveys a reassuring sense of mystery to Western observers. In countless learned and popular allusions, it confirms our deepest conviction about how people with inscrutable Oriental minds ought to act. It is comforting to know — somewhat like "there will always be an England" — that in India spiritual values are more precious than life itself. And at the same time it makes us feel sad. How can we ever hope to understand people so different from ourselves? Westerners find the idea that there might be a practical explanation for Hindu love of cow more upsetting than Hindus do. The sacred cow — how else can I say it? — is one of our favorite sacred cows.

Hindus venerate cows because cows are the symbol of everything that is alive. As Mary is to Christians the mother of God, the cow to Hindus is the mother of life. So there is no greater sacrilege for a Hindu than killing a cow. Even the taking of human life lacks the symbolic meaning, the unutterable defilement, that is evoked by cow slaughter.

According to many experts, cow worship is the number one cause of India's hunger and poverty. Some Western-trained agronomists say that the taboo against cow slaughter is keeping one hundred million "useless" animals alive. They claim that cow worship lowers the efficiency of agriculture because the useless animals contribute neither milk nor meat while competing for croplands and foodstuff with useful animals and hungry human beings. A study sponsored by the Ford Foundation in 1959 concluded that possibly half of India's cattle could be regarded as surplus in relation to feed supply. And an economist from the University of Pennsylvania stated in 1971 that India has thirty million unproductive cows.

It does seem that there are enormous numbers of surplus, useless, and uneconomic animals, and that this situation is a direct result of irrational Hindu doctrines. Tourists on their way through Delhi, Calcutta, Madras, Bombay, and other Indian cities are astonished at the liberties enjoyed by stray cattle. The animals wander through the streets, browse off the stalls in the market place, break into private gardens, defecate all over the sidewalks, and snarl traffic by pausing to chew their cuds in the middle of busy intersections. In the countryside, the cattle congregate on the shoulders of every highway and spend much of their time taking leisurely walks down the railroad tracks.

Love of cow affects life in many ways. Government agencies maintain old age homes for cows at which owners may board their dry and decrepit animals free of charge. In Madras, the police round up stray cattle that have fallen ill and nurse them back to health by letting them graze on small fields adjacent to the station house. Farmers regard their cows as members of the family, adorn them with garlands and tassels, pray for them when they get sick, and call in their neighbors and a priest to celebrate the birth of a new calf. Throughout India, Hindus hang on their walls calendars that portray beautiful, bejeweled young women who have the bodies of big fat white cows. Milk is shown jetting out of each teat of these half-women, half-zebu goddesses.

Starting with their beautiful human faces, cow pinups bear little resemblance to the typical cow one sees in the flesh. For most of the year their bones are their most prominent feature. Far from having milk gushing from every teat, the gaunt beasts barely manage to nurse a single calf to maturity. The average yield of whole milk from the typical hump-backed breed of zebu cow in India amounts to less than 500 pounds a year. Ordinary American dairy cattle produce over 5,000 pounds, while for champion milkers, 20,000 pounds is not unusual. But this comparison doesn't tell the whole story. In any given year about half of India's zebu cows give no milk at all — not a drop.

To make matters worse, love of cow does not stimulate love of man. Since Moslems spurn pork but eat beef, many Hindus consider them to be cow killers. Before the partition of the Indian subcontinent into India and Pakistan, bloody communal riots aimed at preventing the Moslems from killing cows became annual occurrences. Memories of old cow riots — as, for example, the one in Bihar in 1917 when thirty people died and 170 Moslem villages were looted down to the last doorpost — continue to embitter relations between India and Pakistan.

Although he deplored the rioting, Mohandas K. Gandhi was an ardent advocate of cow love and wanted a total ban on cow slaughter. When the Indian constitution was drawn up, it included a bill of rights for cows which stopped just short of outlawing every form of cow killing. Some states have sinced banned cow slaughter altogether, but others still permit exceptions. The cow question remains a major cause of rioting and disorders, not only between Hindus and the remnants of the Moslem community, but between the ruling Congress Party and extremist Hindu factions of cow lovers. On November 7, 1966, a mob of 120,000 people, led by a band of chanting, naked holy men draped with garlands of marigolds and smeared with white cow-dung ash, demonstrated against cow slaughter in front of the Indian House of Parliament. Eight persons were killed and forty-eight injured during the ensuing riot. This was followed by a nationwide wave of fasts among holy men, led by Muni Shustril Kumar, president of the All-Party Cow Protection Campaign Committee.

To Western observers familiar with modern industrial techniques of agriculture and stock raising, cow love seems senseless, even suicidal. The efficiency expert yearns to get his hands on all those useless animals and ship them off to a proper fate. And yet one finds certain inconsistencies in the condemnation of cow love. When I began to wonder if there might be a practical explanation for the sacred cow, I came across an intriguing government report. It said that India had too many cows but too few oxen. With so many cows around, how could there be a shortage of oxen? Oxen and male water buffalo are the principal source of traction for plowing India's fields. For each

farm of ten acres or less, one pair of oxen or water buffalo is considered adequate. A little arithmetic shows that as far as plowing is concerned, there is indeed a shortage rather than a surplus of animals. India has 60 million farms, but only 80 million traction animals. If each farm had its quota of two oxen or two water buffalo, there ought to be 120 million traction animals — that is, 40 million more than are actually available.

The shortage may not be quite so bad since some farmers rent or borrow oxen from their neighbours. But the sharing of plow animals often proves impractical. Plowing must be coordinated with the monsoon rains, and by the time one farm has been plowed, the optimum moment for plowing another may already have passed. Also, after plowing is over, a farmer still needs his own pair of oxen to pull his oxcart, the mainstay of bulk transport throughout rural India. Quite possibly private ownership of farms, livestock, plows, and oxcarts lowers the efficiency of Indian agriculture, but this, I soon realized, was not caused by cow love.

The shortage of draft animals is a terrible threat that hangs over most of India's peasant families. When an ox falls sick a poor farmer is in danger of losing his farm. If he has no replacement for it, he will have to borrow money at usurious rates. Millions of rural households have in fact lost all or part of their holdings and have gone into sharecropping or day labor as a result of such debts. Every year hundreds of thousands of destitute farmers end up migrating to the cities, which already teem with unemployed and homeless persons.

The Indian farmer who can't replace his sick or deceased ox is in much the same situation as an American farmer who can neither replace nor repair his broken tractor. But there is an important difference: tractors are made by factories, but oxen are made by cows. A farmer who owns a cow owns a factory for making oxen. With or without cow love, this is a good reason for him not to be too anxious to sell his cow to the slaughterhouse. One also begins to see why Indian farmers might be willing to tolerate cows that give only 500 pounds of milk per year. If the main economic function of the zebu cow is to breed male traction animals, then there's no point in comparing her with specialized American dairy animals, whose main function is to produce milk. Still, the milk produced by zebu cows plays an important role in meeting the nutritional needs of many poor families. Even small amounts of milk products can improve the health of people who are forced to subsist on the edge of starvation.

When Indian farmers want an animal primarily for milking purposes they turn to the female water buffalo, which has longer lactation periods and higher butterfat yields than zebu cattle. Male water buffalo are also superior animals for plowing in flooded rice paddies. But oxen are more versatile and are preferred for dryfield farming and road transport. Above all, zebu breeds are remarkably rugged, and can survive the long droughts that periodically afflict different parts of India.

Agriculture is part of a vast system of human and natural relationships. To judge isolated portions of this "ecosystem" in terms that are relevant to the conduct of American agribusiness leads to some very strange impressions. Cattle figure in the Indian ecosystem in ways that are easily overlooked or demeaned by observers from industrialized high-energy societies. In the United States, chemicals have almost completely replaced animal manure as the principal source of farm fertilizer. American farmers stopped using manure when they began to plow with tractors rather than mules or horses. Since tractors excrete poisons rather than fertilizers, a commitment to large-scale machine farming is almost of necessity a commitment to the use of chem-

ical fertilizers. And around the world today there has in fact grown up a vast integrated petrochemical-tractor-truck industrial complex that produces farm machinery, motorized transport, oil and gasoline, and chemical fertilizers and pesticides upon which new high-yield production techniques depend.

For better or worse, most of India's farmers cannot participate in this complex, not because they worship their cows, but because they can't afford to buy tractors. Like other underdeveloped nations, India can't build factories that are competitive with the facilities of the industrialized nations nor pay for large quantities of imported industrial products. To convert from animals and manure to tractors and petrochemicals would require the investment of incredible amounts of capital. Moreover, the inevitable effect of substituting costly machines for cheap animals is to reduce the number of people who can earn their living from agriculture and to force a corresponding increase in the size of the average farm. We know that the development of large-scale agribusiness in the United States has meant the virtual destruction of the small family farm. Less than 5 percent of U.S. families now live on farms, as compared with 60 percent about a hundred years ago. If agribusiness were to develop along similar lines in India, jobs and housing would soon have to be found for a quarter of a billion displaced peasants.

Since the suffering caused by unemployment and homelessness in India's cities is already intolerable, an additional massive build-up of the urban population can only lead to unprecedented upheavals and catastrophes.

With this alternative in view, it becomes easier to understand low-energy, small-scale, animal-based systems. As I have already pointed out, cows and oxen provide low-energy substitutes for tractors and tractor factories. They also should be credited with carrying out the functions of a petrochemical industry. India's cattle annually excrete about 700 million tons of recoverable manure. Approximately half of this is used as fertilizer, while most of the remainder is burned to provide heat for cooking. The annual quantity of heat liberated by this dung, the Indian housewife's main cooking fuel, is the thermal equivalent of 27 million tons of kerosene, 35 million tons of coal, or 68 million tons of wood. Since India has only small reserves of oil and coal and is already the victim of extensive deforestation, none of these fuels can be considered practical substitutes for cow dung. The thought of dung in the kitchen may not appeal to the average American, but Indian women regard it as a superior cooking fuel because it is finely adjusted to their domestic routines. Most Indian dishes are prepared with clarified butter known as *ghee*, for which cow dung is the preferred source of heat since it burns with a clean, slow, long-lasting flame that doesn't scorch the food. This enables the Indian housewife to start cooking her meals and to leave them unattended for several hours while she takes care of the children, helps out in the fields, or performs other chores. American housewives achieve a similar effect through a complex set of electronic controls that come as expensive options on late-model stoves.

Cow dung has at least one other major function. Mixed with water and made into a paste, it is used as a household flooring material. Smeared over a dirt floor and left to harden into a smooth surface, it keeps the dust down and can be swept clean with a broom.

Because cattle droppings have so many useful properties, every bit of dung is carefully collected. Village small fry are given the task of following the family cow around and bringing home its daily petrochemical output. In the cities, sweeper castes enjoy a monopoly on the dung deposited by strays and earn their living by selling it to housewives.

From an agribusiness point of view, a dry and barren cow is an economic abomination. But from the viewpoint of the peasant farmer, the same dry and barren cow may be a last desperate defense against the money-lenders. There is always the chance that a favorable monsoon may restore the vigor of even the most decrepit specimen and that she will fatten up, calve, and start giving milk again. This is what the farmer prays for; sometimes his prayers are answered. In the meantime, dung-making goes on. And so one gradually begins to understand why a skinny old hag of a cow still looks beautiful in the eyes of her owner.

Zebu cattle have small bodies, energy-storing humps on their back, and great powers of recuperation. These features are adapted to the specific conditions of Indian agriculture. The native breeds are capable of surviving for long periods with little food or water and are highly resistant to diseases that afflict other breeds in tropical climates. Zebu oxen are worked as long as they continue to breathe. Stuart Odend'hal, a veterinarian formerly associated with Johns Hopkins University, performed field autopsies on Indian cattle which had been working normally a few hours before their deaths but whose vital organs were damaged by massive lesions. Given their enormous recuperative powers, these beasts are never easily written off as completely "useless" while they are still alive.

But sooner or later there must come a time when all hope of an animal's recovery is lost and even dung-making ceases. And still the Hindu farmer refuses to kill it for food or sell it to the slaughterhouse. Isn't this incontrovertible evidence of a harmful economic practice that has no explanation apart from the religious taboos on cow slaughter and beef consumption?

No one can deny that cow love mobilizes people to resist cow slaughter and beef eating. But I don't agree that the anti-slaughter and beef-eating taboos necessarily have an adverse effect on human survival and well-being. By slaughtering or selling his aged and decrepit animals, a farmer might earn a few more rupees or temporarily improve his family's diet. But in the long run, his refusal to sell to the slaughterhouse or kill for his own table may have beneficial consequences. An established principle of ecological analysis states that communities of organisms are adapted not to average but to extreme conditions. The relevant situation in India is the recurrent failure of monsoon rains. To evaluate the economic significance of the anti-slaughter and anti-beef-eating taboos, we have to consider what these taboos mean in the context of periodic droughts and famine.

The taboo on slaughter and beef eating may be as much a product of natural selection as the small bodies and fantastic recuperative powers of the zebu breeds. During droughts and famines, farmers are severely tempted to kill or sell their livestock. Those who succumb to this temptation seal their doom, even if they survive the drought, for when the rains come, they will be unable to plow their fields. I want to be even more emphatic: Massive slaughter of cattle under the duress of famine constitutes a much greater threat to aggregate welfare than any likely miscalculation by particular farmers concerning the usefulness of their animals during normal times. It seems probable that the sense of unutterable profanity elicited by cow slaughter has its roots in the excruciating contradiction between immediate needs and long-run conditions of survival. Cow love with its sacred symbols and holy doctrines protects the farmer against calcula-

tions that are "rational" only in the short term. To Western experts it looks as if "the Indian farmer would rather starve to death than eat his cow." The same kinds of experts like to talk about the "inscrutable Oriental mind" and think that "life is not so dear to the Asian masses." They don't realize that the farmer would rather eat his cow than starve, but that he will starve if he does eat it.

Even with the assistance of the holy laws and cow love, the temptation to eat beef under the duress of famine sometimes proves irresistible. During World War II, there was a great famine in Bengal caused by droughts and the Japanese occupation of Burma. Slaughter of cows and draft animals reached such alarming levels in the summer of 1944 that the British had to use troops to enforce the cow-protection laws. In 1967 *The New York Times* reported:

Hindus facing starvation in the drought-stricken area of Bihar are slaughtering cows and eating the meat even though the animals are sacred to the Hindu religion.

Observers noted that "the misery of the people was beyond imagination."

The survival into old age of a certain number of absolutely useless animals during good times is part of the price that must be paid for protecting useful animals against slaughter during bad times. But I wonder how much is actually lost because of the prohibition on slaughter and the taboo on beef. From a Western agribusiness viewpoint, it seems irrational for India not to have a meat-packing industry. But the actual potential for such an industry in a country like India is very limited. A substantial rise in beef production would strain the entire ecosystem, not because of cow love but because of the laws of thermodynamics. In any food chain, the interposition of additional animal links result in a sharp decrease in the efficiency of food production. The caloric value of what an animal has eaten is always much greater than the caloric value of its body. This means that more calories are available per capita when plant food is eaten directly by a human population than when it is used to feed domesticated animals.

Because of the high level of beef consumption in the United States, three-quarters of all our croplands are used for feeding cattle rather than people. Since the per capita calorie intake in India is already below minimum daily requirements, switching croplands to meat production could only result in higher food prices and a further deterioration in the living standards for poor families. I doubt if more than 10 percent of the Indian people will ever be able to make beef an important part of their diet, regardless of whether they believe in cow love or not.

I also doubt that sending more aged and decrepit animals to existing slaughterhouses would result in nutritional gains for the people who need it most. Most of these animals get eaten anyway, even if they aren't sent to the slaughterhouse, because throughout India there are low-ranking castes whose members have the right to dispose of the bodies of dead cattle. In one way or another, twenty million cattle die every year, and a large portion of their meat is eaten by these carrion-eating "untouchables."

My friend Dr. Joan Mencher, an antropologist who has worked in India for many years, points out that the existing slaughterhouses cater to urban middle-class non-Hindus. She notes that "the untouchables get their food in other ways. It is good for the untouchable if a cow dies of starvation in a village, but not if it gets sent to an urban slaughterhouse to be sold to Muslims or Christians." Dr. Mencher's informants at first denied that any Hindu would eat beef, but when they learned that

"upper-caste" Americans liked steak, they readily confessed their taste for beef curry.

Like everything else I have been discussing, meat eating by untouchables is finely adjusted to practical conditions. The meat-eating castes also tend to be the leather-working castes, since they have the right to dispose of the skin of the fallen cattle. So despite cow love, India manages to have a huge leathercraft industry. Even in death, apparently useless animals continue to be exploited for human purposes.

I could be right about cattle being useful for traction, fuel, fertilizer, milk, floor covering, meat, and leather, and still misjudge the ecological and economic significance of the whole complex. Everything depends on how much all of this costs in natural resources and human labor relative to alternative modes of satisfying the needs of India's huge population. These costs are determined largely by what the cattle eat. Many experts assume that man and cow are locked in a deadly competition for land and food crops. This might be true if Indian farmers followed the American agri-business model and fed their animals on food crops. But the shameless truth about the sacred cow is that she is an indefatigable scavenger. Only an insignificant portion of the food consumed by the average cow comes from pastures and food crops set aside for their use.

This ought to have been obvious from all those persistent reports about cows wandering about and snarling traffic. What are those animals doing in the markets, on the lawns, along the highways and railroad tracks, and up on the barren hillsides? What are they doing if not eating every morsel of grass, stubble, and garbage that cannot be directly consumed by human beings and converting it into milk and other useful products! In his study of cattle in West Bengal, Dr. Odend'hal discovered that the major constituent in the cattle's diet is inedible by-products of human food crops, principally rice straw, wheat bran, and rice husks. When the Ford Foundation estimated that half of the cattle were surplus in relation to feed supply, they meant to say that half of the cattle manage to survive even without access to fodder crops. But this is an understatement. Probably less than 20 percent of what the cattle eat consists of humanly edible substances; most of this is fed to working oxen and water buffalo rather than to dry and barren cows. Odend'hal found that in his study area there was no competition between cattle and humans for land or the food supply: "Basically, the cattle convert items of little direct human value into products of immediate utility."

One reason why cow love is so often misunderstood is that it has different implications for the rich and the poor. Poor farmers use it as a license to scavenge while the wealthy farmers resist it as a rip-off. To the poor farmer, the cow is a holy beggar; to the rich farmer, it's a thief. Occasionally the cows invade someone's pastures or planted fields. The landlords complain, but the poor peasants plead ignorance and depend on cow love to get their animals back. If there is competition, it is between man and man or caste and caste, not between man and beast.

City cows also have owners who let them scrounge by day and call them back at night to be milked. Dr. Mencher recounts that while she lived for a while in a middle-class neighborhood in Madras her neighbors were constantly complaining about "stray" cows breaking into the family compounds. The strays were actually owned by people who lived in a room above a shop and who sold milk door to door in the neighborhood. As for the old age homes and police cowpounds, they serve very nicely to reduce the risk of maintaining cows in a city environment. If a cow stops producing milk, the owner may decide to let it wander around until the police pick it up and bring it to the precinct house. When the cow has recovered, the owner pays a small fine and returns it to its usual haunts. The old age homes operate on a similar principle, providing cheap government-subsidized pasture that would otherwise not be available to city cows.

Incidentally, the preferred form of purchasing milk in the cities is to have the cow brought to the house and milked on the spot. This is often the only way that the householder can be sure that he is buying pure milk rather than milk mixed with water or urine.

What seems most incredible about these arrangements is that they have been interpreted as evidence of wasteful, anti-economic Hindu practices, while in fact they reflect a degree of economizing that goes far beyond Western, "Protestant" standards of savings and husbandry. Cow love is perfectly compatible with a merciless determination to get the literal last drop of milk out of the cow. The man who takes the cow door to door brings along a dummy calf made out of stuffed calfskin which he sets down beside the cow to trick it into performing. When this doesn't work, the owner may resort to *phooka*, blowing air into the cow's uterus through a hollow pipe, or *doom dev*, stuffing its tail into the vaginal orifice. Gandhi believed that cows were treated more cruelly in India than anywhere else in the world. "How we bleed her to take the last drop of milk from her," he lamented. "How we starve her to emaciation, how we ill-treat the calves, how we deprive them of their portion of milk, how cruelly we treat the oxen, how we castrate them, how we beat them, how we overload them."

No one understood better than Ghandi that cow love had different implications for rich and poor. For him the cow was a central focus of the struggle to rouse India to authentic nationhood. Cow love went along with small-scale farming, making cotton thread on a hand spinning wheel, sitting cross-legged on the floor, dressing in a loincloth, vegetarianism, reverence for life, and strict nonviolence. To these themes Ghandi owed his vast popular following among the peasant masses, urban poor, and untouchables. It was his way of protecting them against the ravages of industrialization.

The asymmetrical implications of *ahimsa* for rich and poor are ignored by economists who want to make Indian agriculture more efficient by slaughtering "surplus" animals. Professor Alan Heston, for example, accepts the fact that the cattle perform vital functions for which substitutes are not readily available. But he proposes that the same functions could be carried out more efficiently if there were 30 million fewer cows. This figure is based on the assumption that with adequate care only 40 cows per 100 male animals would be needed to replace the present number of oxen. Since there are 72 million adult male cattle, by this formula, 24 million breeding females ought to be sufficient. Actually, there are 54 million cows. Subtracting 24 million from 54 million, Heston arrives at the estimate of 30 million "useless" animals to be slaughtered. The fodder and feed that these "useless" animals have been consuming are to be distributed among the remaining animals, who will become healthier and therefore will be able to keep total milk and dung production at or above previous levels. But whose cows are to be sacrificed? About 43 percent of the total cattle population is found on the poorest 62 percent of the farms. These farms, consisting of five acres or less, have only 5 percent of the pasture and grazing land. In other words, most of the animals that are temporarily dry, barren, and feeble are owned by the people who live on the smallest and poorest farms. So that when the economists talk about getting rid of 30 million cows,

they are really talking about getting rid of 30 million cows that belong to poor families, not rich ones. But most poor families own only one cow, so what this economizing boils down to is not so much getting rid of 30 million cows as getting rid of 150 million people — forcing them off the land and into the cities.

Cow-slaughter enthusiasts base their recommendation on an understandable error. They reason that since the farmers refuse to kill their animals, and since there is a religious taboo against doing so, therefore it is the taboo that is mainly responsible for the high ratio of cows to oxen. Their error is hidden in the observed ratio itself: 70 cows to 100 oxen. If cow love prevents farmers from killing cows that are economically useless, how is it there are 30 percent fewer cows than oxen? Since approximately as many female as male animals are born, something must be causing the death of more females than males. The solution to this puzzle is that while no Hindu farmer deliberately slaughters a female calf or decrepit cow with a club or a knife, he can and does get rid of them when they become truly useless from his point of view. Various methods short of direct slaughter are employed. To "kill" unwanted calves, for example, a triangular wooden yoke is placed about their necks so that when they try to nurse they jab the cow's udder and get kicked to death. Older animals are simply tethered on short ropes and allowed to starve — a process that does not take too long if the animal is already weak and diseased. Finally, unknown numbers of decrepit cows are surreptitiously sold through a chain of Moslem and Christian middlemen and end up in the urban slaughterhouses.

If we want to account for the observed proportions of cows to oxen, we must study rain, wind, water, and land-tenure patterns, not cow love. The proof of this is that the proportion of cows to oxen varies with the relative importance of different components of the agricultural system in different regions of India. The most important variable is the amount of irrigation water available for the cultivation of rice. Wherever there are extensive wet rice paddies, the water buffalo tends to be the preferred traction animal, and the female water buffalo is then substituted for the zebu cow as a source of milk. That is why in the vast plains of northern India, where the melting Himalayan snows and monsoons create the Holy River Ganges, the proportion of cows to oxen drops down to 47 to 100. As the distinguished Indian economist K. N. Raj has pointed out, districts in the Ganges Valley where continuous year-round rice-paddy cultivation is practiced, have cow-to-oxen ratios that approach the theoretical optimum. This is all the more remarkable since the region in question — the Gangetic plain — is the heartland of the Hindu religion and contains its most holy shrines.

The theory that religion is primarily responsible for the high proportion of cows to oxen is also refuted by a comparison between Hindu India and Moslem West Pakistan. Despite the rejection of cow love and the beef-slaughter and beef-eating taboos, West Pakistan as a whole has 60 cows for every 100 male animals, which is considerably higher than the average for the intensely Hindu Indian state of Uttar Pradesh. When districts in Uttar Pradesh are selected for the importance of water buffalo and canal irrigation and compared with ecologically similar districts in West Pakistan, ratios of female to male turn out to be virtually the same.

Do I mean to say that cow love has no effect whatsoever on the cattle sex ratio or on other aspects of the agricultural system? No. What I am saying is that cow love is an active element in a complex, finely articulated material and cultural order. Cow love mobilizes the latent capacity of human beings to persevere in a low-energy ecosystem in which there is little room for waste or indolence. Cow love contributes to the adaptive resilience of the human population by preserving temporarily dry or barren but still useful animals; by discouraging the growth of an energy-expensive beef industry; by protecting cattle that fatten in the public domain or at landlord's expense; and by preserving the recovery potential of the cattle population during droughts and famines. As in any natural or artificial system, there is some slippage, friction, or waste associated with these complex interactions. Half a billion people, animals, land, labor, political economy, soil, and climate are all involved. The slaughter enthusiasts claim that the practice of letting cows breed indiscriminately and then thinning their numbers through neglect and starvation is wasteful and inefficient. I do not doubt that this is correct, but only in a narrow and relatively insignificant sense. The savings that an agricultural engineer might achieve by getting rid of an unknown number of absolutely useless animals must be balanced against catastrophic losses for the marginal peasants, especially during droughts and famines, if cow love ceases to be a holy duty.

Since the effective mobilization of all human action depends upon the acceptance of psychologically compelling creeds and doctrines, we have to expect that economic systems will always oscillate under and over their points of optimum efficiency. But the assumption that the whole system can be made to work better simply by attacking its consciousness is naïve and dangerous. Major improvements in the present system can be achieved by stabilizing India's human population, and by making more land, water, oxen, and water buffalo available to more people on a more equitable basis. The alternative is to destroy the present system and replace it with a completely new set of demographic, technological, politico-economic, and ideological relationships — a whole new ecosystem. Hinduism is undoubtedly a conservative force, one that makes it more difficult for the "development" experts and "modernizing" agents to destroy the old system and to replace it with a high-energy industrial and agribusiness complex. But if you think that a high-energy industrial and agribusiness complex will necessarily be more "rational" or "efficient" then the system that now exists, forget it.

Contrary to expectations, studies of energy costs and energy yields show that India makes more efficient use of its cattle than the United States does. In Singur district in West Bengal, Dr. Odend'hal discovered that the cattle's gross energetic efficiency, defined as the total of useful calories produced per year divided by the total calories consumed during the same period, was 17 percent. This compares with a gross energetic efficiency of less than 4 percent for American beef cattle raised on Western range land. As Odend'hal says, the relatively high efficiency of the Indian cattle complex comes about not because the animals are particularly productive, but because of scrupulous product utilization by humans: "The villagers are extremely utilitarian and nothing is wasted."

Wastefulness is more a characteristic of modern agribusiness than of traditional peasant economies. Under the new system of automated feed-lot beef production in the United States, for example, cattle manure not only goes unused, but it is allowed to contaminate ground water over wide areas and contributes to the pollution of nearby lakes and streams.

The higher standard of living enjoyed by the industrial nations is not the result of greater productive efficiency, but of an enormously expanded increase in the amount of energy available per person. In 1970 the United States used up the energy equivalent of twelve tons of coal per inhabitant, while the corresponding figure for India was one-fifth ton per inhabitant. The way this energy was expended involved far more energy being wasted per person in the United States than in India. Automobiles and airplanes are faster than oxcarts, but they do not use energy more efficiently. In fact, more calories go up in useless heat and smoke during a single day of traffic jams in the United States than is wasted by all the cows of India during an entire year. The comparison is even less favorable when we consider the fact that the stalled vehicles are burning up irreplaceable reserves of petroleum that it took the earth tens of millions of years to accumulate. If you want to see a real sacred cow, go out and look at the family car.

THE CANADIAN WEST COAST PUNK SUBCULTURE: A FIELD STUDY

Stephen W. Baron

Research in the area of adolescent subcultures in Canada has been sparse. In one of the few discussions of the topic, Brake (1985) argues that Canadian youth subcultures have been overlooked because they do not take on the "dramatic, socially visible form" of the subcultures found in Britain and the United States (Brake, 1985: 152). He also observes that Canada lacks the class divisions that are linked to subcultures in those countries. Moreover, the absence of a unique Canadian culture has led to derivative youth culture in Canada. Yet both Brake (1985) and Shragge (1982) predict that relatively high youth unemployment and increased competition for jobs may lead to an increase in delinquent

From "West Coast Punk Subculture: A Field Study" by Stephen W. Baron, Volume 14(3), 1989. By permission of *The Canadian Journal of Sociology* and the author.

resistance. In short, high youth unemployment may lead to the development of a "significant" youth culture in Canada. More generally, McLaren (1980) points to the increasing similarities between the conditions in the large Canadian cities and their counterparts in the United States and Britain which will carry over into Canadian youth culture as problems of poverty and unemployment become more difficult.

In light of the literature above, certain questions arise concerning the punk subculture that emerged in Canada during the recent recession. It may be the classless derivative form of youth culture found in past studies, or the punks may represent the significant delinquent response predicted by McLaren (1980), Shragge (1982) and Brake (1985). Given the lack of Canadian literature on subcultural formations in Canada, it will be useful to review the theories that have been used to account for this phenomenon in the United States and Britain. The resulting insights will guide our analysis of the Canadian punk subculture.

Theoretical Perspectives on Youth Subcultures

Subcultural theory has its basis in American functionalist sociology, which assumes the existence of a dominant ideology that stresses the achievement of mainly financial goals (A. Cohen, 1955; Merton, 1957; Cloward and Ohlin, 1960). While these goals are seen to transcend class lines, functionalist theorists point out that those in the lower class are at a disadvantage. Their class location restricts their access to the means needed to achieve success. For lower-class youths, this first becomes apparent in the school system. Inadequately socialized to compete with middle-class youths, the lower-class child cannot meet the criteria for status in the school. Youths who fail to secure an education are likely to realize that chances of success in the social

system are limited. Functionalist theorists believe that actors in this position evolve adaptations that will enable them to overcome the goal-means discrepancy. Youth subcultures represent the rebellion adaptation as the frustration over restricted opportunities leads lower-class youths to reject cultural goals and the legitimate means to achieve them. The cultural goals are replaced with those that can be more readily achieved. Subcultural formation takes place when there are a number of youths with similar problems of adjustment. The subculture addresses these problems of adjustment more effectively than any solutions offered by institutional means. It provides an environment where status can be achieved and, furthermore, through the development of group norms and boundaries supports the decision to reject the dominant ideology.

Miller (1958) has argued that this theory underestimates the connection between working-class culture and the subculture. He suggests that subcultural values are extensions of working-class culture. Matza and Sykes (1961), on the other hand, argue that the theory fails to recognize the continuities between working-class culture and the dominant culture. They suggest that the delinquent values of the subculture are shared with those of the dominant culture.

From these arguments British scholars began to reformulate subcultural theory in an attempt to explain British youth subcultures. Although British researchers felt American subculture theory to be culturally specific, the lack of a British tradition led them to draw from American literature. The American literature demonstrated the need to study the effects of working-class culture, the dominant culture, and class inequalities in structuring the social situation of youths and their response to it. What the British theorists added was a Marxist argument.

Neo-Marxists emphasize culture, ideology, and hegemony. Culture is usually defined as the distinct patterns of life developed by social groups, the way in which these groups give expressive form to their "social and material life experiences." Neo-Marxists reason that people are born into sets of meanings, institutions, and relations, which help to locate them in a culture. These structures and meanings tend to reflect the positions and interests of the most powerful class, which supports a dominant ideology. The dominant class attempts to exert authority over other groups through the organization of rules and meanings. When an alliance of groups can exert "total authority" over a group, it is referred to as hegemony. In some measure the subordinate classes resist and struggle against hegemony, thus "negotiating' a redefinition of cultural meanings.

According to Marxist researchers, youth subcultures are an example of this negotiation and redefinition process as they engage in a "struggle over cultural space" (Brake, 1985: 4). Within subcultures the structural contradictions rooted in the wider societal context can be overcome. Thus, youth subcultures take problems that exist in their parent class and attempt to come to terms with them through redefinition of their own experience.

In the school and the family youths resist the class-based ideological codes legitimizing subordinate/superordinate roles. The subculture becomes a positive reference group providing symbolic and social support that allows for the formulation of a counter-ideology. Further evidence of resistance is found in the subcultural style (the appearance composed of costume, hairstyle, jewellery and other artifacts), and the way it is constructed and defined by members.

This form of resistance has inherent limitations because it takes place on the street, not in the institutions where change can be made. Therefore, youth subcultures can be said to offer only symbolic representations and critiques of structural contradictions. Members use the subculture as a vehicle to escape class and occupation in a symbolic manner. British theorists have chosen to refer to these symbolic solutions as "magical." Furthermore, the oppositional nature of the subculture is diluted and neutralized by the media and the popular culture industries. However, neutralizing effects are never totally pervasive because many of the subcultural activities (eg., crime) are not commercially exploited but are dealt with by the police and the courts. Thus, deviance in this case is the "essence of political protest."

Subcultural theories have tended to focus on males. Theorists argue that masculinity has a central focus in subcultures and can be seen as a solution to problems rooted in "structural features." The absence of females in subcultural studies reflects their relationship to production, a sphere where young women are also assumed to be peripheral. Furthermore, the distinctive types of activities that females engage in, and their greater parental supervision, limits subcultural participation. When females do participate, their relations to the dominant order are reproduced. Within the subculture they are still influenced by the ideology of male supremacy. Brake argues that this occurs because "working class girls are not exposed to any alternative concepts of femininity" (Brake, 1985: 174). For females the subculture is likely to have a social focus. The subculture is something to dress for and which enables an escape from home, school, and work.

The literature on the punk subculture is dominated by the above neo-Marxist position but contains little empirical research. There are different views concerning the class content, the political significance, and the style of the subculture. Some scholars argue that the subculture was dominated by working-class youth. Others believe that the subculture contains several strata including middle-class artists. Politically, these theorists argue that punk music, with its social and political comment, raises the political consciousness of those involved in the subculture. However, the punk movement may have only succeeded at a symbolic or "magical" level. The form it took (unintelligable) may have doomed it to failure, while its lack of political impact may be due to the middle-class involvement and libertarianism. Some argue that the style of the subculture reflected its "working-classness" others argue it was an assertion of their bohemian lifestyle. Some suggest that the style reflected members' conditions and attitudes, amplifying everything feared in society.

The above theoretical discussion offers useful analytic concepts that, in a manner reminiscent of the method adopted by British researchers in developing their theory, will be used to guide this study. Consistent with this approach, both the functionalist and neo-Marxist perspectives will be drawn from. This will help to shed light on one Canadian adolescent subculture.

Method

To make sense of the punk rock subculture, I adopted a participant observation approach to gathering data. This method, which has a distinguished history, has been used in other youth culture studies in Britain with great success.

An initial scouting of downtown Victoria (a mid-sized city on Canada's Pacific coast; population 250,000) preceded entry. It revealed that the downtown core was divided up into various subcultural territories. The present study began when I approached a group of punks on the street corner of the city well known to be punk "turf" (and, as I was later to find out, "skinhead" turf). I

introduced myself and explained the nature of the research to the group. No attempt was made to mislead the prospective subjects. I explained that participation in the interviews was voluntary, and stressed that they could withdraw from the interview at any time or refuse to answer any questions. It was explained that the interviews were to be recorded with a microcassette recorder. I also explained that, due to ethical restrictions, I was not interested in any illegal activities. This assurance seemed to put members at ease and resulted in interviews being granted. Consent statements were repeated before each interview. I was permitted to spend time with the group and soon its members came to expect my presence at certain times.

Completed interviews were selectively transcribed within a twenty-four-hour period to ensure against ethical problems. To preserve anonymity subjects were given pseudonyms and identifying information was left out. A total of sixty days were spent in the field interviewing subjects. Time in the field ranged from five to fifteen hours a day, depending on the type of activity. I maintained subsequent contact by returning to the field one day a week for an additional two months, after which contact was then limited to attending the local punk "gigs" (concerts).

In addition to the "punks" street corner turf, data collection took place inside of a restaurant about two blocks away and about four blocks away in front of a fast-food restaurant which was also a gathering place for "skaters." All three of the locations were on the periphery of a fourth subcultural group in the downtown core; the "rockers."

The data were gathered through a combination of unstructured interviews with all thirty-five members of the subculture and field notes kept on members' activities, interactions, and physical appearance. Members were questioned concerning issues of theoretical interest; specifically, goals, school, family, political attitudes, style, music, and status. I also explored unanticipated topics that emerged during field work. There was no consistent sequence of questions in the interviews; I often had to adapt to the flow of the conversation by taking the liberty to explore other facets that the subjects seemed to believe were important. All the interviews were useable, although some subjects chose not to respond to specific questions and occasionally I was unable to ask certain questions.

The strong rapport I developed with members far in advance of an interview facilitated data collection. However, interviewing street youth can be difficult. Subjects usually carried on their daily activities during interviews, resulting in interruptions from other members and panhandling. Subjects sometimes broke off the interview to pursue more exciting activities with other subculture members. The rapport I developed also hampered research in the last phases of the study. I was now considered a member of the subculture and my questions were dissonant with everyday subcultural activities. I therefore resorted to asking a member one or two questions during informal conversation and recording the responses at the earliest opportunity, a method that also provided a reliability check of the members' previous responses. The appearance that I had adopted for the field (long unkempt hair, black leather jacket, torn jeans, work shirts, T-shirts, and high-top runners) also created problems when local police officers assumed I was a member of the subculture. Fortunately, no complications occurred.

Consistent with the "grounded theory" approach (Glaser and Strauss, 1967), data analysis took place through the development of typologies that were divided by gender and social class. The results of this analysis follow a logical sequence: factors relating to entry, subcultural resistance, and apparent resolution of problems leading to entry. First I examined the variables identified above as theoretically relevant to subcultural participation: members' goals, attitudes towards school, and attitudes towards their family. The paper then explores three methods of resistance outlined in previous literature; political, stylistic, and creative. The last section of the paper investigates how the subculture enables members to achieve status in subcultural terms and overcome their problems of adjustment.

Findings

Background

The subculture contained thirty-five members at the time of the field study (twenty-one males, fourteen females) who ranged in age from fourteen to twenty-nine, with a mean and median age of seventeen. Length of participation in the subculture ranged from four weeks to five years, with a mean of approximately two years.

Members' class of origin was determined through questions concerning parental occupations. I resorted to a simple blue-collar/white-collar dichotomy since the subjects did not have extensive knowledge of what their parents' occupations actually entailed. By these criteria, there were eighteen members from blue-collar backgrounds (eleven males, seven females) and fifteen members from white-collar backgrounds (eight males, seven females). Two members withheld this information. Thus, contrary to theoretical predictions, almost half of the members came from white collar backgrounds. The types of occupations cited by those from white-collar backgrounds included four university professors, two top-level bureaucrats, two chartered accountants, a head of a large food firm, a shopping mall manager, a university instructor (without a PhD.), a school principal, and three owners of small businesses. In contrast, parental occupations reported by members from blue-collar backgrounds included mechanics (both car and boat), boat painter, dock worker, cement truck driver, policeman, two career soldiers, labourers, bartender, etc.

Table 1
CLASS OF ORIGIN BY SEX

SEX	BLUE COLLAR	WHITE COLLAR	UN-KNOWN	TOTAL
Male	11	8	2	21
Female	7	7	0	14
Total	18	15	2	35

The majority of the members, however, had established independence from their parents. That is, only twelve members of the subculture resided in their parents' homes. Fourteen members of the subculture rented their own residences. Three of these were supported by their parents, three others supported themselves through low-wage employment and seven members relied on the state for support. One member who rented her own residence would not disclose how she supported herself. Nine members of the subculture lived on the street, did not work, and relied on various methods of survival including illegal activities. The street experience was quite common. Nine of the thirteen members who were renting their own apartments had lived on the street, including four who moved off the street during the field study. Three others living at home at that time had also lived on the street previously. This brings the total to twenty-one members who had at some point in time lived on the street.

Seventeen of the twenty-three members who did not live at home were males, as well the majority of those who had, or were

presently, living on the street. In addition, those who received state support were male. In contrast, eight of the twelve members that lived "at home" were female. In sum, the subculture is male dominated both in terms of numbers and severity of resistance. That is, they adopt the full code of behaviors of the subcultural lifestyle.

These results also indicate that it is not only working-class youth who participate in youth subcultures. This contradicts the expectations of both the functionalist and neo-Marxist theories, but supports some of the British literature on punk subculture. Perhaps Brake's (1985) suggestion that the punk subculture is the sort of classless form of youth culture that one would expect in Canada is the more accurate interpretation of my findings. There is a diversity in socioeconomic backgrounds as opposed to a homogenity in socioeconomic status. However, the marginal class location adopted by members was not anticipated in previous literature. Therefore, the diversity of the members' class origins may not be a result of Canadian "classless" youth culture, but may be a result of the social problems of youth which cut across socioeconomic strata. Members may be rejecting dominant values and norms and as a result adopting a marginal socioeconomic position. On the other hand, membership pressures members to reject dominant norms and material comforts and adopt very poor socioeconomic conditions.

GOALS

Both American and British theorists have focused on the manner in which youth react to dominant goals. Functionalists suggest that lower-class youth who experience frustration when the means to attain goals are blocked will dismiss dominant goals and replace them with goals that can be met through subcultural participation. Neo-Marxists argue that working-class youths negotiate cultural space by refusing to adopt dominant cultural goals. These youths enter the subculture to attain status via subcultural criteria and escape their class and occupation symbolically. To examine this issue, respondents were questioned about occupational goals and about the perceptions of their future. Their answers were readily classified in terms of the classic typology of conformist, rebel/retreatist, and innovator.

About one-third of the respondents could be placed within the "conformist" type. They had goals of attaining positions where there would be some legitimate monetary rewards (n=12). Typical examples of a conformist orientation are the following responses:

Go to Toronto to get a job. A friend of mine I was talking to a couple of nights ago and there's lots of money, a lot of money. Anything I can get right now and maybe save up for college or something.

Get a job, make lots of money, drive a Porsche, snort lots of Cocaine.

Some of these members planned to obtain post-secondary education, believing that education was a route that would enable them to reach these occupational goals. Their responses demonstrate the internalization of the dominant ideology described by functionalist theorists.

Their present school circumstances provide evidence that their expectations may be unrealistic. Half of the "conformists" attended non-diploma granting alternative schools, while the others did not attend school. Both of these situations would seem to disqualify members from attending postsecondary institutions and thus as Downes (1966) suggests, the most obvious means to reach their goals. This discrepancy between expectation and reality may reflect or cause their frustration

leading to subcultural participation. However, contrary to theoretical predictions, these youths have not discarded their cultural goals upon subcultural entry.

Neither class of origin nor present class location was systematically related to the responses of those placed into the "conformist" type. Five members were from blue-collar backgrounds, seven from white-collar backgrounds. Their present class location spanned the spectrum from residing in white-collar homes to living on the street. Similarly, the sexes were equally represented in the "conformist" membership.

The second major type of response, "rebel/retreatist," revealed that an equal proportion of the subculture members, mainly male, were negative about their futures and lacked long-term occupational goals (n=12). Some reported that they were not interested in succeeding. Two members saw themselves as permanent street people. Others described an apocalyptic future. This group have no real cultural goals and no faith in institutional means to attain them. Within the subculture, there is social support for their attitudes and they are able to attain status via alternative subcultural criteria.

Nine of the twelve in this category were in marginal socioeconomic circumstances; only three individuals attended school and resided in their parents' homes. The following are examples of responses made by those placed into this type:

I'm downwardly mobile and proud of it. Like I don't know about the way my parents live. Like get a job, work nine to five, do it for thirty odd years, then get shipped off to some lousy pension. I couldn't handle that. Like my dad worked thirty years to get a pension. You might as well live on welfare.

Panhandling for the dog, scamming a little bit here, scamming a little bit there. It's a living.

Generally, I don't like to think about it. You walk down the street and you see old men crashed out and you just hope that's not you in a few years.

Few respondents could be placed into the "innovator" (n=12) or the "ritualist" (n=12) adaptations. The ritualists held down low-wage employment and did not desire advancement or felt it was unlikely. These members did not subscribe to the achievement ideology, but continued to work through institutional means. For example:

I've got a job. I make five bucks an hour. That's enough to live on. That's all I really need. I don't want an office job. So in ten years dying or doing the same thing I'm doing now.

The innovators saw difficulties with society's emphasis on education as the avenue to upward mobility. They held dominant goals but felt they could not achieve them through institutional means, as the following reveals:

Art if I could. It would take too many years of school but I like marine biology but I'm too lazy. Maybe I'll get my act together some day.

In sum, there is a diversity of future orientations among subculture members. Not all members wish to attain goals, but among those who do, there is evidence that class does not strongly influence the internalization of the success ideology. This applies not only to class of origin, but to present class circumstances as well. Furthermore, it appears that youths of all classes who experience goal blockage may seek a subcultural solution. There is also evidence that some members' expectations of achieving these goals are unrealistic due to their present class and educational circumstances. This discrepancy between reality and expectation may have led these members to seek a subcultural solution. If not,

they may experience this strain in the future. These youths also continue to cling to the hopes of someday attaining goals. For them the subculture might be viewed as an avenue to temporary social and symbolic status with the realization that more permanent status through occupation must be gained as they pass into adulthood.

There is also evidence that a number of members (n=12) do not aspire to the success goals espoused in the dominant ideology or have become alienated from the dominant ideology and therefore reject conventional success goals. These members have adopted counter-norms of their own which lead to their marginal socioeconomic status. They use the subculture to negotiate cultural space within hegemony. The predominance of males in the "retreatist/rebel" category points to the gender differences cited by Benston (1982) concerning occupational success. For those males who perceive their opportunities blocked, the subculture may provide an alternative route to masculinity usually gained through occupation.

The above analysis reveals that members of the punk subculture are socially heterogenous, not homogenous. It is not only the "rebel" who inhabits the youth subculture. Rather, the subculture allows for a number of responses based on the diverse experiences, reactions, and goals of the members. This suggests different levels of resistance to the dominant order, something which theorists have failed to predict.

What the present study cannot tell us is whether individuals already exhibiting characteristics of these "types" are recruited into the subculture or if subcultural membership produces these orientations. Perhaps the process works in both directions depending on each particular case. Considering the number of adaptations I observed, there is room for all three causal interpretations.

SCHOOL

The experience of youth in the school is cited by both the structural functionalist and neo-Marxist theorists as a contributing factor in the formation of adolescent subcultures. For functionalist theorists it is in school that youths recognize that the means to attain goals are blocked. Therefore, the opposition towards school demonstrates the strain deriving from ideological goals. Alternatively, the neo-Marxists consider oppositional behavior as an attack on the dominant order and more specifically, resistance to the ideological nature of the school.

Only seven members of the subculture had school backgrounds that were not marked by expulsion, failure, or departure. Ten members had been expelled from school (eight males, two females), seventeen members had quit school (nine males, eight females) and one female member had failed. Usually expulsion resulted for disciplinary reasons, after a physical confrontation with a teacher or principal in three cases, rather than school performance. Class of origin was not a factor in predicting which members continued school. However, present class location was: during the course of the research, nineteen members of the subculture attended school (eight males, eleven females), most of whom lived with their parents or received parental support. In contrast, all sixteen of the nonstudents (thirteen males, three females) were in marginal socioeconomic locations.

Student members of the subculture were experiencing problems within the school system. Responses to questions concerning attitudes towards school were of three types. Some (n=12) believed the present curriculum was inadequate because it failed to provide them with job skills. Hence, school was seen as a waste of their time because it failed to provide anything

marketable. This response was prominent among males, those with blue-collar backgrounds, those in present marginal economic circumstances, and among those who were not attending school. Typical responses included:

It teaches you to be an educated bum. Your chances are about 30 percent that you're just as much a bum now as you were then. No one needs school anyway. They just teach you how to read or write and if you want more you do more school.

I don't think there's enough kids interested in school. They don't offer what kids want. There is so many drop outs. There's nothing in school . . . I know when I get out of school I won't have to know anything about dead pigs or anything like that. I don't understand why I have to learn it. The courses that they are coming out with now, like work experience courses are really good. You get work experience. They should offer more courses like that and maybe courses that allow kids to get into a field.

A smaller group (n=5) felt that the school system attempts to form their opinions and behaviors. These views were usually held in conjunction with the above criticisms regarding the school's curriculum. The members of this second group saw the education system as preparing them for low-wage menial employment. Again the respondents who fell into this type tended to be males from blue-collar backgrounds and in marginal present class locations. The following are examples of their responses:

I hated it. Teaching you useless stuff. It sucks. You really don't learn anything, all you learn is to follow orders. They don't teach you how to think and survive. They just try to mold you into their little working part of society.

Basically I think the school system is just to teach the kids how to be good followers. Like you're taught all the stuff you're learning is what other people have to say and repeating it back. You're not suppose to think, you're supposed to say yes ma'am, yes sir. The law has been decreed by their standards.

A third group expressed the view that their school education would aid them in gaining employment (n=10). Therefore, continued attendance was important. While members placed into this type did have criticisms of the school system, they realized that their chances of gaining employment without education were slim. It is interesting to note that of these ten, eight attended school and, moreover, that seven had to quit or been expelled from school at some time. Even though they support education, these students did indeed experience difficulties in the school system. Class of origin and present class location was not related to responses. Again these data tend to show that the achievement ideology had been internalized by some respondents from all economic strata as the following reveal:

Well I don't like it but I put up with it. If I want to be intelligent I go to school. There's no such things as iron workers. There's computers and stuff and you got to use your brain. Well the way I see it if we didn't go to school, no one could read or write. Nobody would know how to read or write. You wouldn't know mathematics. We need mathematics now, or we will.

In general I think it sucks shit because in the regular school I can't stand to be told what to do six hours a day; told what to do every single minute of it. But it'll help get you a job because you'll know stuff. You'll be able to prove you can do it.

As with goals, our examination of members' views on education show differing levels of resistance to the dominant order. It appears to be an antischool culture with two sub-groups. The first consists of those who criticize the school system but view education as a means to gain employment and continue to strive for goals while participating in the subculture. A number of the members in this group had histories of school problems suggesting that they experienced blockage and sought a subcultural solution where they could meet the criteria for status. The second group consists of those who dismiss the utility of school and display resistance through absence and rebellious behavior. Education was resisted because it only qualified them for menial low-wage employment or was viewed as an ideological tool to shape their consciousness. Participation offers an alternative route to status defined in subcultural terms. The formation of rebellious attitudes may precede or follow the entrance of youths into the subculture; however, once youths are part of the subculture its counter-ideology encourages, reinforces, and supports resistance towards school.

The rebellion seems to be more prevalent among those from blue-collar backgrounds, marginal present class locations, and males. The result of this rebellion is often the adoption of a low socioeconomic position. Members live on the streets or survive through state income assistance. They have no skills to gain employment other than the low-wage alienating type they abhor, thus their alternatives are restricted.

The school attendance of females is characterized by less resistance. By remaining in school, females increase their chances of gaining access to nontraditional male-dominated occupations. Those who drop out of school adopt a similar resistance to their male counterparts and may meet with the same results.

THE FAMILY

The neo-Marxist perspective focuses on resistance towards the family as an integral part of subcultural participation. These theorists outline the way in which the family relays ideological codes. They predict that youth come to question these codes because the codes contradict their own experience outside of the family. The result is friction between youths and parents. While the functionalists point out that the family is an important component in passing on dominant norms and that members may not be close to the family, these issues are downplayed.

Members' experiences in the family setting can be usefully organized in terms of these three categories: nonfriction, friction, and violence. The nine members in the nonfriction type were able to discuss their problems and their subcultural membership with parents who were apparently understanding. That the majority in this category were from blue-collar backgrounds suggests that blue-collar parents may be more sympathetic to a youthful deviance. Six of the nine reporting good parental relationships were still residing in their parents' homes. The following comments are representative of the nonfriction type:

If I didn't want to live at home, they go well we'd rather you didn't (leave) but we're not going to let you starve to death or nothing, or so you have no money. So they half support me. Not enough to make me comfortable, but enough. They think right on . . . and I'm happy. For some people I know it's caused problems. Problems like you don't fit into society so you're screwed so go away. Like I know a lot of people have been kicked out of the house because they wouldn't conform to what their parents wanted.

I get along with her quite well. I still do. It's not like some of these people, "oh my fuckin' parents kicked me out."

For the sixteen members in the "friction" category, relationships were characterized by "conflict" — i.e., parents questioning members about school work attitudes, friends, involvement in illegal activities, style, as well as other behaviors. These conflicts, in many cases, drove group members out of their parents' residences and onto the streets. Perhaps an indicator of the seriousness of the friction is that ten of the sixteen did not live at home. As two explained:

I just couldn't handle living with them. They're hard to live with. Bugging me about coming in late, about the way I look, 'get your hair cut, change your clothes.' Ragging at me because I don't get A's.

I just didn't want to live with them any more. They were trying to lay down too many rules I thought were just bullshit. So I left.

The "violence" category contained seven males whose parents resorted to violence as a means of punishment or discipline. The incidence of violence may, however, be greater than these data indicate. Some of those reporting "friction" may have been involved in violence and not reported it. Six of these members no longer lived in their parent's homes because of the violence. There was no clear trend in class backgrounds. Typical responses included the following:

Like you get busted and your dad is sitting there. You don't get charged or nothing, you just get tossed around the police station a bit. Then get belted around for humiliating your father. Other than that he was o.k.

My dad once hit me, broke my nose, and I fell into the closet and broke the door. So he beats me up for breaking the door and getting blood on the carpet. Once he beat me and took me to the hospital and told them I fell down the stairs. Meanwhile there's like knuckle prints on my face. He used to tell me never to hit girls, so when he'd get mad at my mom he'd hit me. Oh oh, dad's mad at mom better leave. So one night I locked myself in my room, came out at night with a baseball bat, beat him, stole his wallet and ran away.

Friction may arise from the youth's disagreement with parental views. As neo-

Marxists theorists suggest, the youth questions these views because they contradict his/her experience. These sources involve qualities that functionalist theorists describe as essential for success and in some cases reflecting success. Parents who have assimilated the dominant ideology and have spent time passing it on to their children react strongly to their children's disregard for these values and ideas. They view their appearance, types of friends, school grades, leisure pursuits, and illegal activities as preventing them from "getting ahead." My findings on goals and school show that a number of members are resisting dominant views concerning those two issues. The result of this friction is that many children feel they have no alternative but to leave home.

A number of the points of friction concern, as neo-Marxists believe, the subordinate position of an adolescent in the family. Adolescents challenge parental authority in an attempt to assert their own identity and in the process produce friction. This friction may be a factor in entering the subculture. Alternatively, subcultural participation may itself be a source of friction. The subculture provides an environment in which the youth does have status. Furthermore, it allows members to develop, assert and test their own identities.

Members may be encouraged to leave home by other subcultural members or their leaving home may result in participation in the subculture. The twenty-three members who did not live with their parents tended to adopt a marginal socioeconomic status. This marginal existence may be seen as a conscious attempt to retreat and resist. For some, especially males involved in violence at home, there was little choice. This is further evidence of the male domination of the subculture. They engage in the most extreme resistance and enter the subculture because it offers them an environment to discuss problems and a route to status via alternative criteria defined by members. The street is viable because of the knowledge gained vicariously through the experiences of subculture members.

In contrast, while females did experience friction within the family they did not adopt, for the most part, the street option. The subculture did not provide support for females living on the street. The males in the subculture may discourage this option, or make it difficult. Another possible reason that females may engage in a less severe resistance is their use of the subculture as a social vehicle. As a result they may be less likely to be expelled from parents' homes.

There is less resistance among those members living at home, with half of this group experiencing friction with their parents. Those members who did have good relationships with their parents generally had their parents' support and understanding.

POLITICAL ATTITUDES

The literature suggests that youths encountering problems (be they in the school, family, or social structure) may enter a subculture to address these problems. The evidence presented above is consistent with this view: young people were drawn into the punk subculture because of their attitudes and experience in the school and family. In a number of cases these youth were resisting the ideological nature of these institutions, which raises the neo-Marxist point that subcultures may also contain the potential for political resistance.

Indeed, the political element of the punk subculture has been debated in the literature. Some researchers argue that, on the one hand, punk serves to raise the consciousness of its members, but on the other hand, that the political element of punk fails to confront the individual problems of its members. Questions concerning the members' political attitudes revealed that the "political element" of the subculture was not pervasive. Only some members voiced political opinions and beliefs, but even then not in great detail. At a minimum, the members were very critical of the present federal and provincial governments, but most were unable to articulate their reasons. An explanation for this type of criticism may lie in the limited political knowledge of these youth. The trend appears to be for them to use their available knowledge, based in everyday experience, to form criticisms against targets they believe to be the source of their problems. Hence their responses fail to address the complexity of the problems.

Anti-government attitudes tend to vary, judging from responses to an open-ended question. Opinions were often contradictory, suggesting a fragmentary social consciousness. Political issues mentioned included anarchy, anti-statism, nationalism, endorsement of reform parties, socialism, bureaucracy, and mismanagement of the economy. Fourteen of the twenty-two members who gave this "critical" type of response were living on their own. Fifteen of the twenty-two were males, again pointing to the male domination of the subculture. Typical comments from members included:

Politically I'm an anarchist because I believe that the government that governs the best, doesn't govern at all. Socialism is a good idea but you have to go through a dictatorship of the proletarian. You get that and the group in power aren't going to give that up. Like look at Russia. It's been 70 odd years. I mean I'm sure capitalism has been abolished in Russia by now.

I hate the Canadian politics. They are wimps. They suck Reagan's dick. Vander Zalm would too if he thought he could get two by four's out

of it. And Reagan is a senile retardo. I think the Canadian government is an embarrassment. They do whatever the Americans tell them to do. The things they do are ridiculous.

Generally, little sympathy was expressed for politicians and the tasks they faced. However, three members felt that others should not be so quick to judge politicians because the job was difficult:

I think its hard for any politician to do a good job no matter what country unless they're really savvy and there's not many normal people out there like that so there's not much hope.

A number of the members were politically apathetic (n=10). They took no interest in political affairs, although it later became apparent that some of these respondents expressed opinions during informal discussions. These members, who mainly were in a marginal class location, did not want to involve themselves in politics, perhaps feeling that there was little they could do to foster change. Their experiences at home and school may have taught them that resisting authority is futile. In any case, they made no attempt to change anything:

I really don't get involved in politics. I try to stay away from it. I figure if you get tied into it . . . I don't like to preach to people.

I don't know. It doesn't matter. I don't pay much attention, I haven't got a t.v.

In short, there is no coherent ideology in the punk subculture that would facilitate organized political resistance. Rather political opinions are diverse. The subculture seems to encourage members to be critical of governments, as well as to formulate their own criticisms of which may be influenced by their own backgrounds, experiences, and depth of knowledge. Furthermore, those views expressed rest on a limited knowledge and the criticisms do not provide possible avenues for solution. Thus, political resistance by the subculture is muted. The inability of members to act upon their critiques may reflect their exclusion from, alienation from, and lack of participation in, the major institutions through which political mobilization and change can take place.

If anything, punk ideology is libertarian. The types of resistance engaged in reflect this libertarianism. The members are into "doing their own thing" which means no restrictions. Those most critical withdraw from the institutions that attempt to restrict behavior and attitudes, especially the family and school. There is also an avoidance of and cynicism towards other state institutions that members encounter (e.g., the police, various government ministries).

The degree of depth and sophistication of the responses to my question on politics seemed to correlate negatively with socioeconomic status: those less well off were more expressive. Perhaps they have more to criticize because of personal experience. Alternatively, their resistance may have led to their current circumstances. Those members who expressed "apathetic" responses were also socioeconomically disadvantaged, although this attitude may result from the realization that change is futile. Those members whose responses were not as strong were economically dependent on their parents and thus had not experienced conditions which had led other members to develop political critiques or apathy.

These results help explain the lack of politicization among punks. The significant degree of middle-class participation and libertarian politics are cited by Brake (1985) as possible reasons for this disappointment. This explanation may also apply to the subculture under study. It may be that the classless ideology of Canada encourages all members to adopt a "middle class" resistance. Marchak (1981) notes

that "radicals" in a liberal society tend to become more liberal — i.e., libertarian or anarchist. This aptly characterizes the members' responses documented above. Subcultural resistance is further limited by a fragmented political consciousness. However, while members are not part of a struggle for power, their resistance in the home and school indicates their dissatisfaction with the dominant order and desire to negotiate more space in it. This negotiation allows members to leave behind their problems but not eliminate them. Thus subcultural membership is a symbolic "magical" solution. For a small number of adolescents the punk subculture allows them to temporarily escape concerns about their future adult roles.

SUBCULTURAL "STYLE"

Neo-Marxists suggest that adolescent subcultures demonstrate their resistance to the dominant order through style or physical appearance. Accordingly, style allows members to "display" their opposition in "visual" terms for the general public to witness. My respondents felt that their style was an individual creation, a representation of their feelings and attitudes. There was no admission of imitation.

These punks were very serious about the lifestyle they adopted. Style was not something to be embraced and discarded at certain times of the day, but represented an extension of the member. It became clear from the observation of members discussing new objects of style they would like to obtain and the excitement members displayed as they showed off new objects, that considerable thought was put into the constructing of style. For example:

It's the only fucking thing that I can identify with. I fucking hate people. I don't like people so I segregate myself as much as I can. The only way I feel comfortable about myself is the way that I dress. If I dressed like a preppie I'd feel like a goof because I wouldn't be dressing the way that I believe.

The most creative and intellectual people I've found, and artsy people, are the people that dress differently. Like it reflects their personality. . . . I've found there's more expression in the friends I've chosen around here.

These responses reflect the libertarian "do your own thing" outlook noted above regarding political attitudes. This sense of individuality discourages any group action. However, by refusing to dress in a certain manner, members criticized the dominant order. Punk style is the antithesis of "dressing for success." In fact, their style disqualifies them from even the low wage, menial labour for which most are qualified. They refuse to fulfill the requirements of conventional society. In doing so they resist the dominant order, but in a way that does not depend upon collective solidarity.

The homologous nature of the subculture discussed by neo-Marxists also reflects resistance. "Homology" refers to the adoption of objects that correspond, reflect, or "possess" the values of the members. The members were very conscious of style as a kind of self-representation, particularly as expression of attitudes and feelings regarding school, the family, and politics. Clear evidence of this is found in the slogans that the members decorated their clothes with, the rips and tears that depicted the poverty that many members were experiencing, the dark colors and work shirts that displayed their despair. "Bricolage" was also seen to be taking place. Bricolage refers to the transference of meaning that must occur before an object can be assimilated into that style. Members took objects available in mainstream culture and altered their definitions to suit subcultural style. For example, male members took jean jackets and tore and decorated them with slogans. This process al-

tered the definition of the jacket as a mere clothing item sold for profit to a personal expression of attitudes that at the same time represented the poverty and violence of the subculture. However, the style could only offer symbolic resistance to the dominant order and, further offered no solutions to the problems which members encountered outside the subculture. Like the subcultural participation itself, the solution was, as British theorists argue, "magical." That is, punk style allowed members to escape their structural locations for a period, but offered no real solution to structural problems.

The importance of style to members was revealed through their descriptions of subcultural change. Members characterized the subculture as becoming "trendy" through the fashion industry. However, when questioned if they were "trendy," the response was always negative. There was much criticism from members about "outsiders," referred to as "poseurs," who had adopted the punk style. Poseurs were criticized for adopting the punk style without adopting the accompanying attitudes and lifestyle. The poseurs were seen as adopting the style for reasons of social status rather than commitment to being a "real" punk:

The poseurs and stuff like that kind of bother me. They go yeah, like I'm a punk rocker, go home to mommy and daddy and have dinner, come downtown, change my clothes and be a punk rocker until 9:30 until I have to catch my bus right. I don't know, they miss the whole point of what it's supposed to be.

Then there's the people out here on the street who sit around today, with a haircare. They're there for attention. Oh that's real cool man. They cause shit for everyone else . . . I mean nobody knows them . . . on the whole they don't have any idea what they're doing.

Poseurs embody the sanitization and attempted neutralization of the subculture through popular culture. . . . The products enable youth to adopt the style without actually participating in the subcultural lifestyle. The sanitized style leads them to be labelled poseurs, to be denied membership and to be made targets for abuse. Thus, the potential dilution of punk by popular culture industries is resisted by subculture members.

A central aspect of the punk style is punk music. Lyrically, punk rock or "hard core" describes the problems and expresses the anger of youth while at the same time offering a critique of the dominant order. The music itself appears to represent the anger and frustration of its listeners. Neo-Marxists point to punk music as an important element in raising the political consciousness of youth. Members of the local subculture also listen to speed metal (sometimes referred to as thrash or speed core) and death rock. The former can be described as a hybrid between punk and heavy metal. Like punk it is loud and fast, although it dwells on satanic themes as well as social issues. These themes, as with those in punk, can be seen as an attempt to offend, shock, and attack the mainstream. Death rock, sometimes called funeral music, is slower and dwells on more melancholy themes. Every member of the subculture responded that they had a great interest in music. They also felt that music was a central aspect of the subculture. The following are examples of members' responses:

Well it's really powerful and straight forward. It's got something to say, most of it. I mean if it doesn't have something to say then it's humourous or stupid. I'm pissed off everyone listens to hard core now. They don't know what its about.

I like hard core a lot . . . I don't like idiotic stuff though, like Venom and stuff. I like lyrics that actually say something and music that makes you want to beat up somebody.

The responses indicate that the music was homologous with members' attitudes. However, given the previous discussion of political views, the channelling of dissent through music may be able to raise or reflect political consciousness, but cannot precipitate political action.

Also part of subcultural style is a creative element. Most members were involved in some sort of creative activity, such as music, art, poetry, and short stories. Members developed individuality and expressed feelings through this nonalienating creativity. Creative expression was also another form of resistance, allowing members to display their displeasure with the dominant order. Again this mode of resistance is individualized and libertarian, each member tackles his/her experience his/her own way, and thus does not encourage collective politics. This results in a muted resistance expressed almost exclusively to other members:

I think a lot of it comes out more. I figure a lot of the people that hang out here have problems in their life or you know. Or they feel they have problems and it's a way of getting rid of them or explaining them by drawing or writing music or whatever.

They have an outlet I can relate to. I may not be able to do it, like art, but I can relate to it because its an outlet of what someone is trying to say and that's why people are so tight. We do have a family because everyone is showing what they're feeling inside by their art work or their music or whatever, right.

. . . Certainly the members of the local subculture display a libertarian resistance. However, the delinquent behaviors of some members (including theft, scams, violent crimes, and violence against other subcultures) makes the bohemian label inappropriate. The fact that for many of the members, the street is, or has been, their home again suggests that the bohemian interpretation is flawed.

Since punk appears to contain both delinquent and bohemian elements, it seems more accurate to interpret it as a hybrid of "bohemian youth culture" and "delinquent youth culture." Scholars have tended to make clear distinctions between these two types of culture. "Delinquent youth culture" focuses on leisure because the members are marginal to the labour market (Young, 1971: 144). "Bohemian youth culture" is focused on leisure because its members reject the labour market (Young, 1971: 147). Certainly the members of the punk subculture refuse the opportunities available, but many have restricted opportunities. Further, those members whose opportunities do not appear restricted in real terms have adopted delinquent patterns in their resistance that go well beyond "artistic" rebellion. In sum, although members resort to a libertarian resistance, and display this resistance through creative means, the delinquent aspects point to a cross between delinquent and bohemian cultures.

ALTERNATIVE STATUS

I have demonstrated that the members' problems, objectively rooted at a macro level, cannot be solved because of subculture's individual, often idiosyncratic, methods of resistance. The problems are addressed only at the "magical" level. That is, members do not attempt to address their problems in a manner in which change could be fostered but rather through symbolic resistance. However, the importance of status through membership, and the support for resistance within the subculture cannot be underestimated.

Both the functionalist and neo-Marxist theorists believe that the counternorms developed in subcultures, and the criteria for status that emerge from these, enable members to gain a positive self-image. My findings show that the achievement of status and support for resistance occurs in a variety of ways. Members' attitudes towards other subcultural groups displayed their feelings of superiority, reflecting a positive collective sense of identity. Similarly, the selective initiation that the subculture used to control membership implied that membership was something to be achieved. Not everyone could be a punk. The members also believed that participation was personally beneficial because other members understood their problems. This support allowed members to develop and test identities without fear of rejection, in the process providing them with status via membership. It allowed members to reject the dominant ideology and formulate their own counter-ideology at a personal level.

This is further reinforced by discussions among members about daily survival. The problems that tend to be dealt with inside of the subculture are those concerned with school, relationships with parents and others, housing, and financing. Members could count on others for shelter and money. They realized that it was easier to live in groups than to survive alone. It was not uncommon for those members who received money to use it to feed others. When members moved into residences of their own, this usually meant a number of guests (members) sleeping on their floor when other places to sleep could not be found. The members also provided physical protection for each other.

Participation in violence (and the threat of it) was also a source of status, strengthening members' allegiance for the subculture. It made being a punk even more prestigious and added another requirement for membership. Further, fighting may be seen as a display of masculinity in the male-dominated subculture. Violence may confer status on members that they cannot get through occupational success.

Discussion

The results of this study provide insights into neglected aspects of Canadian adolescent subcultures. As some scholars have speculated, the Canadian punk subculture appears to be a "classless" form of youth subculture. However, it is also a significant delinquent youth culture. Some observers have speculated that Canadian youth subcultures would develop this tendency as economic conditions worsened. While British Columbia has suffered through a severe recession, Frith (1985) argues that youth unemployment cannot be understood only in economic terms. Frith suggests that youth unemployment is an age or generational problem. He notes that employers do not want young workers because they lack the personal qualities (responsibility, self discipline, flexibility, and punctuality) that adult workers have learned through experience. The result is that there is a growing differentiation between adult and young workers. Youths become a cheap labour source with low status. Data on work opportunities in Canada indicate that youths are heavily concentrated in low wage, service sector job ghettos (Myles et al., 1988). Furthermore, the wages for workers aged 15–24 decreased during the recession and the period of recovery. This occurred across industrial sectors, occupational groups, regions, and levels of education (Myles et al., 1988). This age and generational effect of youth employment opportunities provides some explanation for the classless delinquent youth culture that we have studied. It is youths who do not have the experience for better jobs and who do not wish to take the low status, low wage employment that participate in the punk subculture.

These youths are reacting to their structural location based on age and generation. Their attitudes reflect "levels of resistance" to the dominant order. Some members are totally committed to a lifestyle of resistance. They are alienated from dominant goals, rebel at home and school, and live on the streets engaging in illegal activities to survive. At the other end of the spectrum are those who display resistance in only one of these areas, (e.g., school) or whose resistance is muted (e.g., live at home).

While the members share common problems that emanate from their location in the labour market, the manner in which they carry out resistance provides few prospects for change. The style of the subculture only displays members' dissatisfaction with their position. The "libertarian consciousness" that fuels resistance is self-muting. Furthermore, the members do not participate in political institutions where change can be fostered. What the subculture does offer is an environment where youths experiencing similar problems can interact. The subculture offers them status where school and employment does not. It allows them to escape their low status location for a period of time in what neo-Marxist theorists have termed a "magical" manner.

Subcultural resistance is not without consequences. For many members it means the adoption of marginal socioeconomic locations. Members were forced into squatting, scamming, rolling (i.e., mugging), panhandling, and violence. The harshness of these consequences demonstrate the depth of commitment to the subculture. It also brings to light problems associated with high levels of youth unemployment.

Males tend to adopt the more severe forms of resistance. They have little work experience and few skills, and face a labour market where there is a declining demand for manual labour. At the same time, they do not desire the employment that is available since the pay is poor, provides little status, and is alienating. For the male, the subculture is an alternative source of status. The others share his problems and by dismissing the dominant ideology he can attain status via subcultural criteria.

Female participation was less severe perhaps because the service sector areas where they are most likely to be employed are still in need of cheap labour. Furthermore, they are still likely to be subject to parental supervision and view the subculture as a social vehicle.

This paper shows that historical conditions have produced significant delinquent subcultures in Canada. However, the membership in these subcultures is still relatively small in comparison to the number of youths who are exposed to the same problems. If the trend in youth unemployment continues, one would expect that the number of youths participating in delinquent subcultures would increase. Not only should there be more youths who exhibit the severe forms of resistance but an even greater number who exhibit the less extreme forms. However, it is likely that even when conditions worsen, the majority of youth will not enter a delinquent subculture. What may begin to happen is that the young might start to reinterpret their situation. As Frith (1985) notes, one effect of unemployment is that more people than ever are returning to school. This "student" experience allows for the possibility of organization. The alternative to the delinquent subculture may be groups of youths organizing themselves in political interest groups. It may be in this manner that youth realize the political potential that the new subcultural theorists had predicted for delinquent youth subcultures.

HISTORICAL TRADITIONS AND NATIONAL CHARACTERISTICS: A COMPARATIVE ANALYSIS OF CANADA AND THE UNITED STATES

Seymour Martin Lipset

There is much to be gained, both in empirical and analytic terms, from a systematic comparative study of Canada and the United States. They have many of the same ecological and demographic conditions, approximately the same level of economic development, and similar rates of upward and downward social mobility. And alongside the obvious distinctiveness of francophone Quebec, anglophone Canadians and Americans have much in common in cultural terms as well. Yet, although overall these two people probably resemble each other more than any other two nations on earth, there are consistent patterns of difference between them. To discover and analyze the factors which create and perpetuate such differences among nations is one of the more intriguing and difficult tasks in comparative study.

In this essay I shall focus on value differences between the two countries, that is, differences in that set of attitudes which tends to characterize and permeate both the public and private ethos in each country. The central argument of the paper is that Canada has been a more elitist, law-abiding statist, collectivity-oriented, and particularistic (group-oriented) society than the United States, and that these fun-

From "Historical Traditions and National Characteristics: A Comparative Analysis of Canada and the United States." Appearing in *The Canadian Journal of Sociology*, Volume 11(2), 1986, By permission of the publisher and the author.

damental distinctions stem in a large part from the defining event which gave birth to both countries, the American Revolution. The social effects of this division have been subsequently reinforced by variations in religious traditions, political and legal institutions, and socio-economic structures, among other factors.

A brief characterization of the essential core, or organizing principles, of each society may help clarify the type of difference being referred to here. With respect to the United States, the emphasis on individualism and achievement orientation by the American colonists were an important motivating force in the launching of the American Revolution, and were embodied in the Declaration of Independence. The manifestation of such attitudes in this historic event and their crystallization in an historic document provided a basis for the reinforcement and encouragement of these orientations throughout subsequent American history. Thus, the United States remained through the nineteenth and early twentieth centuries the extreme example of classically liberal or Lockean society which rejected the assumptions of the alliance of throne and altar, or ascriptive elitism, of mercantilism, of *noblesse oblige*, of communitarianism. Friedrich Engels, among other foreign visitors, noted that as compared to Europe, the United States was "purely bourgeois, so entirely without a feudal past" (Engels, 1942: 467).

By contrast, both major Canadian linguistic groups sought to preserve their values and culture by reacting against liberal revolutions. English-speaking Canada exists because she opposed the Declaration of Independence; French-speaking Canada, largely under the leadership of Catholic clerics, also sought to isolate herself from the anti-clerical, democratic values of the French Revolution. The leaders of both, after 1783 and 1789, consciously attempted to create a conservative, monarchical and ecclesiastical society in North America. Canadian elites of both linguistic groups saw the need to use the state to protect minority cultures, English Canadians against Yankees, French Canadians against anglophones. In the United States, on the other hand, the Atlantic Ocean provided an effective barrier against the major locus of perceived threat — Britain — which helped sustain the American ideological commitment to a weak state that did not have to maintain extensive military forces. As with the United States, however, these initial "organizing principles" in Canada served to structure subsequent developments north of the border. Although the content and extent of the differences between the two countries have changed over time, the contemporary variations still reflect the impact of the American Revolution. . . .

The effort to relate variations in the value systems and institutions of nations to the differences in their key formative experiences provided a good illustration of Max Weber's methodological dictum that current differences among social structures may often be linked to specific historical events which set one process in motion in one nation or unit, and a different one in a second. Weber, in fact, used the analogy of a dice game in which each time the dice came up with a certain number they were loaded in the direction of coming up with that number again. That is, a decision in a certain direction tends to reinforce those elements which are congruent with it. In other words, historical events establish values and predispositions, and these in turn affect later events.

One illustration of how, in concrete terms, this process can unfold can be seen by looking at the broad sweep of Canadian history from the time of the American Revolution through to the establishment of Canadian independence in 1867. It was not just in 1776 that those to the north opted for the more conservative path. Canadian historians have noted that the democratic or populist elements lost their battle on many occasions. . . .

. . . As a result of the American Revolution, many Loyalists — those most opposed to the populist egalitarianism of the Revolution — emigrated to Canada. As J.M.S. Careless, another Canadian historian, has noted, they formed the "backbone of . . . resistance" to American invasion in 1812 (Careless, 1963: 113). The dice were loaded in this instance in the direction of a more conservative posture in Canada than in the United States by virtue of the Revolution and the subsequent migration north by those opposed to the values embodied in this historic event. Interestingly enough, . . . it may be argued that the values inherent in a monarchically rooted conservatism such as those which developed in Canada and much of Europe give rise in the modern world to support for social democratic redistributive and welfare policies. Conversely a dominant *laissez-faire* Lockean tradition which has been characteristic of the United States for much of its history is antithetical to such programs. Northrop Frye, Canada's leading literary critic, called attention to this alliance of opposites when he stated in 1952: "The Canadian point of view is at once more conservative and more radical than Whiggery [the liberal ideology of the American Revolution], closer both to aristocracy and to democracy [equality] . . ." (Frye, 1953: 273).

The attitudes and values characteristic of a people do not exist in a vacuum, however. It is important to recognize that one of the major factors explaining the persistence of particular orientations is that they become embodied in institutions which help perpetuate them. An illustration of this interaction between values and institutions can be found by comparing religious institutions and attitudes in Canada and the United States, which have consistently differed. The American tradition and law have placed much more emphasis on separation of church and state than has the Canadian. A large majority of Americans have adhered to Protestant sects, which had opposed the established state Church in England. These largely have a congregational structure, and foster the idea of an individual relationship with God. Most Canadians have belonged to either the Roman Catholic or the Anglican churches, both of which have been hierarchically organized state religions in Britain and Europe. While efforts to sustain church establishment ultimately failed in Canada, state support of religious institutions, particularly schools, has continued into the present. Hence religious institutions have both reflected and contributed to anti-elitist and individualist orientations in the United States and countered them in Canada.

It should be noted that a great deal of debate has been generated over the question of the relative significance of Canadian-American value differences. The argument essentially has been between those like myself, who emphasize the distinctiveness of the *values* of the two countries, and the ways these in turn affect behaviour, beliefs and institutional arrangements, and those who place primary importance on various *structural* differences, particularly geographic, economic, and political factors. It should be stressed, however, that a concern with the influence of economic, ecologic, and value elements in determining given national developments or traits is not a matter of dealing with alternative mutually exclusive hypotheses. Rather, as in the case of Weber's discussion of the relative contribution of economic and value factors in the rise of capitalism, one may conclude that different variables are each necessary but not sufficient to produce the results sometimes credited to one of them alone.

And, in fact, when the arguments of those identified as adhering to one or the other interpretation of the sources of Canadian-American differences (values or structure) are carefully examined, it becomes apparent that most of the distinctions really are ones of emphasis. For example, my own analysis takes into account that the two nations do vary in their ecology, demography and economy, and that these differences have exerted an important influence on the development of values and attitudes on both sides of the border. Canada controls an area which, while larger than her southern neighbor's, is much less hospitable to human habitation in terms of climate and resources. Her geographical extent and weaker population base have contributed to an emphasis on direct government involvement in the economy to provide various services, for which sufficient private capital or a profitable market have not been available. South of the border, the anti-statist emphasis subsumed in the revolutionary ideology was not challenged by the need to call upon the state to intervene economically to protect the nation's independence against a powerful neighbor.

In a similar way, those whose analysis emphasizes the significance of structural factors also acknowledge the role that values play in affecting the development of political and economic differences across the border. A good example can be found in the writing of Friedrich Engels, the cofounder of the most influential structural approach of all. He was one of the first writers to contend that Canada's economic backwardness compared to the United States is primarily a function of her value system. Following a visit to both countries in 1888, he wrote: "Here one sees how necessary the *feverish speculative spirit* of the Americans is for the rapid development of a

new country" and looked forward to the abolition of "this ridiculous boundary line" separating the two countries (Engels, 1953: 204, emphasis mine). More recently, Harold Innis, Canada's preeminent economic historian who has strongly emphasized structural factors, such as the "hard" character of the Canadian frontier in affecting national orientations, has also noted the importance of "the essentially counter-revolutionary traditions, represented by the United Empire Loyalists and by the Church in French Canada, which escaped the influences of the French Revolution" (Innis, 1956: 406).

A comparison of the frontier experiences of the two countries encapsulates the ways in which values and structural factors can interact to produce different outcomes. Inasmuch as Canada had to be on constant guard against the expansionist tendencies of the United States, it could not leave its frontier communities unprotected or autonomous. "It was in the established tradition of British America that the power of the civil authority should operate well in advance of the spread of settlement" (McInnis, 1942: 306–307). Law and order in the form of the centrally controlled North West Mounted Police moved into the frontier before and along with the settlers. This contributed to the establishment of a much greater tradition of respect for the institutions of law and order on the Canadian frontier as compared with the American, meant the absence of vigilante activity in Canada, and enabled Canada to avoid the Indian Wars which were occurring south of the border.

The pervasiveness of government legal controls on the Canadian frontier seriously undermined the development of an excessive emphasis on individualism which characterizes the United States. The development of the Canadian frontier, in fact, did not simply follow on population movements impelled by natural social pressures, as occurred in the United States. Rather, the Canadian government felt the need deliberately to plan for the settlement of the West.... And this history of active state involvement in the political and economic development of the country is reinforced by the population and geographic factors that today encourage a continued state role in economic investment and the provision of industrial infrastructure. Thus it may be argued with Weber that the appropriate structural environment for a given development requires the emergence of facilitating values, or that necessary values will not result in the anticipated changes unless the structural conditions are propitious.

Given all of the differences distinguishing the Canadian historical experience from the American, it is not surprising that the peoples of the two countries formulated their self-conceptions in sharply different ways. As an ideological nation whose left and right *both* take sustenance from the American Creed, the United States is quite different from Canada, which lacks any founding myth, and whose intellectuals frequently question whether the country has a national identity.... Although interpreted in a variety of ways by different groups and individuals, the ideology of the American Revolution provides for each of them a *raison d'être* for the Republic — it explains why the United States came into being, and what it means to be American.

The contrast with Canada is a sharp one. Canada could not offer her citizens "the prospect of a fresh start, . . . because (as the Canadian poet Douglas Le Pan put it) Canada is 'a country without a mythology'" (Bercovitch, 1981: 24). To justify her separate existence, both linguistic cultures deprecated American values and institutions. As Frank Underhill once noted, Canadians are the world's oldest and most continuing anti-Americans (Underhill, 1960: 222). This stance was reflected in the writings of various Canadian observers in the 1920s, who

"discerned and condemned an excessive egalitarian quality derived from notions of independence and democracy that had been set free during the [American] Revolution" (Weaver, 1973: 80). Further evidence of such attitudes was gathered during the 1930s when the first efforts at a systematic sociological investigation of opinions in Canada concerning themselves and Americans were launched. One of the most important and prolific contributors to the research was S.D. Clark, then starting his scholarly career. He summarized the findings in the following terms:

Canadian national life can almost be said to take its rise in the negative will to resist absorption in the American Republic. It is largely about the United States as an object that the consciousness of Canadian national unity has grown up. . .

Constantly in the course of this study we shall come across the idea that Canadian life is simpler, more honest, more moral and more religious than life in the United States, that it lies closer to the rural virtues and has achieved urbanization without giving the same scope to corrupting influences which has been afforded them in the United States. (Clark, 1938: 243, 245)

As Clark suggests in this passage, Canadians have tended to define themselves, not in terms of their own national history and tradition, but rather by reference to what they are *not*: American.

These differences between Canada and the United States can be seen, not just in history or in the findings of social science research, but also in the novels, poems, and stories created by writers in each country. In fact, of all artifacts, the art and literature of a nation should most reflect, as well as establish, her basic myths and values. And many analysts of North American literature have emphasized the continuing effects of the "mythic and psychic consequences of founding a country on revolution or out of the rejection of revolution." "Brown (n.d.). . . .

One of Canada's foremost novelists, Margaret Atwood, has vividly captured . . . what she sees as the central symbol of each of these two countries and their cultures. She suggests that the symbol for America is "The Frontier," which implies "a place that is *new*, where the old order can be discarded" and which "holds out a hope, never fulfilled but always promised, of Utopia, the perfect human society." She notes that most twentieth-century American literature is about the "gap between the promise and the actuality, between the imagined ideal . . . and the actual squalid materialism, dotty small town, nasty city, or redneck-filled outback" (Atwood, 1972: 31–32). Such an image both reflects and encourages a belief that one ought to *strive*, to seek out the better in life.

The central symbol for Canada, by contrast, based on numerous examples of its appearance in French and English Canadian literature, is "Survival, *la Survivance.*" The main meaning of survival in Canadian literature is the most basic one, "hanging on, staying alive." Atwood notes the continued Canadian concern with Canada: does it exist? will it last? what does it mean to be a Canadian? do we have an identity? etc. As she puts it: "Canadians are forever taking the national pulse like doctors at a sickbed; the aim is not to see whether the patient will live well but simply whether he will live at all" (Atwood, 1972: 33).

Atwood points out other national differences which are reflected in the literature of the two countries; one of the most important of these is the difference in the way the two societies look at authority. She argues that Canadians, unlike Americans, do not see authority or government as an enemy. "Canada must be the only country in the world where a policeman [the Moun-

tie] is used as a national symbol." It is not surprising, then, to find that rebels and revolutionists are not heroes in Canadian literature (Atwood, 1972: 171).

The study of a nation's arts and literature is important to any effort to *understand* her values. But as Ronald Sutherland has suggested, literature also helps *form* national values: "The greatest writers of a nation . . . respond to the forces that condition a nation's philosophy of life, and they in turn condition that philosophy" (Sutherland, 1982: 402). Literature is, of course, not alone or even predominant in these respects. As we turn now to a systematic comparison of a number of facets of the two societies, ranging from law and crime to center-periphery relations, we shall continue to observe this mutual interation between the values predominant in a nation and the institutions which both reflect and shape them.

Religion

One sphere of life in which this relationship is clearly observable is that of religion. As far as understanding the ways in which religious tradition in Canada differs from that in the United States is concerned, Harold Innis may have said it all when he wrote that a "counter-revolutionary tradition implies an emphasis on ecclesiasticism" (Innis, 1956: 385). As previously mentioned, the majority of Canadians adhere to the Roman Catholic or Anglican churches, both of which are hierarchically organized and continued until recently to have a strong relationship to the state. On the other hand, most Americans have belonged to the more individualist "nonconformist" Protestant sects. . . .

The abolition of established religion in the United States fostered a strong commitment to voluntarism which, as Tocqueville argued, has been an important factor strengthening religion in the United States. In his view, voluntary competitive institutions which rely on their membership for funds and support are likely to be stronger than institutions supported by the state. Moreover, this commitment to voluntarism, together with the considerable strength of the dissenting and anti-statist Methodist and Baptist denominations, meant that religion not only contributed to the economic orientations of the people, but also reinforced the egalitarian and democratic ethos. Tocqueville pointed out that all American denominations were minorities and hence had an interest in liberty and a weak state (Tocqueville, 1945: 312).

By contrast, both the Church of England and the Roman Catholic Church received overt government support and, in return, gave strong support to the established political and social order. Hence one found mutually reinforcing conservative forces at the summits of the class, church and political structures (Clark, 1950: 388). In comparing French and English Canada, Roger O'Toole emphasizes that until recently in Quebec the Roman Catholic Church has retained the informal role of the state church of French Canada. And, although the Anglican Church failed in its effort to become a "national" church in English Canada, it helped establish the founding ethos of the country and to legitimate "monarchy, aristocracy, and British constitutionalism [as] part of a sacred scenario.... [I]ts condemnation of mass democracy, egalitarianism, republicanism, and revolution as the work of the devil, left an indelible mark on English-Canadian political life" (O'Toole, 1982: 184–185).

Just as religious practices and institutions can reinforce general value orientations prevalent in a national community, so too can the latter influence the former, as is demonstrated in Kenneth Westhues' comparative study of the American and Canadian Catholic churches. He suggests that there has been an "acceptance by the American [Church] of the role of voluntary association ... as the most it could hope for" (Westhues, 1978: 251). Thus, the Catholic Church in the United States has taken over many of the characteristics of Protestantism, including a strong emphasis on individual moralism. As a result, the Vatican has frowned on the American church and has, in fact, not treated it as well as the Canadian affiliate. . . .

And Westhues argues, the "major question always before the Catholic church in the United States has been how far to assimilate to the American way of life." This question "has never arisen in Canada, basically for the lack of a national ideology for defining what the Canadian way of life is or ought to be" (Westhues, 1978: 254–255).

Religion in both countries has become more secularized in tandem with increased urbanization and education. For instance, Canadian Catholicism, particularly in Quebec, has modified the nature of its corporatist commitment from a link to agrarian and elitist anti-industrial values to a tie to leftist socialist beliefs. These variations, of course, parallel the changes in French Canadian nationalism. Public opinion research suggests that francophone Catholics have given up much of their commitment to Jansenist puritanical values, particularly as they affect sexual behaviour and family size. This secularizing trend, although generally observable in both countries, has been less noticeable in the United States, particularly among evangelical Protestants. Americans, according to data from sample surveys, ... are much more likely to attend church regularly than Canadians, and to adhere to fundamentalist and moralistic beliefs. And the continued strength of Protestant evangelical, sectarian and fundamentalist religion south of the border has meant that traditional values related to sex, family and morality in general are stronger there than in Canada. . . .

There is a consistent pattern in these data: Americans far outnumber Canadians generally in giving expression to Protestant fundamentalist beliefs, with anglophones more likely to hold such views than francophones. And, congruent with the variation in religious practice and belief, Americans appear to be more puritanical than Canadians, with francophones the most tolerant with respect to sexual behavior.

Institutionally, national values should be clearly expressed in a nation's system of laws and the way individuals are treated under and react to them and, in fact, this is what we find in examining these aspects of Canadian and American society.

Law and Deviance

The difference in the role of law in the two countries is linked to the historical emphases on the rights and obligations of the community as compared to those of the individual. The explicit concern of Canada's founding fathers with "peace, order, and good government" implies control and protection. The American stress on "life, liberty, and the pursuit of happiness" suggests upholding the rights of the individual. This latter concern for rights, including those of people accused of crime and of political dissidents, is inherent in the "due process" model, involving legal inhibitions on the power of the police and prosecutors, characteristic of the United States. The "crime control" model, more evident in Canada, as well as Europe, emphasizes the maintenance of law and order, and is less protective of the rights of the accused and of individuals generally. . . .

The Canadian government has greater legal power to restrict freedom of speech and to invade personal privacy. Acting through an order-in-council, it may limit public discussion of particular issues and, as in 1970 during the Quebec crisis, impose a form of military control. . . . Comparing American and Canadian public reaction to violations of privacy by the government, Alan Westin writes:

[I]t is important to note that in Canada there have been some incidents which, had they happened in the United States, would probably have led to a great causes célèbres. Most Canadians seem to have accepted Royal Canadian Mounted Police break-ins without warrants between 1970 and 1978, and also the RCMP's secret access to income tax information, and to personal health information from the Ontario Health Insurance Plan. If I read the Canadian scene correctly, those did not shock and outrage most Canadians. (Westin, 1983: 41)

That Canadians and Americans differ in the way they react to the law is demonstrated strikingly in the aggregate differences between the two with respect to crime rates for major offenses. Americans are much more prone than Canadians to commit violent offenses like murder, robbery, and rape and to be arrested for the use of serious illegal drugs such as opiates and cocaine. They are also much more likely to take part in protest demonstrations and riots. . . . Although the United States population outnumbers the Canadian by about ten to one, the ratios for political protest activities have ranged from twenty to one to forty to one.

Evidence from national opinion surveys in the two countries indicates that lower rates of crime and violence in Canada are accompanied by greater respect for police, public backing for stronger punishment of criminals, and a higher level of support for gun control legislation. For example, when asked by the Canadian Gallup poll in 1978 to rate the local, provincial, and Royal Canadian Mounted Police, a large majority (64 percent, 64 percent, and 61 percent, respectively) said "excellent" or "good." The corresponding percentages reported by Harris survey for local, state and federal law enforcement officials in 1981 were 62, 57, and 48. In the early eighties, the CARA surveys conducted by Gallup found more Canadians (86 percent) than Americans (76 percent) voicing a great deal or quite a lot of confidence in the police. There was no significant difference between the two Canadian linguistic groups on this item.

In the United States, gun ownership has been regarded as a "right," one linked to a constitutional guarantee established to protect the citizen. Canada's policy is based on the belief that "ownership of 'offensive weapons' or 'guns' is a privilege, not a right" (Thomas, 1983: 40). It is not surprising, then, that Canadians have consistently been much more supportive of gun control legislation than Americans and have been much less likely to own guns (Thomas, 1983: 6). When asked by the Gallup Polls in 1975, "Would you favor or oppose a law which would require a person to obtain a police permit before he or she could buy a gun?" 83 percent of Canadians voiced support compared to 67 percent of Americans.

The lesser respect for the law, for the "rules of the game" in the United States, may be viewed as inherent in a system in which egalitarianism is strongly valued and in which diffuse elitism is lacking. Generalized deference is not accorded to those at the top; therefore, in the United States there is a greater propensity to redefine the rules or to ignore them. The decisions of the leadership are constantly being questioned. While Canadians incline toward the use of "lawful" and traditionally institutionalized means for altering regulations which they believe are unjust, Americans seem more disposed to employ informal and often extralegal means to correct what they perceive as wrong.

The greater lawlessness and corruption in the United States may be attributed in part to the greater strength of the achievement value in the more populous nation. As Robert Merton has pointed out, a strong emphasis on achievement means that "[t]he moral mandate to achieve success thus exerts pressure to succeed, by fair means if possible and by foul means if necessary" (Merton, 1957: 169). Merton accounts for the greater adherence to approved means of behavior in much of Europe compared to the United States as derivative from variations in the emphasis on achievement for all. And the same logic implies that since Americans are more likely than their Canadian neighbors to be concerned with the achievement of ends — particularly pecuniary success — they will be less concerned with the use of the socially appropriate *means*; hence we should expect a higher incidence of deviations from conventional norms in politics and other aspects of life south of the forty-ninth parallel.

Although the cross-national behavioral and attitudinal variations with respect to law and crime have continued down to the present, Canada has been involved since 1960 in a process of changing her fundamental rules in what has been described as American and due process directions. The adoption of a Bill of Rights in 1960, replaced by the more comprehensive Charter of Rights and Freedom in 1982, was designed to create a basis, absent from the British North American Act, for judicial intervention to protect individual rights and civil liberties.

While these changes are important, it is doubtful that they will come close to eliminating the differences in legal cultures. Canadian courts have been more respectful than American ones of the rest of the political system. . . .

Beyond these general distinctions there are specific provisions in the new Charter of Rights and Freedoms which set it apart from the American Bill of Rights. For example, to protect parliamentary supremacy, the Canadian constitution provides that Parliament or a provincial legislature may "opt out" of the constitutional restrictions by inserting into any law a clause that it shall operate regardless of any part of the Charter. In addition, the new rights do not include any assurance that an accused person shall have a lawyer, nor that he has the right to remain silent, nor that he need not answer questions which may tend to incriminate him in civil cases or in investigatory proceedings.

Just as the legal system has aspects which are relevant both to our private lives and public realm, so too does the economy. Thus the next task is to examine the relationship between values and structure in the two North American states in this sphere of activity.

The Economy: The Private Sector

The United States, born modern, without a feudal elitist corporatist tradition, could create, outside of the agrarian South, what Engels described as the purest example of a bourgeois society. Canada, as we have seen, was somewhat different, and that difference affected the way her citizens have done business. . . .

. . . [A]ccording to Hardin (1974), Canadian entrepreneurs have been less aggressive, less innovating, less risk-taking than Americans. Hardin seeks to demonstrate that private enterprise in Canada "has been a monumental failure" in developing new technology and industry, to the extent that Canadian business has rarely been involved in creating industries to process many significant inventions by Canadians, who have had to go abroad to get their discoveries marketed.

This has been partly due to traditional management values and organizational

process. Also important is the fact that, compared to Americans, Canadian investors and financial institutions are less disposed to provide venture capital. They "tend consistently to avoid offering encouragement to the entrepreneur with a new technology-based product . . . [or to] innovative industries." . . .

Data drawn from opinion polls reinforce the comparative generalizations about the greater economic prudence of Canadians. Studies of English and French speaking Canadians indicate that on most items, anglophones fall between Americans and francophones. When asked by the American and Canadian Gallup Polls in 1979 (U.S.) and 1980 (Canada) about usage of credit cards, 51 percent of Canadians said they never used one, as compared to 35 percent of Americans. The latter were more likely than Canadians to report "regular" usage, 32 percent to 16 percent. Francophones made less use of credit cards (64 percent, never) than anglophones (44 percent, never). English speakers were also more likely to be regular users than French speakers.

If Canadians have been more conservative than Americans in their behavior in the private sector, they have been much more prone to rely on the state to handle economic and other matters, as the next section indicates.

The Economy: The Public Sector

As mentioned earlier, and as will be further elaborated below, the stronger conservative orientation north of the border historically has meant a larger role for the state in the Canadian economy. For example, the proportion of the Canadian GNP in government hands as of the mid-seventies was 41 percent, compared to 34 percent in the United States; as of 1982 the ratio was 44 to 38 percent. Subtracting defense spending, roughly 2 percent for Canada and 5 to 6 percent for the United States, widens the gap between the two countries considerably. Taxes as a share of total domestic product were 35 percent in Canada as compared to 30 percent in the United States in 1982. Unlike "the United States, [Canada] has never experienced a period of pure unadulterated *laissez-faire* market capitalism." The period since 1960 has witnessed a particularly rapid expansion in the number of crown corporations: fully 70 percent of them were created in the past quarter of a century (Chandler, 1983: 187). . . .

Research based on opinion poll interviews indicates that Canadians, at both elite and mass levels, are more supportive than Americans of state intervention. . . .

Mass attitudinal data reinforce the thesis that Canadians are more collectivity-oriented than Americans and therefore are more likely to support government intervention. In the 1968–70 studies of American and English Canadian attitudes . . ., Stephen Arnold and Douglas Tigert found that, compared to Canadians, Americans are more opposed to big government and less likely to believe that government should guarantee everyone an income. . . . They also reported that Americans are more likely than Canadians to take part in voluntary communitarian activities which, according to the authors, contradicts my assumption that Canadians are more collectivity oriented (Arnold and Tigert, 1974: 80–81). However, I would argue that the findings support this contention, since they demonstrate that Americans are more likely to take part in voluntary activity to achieve particular goals, while Canadians are more disposed to rely on the state. And in fact, an . . . article by Stephen Arnold and James Barnes . . . concluded: "Americans were found to be individualistic, whereas Canadians were more collectively ori-

ented," more supportive of state provision of medical care or a guaranteed minimum income (Arnold and Barnes, 1979: 32).

Elitism and Equalitarianism

From a consideration of the role of the state with respect to economic policies, it seems appropriate to turn to aspects of stratification. In earlier writings on this subject, I suggested that Canada and the United States vary with respect to the values of equalitarianism-elitism and achievement-ascription (Lipset, 1970: 38–39). Elitism is presumed to be reflected in diffuse respect for authority, and in Canada contributes to the encouragement of a greater role for the state in economic and social affairs. Equalitarianism can be perceived as the polar contrast to elitism, in Tocquevillian terms as generalized respect for "all persons . . . because they are human beings" (Lipset, 1970: 38). Equalitarianism, however, has many meanings, not all of which are incompatible with elitism. Conceptualized as "equality of result," it enters into the political arena in efforts to reduce inequality on a group level. And, reiterating the arguments just presented, it may be said that Tory stimuli, elitist in origin, produce social democratic responses, efforts to protect and upgrade the position of less privileged strata.

Conceptualizing equalitarianism in this fashion leads to the expectation that nations which rank high with respect to the value of achievement, "equality of opportunity," will be less concerned with reducing inequality of condition. If the United States is more achievement oriented and less elitist than Canada, then she should place more emphasis on educational equality as the primary mechanism for moving into the higher socio-economic positions. Canada, on the other hand, should be more favorable to redistributive proposals, thus upgrading the lower strata, as, in fact, she is.

Robert Kurdrle and Theodore Marmor note that "the ideological difference — slight by international standards — between Canada and the United States appears to have made a considerable difference in welfare state developments" (Kudrle and Marmor, 1981: 112). Canadian programs were adopted earlier, "exhibited a steadier development," are financed more progressively and/or are more income redistributive in the areas of old age security, unemployment insurance, and family allowances (non-existent in the United States), and medical care (Kudrle and Marmor, 1981: 91–111). Similarly, a recent study of health care practices notes that "the equity objective in health has a much higher priority in Canada than in the United States . . ." (Weller, 1984: 12).

The main evidence which bears on the relationship between elitism and equality of opportunity in my earlier essay concerns education. As of 1960, the proportion of Canadians aged 20–24 in higher education (16 percent) was much lower than that of Americans (32 percent). The educational literature of the time also called attention to the more elitist character of the Canadian system, the fact that education in the north was more humanistic and less vocational and professional in orientation.

The numbers of people attending higher education have increased greatly in both North American societies during the past two decades, although there is still a considerable gap. As of 1979, the percentage of Canadians aged 20–24 in higher education had risen to 36, but the comparable American figure had increased to 55. The proportion of Canadians enrolled in tertiary education jumped by 125 percent; that of Americans by 27 percent. Americans, however, moved up more in absolute terms, 23 percent to 20 percent for Canadians.

Some analysts of recent changes in Canadian universities have referred to them as "Americanizations" (Bissell, 1979: 198). Canada not only sharply increased the number of universities and places for students, but her higher education institutions, following public policy, have changed. They have incorporated practical and vocationally relevant subjects, expanded the social sciences and graduate programs, and placed greater emphasis on faculty scholarship. As Claude Bissell, former President of the University of Toronto, emphasizes, his country has been moving away from an elitist conception of higher education. . . .

The changes in the size and content of higher education in Canada should lead to a reduction in the proportion of persons without professional training who hold top jobs. Comparative data indicate that Canada has differed from America, and resembled Britain, in disproportionately recruiting her business and political administrative elites from those without a professional or technical education. As Charles McMillan reports, "Canadian managers tend to be less well educated than their counterparts in any other industrialized country with the possible exception of Britian" (McMillan, 1978: 45).

This conclusion is documented by Wallace Clement's studies of business elites which reveal that the Canadians not only have less specialized education than the Americans, but also that the former are much more likely to have an elitist social background. As Clement reports, "entrance to the economic elite is easier for persons from outside the upper class in the United States than it is in Canada. . . . [T]he U.S. elite is more open, recruiting from a much broader class base than is the case in Canada" (Clement, 1977: 183, 209). Sixtyone percent of the Canadian top executives are of upper class origin compared to 36 percent of the Americans (Clement, 1977:

215–250, esp. 216; see also Safarian, 1969: 13). . . .

As with many other Canadian institutions, the civil service has been changing. A more recent survey of bureaucrats in central government agencies by Colin Campbell and George Szablowski finds that in "the past decade Canada has seen a remarkable influx of bureaucrats representing segments of the populace traditionally excluded from senior positions in the public service," and that many of those interviewed had "experienced rapid upward mobility" (Campbell and Szablowski, 1979: 105, 121). These developments may reflect the documented decrease in educational inheritance in Canada as the higher education system has grown (Manzer, 1974: 188–206).

Cross-national surveys conducted in recent years have explicitly sought to estimate support for meritocracy when contrasted with equality of result. Their findings point to strong differences between Americans and Canadians on these issues. In the fall of 1979, national samples in the two countries were asked by a Japanese research group to choose between the two in fairly direct fashion:

Here are two opinions about conditions existing in our country. Which do you happen to agree with?

A. There is too much emphasis upon the principle of equality. People should be given the opportunity to choose their own economic and social life according to their individual abilities.

B. Too much liberalism has been producing increasingly wide differences in people's economic and social life. People should live more equally.

Forty-one percent of the Canadians chose the more egalitarian and collectivity-oriented option B. The proportion of Americans responding this way was 32 percent. Clearly the pattern of responses suggests that Canadians value equality of result more than Americans, while the latter are more achievement oriented. . . .

If greater commitment to equality of result leads Canadians to voice a higher preference for equality over freedom or liberty, the assumption that Canada is more elitist than the United States implies, as I noted in an earlier comparison of the two societies, that Canadians should be more tolerant towards deviants or dissidents than Americans (Lipset, 1970: 46–48). I suggested that even without a due process system, the greater tolerance and civil liberties for unpopular groups in elitist democracies, such as Britain and Canada, as compared to populist ones reflected the ability of elites in the former to protect minority rights. Opinion studies from many democratic societies indicate that educated elites invariably are more tolerant than the less educated; hence the tyranny of the majority is less of a problem in a more elitist system. And the CARA data bear out the anticipation that Canadians would, therefore, be more tolerant than their southern neighbors. When asked about various kinds of unpopular people, which of them you "*would not* like to have as neighbors," Canadians, the francophones particularly, were more accepting than Americans. The latter were more likely (49 percent) than English Canadians (40 percent) or French Canadians (30 percent) to say that they were opposed to having "people with a criminal record as neighbors." Americans also were more disposed to find "emotionally unstable people" offensive as neighbors (47 percent) than English Canadians (33 percent) or French Canadians (13 percent). Not surprisingly, Americans exhibited less tolerance for people described as "extremists." Thus, "left-wing extremists" were rejected as neighbors by 34 percent of the Americans, 31 percent of the English Canadians, and only 20 percent of the French Canadians; while "right-wing extremists" were turned down by 26 percent of the Americans, 24 percent of the anglophone Canadians, and 14 percent of the francophones.

As a final subject, this analysis turns to national unity, to the ways that subgroups, ethnic and regional, behave in the two societies.

Mosaic and Melting Pot: Center and Periphery

In an earlier paper, I asserted that "Canada is more particularistic (group-attribute conscious) than the seemingly more universalistic United States" (Lipset, 1970: 55). These differences are reflected (a) in the Canadian concept of the "mosaic," applied to the right to cultural survival of ethnic groups, as compared to the American notion of the "melting pot"; (b) in the more frequent recurrence and survival of strong regionally based third parties in Canada than in the United States; and (c) in the greater strength of provinces within the Canadian union, compared to the relative weakness of the states and the nationalization of politics, i.e, the decline of regionalism, in America.

The origin of these cross-national differences, as with those previously discussed, can be traced to the impact of the Revolution. American universalism, the desire to incorporate diverse groups into one culturally unified whole, is inherent in the founding ideology, the American Creed. Canadian particularism, the preservation of sub-national group loyalties, an outgrowth of the commitment to the maintenance of two linguistic sub-cultures, is derivative from the decision of the francophone clerical elite to remain loyal to the British monarchy, as a protection against the threat posed by Puritanism and democratic populism from the revolutionary south. Given the importance of the French-speaking areas to British North America, the subse-

quent Canadian federal state incorporated protections for the linguistic minority, and the provinces assumed considerable power.

These differences could be expected to decline with modernization. Most analysts have assumed that industrialization, urbanization, and the spread of education would reduce ethnic and regional consciousness, that universalism would supplant particularism. As Nathan Glazer and Daniel P. Moynihan noted, it was generally believed that "divisions of culture, religion, language [and race] ... would inevitably lose their weight and sharpness in modern and modernizing societies, ... that common systems of education and communication would level differences" (Glazer and Moynihan, 1975: 6–7). Samuel Beer argued that modernization inherently led to a growth in authority at the center and a decline in state and provincial power as the different parts of federal countries became more differentiated and interdependent. As he put it: "In the United States, as in other modernizing societies, the general historical record has spelled centralization. ... [T]he main reasons for this change are ... to be found ... in the new forces produced by an advanced modernity" (Beer, 1973: 52).

The validity of the assumption that structural modernizaton would sharply reduce ethnic and regional diversity and the power of federal sub-units has been challenged by developments both within and outside of Canada. From the sixties on the world has witnessed an ethnic revival in many countries. In Canada, even prior to the revival, the values underlying the concept of the "mosaic" meant that various minorities, in addition to the francophones, would be able to sustain a stronger group life than comparable ones in the United States. ...

The differing organization of Jews in Canada and the United States also shows how the structure and behavior of an ethnic-religious group may vary with national environments. Canadian Jewry is much better organized as a community than its American counterpart. A single national organization, the Canadian Jewish Congress, represents all Jews in Canada, while there is no comparable group in the United States. A much higher proportion of Jewish youth is enrolled in day schools in Canada than in the United States, while the intermarriage rate is lower north of the border in spite of the fact that the Canadian Jewish community is much smaller than the American. The size factor should have led to greater assimilation in Canada, but the emphasis on particularistic group organization subsumed in the mosaic character of Canada seemingly helps to perpetuate a more solidaristic Canadian Jewish community (Schenfeld, 1978).

The greater autonomy and coherence of ethnic groups north of the border is the result, not just of a different set of attitudes, but also of explicit government policies which reflect them. Ever since the publication in 1969 of the fourth volume of the *Report of the Royal Commission on Bilingualism and Biculturalism*, the country has been committed to helping all ethnic groups through a policy of promoting "multiculturalism." The extent of the government's willingness to support this policy was reflected in the 1973 establishment of a cabinet ministry with the exclusive responsibility for multiculturalism. In addition, the government has provided funding to ethnic minorities for projects designed to celebrate and extend their cultures.

During the past two decades blacks have assumed a role within the American polity somewhat similar to that which the Québécois play in Canada. They call for "Black Power," in the context of demands for group, as distinct from individual, rights through affirmative action quotas and other forms of aid, has led the United States to explicitly accept particularistic standards for dealing with racial and ethnic groups. Much as francophones have legitimated cultural autonomy for other non-Anglo-Saxon Canadians, the changing position of blacks has enabled other American ethnic groups and women to claim similar particularistic rights. In effect, the United States has moved toward replacing the ideal of the "melting pot" with that of the "mosaic." Nevertheless, as John Porter argued at the end of the seventies, these changes still leave the United States a more universalistic society than Canada (Porter, 1979: 160).

If the two North American countries have reduced some of the variation in the ways they define the position of minorities, they are more disparate than before with respect to the importance of the center and the periphery — the national government versus the regions, states, and provinces. Regional differences have steadily declined in the United States; they have remained important or have even increased in Canada. . . .

The sharp discrepancy between Canadian and American developments, on the one hand a weakening of the power of the national government, on the other a strengthening of it, has led political scientists to ask "what has accounted for these contradictory developments?" The answers suggested are manifold. Few Canadian scholars are ready too agree, as John Porter was, that the difference is derived from the continued influence in Canada of counterrevolutionary traditions and institutions, or that the variations represent a "choice of different sets of values, as the choice between a preference for the maintenance of group identities or for the diffusion of individual universalism" (Hueglin, 1984: 22). Rather, they discuss a variety of relevant factors: "*societal* (economic, demographic, and international forces) and *institutional* (the formal or constitutional structures of the state)."

Two variables, both of which may be linked to the outcome of the American Revolution, appear to be most important. One is the role of the French Canadians discussed earlier. The other is the effect of the variation between the Presidential-Congressional divided-powers American system and the British parliamentary model. As Roger Gibbins emphasizes, "the Quebecois ... have used the Quebec provincial government as an instrument of cultural survival and, because the stakes are so high, provincial rights have been guarded with a vigor unknown in the United States" (Gibbins, 1982: 192). Smaller provinces, seeking to protect their autonomy, have been able to do so because Quebec has always been in the forefront of the struggle.

The much greater propensity of Canadian provinces as compared to American states to engage in recurrent struggles with the federal government and to support a variety of particularistic third parties may be explained by the fact that regional interests are much less well protected in Parliament than in Congress. As I argued three decades ago: "Given the tight national party discipline imposed by a parliamentary as compared with a presidential system, Canadians are forced to find a way of expressing their special regional or other group needs. ... [T]he Canadian solution has been to frequently support different parties on a provincial level than those which they back nationally," so that provincial governments may carry out the representation tasks which in the United States are fulfilled by Congressional interest blocs. Or, as Donald Smiley puts it, "[C]ongressionalism appears to inhibit the direct confrontation of federal and state governments, while the parliamentary forms in their contemporary Canadian variant sharpen the conflict between federal and provincial jurisdictions" (Smiley, 1984: 55).

Conclusion

Without succumbing further to the temptation of discussing other Canadian-American differences, there can be little doubt that regardless of how much emphasis is placed on structural or cultural (value) factors in accounting for variations, that Canada and the United States continue to differ considerably along most of the dimensions suggested in my previous work.

Some critics of the cultural approach, such as Arthur Davis and I.L. Horowitz have contended that the differences between the two nations have largely been a function of "cultural lag," that Canada, traditionally somewhat less developed economically than the United States, has been slower to give up the values and life styles characteristic of a less industrialized, more agrarian society (Davis, 1971; Horowitz, 1973). Presumably then, as the structural gap declines, Canada should become more like the United States. A similar thesis, on a broader scale, has been enunciated by various proponents of world system or convergence theories, who see national cultural differences diminishing, if not vanishing, as the industrial systems of the developed countries come to approximate each other. In the specific case of Canada and the United States, the two should become even more similar since the "American connection" has resulted in increased domination by American companies over broad sections of Canadian economic life, while Canada has also become more culturally dependent on its southern neighbor through the spread of the American mass media, particularly television, as well as various forms of journalism. Since World War II, substantial changes in economic productivity, education — quantitatively and qualitatively — , and in rates of upward social mobility, that have been described in Canada, particularly Quebec, as the "quiet revolution" and in the United States as "the post-industrial revolution," have clearly reduced the structural gap. But there has been no consistent decline in the patterns of differences in behavior and values. As has been elaborated in the preceding pages, significant variations remain across the border with respect to a broad range of societal conditions.

I have paid more attention here than in my earlier writings to variations between the two Canadian linguistic cultures. The evidence indicates that francophone Canadians vary more from their anglophone co-nationals than the latter do from Americans. Quebec, once the most conservative part of Canada, has become the most liberal on social issues and had a quasi-socialist provincial government from 1976 to 1986. Clearly, as John Porter and others have emphasized, there are Canadian styles and values that differentiate both linguistic cultures from the American one.

The cultural and political differences between the two North American nations suggest why they occasionally have some difficulty understanding each other in the international arena. There are the obvious effects of variations in size, power, and awareness of the other. Canadians object to being taken for granted, and to being ignored by their neighbor. As citizens of a less populous power, they sympathize with other small or weak countries who are pressed by the United States. But beyond the consequences of variations in national power and interests, Canadians and Americans, as I have tried to spell out here, have a somewhat different *Weltanschauung*, world-view, ideology. Derivative from their revolutionary and sectarian Protestant heritages, Americans, more than other western peoples, tend to view international politics in non-negotiable moralistic and ideological terms. Canadians, like Europeans, with whom they share a Church

rather than a sectarian religious tradition, and a national self-conception drawn from a common history rather than a revolutionary ideology, are more disposed to perceive foreign policy conflicts as reflections of interest differences, and therefore subject to negotiation and compromise.

In trying in the early fifties to answer the question what is "distinctively Canadian," Frye noted that "historically, a Canadian is an American who rejects the Revolution" (Frye, 1953: 273). By the mid-sixties, I suggested that the national self-images were changing as a result of varying perceptions of international events, that "[m]any Canadians now view their country as more 'leftist' or liberal in its institutions and international objectives than the United States" (Lipset, 1970: 74). Since then, many Canadians, including Conservatives, have supported the "revolution" in various places, such as Vietnam, Nicaragua, and El Salvador, while the United States has backed the "counterrevolution," the "contras." (Americans, it should be noted, often take this position in the context of a belief that they are backing democracy, the people, against actual or potential tyrants.)

The United States and Canada remain two nations formed around sharply different organizing principles. As various novelists and literary critics have emphasized, their basic myths vary considerably, and national ethoses and structures too are determined in large part by such myths. However, the differences in themes in the two national literatures have declined in the past two decades. Ronald Sutherland and A.J.M. Smith, two Canadian literary critics, have both called attention to a new nationalism north of the border, one which has produced a more radical literature (Sutherland, 1977: 413; Smith, 1979: 236–237). But ironically, as Sutherland points out, these changes are making Canada and her fiction more American, involving a greater emphasis on values such as pride in country, self-reliance, individualism, independence and self-confidence.

It may be argued, however, that these changes, while reducing some traditional differences, have enhanced others. The new nationalism, often linked among intellectuals both to socialism and Toryism, seeks to resist takeover of Canada's economy and increased cultural and media influence by Americans, and its weapon in so doing is the remedy of state action. As Christian and Campbell have observed in this context: "Toryism, socialism, and nationalism all share a common collectivist orientation in various forms" (Christian and Campbell, 1983: 209).

Although some will disagree, there can be no argument. As Margaret Atwood has well put it: "Americans and Canadians are not the same, they are the products of two very different histories, two very different situations" (Atwood, 1984: 392).

chapter

4

Social Structure

Sociologists generally describe social structure as patterns of behaviour and distribution of resources that stand outside of and constrain individuals. All the readings in this chapter deal with people's experiences of social structure. The first selection, by Marion Pirie of York University, explains how feminist theory can help us show that medical knowledge is a social product and that a medical condition is a label created and applied by medical professionals who are also members of the medical-industrial complex. Here, in investigating the medicalization of menstruation, Pirie shows how women's premenstrual experience is shaped by culture and social structure and comes to be defined as an illness. And, in focusing on those with the power to label a condition as

an illness, Pirie is also making a contribution to labelling theory, an important perspective in the sociology of deviance and social control.

The second selection, by Elliot Leyton of Memorial University, follows very much in the tradition of Emile Durkheim's classic study of suicide. In this excerpt from his book, *Hunting Humans*, Leyton shows how even the most bizarre, frightening and apparently idiosyncratic actions can only be understood within the context of social structure. Even multiple murderers draw their motives and choose their targets in a way that reflects the influence of social structure.

The final selection, by Peter Clark of Dalhousie University and Anthony Davis of St. Francis Xavier University, might perhaps have fitted better in the preceding chapter on "Culture." We include it here because it seemed to us that this rather fascinating, somewhat bizarre and, we must admit, in terms of its subject matter, what we find a repugnant research topic, does demonstrate how even such taken-for-granted aspects of everyday life as our notions of what is clean and what is dirty are shaped by social structure and, in this particular case, by partriarchy and male supremacy. Moreover, the authors have, in our view, used effectively anthropological concepts developed to examine nonindustrial societies as well as our own industrial society. While we, of course, include this selection because we think it provides an insightful view of another dimension of social structure, it is also possible that, at a more mundane level, you may learn more about why, come end of the second term you want to get rid of a particular roommate or, turning it round, there seems a desire to get rid of you.

RELATED READINGS

C. Wright Mills: "The Promise." (Chapter 1)
Emile Durkheim: "What is a Social Fact?" (Chapter 1)
Karl Marx: "The Materialist Conception of History." (Chapter 1)
Rhonda Lenton: "Homicide in Canada and the USA: A Critique of the Hagan Thesis." (Chapter 7)

WOMEN AND THE ILLNESS ROLE: RETHINKING FEMINIST THEORY

Marion Pirie

In discussing the relevance of feminist theory to the sociological study of women and health, it is instructive to recall something of the aims, content, and spirit of discovery involved in the feminist research enterprise. In the social sciences, feminist research incorporates two distinct but complementary goals. The first is a humanistic, value oriented one, where political change and a commitment to social justice are primary (McCormack, 1981b: 2). As Margrit Eichler in a recent review of the topic asserts: "At the most fundamental level, feminist scholarship is committed to understanding and improving the situation of women" (Eichler, 1985: 624). At the same time, feminist research has increasingly embraced what are often called the "soft paradigms"; models which emphasize reflexivity (of both the researcher and her subjects), subjective experience, cognitive structures, intuition, personal biographies, and perhaps most controversially for the social sciences, feelings. Feminist theory has long rejected the value of processing lifeless variables in favour of attempting to understand the subjective experience of human beings. The preferred epistemology among feminist scholars is and has long been "characteristically phenomenological" (McCormack, 1987: 2) and its preferred modes of investigation have remained characteristically qualitative. (See Baumrind, 1980; Oakley, 1981; Stanely and Wise, 1985; Eichler, 1985; McCormack, 1987; for a discussion of feminist applications of qualitative research).

From "Women and the Illness Role: Rethinking Feminist Theory" by Marion Pirie. First published in Volume 25:4, 1988. By permission of *The Canadian Review of Sociology and Anthropology*.

The complementarity of these aims is suggested by the argument that it is not largely, but *only* through the phenomenological investigation of women's subjective experience that 1) identity and credibility will be restored (McCormack, 1987) and that 2) women's understanding of their own political efficacy in an oppressive society would be revealed (often via the research enterprise itself). Incorporating these aims, then, the spirit of feminist research involves not only a consciousness-seeking, but a consciousness-raising process, as well. Lillian Rubin's combined phenomenological humanistic approach (1975; 1979; 1981) stands out as an exemplary model of the feminist research enterprise.

The phenomenological orientation of feminist research in the area of women and illness behaviour, however, has not been as fully utilized as it might be. In terms of empirical research, quantitative studies far outweigh qualitative studies; structural variables are preferred over process variables as modes of measurement. Indeed almost no studies on gender and health exist which address the way in which symptoms are labelled and the severity of illnesses assessed by individuals (Verbrugge, 1985: 156).

Similarly, theoretical discussions tend to reject phenomenological approaches to the study of women and illness behaviour. The preferred orientation here is to develop macro analyses which are largely directed towards identifying agents of social control and the strategies of medical labelling in which they engage. While such discussions are useful in their ability to identify the non-medical motives influencing the medical labelling process, there is no attempt to explain how medical labels themselves become internalized by the subjects involved.

Most such analyses tend to focus on the particular problems of the female reproductive role, an aspect of women's experience which would seem to lend itself most fruitfully to phenomenological investigations. These arguments generally comment on how "patriarchal discourses" of illness foster negative labels of menstruation, menopause, and childbirth, as ways of restricting women's participation in society. The tone such discussions often take is exemplified in the following passage by Paula Weideger in her widely cited book *Female Cycles* (1982). As explanation for the relationship between cultural views of menstruation and the position of women in society, Weideger argues that

A committed misogynist will use any example of women's 'weakness' to bolster his prejudice. He already uses the very existence of menstruation and menopause to prove that woman is unpredictable and unfit for positions of trust and responsibility. (Weideger, 1982: 13)

She then goes on to explain that it is through these patriarchally fostered cultural views that women so readily embrace natural events such as menstruation and menopause as illness constructs.

What is problematic about the typical feminist analyses of women and illness behaviour is that the relationship between the construction of illness labels and their subsequent adoption as illness role behaviour is assumed but never explained. There is no exploration of how women themselves interpret bodily events associated with the reproductive function. There is no exploration of the generative properties of the social interaction within which illness labels are adopted by individuals. There is no exploration of the social and cultural context within which certain illness labels, such as the premenstrual syndrome are credited with plausibility by large numbers of people, while others, such as the Epstein Barr Virus Syndrome, receive comparatively less notoriety. Ultimately, there is no attempt in analyses such as Weideger's to explain the relationship between abstract categories of knowledge and their internalization as part of one's personal biography.

What may be said of such studies as Weideger's, then, is that however humanistically oriented, the rhetoric of feminism is continually cited, but the voice of women seldom heard. The result is a somewhat simplistic causal model which argues that ideological forms of knowledge flow in a more or less undiluted form from patriarchal structures of control and deposit themselves unproblematically on unwitting, passive subjects. Such models are appealing in their ability to identify the politics of medical labelling, but in assuming that the construction of a label ensures its collective adoption, these analyses ignore the central fact that illness is a world made meaningful only through culturally situated social interaction. In point of fact, if the "essence" of feminist research is its insistence on beginning from the point of view of women's reality; its insistence on asserting the validity of women's experience (often *over* the validity of theory); its insistence on exploring the contradictions between women's involvment in everyday experience and the "language of theory" (Stanley and Wise, 1985: 135, 163), then feminist analyses of women and the illness role fall far short of the stated goals of the feminist research enterprise.

It is in the context of such questions and issues that the present discussion is formulated. It is the purpose of this paper to suggest a preliminary conceptual schema of illness behaviour which reaffirms the commitment to exploring the subjective experience of the actor as she attempts to make sense of a culture-bound world of illness. Both the emphasis on subjective experience and the emphasis on illness as a culture-bound category of knowledge are essential to a research enterprise committed to exploring the way in which women make sense of a world largely designed by and for men.

Agreeing with the position that illness labelling can constitute an ideological form of social control, the rationale for incorporating a phenomenological orientation is based on the premises that 1) there exists a determinate relationship between ideology and individual experience; and 2) this relationship is discoverable ultimately through phenomenological forms of investigation (Wuthnow, 1985). The rationale for emphasizing the importance of regarding illness as a culture bound syndrome is based on the premise that the meaning illness holds for any individual is grounded in, *though not reducible to*, the network of meanings any illness has in a particular culture; the metaphors associated with disease; the basic values, practices, and cultural preoccupations which determine how some bodily states and events and not others become coded and subsequently adopted as "illness" states (Good and Good, 1981: 176).

The central position of this paper, then, is that a full exploration of the illness labelling process involves examining three (but by no means sequential) phases of reality construction processes. First of all, the social construction of medical knowledge must be traced to the productional activities of dominant groups with commercial and/or political self-interests. This is essentially the mode of analysis adopted by the current feminist models. Secondly, the social construction of medical knowledge needs to be investigated at the level of the productional activities of the subjects themselves; the face-to-face encounters where the world of illness is made meaningful to the actor. And thirdly, this reality construction process needs to be investigated in terms of the cultural determinants which predispose the collective adoption of some illness categories, and not others.

This paper will begin by reviewing the labelling theory and social control literature out of which the more recent feminist critiques of women and illness behaviour have emerged. From there, a new conceptual framework incorporating a phenomenological and cultural orientation will be presented. The paper will conclude with a discussion of how such a framework may be applied to the study of women and illness behaviour by referring to the author's own research on the premenstrual syndrome.

The Sick Role: From Functionalism to Labelling Theory

The labelling/social control models of illness behaviour emerged in response to the essentially conservative position at least implied in the original Parsonian conceptualization of the sick role. While Parsons' model of the sick role is well-known to most sociologists, it is worthwhile to review certain of those premises contained in his theory, since that model provided the major impetus for exploring the question of social control and illness labelling strategies as political processes.

Essentially, Parsons argued that while malingering was to be considered deviant, the illness role in general should be regarded as a predictable, indeed adaptive response to social life. Illness allows the individual temporary but legitimate exemption from normal obligations and duties, or, as the following citation illustrates, legitimate, non-disruptive (albeit displaced) expressions of social discontent.

Parsons, for example, once claimed that women "often seize upon illness as a compulsively feministic way of reacting to (their) exclusion from the life open to a man," or as an "institutionalized way out of the burdens of her heavy 'human relations management'" (Parsons and Fox, 1968: 380–1). And while Parsons in no way *endorsed* illness as an adaptive response to the burdens of responsibility, he did ultimately view the sick role as both a predictable, but at the same time potentially

abusive strategy of coping with the pressures of social life. In order to counteract the potential disruptions malingering might engender, Parsons recommended that all sick individuals should attempt to regulate the illness role by seeking out competent and objective, (i.e., *professional-medical*) help. The illness role, then, was seen by Parsons as a socially predictable but potentially deviant form of institutionalized interaction, the function of which was to allow a legitimate respite from social obligations.

At a very general level, Parsons' theory of the sick role has been criticized for being politically conservative; normative in content, if not ideological in intent. By the very nature of what Parsons' theories investigate (namely the forces securing social harmony and stability), the status quo is ultimately, if not intentionally, legitimated. Following this line of critique, McCormack argues, for example, that Parsons' emphasis on micro role behaviour and not the larger macro processes of social relationships automatically removes the larger socio-political spheres from scrutiny. She points out, as well, that "if work were fulfilling and secure, if interpersonal relationships provided for self-development and personality growth, if community life gave citizens a sense of political efficacy, few would prefer illness to health . . ." (McCormack, 1981a: 41, 42).

Parsons' theory of the sick role provided the stimulus for the development of a body of research interested in how medical knowledge operates as a vehicle of social control. For many of the reasons cited above, this school was particularly concerned with the way in which Parsons' theory reinforced the status quo, particularly the elitism and authority of the medical profession. Social control theorists argue that both the select social positions and training programs of physicians cannot help but engender a certain propensity to preserve the status quo. This school is quick to point out that medical labelling and action may be rationalized in terms of the dominant political and cultural biases of a given system. As the most profound example of such abuse of the power to define health and illness, social control theorists point to the Soviet countries (see, for example, Szasz, 1974).

The Social Control/Labelling theories of illness are represented by such researchers as Thomas Szasz (1974), Irving Zola (1971), Eliot Freidson (1970) and Peter Conrad (1975) although European thinkers such as Michel Foucault (1965, 1975) have also explored the relationship between the identification and treatment of mental illness and social context. Both Zola and Szasz are more interested in how social control operates *through* the medical profession, (largely regarded as a handmaiden of larger socio-political forces). Eliot Freidson focuses more specifically on the professional dominance of doctors, per se. Peter Conrad examines the political and social conditions under which the "discovery" of disease entities have occurred, and what self-interests are being served by that discovery. All are concerned, however, with the way in which the creation and regulation of medical knowledge serves self-interests other than those of the patients. The models proposed by Eliot Freidson and Peter Conrad have been the ones most often adopted in feminist analyses, and for that reason are being reviewed here.

Freidson, like all social control theorists views the absolute power doctors have in defining health and illness as inherently problematic. He argues, for example, that the nature of the doctor-patient relationship is fundamentally hierarchial and essentially demeaning to the majority of patients. The key characteristic facilitating the power doctors have over patients, according to Freidson, is information control, a self-imposed state which eventuates in doctors being loath to give even per-

functory information to patients whom they regard at best as "management problems"; and at worst as "little more than a nuisance" (Freidson, 1970: 142). Freidson's proposed remedy to this situation is to have patients take a more active role in the delivery of healthcare services, both at the personal and at the political level.

It is not surprising that feminist theories of women and illness behaviour have found Freidson's model appropriate to the phenomena they address. In the first place, Freidson's attack on the hierarchical nature of the doctor patient relationship cannot but strike an all too familiar chord of recognition in most women. Tired of a male-dominated medical profession's appropriation of definitions of health and illness for women, the edict that women need to "reclaim their bodies" has become not only the basis of the women's health movement, but the main stimulus underlying most feminist theoretical discussions of women and health, as well. Feminists often explain the question of women's "excess" morbidity and "abuse" of healthcare services, for example, often by referring to the professional dominance thesis. The feminist position here argues not that illness is a predictable response to an oppressive social order, but rather that many of the typical "female" illnesses are the result of a coercive and highly effective labelling process exercised by the medical profession operating not only in its own self-interest (in insuring its monopoly over healthcare) but in those of the state and other agents of control eager to restrict women's equal participation in society. According to this tradition, if a male-dominated healthcare system did not impose categories of illness on ordinary bodily events such as menstruation, menopause, pregnancy and childbirth, the differential morbidity rates between men and women, it is argued, would diminish substantially. (See Trypuc, 1984; Weideger, 1982; Delaney, et al., 1976;

McRae, 1983; Weitz and Sullivan, 1985, for discussions of professional dominance.) Freidson's exhortation to exercise more control over the labelling and treatment of illness has since become the cornerstone of the women's health movement, best expressed by the title of the Boston Women's Health Collective's medical manual for women, *Our Bodies, Ourselves* (1976, see also 1984).

A second direction taken by social control theorists interested in the social construction of medical knowledge comes out of the labelling school in deviance. This orientation, exemplified in the work of Peter Conrad (Conrad, 1975; Conrad and Schneider, 1980), for example, is less concerned with the professional dominance of doctors acting in their own self-interest and more concerned with how medical knowledge operates indirectly as an ideological strategy of social control. Conrad and others writing in this tradition investigate how certain overt behaviours acquire the status of disease and what self-interests are evident in the labelling processes involved. The main premise here is that when individual (or collective) behaviour becomes socially disruptive, labelling that behaviour as illness (as opposed to deviance) has the effect of mitigating the stigmatizing properties of that behaviour. When "badness" is seen as "illness," the individuals concerned are no longer responsible for their action; a condition which ultimately results in the depoliticization of that same behaviour. Aptly termed the "medicalization of evidence" this labelling would look at alcoholism or hyperkinesis, for example, as cases in point. Alcoholism is often seen as a problem of the individual's biochemical makeup (thereby removing from the individual any responsibility for the disease). At the same time, this medical definition of a social behaviour removes from scrutiny the kinds of social pressures (including media programming) which

motivate people to engage in substance abuse in the first place. Labelling theorists argue that by locating the pathology within the individual rather than society, social problems are effectively translated into individual problems, through means which are normally regarded as humanitarian, altruistic and, subsequently, apolitical.

The dominant labellers, then, although often facilitated by the medical profession, may not, in fact, be physicians themselves. Rather, those with the power to define illness could be anyone with particular commercial or other non-medical motives and self-interests. Labelling theory proceeds by examining the social circumstances under which certain diseases are "discovered" and subsequently exploited by groups with a vested interest in commercial gain or power consolidation of some type. One way of exploiting the power to define health and illness is to engage in profit-seeking commercial enterprises by promoting and marketing "cures" or treatments. Other forms of exploitation involve authority figures in society, such as teachers and parents, attempting to "regulate" behaviour through medical labelling processes. Such was the case, according to Conrad (1975) with the "discovery" of hyperkinesis and the widespread usage of ritalin in an attempt to control disruptive behaviour in school-age children. According to this school of thought, the dominant labellers of disease are not necessarily, (indeed, not often), doctors, but any group or individual who has acquired the morally legitimated authority to impose definitions of health and illness on groups of lesser power. Such labellers are aptly referred to as "moral entrepreneurs," a term well-known to sociologists acquainted with the work of Howard Becker.

A recent feminist adaptation of this model is found in Frances McRae's study of the "discovery" of menopause as a disease entity (McRae, 1983). McRae traces the "discovery" (or medicalization) of menopause to the commerical interests responsible for promoting the dissemination of synthetic estrogen in the early 1960s. The author discovered that a program originally (and one may say ironically) aimed at curing male impotence created a market for, and an interest in, hormone replacement therapy. Among the promoters of estrogen replacement therapy was Robert A. Wilson, who founded an institution to promote research on estrogen with the assistance of a 1.3 million dollar grant from the pharmaceutical industry. The ultimate "discovery" of menopause as a "deficiency disease," according to McRae, came with the publication of Wilson's *Feminine Forever* (1966, cited in McRae, 1983) where he describes menopausal women as "living decay." McRae's central thesis is that by "individualizing" the problems of menopause, physicians and other "moral entrepreneurs" turn attention away from social structural interpretations of women's conditions, and more importantly from the power structures in society which facilitate medical labelling. By accepting a medical model of menopause, McRae argues that the locus of the solution, then, becomes the medical/industrial complex itself, ever ready to exploit women's passivity, dependency, and culturally conditioned fear of loss of femininity, where the "vulnerable status of women makes fertile ground for medical imperialism" (McRae, 1983: 120).

In adopting this model, McRae and other feminists writing in this tradition have indeed identified power relations in society which influence the medical labelling process. Moreover, these analyses do place the sick role in a larger social, political and historical framework, a theoretical strategy which, as pointed out earlier, is distinctly lacking in the original Parsonian model.

There are major problems, however, in limiting analyses to the identification and

exploration of those who create medical knowledge. This problem may be conceptualized as an inability to distinguish between "naming" and "explaining"; which, in feminist theories of illness labelling involves "naming" the ideological strategies of a patriarchal elite, without proceeding to explain how those strategies actually work. We need only pause to reflect on the tautologies present in an argument which infers abstract concepts such as patriarchy, misogyny or even commercial self-interest from observations of social life, and then imposes them back as explanations for the ordered phenomena out of which they were inferred in the first place. In other words, in the process of abstraction, abstract concepts and categories are given causal force. What is not taken into consideration in the analyses cited above, is the fact that women are, as Margrit Eichler points out (1985: 622) historical actors as well as "the acted upon"; subjects as well as objects. While the dominant medical labellers are named, what is not explained is the process by which women themselves adopt certain illness categories at certain periods in social history, while rejecting others. As mentioned earlier, it has never been adequately explained why at this time in the history of our culture, the premenstrual syndrome has gained such immediate and pervasive notoriety when equally obscure and undifferentiated (and therefore potentially exploitable) syndromes, such as the Epstein Barr Virus Syndrome, or even the Toxic Shock Syndrome have received little attention, by comparison. It has never been adequately explained why young adolescent women, and not older or prepubescent women, or men of any age, tend more readily to succumb to anorexia nervosa. This is not to say that attempts have not been made to explain the differential adoption of illness roles and categories of disease by age, class and gender. But many such attempts merely speculate on the role of the media and other social forces as "illness socializing agents," often operating on behalf of agents of social control. For example, a typical "explanation" of the social distribution of anorexia nervosa argues that young women are forced to compare themselves to unrealistic aesthetic standards in our culture, and hence, fetishize thinness to the point of distorting their own sense of bodily realities. While there may be a certain degree of truth in these speculative discussions, the *process* by which ideology becomes translated into personal biographies is left unexplained.

Until we attempt to understand the intervening reality construction and selection processes linking the production of categories of knowledge to their eventual adoption as personal biography, much of the phenomenon of illness labelling will remain steeped in tautological reasoning. The following discussion is directed towards suggesting a preliminary conceptual schema capable of delineating those processes.

Phenomenology, Correspondence Theory and Culture-Bound Illness Categories

At present, the most effective paradigm capable of investigating the link between categories of knowledge and personal biographies is the phenomenological approach articulated in the work of Berger and Luckmann (1967) and Berger and Kellner (1970). Berger and Luckmann's *The Social Construction of Reality* (1967) develops a general epistemology of the nature of reality construction. Berger and Kellner's widely cited study entitled "Marriage and the Construction of Reality" (1970) emphasizes a more situated context for reality construction processes, and in that respect provides a useful starting point for building

a more comprehensive paradigm of illness behaviour.

Berger and Kellner's central premise is that marriage is the key milieu or social context in which prevailing cultural categories and social arrangements become translated into personal biographies. Since we cannot perceive the world as a whole, Berger and Kellner argue, we need to "mediate" this larger reality through face to face encounters with our intimates. This mediation process involves daily conversations where the social world becomes "our world," duly translated and personalized to the extent that we no longer recognize a clear-cut distinction between the public and private spheres of meaning. While we construct personal meanings as social reality during the course of interaction, we simultaneously experience this reality as somehow "out there" awaiting our arrival on the scene. When this privately constructed, but externally perceived, reality is presented to us for validation, the final legitimation process is secured almost exclusively through daily conversations with our spouses (Berger and Kellner, 1970). The authors emphasize, moreover, that the reality bestowing force of social relationships depends not on proximity *per se*, (as Goffman, for example, would argue) but on those face to face encounters which are "credited with primary significance" (Berger and Kellner, 1970: 53), where an investment in the relationship influences the reality construction processes (even to the extent to where spouses often "rediscover" and reconstruct their past).

Berger and Kellner's paradigm of marriage as the central reality bestowing context of social life remained virtually unchallenged until very recently. In an attempt to make the Berger and Kellner thesis relevant to current social relationships, Norbert Wiley (1983) argues that their model of the marital conversation was grounded too much in a post-war version of an "unusually talkative" family. Wiley suggests, rather, that family structures have changed to include single as well as dual parent families; other social contexts often take the place of (or compete with) the marital dyad as primary groups charged with emotional investments and narcissistic involvements with self esteem and identity formation. Moreover, Wiley (1967: 27) argues that because of these narcissistic involvements, marital conversations are more highly invested with emotional, irrational, unconscious needs; characteristics of reality construction processes which are receiving long overdue attention in non-clinical modes of investigation.

The social-phenomenological models, then, argue that marriage or some other social context capable of continued face to face encounters and credited with primary affective investments provides the key reality-bestowing context for making sense of social life. Given that the inner world of illness requires as much "mediation" or "making sense" as the outer world of social action, then the family or some parallel primary group, according to this model, would be essential to that reality bestowing process. Since the adoption of an illness role is central to one's identity, self-esteem, and strategies of relating to intimates, it seems worthwhile to explore the influence that groups credited with primary significance have on the way in which the meaning of illness is negotiated and ultimately adopted by individuals faced with the necessity to code or recode certain bodily events as health or illness. The phenomenological orientation inherent in the Berger and Kellner thesis provides a logical corrective to the social control/labelling theories of illness behaviour.

The implications of incorporating a more phenomenologically oriented approach, while providing a corrective to current models on the one hand, challenge certain

central assumptions contained in those models, on the other. Essentially, in grafting the Berger and Kellner thesis to the social control model, the doctor/patient relationship may no longer be regarded as the *central* reality bestowing context in determining illness categories. Rather, the "labelling role" of the physician might best be regarded as one of providing an external reference point which merely poses the category, so to speak. In other words, the labelling processes characterizing the doctor/patient interaction might be conceptualized as relevant only to one phase of the reality construction process; that phase which presents the possibility of either adopting or rejecting a medical label. Indeed, in support of incorporating a phenomenological orientation as a corrective to the current emphasis on doctors as the dominant labellers in society, one need only refer to the extensive literature on patient non-compliance with medical advice (Mumford, 1983: 515).

As further evidence of the role primary groups play in central reality bestowing contexts determining illness roles, one may refer to the more clinically oriented literature on family scapegoating (Vogel and Bell, 1968); family symptom carriers (Minuchin et al., 1978) and family identified patients (Satir, 1964). These models examine how family members come to be labelled ill, particularly when the illness state appears to have no organic cause. There is considerable empirical evidence, for example, documenting how irrational processes characterizing family interaction operate to create "identified patients." In such families, less powerful members often acquire an illness state which, upon clinical examination, is seen to symbolize conflicts felt by more powerful members. For example, if status achievement was an issue which caused spousal conflict and disillusionment, it was often observed that a child in the family would acquire a condition or disability which affected his or her academic achievement. This designation of the "identified patient" is a process which Good and Good (1981: 179) suggest is much the same as dream symbolization where the illness labels, like dreams, come to condense "a network of significant experiences and symbols" signifying highly affect-laden events arising in the patient's life. Family theorists, such as Vogel and Bell (1968), argue that these labels derive, not out of individual experiences, but out of group conceptualizations, values, and meanings associated with the symptoms.

A case in point is anorexia nervosa. Refusing to eat always involves issues of control (either self-control, or parental control and manipulation) at some level. The anorectic symptom as expressed in the child may embody (and therefore absorb) the meanings and feelings attached to issues of control which plague the entire family. In such cases, the husband may not feel he exerts appropriate control over his wife's behaviour; she over his; they over their children. The resultant feelings are lack of self-esteem, fear of loss of control, and general disillusionment with the ability to participate effectively in intimate relationships. Because these issues are often too conflict laden and emotionally charged to be confronted openly by the adult members, the symbolic content of the illness category, anorexia, invites expression of these feelings in less threatening and more easily contained interactional circumstances. (See Minuchin et al., 1978, for a discussion of how these illness labelling processes operate within families.)

The clinical phenomenological models of reality construction, then, provide an important corrective to the emphasis placed on the centrality of the medical profession as the dominant labellers of illness. Although these models are outside what one may regard as "mainstream" sociology, they do provide empirical evidence of the key role families and other primary groups play in organizing the way in which the meaning of illness becomes negotiated. Moreover, and perhaps of even greater value to medical sociology, the clinical approaches provide a highly refined qualitative methodology designed to observe and code the structure of meaning embedded in interaction.

The influence of culture and its impact on the illness labelling process, however, requires further refinement within these models. While the clinical/phenomenological models acknowledge and often discuss the importance of cultural background in the illness construction processes, they have not developed a systematic model for examining the selection processes involved in the way certain social groups afford certain disease categories credibility, while ignoring others. In other words, the clinical/phenomenological frameworks emphasize the important aspect of reality *construction* processes, but pay less attention to reality selection processes. These models do not attempt to account for the intervening structural and cultural conditions which afford some categories of illness *plausibility*, while others remain relatively unacknowledged, despite their "discovery" by moral entrepreneurs or other agents of social control. It is the selection process discussed earlier as an important third step in the social construction of medical knowledge which requires much stronger theoretical development in both medical and clinical sociology, and most particularly feminist analyses developed within these sub-disciplines.

The process by which categories of knowledge are selectively credited with plausibility is best addressed by what Robert Wuthnow (1985) calls "correspondence theory." The major proponents of this model are most interested in how ideology becomes legitimated and subsequently experienced as normal, day-to-day, social life. The central premise of the correspondence model is this: the extent to which new forms of knowledge will be collectively internalized or credited with plausibility will depend upon the extent to which they are dramatized by both existing social beliefs and existing social practices — what Wuthnow terms, "vital aspects of collective life" (Wuthnow, 1985: 800). Accordingly, Weber (1958) has argued that the modern concept of capitalism derives, at least in part, from earlier practices of Calvinism. More recently, Wilson (1977) argued that the contours of American ideology with its inherently unreflexive view of social life derives not merely from a commitment to, but the actual practice of, scientific rationalism (thus demonstrating Wuthnow's point (1985: 801) that a rational ideology will be more likely to emerge within a "rationally organized society").

The correspondence model argues further that the genesis of new ideological forms can be traced by examining the social and cultural filtering processes (what Wuthnow terms "plausibility structures") through which they have been disseminated — often randomly, and often without apparent conspiratorial intent. Medical anthropologists, for example, have long recognized the importance of examining the influence of plausibility structures or cultural pathways on the selection of illness categories among non-western world cultures. This school argues that illness categories often condense meanings and symbolize a number of culturally-specific experiential currents in a patient's life. Medical anthropologists, Good and Good (1980) have discussed obesity as a culture-bound pathology in western world societies. In our society, Good and Good argue, we place a high premium on mastery, instrumentality, and rationality. To be overweight denotes a lack of control, self-indulgence, and an irrational tendency to

engage in non-instrumental (indeed, self-destructive) behaviour. Obesity, then, may be regarded as a physiological pathology which mirrors a social pathology. Consquently, the labelling of obesity as an illness category is more likely to occur in a society such as ours where self-control and self-mastery have become strong cultural preoccupations.

To summarize the argument thus far: social control models provide a framework for identifying the conditions under which categories of medical knowledge become introduced and promoted in our society. Social control theory, therefore, has provided an important contribution to the sociological and anthropological study of illness labelling. However, a more comprehensive framework as suggested by correspondence theory is required to accommodate the phenomenological component of illness labelling, and to investigate the plausibility structures through which illness categories become duly disseminated. Such a model would 1) acknowledge and discuss the primary role the medical/industrial process plays in introducing *and* promoting illness categories; 2) provide some conceptual schema and method for determining how those illness categories become *selectively* chosen by some and not others; and 3) incorporate a conceptual and methodological framework capable of examining the information processing dynamic wherein illness categories become translated into personal biography at the level of small, primary group interaction. In other words, the social production of any form of knowledge involves three fundamental steps: 1) the introduction or provision of abstract categories of knowledge; 2) the selection process by which some categories (and not others) are entertained as relevant to one's own social situation; and 3) the meaning negotiation processes which endow abstract categories of knowledge with pesonal meaning, such that the social world of illness becomes "our world."

My own research on the medicalization of menstruation was instrumental in suggesting the need for a more comprehensive model of illness behaviour in women than the current feminist analyses have provided. First of all, it became obvious from the findings that the medical profession was not as influential in "promoting" the disease known today as the premenstrual syndrome as social control models would predict. Indeed, in a sample of 244 licensed female dental hygienists (a profession with a higher than average knowledge of anatomy and biology) only 8.15 per cent (approximately 30) reported that they first heard of the premenstrual syndrome from a doctor. The sources most often cited as the initial purveyor of information on the premenstrual syndrome were women's magazines, accounting for 26.6 per cent of the responses. Other labelling sources cited were randomly dispersed among friends, family members, women's groups, and television shows. Despite the lack of medically legitimated knowledge of this illness state, 43 per cent of the sample labelled themselves sufferers of the premenstrual syndrome — a finding which suggests that doctors are not as influential in the medical labelling processes as many feminist analyses assume. It seemed obvious from these data that other intervening interactional variables beyond the doctor patient relationship were influencing the medical labelling process within this sample of women. It therefore became important to re-examine the efficacy of the current theoretical models attempting to explain the social construction of medical knowledge.

Furthermore, a preliminary analysis of the interview data suggested that the interactional dynamics contained most particularly within the family context had more to do with the adoption of pms as an illness state than either the medical profession or the media. The interview data tended to support the clinical phenomenological premise that under certain conditions illness states may be socially constructed and sustained out of family interactional needs to absorb more conflict laden and disruptive issues that threaten the stability of the spousal and parent dyads. It became evident from certain of my interviews that the premenstrual phase absorbed a number of conflicts which would otherwise have been disruptive to family functioning. For example, the "meaning" of much of the discontent these women experienced with regard to their marriages, and dual career obligations, became condensed under the general heading of an "illness," and came to be understood as the result of a temporary biological aberration rather than the manifestation of an enduring social problem. In other words, many of the respondents in this study could only legitimate feelings of anger and frustration (largely arising out of dual career obligations) when they were understood to be biological rather than social relational responses. The concept of "identified patient" introduced earlier appeared to be operative in some of the primary group contexts of the women interviewed. Hence, despite their almost exclusive clinical usage, the data suggest that this concept is one which deserves more attention in nonclinical, phenomenological studies of similar phenomena.

The very topic of my research — the medicalization of menstruation — suggested the need to investigate models which were more sensitive to the impact of culture (and not merely the political culture) and social structure on the social experience of illness. The role of culture in facilitating the widespread adoption of pms as an illness state becomes apparent, as well, when one explores how the contradictions and inconsistencies surrounding the research on causes and cures of pms reflect the broader social and cultural ambivalences held with regard to menstruation and fertility. One has only to peruse current advertisements for menstrual products to ascertain that the "aesthetics" (indeed, the reality) of menstruation borders on denial rather than full expression of womanhood. One has only to peruse current cultural stereotypes of the sexually attractive woman to see that the *pre*pubescent "infantilized" look continues to represent an idealized form of femininity. Yet, alongside these symbolic representations, stands a paradoxical celebration of fertility with the support of the pro-family movement in Canada, and with the symbolic support of large families through such media representations as "Family Ties," "Eight is Enough" and "The Cosby Show." Perhaps the strongest example of our own cultural ambivalence towards fertility is the long-standing debate, despite the current legislative changes, on abortion on demand. These ambivalences we hold with respect to the cultural value of fertility may be seen to be reconstituted in the contradictions and inconsistencies characteristic of premenstrual syndrome symptom-reporting.

Distinct differences in the way in which the premenstrual illness state was expressed *and* experienced in the workplace and the home, were found, as well. No existing theory in the traditional labelling/social control models could account for these differences. For example, where one woman was constantly experiencing problems with physical co-ordination at home during her premenstrual phase, she experienced no problems with manual dexterity while working with patients in the dentist's office; a situation for which she herself had no explanation. Others who routinely shipped children out to neighbours, family and friends during the premenstrual phase (when mood shifts and feelings of loss of control were at their peak) reported no changes in interactional, affective-expressive, or affective-experiential patterns involving even the most difficult clients (generally referred to as the "nervous types" and "chronic complainers"). Again, no explanations were offered, and when this anomaly was pointed out, it was as if the contradiction were being noted for the first time.

It therefore became necessary to investigate theories which could account for these inconsistencies in the social experience of illness. A correspondence orientation which investigates the link between social structure, including cultural preoccupations and practices, and the social experience of illness was deemed the most appropriate. For example, an important corollary to the correspondence thesis is the notion that symptoms experienced at different times and in different social contexts within the same culture will be understood and labelled differently. What could then be inferred from my observations is not merely the commonplace observation that social context affects reality construction processes but that different social contexts provide different cultural "pathways" which allow for the legitimation and subsequent integration of the illness role. The metaphors associated with the illness state known as the premenstrual syndrome simply do not prevail in work settings where the interactional dynamics that both shape and sustain the meaning of illness do not allow for its structural integration in these contexts. As Good and Good (1981) point out, ours is a culture which places a high value on self-determination and self-mastery. One may add that ours is a culture which values self-discipline and control, largely *in its public domain*, while the family, our "Haven in a Heartless World," is the domain where the irrational, affective needs of which Wiley spoke, can be more appropriately expressed. Menstruation, with its often unpredictable emotional and endocrinological disruptions, represents the physiological obverse of the social values described by Good and Good: self-mastery, control, self-discipline. Hence, in the private sphere of the family, where emotions may run high, where irrational needs are more likely to be acted out, where lack of predictability and control are more often the rule than the exception in characterizing family relational patterns, and where the meanings of day-to-day encounters of family life are likely to become condensed in an illness role, the premenstrual syndrome has a much greater chance of becoming structurally integrated as a credible and appropriate illness state. In the more rationally ordered public domain of the workplace, however, illness states which incorporate an affective component and which appear to express or to mirror uncontrolled, irrational, affectively-charged needs, are much less likely to be afforded credibility and gain legitimacy not only of expression, but of meaning and experience as well.

Summary

The foregoing discussion has presented a conceptual schema to augment the current feminist analyses of illness behaviour in women. It has suggested that the social construction of medical knowledge and its subsequent adoption by social groups involves a three step process. The first stage of this process involves the productional activities of those we generally consider the dominant labellers or social control agents in society; the medical profession, members of the medical-industrial complex, such as pharmaceutical companies, the state, and other groups with commercial, professional and political self-interests. The current analyses of illness behaviour generally focus the discussion on this aspect of the labelling process alone. Two other stages in reality construction processes, however, need to be explored to account for 1) the selective adoption of certain illness categories over others and 2) the translation of those categories into personal biographies of illness. The latter stage of this labelling process requires a strong phenomenological orientation which feminist theory has always upheld as one of its primary mandates. The former stage of this process requires integrating a correspondence model into the existing social control theories in order to detect the structural arrangements and cultural preoccupations which facilitate the legitimation of new illness categories such as the premenstrual syndrome. The author's current research on the premenstrual syndrome was then discussed in terms of its relevance for the conceptual schema suggested here.

THE MODERN MULTIPLE MURDERER
Elliott Leyton

"For murder, though it have no tongue, will speak
With most miraculous organ."

Hamlet

Are multiple murderers merely "insane"? Can such bizarre behaviour be dismissed as simple psychiatric or genetic freakishness? There is an ancient chord in our civilization which insists that such terrible acts be interpreted in terms of possession by evil spirits, or witchcraft (an explanation which reverberates today in

From *Hunting Humans: The Rise of the Modern Multiple Murderer* by Elliott Leyton. Used by permission of the Canadian Publishers, McClelland & Stewart, Toronto.

the press's frequent, and inaccurate, speculation that occultism is a motive for these crimes); and a more modern variation of this theme similarly dismisses the acts with notions of possession by "mental disease." It would be most comforting if we could continue to accept such explanations, for they satisfyingly banish guilt beyond our responsibility; yet to do so would beg the question — why does modern America produce proportionately so many more of these "freaks" than any other industrial nation? Moreover, if the killers are merely insane, why do they in fact so rarely display the cluster of readily identifiable clinical symptoms (including disorders of thought and affect) which psychiatrists agree mark mental illness? In one important sense, of course, any person who murders another human being has abandoned all reason and sanity; yet such a position is essentially *moral*, and does not help us in an objective attempt to understand the cause and meaning of such a phenomenon.

I first embarked upon this journey into the souls of modern multiple murderers because I was unable to understand the profound personal fulfillment they seemed to derive from their killings. Now, after four years of total immersion in the killers' diaries, confessions, psychiatric interviews, statements to the press, videotapes, and photographs, I see their motives as so obvious and their gratifications as so intense that I can only marvel at how *few* of them walk the streets of America. Nevertheless, their numbers do continue to grow at a disturbing rate: until the 1960s, they were anomalies who appeared perhaps once a decade; but by the 1980s, one was spawned virtually each month. Today, according to unofficial U.S. Justice Department estimates, there may be as many as one hundred multiple murderers killing in America, stealing the lives of thousands. The uncomfortable conclusion reached in this book is that there will undoubtedly be many more

before this epoch in our social history draws to a close. They may still be statistically rare, but I shall try to show that they are no freaks: rather, they can only be fully understood as representing the logical extension of many of the central themes in their culture — of worldly ambition, of success and failure, and of manly avenging violence. Although they take several forms — the serial killer whose murders provide both revenge and a lifelong *celebrity career*; and the mass killer, who no longer wishes to live, and whose murders constitute his *suicide note* — they can only be accurately and objectively perceived as prime embodiment of their civilization, not twisted derangement.

The mid-1980s were years of unprecedented growth, experimentation, and innovation among multiple murderers, years in which all previous "records" were broken and sacrosanct social barriers were pierced. In 1984 alone, a fortyish drifter named *Henry Lee Lucas* delivered his confessions in which he claimed to have tortured and murdered hundreds of women, a number far in excess of any previous claimant's. Lucas lived with his fifteen-year-old common-law wife in a trailer parked in The House of Prayer For All People campground, a former chicken farm operated as a Pentecostal retreat in a small town in Texas. His eight-year killing spree was terminated only when he murdered an elderly local woman who had befriended him, which provoked his close scrutiny by the local police. Jailed on little more than suspicion, he passed a note to a deputy, claiming that "I have done something terrible, and I want to talk to sheriff." It was only then that inquisitive police began the lengthy interrogations and checking of his claims. Lucas outlined his story to a largely disbelieving audience, spinning an unrivalled tale of rape, torture, dismemberment, and murder, while conceding only that "I know it ain't normal for a person to go out and kill a girl just to have sex with her."

The thirteenth child of a prostitute mother, Lucas began his career in 1960 when, at the age of twenty-three, he stabbed his mother to death in her bed. He spent the following fifteen years in prisons and mental hospitals in Michigan, without obtaining any relief from his homicidal "needs." "I have been to the Ionia State Hospital for the Criminally Insane in Michigan," he told a Texas judge. "I have been to a mental hospital in Princeton, West Virginia. And I tell them my problems, and they don't want to do nothing about it, but there is a hundred, oh, about a hundred women out there that says different." Despite his protestations, he claims, he was released: "I told them before I ever left prison that I was going to commit crimes, told them the types of crimes I was going to commit, and they wouldn't believe it. They said I was going regardless of whether I liked it or not. And the day I got out of jail is the day I started killing." He says he killed two women that day.

"I was death on women," he told a television reporter in his disconcertingly genial manner. "I didn't feel they need to exist. I hated them, and I wanted to destroy every one I could find. I was doing a good job of it. I've got [killed] 360 people, I've got 36 states, in three different countries. My victims never knew what was going to happen to them. I've had shootings, knifings, strangulations, beatings, and I've participated in actual crucifixions of humans. All across the country, there's people just like me, who set out to destroy human life." For eight years he criss-crossed the continent, looking for women alone and defenceless — hitchhikers, runaways, women whose cars had broken down on lonely roads. He explained his behaviour in intellectual constructs borrowed from his culture, which is to say in terms of his childhood. "That's the way I grew up when I was a child —

watching my mom have sexual acts. She wouldn't go into different rooms, she'd make sure I was in the room before she started anything, and she would do it deliberately to make me watch her, you know. I got so I hated it. I'd even leave the house and go out and hide in the woods and wouldn't even go home. And when I'd go home, I'd get beat for not coming home. I don't blame mom for what she done, I don't blame her for that. It's the idea of the way she done it. I don't think any child out there should be brought up in that type of environment. In the past, I've hated it. It's just inside hate, and I can't get away from it." What Lucas says *seems* to explain it all: yet he killed his mother first, when he was only twenty-three, and that should have finished her. Why did he have to spend decades in exorcising her ghost by killing "her" over and over again? His explanation seems most imperfect.

If Lucas established the modern record for serial murder (killings spread over time), 1984 was also the year in which the mass-murder record (killings in one explosive burst) was broken in America. It was then that *James Oliver Huberty* burst into a McDonald's restaurant in San Ysidro, California, and began to kill. Before the afternoon was out, during the course of an eighty-two-minute siege, he fired some 245 shots at terrified and dying restaurant customers and at passersby, killing twenty-one and wounding nineteen more, before a police bullet struck him in the chest and killed him. Unlike Lucas, Huberty was no homeless and uneducated drifter. It is true that he did come from a broken home, and that his only friend during his lonely childhood had been his dog; but such minor anguish has been the lot of millions. His mother, who abandoned her son and his only sister when they were very young, could only say that "I knew he needed help."

The adult Huberty was married and had two daughters. Reportedly, he was a graduate in sociology from a small Quaker college in Ohio, and he owned his own home; which is to say that he possessed some of the exterior hallmarks of the stable family man. Nevertheless, he lost his job as a welder when the plant closed (and he never practised embalming, for which he had received a licence in 1965 from the Pittsburgh Institute of Mortuary Science). According to one news magazine, many of his friends thought he was a communist when he blamed the capitalist system for the closure of his plant. However, his wife said: "If anything, he was a Nazi." Huberty decided to move west and start a new life, but he lost a great deal of money on the sale of his home. Then, inexplicably, he moved to the Mexican border town of Tijuana where, unable to speak the language and feeling (according to his wife) "hopeless, lost and rejected," his hatred of Hispanics began to grow. He then moved back to the U.S., settling in San Ysidro within sight of a McDonald's restaurant much frequented by young Hispanics. He found work as a security guard, but was laid off within a few weeks.

In what seems to have been a last attempt to salvage what remained of his life, he tried to obtain an appointment at a mental health clinic, but was unable to obtain one. The day of the killings, he visited the San Diego Zoo with his family. Staring at the caged animals, perhaps feeling not unlike them, Huberty told his wife, "Society's had their chance!" He drove his family to their home and, announcing that "I'm going hunting . . . hunting humans," he armed himself and drove to the nearby McDonald's in his battered Mercury.

The reaction of the state following the massacre was almost as tragic and misguided as the event itself. If television coverage can be taken as meaningful (and it is surely *the* prime cultural disseminator in modern America), the state and its agencies intervened only to express bewilder-

ment regarding the killer's motive, and to offer the services of therapists who would help victims (present and future) to "adjust" to the shock of such tragedies. The state thus moved to avoid the question: are such killings truly inevitable? Why did Huberty choose to kill and die among the predominantly Hispanic customers of that restaurant? Was there in fact any connection between his precipitous decline in the social hierarchy and his assault on the bottom dwellers, the struggling Hispanics who moved too freely in "his" white, middle-class restaurant? Was there deep social meaning to this act, or only bizarre psychopathology? As I write this, scientists were dispatched to find answers to the Huberty case. Typically, however, they were instructed to look in the wrong direction, and told to dissect his brain to search for mysterious "lesions" among its folds, rather than analyzing the social content of his acts.

If Lucas and Huberty raised the murderous ante of lives destroyed and minds and bodies maimed, *Christopher Wilder* raised the social ante, for he was the first to prey exclusively on upper-middle and upper-class targets other than the "usual" university women. Wilder's case is especially fascinating, although it must remain an enigma since he was killed during his capture and he left nothing behind to explain himself — except his murders. Yet, he was no enraged lumpen proletarian like Lucas, taking out his rage upon the class that suppressed him; nor was he a dispossessed petit bourgeois like Huberty, protesting his disenfranchisement. Born to reputedly wealthy Australian parents, Wilder emigrated to the United States in 1970 and established his own successful contracting business. He owned Florida real estate worth at least a half million dollars, skied in chic resorts, raced cars, and kept a luxury home — according to all reports. Yet there are many suggestive contradictions in his life. His business partner has disputed the authenticity of his wealth, claiming that Wilder's diamond rings were fakes, his Porsche seventeen years old, and his home a "junk-heap" that he repaired with the construction company's left-over materials. His partner insisted that Wilder was "just an easy-going quiet guy who watches a lot of TV because he has nothing else to do." As the contradictions multiplied during the investigation, Wilder was found to be an animal lover: this rapist torturer and murderer had made donations to Save The Whales and the Seal Rescue Fund. Moreover, he always braked when turtles crossed the road. Nevertheless, after an international career in sexual assault (for which he went virtually unpunished) this easy-going watcher of television, this lover of whales, seals, and turtles, abducted eleven beautiful and elegant women, only three of whom survived the ordeal. Using a standard ruse, he approached young women, some of whom were aspiring models, and offered them careers in modelling. If they refused to accompany him "for photographs," he would forcibly abduct them and subject them to electric shocks and other tortures before killing them. Not unlike Theodore Bundy, whom we examine in great detail later on in this book, Wilder began his cross-country rampage shortly after a beautiful young woman, a teacher of mentally disturbed children and herself a member of an established Florida family, refused his offer of marriage. The authorities were bewildered by the entire case, but a racing partner of Wilder's put the critical question when he insisted there was no logic to Wilder's sex crimes: "If you want to act out a pornographic scene, you just go out and hire a bunch of hookers. He had no reason to subject himself to this." Precisely. Why should Wilder indulge in such life-destroying activities when, if his motivation was only 'sexual, he could have safely reproduced it on a commercial basis? This book is an attempt to answer

that inelegant question in full, and to follow its ramifications wherever they might lead us. We must study them well, for there will be many more such killers in what remains of this century — and it should be clearly understood that their intent is to steal our daughters and sons, and to snuff out their lives.

How can we begin to explain these modern multiple murderers who, whether in a campaign lasting many months or in one that can be measured in hours, launch premeditated assaults upon a single social category? The killers appear to defy the social laws by themselves coming from the middle and lower classes. Perhaps they are victims — as psychiatry and the courts argue so vociferously — of obscure mental disorders? Perhaps they are, but if so, why should there be so many more victims of this particular type of mental disease in the 1970s and 1980s than ever before in human experience? Is there something in our modern toilet-training practices, or some strange change in our biochemistry, which is producing so much of this disorder? Perhaps not, for the whole notion of mental disease as latterly defined by psychiatry (which teaches that mental illness is a disease much like, say, tuberculosis) becomes quite untenable when subjected to the anthropological, cross-cultural evidence. The apparently immutable mental diseases of "schizophrenia," "manic-depression," and so on, often disappear or take quite different forms in other cultures. Thus a troubled person's leave-taking from conventional reality (which we call "psychosis") takes a form that his or her culture prescribes. For example, in Ojibwa traditional culture — which taught that persons could be possessed by spirits and that the possessed ones would have an uncontrollable desire for human flesh — madness took the form of Windigo Psychosis. Believing what they were "taught," the victims would kill humans, often their own families, and devour their flesh. Similarly, in that pressure cooker that was Eskimo life, the madness took a special northern form known as Arctic Hysteria, in which the victim would rip off his or her clothes and, insensible to danger, race out onto the ice floes.

In his splendid but little-known study of a schizophrenic, *Oscar*, Peter J. Wilson (1974) concluded that madness is the individual's response to the obliteration of his identity by others. "The only recourse available to those who are so overwhelmed is to banish such tyranny from their lives — to a hospital, an asylum, any ship of fools." Thus madness is both a creative, self-protecting act, and a program of the culture, for South American "primitives," the *Yanomamo*, do not experience Arctic Hysteria and Americans do not encounter Windigo Psychosis. In our own society, an increasing number of people kill for the pleasure it appears to give them. Are they mad, or are they acting out some analogous social message? The lesson here is that the psychiatric analogy is a false one: madness is not like cancer or any other physical ailment. Rather, it is a culturally programmed dialogue. It should not therefore be surprising that no matter how hard our psychiatrists search, they are unable to discover much mental disease among our captured multiple murderers (except in the nature of their acts). Therein lies the special horror, for the killers are as "normal" as you or me, yet they kill without mercy, and they kill to make a statement.

If they cannot be dismissed as biological or psychological freaks, neither can they be regarded as mere manifestations of America's astonishingly high homicide rate (the highest in the western industrial world, and by a huge margin). The evidence for this assertion is clear: a rise or fall in the overall homicide rate is not necessarily related in any way to a rise or fall in the multiple-murder rate. Indeed, in the early 1980s, when the ever-rising U.S. homicide rate fi-

nally began to abate, the multiple-murder rate continued its meteoric rise. In Canada, where the overall homicide rate has been curiously stable for years, the multiple-murder rate seems similarly stable (if periodically and artificially inflated by the presence of foreign killers — a tradition that began with Winnipeg landlady-killer Earle Nelson in the 1920s and continues into the present: with claims by Henry Lucas that he was killing in Canada, with attempts by Christopher Wilder to escape to Canada, with Ted Bundy's occasional visits to Vancouver, and with the recent capture of alleged torturer and serial killer Charles Ng in Calgary). More interestingly, nations such as Britain or Germany, which have very low homicide rates, appear to have high multiple-murder rates; while nations such as Switzerland have low overall homicide and multiple-murder rates. The point should be clear: these are different and almost unrelated phenomena. The multiple murderer, who sacrifices his own life to make an art form out of killing strangers, is qualitatively a very different man from the slum husband who, driven beyond endurance by poverty and humiliation, beats his wife or neighbour to death in some drunken brawl. A sophisticated quantitative debate currently rages in social science over whether the ultimate cause of homicide lies in absolute poverty, relative inequality, or in regional subculture; but clearly all three embrace their share of truth, for *all* deprivation (be it absolute or relative) provokes frustration, and culture is ever the programmed maze instructing individuals how best to display their emotions. In any case, the multiple murderer is quite a different person: most often on the margins of the upper-working or lower-middle classes, he is usually a profoundly conservative figure who comes to feel excluded from the class he so devoutly wishes to join. In an extended campaign of vengeance, he murders people unknown to him, but who represent to him (in their behaviour, their appearance, or their location) the class that has rejected him.

With varying degrees of explicitness, multiple murderers see themselves as soldiers: small wonder then that they feel neither remorse for their victims, nor regret for launching their bloody crusades. Moreover, the public treats them as major celebrities. No one ever became famous by beating his wife to death in an alley; but virtually all our multiple murderers achieve true and lasting fame. They are the subjects of articles and books, radio and television shows — for the remainder of their lives — and they thus attain an immortality denied the unenterprising common man. During their trials, they will almost certainly be surrounded by admiring women who press their affections upon the killer, radiating toward him little but admiration and love. Sometimes, as with Theodore Bundy, a reverent member of the public will marry the multiple murderer during his trial — and even conceive his child during his incarceration. He will be besieged with letters and communications from special-interest groups who will see in him some weighty philosophical point or an opportunity to test their theories of rehabilitation. The Son of Sam was not so very wrong when he thought the public was urging him on during his killing spree, for the media chronicled his every deed in a state of mounting excitement. Should any potential killer fail to grasp the cultural message that this is a certain route to celebrity and fulfillment, a popular song of the mid-1980s spells it out:

Once that you've decided on a killing
First you make a stone of your heart
And if you find that your hands are still willing
You can turn a murder into art

Well if you have a taste for this experience
You're flushed with your very first success
Then you must try a twosome or a threesome
Before your conscience bothers you much less

Then you can join the ranks of the illustrious
In history's great dark Hall of Fame
All our greatest killers were industrious
At least the ones that we all know by name*

Murder for Profit

It is not my intention in this book to study all forms of multiple murder. A paucity of data made it impossible for me to examine the "Tylenol" murders, the many recent hospital murders, the plunging of automobiles onto crowded sidewalks, or even the common homosexual multiple murderers (for they rarely leave any confessions behind them): one can only speculate that they might be similar to those studied here. Additionally, I rule out of our province those who kill for profit, like Charles Sobhra who was implicated in 1978 in the murder and robbery of dozens of tourists in Asian resorts. This multiple murderer for profit is merely one form of making a living, one in which the murder is incidental to the goal. Those who practise this "profession" would undoubtedly follow another if they were offered more money. We are concerned only with those who appear to kill *for its own sake*, those for whom killing alone is the apparent goal.

Neither are we studying the professional state-employed torturers and murderers who are essentially bureaucrats, wreaking havoc on their fellows on behalf of the rulers of modern governments. They are far more effective in killing than those we study here, for these bureaucratic killers are *apparatchiks*, killing with the latest technology as part of their career strategies and, primarily (or even entirely) for career advancement. Transfer them with a solid promotion to the Board of Weights & Measures and they might be just as happy, al-

---

* From one of the best-selling albums of the mid-1980s, *Synchronicity*, by The Police, A & M Records of Canada, © copyright 1983, Magnetic Publishing Co.

though some would miss the shuddering of their victims. These joyless bureaucratic killers find their perfect embodiment in Adolf Eichmann, the efficient ruler of the Nazi death camps, but his emulators have appeared everywhere in the second half of this century. Modern death squads pursue their terror on behalf of ruling elites, and sometimes do so with the enthusiastic assistance of the general population, but they are not the individual entrepreneurs pursuing their private goals who are the object of our study.

Perhaps the most successful government-sponsored mass-murder programs since the Second World War have been in Indonesia, where right-wing Islamic fundamentalists annihilated the political left; and in Cambodia, where left-wing revolutionaries destroyed virtually everyone. In Indonesia, where a conservative estimate puts the murdered at half a million, an Islamic government's decision to eliminate the opposition communist party (PKI) began in 1965 with mass executions by government troops, and then spread to a general slaughter of all party members and their families. Amnesty International's *Political Killings By Governments* records in its dry prose how in many regions "local army commanders loaded lorries with captured PKI members — their names checked off against hastily prepared lists — and drove them to isolated spots nearby for execution, usually by bullet or knife." Elsewhere in Indonesia, however, "most people were executed with long sugar-cane knives and sickles [and] the slaughter often assumed a ritualistic and ceremonial character. In several places the killers held feasts with their bound victims present. After the meal each guest was invited to decapitate a prisoner."

In Cambodia, the slaughter was conceived by the communist government as a means of stopping any potential counter-revolutionary activity. Only high-ranking officers were killed until early 1975, but death was soon extended to any merely *suspected* of resistance to the new regime. One Khmer Rouge soldier, who tired of the killing, testified: "In 1975, we were made to change policy: the victory of the revolution had been too quick. If the population was not wiped out immediately, the revolution would be in danger because the republican forces, the forces of Sihanouk, the capitalist forces would unite against it. It was therefore necessary to eliminate all these forces and to spare only those of the Communist Party of Kampuchea. It was necessary to eliminate not only the officers but also the common soldiers as well as their wives and children. This was also based on revolutionary experience. In the past, Sihanouk had killed revolutionaries, but their wives, children and relatives had united against him and had joined us. That must not be repeated against us now. At the beginning of 1976, however, the families of common soldiers were also killed. One day at Choeung Prey, I cried for a whole day on seeing women and children killed. I could no longer raise my arms [to kill]. Comrade Saruoeun said to me: 'Get on with it.' I said: 'How can I? Who can kill women and children?' Three days later I was arrested." But these wretched creatures with their extermination camps, all prisoners of their own systems and of the empires that manipulate them, are not the stuff of this book.

For Its Own Sake

The men of whom I write seek neither profit nor bureaucratic advancement. On the contrary, they are what the Germans call the practitioners of *lustmord*, joy-murderers who act quite independently, killing simply because of the personal satisfaction they seem to derive from the act. However, I shall try to show that their killings are far more than mere pleasure: that they are a kind of sub-political and conservative protest which nets the killer a substantial social profit of revenge, celebrity, identity, and sexual relief. They conceive of the killings as a kind of mission, task, or crusade — sometimes only dimly perceived (as with DeSalvo and Berkowitz), and sometimes expressed with great clarity (as with Essex, Panzram, and Starkweather). In either case it is the same phenomenon, a kind of primitive rebellion against the social order which has become an increasingly fashionable form of social art. If the murders can only be understood as a personalized social protest, it must be emphasized that these killers are no radicals: they have enthusiastically embraced the established order only to discover that it offers them no place they can endure. Their rebellion is a protest against their perceived exclusion from society, not an attempt to alter it as befits a revolutionary. This fundamentally rebellious, not revolutionary, nature of their protest is undoubtedly why so few government and police resources are allocated to the capture of these killers (compared, say, to the huge police apparatus that monitors political dissidents), for they pose no threat to the established order — neither in their ideology nor in their acts. Thus, in this book, we discuss Huberty the "Nazi"; Essex the racist; Kemper of the Junior Chamber of Commerce; Bundy the Young Republican; Panzram the nihilist; Nilsen the professionally perfect person; Berkowitz the avenger; DeSalvo the social climber; and Starkweather who slaughtered the aristocratic inhabitants of a mansion. These were no more "blows for the people" than they were the acting out of some dreaded mental disease. To the contrary, they were the natural revenge of those who had looked upon their lives and pronounced them unlivable, and then made the decision to exact a fearful revenge, for which they were willing to sacrifice their lives.

The killings are thus also a form of *suicide note* (literally so with most mass murderers, who expect to die before the day or week is out; metaphorically so for most serial murderers, who sacrifice the remainder of their lives to the "cause"), in which the killer states clearly which social category has excluded him. Our task is to learn to read the note, to pore over the killings and the speeches of the killers, searching for meaning. We must not be content with superficial explanations which focus merely on personal and short-term satisfactions, however compelling they may appear to be, for they avoid coming to terms with the ultimate cause of these abominations. This warning is necessary, for even society's most perceptive spokesmen can fall into this error — as when the astute Judge Ronald George, who presided over the Hillside Strangler trials, confused cause with reward when he concluded that "Angelo Buono and Kenneth Bianchi terrorized this city for several months, haunting the community like the ultimate in evil spirits as they abducted children and young women, torturing, raping and sodomizing them, and finally depriving their families and friends of them forever . . . and all for what? The momentary sadistic thrill of enjoying a brief perverted sexual satisfaction, and venting their hatred of women." While this book must *not* be taken as a plea for the serious consideration of the killers' "philosophies," it does argue that if we are to understand the forces that create them, we must look beyond their vile pleasures to the source of their deformation.

The Settling of Accounts

"There comes a point when the only way you can make a statement is to pick up a gun."
                                        Sara Jane Moore

I thus intend to argue the case that these killers are not alien creatures with deranged minds, but alienated men with a disinterest in continuing the dull lives in which they feel entrapped. Reared in a civilization which legitimizes violence as a response to frustration, provided by the mass media and violent pornography with both the advertising proclaiming the "joy" of sadism and the instruction manual outlining correct procedures, they grasp the "manly" identity of pirate and avenger. If they no longer wish to live, they will stage a mass killing whose climax is their execution; but should they wish to live, and to achieve notoriety — even celebrity — they will prepare their careers in serial murder. In doing so, they settle old scores in a manner which often yields a double dividend of sexual pleasure and defiance of the authorities. The killings are a kind of vituperative monologue with the social order — sometimes *literally* so, as when the macabre British homosexual serial murderer, *Dennis Nilsen*, stood in front of the corpses of the young men he had killed and tied to chairs in his apartment, and lectured at them for hours, apparently on subjects as diverse as civil service regulations and modern social issues. More often, however, the killers' message is whispered too low for the human ear to comprehend unassisted, or it is expressed in garbled riddles. What did Nilsen mean when he wrote to the investigating officers after his arrest that, "The evil was short-lived and it cannot live or breathe for long inside the conscience"? The evil was nothing of the kind, for he would have continued to kill indefinitely had he not been unmasked. "I have slain my own dragon," wrote this killer of sixteen defenceless young men, but he offered no further explanation when asked what form the dragon took, or precisely why he killed. "I don't know," he told police. "I've been trying to work it out. I'm not a headshrinker but everyone keeps walking out on me [a reference to the fact that his friends invariably abandoned him]. There might be a lot of individual reasons. Being a professionally perfect person I hate the establishment. I am under great pressure. I drink to relieve the pressure." Is this mere madness, or

some garbled message delivered in an indecipherable code by this professionally perfect person?

Perhaps the most disturbing (yet the most vital) act the killers perpetrate is when, after their apprehension, they so often indulge in the cheapest kind of moralizing — lecturing society, or even the families of their victims. The records of the trial of the fifteenth-century pedophile torture-murderer, *Baron Gilles de Rais*, document the manner in which he instructed the parents of those he had murdered on how best to raise their surviving children. And Nilsen insisted that, "It was my morality and sense of justice which revealed all," when it was nothing of the kind. As I write, the Canadian child-murderer *Clifford Olson* sits in prison and composes philosophical essays, and sends letters to professors of sociology: "I have always enjoyed sociology myself," he writes, "as its [sic] a science of human society. In the last 18 months I have been doing some extenive [sic] writings on a vast amount of my own personal reflections on my own views on many subjects which I believe in myself. . . . Some of my topics [sic] and papers I have completed . . . are as follows. (1) immortality: (2) good and evil: (3) beauty: (4) emotion: (5) love: (6) logic: (7) happiness: (8) family: (9) knowledge: (10) art: these have all been completed." We do ourselves a great disservice if we simply dismiss this for the pretentious prattle it is — the same disservice that a mediocre general does his army if he ignores the thinking of his enemy (for whom he has too much contempt) — for we ensure the killers' triumph if we do not struggle to understand their motives and goals. If we are to excise this abomination from the universe, we must listen studiously to what they say, despite their insufferability. Some of the killers speak a form of truth.

Who are these modern American multiple murderers? They refuse to meet our expectations. I have already stated that very few of them are "mad," or delusionary in any observable way. They are usually white and male, and from the solid working class or lower-middle class. Most important, in their thoughts and behaviour, they are among the most *class conscious* people in America, obsessed with every nuance of status, class, and power. This "sensitivity" expresses itself variously among different types of multiple murderers. Among serial murderers, their truncated sense of self and identity (a reflection of the fact that the vast majority of them are adopted, or illegitimate, or have spent a major portion of their childhoods or adolescences in institutions such as orphanages or juvenile homes) pushes them toward finding their identity and their personal fulfillment in the killings, and all their ambitions in the international celebrity that most often attends their capture. This contrasts strikingly with mass murderers like Essex and Huberty and Starkweather, who are much more likely to come from relatively solid familial situations but find themselves unable to maintain their social position: the gap between their expectations and their realities is so wide that they can only vent their rage upon the hated group in one brief suicidal purple explosion. Huberty felt himself too annulled to yearn for the public spotlight that so bedazzled Berkowitz. Yet both serial and mass murderers are overwhelmed with a profound sense of alienation and frustration stemming from their feelings that no matter how fierce their ambitions may be (and they are, most often, among the most ambitious of men), no matter what they might do, they could not achieve the place in society to which they aspired. They aim high, these multiple murderers: they have not, like Durkheim's contented man, accepted their station in life. Sometimes, as with Bundy and perhaps Wilder, they *do* achieve the position they covet, but their uncertain social origins and their upward social mobility render them unable to feel at ease with themselves while

sitting on this lofty throne. In such a milieu, a sense of personal mission begins to incubate.

Typically, their victims are drawn from a single social type or category. Usually this takes the form of those who are members (or who appear to be) of a specific social class, most often one or two narrow social bands above the killer. Typically too, unless their sexuality is undeveloped (as was Berkowitz's) or overwhelmed by their urgent anger (as with Essex and Huberty), they select members of that social class whom they find beautiful, adding the joy of sex to their adventure. Sex is not the prime motivator, but it is vital to the enterprise: a delicious by-product, or extra dividend, to their adventure. Despite the facts that neither Essex nor Berkowitz touched their victims, or that Starkweather made only a few fumbling attempts to do so, we should not dismiss the sexual component of the sprees, but merely emphasize its *secondary* position to the "Prime Mission," which is to wreak vengeance upon the established order. Thus the Boston Strangler was "putting things over on high class people"; Starkweather was showing how "dead people are all on the same level"; Kemper was making "a demonstration to the authorities"; Bundy was stealing the most valuable possessions of the established classes, their beautiful and talented young women; and Essex was killing white people who, he had decided, were the "beasts of the earth." In this special sense then, the killers know precisely what they are doing and why they are doing it. If we are to understand them, rather than dismiss them, their acts must be seen as a kind of deformed creativity, not a consequence of some drooling derangement.

Our purpose in this book is to determine the source of this deformation, demonstrating through the intensive examination of illustrative cases the fundamentally social nature of their creation and the deep social meaning of their acts. Along our path we shall encounter many lies and half-truths — as often from the professionals who must deal with the killers as from the killers themselves — but we shall attempt a dissection with surgical precision. Enroute, we will occasionally assess the behaviour of the social institutions charged with the responsibility for dealing with multiple murderers: here too we shall encounter surprises, for the police, who are commonly regarded as stupid and brutal, often appear in these pages to possess more intelligence and insight into the killers than do the "professionals." Moreover, as the distinguished American psychiatrist Willard Gaylin (1983) has freely admitted, "Most of us are aware how trivial, ephemeral, descriptive, and meaningless are psychiatric diagnoses." Sadly, the evidence in this book is that many of his colleagues are not aware of this problem and that they allow themselves to be used, in the crassest imaginable way, by any legal team that hires them.

Caveat

A warning should be issued here. There is a pitfall which entraps researchers and readers alike when venturing into this kind of territory. I refer to the propensity, recently attacked by Willard Gaylin, to become so emotionally involved with the killers as to minimize, or even entirely forget, the evil that these men have done. This selective amnesia takes many forms, but all are pernicious. I do not speak here only of the kind of sycophantic and grotesque affection that Flora Rheta Schreiber oozes over her informant, the torture-murderer Joseph Kallinger, in her book *The Shoemaker* (a syrup so thick that it inspires the killer to send poems to his biographer). I also refer to the kind of shift of sympathy that warps books even as beautifully crafted as Daniel Keyes' *The Minds of Billy Milligan*. Keyes, so en-

raptured by his subject, was unable to control his righteous rage at the "rednecks" who interrupted the multiple rapist's "rehabilitation" by shooting at him as he walked along the grounds of the mental hospital. I do not wish to go on record as approving the shooting of mental patients, or anyone else, but author and reader must maintain their perspective, reminding themselves that Milligan was a brutal rapist who destroyed the peace and contentment — and very possibly the sexuality — of many of his victims. Moreover, it is rather likely that the avengers were friends or relatives of the victims (or perhaps the victims themselves). They deserve more sympathy than Billy, and a society that does not understand this provides fertile ground for the sowing of more rapists and murderers.

Willard Gaylin has written with much insight of the process whereby the victims, not the killers, are diminished and denied their humanity in order to put the killer on trial in the best possible light. A similar infection invades the description of the killer and his works, and scholars are no more resistant to this disease than anyone else. If we insist upon the right to understand the dark forces that propel a person into launching a war upon the innocent, we must also assume the responsibility of recognizing the unholiness of his acts, and the tragedies he perpetrates. A cultural system which does otherwise, as does our own, is guilty of much more than misplaced tenderness: it must be charged with encouraging the repetition of such acts. Conversely, a legal system such as ours that consistently makes a mockery of natural justice for violent offenders, releasing them back into society (or not incarcerating them at all) without any sense of wrong-doing, may occasionally benefit from a dash of free-spirited public intervention. To avoid all these problems, I have tried very hard, while seeking to sympathetically understand the motives of the killers, to deglamorize their acts and to humanize their victims. We are all human beings, but the innocent deserve more than the guilty.

An additional problem is that those who argue from ideological positions sometimes find themselves painted into tiny ideological corners. I have never placed too much trust in the judgment of intellectuals, for too often they love their logical systems more than gritty reality. In such a spirit of closed minds and closed systems of thought, gentlepersons of the left sometimes insist that to devise mechanisms for the apprehension and control of the killers is merely to act as agents for the oppressive system that created the killers. Arguing that since the system created them, it has no moral right to punish or control them is as absurd as arguing that a zoologist has no right to destroy some laboratory culture that has turned poisonous. In consistently making such a case, however, the political left parades its moral bankruptcy, for societies that tolerate the commission of these acts (and I believe that ours do) are doomed. The ideologues of the right err just as grievously when, in their fervent attempts to exonerate the ruling class of all blame, they too often act like simpleminded pollyannas, resolutely tending to the bright side and closing their eyes to a causal reality that cannot exonerate society. In arguing, as they so often do, that we should avert our gaze from the darker consequences of the social and economic formations which pattern our lives, they parade their intellectual bankruptcy.

The fact of this very human matter is that, as Willard Gaylin has observed, "in our unconscious we are all killers, rapists, incestual, exhibitionistic, voyeuristic, aggressive, and homicidal." Many of us are programmed still further by our social system to displace our rage upon others: but why do individuals with equally tragic (or far more so) backgrounds choose not to kill? The fundamental act of humanity is to refuse to kill. Our murderers have consciously rejected that humanity. They are not robots programmed by some machine to do exactly what they do: they know precisely what they are doing. For their betrayal of humanity, they deserve no better fate than to be permanently excised from the social order. Their only value is as objects of study.

THE POWER OF DIRT: AN EXPLORATION OF SECULAR DEFILEMENT IN ANGLO-CANADIAN CULTURE

Peter Clark and Anthony Davis

Introduction

The one who can defile others, whether clean himself [sic] or not, is the boss. (Enzensberger, 1972: 47)

In the 20 years since Mary Douglas' groundbreaking work *Purity and Danger: An Analysis of Concepts of Pollution and Taboo* (1966) introduced the concept of "dirt" to the social science community, the reaction has been largely one of curiosity coupled with avoidance. Empirical inquiry concerning this topic has been similar in character to the phenomenon itself — a furtive fascination but a reluctance to engage in any "hands-on" research. It is not our view that Douglas' treatment of secular defilement is fundamentally wrong-headed or that this area of research constitutes a scholarly

From "The Power of Dirt: An Exploration of Secular Defilement in Anglo-Canadian Culture" by Peter Clark and Anthony Davis. First published in Volume 26:4, May 1989. By permission of *The Canadian Review of Sociology and Anthropology* and the authors.

"dry hole." Rather, we suspect that the fear of snickering colleagues and disapproving administrators has dampened research involvement, thereby retarding development in this promising field of inquiry. In an effort to correct for these past errors of omission, we have initiated a preliminary investigation, albeit modest in scope, of beliefs regarding uncleanness in Anglo-Canadian culture with an analytical focus on cultural processes and gender differences.

Like Douglas, we contend that the rules and conditions surrounding the specifications and processes of defilement constitute a cornerstone in the construction of culturally defined forms of identity and solidarity for individuals and social collectivities in any and every culture. However, unlike Douglas, we contend that these rules and conditions contain elemental qualities underwriting the distribution of power and advantage in societies and cultures characterized by structural social inequality. Culture becomes a vehicle for the maintenance and reproduction of dominant-subordinate relations in so far as it extends, through enculturation and identity construction processes, differential sensibilities and vulnerabilities in relation to defiling situations and substances. Such differentials provide the dominant with a means to distinguish itself from the subordinate while also providing the dominant with a device to control and manage dominant-subordinate relations. In order to explore these ideas we begin by tracing out theoretical and conceptual considerations regarding secular defilement. This is followed by the presentation and analysis of some data which permit a preliminary delineation of conditions and characteristics definitive of secular defilement in Anglo-Canadian culture. We then proceed to a description and discussion of gender in regard to differential sensitivities and vulnerabilities to defilement as revealed in the data.

Theoretical and Conceptual Considerations

Following Douglas (1966), we begin by defining secular defilement as a state of perceived uncleanness resulting from sensory contact between a person and an object or activity believed for reasons unrelated to religion to be "dirty" or polluting. Secular defilement is frequently confused with the related notion of "ritual pollution" which plays a very minor role in our culture. In ritual pollution a set of rules of uncleanness is prescribed in a religious doctrine. These rules identify unclean substances and activities, the conditions under which they have the power to defile, and often the purification rituals required to nullify the effects of the pollutant. To cite a few random but well known examples, menstrual discharge is specifically cited as unclean in the Bible (Leviticus, 15: 19) and may, in part, account for the avoidance of sexual intercourse during menstruation which is still a strong taboo among North Americans (Delaney et al., 1976: 14-23). Certain foods are commonly specified as unclean. For example, religious Jews and Moslems define pork as an unclean food; Christian Copts forbid the consumption of camel flesh; upper caste Hindus regard fowl and eggs as polluting; and mediaeval European Catholics avoided horsemeat (Simoons, 1961: 84).

The notion of secular defilement is distinguished from ritual pollution by the absence of a religious doctrine. The concept of secular defilement is more appropriate to contemporary Western industrial societies where the impact of religion on diet and personal hygiene is rather insignificant. However, in saying this one should always remember that even in the industrial context, religious and ethnic minorities routinely distinguish themselves from the surrounding society by invoking a unique set of pollution rules.

In her discussion of secular defilement, Douglas defines "dirt" or the defiling object as being "matter out of place."

Shoes are not dirty in themselves, but it is dirty to place them on the dining table; food is not dirty in itself but it is dirty to leave cooking utensils in the bedroom, or food bespattered on clothing; similarly bathroom equipment in the drawing room; clothing lying on chairs; out-door things indoors; upstairs things downstairs; under-clothing appearing where over-clothing should be, and so on. (Douglas, 1966: 36)

Presumably anything which breaks an ordered arrangement becomes dirt and, as such, can become a potential pollutant. But surely a prima facie case can be made against the claim that dirt equals disorder. As Harris puts it,

Even Douglas might not be willing to accept disorder as the sole or principal component of dirt if she was obliged to tidy up a lawn strewn with gold watches and diamond rings. (Harris, 1979: 197)

Meigs (1978: 317) makes the additional point that a cultural distinction is made in the North American context between "dirty things" which have the power to defile and "messy things" which may annoy but do not pollute. The cultural categories "the messy" and "the dirty" correspond to Douglas' famous definition. Her definition is not sufficiently restrictive, for although dirt may always be something out of place, not all things out of place become dirt. Meigs has her own view of what constitutes "the dirty" in the North American context. She offers a definition which we suspect is even more faithful to Douglas' own substantive descriptions. Meigs defines "the dirty" as,

. . . substances which are perceived as decaying, carriers of such substances and symbols of them in those contexts in which the substances, their carriers, or symbols are threatening to gain access to the body where that access is not desired. (Meigs, 1978: 313)

In her view, the finicality North Americans express when confronting body emissions derives primarily from their imminent decay. Sexual fluids, feces, urine, sweat, and blood are, once they have been cut off from the vitality of the body, all well on the road to decay. This decay is thought to lead to some ill-defined sickening, hence our finicalness when in contact with the bodily emissions of another (Loudon, 1977).

While Meigs' definition is overly restrictive, our data show that she has succeeded in identifying that which is almost invariably considered defiling in our culture; namely, the unwanted physical contact with the bodily emissions of others. During the course of the day, our bodies leave in their wake an astonishing variety of castings and leavings such as dandruff, ear wax, nasal discharge, saliva, perspiration, urine, semen, fecal matter, vomit, menstrual discharge, and intestinal gas. One of the most central themes governing the notion of civility in Anglo-Canadian culture is the personal responsibility to dispose of these emissions in a manner which minimizes the possibility of soiling others. Facial tissues, bath tubs, wash basins, urinals, toilet bowls, garbage pails and even our under-clothing serve as carriers of our emissions. As Meigs notes even these carriers themselves, if thought to carry the bodily emissions of others, can be regarded as polluting.

One could conclude that finicality is simply a rational response to the potential of infection inherent in decaying body emissions. However, this fear of infection cannot fully account for the abhorrence felt towards these objects. Consider the following thought experiment suggested by Smith (1979: 22). Imagine examining the bath tub in your newly rented hotel room and finding either a) a ball of hair clinging to the side of the tub near the drain, or b) a dirty footprint on the bottom of the tub. If you had a choice between these two objects as a bathing companion, which one would it be? Reason should tell you that whereas the muddy footprint may carry a variety of pathogens, the ball of hair has undoubtedly been washed clean. However, virtually no one finds the footprint dirtier than the hair, for the hair is considered a "dirty thing" whereas the footprint is merely a "messy thing."

The existence of urban defilement legends illustrates the importance which our culture places on the threat to our purity posed by the putrification and decomposition of bodily wastes. These myths usually take the form of a short "gross-out" story which is passed on by word of mouth as if it were a well-documented newspaper story. Perhaps the most famous of all urban legends is the "Death Car" myth. The basic outline of this legend runs as follows. A "nearly new" expensive model automobile is reported as being for sale in a used car lot across town at a bargain price. There has been a long succession of customers interested in the car but they inevitably return it within a day or two. The problem appears to be that the previous owner committed suicide in the car in some remote location, leaving the body undetected for several months. The car was completely fumigated, repainted, recarpeted and reupholstered by the dealer. However, the storyteller concludes, it was to no avail because "the smell of death would simply not go away." Another myth with defilement as a punishment for a crime is the story of the "hoser" who mistakenly attempted to siphon gasoline out of the holding tank for the toilet of a camper trailer and was found the next morning in some adjacent bushes "still barfing his guts out." Finally, the most ubiquitous stomach-churner of them all, the

dead mouse in a coke or beer bottle, again has pollution as its message.

The pervasiveness of these and countless other pollution myths (Brunvand, 1983) suggests that they contain a message of importance to the listener. We accept Meigs' claim that unwanted bodily emissions and other decaying material which threaten to gain access to one's body are defiling. Many of these items are so powerful that defilement by them creates nausea in some and a sense of disgust in others. Although the set of pollutants identified by Meigs certainly includes some of the most salient ones, these are not the only defiling agents. Our study demonstrates that some Anglo-Canadians report being defiled in situations which involve no bodily emissions, carriers, or the symbols of such.

Methodology

In an attempt to examine some of these ideas, we constructed and distributed a self-administered questionnaire to university students at Dalhousie, St. Francis Xavier, and Saint Mary's universities. Altogether 57 students (30 females and 27 males) volunteered in the pre-test and 212 students (140 females and 72 males) volunteered to complete the final modified questionnaire. The nature of our sample imposes severe limitations on the claims which can be made about the culture as a whole. For example, a university student population limits examination of such social dimensions as age, ethnicity, education level, occupation and other social characteristics which differ from the surrounding population. Nevertheless, we accepted this limitation on our study because we concluded that the questionnaire would be regarded as too offensive for distribution beyond the bounds of the university.

After being asked a standard set of demographic questions, the student volunteers were given the following instruction:

In our society, there are some objects and activities which are regarded as having the power to defile or make one feel dirty. For some people the idea of defilement is highly developed, such that any form of contact with an object thought to be unclean makes them feel nauseous. This can be coupled with an overpowering desire to purify or rid themselves of the unclean object (e.g. wash yourself, spit it from your mouth, change your clothes and/or flee from the scene). Other people are only mildly distressed by such an encounter, and there are some who are almost completely unaffected by this type of encounter. We are interested in learning where you stand on this matter. On the next few pages, you will find a number of lists of items. You are requested to indicate your reaction to each item by circling the number which best reflects your feelings on the following scales:

Does not *make me feel sick [1 2 3 4 5] Does make me feel* very *sick.*

You would circle number 5 if the item presented makes you feel very sick. You would circle number 1 if you are in no way made to feel sick. You would circle numbers 2, 3, and 4 if you felt that the item was somewhere in between these two extremes.

Ten separate lists of items followed this general instruction. These were: food items, toiletries, discarded items of strangers, bodily emissions, types of people, pornography, violations of privacy, gestures, violations against the person, and table manners. Each of these lists was preceded by a possible cultural scenario within which defilements could occur.

Over All Defilement Reactions

Data presented in Table I clearly support Meigs' thesis that those bodily emissions which have a high propensity to decay are generally thought to be highly defiling. Vomit, feces, nasal discharge, urine and semen are almost unanimously considered to be defiling by our sample. At the opposite end of the defilement spectrum can be found a bodily emission which appears to be hardly at all defiling, namely tears. Douglas recognized this exception:

But admittedly clear, fast-running tears are the stuff of romantic poetry; they do not defile. This is partly because tears are pre-empted by the symbolism of washing. Tears are like rivers of moving water. They purify, cleanse, bathe the eyes, so how can they pollute? But more significantly tears are not related to the bodily functions of digestion or procreation. (Douglas, 1966: 149)

Similar patterns are evident in the response reactions to discarded toiletries and other items of personal hygiene. With the exception of the scab (which should in retrospect have been included among bodily emissions), contact with these items is on the whole less defiling than is the case with bodily emissions. This outcome conforms to the theoretical position which we have discussed above, since none of these items are related to either sexual or excretory functions and none (except the scab) are prone to obvious decay. Consistent with the previous results is the finding that the three most potent defilers among the discarded possessions of strangers (used toilet paper, sanitary napkins, and condoms) are all objects which contain potentially putrifying emissions associated with their excretory or sexual functions. It is now apparent that uninvited contact with sexual and excretory emissions of strangers will always defile in our culture. Although other objects may defile to a lesser degree, sex-elimination objects are clearly more potent. It appears that very little can be more devastating to our identity than the public display or suggestion that one's body has been bespattered by sexual fluids or excrement. We assume that a person's identity or self-image is largely a cultural entity. That is, it is socially constructed in such a way as to be meaningfully inter-

TABLE I
DEFILEMENT REACTIONS TO BODILY EMISSIONS, TOILETRY DISCARDS,
AND THE DISCARDED POSSESSIONS OF STRANGERS

DEFILEMENT REACTIONS
DOES NOT MAKE ME SICK   DOES MAKE ME FEEL VERY SICK

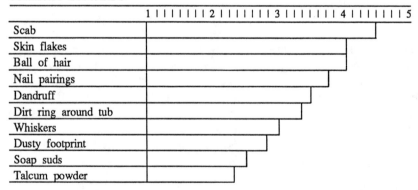

BODILY EMISSIONS [a]

1 | | | | | | | | 2 | | | | | | | | 3 | | | | | | | | 4 | | | | | | | | 5

Vomit
Feces
Urine
Nasal discharge
Semen
Saliva
Earwax
Blood
Perspiration
Human mother's milk
Loose hair
Tears

[a] Wording: "This list consists of a variety of human excretions of strangers. You are to imagine yourself accidentally sitting on the following items while changing your clothes in a locker room."

TOILETRY DISCARDS [b]

1 | | | | | | | | 2 | | | | | | | | 3 | | | | | | | | 4 | | | | | | | | 5

Scab
Skin flakes
Ball of hair
Nail pairings
Dandruff
Dirt ring around tub
Whiskers
Dusty footprint
Soap suds
Talcum powder

[b] Wording: "This list consists of toiletries and other items frequently discarded during grooming and other forms of personal hygiene. You are to imagine yourself in the following setting. You have a relaxing bath. However, just when you have lowered yourself into the water you see the following object clinging to the side of the tub."

DISCARDED POSSESSIONS OF STRANGERS [c]

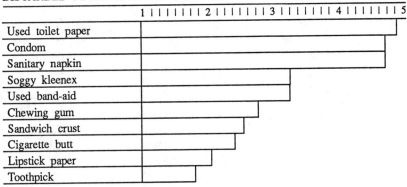

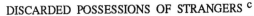

c Wording: "This list consists of discarded possessions of strangers. You are to imagine that you and a friend have just spent a glorious day sunning yourselves on the beach. As you rise to go home, your friend points out that the following object is sticking to the back of your bathing suit."

preted by others in that culture (Strauss, 1959). It conveys information concerning the bearer's disposition, intentions and, most importantly, his or her current social role. The maintenance of a self-image which is not only culturally interpretable but which also reflects positively upon us is a necessary precondition to full participation in the social order. It is to be expected that the individual will strenuously resist anything which threatens to destroy this elaborately constructed image. It is our view that in a number of very significant ways, secular defilement threatens to destroy the integrity of one's self-image. At the most basic level upon which all other identity constructions are built is the message that the identity holder is a living, socialized human being. Consequently, the uninvited intrusion of things which indicate that we are in a dying state will be regarded as extremely defiling. To carry on our face, hands, or clothes, putrefying flesh or decaying bodily emissions indicates to others a possible loss of vitality and entrance into a necrotic state. This explains Meigs' observation that bodily emissions, especially those in a state of decomposition, are considered to be extremely defiling.

Only slightly less central to our culturally constructed identity is our ability to identify with the rest of the human species. Again, if uninvited objects or actions succeed in indicating to others a lack of humanness and an animal-like image, then we will find that very defiling. Some obvious examples are the consumption of foods which are culturally defined as being fit only for animals, or the implication deduced from telltale signs that one has copulated or defecated publicly.

Our identity as socialized members of society with a developed level of cultural competence counts as a very salient identity component. One would be defiled by objects and activities which suggested an unsocialized person such as an infant, a retarded person or someone not fully sane. A complete list of salient identity components will not be attempted here, but two closely linked types, namely, gender identity and sexual preference ought to be mentioned. Objects and activities which succeed in suggesting to others that a male is a female or vice versa, or that a heterosexual is a homosexual are usually greeted with horror. Other identity components such as occupational role, nationality, ethnicity, religion, etc. will not be considered because they are less broadly based and less salient. Unlike those previously discussed, they are not operative in every social situation. One might be humiliated and embarrassed by having one's occupational identity sullied, but one is unlikely to be nauseated by it.

In general, it appears that very little can be more devasting to one's self-image than public bespattering with rotting sexual emissions and excrement. Our worst terms of insult and abuse almost invariably involve the language of sex and elimination. Terms such as "shit head," "shit face," "ass wipe", "asshole," "prick," "fuck-up" and "cunt" all involve the sex-elimination amalgam to characterize someone's identity.

Why should this be the case? There does not appear to be any instinctive aversion to our sex-elimination products and by-products. Young children have no sense of defilement. Both coprophilia and urolagnia are exceedingly common, with young children handling excreta much as they would any other object in their environment. Nor does it appear that adults are as fastidious in their concern with defilement when they think that it has gone undetected by others. For example, Kira (1976: 14) in his research on excretory facilities, reports that perfunctory purification practices such as hand washing after defecation or urination in a public restroom is typically only carried out when one is conscious of being observed. As further evidence that "dirt" and defilement only exists when there is a significant other (or even an insignificant other) to behold it, Kira cites a German study of perineal practices. It was discovered that:

. . . even the most apparently elegant and fastidious are often to be found wearing underdrawers soaked in urine and smeared with fecal matter. (Kira, 1976: 14)

In our culture, complete privacy is considered a necessary condition for the acceptable performance of sexual and excretory activity. Public copulation and defecation or even the suggestion of such is considered damaging to one's reputation. According to Kira,

. . . we tend to want to hide and disguise our involvement with [sex and elimination]; in other words, we seek privacy for it. We seek this privacy beginning with our language usage; we cannot even state directly what our needs are or where we wish to go, and once there we resort to all sorts of strategems to avoid anyone's knowing where we are and what we are about. Even nudists, who otherwise are relatively relaxed with respect to the body, apparently still insist on privacy for elimination as well as sexual relations. (Kira, 1976: 107)

Signs of having made these "private" activities "public" such as the unzippered fly, urine splatters on one's pant leg or used toilet paper clinging to one's shoe can be extremely subversive to the successful presentation of self. We hypothesize in accordance with a theory put forward by Elias (1939) that public defecation and copulation has come to be considered the prerogative of animals in our culture. Humans engaging in such activities are viewed as being "no better than animals." Indeed, in his history of manners from the 13th century to the present century, Elias documents a continuous lowering of the threshold of repugnance over time. The overriding theme of this propensity towards greater finicality is a tendency for Westerners "to suppress in themselves every characteristic which they feel to be 'animal' " (Elias, 1939: 120). Although the data presented thus far support this hypothesis, it should not be assumed that sex-elimination products and by-products possess the exclusive power to defile.

TABLE II
DEFILEMENT REACTIONS TO VIOLATIONS OF PRIVACY, GESTURES AND
VIOLATIONS OF TABLE MANNERS

DEFILEMENT REACTIONS
DOES NOT MAKE ME SICK   DOES MAKE ME FEEL VERY SICK

VIOLATIONS OF PRIVACY [a]

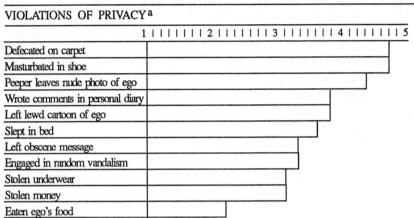

	1	2	3	4	5
Defecated on carpet					
Masturbated in shoe					
Peeper leaves nude photo of ego					
Wrote comments in personal diary					
Left lewd cartoon of ego					
Slept in bed					
Left obscene message					
Engaged in random vandalism					
Stolen underwear					
Stolen money					
Eaten ego's food					

[a] Wording: "The following list consists of violations of privacy. You are to imagine that you have arrived home from work and that as you open the front door you discover that your home has been broken into. You find that the intruder has left signs of having done the following to your home."

GESTURES [b]

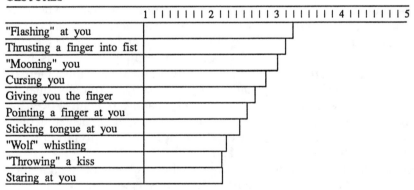

	1	2	3	4	5
"Flashing" at you					
Thrusting a finger into fist					
"Mooning" you					
Cursing you					
Giving you the finger					
Pointing a finger at you					
Sticking tongue at you					
"Wolf" whistling					
"Throwing" a kiss					
Staring at you					

[b] Wording: "This list consists of gestures. You are to imagine that you are walking by an apartment building when you suddenly catch sight of a person partly hidden (you are unable to determine the gender) on one of the balconies doing the following."

TABLE MANNERS [c]

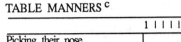

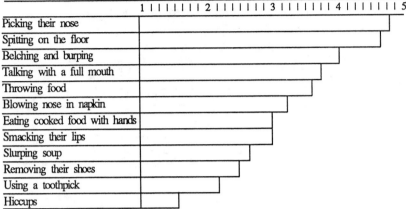

	1 2 3 4 5
Picking their nose	
Spitting on the floor	
Belching and burping	
Talking with a full mouth	
Throwing food	
Blowing nose in napkin	
Eating cooked food with hands	
Smacking their lips	
Slurping soup	
Removing their shoes	
Using a toothpick	
Hiccups	

[c] Wording: "This list consists of possible violations of table manners. You are to imagine yourself dining at a restaurant and observing the following scene at an adjacent table."

Table II relates to various violations of privacy. Unlike the previous table, this list does not involve direct contact with bodily emissions and their carriers. In reactions to violations of privacy the two most potent defilers involve sex-elimination products being left by the intruder. Although no direct physical contact is made with these substances, a home may be considered an extension of the self in terms of impression management. Information is conveyed to others about the self, not only by means of the body, but also by one's place of residence. Sex-elimination products left on the floor convey the impression that the resident behaves "like an animal" or at the minimum is insane or malsocialized. However, vandalism which leaves the home in a "mess" appears significantly less defiling. Violation of one's home for personal gain such as money or food, although it may result in a material loss, is far less defiling than image threatening violations. Violations considered highly defiling all involve a threat to the image one wishes to convey to outsiders, either by attempting to sabotage one's image directly (the lewd cartoon and obscene message) or by making that which is private (not part of the public image) public. The last type of threat to one's identity is illustrated by the voyeur who leaves photos of ego in a state of undress. The voyeur has defiled ego because a completely private act has become part of the public domain and beyond ego's control. Again something private has been made public with the theft of the undergarments and the reading of the personal diary. Ego suffers a loss of control over the release of this information, the extent of its circulation and the interpretation of its meaning.

Although the level of defilement associated with gestures is well below that found in direct contact with sex-elimination products and their carriers, the findings show that the most defiling gestures symbolize sexual and/or excretory functions. Public cursing may appear to be an exception; however, as Flynn (1977: 30) points out, most curses make some allegation concerning the recipient's non-conforming sexual or excretory behavior, thus sabotaging his or her public image. The activities which receive the highest defilement ratings in reactions to violations of table manners all involve something exiting from a body orifice rather than entering it at a meal. Belching, spitting, nose-picking are all of this nature.

As the data concerning violations of personal space illustrate, the most defiling invasions are those which involve attempts to gain access to and use one's genitalia in a public place when that access and use is not desired. The most interesting departure from the sex-elimination syndrome is the act of spitting. Although spittle is a bodily emission, it should be noted that the act of being spit upon is more defiling than simply coming into contact with saliva (See Table I). We suspect that spitting is a special case. It is itself a reaction to defilement in our culture. Spitting indicates that one's mouth has been defiled by an "unclean" object. Cleansing is gained by the forceful ejection of that object from the mouth. The ejection of saliva from the mouth has come to symbolize the identification and purification of defilement in general. Thus, when one is spit upon, one is contaminating the recipient with "dirt" symbolically located in the saliva. It may also be the case that the defiling object which provokes the spitting is the recipient himself or herself — the defilers having their defiling selves thrust back at them.

The examination of pornography as a form of defilement appears to have been almost completely ignored in the large and rapidly expanding literature on pornography and erotica. With the exception of Davis (1983), very few academics appear to have taken seriously the folk classification of pornography with "dirt." Common folk categories such as dirty books, filthy pictures, smut, and trash, and slime certainly suggest such a connection. Even the word "obscene," whose Latin derivation means "filthy or dirty," is often used as a synonym for "pornographic" by the general public.

Our results clearly show that the defilement reactions to certain types of pornography (snuff, necrophilic, coprophilic and urophilic films) are of the same order of magnitude as direct contact sex-elimination excretions of strangers. This finding may seem somewhat counterintuitive because, unlike the previous examples, the defilement by films is "second-hand." Of course, it is not the celluloid but the projection of the viewer into the depicted activity which results in the defilement reactions.

If we examine the nature of the most defiling types of pornography, we find that the sex-elimination products featured in the preceding analysis get top billing here as well. Snuff movies typically feature a woman being tortured, disembowelled, and dismembered. Although the erotic content is "soft-core" (Davis, 1983: 198), with the violence obviously simulated and less convincing than in regular Hollywood feature films, the idea clearly disgusts most people. The anti-pornography movement certainly regarded the first snuff movie as a watershed. According to Beverly LaBelle (1980: 274):

"Snuff" was one of the very first pornographic films to elicit strong protest from the feminist sector of the population. It marked the turning point in our consciousness about the meaning behind the countless movies and magazines devoted to the naked female body. "Snuff" forced us to stop turning the other way each time we passed an X-rated movie house. It compelled us to take a long, hard look at the pornography industry. The graphic bloodletting in "snuff" finally made the misogyny of pornography a major feminist concern.

In our view, it is not simply the "graphic bloodletting" referred to by Labelle which nauseates, but rather the grisly mutilation, the violent intermixing of blood, excretia, and semen, and the mangling of sexual organs. In Anglo-Canadian culture simulated bloodletting is considered an attrac-

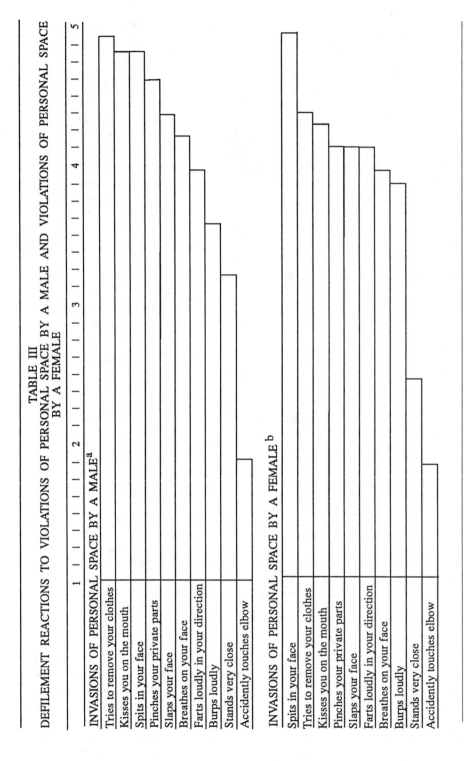

TABLE III
DEFILEMENT REACTIONS TO VIOLATIONS OF PERSONAL SPACE BY A MALE AND VIOLATIONS OF PERSONAL SPACE BY A FEMALE

INVASIONS OF PERSONAL SPACE BY A MALE[a]

Tries to remove your clothes
Kisses you on the mouth
Spits in your face
Pinches your private parts
Slaps your face
Breathes on your face
Farts loudly in your direction
Burps loudly
Stands very close
Accidently touches elbow

INVASIONS OF PERSONAL SPACE BY A FEMALE[b]

Spits in your face
Tries to remove your clothes
Kisses you on the mouth
Pinches your private parts
Slaps your face
Farts loudly in your direction
Breathes on your face
Burps loudly
Stands very close
Accidently touches elbow

[a] Wording: "This list consists of possible violations against the person. You are to imagine that you have just entered an elevator in which there is a solitary male passenger. This passenger suddenly does the following to you."

[b] Wording: "This list concerns the same situation as that in the previous list except that there is a woman on the elevator instead of a man."

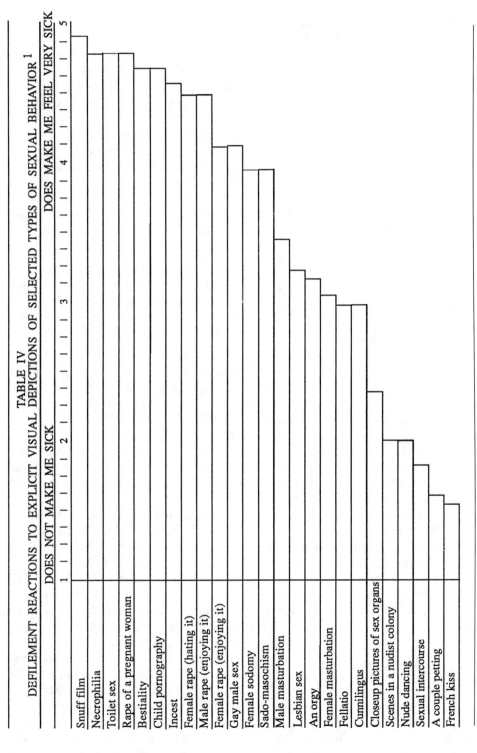

TABLE IV

DEFILEMENT REACTIONS TO EXPLICIT VISUAL DEPICTIONS OF SELECTED TYPES OF SEXUAL BEHAVIOR [1]

DOES NOT MAKE ME SICK — DOES MAKE ME FEEL VERY SICK

[1] Wording: "This list consists of scenes from sexually explicit films. You are to imagine that you have been invited over to a friend's place to watch a recent movie which your friend has just rented from a video outlet. However, instead of the movie which you and your friend expected, you find yourself watching explicit scenes of the following sexual activities."

tive form of entertainment readily available on television and in movie theatres. What makes the "snuff" film different from the "splatter" film is that in the former sex-elimination products constitute the splatter rather than simply blood and "guts." Every substance which played a major role in defilement according to our previous findings can be found in the snuff film.

Necrophilia, toilet sex and bestiality are all predictably highly defiling. However, it should be noted that incest and child pornography receive high scores yet both activities involve no greater contact with sex-elimination products than regular sexual intercourse. Yet, both incest and child pornography were considered to be much more defiling than intercourse. Both incest and sexual intercourse with young children are strongly tabooed activities in our culture. Depictions of these activities are also tabooed. These cases are clearly exceptions to our hypothesis and are not explicable in terms of it. We suspect that reactions to pornography consist of a combination of a feeling of defilement and a disapproval of tabooed sexual practices.If we examine the middle range of defilement reactions, the same mixture can be observed. Common practices which are not strongly condemned such as male and female masturbation, fellatio and cunnilingus receive similar defilement reactions as homosexual and sadomasochistic practices. The reactions to the former may have more to do with the hands on and mouth on contact with sexual emissions than with general societal approval/disapproval.

Social Class and Gender

Elias argues that the degree of finicality or the threshold of repugnance will vary by social class. The upper class will exhibit a much lower nausea threshold than people beneath them in the social hierarchy. This is the case because these highly elaborate notions of "refinement" and "delicacy of taste" serve as cultural exclusionary devices used by the upper class to distinguish themselves from the lower classes. A highly developed finicalness is a form of cultural capital, such as an upper class accent, which can be passed on like an heirloom from one generation to another, serving as a mark of distinction in a stratified society. However, the upper classes must constantly "up the ante" because of adoption by the lower classes of upper class standards of taste. According to Elias (1939: 100–1):

They thereby lose, to some extent, their character as means of distinguishing the upper class. They are somewhat devalued. This compels those above to further refinement and development of behaviour. And from this mechanism — the development of courtly customs, their dissemination downward, their slight social deformation, their devaluation as marks of distinction — the constant movement in behaviour patterns through the upper class receives part of its motivation.

Although we find the evidence put forward by Elias in defence of his thesis to be entirely convincing, we were unable to detect any evidence for its existence in the Anglo-Canadian context. Because of the importance of Elias' theory in this field of inquiry we measured our respondents' objective socio-economic status (based on occupation) (Blishen and McRoberts, 1976; Blishen and Carroll, 1978) and their subjective status (their notion of where they stood relative to others in the community). Neither of these two measures of status were significantly related in any way to the level of defilement reactions. It should be pointed out, however, that our inability to find a class dimension to finicality may be in part the result of the non-representativeness of our student sample. Since university students are over-represented in the upper end of the social hierarchy, this may have weakened the connection between finicality and social class in our data. However, using Pearson's coefficient of correlation we were unable to find *one* statistically significant correlation between either of the two measures of social class and any of our defilement reactions. It is our view that defilement and social power *are* intimately connected in Anglo-Canadian culture but not in the class based manner which has been historically the case in Europe or, for that matter, in the caste related system found in India. Instead, we contend that the relation between defilement and social power is located in the structure of gender identity and gender relations.

The anthropological sense of culture most frequently stresses its integrative qualities. Culture is most often conceived of as the distinctive learned behaviors, values, beliefs, feelings which constitute a way of life of a people. The array of organizational forms, social structures, institutions, technologies, world views, symbolic systems, and so on, particular to any culture is generally viewed as the way a specific people have developed to satisfy the imperatives of survival, reproduction, and the like. In this view, culture is more or less homogeneous, only containing diversity for the purpose of forming a division of labour needed for integration. Typically culture has not been conceptualized as a vehicle whereby certain groups or individuals attempt to express their advantage and entrench their power over others. Indeed, the emphasis on universally shared values and integrative qualities within a culture has underwritten the recent abandonment of culture as a useful analytic concept by many in social anthropology, particulary among those concerned with the study of structured social inequality, class systems, and intergroup conflict. Even the early efforts to keep the notion alive by attempting to reconcile the inte-

grative approach with conflict and inequity through such notions as subculture and biculturalism have proven unsuccessful (Valentine, 1968; Valentine and Valentine, 1975).

Some recent work, however, is breathing life back into the concept of culture and enabling researchers to account for such phenomena as inequality and conflict. Feminists, in considering the origins and character of patriarchy, focus on the cultural construction of gender identity and the enculturation processes whereby males and females acquire the behaviors and psychologies of superordinates and subordinates. Essentially this argument insists that patriarchy, the dominion of men over women, is expressed both institutionally and, more significantly, culturally, especially in the enculturation and gender identity construction processes (Brownmiller, 1984; Miles, 1983; Reynaud, 1983). From this perspective, patriarchal culture is the vehicle which entrenches, legitimates, maintains, and reproduces the inequitable distribution of power and advantage between the genders. In this view, women acquire a culturally derived identity, emotionality and temperament consistent with their position as subordinates. Women express the "weaknesses" of emotionalism, sensitivity, submissiveness, and modesty against which are counterpoised the acquired male "strengths" of rationalism, insensitivity, aggressiveness, and brusqueness. Patriarchy situates men and women with culturally derived personal and social characteristics consistent with the symbolic and actual expressions of domination and subordination.

In our data males and females tend to react differently to defilement. In general, females have a lower nausea threshold than men. Only in seven out of 110 defilement incidents did males react more strongly than females. In none of these seven incidents was the difference between

Table V
DEFILEMENT REACTIONS WHERE MALE MEAN REACTIONS SIGNIFICANTLY EXCEED FEMALE MEAN REACTIONS

CATEGORY	DEFILEMENT REACTIONS	
	SIGNIFICANCE LEVEL OF $\leq$ .001 (STUDENT'S T-TEST)	SIGNIFICANCE OF $\leq$ .01 (STUDENT'S T-TEST)
Bodily emissions	Sweat, blood, saliva, earwax, nasal discharge, feces	Urine, vomit
Toiletry discard	Whiskers, tub ring, dandruff, hairball, skin flakes, nail pairings, dusty footprint, scab	
Discarded possessions of strangers	Used sanitary napkins, used condom	Used band-aids, cigarette butt
Violations of privacy	Left lewd cartoon of ego, left obscene message, peeper leaves nude photo of ego, stolen underwear	Wrote comments in personal diary
Gestures	Flashing	Finger thrusting
Invasions of personal space by a male		Slaps your face, Spits in your face
Invasions of personal space by a female	Kisses you on the mouth, pinches your private parts, tries to remove your clothes, stands very close, breathes on your face, slaps your face, accidently touches elbow, spits in your face	
Violations of table manners	Picking their nose	Throwing food, spitting on the floor, eating cooked foods with hands, uses a toothpick
Explicit visual depictions of sexual activity	Lesbian sex, female masturbation, an orgy, female sodomy, female rape (enjoying it), cunnilingus, fellatio, sado-masochism, nude dancing, intercourse, incest, scenes from a nudist colony, child pornography, necrophilia	Toilet sex, bestiality

the genders statistically significant. In 94 incidents females reacted more strongly than males. In 58 of these the difference was statistically significant. What accounts for this difference?

The observation that females in our culture have more delicate sensibilities than males is common enough. Males are viewed as being more insensitive, less finicky, and generally less "refined" than females. Henley (1977: 14) argues that females in our culture are more sensitive to all manner of nonverbal socio-cultural stimuli. She argues that women's nonverbal sensitivity is a result of their weaker power position in society. That is, their inferior status position sensitizes them to react more strongly to techniques used by status superiors to further degrade them. In an earlier paper (Clark and Davis, 1984: 35) we found that defilement was almost invariably thought to be status lowering. The consequence of a ruined or spoiled identity resulting from defilement is, of course, a vastly inferior identity.

There is little doubt that defilement can be used as a resource by men to maintain or even enhance their position of dominance over women. We are not suggesting that defilement is only used in the "battle of the sexes." It is a common enough practice in the battle of men against men as well. For instance, political prisoners frequently report being urinated on being forced to eat their own excrement, being raped, and so on. Here defilement is being used as a weapon in a power struggle to enhance further the power position of the victor and to "mark" the completeness of the conquest. Nor should it be thought that the relatively powerless are incapable of using defilement in an attempt to bring down the powerful. To quote Henley (1977: 83),

Anyone who has seen young boys deliver soulful belches one after another at a family gathering's elaborate meal, or seen the angry look directed at them for uncontrolled flatulence, has seen this phenomenon in action.

Although defilement is a resource which can be appropriated by the powerless (Corbin, 1986: 215), it is likely to achieve little more than momentary disruption. However, in the hands of the powerful it can be more effectively used to consolidate and symbolize their power position over subordinates.

In Table V two types of defilement account for nearly all of the incidents listed, namely, cutaneous and sexual defilement. Exudations of the skin such as dandruff, skin flakes, sweat, ear wax, and so on are body products which males generally dismiss as undefiling, yet females find them very defiling. This gender difference, is, in part, explained by the fact that females in our culture are much more body hygiene conscious than males. Stone (1978: 127) notes that females in Western industrial societies spend nine more minutes per day on personal hygiene (grooming, brushing teeth, bathing, applying cosmetics, etc.) than men. The difference between North American men and women is even greater, approximately 17.5 minutes. Stone notes that some of the non-Western societies surveyed do not exhibit such a time differential in personal care. As Lakoff and Scherr (1984) argue, this hygiene consciousness on the part of women in Western culture is indicative of their greater concern, not so much with health, but with beauty. They conclude that in Western culture,

. . . the desire for beauty, or at least attractiveness, possesses every woman, that every woman considers her looks a vital part of herself, that to fail to realize one's full potential for beauty is to feel oneself a failure as a woman and a human being. (Lakoff and Scherr, 1984: 12)

Although Lakoff and Scherr may overstate their case somewhat, it is very clear that most men in Western culture do not currently place such a high value on their own beautification (Hatfield and Sprecher, 1986: 125–30). The authors emphasize that beauty is a source of influence in the same way that money, political position, and physical strength can be. It can be used as a means of controlling and manipulating others to serve one's own interests. For women the ruination of one's beauty is the destruction of one's source of influence over men, albeit, a temporary and somewhat limited basis for leverage. Men, because their bases of power lie elsewhere, are not as vulnerable to cutaneous defilement as women.

The other area in which women react more strongly than men is towards sexual defilement. Three very important patterns should be noted in these data. Firstly, females react with repugnance to violations of the person by perpetrators who are of both genders, while males only react in this manner if the perpetrator is another male. Secondly, females are much more upset by carnal knowledge being made public than males. Thirdly, unlike males, females more commonly find all types of pornography repugnant. Sociobiologists (e.g., Symons, 1979) argue that gender differences such as these are closely linked to the differential biological and social costs associated with the two reproductive systems. The greater investment on the part of the females in their reproductive system leads to greater fearfulness and aversion to any potential violation to the integrity of that system. Even though we differ profoundly with the sociobiologists when they attribute this phenomenon to genetic factors and with their tendency to reify and universalize Western cultural practices, we nevertheless think that they have managed to identify an important tendency.

In the presentation of their selves, Anglo-Canadian women are socialized to display greater coyness towards public erotic ac-

tivity. This consists of publicly proclaiming the exclusivity of their sexual equipment, a condition key to male interests within patriarchy. To be perceived as being "a loose woman" or promiscuous means that one loses value. Influence over men based on the maintenance of sexual organs for the exclusive use of one male or possibly two or more mutually unacquainted males, is similar to influence based on beauty. Both are vulnerable to defilement, both are male dependent sources of influence and neither are used with the same degree of obsessiveness by men. Both sexual modesty and beauty constitute core components of what is often referred to as "femininity" in Anglo-Canadian culture. The nausea displayed by women towards the defilement of their femininity not only indicates a loss of a source of influence but also signals to men women's greater vulnerability. Men's ability to "keep their cool" in the face of similar defilement reflects the insignificance of their loss and their relative immunity gained by having other unviolated sources of power.

Conclusions

The strength of the female-male differences apparent in the defilement data suggests that, in an important sense, men and women live and experience a dissimilar relationship to defiling substances and situations. In order to account for and explain this difference between the genders, we found it useful to consider notions of culture, self-identity, power and patriarchy. Substances and situations which defile, sully or dirty are rooted in the specifications and structure of culture. In Anglo-Canadian culture this is primarily, although not exclusively, sex-elimination body products, their carriers or their symbols. Direct and persistent association with cultural "dirt" is felt to ruin or place in jeopardy one's self-identity within a given culture. These self-images, culturally constructed, are significantly different for men and women. To understand the nature of these gender based differences in self-identity, it is essential that we understand the role of power in their construction. To do this we must move beyond the static, integrative and inclusive conception of culture and adopt a more conflict oriented, more dynamic, and more fractioned conception. It is our contention that the differences between male and female defilement reactions can only be fully understood from the point of view of cultural hegemony. Sider (1986: 119) has defined the notion of cultural hegemony as a conception which:

. . . goes beyond both the concept of culture and the concept of ideology. It is more specific than culture in that it relates whole social processes in which people "define and shape their lives," to specific distributions of power and influence.

In hegemonic patriarchal culture or male supremacist culture, one would expect to find the maintenance and reproduction of male advantage manifest itself in the enculturation of both males and females. Sexual modesty and beauty, two pillars of femininity which constitute central features in the self-identity of women, are examples of this. Both sexual modesty and beauty are male focussed attributes expressive of male interests. Although used by women to attain a modicum of influence over men, both beauty and sexual modesty are directed towards males and dependent upon male approval. Because of the nature of the feminine self-image, females find themselves more vulnerable than males, and thus react more strongly to threats of defilement. Being significantly less sensitive and less repelled by cultural "dirt" than females, men are positioned to employ, intentionally or unconsciously, defilement as a device in the legitimation and

management of their domination over women.

Everyday instances of this are commonplace, ranging from the seemingly benign situations in which men express behaviours considered "natural" for their gender, such as frequent spitting, flatulence, "grubbiness," and public genital self-manipulation, to the consumption of pornography and, most likely, sexual assault. These actions are all the more powerful because they are thought to be "natural" and beyond the realm of manipulated self-presentation. These acts of defilement are micropolitical acts which signal to females the supremacy of males. Women's sensitivity to the spoilation of their more vulnerable and fragile self-identities is taken as an indication of their weakness. One consequence is that females will attempt to forestall male "grossness" by acts of subservience towards males. Another, far more ironic consequence, is that women, because of the lower female threshold of repugnance coupled with their lowly power position, find themselves laboring as housewives and commercial cleaners in close association with dirt. Here we see little of the dirt tolerant male as the dirt sensitive female scrubs the toilet and cleans the dirt of others.

chapter

5

Socialization and Interaction

The selections in this chapter are concerned with issues of everyday life, of how we perceive the world and act upon our perceptions, while at the same time we are constrained by the world. The first question addressed in this chapter is how infants are transformed into human beings through a process called socialization. Some sociologists object to this depiction of socialization, arguing that the infant already possesses the full range of potentialities and socialization is a selection of some of these potentialities at the expense of others. Some would say that socialization in an unequal, exploitative society is a process of alienation whereby the infant is transformed from a naturally social and cooperative being to something competitive, a self-aggrandizing creature. Yet others, following Freud, would view socialization

as the never fully successful process of controlling and harnessing our nasty energies toward socially constructive activities.

Clearly, the meaning of socialization varies with the assumptions we make about the children undergoing the process. In the first selection, Anthony Synnott of Concordia University reviews the assumptions we make about children and holds these assumptions up for inspection. As he shows, our conception of children and childhood is neither fixed nor linear and that while the debates about the proper way to socialize children take many guises, underlying them all are fundamental disagreements about human nature.

The second selection by Esther Greenglass of York University is an excerpt from her book *A World of Difference.* It deals more concretely with one of the most important, if not the most fundamental, aspects of socialization: learning to be "male" or "female." She illustrates not only how we learn these traditional roles but also how they constrain us. And, the fact that Greenglass has been able to stand outside this process is, perhaps, an important illustration of a way, at least subjectively, out of such constraints.

The third selection, by Michael Petrunik of the University of Ottawa and Clifford Shearing of the Centre for Criminology, University of Toronto, builds on the work of George Herbert Mead to examine adult interaction. Their focus on the disrupted interaction of stutterers demonstrates two key principles of symbolic interactionism: first, that human interaction is creative work; and second, that while we often take for granted this work, it becomes visible when our interaction is problematic. In other words, we can learn a good deal about interaction by studying those instances in which it does not flow smoothly.

The final selection in this chapter, by Cheryl and Daniel Albas of the University of Manitoba, also looks at the work involved in social interaction. Their study of a situation familiar to most readers, the exam, shows how people do work to cope with and manage emotion. Their paper reminds us that there are social rules governing the experience and display of emotion and people develop creative strategies for interpreting and living up to these rules. Human interaction is always an accomplishment.

RELATED READINGS

Marion Pirie: "Women and the Illness Role: Rethinking Feminist Theory" (Chapter 4)
Roberta Hamilton: "Women, Wives and Mothers" (Chapter 6)
Susan Russell: "The Hidden Curriculum of School: Reproducing Gender and Class Hierarchies" (Chapter 12)
David Stymiest: "Ethnics and Indians" (Chapter 13)

LITTLE ANGELS, LITTLE DEVILS: A SOCIOLOGY OF CHILDREN

Anthony Synnott

"Our world is obsessed by the physical, moral and sexual problems of childhood," wrote Philippe Ariès in his well-known *Centuries of Childhood* (1962: 411). Obsessions may be too strong a word, but certainly concern is not new. Plato and Aristotle debated the subject of children at length.

In this paper, we shall explore some of the themes in the development of thinking about children and childhood from the early modern age to the present, not as fixed paradigms of childhood reflecting specific interests, but as a set of interrelated themes, each composed of residual, dominant and emergent elements. Certain elements appear, disappear and reappear over time — yesterday's residual elements may become dominant tomorrow to be succeeded by new, emergent elements and so on. We shall attempt to describe the variations and explain why they changed over time.

Laslett has cautioned that "We know very little indeed about child-nurture in pre-industrial times" (1965: 104), but we do know a little about what people thought about children in general, and their own children in particular.

Indeed, the early moderns regarded children in five conceptually distinct ways

Reprinted from *The Canadian Review of Sociology and Anthropology*, Volume 20:1, February, 1983. By permission of *The Canadian Review of Sociology and Anthropology* and the author.

or, to rephrase this, entertained five distinct beliefs about the nature of the child and, more broadly, about human nature itself (cf. Stone, 1977: 245 ff.).

Perhaps the most influential essayist of the Renaissance was Michel de Montaigne (1533-92). He discussed children in two interesting essays, and perhaps a few brief excerpts will give the flavour of his extremely important ideas. In one essay, "On the Affection of Fathers for Their Children," he discussed how to raise children: "I would try, by kindly dealings, to foster in my children a warm friendship and unfeigned good feeling towards myself; which from noble natures are not hard to win. But if they are savage brutes, such as our age produces in profusion, they must be loathed and shunned as such" (1979: 146).

This humanist believed that there are two kinds of children, some noble and some savage, some good and some evil, yet, on the whole, he believed in the former; his advice is for parents to treat their children openly and without violence. "I am open with my family, to the extent of my powers" (1978: 150), adding that "It is a very poor father that has no other hold on his children's affection than the need they have of his assistance — always supposing that this can be called affection at all. He should win their respect by his virtue and abilities, and their love by his goodness and sweetness of character" (1978: 141).

Unlike many who followed him in time (Locke, Calvin, Wesley, even Spock), Montaigne was opposed to violence: "I condemn all violence in the education of a tender soul" (1978: 142; cf. p. 72). And his essay "On the Education of Children" is a remarkable critique of the traditional, formal education system, which in many respects anticipated Montessori, Ivan Illich and A. S. Neill by almost 400 years; Montaigne's essays first appeared in 1580.

Montaigne's urbane, reasoned and almost modern views on children are in sharp contrast to those of the contemporary Calvinists, and then the Puritans, who regarded children as born with sin, prone to evil and requiring strict restraint, strong guidance and salutary punishment. Calvin (1535) remarked concerning children: "their whole nature is a certain seed of Sin, therefore it cannot but be hateful and abominable to God" (Muir and Brett, 1980: 3). And almost 100 years later the American Puritans Robert Cleaver and John Dod reiterated these views: "The young child . . . is altogether inclined to evil . . . Therefore parents . . . must correct and sharply reprove their children for saying or doing ill" (deMause, 1975: 316–17; cf. Gordon, 1978: 158–9).

This view of human nature and children's nature had clear political implications which were drawn by Thomas Hobbes in *Leviathan* (1651). His views on the nastiness of man in the state of nature and the necessity for strong government are well known. He was no Puritan but his perception of people by nature as "in that condition which is called Warre; and such a Warre, as is of every man, against every man . . ." was in line with the Puritan concept of children as, literally, "little devils." The Puritan view declined with Puritanism and, in England, this can be dated to the Restoration of the Stuarts (1660).

A third view was environmentalist: the child is a "tabula rasa," a blank slate that is neither good nor evil intrinsically. The idea can be traced back to Aristotle, who was cited as stating: "The soul of a child is like a clean slate on which nothing is written; on it you may write what you will" (Beekman, 1977: 20). John Early repeated this in 1628: "A child is a man in a small letter, yet the best copy of Adam before he tasted of Eve or the apple . . . His soul is yet a white paper unscribbled with observations of the world . . . he knows no evil" (quoted in Illick, ibid.: 317; and c.f. p. 342, fn. 75).

This view was popularized by John Locke in his book, *Some Thoughts Upon Education* (1693). Locke's most famous saying, repeated in his *Essay on Human Understanding* (1690), is that a child's mind is like "white paper, or wax, to be moulded and fashioned as one pleases." He suggests that "the difference to be found in the manners and abilities of men is owing more to their education than to anything else"; in his first paragraph he states: "I think I may say that, of all the men we meet with, nine parts of ten are what they are, good or evil, useful or not, by their education."

However, Locke was not a complete environmentalist. Even in the seventeenth century, the nature-nurture, genetic versus environmental determinism debate may be seen in embryonic form. Locke admits that "God has stamped certain characters upon men's minds . . . Everyone's natural genius should be carried as far as it could, but to attempt the putting another upon him, will be labour in vain" (paragraph 66).

This biological determinism had been briefly anticipated by Francis Bacon (1561–1626), Lord Chancellor under King James I, and a contemporary of Montaigne's. He rather disliked children, regarding them, like wives, as "hostages to fortune; for they are impediments to great enterprises" (1957: 12). He half practised what he preached for he was married, but childless. However, where Montaigne had described the "age" (i.e. environment) as producing noble or savage children, Bacon stresses forces outside human control: "A man's nature runs either to herbs or weeds; therefore let him seasonably water the one and destroy the other" (Bacon, 1957: 72). Thus, in Bacon's view biological or theological determinism (it is not clear which) is not complete, but may be modified.

The view that children's natures varied and were determined naturally (genetically, as we would say) or by divine will or by the stars also implies an element of fatalism. There was little or nothing that family or education (despite Locke) could do about it; and this view seemed to gain credence in the eighteenth century.

Lady Hervey (1744) explained that children "acquire arts but not qualities; the latter, whether good or bad, grow like their features; time enlarges but does not make them" (Stone, 1977: 255). A more direct statement came from Enos Hitchcock (1790) in the newly independent United States: "We must take children as they are, induced with a variety of humors, dispositions and propensities" (Beekman, 1977: 74). This was a far cry from Locke's "tabula rasa" theory of only 100 years before, or the rigid controlling ideas of the Puritans and Calvinists.

Finally, some believed that children, and indeed all human beings, are intrinsically good. This Romantic view had been broached during the Renaissance but was given widest currency by Jean-Jacques Rousseau in the middle of the eighteenth century, particulary in his most acclaimed work, *Emile* (1762). "God made all things good, man meddles with them and they become evil," was the opening sentence to that work (1969: 5). He attacked the views of the Puritans and the fundamentalists, observing that "there is no original sin in the human heart" (1969: 56). He turned Hobbes on his head, arguing that the origins of war and other evils lie in society, not in man; and he disagreed with Locke, Bacon and Montaigne on a number of points: "Use force with children and reasoning with men," he suggested (1969: 55) in a debate reminiscent of the on-going discussion about permissiveness and discipline.

Unfortunately, Rousseau was unable to practise what he preached and ended by dispatching his five children to an orphanage. Nonetheless, his ideas on children and education exercised considerable influence, particulary over the English Romantics in the nineteenth century. The belief that man is naturally good, free and equal was a powerful force in European and North American history, facilitating the American and French revolutions and reform in Britain.

Nonetheless, it was not unchallenged. There were, as we have seen, four other views about children circulating at the time. However, the principal contemporary challenge to Rousseau came from the Methodists, and a sermon of John Wesley's indicates that his ideas were close to Calvin's and the Puritans': "break the will if you would not damn the child . . . let a child from a year old be taught to fear the rod and cry softly . . . Let none persuade you it is cruelty not to do it. Break his will now and his soul will live" (Muir and Brett, 1980: 101).

William Wilberforce, the great abolitionist, states: "Remember that we are fallen creatures, born in sin and naturally depraved, Christianity recognizes no innocence or goodness of heart" (Thompson, 1968: 440). And Hannah More writes in 1799 that it is a "fundamental error to consider children as innocent beings" rather than as beings of "corrupt nature and evil dispositions" (Thompson, 1968: 440). These Puritan and Methodist views spanning two centuries hark back to the Biblical adage "He that spareth the rod, hateth his son" (Prov. 13: 24), more usually rendered in Butler's aphorism, "Spare the rod and spoil the child."

But both are a far cry from the words of Christ in the New Testament: "Verily I say unto you, except you be converted, and become as little children, ye shall not enter the kingdom of heaven" (Matt. 18: 3) and "Suffer the little children to come unto me, and forbid them not; for of such is the kingdom of God" (Mark 10: 14).

The early modern age, therefore, was not static and uniform but rich, varied, confusing and moving fast. And the conflicting ideologies of various ages — the humanism of Montaigne, the repressiveness (as we would see it) of Calvin, the Puritans and Wesley, the environmentalism of Locke, the genetic determinism of others, and the romanticism of Rousseau — not only stimu-

lated debate about the nature of children, and humanity generally, but also about the practices of raising children.

Perhaps the most important changes in the lives of children in the pre-industrial era were: the rise of education, with the school creating modern childhood (Ariès, 1962: 369); the increasing transfer of functions to the state (notably education) (Stone, 1974: 27); and the growth of what Stone calls "affective individualism" (Stone, 1977; 221 ff.). This brings us to the question of love; Ariès warns us that the pre-industrial family was an economic rather than a sentimental reality. "This did not mean that parents did not love their children, but they cared about them less for themselves . . . than for the contribution those children could make to the common task" (1962: 368). A delicate balance hesitated between the child as producer and consumer.

There was a constant awareness of death that must have affected love; both fertility and mortality rates were higher, so love was "spread around" more children, who were more likely to die. Emotional involvement was likely to have been less, simply out of self-protection, but such things are impossible to measure. Perhaps children, and adults, were not loved any less, but differently.

A medieval villager in Montaillou cries out when his only son dies: "I have lost all I had through the death of my son Raymond. I have no one left to work for me" (Ladurie, 1980: 210). A modern father would not speak like this, but, of course, the implications of the death of an only son would be different. The thirteenth-century villager, without a son, was probably condemned to poverty and an early death. Nor would a woman console a new mother like this seventeenth-century woman does: "Before they are old enough to bother you, you will have lost half of them, or perhaps all of them" (Ariès, 1962: 38).

Among the wealthy and the secure, the gentry and the squirearchy, however, such seemingly cold attitudes were not so common. We can see Henry VIII playing with his son Edward with "much mirth and joy, dallying with him in his arms a long space" (1538) (deMause, 1975: 240). Mme de Sevigné writes about her 18-month-old granddaughter in 1670: "I am very fond of her ... she does a hundred and one little things — she talks, fondles people, hits them, crosses herself, asks forgiveness, curtsies, kisses your hand, shrugs her shoulders, dances, coaxes, chucks you under the chin: in short she is altogether lovely" (deMause, 1975: 21).

Emotional attitudes varied, therefore, as did child-rearing practices. Swaddling clothes were being discarded, and babies were now dressed in looser clothes. As they grew older specific costumes were developed: children no longer dressed as miniature adults; mothers began to breast-feed their children instead of giving them to wet-nurses; control was maintained less by the rod and by breaking the will and more by sweet reason and sweet talk; formal distance between parents and children began to decline, as did a certain religious fatalism or acceptance of the Divine Will, to be replaced by a new practicality and eventually a scientific spirit. These gradually changing practices indicated gradually changing ideas about children. In sum, a world, or several worlds of childhood coexisted in the early modern period, with enormous variations by class and by philosophical or religious orientation.

Industrialization, in the conventional sociological wisdom, changed all this. The classical distinctions: Tonnies' Gemeinschaft-Gesellschaft typology and Redfield's folk-urban dichotomy emphasize the all-embracing impact of modernization on the family, specifically the shift from the extended family to the nuclear family. Neil Smelser states one consequence of mod-

ernization: "The direct control of elders and collateral kinsmen weakens. This marks in structural terms the differentiation of the nuclear family from the extended family" (1964: 263).

Yet, obvious as this may seem in traditional sociology, many scholars have recently come to question this simple cause-effect relation. Laslett, for instance, has argued that the change from the extended to the nuclear family was not caused by industrialization, for the nuclear family was typical of life in seventeenth-century England, and industrialization did not begin until the second half of the eighteenth century. The change in the family (if any) therefore preceded, and did not follow, industrialization (1972: 1–89, 137–9).

Sidney M. Greenfield, a sociologist, has pointed out that industrialization and the nuclear family are not necessarily related: the extended family has persisted in urbanized, industrial Brazil, Québec, England (parts) and Japan, while the nuclear family exists in Barbados without either industrialization or urbanization. He argues that New England was founded by, and on, the nuclear family before industrialization (Greenfield, 1961; Schulz and Wilson, 1973: 46–60). Anderson has even shown that the extended family was strengthened, not destroyed by industrialization in Lancashire (Anderson, 1975: 78–96).

Historians and sociologists may agree that childhood has changed, but while sociologists tend to favour dichotomous typologies, as Lee does, historians seem to emphasize that change has not been unilinear, has not been caused simply or primarily by modernization, and may proceed at different rates, in different directions, for different reasons, in different countries or parts of the country at different times.

Through industrialization and urbanization, modernization had tremendous, if varied, effects on children; many did not survive it. The infant mortality rate (0–1 year) soared from an English average in the second half of the seventeenth century of between 118 and 147 per thousand to a rate of about 250 per thousand in Sheffield in 1837–42. The child mortality rate (0–5) was at least 506 per thousand. The situation was similar in Manchester. And these figures, in Thompson's view, "underestimate – and perhaps seriously underestimate – the actual child mortality rate" since they probably exclude deaths among the unregistered immigrant populations (de-Mause, 1975: 305; Thompson, 1968: 316).

These figures are averages only; a House of Commons Select Committee on the Protection of Infant Life reported as late as 1871 that the infant death rate in "baby farms" in large towns was "70, 80 and even 90 per cent" (1871: 610). This was attributed mostly to carelessness, but sometimes to criminal intent. Infanticide was not uncommon. The committee reported that 276 children, mostly under a week old, had been found dead in London in 1870, with another 105 up to 19 May 1871 (1871: 610).

Urban working class life was difficult for children and adults, and perhaps no one documented this better than Henry Mayhew, who anticipated Studs Terkel and oral history by 100 years. He interviewed one fourteen-year-old lad — a "mud-lark" for three years:

He worked every day, with 20 or 30 boys, who might all be seen at day-break with their trowsers tucked up, groping about, and picking out the pieces of coal from the mud on the banks of the Thames. He went into the river up to his knees, and in searching the mud he often ran pieces of glass and long nails into his feet. When this was the case he went home and dressed the wounds, but returned to the river-side directly, "for should the tide come up," he added, "without my having found something, why I must starve till next low tide." In the very cold weather he and his other shoeless companions used to stand in the hot water that ran down the river side from some of the steam-factories, to warm their frozen feet (Mayhew, 1968, vol. 3: 357).

It was quite normal for the young lads to soon turn to crime, their sisters to prostitution.

Industrialization also had a tremendous impact on children's lives. Children's labour was not new but the *conditions* of labour were new. Conditions in the British coal mines, the cotton mills and factories were appalling. Investigation after investigation, Blue Book after Blue Book documented atrocities of child labour and, as we shall see, ultimately generated a romantic reaction to capitalist reality. Yet reform was slow: the first Factory Act (1833) prohibited labour, but only for children under six; children under ten years were not permitted to work more than sixteen hours a day.

The situation was similar in the United States and British North America, although there was considerable regional variation. The New England Workingmen's Association declared in 1833 that "children should not be allowed to labor in the factories from morning till night without any time for healthy recreation and mental culture." The first child labour law was passed in Massachusetts (1842) limiting the number of working hours to ten for children under twelve; like much other legislation, however, it was more a statement of principle than reality for it contained the qualifier that only manufacturers who "knowingly" employed such children were to be fined (Lumpkin and Douglas, 1937: 247–8; cf. also Kaestle and Vinovskis, in Harevan, 1978: 138–9). Furthermore, slavery was not abolished in the U.S. until 1865.

Manufacturers in the days of high capitalism tended to regard children without romance or sentimentality as grist for the proverbial mill, i.e. as *young adults*; even into the 1920s some protested that they were against exploitation (which they presumably defined differently from the labour unions and the reformers): "We join in the condemnation of the exploitation of children . . . and we insist that our growing youth shall be taught the dignity, duty and necessity of labour" (National Association of Manufacturers, 1924). "The Savior has said, 'My Father worketh hitherto, and I work' ... May not the child follow the footsteps of the Savior in this?" (Lawyer, 1924; Lumpkin and Douglas, 1937: 219).

And yet, at the same time as the children of the industrial and agricultural proletariat died in North America and Western Europe, the middle classes of the Victorian era were building nests for their children. Mrs Beeton, a popular advisor of the time, could write: "It ought ... to enter the domestic policy of every parent to make her child feel that home is the happiest place in the world; that to imbue them with this precious home-feeling is one of the choicest gifts a parent can bestow" (quoted by Robertson, in deMause, 1975: 413). Her contemporary Mrs Ellis informed mothers in 1844 that the best preparation possible for the realities and hardships of life was a happy childhood (deMause, 1975: 413).

This was the Golden Age of Victorian childhood (for the middle class); childhood was the age of innocence. The child was idealized as pure, trusting and carefree. The child was a little angel, despite Calvin, and was epitomized by the famous advertisement for Pears Soap, "Bubbles." Wordsworth's "Ode on Intimations of Immortality" captured the spirit of this innocent angel:

Not in entire forgetfulness,
And not in utter nakedness,
But trailing clouds of glory do we come
From God, who is our home:
Heaven lies about us in infancy!

The idealized child of the Romantics and of Victorian sentimentality arose like Tiny Tim, Oliver Twist, Little Nell and Pip from the debris of industrial labour. The Golden Age of Innocence and child labour, however, go ill together, and a contemporary of Queen Victoria and Charles Dickens, Karl Marx, observed in *The Communist Manifesto* (1848): "Society as a whole is more and more splitting up into two great hostile camps, Bourgeoisie and Proletariat," Bubbles and Tiny Tim.

The exploitation of child labour and the related sentimentality of the Romantics were two of the most salient features of childhood in the nineteenth century; in the second half of the century, Charles Darwin published, successively, *On the Origin of Man* (1859) and *The Descent of Man* (1871), which, although bitterly contested on theological grounds, soon transformed contemporary thought about humanity and, of course, children. To put it simply, perhaps too simply: Victorians had three perspectives on children — little workers, little angels and little animals, especially little monkeys (still a favourite phrase today) — depending on whether they were high capitalists, Romantics, or scientists.

The Victorian age ended with the death of the old Queen in 1901; and much of what the age symbolized died with her or on the battlefields of World War I. A new world of childhood dawned with the new century. Certainly Freud tolled the death-knell on the ideology of childhood as innocence; little angels do not have Oedipus or Electra complexes; nor do they pass through successively oral, anal, and phallic phases of psycho-sexual development, with both sadistic and masochistic impulses! Freud's attitude to childhood, like Darwin's was unsentimental, and clinical. He introduced entirely new ways of regarding children and if Wordsworth cannot be mistaken for Calvin, nor can Freud.

Both sexes seem to pass through the early phase of libidinal development in the same manner. It might have been expected that in girls there would already have been some lag in aggressiveness in the sadisticanal phase, but such is not the case. Analysis of children's play has shown our women analysts that the aggressive impulses of little girls leave nothing to be desired in the way of abundance and violence. With their entry into the phallic phase the differences between the sexes are

*completely eclipsed by their agreements. We
are now obliged to recognize that the little girl
is a little man (Freud, 1977: 151).*

Little girls as aggressive, violent and,
anal-sadistic and, even, little men! Calvin
and Wesley might have recognized their
agressiveness, and described it as sin-
fulness, and Hobbes would have felt vindi-
cated; but none would have understood the
sex change. And this was just the tip of the
iceberg, to embrace an appropriate image.
Freud's discussion of masturbation, castra-
tion complexes, erotogenic zones, and
penis-equivalents in children created a totally different view of childhood. Psychoanalytic theory, which has had such an
impact on contemporary world views, was
not the world of Bubbles or Tiny Tim or
Emile. Thanks to Darwin and Freud, rather
than to industrialization, I would suggest,
the Victorian little angels became more like
little sex-maniacs — devils, but not devils
in the Calvinistic mode. Furthermore, in
stressing the importance of the first three
years of life, Freud reversed the traditional
view of aging. Locke had argued that a person is 90 per cent the product of education;
Freud suggested people were principally
the product of their first three years. Children were therefore no longer "only" mini-
adults, to be seen and not heard. Adults
were now "only" children grown older,
merely *consequences* of their childhood.

Nonetheless, despite the impact of evolutionary and psychoanalytic theory in the
nineteenth century, the later studies by sociologists and anthropologists on the socialization of children demonstrate that
childhood in twentieth-century Western
society is neither homogeneous nor static;
nor is the thinking about childhood. Beekman (1977) and Stendler (1950) have reviewed the advice given to parents on how
to bring up children, and have shown the
dramatic changes in advice over the century. After analyzing articles in such middle-class magazines as the *Ladies Home*

Journal, Women's Home Companion and
Good Housekeeping, Stendler concluded
that:

*Three different schools of thought have
prevailed with regard to how children should
be raised. The 1890s and 1900s saw a highly
sentimental approach to child rearing; 1910
through the 1930s witnessed a rigid
disciplinary approach; the 1940s have
emphasized self regulation and understanding
of the child. These sixty years have also seen a
swing from emphasis on character
development to emphasis on personality
development (quoted in Gordon, 1978: 150).*

Each age seems to instruct its parents
differently, and to hold different beliefs
about children. Reacting, perhaps, against
the sentimentality of a Dickens or a Mrs
Beeton in Britain, or the "romance" of Tom
Sawyer and Huckleberry Finn in the U.S.,
the experts advised discipline and regularity in the 1920s. A typical work from
1921 states:

*If a young mother were to ask me what I
consider the keynote of successful baby
training, I should say, without hesitation,
regularity.*
   *This means regularity in everything, eating,
sleeping, bathing, bowel habits, and exercise.
Each event in a baby's daily life should take
place at exactly the same hour by the clock
until the habit is established.*
   *It is possible to train the baby to be an
efficient little machine, and the more nearly
perfect we make the running of this machine,
the more wonderful will be the results
achieved and the less trouble it will be for the
mother (quoted in Beekman, 1977: 109–10;
emphasis added).*

This mechanistic view of the child not
only ignored or denied the possibility of
variability, which Locke had commented
on so much earlier, but also made the
mother's needs paramount over the
child's.

The most popular book on child care for
years was Dr Luther Emmelt Holt's *The*

Care and Feeding of Children, first published in 1894 and re-issued dozens of times, even after his death, until 1943. Holt's attention was directed principally to the technical or "mechanical" aspects of child care — nutrition, formulas, schedules, hours of sleep, bowel movements and so on. Physiology and routine were all. Emotional involvement was to be minimal: "Babies under six months old should never be played with, and the less of it at any time the better." Holt also recommended: "Never give a child what it cries for; let the child 'cry out' and *break* the habit" (Beekman, 1977: 116, 117). The idea of breaking takes us back to Calvin and Wesley.

Holt's ideas and beliefs were challenged by a behavioural psychologist, John B. Watson, who published *Psychological Care of Infant and Child* in 1928. The shift in emphasis from physiology to psychology is evident in the first two paragraphs of his book:

Ever since my first glimpse of Dr Holt's The Care and Feeding of Children, I hoped some day to be able to write a book on the psychological care of the infant. I believed then that psychological care was just as necessary as physiological care. Today I believe that it is in some ways more important. Healthy babies do grow up under the most varied forms of feeding and bodily care. They can be stunted by poor food and ill health and then in a few days of proper regimen be made to pick up their weight and bodily strength.

But once a child's character has been spoiled by bad handling which can be done in a few days, who can say that the damage is ever repaired? (quoted in Beekman, 1977: 147).

But equally evident and more ominous is the idea that the child is a problem — the threat of irreparable damage to the child due to "bad handling" is absolutely clear. The age of the expert, with all of his sanctions, has arrived. Indeed, Watson makes the astounding statement: "No one today knows enough to raise a baby." The implication, "except me," is obvious. He continues:

Give me a dozen healthy infants, well-formed, and my own specified world to bring him up in and I'll guarantee to take any one at random and train him to become any type of specialist I might select — into a doctor, lawyer, artist, merchant-chief, and yes, even into beggar-man and thief, regardless of his talents, penchants, tendencies, abilities, vocations and race of ancestors (quoted in Beekman, 1977: 146).

Such promises were very American congruent not only with Locke's "tabula rasa" theory, but also with democratic egalitarian theory, with the Horatio Alger myth and the Dale Carnegie ethic, although it was not the individual working virtuously for himself who achieved, but the parent who achieved for the children. "Treat them as though they were young adults," he advised, "never hug and kiss them, never let them sit in your lap. If you must, kiss them once on the forehead when they say good night. Shake hands with them in the morning" (Beekman, 1977: 151).

Watsons emphasis on training, discipline and the minimum of emotional involvement — childhood as apprenticeship — was challenged by various doctors who focused increasingly on the needs of the child. None was more popular than Dr Spock's *Baby and Child Care*, first published in 1946. It was comprehensive, inexpensive, well-written and began reassuringly: "Trust yourself, You know more than you think you do" (1958: 15). Precisely the opposite of Watson, it showed that much had changed in only thirty years.

The fact that the dominant ideas in the middle class have changed over time does not necessarily mean that practice has changed equally, still less that family practices and the roles of children conform to the advice given. John and Elizabeth Newson conducted interviews in the 1950s with over 700 mothers in Nottingham, England, dealing with their manner of raising children; they found an enormous range of attitudes, and behaviour, both by class and within class, with respect to weaning, spanking, sleeping patterns, toilet training, coping with temper tantrums, breast-feeding, permissiveness, the father's role and so on (1965).

The Newsons, however, only interviewed parents. Devereux, Bronfenbrenner and Rodgers surveyed children themselves in an extensive international comparison. Questions about fourteen aspects of parental behaviour were asked of 741 English children and 968 American children in matched samples. On ten of these items the differences were significant. While these findings should be taken as indicative rather than conclusive, they are generally supported by other studies. Curiously, Harriet Martineau, an Englishwoman who visited the United States, described some of these same differences in 1837 — a hint that practices have changed very little, despite increased industrialization, Queen Victoria, Darwin and Freud (in Larson, 1976: 241–610).

Childhood in the eighties may differ again from the fifties or even the sixties; most of us would agree that the difference is not only quantitative but qualitative as well. The innocence is shot. The "romance," as the Victorians would have said, has disappeared.

The lead article in *Homemakers' Magazine*, in a special issue to commemorate the Year of the Child, asks the extraordinary questions: "Why do we continue to fail children? Who listens to what the child has to say?" (Morris, 1979: 8). Even allowing for journalistic exaggeration and alarmism, these questions seem to indicate an amazing self-doubt, lack of self-confidence, and guilt. It is not just childhood that has changed; so has parenthood.

The lead article in a recent *New York Times* describes contemporary children as "children without childhood," arguing that children are now, in many ways, little

adults, far more politically and emotionally aware than we, or their parents, ever were at their age (Winn, 1981). Such articles would have been impossible twenty years ago.

A symbol of the new child, or the new loss of childhood, is perhaps Brooke Shields. A high school student who earns more than the president of the United States, she has recently appeared on the cover of *Time*, has featured in nine films, played a twelve-year-old prostitute when she was twelve, has worked for sixteen years, and is now sixteen. Brooke Shields is not, of course, a typical sixteen-year-old, but ten years ago she would have been impossible. Eileen Ford, head of the world's largest modelling agency, says of Shields: "She is a professional child and unique. She looks like an adult and thinks like one" (*Time*, 9 February 1981). There have been child stars before, like Shirley Temple; the earlier star was marketing innocence, however, while Brooke Shields is selling sexuality. And Shields is not alone. Jodie Foster played a child prostitute in *Taxi Driver* and a murdering nymphet in *The Little Girl Who Lives Down the Lane*. Kristy McNichol and Tatum O'Neal race to lose their virginity in *Little Darlings* and Tatum O'Neal tries to seduce Richard Burton in *A Circle of Two*.

Pretty babies become cover girls; prepubescent girls become sex symbols, and while parents and school boards debate sex education in schools, their children identify with their "active" peers. Child sex is no longer taboo, at least in the movies. Kiddie porn magazines abound; pedophiliac organizations are springing up, the slogan of one being "sex before 8, or else it's too late" (*Time*, 7 September 1981).

Children are being "sexualized" younger; adults are being socialized to children's sexuality. Children are the last sexual frontier and the barriers are coming down — the taboos are being broken on the screen daily. The parents consent, indeed compete; the media, the fashion magazines, the garment industry (Calvin Klein jeans), the advertising industry cooperate in this redefinition of children as adults. Kids have money.

It is too early to see the consequences; crimes *by* children and crimes *against* children appear to be increasing, although this is not entirely the result of the sexualization process. However, the mass sex killings of *children* in Atlanta and British Columbia are a new phenomenon. The spillover of child sex and child violence from media fantasy to reality should be expected. Children are becoming sex objects — fair game and therefore potentially victims. One should not over-estimate the media-hype, nor should one under-estimate it. Brooke Shields is not typical, but there is a broad pattern of factors that affect the contemporary world of childhood.

Much has changed even since the fifties. Enid Blyton and the Hardy Boys are light years away from Judy Blume and Norma Klein; Anne of Green Gables bears no resemblance to twelve-year-old *Lolita* (1956); the Mad Hatter has been transformed into the satirical *Mad Magazine*. Television has exposed children of all ages not only to children's programs but also, and perhaps principally, to the adult worlds of soap operas, documentaries on famine, war, energy crises and scandals, and adult fantasy worlds of explicit sex and violence, for hours at a time. In this sense, therefore, children are being socialized into an adult world prematurely.

Children's values and the structure of childhood have changed and so, naturally enough, have ideas about children. More couples want no children, and many want fewer children than they did in the past. The birthrate has fallen dramatically in the last 100 years and roughly halved since the baby boom of the fifties in North America, to below replacement level. The abortion rate has increased steadily, doubling in the U.S. from 1973–9 (*Time*, 6 April 1981).

Children are now being seen, perhaps for the first time in history, as unnecessary, both economically and psychologically. They are regarded as expensive luxuries, or as hindrances to personal growth and career development, especially for women. (Shades of Bacon!) Indeed, Pogrebin refers to "the *flight* from motherhood" (1981: 143; emphasis in original). Even those who do have children are, like children themselves, under fire. Bronfenbrenner describes the major change in the family crisply: "Children used to be brought up by their parents" (1972: 95). Now schools, television, peer-groups, baby-sitters, and day-care centres more often do the job. Christopher Lasch argues that children are no longer the centre of the family: with the "me" generation, parents no longer sacrifice themselves for their children, but sacrifice children for themselves (1979). Margaret Mead states firmly that "we have become a society who neglect our children, are afraid of our children, find children surplus instead of the raison d'être of living" (Gross and Gross, 1977: 154).

The pathology of childhood perhaps confirms these definitions of children as, increasingly, a social problem. Child homicide and suicide rates, alcoholism, crime rates, and abortion rates are all rising. Child abuse is prevalent. A grim picture of childhood as violent, unhappy and self-destructive is emerging — perhaps not accurate for all, but accurate for many and, more to the point, becoming increasingly prevalent.

In sum, ideas about children and childhood are quite confused today. Children's liberationists claim that children have no rights, and some say that they never had it so bad (Gross and Gross, 1977). Others say children have never had it so good, with too many rights and not enough duties and responsibilities (the Tough Love Movement). Some describe children as bereft of childhood (Winn, 1981); others observe that children lack parents (Bronfenbrenner, 1972; Lasch, 1979). Some identify children as a social problem; others identify parents as the problem, one that is causal in nature. Still others identify other factors. However, despite the contradictions, there is very clearly a new trend emerging: the belief that children are not necessary, either psychologically or socially, and that they are an increasing social problem. It is not a happy perspective.

Historically, there has been little consensus. Both ideologically and structurally, many worlds of childhood have been constructed, and many theories developed. Locke's theory of children as a "tabula rasa" contrasts strikingly with the beliefs of such contemporary fundamentalists as Calvin and, later, Wesley, who viewed the child as a little devil. The interests of high capitalists in children as little workers evoked the Romantics' description of children as little angels. Each construction of the nature of children (and, implicitly, humanity) may imply radically different theories of education, social control, politics and so on.

Darwin's theory of evolution and Freud's theories of psycho-sexual development not only contradicted the Romantic view but added new and startling dimensions of thought — children as little animals and children as rampant ids. But not everyone changed their ideas. Durkheim entertained a sponge-theory of childhood, not far removed from Locke's "tabula rasa":

The child is naturally in a state of passivity quite comparable to that in which the hypnotic subject is found artificially placed. His mind yet contains only a small number of conceptions able to fight against those which are suggested to him; his will is still rudimentary. Therefore he is very suggestible (1965: 87).

On the other hand, Maria Montessori states that "children are human beings to whom respect is due, *superior* to us by reason of their 'innocence' and of the greater possibilities of the future" (1965: 133; emphasis added). And she even compares the child to the child Jesus (1975: 67 ff.).

Not everyone agreed with Montessori: Dr Edward Glover, the distinguished British psychoanalyst, stated in 1922 that the normal baby is "a born criminal" (Montagu, 1981: 118).

Expressing these technical discoveries in social terms we can say that the perfectly normal infant is almost completely egocentric, greedy, dirty, violent in temper, destructive in habit, profoundly sexual in purpose, aggrandizing in attitude, devoid of all but the most primitive reality sense, without conscience of moral feeling, whose attitude to society (as represented by the family) is opportunist, inconsiderate, domineering and sadistic. And when we come to consider the criminal type labeled psychopathic it will be apparent that many of these characteristics can under certain circumstances persist into adult life. In fact, judged by adult standards the normal baby is for all practical purposes a born criminal.

This view is perhaps a logical development from Freud's ideas, and is not far removed from the Puritan and Calvinist views of the child as a born sinner, although Glover's context is secular. But it is exactly the opposite of the Victorian view of the child as innocent, and Montessori's view of the child as superior. Glover's view co-existed with those of other experts in the twenties who compared the child to a little machine, insisting that "bad habits" be broken (a phrase reminiscent of the fundamentalists 250 years before who insisted that the child's "spirit" should be broken). Watson even said that children should be regarded as little adults (Beekman, 1977: 151). Contradictions abound. Of course, children could also be regarded as sponges, clean slates, little angels, little devils, little monkeys, unrestrained ids or like the child Jesus. Romance, however, is not yet dead. Recall the Lord Mayor of London's remark when he heard that Lady Diana was pregnant: "Babies are bits of Stardust blown from the hands of God" (*Gazette*, 6 November 1981). Calvin, Wesley, Darwin and Freud would have shuddered.

Surely these constructions of childhood tell us more about the constructors than they do about childhood. Childhood is not given; it is not a "natural" category. There are no natural categories, only social categories with different meanings imposed and developed by every age, and by different populations within every age. Educators, doctors, sociologists, religious leaders, parents, and philosophers have all put forward their ideas; no doubt it is trite to remark that none are likely to possess the truth, the whole truth and nothing but the truth about childhood, or more broadly, humanity. Nonetheless, it is perhaps instructive to consider the scope and range of the views, the implications of these views for praxis and some explanations for the variations. The emphasis on the range of historical perspectives should not blind us, however, to the range of our own personal and changing ideas, as John Wilmot, Earl of Rochester (1647–1680) so aptly commented: "Before I got married, I had six theories about bringing up children; now I have six children and no theories" (Muir and Brett, 1980: 99).

SOCIALIZATION OF GIRLS AND BOYS: HOW GENDER ROLES ARE ACQUIRED

Esther Greenglass

A person's gender role is a significant social fact. It is important because it has predictable consequences, not only for the individual, but also for the individual's re-

From *A World of Difference: Gender Roles in Perspective* by Esther Greenglass. By permission of John Wiley & Sons Canada.

lationships with others. Gender roles are so tightly woven into the fabric of society that no individual's development is free from their influence. In view of their importance — both psychologically and socially — it is relevant to raise certain questions about their development. For example, at what stage are gender roles acquired and what are the processes involved in their acquisition? What is the nature of these roles?

In the acquisition of gender roles, socialization is a key concept. As used here, socialization refers to the process by which an individual acquires the attitudes, language, norms, and values necessary to function in a given society. It also involves continuous learning to perform various social roles throughout one's lifetime. Gender-role socialization refers to the processes by which an individual acquires the behaviours, attitudes, values, emotional responses, and personality characteristics defined as appropriate for his or her gender role. These vary from one culture to another.

As Margaret Mead (1935) has demonstrated in her now-classic study of three New Guinea tribes, there may be marked differences in the specific behaviours and personality characteristics ascribed to males and females in different cultures. Among the Arapesh, for example, one of the cultures she describes, both males and females are socialized (and expected) to be loving, caring, gentle, nurturant, responsive, co-operative, and willing to subordinate themselves to the needs of others. Therefore, the personality characteristics that are inculcated in members of the Arapesh society are those defined as "feminine" traits in North America. Compare this culture with another New Guinea tribe, the Mundugumor, or headhunters, who expect their women and men to be aggressive, not nurturant. Additional predominant personality characteristics among these people are hostility, hatred, and suspicion. In a third culture, the Tchambuli, the women are typically dominant, impersonal, and managing, and the men are usually less responsible and more emotionally dependent — something of a reversal of stereotypes associated with the roles assigned to women and men in North American society. Aside from demonstrating the malleability of the human personality, Mead's study provides evidence that environmental (socialization) factors carry more weight than biological ones in determining what characteristics are considered to be masculine and feminine. Through the processes of selective reinforcement, personality can be shaped during socialization to conform to the expectations of a society's members. The demonstration of the importance of environmental factors as contributors to the shaping of personality does not, of course, rule out the influence of biological factors whose contribution to personality may not always be immediately obvious.

While Mead's study has been repeatedly cited as evidence of the plasticity of human personality and behaviour, other research findings dispute her results. For example, one investigator (Fortune, 1939) has argued that even among the Arapesh, it is the male who not only retained ultimate power in that society, but who also was solely responsible for organizing collective aggressive activity, including waging war. The same investigator has disputed Mead's original findings that similar gender roles existed for women and men among the Arapesh.

Cross-cultural studies of gender roles can be very informative. Despite the tendency of most cultures to make their own definitions of gender-role-appropriate behaviour, there are some regularities in the definition of gender roles among various cultures. For example, most societies organize their social institutions around men and, as was discussed earlier, men in most cultures tend to behave more aggressively and to have greater authority than women. In many cultures, the division of labour falls along gender-role lines: men are most often assigned the physically strenuous and dangerous tasks, and they are often required to travel long distances from home to their various tasks. Women usually carry out domestic routines, look after the children, and minister to the needs of others. In most societies, cross-cultural regularities also exist in the personalities of boys and girls: while boys tend to engage in conflict and overt, observable aggression, girls are more frequently found to be affectionate, co-operative, responsive, and sociable (D'Andrade, 1966).

These cross-cultural regularities in behaviour may be partly the result of biological differences between females and males. For example, it is usually the male who possesses the potential for greater physical strength. The biological facts that only females can give birth and nurse the young caused females (in many societies) to remain close to home, at least while their offspring were young. Of course, while it is true that only the female can give birth to the young, even a nursing mother need not stay close to home all the time today. The combination of breast and bottle (to provide food while the mother is away from the infant during the day) can work remarkably well should the mother wish to return to her employment shortly after she gives birth. Within only a few weeks, the breasts adjust their milk supply to the needs of the mother-baby couple.

However, there are cultures, such as that of the Tchambuli, where the usual gender-role assignments do not apply or may even be reversed. And in many cultures, including our own, there are "normal" individuals who possess traits most commonly ascribed to another gender role than their own. Depending on factors in the person's environment, including others' expectations regarding gender-role-appropriate behaviour, personality can be shaped to develop in any of several directions.

An individual develops a gender role not within a vacuum, but within a dynamic social system which exerts a powerful influence on the direction that development takes. In order to get a comprehensive picture of how individuals acquire their gender roles, it is important to understand the influence of various social institutions, social forces, and groups of various kinds that make up this social system. These various influences gradually shape appropriate gender-role behaviour through the systematic application of positive and negative sanctions. While the influence of the social system is lifelong, much of our discussion of gender-role socialization will focus on the individual's early years (up to adolescence), since gender-role identity develops in the early years and stays with the individual throughout life. In this regard, the family must be viewed as one of the most significant agents of gender-role socialization.

The Family as an Agent of Gender-Role Socialization

It is in the family that society's expectations of gender-role-appropriate behaviour, as mediated by the parents, are first impressed upon the child. The child depends on its parents over a relatively long period not only for the satisfaction of its basic needs, such as food and shelter, but also for the fulfillment of its psychological needs, including the needs for acceptance and approval. This results in the parents being invested with an unparalleled amount of power. They control virtually all the child's resources, at least in early life. The parents' possession of such power over the child's material and psychological resources renders it relatively easy for them to shape their children's behaviour in the direction

of their expectations, including those relating to gender-role-appropriate behaviour. And parents have certain preconceived ideas of how males and females should think, behave, and be. Based on social stereotypes, these ideas frequently act as guides for the parents' behaviour when they are interacting with their developing children. Parents also serve as role models for their children. Through their teaching and their examples, parents are preparing their children for the roles which they think the children will enact as adults. The discussion of the family as an agent of socialization will focus on the parents as role models, parent-child interactions, and the influence of toys and activities designated as appropriate for girls or boys.

PARENTS' SEX PREFERENCE

Long before the child's birth, parents start to discuss their preference for a girl or a boy, and frequently they discuss possible names for the child. "Pregnant couples" delight in predicting the sex of the child on the basis of such things as how high the woman is carrying and how hard the foetus is kicking. If, in the last trimester of pregnancy, the foetus is active, kicking, and moving a great deal, mothers have been reported to interpret these as signs that the child was a male (Sontag et al, 1969). But the wish to be surprised by the sex of the child when it is born is so strong in some couples that even when they can be informed of its sex beforehand by a procedure called amniocentesis, many couples choose not to be told. Amniocentesis involves withdrawing some amniotic fluid, which contains cells cast off from the foetus. The cells of the amniotic fluid are cultured and analyzed, and the resulting chromosomal study allows prenatal diagnosis of various chromosomal defects associated with the foetus, including Down's syndrome (also known as mongolism), which results in some degree of mental retardation. The child's sex is also evident from the arranged set of chromosomes.

At birth, the most dominant characteristic used to describe the baby is its sex. While some birth announcements provide information on other physical characteristics of the infant (such as its weight) virtually all of them announce whether "it's a boy!" or "it's a girl!". Even before the child is born and certainly afterwards, parents, friends, and the social community are labelling and then responding to the child in a sex-differentiated fashion.

Parents do not want boys and girls to the same extent. Prospective parents tend to prefer boys, although this trend is less frequent now than it was in the past. In an American national-sample study reported in 1977, over 1500 married women under 40 and 25% of their husbands were asked whether they wanted to have boys or girls (Hoffman, 1977). While most wanted children of either sex, the preference was still clearly for boys. Almost twice as many of the women preferred boys as preferred girls, and three to four times as many men preferred boys to girls. In the same study, prospective parents were asked why they wanted a boy or a girl. This type of question should yield information on the kinds of expectations people have for a son and a daughter. Some of the reasons given by the women for wanting a boy were to please their husbands, to carry on the family name (the husband's family name), and to be a companion to their husbands. Women wanted a girl in order to have a companion for themselves, and many of them said it would be fun to dress up a girl. They also said that girls are easier to raise, they are more obedient, and girls can help with the housework and the care of other children. Many agreed that girls stay closer to their parents and are sweeter and cuter. In view of prospective parents' preference for boys, as well as their different expectations

for male and female children, it should not be surprising to learn that parents treat boys and girls differently.

BABIES

All babies cry. This is a fact that can be verified by asking parents anywhere in the world. But how do people interpret crying behaviour? There is reason to believe that people may interpret a baby's crying differently depending on whether the baby is a boy or a girl. In one study (Condry and Condry, 1976), for example, a videotape of a nine-month-old crying baby was observed by a group of people, some of whom were led to believe it was a boy, while others were told it was a girl. The baby was videotaped reacting to a series of four stimuli: a teddy bear, a jack-in-the-box, a doll, and a buzzer. The results were that people attributed the baby's crying to different causes, depending on what they perceived was the sex of the baby. When the baby cried, the observers who thought it was a boy said that the baby was angry; those who thought it was a girl said that the baby was afraid. These impressions have important implications for how people would have treated the baby. Those who thought the baby was afraid, would have been more likely to hold and cuddle it than those who thought the baby was angry. In the latter case, people would likely have tried to restrain, discipline, or ignore the baby, rather than comfort it.

This raises the question of how parents view the behaviour of their male and female infants. Research suggests that as early as the infant's first day of life, parents tend to perceive their male and female babies in stereotyped ways. In one study (Rubin et al, 1974), 30 sets of parents of newborns were asked to describe their infants. The daughters were described more often as little, beautiful, cute, weak, delicate, and as resembling their mother. Sons were described more often as firmer, larger-featured, better co-ordinated, more alert, stronger, and hardier. It is important to note, however, that because the male and female babies were equal in body dimensions and activity level, the actual viewing and holding of the babies could not have produced such different descriptions. This study illustrates well how preconceived gender-role stereotypes lead to different kinds of descriptions of male and female babies.

Do parents treat male and female infants differently? Research has shown that, in some ways, they do. For example, parents tend to play more roughly and vigorously with their infant sons than with their infant daughters. In other words, both mothers and fathers seek to elicit gross motor behaviour more in their sons than in their daughters. It would seem, then, that parents perceive their infant sons as sturdier or more able to withstand rough treatment than their infant daughters. The evidence, however, supports the opposite conclusion. Female neonates have been found to be physiologically more mature and more resistant to disease and injury (Garai and Scheinfeld, 1968). Nevertheless, people, parents included, seem to persist in the belief that infant girls are more fragile. This assumption appears to extend beyond infancy into early childhood when parents of toddlers have been reported to be more apprehensive about their daughters' physical well-being (Minton et al, 1971). From these observations, it does appear that parents' treatment of their female and male offspring is affected to some extent by cultural stereotypes or beliefs as to what girls and boys are supposed to be. It is interesting to note that differential parental behaviour toward sons and daughters has been recorded so early in the child's life.

For years psychologists and nonprofessionals alike have held the belief that parents talk to their daughters more than to their sons, beginning in infancy. It has been further assumed that, having received more verbal stimulation, girls' verbal development is more rapid during the early years. Recent evidence does not clearly support either of these beliefs, however. In Maccoby and Jacklin's (1974) review of 22 studies which recorded parent-child verbal interaction, mainly with babies and preschoolers, no differences were found in either the kind or the amount of parents' vocalization to daughters and sons. As with vocalization, there is no clear-cut differential treatment of infant sons and daughters when parental warmth and nurturance are examined. Sometimes mothers are reported holding their three-month-old infant sons more (Lewis, 1972); but others have found that mothers touch their six-month-old daughters more frequently (Goldberg and Lewis, 1969). Maccoby and Jacklin examined nine observational studies involving mainly mothers and babies or small children. They found no sex differences in six of these studies in affectionate contact. Measures that were used include smiling, rocking, holding, and touching the child. In infancy, then, there does not appear to be any difference in parental warmth expressed toward children of the two sexes.

There are few consistent differences in the way parents treat their infant sons and daughters. One of the reasons more differences have not been found is that at this early stage, infants seem to be treated more as babies than as boys and girls. There are, after all, limitations to what parents are able to do with infants, simply because of their physical and intellectual immaturity. Parental handling at this early stage would centre more around basic caretaking activities and include some limited forms of play. As the child develops language skills and greater mobility, and asserts its independence more, parents and other caretakers find that they have to exert more control over the child, frequently for the child's safety. Consequently, as the child develops, its changing forms of behaviour often serve as cues to the parents who, in turn, must respond in an appropriate fashion. What is more, there are fairly clear-cut stereotypes regarding the behaviour parents expect in their male and female children. Throughout the child's development, these stereotypes appear to become increasingly salient as determinants of parental behaviour toward children.

CHILDHOOD

Boys' and Girls' Rooms: Is There Any Difference?

In their efforts to assess how parents view and treat their developing youngsters, the majority of investigators use standard techniques of assessment, which include questionnaires, interviews, and observations of the parent and child interacting. Another, rather novel technique of assessing parental attitudes toward male and female children consists of looking at the furnishings and contents of the rooms parents provide their children. How parents furnish the rooms of their sons and daughters, including the toys they provide, are indices of their expectations for their children's behaviour. If parents tend to furnish a child's room with dolls and stuffed animals, the behaviour expected of that child probably includes caretaking, nurturing, and playing house. On the other hand, when a child is provided with toys that consist primarily of blocks, puzzles, and toy tools, for example, the child can be said to be expected to engage in intellectual and physical manipulation of various elements of the environment.

These were the premises of a study examining how parents furnished the rooms of 48 boys and 48 girls, who ranged in age from one month to six years (Rheingold and Cook, 1975). The boys' rooms contained toys that tended to fall into a re-stricted group: vehicles of all kinds, depots, educational-art materials, sports equipment, machines, and military toys. The toys in the girls' rooms formed a completely different group. Girls most often had dolls, doll houses, and domestic toys of all kinds. Notable by their absence in the girls' rooms were wagons, boats, and buses, while in the boys' rooms, there was an almost total absence of baby dolls and domestic toys. It would seem, then, that boys were provided with toys that encourage activities directed *away from* the home, while girls' rooms were furnished with objects that encourage activities *within* the home. By restricting their children's toys, depending on their sex, parents are conveying quite unambiguously just what their behaviour expectations are for their children. This is particularly true when children are young — under six years of age. While children may express their preference for certain toys, it is still usually the parent who makes the final decision about which toys to buy and how to furnish children's rooms. It is worth noting, however, that since the families in this study could afford to provide the children with their own rooms, they had probably achieved a fairly high socio-economic level. As such, it could be said that the sample was a select one and hardly representative of most of the population in terms of socio-economic class.

The fact that parents encourage different kinds of play in their sons and daughters by providing them with different types of toys is but one manifestation of the larger process of gender-role typing by which parents encourage their children to behave, think, and feel in ways defined by society as appropriate to a particular gender role.

Encouragement of Gender-Role Typing: Unequal Pressure on Boys

Tommy, the three-year-old son of a colleague of mine, is going to the zoo with his father. Just as the two prepare to leave, Tommy tells his

*father he has forgotten something and scurries
up to his room. A few moments later, Tommy
reappears with a pink ribbon in his hair. His
father is aghast and shouts, "Take that thing
out of your hair. No son of mine is going to the
zoo with a ribbon in his hair." Tommy then
bursts into tears and runs out of the room.*

We would be hard-pressed these days to
come up with an analogous anecdote about
a three-year-old girl. Parents are much
more likely to be found encouraging "masculine" behaviour in their sons than they
are found insisting on "feminine" behaviour in their daughters (Lansky, 1967;
Fling and Manosevitz, 1972). A boy is generally found to be subjected to more disapproval for being a "sissy" than a girl is for
being a "tomboy". Not only do little boys
experience greater pressure to behave in a
gender-role-appropriate way, but also this
pressure is often enforced rather harshly
(Block, 1978). In their review of close to 200
published studies dealing with the socialization of girls and boys, Maccoby and
Jacklin (1974) found that parents tend to
use more physical and nonphysical negative reinforcements, as well as more praise,
in pressuring their sons to behave in a
"masculine" way.

Despite the well-known observation that
fathers do not spend much time with their
children, particularly when the children
are young, fathers play an important part in
the development of a boy's gender role.
Some have argued that fathers are much
more concerned that their children develop appropriate gender-role behaviour
than are mothers. For example, fathers
have been reported to worry when their
sons appear unaggressive and unwilling to
defend themselves (Goodenough, 1957).
However, they rarely express concern
when their daughters appear unaggressive.
While others maintain that mothers do not
feel very strongly about their children be-
having in a gender-role-appropriate manner, there is reason to believe that mothers,

just as much as fathers, may be concerned
about their *sons* growing up to be masculine. This comes from a study (Van
Gelder, 1975) of attitudes towards child-
rearing practices among mothers who were
also feminists. The sample included
women who held leadership positions in
feminist organizations, as well as those who
said they had personally been touched by
the Women's Liberation Movement. In interviews, about one-third of the mothers
said they had never given any serious
thought to the application of nonsexist
childrearing to boys. Even among the
women who did not particularly disapprove of homosexuality, there was a lot of
apprehension that their sons could become
"unnecessarily" homosexual because of
them. Interestingly, none of the women
who also had daughters feared that a "liberated" upbringing would transform a girl
into a lesbian. Despite their ideological beliefs, these mothers were unable to extri-
cate themselves from a belief system that
emphasizes the importance of masculinity
in boys and tolerates little deviation from
this norm. The results of the study are all
the more compelling when one considers
that these women were drawn from among
people who have espoused equality between women and men. It may be inferred
from this study that a survey of more conventional families would reveal that they
would be even more likely to subscribe to
the stereotype that a "liberated" upbringing may lead to reduced masculinity and,
thus, homosexuality, in males. But . . . gender-role behaviour and sexual preference
(male or female) are really independent
dimensions of personality. Gay people may
engage in the same range and diversity of
gender-role behaviours as heterosexuals.

What Do Parents Expect of Their Sons and Daughters?

On the basis of their review of research in
the area of childhood socialization, Mac-

coby and Jacklin (1974) conclude: "Our survey of the research on socialization of the two sexes has revealed surprisingly little differentiation in parent behaviour according to the sex of the child. However, there are some areas where differential 'shaping' does appear to occur." Nevertheless, the authors state that they found evidence that parents have a tendency to "shape" the behaviour of their sons and daughters in gender-role-appropriate ways by dressing them differently, by assigning them gender-role-differentiated chores and toys, and by encouraging interests along gender-role lines. This is most significant information, which children utilize in the development of their gender-role identity, as well as in their cognitive construction of their gender role. In effect, then, through experience with parents, peers, and the outside world, children learn the behaviours, interests, and tasks associated with these roles.

The conclusion that parents do not differentially socialize their sons and daughters has not gone unchallenged. For example, Block (1976 and 1978) has re-analyzed many of the studies summarized by Maccoby and Jacklin and has come to different conclusions about many of the same issues. For one thing, Block argues, the studies that Maccoby and Jacklin considered involved primarily very young children for whom many of the measures were inappropriate because of their youth. Other researchers have found that in guiding their children in specific behaviours appropriate to their age group, parents clearly treat boys and girls differently. For example, in one study, sons were encouraged *more* than daughters to explore their environment independently (Fagot, 1977). When mothers of four-year-olds were asked in another study at what age they thought parents should expect or permit certain behaviours in their children, mothers of boys gave *younger* ages than mothers of girls for "independence-granting" items (Callard, 1964). These included such things as crossing the street alone, being allowed to play away from home for long periods of time without first telling their parents where they would be, and using sharp scissors without adult supervision. But, interestingly, boys are *not* more advanced in many of the skills involved here and, if anything, are frequently more impulsive and less mature (Hoffman, 1977).

Parents also see their female toddlers as needing help more than their male counterparts. Female toddlers are encouraged more to ask for help from parents and are rewarded more for following their parents around the house. Parents have also been reported to feel that their daughters need more warmth and, in general, to feel more fear for girls than for boys. These parental preconceptions are not restricted to very young children, but seem to continue to be an integral part of the parents' relationship with their daughters throughout their development. For example, parents whose children ranged in age from 3 to 20 years have reported that they feel greater warmth for and closeness toward their daughters, and they tend to restrict and supervise their daughters more (Block, 1978). Since it would seem that parents see their daughters as needing more guidance, protection, and warmth than their sons, it is not surprising to learn that girls and boys are treated differently by their parents in ways that coincide with these differential perceptions.

Implications for the Child

While parents are preparing and training their sons to mould their world, they train their daughters to be moulded by it. Not only are girls expected to be more dependent than boys, but their parents actually reward them for dependency behaviour, while depriving them of the independence training that boys receive. Boys experience a different form of deprivation in their training. The socialization of boys is directed more toward the encouragement of the development of a sense of independence. There is less emphasis in boys' socialization on the development of skills needed to express interpersonal needs, particularly in emotional relationships, and to relate meaningfully to others in interpersonal relationships — characteristics associated with interdependence.

As a result of gender-role differences in independence-dependency and interdependence training, the young girl is not as likely as the young boy to establish an early and independent sense of self. While both boys and girls form their first attachment to the mother, the girl's identification with her mother is consistent with both her sex and her gender role. The boy, on the other hand, has to be encouraged to separate from his mother, identify with his father, or learn some abstract concept of the masculine gender role. The desired behaviour that the boy must acquire is rarely defined as something he must do. Instead, undesirable behaviour is indicated negatively as something he should *not* do or be — anything, that is, labelled "feminine." Another factor contributing to the boy's separation from his parents, particularly his mother, is his greater tendency to be aggressive, which increases the likelihood of his coming into conflict with them. Pressure to separate his identity from that of his mother, combined with independence training, pave the way for the development of independence coping skills that are seen to be necessary for effective enactment of the masculine gender role in our society. Presented in this fashion, the very methods that train the boy to act independently prevent him from developing a greater sense of interdependence. If interdependent qualities are labelled "feminine" and associated only with the mother, the boy will find it less likely that these traits could exist in himself alongside his independent qualities.

Since girls are expected to be dependent and are often rewarded for dependent behaviour, they are likely to develop an inadequate sense of personal competence. They have probably received less encouragement than boys to "try their own wings." Girls are more likely to underestimate their own ability and more apt to lack confidence in their judgement when it is contrary to that of others. What is more, fathers have been found frequently to respond to their daughters in a gender-role-stereotyped manner (Lynn, 1974). This type of behaviour on the part of the father may actually impede a young girl's intellectual growth and independent achievement if the father sees these as masculine qualities not to be encouraged as much in girls. A father who treats his daughter in a fashion that elicits traditionally feminine behaviours may thus hinder her intellectual and academic development.

If girls are to be given equal opportunity with boys to become independently competent and self-confident, not only do they need encouragement and positive reinforcement of their independence strivings, but they may also need some maternal rejection to achieve a greater sense of separate self. This is not to imply, however, that mothers should be hostile to their daughters. One can encourage separation and independent functioning, even among toddlers, in a warm and loving relationship. Through gentle guidance and reinforcement of the young girl's independence efforts, she should come to value herself as a competent being. Conversely, if boys are to accept dependency needs both in themselves and in others and if they are to learn how to relate sensitively in interpersonal relationships, independence, dependency and interdependence cannot be presented as mutually exclusive characteristics. By encouraging and rewarding independent behaviours, *as well as* those that promote meaningful relationships, parents will be teaching their sons that they do not have to reject their own and other people's emotional needs in order to be independent.

In summary, if parents try to establish relationships with *both* their sons and daughters in which the youngsters can model their parents' independence efforts and be rewarded for them, they will have gone a long way towards fostering independence and self-confidence in their developing children. At the same time, if sons, as well as daughters, are not punished for showing dependent and interdependent qualities, parents will demonstrate that awareness and expression of emotional needs and independence can coexist in one person, and they will have had a great part in furthering the development of complete human beings. . . .

THE "I," THE "ME," AND THE "IT": MOVING BEYOND THE MEADIAN CONCEPTION OF SELF

Michael Petrunik
Clifford D. Shearing

Introduction

While the reality referred to by the phrase "social construction of reality" presents itself, or is experienced, as both "objective" and "subjective" (Berger and Luckmann, 1967) sociologists have tended to limit the boundaries of their analysis, at least im-

From "The 'I,' The 'Me,' and the 'It': Moving Beyond the Meadian Conception of Self": appearing in *The Canadian Journal of Sociology*, Volume 13(4), 1988. Reprinted by permission of *The Canadian Journal of Sociology* and the authors.

plicitly, to objects of experience that are socially accessible and thus have a public status. Consequently, subjective experience has generally been regarded as essentially a psychological domain about which sociology has little to say beyond perfunctory references to Mead, Cooley, and sometimes Schutz. Higgins (1980) makes this point with respect to the deaf, Scott (1968) the blind, Schneider and Conrad (1980) epileptics, Kotarba (1977) and Hilbert (1984) pain, and Manning and Fabrega (1972, 1973) physical illness.

This aspect of the Durkheimian legacy which limits sociological analysis to external social fact, is evident even in the work of sociologists whom one might expect would address subjective experience directly. An example is Scheff's *Being Mentally Ill* (1966), a book whose content belies its title. A more accurate title would have been *Becoming a Mental Patient* as Scheff's central concern is the effect of societal reaction on the status and behaviour of those labeled "mentally ill" and not on the subjective experience of mental illness. This sociological neglect of experience is noted by Siegler and Osmond (1974: 70) with reference to labeling theory:

Those using the conspiratorial model [Siegler and Osmond's pejorative term for the labeling perspective], while filled with righteous indignation about abuse of mental patients have shown very little interest in finding out how psychiatric diseases appear to those who actually have them.

The best known sociological approach to subjectivity is George Herbert Mead's analysis of the structure of consciousness, in particular his description of the way in which intentionality is experienced. In identifying the "I" and the "Me" as fundamental "parts" of consciousness Mead provided for the notion of an internal dialogue that has been used in the work of symbolic interactionists as a theoretical basis for the construction of social action (Blumer, 1969). In this use of Mead's ideas the implicit assumption has been that while the "I," or the experience of the self as subject, provides the basis for the construction of social reality this "I" is itself unconstituted. Such a conception is also fundamental to the philosophy of Edmund Husserl whose work has become the basis for a second critical line of thought on the structure of conciousness.

While the Meadian terminology used here — "I," "Me," and "It" — does overlap the Freudian tripartite framework ("ego" means "I" and "id" means "it"), their conceptual status is significantly different. Freud's framework is a "scientific" device for making sense of subjectivity. Bettelheim (1982: 53) notes that to refer to the aggregate of drives which he regards as the ultimate source of motivation, Freud chose the personal pronoun "it"(*es*) and used it as a noun (*das Es*). He goes on to say that "What he [Freud] called the "I" refers primarily to the conscious, rational aspects of oneself" (1982: 55). Although Bettelheim criticizes the choice of the Latin terms "ego" and "id" in English translations as unnecessary and unfortunate jargon this usage does capture the analytic character of the terms. In our view, the Meadian tradition better reflects subjective experience than does the Freudian tradition. The "I" and the "Me" refer to the experience of a locus or source of action (subjective) and identity (objective) respectively.

While an analysis based on the Freudian tradition might be possible and useful, we have chosen in this paper to build on the Meadian framework. By noting that people can and do *experience* an interior source of action and locus of control that is "not-I" and that is in conflict with "I" we seek to expand on Mead's experiential analysis. The "It" is given a conceptual status similar to the "I." Both are viewed as sources of action. What differentiates the "I" and the

"It" is the experience of the "It" as an alien source of action that struggles with the "I."

While our conception is analytically different from Freud's it parallels certain neo-Freudian ideas such as Schachtel's notion of alienation. Schachtel (1962: 78) writes:

By making some quality or circumstances real or exaggerated or imagined the focal point of a reified identity, I look upon myself as though I were a thing (res) and the quality or circumstance were a fixed attribute of this thing or object. But the "I" that feels that I am this or that, in doing so, distances itself from the very same reified object attribute which it experiences as determining its identity and very often as a bane on its life. . . . I do not feel that I am doing this or that or failing to do it but that there is something in me or about me, or that I lack something and that this, once and for all, makes me this or that, fixes my identity.

In this paper we examine stutterers' experience of stuttering to show how they structure conciousness as they struggle to make sense of their speech behaviours. In doing so we extend earlier work (Petrunik, 1974, 1982; Petrunik and Shearing, 1983) in which we developed the ideas of Lemert (1967) and Goffman (1963, 1967) to examine how stutterers manage the awareness that others have of them.

After describing our research strategies and data, we examine, in turn, stuttering as behaviour and experience, stuttering as the expression of an autonomous inner force or "It," and the self-definition and management practices of stutterers. We conclude with a discussion of the implications of our analysis for a sociological analysis of the structure of subjective experience.

The Research

The evidence for this paper is based on data gathered from an earlier study (Petrunik, 1977) which involved participant observation of stutterers in a variety of social settings, focussed interviews, and research diaries kept by several informants. To update this research we have made use of our own experience with stuttering and observations of other stutterers in a variety of settings. We have also collected autobiographical accounts of stuttering in books, the press, and other publications. These published accounts . . . have a special value for they provide highly articulate and sensitive statements of experiences stutterers share. Throughout the research our own personal experience of stuttering, apart from being a source of data, has proven invaluable in allowing us to identify and understand the experiences of others.

STUTTERING AS BEHAVIOUR AND EXPERIENCE

Stuttering has an external aspect for both stutterers and their audiences. It is external in the sense that it is visible behaviour which non-stutterers recognize as stuttering. For stutterers, however, this external aspect is only the "tip of the iceberg." Beneath it there is a vast interior experiential domain that is not directly accessible to observers. Both the exterior and the interior aspects are experienced by the stutterer as obdurate and given.

As *behaviour*, stuttering is typically associated with speech that is characterized by blocks, repetitions, prolongations, or hesitations. "Blocks" are stoppages in the flow of speech. Some examples of blocks might be transcribed as follows:

I went to the ..... store.
I went to the st ..... ore.
I went to the ss ..... tore.

In the course of a block stutterers frequently freeze whatever other action they are engaged in, thereby extending the block from speech to other movements of the body. For example, one stutterer we observed blocked as he was about to tap ash off his cigarette with his finger. During the few seconds he was engaged in his block, his finger remained poised an inch or so above his cigarette. The finger came down and tapped the ash into the ash tray the moment he continued with the rest of the word.

"Repetition" and "prolongation" refer to the repeating of sounds, syllables, words, or phrases more than the "normal form," requires (for example, "pllllease," "nnnnnow," "goooood"). "Hesitations" are pauses or breaks between words or sounds that are sometimes accompanied by filler sounds or words (for example, "ah," "er," "um," "like," "well").

Although stuttering varies considerably, both temporally and situationally, several patterns have been identified (Petrunik, 1977: 34–37; Schwartz and Carter, 1986: 21-23):

1. Stutterers invariably speak fluently when they speak in unison with others including other stutterers.
2. Stuttering typically does not occur when a stutterer sings.
3. Most stutterers are fluent when they speak to themselves, to animals, to infants and very young children.
4. Most stutterers tend to stutter more frequently, and more severely, when they speak before large audiences.
5. Many stutterers stutter more when speaking to people they perceive to have higher status or authority than themselves.
6. Many stutterers stutter more under the stress of fatigue or illness and less under the influence of alcohol, certain drugs, and hypnosis.

As *experience*, stuttering's most fundamental feature is its unintentionality: stutterers experience stuttering as something that happens to them rather than as something they do. The nineteenth-century poet, Martin Tupper, captures this strikingly in his poem, "The Stammerer's Complaint" (Hunt, 1863: 3).

Has't ever seen an eagle chained to the earth?
A restless panther to his cage immured?
A swift trout by the wily fisher checked?
A wild bird hopeless strain its broken wings?
Or ever felt, at the dark dead of night,
Some undefined and horrid incubus,
Press down the very soul, and paralyse
The limbs in their imaginary flight
From shadowy terrors in unhallowed sleep?

The constant galling, festering chain that binds
Captive my mute interpreter of thought;
The seal of lead enstamped upon my lips,
The load of iron on my labouring chest,
The mocking demon, that at every step,
Haunts me, and spurs me on — to burst in
silence.

One of our respondents expressed this sense of lack of control as follows:

I was in French class and getting along quite well. I stuttered but not too badly. The word came out without too many contortions. Then one day it just hit me from out of the blue. I had to read a passage in class and the words literally would not come out. It was like being suddenly gripped by a strange force. The next day I was okay again.

STUTTERING AS AN AUTONOMOUS INNER FORCE

Central to this experienced absence of intention is the sense that the interruptions in speech are caused by some mysterious magical force. This sense arises as stutterers search for an account which will make sense out of their failure to control speech. The experience of loss of control over speech is, for stutterers, profoundly puzzling. "Why," they ask themselves, "can I not do what most other people have no trouble whatever doing? What is it that makes me different?"

This process is most visible when children first become aware that they cannot properly control their speech. For example, Shearing's son, after a period of minor repetitions that he appeared barely to notice found quite suddenly, when he was

seven years old, that words and sounds were not forthcoming on demand. Afraid and bewildered he turned to his parents to ask: "What's happening? Why can't I speak? I want to speak but I can't."

Such questions are posed in the cultural and experiential context in which actions that normally are intentional are expected to have a subjective locus. That is, these questions "are located in the procedures people employ to understand their experiences, and in the cultural resources, categories, and folklore they summon to do so" (Hilbert, 1984: 369). This framework directs stutterers to seek a subjective locus for stuttering in attempting to make sense of what is happening. Their search can be expressed as follows: "What is taking over my speech mechanism? What is this force that I have to struggle against to speak? If 'I' am not doing this what is?"

The conclusion stutterers reach in dealing with this puzzle is that there is another locus of action within consciousness which is "not I." Stutterers thus often come to conceive of, and experience, their unintended interruptions in speech as the work of an *inner* force which possesses them and, somehow, wrests control of speech away from the "I." One stutterer vividly described the experience of possession that this account produces as follows:

What really scares me is when I start to say a word and find myself saying the same syllable over and over again and I can't stop or when I find myself making a yard of an s sound when I only want a quarter inch of it. I get petrified when I fear this sort of thing is going to happen. I feel as helpless as a ventriloquist's dummy. Something, somebody else is in charge of my mouth and I can't do anything about it. (Van Riper: 1971: 158–9)

This sense of stuttering as an autonomous inner "thing" was also revealed in the remarks of a six-year-old boy. "When I stutter . . . the feelings are in my head . . . that's where the stutter is. . . ."

Although this "thing" or "It" is experienced as alien to the "I" (or the self as subject) its relationship to the "me" (or the self as object) is more problematic. The "It," while frequently disowned, comes, by force of its periodic intrusiveness into the stutterer's life, to be incorporated into the stutterer's consciousness as the basis of a central, if unwanted, identity or master status. Evidence for the inclusion of stuttering as a central identity is found in some stutterers' reports of discomfort during intermittent periods of fluency. For example, the comment of a stutterer who relapsed after a fluent period.

I'm glad that period of false fluency is over and I'm my old stuttering self again. Every new sentence, every new word I spoke, I thought would suddenly come out in the horrible stuttering way and when they didn't the pressure grew. I felt like a fake talking so easily and I knew it couldn't last. Odd as it may seem, now that I've relapsed, I feel calmer, more of a peace, though I'm sorry it's gone. (Van Riper, 1971: 213)

In summary, for stutterers the self is experienced as consisting not only of an "I" and a "Me" but an "I," a "Me," and an "It." This "It" is for them every bit as real as the "I" and the "Me." Like the "I" it is a source of action but one which is both independent of and antagonistic towards the "I."

When stutterers refer to "their stuttering" they have two references in mind: the social object, the unintended external behaviour of stuttering that they share with others generally and an experience of an alien source of agency that they share with other stutterers. The *behaviour* called "stuttering" is, for the stutterer, the expression of the work of the "It" as it takes control of speech.

This "It" is experienced as a strangely intangible beast, which sometimes lies dormant in some unknown lair of the body or mind, allowing the "I" to take control over speech. When this happens words and phrases flow freely and effortlessly. At any moment, however, the "It" may leave its lair, and inexplicably seize control, overpowering the "I" with such force the stutterer can only blink and splutter wordlessly.

But have you ever begun to speak and found a word stuck in your throat, your tongue paralyzed, unable to move? You see those around you give looks that say, "Spit it out! Say something!" You try to force the word past your lips, but it lodges deeper and deeper. Finally, after an age, you utter a sound . . . not a word, but something, anything, that will pass for an answer and let you relapse into an aching silence. That is the world of the stammerer, a world I knew so well. (Lapidus, 1981: 10)

This description has implications for our understanding of the structure of the self and consciousness. The first is that the structure of the self reflects the experience of intentionality; as this changes so does the self. The second, is the relation between the experience of self and culture. The experience of self as agent should not be conceived as simply given. Rather it is experienced in terms of the interpretive frames culture provides. Yet the experience of self is not simply a reflection of culture. Experience and culture are inextricably related. Each is ground for the other.

The notion of the self as having, under certain circumstances, an alien and latent locus of action — an imp in a bottle as it were — has implications for self-definition, the management of "illness," "disability," and other "conditions" and thus for "deviance" as a theoretical category.

SELF-DEFINITION AND MANAGEMENT

The experience of stutterers we have described is as fundamental to their self-definition as the behaviour which led others to label them as stutterers. Most stutterers have had the experience of being accepted by others as fluent speakers while at the same time feeling that their fluency was a façade, a denial of their "true" stuttering self, which they accomplished through a variety of artifices (word and situation avoidance, word substitution, fillers, and so on). The experience they report is one of the "I" managing to get the better of, and for a period, outsmarting the "It." Some stutterers, whom clinicians refer to as interiorized (Douglass and Quarrington, 1952), use these artifices with such skill that they are rarely identified by others as stutterers; even by close intimates, such as husbands, wives, and children.

Dr. A., a surgeon in his late 20's, was married for over a year and eventually divorced without ever telling his wife about his stuttering. He stated that he took great pains to conceal his stuttering with his colleagues and patients because he felt they would see his stuttering as a sign of nervousness and question his competence as a surgeon. (Petrunik, 1977: 75)

This phenomenon of people who do not stutter, but who nonetheless see themselves as stutterers because they experience an "It" within the self that seeks to take control of speech away from the "I," provides evidence in support of the argument that it may not be rule-breaking that is critical in the definition of deviance but the perception of an inner essence or presence which may be expressed through visible deviance. It goes further than Katz (1972), however, in suggesting something about the nature of this presence, the way in which it is experienced and how this experience is communicated to others.

The experience of "stuttering" as an inner presence lies at the heart of stutterers' management practices. In managing stuttering, by concealing, avoiding, or struggling with the "It" what stutterers do, in

part, is to engage in a process of self-interaction. This is akin to the process of communicating with oneself that Mead and Blumer (1969: 5) describe except that, instead of the interaction being between the "I" and the "Me," it takes place between the "I" and the "It." This is a critical distinction because, in the latter case, the interaction is between two acting parts of the self rather than between an active and a passive element (the subjective "I" and the objective "Me"). As an interaction between two loci of action it is not so much a "conversation" as a battle in which the spoils are the control of speech.

What's it like to stutter? Think of yourself on the highway. It's dark. You're in a hurry. No traffic. You step on the gas. Suddenly, out of nowhere, directly in front of you, looms the terrifying back of a huge truck. Horror.
Slam on the brakes. Spin the wheel, swerve, pray.
Anything — anything to keep from colliding. The truck is the word that looms ahead of a stutterer. You can't always tell what word it will be. But suddenly you see one that could spell trouble. It is too late to dodge? The collision doesn't kill. But you die a little. Because it produces the worst feelings of . . . shame.
I remember the time in high school more than 20 years ago, when, as president of the honor society, I had to address a school-wide assembly. . . . The first sentences went smoothly enough. Then came the truck, driven by my spiteful imp. A mad, spittle-drenched collision before 500 awed witnesses. (Patrusky, 1976: B-8)

Managing stuttering is a process in which the "I" attempts to outwit, outmanoeuvre, and/or overpower the "It." Normal speech is thus, for the stutterer, a fragile façade which depends on the "I's" ongoing ability to subjugate or elude the "It."

Always, danger lurks. Somewhere that dread, mocking imp crouches, ever ready to pounce and deliver an exquisitely timed kick to the shins, certain to screw things up, then to disappear. So I remain a shade off balance. I can never be sure. (Patrusky, 1976: B-8)

To communicate more effectively, and influence the identity imputations of others, stutterers attempt to develop an understanding of the circumstances in which the "It" is likely to take over speech. This frequently involves classifying words, sounds, and situations in terms of whether they are likely to be troublesome. Thus, stutterers identify certain words and sounds as "hard" and certain situations as "difficult." They also identify circumstances and contexts that seem to make the "I" more vulnerable to the "It." For example:

When I'm tired I always stutter. Whenever I'm sick or run-down I stutter more. If I have to introduce myself in front of a group, I just freeze up and can't get a word out. Using the telephone, especially when someone else is present, is murder. My heart just pounds.

On the basis of this self-knowledge of how the "It" behaves stutterers plan their lives so that they will be able to avoid words, situations, and circumstances associated with stuttering.

Such premeditated management is, however, inherently limited both because most stutterers typically feel that the "It" is not entirely predictable and because they constantly encounter situations in which avoiding "It" proves to be difficult. As a result, in addition to the pre-planned strategies for dealing with "It," management typically takes the form of moment-to-moment encounters between "I" and "It" (Petrunik and Shearing, 1983). Ben Patrusky eloquently describes the stutterer's daily experiences:

If you met me, you wouldn't necessarily find out I stutter, or whatever it is that I do. I've fooled people. I know how to camouflage. A dangerous word is coming up? Quick, use another one. Experts say some stutterers have

pretty good vocabularies. Surely, dodging, substituting, is the reason. If speaking were tennis, I'd dance around my weak backhand to favour my more sure forehand. (1976: B-8)

Implications

In assessing the significance and generality of our analysis of the experience of stuttering, it is useful to consider other instances in which people experience a lack of control over their bodies. These fall along a continuum where one pole is occasional and slight loss of control and the other regular and substantial loss of control. At the lower end of the continuum are the experiences most people have in which they momentarily lose control over some part of their body and do something they had not intended, for example, tripping on a stair, letting a glass slip from their hands, accidentally knocking into something, forgetting what they planned to say. Such incidents are typically accounted for as momentary clumsiness, being under pressure, exhaustion, stage fright, and so on. In such accounts what is suggested is that "I" failed to give proper attention to its activity and as a result something happened which was not intended. Given the occasional nature of this loss of intentional control this account makes sense within the context of cultural assumptions about the nature of the self. At the other end of the continuum where losses of control are substantial and chronic (e.g., a neurological disorder), the accounts provided suggest, not inattentiveness on the part of the "I," but some other alien force that confronts the "I." The way in which this force is conceptualized depends on the cultural context and the range of available interpretive frames. For example, in contemporary western societies the categories of epilepsy, psychosis, Latourrette's syndrome, "phantom limbs," and a variety of other disorders

(Sacks, 1983, 1984, 1985) are used in constructing scientifically legitimate, "rational" accounts indicating that this troublesome, disruptive force has a physical basis. In the absence of clear physical indicators notions such as functional psychosis or multiple personalities may be used to impute a scientifically legitimate cause (Crabtree, 1985). Alternatively, more controversial explanations which stretch outside the western scientific frame may be used, for example, the force may be conceptualized as an evil spirit which possesses the self or a non-western theory of physical causation may be drawn upon, for instance, acupuncture theory. While such interpretations have received little sociological attention they have been widely acknowledged in popular and occult literature, oriental philosophy, and in such marginal and controversial scientific disciplines as parapsychology.

Stuttering, as a type of "socio-motor disorder," is located somewhere near the midpoint of the above continuum. Although the language of personal accounts sometimes suggests a possession-like experience, stutterers usually report experiencing the "It" as an aspect of the self that has partial control over their speech rather than as a distinct and separate personality. This experience of self is both grounded in the experience of stuttering and constructed in the context of cultural assumptions about stuttering, the nature of the self, and intentionality (Johnson, 1944a; 1944b). A framework is provided which gives meaning to both the failure of stutterers to control speech and the practices they use — both reflexively and deliberately — to cope with their inability to speak.

A final implication has to do not with the experiencing of stuttering per se, but with how this experience informs our understanding of self-construction generally. In the view of Mead, Schutz, and Garfinkel we become most fully conscious of objects in our environment when they become problematic in some way. They surprise us, creating an impulse which is resolved via conscious thought and definition. The stutterer experiences multiple loci of subjective control (agency) when control of speech is problematic. Those of us without stuttering, or some kindred disorder, are likely to be less aware of our own sense of agency and how we construct it because it is not usually problematic. What stuttering demonstrates is how closely tied the subjective experience of agency is to control over conduct. When this control is problematic the process whereby our sense of self agency is constructed can become visible.

Conclusion

What generalizations should we draw from our analysis? First, stuttering draws attention to the importance of considering the subjective experience of deviance as well as its symbolic designation by the self and others, in understanding the development of deviant identities and deviant life styles. The dialectic of the stutterer's experience and the construction of inner essences or agents within the self are, in the framework we present, as much the purview of the sociologist as behaviour or externally located social facts.

Second, our analysis provides insights into the experience of self associated with a variety of phenomena where the locus of subjective control is problematic.

Finally, this analysis of problems of agency or locus of subjective control helps provide a better understanding of the process of self-construction generally. The study of the "unusual" illuminates that which is "usual."

MODERN MAGIC: THE CASE OF EXAMINATIONS

Daniel Albas
Cheryl Albas

Magic and Success: The Case of Examinations

In a comprehensive study of university student life (Albas and Albas, 1984), still ongoing, we identify a number of practices designed to allay anxiety and so increase chances for success in examinations. We set out to analyze these common but yet to be systematically studied unusual practices as a kind of "modern day" magic.

Magic seems inevitably to be associated with anxiety-causing events, whether its function is to allay the anxiety, as Malinowski suggests, or to generate anxiety where it does not exist and for societal reasons should, as Radcliffe-Brown suggests (Homans, 1941). Examinations are highly tense and anxiety-causing events, and the practices described in the article as magic are essentially anxiety-coping mechanisms.

The examination arena is one in which students, no matter how well prepared, encounter a number of uncertainties. These include, for example, whether they have interpreted the questions correctly; whether the professors will interpret their answers as they intend them; and not least, whether they themselves are "up" for the contest in terms of the sharpness of their memories, organizational abilities, and ability to complete the task on time. Accordingly, it is not surprising to find sur-rounding the examination a number of practices by students that are clearly intended as uncertainty-coping mechanisms and which could be called magic, if magic is defined as *an action directed toward the achievement of a particular outcome with no logical relationships between the action and the outcome or, indeed, any empirical evidence that the one produces the other.* In effect, this is nonrational behavior in a setting where one might expect maximum rationality. Clearly we are not dealing with the magic of the sleight-of-hand professional magicians intend for entertainment, nor with that of preliterate shamans or urban gypsies (i.e., cultic magic). Such behavior is directed toward achieving an outcome, involves many everyday and commonplace acts, yet does seem to rely for the achievement of the outcome on some mystical element.

In this article we attempt to depict and analyze magical practices students use to allay anxiety and so increase their chances for success. It must be clearly understood that what we are describing as "magic" is behavior that falls on a continuum between the "heavy magic" of preliterate peoples and superstition (Jahoda, 1969). Student magic is more like the kind of superstition practiced by athletes (Gmelch, 1971), soldiers under battle conditions (Stouffer et al., 1949), miners (Wilson, 1942), and gamblers (Henslin, 1967). It is being described here for its ethnographic interest. We realize that magic among students has been observed in the past, but we are not aware of any previous effort to examine it systematically.

A description of how the study was carried out is followed by a discussion of general and specific characteristics of student magic. In the final section we suggest implications of this modern adaptation of an ancient technique for the wider societal context.

From *The Sociological Quarterly* 30(4) 1989, pp. 603–13. "Modern Magic: The Case of Examinations" by Daniel Albas and Cheryl Albas. By permission of JAI Press, Inc.

Method

We gathered the data over the last thirteen years from over 300 students in our own and others' classes in the province's largest university (now enrolling 24,000 students). The sample represents a complete spectrum of student background as to age, sex, marital status, and social class. We observed and interacted with students as they studied in libraries, took study breaks, and made last-minute preparations before making their way to their respective exam sites. We continued our tracking as students gathered outside the exam centers, entered, chose their seats, and wrote their exams. Finally, we monitored students as they again congregated outside the exam sites and even as they gathered in pubs and local restaurants for the traditional "post-mortems." As a result we were able to record the increased frequency of magical practices as they neared culmination on the day of the exam and dropped dramatically (though not entirely) immediately upon completion of the exam.

The methodological process involved triangulation: data of different kinds were collected from a variety of sources in such a way that the weaknesses of one data-collecting technique were compensated for by the strengths of another, thus better ensuring reliability and validity. The four sources employed were: (1) exam logs, (2) surveys, (3) observation and probing for meaning, and (4) student accounts to explain failures.

THE LOGS

A source of data that proved rich in subjective detail was the exam logs which students were asked to keep over the thirteen-year period. These logs included descriptions of thoughts, sentiments, and behavior that they considered significant, from the first day of classes up to and including the return of their examination grades. Over time, such logs were collected from approximately 300 students of all ages, grade levels, achievement levels, and marital statuses. These records served as a valuable source of information about the inner-life of students and other aspects that we were in no position to observe. Although the word *magic* was never mentioned, approximately one-fifth of the students mentioned practices that could be classified as magical.

THE SURVEY (INTERVIEWS)

In checking these accounts, we asked different students who had never submitted logs whether they had employed any of the forms of magic that were listed in the logs provided by other students. The general form of the question was, "Do you engage in any practices designed to enhance 'good luck' or to ward off 'bad luck'? About one-third of the approximately 65 students interviewed indicated that they had done so at one time or another.

OBSERVATIONS AND PROBES

Sensitized to the variety and prevalence of magic, we "probed" by asking for explanations whenever we observed some unusual behavior. A student suddenly breaking the rhythm and length of his stride as he walked into the exam room was avoiding walking on a line (of the basketball court in the gym). Another, rolling his study notes into a cylinder and squeezing them, sought to wring knowledge from his notes. We did not code all explanations given for unusual behaviors as descriptions of magic in our sense. Where explanations showed any sort of plausible empirical connection between the practice and the result sought, the practice was not coded as magical.

ADDITIONAL STUDENT ACCOUNTS (WRITTEN AND VERBAL)

Another data source was the accounts given by students in about a dozen counseling sessions subsequent to the exams to explain their failures on examinations. On such occasions some students would sheepishly admit to having neglected some important practice which they had come to regard as necessary for success.

General Characteristics of Student Magic

We found that from one-fifth to one-third of our students used magic, predominantly of the kind intended to bring good luck rather than to ward off bad luck. In Frazer's (1958) terms, it was largely "contagious" magic rather than "imitative" (no more than half a dozen cases of the latter), and there was only a handful of cases in which "omens" were given credence. The descriptions of magical behaviors and material items employed by students fall into the two major categories of Material Items (Figure 1) and Behavior (Figure 2). In turn, these categories are further divided into Prescribed for Luck, on the one hand, and Unlucky or Tabooed, on the other. Focusing first on Material Items Prescribed for Luck, these can be sub-classified as Favorite Oldies and Oddities, Lucky Locations, and Miscellaneous. Favorite Oldies and Oddities are represented by Items of Appearance, Books and Pens, and Food. Items of Appearance include not only Clothing but also Jewelry, Perfume, and Modes of Wearing the Hair. Thus, Items Prescribed for Luck exhibit a variety of at least seven different classes of items. If one distinguishes between Dressing Up and Dressing Down, the number of different classes of Items Pre-

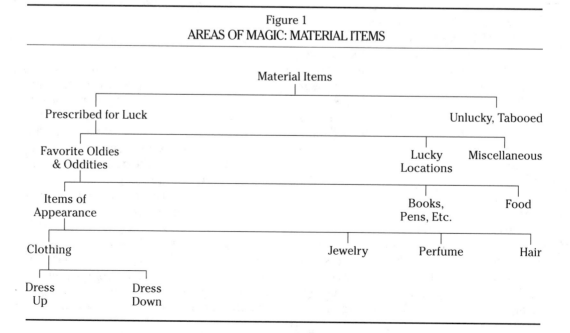

Figure 1
AREAS OF MAGIC: MATERIAL ITEMS

scribed for Luck increases to eight. It did not seem feasible to classify Unlucky Items. Accordingly, the total variety of classes into which magical Material Items fall is nine — eight Prescribed for Luck and an unclassified miscellany of Unlucky Items.

Within the other major category, Behavior, there are five distinct classes prescribed for Luck: Secular Rituals, Religious Rituals, Grooming, Special Music, and a Miscellany of Behavior Directed Toward Others. Under Tabooed Behavior, in regard to both Behavior Directed Toward Self and Behavior Directed Toward Others, is the twofold classification of Secular Rituals and Religious Rituals. This brings the total number of distinct classes of magical Behavior to nine. We now turn to specific descriptions of bottom-line Items and Behavior (those that appear on the bottom line of each of the two figures are not further subclassified).

MAGICAL ITEMS

Items Prescribed for Luck

In regard to Clothing, most students at exam time dress down (i.e., untidily, sloppily), though there are a few who dress up. Among the notable down dressers were: a young woman who always wore to exams her boyfriend's sweatshirt "which was in a deplorable condition with holes everywhere, stretched out of shape and much too big for me"; a science student who always wore an ancient scarf that he insisted "carries parts of my brain in it"; and an engineering student who wore a pink sweatshirt with purported magical qualities. An example of dressing up is the case of a student who always wore a three-piece suit that he had found particularly efficacious when he wore it on one occasion to a job interview. As he indicates, "It's not a very logical thing to wear to an exam

Figure 2
AREAS OF MAGIC: BEHAVIOURS

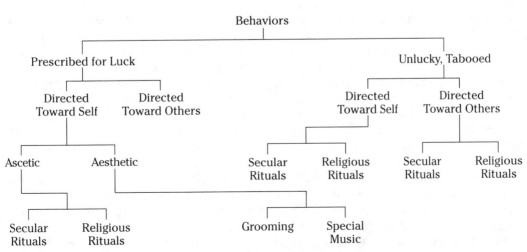

because it's hot and restricting." Nevertheless he persists because of his belief in the continuing efficacy of his suit.

Notable items of Jewelry listed by students as bringing them luck were mother's wedding ring, mother's R.N. pin, and father's class ring. In all of these cases, the students mentioned that the parent was particularly bright and successful, thus implying a faith in magic by contagion.

Under the heading of Perfume, which includes one case of burning incense, all of the accounts suggest a conviction on the part of the students that association with success has the magical power to produce success. One woman wears the perfume that she wore when she met her boyfriend (a lucky event) — "I feel it brings me good luck, as it was luck that brought us together."

Hair is felt by our sample population to possess magical qualities both by its presence and by its absence. One student always has his hair cut short before an exam to permit, as he says, "knowledge to flow freely around my head." Another student, like Sampson, always allows his hair to grow long before exams "in order to keep the knowledge in."

The general impression is that certain favorite items provide a "security blanket" even if students can only see them (e.g., at the front of the room on the floor) and not actually handle them during the examination. Some "special pens" have written previous successful examinations and, without them, students would have less confidence in their ability to do well. For example, an advertisement in a student newspaper read, "Help! I've lost my silver Cross pen. Deep psychological and sentimental value; never written an exam without it. Lost last Friday. If found contact Anna (phone number)." In another instance, the pen had been used to write all of the notes for the course and the student believed that it "knew" the material. Books and notes, although strictly prohibited from use during the exam, are often placed in heaps at the front and along the walls of the room, where students can see them. Many students claim that, in merely looking at the books, "summaries come up through the covers" to them. One student said that on the infrequent occasions she is allowed to take her books with her to her seat, she puts them on the floor and then puts her feet on them. She swears that the knowledge comes up to her through her legs. She adds the disclaimer that she is not crazy and that "it is true."

The magical properties of certain foods or food eaten in a special way at a special time or bought from some particular vendor — all have been claimed to bring good luck. One student insists that the purchase of a *carrot muffin* (no other kind) at the "*patty wagon*" (no other vendor) on the way to the examination room is most potent. Failure to secure the right muffin at the right place is an ill omen for her. Another student insists that on examination days she has to have the following breakfast in the following manner: one sausage placed vertically on the left of the plate and beside it two eggs sunny side up to make the configuration "100" (percent). Still another student stirs his coffee exactly 20 times on examination days. His rationale was that he was taking 5 courses and aspired to an A in each (which is the equivalent of 4 grade points), and 5 times 4 equals 20. This student attained a straight A average over his university career. These student practices resemble what Frazer (1958) refers to in *The Golden Bough* as imitative magic, where the magical method imitates the desired effect.

Examples of Lucky Locations are specific zones of the examination room and may include the back, sides, front, or middle. Students arrive early to secure these Lucky Locations because to sit anywhere else is to court confusion and disaster. Some students insist on a specific seat number that has proved lucky in the past. Some are not particular about the region of the room or a specific seat but they feel they must be in the same cluster with, and close to, those with whom they studied during the term.

Miscellaneous Items include the usual rabbit's feet, dice, coins, as well as tiny teddy bears, kangaroos, and other cuddly toys. One young medical student, very much a positivist in other areas of her life, must, like Christopher Robin, have "Roo" along when she writes her examinations. A young male student is reluctant to write an exam unless he has "found" a coin, which he takes as a sign of "luck." He searches for a coin on the day of the exam, often using up precious study time by "scrounging around bus stops" until he is successful, even at the risk of being late. Another student carries around a lock of his ex-girlfriend's hair in the hope that her extraordinary brightness will illuminate his own efforts.

Unlucky, Tabooed Items

Unlucky Items, interestingly enough, often turn out to be Oldies and Oddities once thought to be lucky but which have failed the owner and so become Tabooed Items. For example, a pink shirt (not the same one mentioned earlier) that had been a lucky talisman was found to be unlucky and thus shunned ever after. What is more, any other student at the same exam who wore a pink shirt was also to be shunned. Another example is the student who reported that in high school he once "crammed" for an exam at home the same day he was to write it and, when he was hungry, heated up a frozen TV dinner. He did unusually well on that exam, so he repeated the pattern of "cramming" at home the day of the exam and eating frozen waffles for breakfast and a TV dinner for lunch. However, when this student arrived at the university he found that studying only on the day of the exam was woefully inadequate and his performance was dreadful. Instead of changing his study habits he changed his "faith" in his lucky food: "It was to the point that even if I ate a whole freezer full of frozen food I would still do poorly on the exam. . . . I not only stopped eating frozen TV dinners before exams, I now make a point of always avoiding them." Other items, such as a bra (which the student believed to be repressive) and anything new or borrowed, are avoided. (Note the inconsistencies across the sample: one student always borrows her boyfriend's sweatshirt while another will not borrow even a pen.)

MAGICAL BEHAVIORS

Turning now to Magical Behavior, by far the most prevalent practices — whether directed toward self or others, whether lucky or unlucky — are those which could be termed *rituals.* In turn, these rituals can be subclassified as secular or religious.

Behaviors Directed Toward Self Prescribed for Luck

Examples of Secular Rituals Directed Toward Self include: knocking on the exam room door three times before entering the room (cf. knocking on wood); stepping over the threshold of the exam room with the right foot first (right in both senses); and making a circuit of the exam building, whatever the weather. However, behaviors Directed Toward Self Prescribed For Luck consist almost entirely of prayer, even in cases where students by their own admission are not particularly religious. Such students nevertheless express a dread of offending God, particularly around examination time, and become compulsively scrupulous in their prayer life and penitent if they forget this duty. There is also, at exam time, an emphasis on virtuous behavior, particularly toward members of the immediate family, but often also even toward people met on the street. There is a distinct "minding of p's and q's" in the fear that any deviation from the path of righteousness (no matter how occasionally trodden) will be punished. Accordingly, whatever the strength of one's belief, it is not worth taking chances with inexorable fate.

Both the Secular and Religious Rituals Directed Toward Self described above could be classified together as being Ascetic in that they involve an element of sacrifice and self-discipline, however unusual. The two other behavior practices directed toward self, namely Grooming and Special Music, may be classified as Aesthetic in that they have to do with effects that are pleasing to the senses.

Another example of Behavior Directed Toward Self Prescribed for Luck involves students who report that being well groomed contributes to good performance. This in itself may not be magical even by our broad definition. However, when one student states that she puts special care into the manicuring of the three fingers that hold her pen, this begins to seem like magic, certainly the *imitative magic* described by Frazer (i.e., polished fingernails produce polished answers).

A number of students report a Behavior Directed Toward Self Prescribed For Luck which involves "lucky tunes" to which they always listen prior to writing examinations: ". . . then twenty minutes before the exam I drive to school listening to 'Money Changes Everything.' I consistently follow this strategy before I write any exam." The following account is worthy of mention, though not technically a tune nor even magic according to our definition (in that there is clearly a thread of empirical connectedness between the act and expected result). One student states that before every exam he listens to a tape by Martin Luther King in which the Reverend King speaks about "his dream" and reiterates the refrain "We shall overcome." Clearly the dream for the student is life success and overcoming this particular exam.

Behaviors Directed Toward Others Prescribed for Luck

The category, Behaviors Prescribed For Luck Directed Toward Others, might better be descibed as behavior required of others by the student. However, since in most cases students go to great ends to elicit such behavior from family and friends, they may be said indeed to engineer specific forms of behavior in others. Examples of this are students who insist that before leaving for an examination they be wished good luck by various members of their families according to a formula of specific wording and at a high volume. Quite often it is not sufficient for the formula of the wishes to be secular; they must be invoked by prayer. "At the moment before I walk out of the door I make sure that my parents wish me good luck and especially add 'God Bless You.' The good luck part I could probably do without, but not hearing 'God Bless You' leaves me feeling I'm not getting all the help I could for an exam." In some cases the others who are expected to tender good luck wishes are non-human others. For one student, it was essential for her dog to sit upon his haunches, offer a paw, and "woof" her good luck.

Much as in the case of Lucky Locations, some students seek out lucky people to sit near during the examination (i.e., people whom they think are likely to be star performers). One interesting case of this is a student who stated that he always sought out the ugliest girl to sit next to. By his reasoning, she would not have a boyfriend and would devote all her time to study and be thoroughly well prepared which, in turn, would rub off on him. The magic of course, is implied in the term "rubbing off" and could best be classified as magic by contagion.

Tabooed Behaviors Directed Toward Others

Secular examples of this include refraining from sexual intercourse even, in some cases, by married partners; refraining from discussing the exam, particularly joking about it; and, above all, in this context, avoiding well-wishing. This is particularly interesting since it seems to contradict the notion of imitative magic that we saw in the case of the student with the manicured pen fingers. Some students avoid others, even lovers and spouses, who are liable to wish them luck. One student who followed this taboo emphatically avowed that he did not believe in luck. He was nevertheless very upset if someone wished him good luck, and he therefore went out of his way to avoid being so wished.

A few activities were classified as rituals tabooed for religious reasons; for example, refraining from gossip about other people because it is offensive to God, and staying away from entertainment and other secular pursuits because by so doing one acquires virtue which will be rewarded. These practices, in regard to both items and behavior, would seem to be most intense when anxiety for the student is at its highest. Similarly, the magic wanes and disappears as the cause for anxiety passes.

Discussion

Examining Figures 1 and 2 suggests that, among our college students, luck-bringing magic is more prevalent than magic to ward off bad luck. This is particularly the case in Figure 1. It is not as immediately apparent in Figure 2, but does emerge when one notes that most of the tabooed behavior described is really directed toward bringing luck rather than warding off misfortune. The point becomes especially clear when we note the prevalence of active manipulative behavior over passive behavior, implying the existence of a feeling among the students of being in command of their destinies rather than succumbing to the fate of omens. Of all the accounts of Magical Items and Behaviors, only about 10 mentioned the significance of omens. This aspect of student magic is in strong contrast to preliterate magic where so much credence is placed in omens. Another contrast is that whereas Frazer found imitative magic to be the more prevalent form among preliterates, we found that among students contagious magic is more prevalent.

Another pattern that emerges from these accounts is that items employed and behaviors exhibited are highly private and idiosyncratic. That is, what may be used and considered efficacious by one student may be tabooed by another (e.g., the pink shirts mentioned earlier and careful grooming versus the disheveled look). This in turn would seem to be related to the fact that student magic is largely invented by the practitioners themselves. It is not traditional or socially shared as is preliterate magic. Student magic is, above all, entirely directed toward self enhancement, and there is not a single case of magic directed toward the detriment of another, quite unlike the cultic magic of preliterates. Finally, student magic, quite unlike that of preliterate groups, is pragmatic, in that students are willing to abandon any item or behavior that does not work.

TOWARDS A THEORY

On the basis of our information it appears that student magic can be thought of as being at one end of a continuum that began with preliterate magic and emerged through other forms such as those practiced by soldiers in warfare, miners, and sports competitors. At the preliterate-magic end of the continuum, magic is a communal, cooperative enterprise in which the participants have shared meanings in regard to the practices and are motivated by a strong collectivity orientation. Among the soldiers, miners, and athletes, magic is still practiced in a community in which there are, to some extent, shared meanings and also, to some extent but considerably less than among preliterate peoples, a collectivity orientation. When we come to students writing exams, we have reached the near end of the continuum of magical practices. Here we find magic practiced individually and in isolation, without shared meaning (even, to some extent, with contradictory meanings), and completely self-oriented in its motivation. In an attempt to understand these differences along the continuum, it might be suggested that for preliterate peoples living in a less complex and completely homogeneous society, one would expect shared meanings in a way that is not to be expected among heterogeneous, largely anonymous groups of students in contemporary urban society. However, even in contemporary society it is reasonable to expect that, within a group of soldiers who have been trained together to act in unison and whose very lives depend upon the actions of every other one in the group, there would tend to be more of a collectivity orientation than among university students writing exams (although perhaps not as much as within more homogeneous, preliterate groupings). The phenomenon of shared meanings would also be expected to be in an intermediate position, since even though soldiers, miners, and athletes are the products of a heterogeneous socialization compared to preliterate peoples, they nevertheless work together and constitute communities to a greater degree than do exam-writing students. As such, this "middle category" has developed many well-known agreed-

upon magical rituals such as "break a leg," "three on a match," not referring to a "winning streak," and "the fatal last shift." In effect then, the particular aspects of student magic that we described earlier, which may seem atypical of magic in the past and in some ways inexplicable, may be partially explained in terms of increasing societal complexity and heterogeneity as well as shifts in cultural values.

In sum, as society moves from preliterate to contemporary, increasing in complexity as well as scientific sophistication, we might expect magic to be transformed from: (1) being publicly performed to being privately and individually performed; (2) being culturally transmitted to being spontaneously generated; (3) being completely shared by the whole community to being utilized privately by individuals; and (4) being unvaryingly uniform and consistent in its rituals to being highly variable and even contradictory. Clearly, with an ideal-type polar construct of this kind, no actual case of magic (including student magic) will in all respects conform to the characteristics of either pole. The burden of this article, however, is that students' magic falls rather toward the latter end of each of these four continua.

chapter

6

The Changing Family

The past two decades have been ones in which there have been not only debates and controversies about family and marriage but also a major rethinking of the sociology of the family. There has, for example, been a long-standing theoretical and historical debate around the issue of what exactly has been the impact of capitalism and industrialism on marriage, family and the situation of women. This is a debate that spills over into considerations of the changing nature and meaning of work, the theme of most of the articles in Chapter 10, "Economic Perspectives." Rethinking of the sociology of the family has, as you might expect by now, come almost exclusively from feminist perspectives in both sociology and social history. Feminist theory and research has had a profound impact not only on our sociological think-ing about the family but also on family law and social policy generally. The rethinking of the sociology of the family has taken place in the context of major and probably enduring demographic and structural changes in the family as it has become more and more apparent that there is not one family form in Canada but a diversity of family-type relationships. Simply, the reality in Canadian society, as in other Western societies, is increasing numbers of single-parent families, female-headed families, dual-income and dual-career families, intentionally childless families and remarriage families, same sex partnerships, as well as a broad range of ethnic variations. And there has been considerable pressure for these various familial arrangements to be given social and legal legitimacy through social policy.

The first selection is an excerpt from a recent Statistics Canada monograph that presents a demographic analysis of Canadian patterns of marriage, family formation, fertility, divorce and remarriage. We have, here, spared you the many tables and statistics included in the monograph and have, rather, extracted the introduction and conclusion. The first part, written by Bali Ram, a demographer with Statistics Canada, provides you with a brief background on some of the controversies surrounding our understanding of the contemporary family. In the latter part of the selection, A. Romaniuc, also a demographer at Statistics Canada, summarizes the demographic changes and trends with respect to the Canadian family and considers their social and policy implications.

The second selection, by Roberta Hamilton of Queen's University, is broadly speaking, historical in nature. But, it is not a standard history of the family in Western society. Rather, Hamilton here draws upon both feminist and Marxist perspectives to explore and explain the impact of capitalism and industrialism on the role of women in society and within the family and the impact of changing economic relationships on family relationships. In doing so, Hamilton not only provides you with perhaps a different way of thinking about the family and the women's movement but also with a very clear description of the economic and social changes accompanying the rise of capitalism and the meaning of these in the everyday lives of people experiencing these changes. Later, as you attempt to understand something of the complexities of the rise of capitalism and industrialism (Chapter 10), you may want to return to this selection.

The third selection, by one of your authors, is an abridged and edited version of a paper originally prepared to assist the Department of Justice, Canada in setting research priorities in the area of family law in the 1990s. In writing the paper, Richardson was drawing on his experience of conducting applied and evaluation research on various aspects of family law over the 1980s. In this selection he describes the formal and informal changes in family law and how these have been shaped by both changing and competing ideologies about marriage, family and divorce. What has sometimes been referred to as "the war over the family" nicely reflects the various responses of groups to social change more generally: some seek radical reform; some wish for piecemeal reform and some, in wishing family law and policy to strengthen traditional values, clearly seek Utopia in some perhaps mythic past.

The final selection, our second one by Margrit Eichler, could easily be included in Chapter 14, which focuses on social change. This is because Eichler uses the family as a focus for examining some of the major pressures and movements for social change. Specifically, she examines the patriarchal family movement and feminism as two major movements that will help shape how Canadians respond to such issues as abortion, homosexuality, divorce, daycare, sex equality and reproductive technology. And she nicely captures how the very different assumptions and ideologies of the two movements mean that debates about these issues often consist of people talking past one another. However we may define it and think about it, it is evident that the family matters to Canadians.

RELATED READINGS

1. **Anthony Synnott**: "Little Angels, Little Devils" (Chapter 5)
2. **Roderic Beaujot**: "The Family in Crisis?" (Chapter 8)
3. **Marilyn Porter**: "Women and Old Boats" (Chapter 10)

NEW TRENDS IN THE FAMILY

Bali Ram and A. Romaniuc

In recent years there has been an upsurge in the popular, journalistic and scientific literature on the family. Although it is generally agreed that the family, as an institution, is in transition, there is a lack of agreement as to the exact nature of this transition, and more importantly, as to what the implications of the changes are for individuals and society.

A wide range of views on family issues may be abstracted from the extensive literature which has accumulated over the years. From one end of the spectrum, the family is seen as obsolete, declining and heading for extinction, from the opposite end, the family is seen to be as strong as ever and *Here to Stay*, to use the title of a book by Mary Jo Bane. Both views have their proponents, and there is much room for reconciliation. But such is not the express aim of this study. Rather the focus is on describing recent changes in the demographic profile of the family in Canada.

The intention is to gain some understanding of the changes that have occurred in recent years with respect to both the formation and the structure of the family. The very least that will emerge from this analysis is that the living arrangements of Canadians are more diverse and to some extent less stable than they were two or three decades ago. Certain previously marginal living arrangements have evolved into a prominent feature of our society's family and household organization.

But before going into the actual analysis of the Canadian data on the family, we shall briefly review the literature and thus gain a

From "Statistics Canada." *Current Demographic Analysis: New Trends in the Family* Catalogue No. 91-535, 1989. Reproduced with the permission of the Minister of Supply and Services, 1991.

broader perspective on the controversies surrounding the subject of the contemporary family.

Arguments and Counter Arguments

There is no doubt that, during the twentieth century and more so in the last couple of decades, the family has changed in both form and function. This is not in dispute. What is in dispute is what these changes mean for the individual and society at large. Looking back through history at the instrumental and indispensable role that the family institution has played in society has led some to voice deep concerns over the declining marriage rate, the rising divorce rate, the persistence of below-replacement fertility, the growing proportion of unwed mothers, increasing participation in the labour force by mothers of young children, the rise of individualism, the proliferation of one-person households, and many other emerging trends, all of which seem to point to the decline of the family. Victor R. Fuchs (1983: 3–4), in addressing these issues in his book entitled *How We Live*, is quite forceful in his conclusion:

Several recent studies . . . claim that the family is as strong as ever; but such claims lack credibility when . . . the birth rate has been below replacement level for a decade, when almost 25 percent of children live in one-parent or no-parent households, when two out of five marriages end in divorce, and when most of the elderly depend on the government for their daily sustenance. My reading of the data leads to a more troubled conclusion about American families. In describing the decline in importance of the conjugal family, however, I am not predicting its disappearance; neither am I denying others the right to redefine the term "family" as they wish. But there is overwhelming evidence that individuals rely less on their families today

*than in the past for the production of goods
and services and as a source of financial and
psychological support in time of need.*

Such interpretations, portending decay,
imply that the family was at one time more
stable and harmonious than it is now. Historical research, however, has uncovered
no "Golden Age" of the family. Adultery,
illegitimacy, marital conflict and many
other deviations from "Victorian family
norms" are not unique to the twentieth century. Accordingly, those who view family
issues from the opposite perspective tend
to argue that the decline of the family is a
myth. Indeed, according to some social scientists, history shows that the family —
because of its flexible and adaptive nature
— has always been able to withstand the
forces of social upheaval. "Of all social institutions," Kingsley Davis (1972) maintains, "the family shows least evidence of
change." He even finds the family in industrial society to be very similar to the family
in primitive society: "In fact, in many ways
the modern family is more primitive in the
sense of being elementary, than the family
in primitive societies."

Such was the thesis expounded in the
book *Middletown Families* by Theodore
Caplow and associates. Following an intensive analysis of family life in the United
States (based primarily on the population
of Muncie, Indiana), Caplow (1983: 321)
concludes:

*The standard family package itself appears to
have high survival value since it is the product
of the selective continuity and change that
renewal in each generation facilitates. Indeed,
the future development and elaboration of the
family within the relatively affluent and
beneficent environment of urban industrial
America seems almost assured when viewed
against the backdrop of the vicissitudes
experienced by families in America's first 300
years. Certainly, American society with its
familistic values is far from turning hostile
toward marriage and family institutions. I do*

*not think that our successors, in writing about
the American family, will mark the 1970s as a
watershed of change away from the family as
we know it. I think, too, that they will report
the American family of the year 2000 to be
minimally changed in form and structure but
more successful, especially for women and
children, than the family of today.*

Others, ranged behind this "positive"
viewpoint, have gone as far as to predict a
bright future for the family. While they acknowledge that the divorce rate is increasing, they point out that marriage is not yet
obsolete, since most divorced people
marry again. When informed that the extended family seems to be disappearing,
they reply that, historically, it has never
been the predominant form. When informed that out-of-wedlock births are on
the rise, they reply that the number of unwanted births is decreasing. When faced
with evidence that the economic independence of women who work outside the home
generates stress within the family, they
contend that women's earnings enhance
both the family's well-being and, particularly, the resources devoted to child
care. Hence, they maintain that these
changes, so often characterized as harmful
to adults and children alike, are in fact beneficial, and help to sustain the family unit.
They agree that there may be fewer traditional family units in the future, but at the
same time they believe that the quality of
family life will improve substantially. As
Betty Yorburg (1973: 191) sees it:

*. . . the nuclear family will not only persist into
the twenty-first century, but it will be stronger
than ever. We live in a time of rising
psychological as well as economic
expectations. The family as an institution will
not be abolished because people expect more
of it and are more apt to express and act on
their dissatisfactions. This is more likely to
preserve than to destroy the institution of
marriage, which is the basis of the nuclear
family. Other forms — homosexual marriages,*

group marriages, single parent households, communes — will probably become more prevalent with the increased tolerance of individual choice and cultural pluralism in less ethnocentric, more educated, and more permissively reared citizens. But ultimately for biological reasons, the pairing husband and wife relationship and the exclusive parent-child relationship will endure.

Between these two opposing viewpoints is a fertile, middle-ground body of thought, well exemplified in Arlene Skolnick's poignant assertion that the nuclear family is "alive, but not well." Future-shock theorist Alvin Toffler is no less convinced about the "fractured" nature of the modern family. He suggested, however, that the two opposing camps may both be wrong, and that the family in its present form may disintegrate into fragments that will reassemble into a new type of social unit. An example of the changes that Toffler foresees in family life is temporary marriage, which will, he argues, become commonplace.

Various theorists envisage the evolution of alternative family structures that will supersede the husband/wife/child conjugal family as we know it today. A re-examination of the family in light of these postulations is warranted, and is what prompts this analysis of the family itself, and its social importance.

Importance of the Family

In one form or another, the family has existed in every society. According to Berger and Berger (1983: 204):

The family, and no other conceivable structure, is the basic institution of society. If we have learned anything from the tumultuous activities surrounding the family in recent decades, it is that there are no alternatives or substitutes, no matter how well intentioned or attractive they may appear at first sight.

Framed in this perspective, it is not the survival of this "basic institution of so-ciety," per se, that is at issue in the wide-ranging debates over the family. What is at issue, rather, at least in the Western industrialized countries and particularly in North America, is the future of the "nuclear family." What is the fate of this particular form? Is it essential to society? A quick survey of theory may help to understand, if not resolve, the issue.

According to the "structural-functionalist" school of thought, the nuclear family is essential because it is posited to be a vital sub-system of society. Such sub-systems cannot be removed or replaced without disrupting all the other constituents of society — thus resulting in severe upheaval. Its potential to cause such upheaval is what makes it vital. Though controversial owing to its apparent tautological nature, this notion provides a springboard for discussion.

Indeed, structural functionalism is not based on a purely deductive process; it was founded by field-work researchers whose investigations led them to reject the evolutionary theory of marriage and the family. It was probably Malinowski who laid the groundwork for this approach in his book *The Family Among the Australian Aborigines*, published in 1913. Malinowski's anthropological research led him to challenge the conventional wisdom of the time, which held that a family unit made up of parents and children could not function among sexually promiscuous, primitive people. He found that aborigines had rules governing sexual intercourse, and that children had specific mothers and fathers even if both parents occasionally engaged in sexual relations with other members of the community. He concluded that the family existed among primitive people because it fulfilled a fundamental human need — the nurturing of children.

Malinowski's thesis was later echoed in the writings of other anthropologists and sociologists who gradually came to see the family as an essential institution for society. After studying some 250 societies, anthropologist George Peter Murdock (1949: 2) wrote:

The nuclear family is a universal human social grouping. Either as the sole prevailing form of the family or as the basic unit from which more complex familial forms are compounded, it exists as a distinct and strongly functional group in every known society.

Citing another anthropologist, Lowie, he continues:

It does not matter whether marital relations are permanent or temporary; whether there is polygyny or polyandry or sexual license; whether conditions are complicated by the addition of members not included in our family circle: the one fact stands out beyond all others that everywhere the husband, wife and immature children constitute a unit apart from the remainder of the community.

In this research, Murdock shows that the nuclear family is not only a universal social institution, but that it is also necessary for the continuation of any human society. He lists its four basic, interrelated functions — sexual, economic, reproductive and educational/socializational. He argues that the provision for regulated sexual relations between men and women, usually through marriage, is necessary for maintaining co-operative relationships between individuals and groups. The regulations governing sexual relations between husband and wife are, in turn, reinforced by economic co-operation and the division of labour. The first two functions of the nuclear family were encapsuled by Murdock in the following aphorism:

Marriage exists only when the economic and the sexual are united into one relationship, and this combination occurs only in marriage.

The family's primary function is reproduction; and reproduction is imperative, for without it, society becomes extinct. Even if parents, per se, do not at-

tach great importance to this function, ". . . society as a whole has so heavy a stake in the maintenance of its numbers as a source of strength and security that it will insist that parents fulfil these obligations."

The fourth function is a logical consequence of the third: in every society, the family is responsible for the socialization of children. The family is the first social institution to which the child is exposed, and therefore, the institution that imparts and inculcates society's basic values and norms. It is also a source of love, affection and intimacy between parents, children, spouses and other members, and its strength depends on the strength of the emotional bonds it creates.

According to structural-functionalist theory, the nuclear family is the only institution capable of performing all these functions independently and efficiently. But structural functionalism has its opponents. Their objections centre on two interrelated issues. The first issue is that the four functions which underpin the structural-functionalist theory of the family are not unique to the context of the nuclear family. These same functions can be performed by family structures other than nuclear, or even by individuals living outside any semblance of a family structure. The communal family of the Israeli kibbutz in the early stages of that country's history; the matriarchal family system of the 19th century Nayers in India; and the visiting and common-law unions of West Indians are examples that seem to refute the contention that the nuclear family, as such, is a fundamental institution of society writ large. On this first issue, then even those critics who admit that Murdock's functionalist theory may be generally valid for Western societies, do not accept its pretense to universality.

The second issue has to do with the functions themselves. Some critics of structural functionalism argue that the family may exist even if it does not serve to fulfil all the aforementioned functions. Industrialized societies, the critics observe, are capable of organizing themselves in such a way that some of the roles traditionally played by the family are shifted to other institutions. They note that an increasing proportion of women are sexually active before marriage. They interpret this to mean that the family institution can no longer be construed as the *sine qua non* for societal continuity: without the family, society does not become extinct. Similarly, to critics of the structural-functionalist school, the presence of more and more women in the labour force signifies that the economic function, with its division of labour on the basis of sex, is no longer pertinent.

This leaves socialization, and perhaps affection-giving, as the only two undisputed functions of the family. Despite the encroachment of various external forces, historian Carl Degler maintains that the basic principles upon which the family is based have remained unchanged for the past 200 years. The family has been highly flexible, and has successfully adjusted to major social alterations. Focussing on the four functions identified by Murdock, he says of the family:

It is today, as it was 200 years ago, the primary institution for the nurturing of children, and its essential interest for adults is that it provides affection, sexual expression, and companionship. (Degler, 1980: 452)

Degler is not alone. In fact, others argue that because the family was required to perform so many functions — a "jack of all trades and master of none" — it may have been on the verge of extinction. Having been stripped of some of these functions, it may now be able to better fulfil its primary role — "... to provide love, support to children and affection between spouses."

There are those, however, who assert that even the latter two functions are in

jeopardy. Social historian Christopher Lasch (1977) espoused this view when he pointed out that the family no longer provides "... emotional security when marriages end so often in divorce and are conducted according to principles of business — 'one leaves a position as a better one offers itself.' ' What's more, when both parents work, it is difficult for them to devote much personal attention to the children. Sociologist Alice Rossi (1977) takes up the argument, stating that, in view of the current structure of the work world and the biosocial aspect of parenting, reconciling employment with child care has become problematic for women. And Lasch adds:

The only function that matters is socialization; and when protection, work and instruction in work have all been removed from home, the child no longer identifies with his parents or internalizes their authority in the same way as before, if indeed he internalizes their authority at all.

All these writings deal with the functional aspect of the family, but are restricted to the conjugal form consisting of husband-father, wife-mother and children. The emergence of other structures and other living arrangements, however, suggests that the status of the traditional family is indeed in question. For most people, in fact, the traditional nuclear family is the predominant form for much of their life, although the enticement of other forms — such as living alone, marrying or living common-law but with no intent of having children, having children but opting to remain single, and so on — is by no means insignificant.

... This study analyses the contemporary Canadian family from a demographic perspective. Demographic aspects of family trends and patterns examined by using historical and contemporary census and survey data as well as other pertinent information from existing studies. The bulk of the analyses covers the 1951 to 1986 period, although in some cases data are presented for a longer period.

Major Changes

The evolution of families and households since the closing of the baby-boom period in the early 1960s has been marked by an increasing diversity and instability of living arrangements. The traditional, husband-dominated, two-parent family, founded on formal marriage, is increasingly challenged by: (a) marital instability and conjugal mobility; (b) two-wage-earner families; (c) informal, non-marital cohabitation; and, (d) lone-parent families.

Prima facie evidence suggests that the "traditional" husband-wife family still retains its dominant position in Canadian society. In terms of all families combined, the proportion accounted for by husband-wife families fell only slightly between 1961 and 1986 (from 92 to 87 percent). But, as a result of the sharp rise in the divorce and remarriage rates manifested since the 1970s, one would expect a growing proportion of such families to be made-up of so-called blended, or reconstituted, families. Though it is not known how many children are living in families with one natural and one step-parent, or how many of them are under the custody of one parent or are under the shared custody of two parents who live apart, their numbers are presumed to be on the rise.

A notable feature in the current changes is the growing number of families in which both the father and the mother are employed. The labour force participation rate of currently married women with at least one child under 6 years of age jumped from 27.1 percent in 1971, to 59.5 percent in 1986. While this has meant an increase in the family's revenue earning capacity and greater economic independence for the spouses, it has perhaps also made divorce a more viable option for some.

A landmark development in the recent history of the family is the rise in non-marital cohabitation. Statistically hardly noticeable only two decades ago, the prevalence of common-law cohabitation stood, according to the 1986 Census, at 8.3 percent of all couples. It is among those in their late teens and in their twenties that the practice is most prevalent. Among cohabiting 20–24 years old, 38 males and 30 females in every 100 were in a common-law union. But those in common-law partnerships are by no means an homogeneous group. For some, it represents an extension to young adulthood without deep marital commitments, a matter of casual convenience. For others it acts as a prelude to marriage, while for others still it provides a permanent alternative to marriage. Compared to formal marriages, common-law unions are less stable and produce fewer children.

The number of lone-parent families more than doubled between 1961 and 1986 — from 347,000 to 854,000 — as a result of significant changes in the factors precipitating the formation of such families. The proportion of lone-parent families with a widowed head plummeted from 62 to 27 percent between 1961 and 1986, whereas those with a divorced head grew from just over four to almost 30 percent. The proportion of never-married mothers rose from about three to just over 13 percent, or in absolute numbers, from 9,000 to 114,000. There is evidence that fewer children borne to single mothers are being given up for adoption. By far the largest proportion of lone-parent families — 82 percent in 1986 — are headed by mothers.

Along with greater plurality and instability, family size has steadily decreased from an average of 3.9 persons in 1961 (at the height of the baby-boom) to 3.1 in 1986. The effect on family size of a sharp drop in the fertility rate has been compounded by the fragmentation of families caused by more frequent marital breakdown. Remarriage has not quite kept pace with the rising divorce rate.

In addition, the rate of family formation has declined. Fewer people have married, or they have done so at a later age. Some have delayed, while others have forgone having children. The fact that 30.0 percent of 25 to 29 year old ever-married women reported themselves as childless in 1981, compared to less than 14 percent in 1961, may well reflect the tendency to postpone parenting. It could also mean, however, that some of them will utlimately remain childless either by choice or because of involuntary age-related sterility.

Finally, more youths in their late teens and early twenties have opted for an independent household, creating an extended hiatus, or transition, between childhood and adulthood. Although they have left their parents' home, they are not yet ready to establish a family of their own. At the opposite end of the age spectrum, living alone has increased significantly among those aged 65 and over. This is especially true among women, where the number increased from 15 percent in 1961, to almost 34 percent in 1986. Seventy-seven percent of the elderly who live alone are women — clearly the result of the female advantage in longevity and their lower rate of remarriage.

The Social Context of Change

A host of factors have combined to bring about increasing diversity and instability in living arrangements as well as a diminishing number of people living in a family situation. Some have their origins in the economy, others in the social context of the family, and still others in contraceptive technology.

In terms of economics, two major developments have made the strongest inroads into the family — the growth of women's employment and the rise of consumerism. On the one hand, an expansion of the traditionally female-dominated activities, particularly services, and a breakdown of the barriers to entry into the former occupational preserves of males, have created unprecedented employment opportunities for women. More women have taken up permanent jobs that require higher skill and greater work commitment. On the other hand, the rise of consumerism — the tremendous expansion in the range of goods, services and leisure, as well as greater expectations triggered by aggressive advertising and assisted by a credit system designed to sustain consumers' demands — has made the two-wage-earner family almost a necessity.

In the social context of the family, changes in the relationship between husband and wife, and parent and child, should be singled out. The traditional husband-dominated relationship has given way to a more egalitarian partnership between the spouses. It is argued by some that the rising primacy of personal gratification and individualization of the marital partnership over the institutional context of the marriage has made the latter more vulnerable to internal strains and external pressure. The transfer of old age security from family to society has long since reduced the economic incentive for having children. Now, the continuing erosion of the parental role in child socialization may be undercutting the psychological drive for parenthood. The generative function of the family has thus diminished. Children themselves are veering away from parents and towards peer groups for companionship and socialization, thus perhaps weakening their own aspirations to become parents.

Finally, attitudes toward marriage and the family, and the actual behaviour of couples, have no doubt been influenced by the contraceptive revolution — the pill in the 1960s and sterilization in the 1970s. The link between sex, marriage and procreation has been weakened — if not broken. The much-celebrated sexual revolution of the 1960s might not have taken hold under conditions of less effective contraceptive technology. Many marriages that would formerly have been prompted by pre-marital pregnancy can henceforth be avoided or postponed, and unwanted pregnancy within marriage has been virtually eliminated. Along with greater employment opportunities for women, effective contraceptive techniques have made alternatives to parenting more readily available.

But the relationship between family and the factors mentioned above is not necessarily unidirectional; it is likely to be reciprocal and interactive in nature. Thus it has been noted that the sharp drop in nuptiality and the rise in divorce followed by several years, rather than preceded, the onset of the baby bust.

The fragility of marriage may not necessarily have been caused by the greater economic independence of spouses, as often claimed. The increasing propensity for women to engage in salaried work could well be seen as a rational option to a marriage which no longer provided insurance for the future. With the sharp decline in fertility and family size, child-related commitments were no longer sufficient to justify women staying at home. This "home-bound" energy has thus been released and redirected toward revenue-generating activities outside the home, making women's economic independence more real.

Impact Areas

The significance of the changes affecting the family become all the more apparent by identifying a few areas of public policy where they can exert an influence.

One such area is family legislation and the administration of justice in family matters. In this regard, among the developments taking place, two stand out prominently: the widespread incidence of non-marital cohabitation (common-law unions); and, marital disruption (divorce, separation, desertion). Situations such as those in which people are legally married but living in a common-law relationship, or conflicts arising from the custody of one spouse or shared custody of both former spouses involving a growing number of children, are bound to present new challenges to the administration of justice.

To the entire field of the administration of work-related legislation, the growing phenomenon of both parents (and would-be parents) working poses problems for which solutions are of the utmost importance to the individuals concerned, their employers, and to society at large. Granted that there is perhaps now more sharing of household work between spouses, child rearing still remains an occupation exacting in time and energy even in this era of reduced family size and modern household facilities. The transfer of child care to private and public agencies can be helpful, if it can be afforded, though it is not without problems when observed from the angle of child socialization. Special work arrangements such as flexible hours and maternity or paternity leave allow parents to spend more time with their children. But if the family is to continue assuming its function of bearing and rearing the nation's future citizens, the quest for institutional solutions to ease the pressure on parents arising from their dual pursuits of family and employment, without undue work disruption and loss in efficiency to employers, will remain an important research and policy issue. With a fertility rate no longer sufficient to ensure the replacement of generations (and in the longer run that of the population), the issues have recently gained considerable public prominence.

There are two other groups that are bidding for public attention. One is single parents, while the other is elderly people living alone. Both groups are cut-off. Direct income subsidies and indirect subsidies through fiscal adjustments, accessible housing and childcare for single parents, and health services geared towards the special needs of the elderly living alone all stand to be important issues on the welfare policy agenda. The expected further growth of these groups and what is often called the "feminization" of poverty makes them all the more important policy issues.

Beyond the domain of public policy, trends and changes in families and households should be watched by business. Those industries catering to the family or household as a consumption unit will have to keep two developments in mind. The first is shrinking size, while the second and probably more important in the long run, is the slowdown in the growth of families and households. The number of Canadian households grew at the impressive rate of 3.5 percent per annum in the 1970s, and by 2.2 percent in the 1980s. But as the baby-boom generations phase out, and the baby-bust generations enter the age of family formation, growth will slow down to roughly one percent by the turn of the century according to the most recent Statistics Canada projections.

WOMEN, WIVES AND MOTHERS

Roberta Hamilton

In the last 20 years, the feminist movement has challenged every aspect of social life in Canada, as it has throughout the world. No arena has been too public, too intimate, or too scholarly to remain untouched by this

From *Reconstructing the Canadian Family: Feminist Perspectives*, pp. 3-20 by Mandell and Duffy. By permission of Butterworths.

latest and most widespread resurrection of the centuries-old struggle for sexual equality. Juliet Mitchell called this struggle "The Longest Revolution" (1966). As in earlier periods, though never so profoundly, this struggle threatens the interests and unleashes the anxieties of so many people in so many ways that the backlash it has provoked could be called "The Longest Counter-Revolution."

This chapter explores the relationship between this struggle and the family. Families, in a capitalist society, comprise a changing set of relationships which take their shape from and exert influence upon that society. The argument here is that the particular nature of the contemporary family, as it emerged as part of the developing relations of capitalist society, provided the important preconditions for the women's movement. This movement produced, as a central part of its analysis, a critique of the relationships between men, women and children within the family. At the same time, the women's movement exposed the dialectical interplay between social institutions. This textbook, a feminist text on the family, results from and contributes to that critique.

Most feminist anthropologists now argue that the relationship between men and women (throughout almost all of human history) has been one of domination and subordination of women (Reiter, 1975). If that is so, the question then arises, Why have there been mass movements of women to fight against oppression only during the last 125 years? The question is not, Why do we have a women's movement now? but, Why did we not have such movements very much earlier in history? The second question is, Why has the struggle for women's liberation encountered such resistance from large numbers of men, and women too?

These questions direct our attention to the family and household: its location within the broader social structure, on the one hand, and the relationships between men, women and children within the family, on the other. For wherever else women have been, historically and in the present, they are centrally located within family households. What they do there, how they do it, and how all this relates to the rest of the society varies enormously. But if we are to understand why women have behaved as they did, why they have accepted or resisted their subordinate position, and why that position has been challenged so pervasively in the last 20 years, we must begin with the family.

Yet, as feminists have emphasized, families both take their shape from and in turn condition economic, political and social relationships. Family structures, functions and roles emerge from a dynamic interchange among individuals and social forces. In the end, consequently, the society as a whole must be taken on as a dynamic set of processes. To understand what we have become, or more precisely, what we are becoming, we must understand from where we have come. This is the task of historical sociology.

We are born into relationships which are so systematic and pervasive that they appear unalterable. We talk about the family, the economic system, the government, almost without believing that it is men and women, in relationship with each other, who create and reproduce them. The new social history calls these "inevitable" relationships into question (Abrams, 1982; Tilly and Scott, 1978; Stone, 1977; Phillips forthcoming; Parr 1982; Trofimenkoff and Prentice, 1977).

This historical approach is especially useful in understanding those areas of human life that appear natural, or pregiven. For we experience ourselves as male or female so profoundly that to be told that this too, this male and female identity, is also socially constructed, in time and

space, can be quite astounding, if not threatening. The anxieties unleashed by what appears to be an attack on the natural family and the natural relations between men and women have led many to contribute to the backlash against the women's movement.

Until the development of feminist theory, philosophers, sociologists and historians tended to accept the relations between the sexes as given — part of the natural order of things. Those who questioned the conventional wisdom were pretty much ignored (de Beauvoir, 1949; Myrdal, 1944; Hacker, 1951).

Sociology students learned that the nuclear family and its sex-based division of labour was functional to society. Talcott Parsons, the most influential of these functionalist sociologists, explained that men played the instrumental role within the family — that is, they went out to work "to bring home the bacon" — and women played the affective role — that is, they cooked it (all the while running emotional interference between father and children to ensure some modicum of peace). Such a division of labour, Parsons argued, was necessary in a highly mobile, competitive society to permit the family to behave as a unit, so that husband and wife would complement each other, not compete. Yet Parsons (1959) was sufficiently astute to point out that these arrangements could be quite constricting for women.

As a description, particularly of white, middle-class American families in the 1950s, this formulation had some plausibility. Students who read this work but came from families that did not conform to the model assumed either that sociology was irrelevant for understanding social life, or that their particular family/household was deviant or at least idiosyncratic. So even though the model did not describe what their families were really like, it described what they thought they *should* be like. Functionalism was more like normative philosophy than sociology.

How then, less than 20 years later, could there appear a feminist textbook on the family, a text that argues systematically that relations between men and women within the family, as elsewhere, are socially constructed, and that the family is a prime site for the reproduction of the relations of domination and subordination between the sexes? This question leads us back to the women's movement. For the feminist critique of the family developed within this social movement, not within the learned academies or within the established disciplines.

The impetus to examine and change oppressive conditions hardly can be expected to come from those who are privileged by those conditions, from those who are part of the dominant or established order. If your mother has always washed your clothes, cooked your meals, and generally cleaned up after you, do you think it likely that one day you would throw up your hands in horror and insist on developing a more equitable division of labour? We should not be surprised that the motivation for examining these practices came not from men, but from women. It was not male sociologists teaching and writing in the universities (who, after all, were also fathers, husbands — and sons), but women, many of them young, who felt dismayed that their education was leading directly to two full time jobs: low-paid waged work and unrelieved domestic labour. The women's movement provided the social basis for initiating a critique of the dominant sociological paradigms. This critique, against considerable resistance, eventually became incorporated into the university curriculum.

It is clear, therefore, that many reasons exist to prompt a most important question: if societies have been patriarchal since time out of mind, as pre-industrial people would say, why are the movements of women for social, economic, and political justice such recent historical developments?

Asking this question does not suggest that patriarchal relations are ahistorical. Indeed, the variety of ways in which sexual inequality occurs boggles the mind. Patriarchal relations are constructed historically, as are those of race and class. Yet the concept of "patriarchy" draws our attention to the systematic, sustained and pervasive production and reproduction of inequality between men and women. This does not mean that all men have had a better time of it than do all women. As the late feminist historian Joan Kelly (1984: 4) explained: we must look at the *relation* between men and women *within* any particular society if we are to understand whether and how history has dealt uneven hands to women and men. In comparison with the majority of men, women and children living today, for example, most of us in Canada, certainly those of us at university, in one capacity or another, are enormously privileged. Sexual inequality, like other socially constructed hierarchies, however, is alive and well within our own milieu.

History is constantly in the making. Yet some historical changes have been so dramatic that they transformed the social landscape. To really understand the peculiarities of our own environment, we must return to these periods. This kind of history requires what Raymond Williams (1977: 121) has called "epochal analysis" because we concentrate upon "dominant and definitive lineaments and features." Here we sacrifice important variations and exceptions for broad contours. In a certain way we compare two photographs, instead of running a moving picture. This kind of history has two advantages: it provides us with distance from our common-sense worldview, and it highlights the inter-relatedness of our current social practices. The last great transition in human history — some would say the greatest there has ever been — was the transition from feudalism to capitalism (Giddens, 1981) which began in England at the end of the sixteenth century. A new set of economic relations was emerging on the world stage, and with them, as an intrinsic part, new forms of the family, and new kinds of relations between men and women (Dobb, 1963; Hilton, 1986; Brenner, 1986; Hamilton, 1978).

The Feudal Family

At the end of the sixteenth century, the majority of people in Europe lived in small households on land which they possessed, but did not own outright. They yielded a living from this land, at least in years when there were good harvests, with some people doing better than others. There were several ways people enhanced their chances of survival: by sending children out as servants to better-off neighbours, thus leaving more food for family members; by selling surplus produce at local markets, thus producing some income; by gathering wood for fuel from the common land to which they had access; and by wage-labouring for small businessmen.

These particular property arrangements had important consequences for the relations between the sexes, or more especially for relations between husband and wife. For marriage was as necessary for men as for women. Husband and wife required the labour of the other to survive and to feed their children who also contributed once they turned four or five. As a result, widowers, after what we might consider an indecently short period of mourning, remarried. "To thrive the yeoman must wive" wrote a practical poet of the time, and most did, some several times (Tusser, 1557). Historian Eileen Power (1965: 410) argued that the interdependence of husband and wife produced a kind of rough and ready equality between them. In addi-

tion, a fair amount of physical abuse was directed from husband to wife. The main point here is that the labour of each was interrelated, and embedded within the network of relations between them and their children.

The family was an economic unit, predicated on what Marx (1973) called "a unity of capital and labour." That is, the essential components needed for survival — land, tools and labour — were present within each household. The enormous relevance of this relationship between kinship, capital and labour becomes clear when we compare it with the situation of men and women in our society. Here there is not "unity" between labour and capital. All that most people own is their labour power — that is, their ability to labour. This they must sell for a wage in order to provide a living for themselves and their children. Indeed, the desperation of the unemployed is directly attributable to this historically particular and very peculiar arrangement in capitalist society. Willingness to labour is not enough. There is nothing to labour upon unless someone gives you a job: a job which he or she, but almost always he, can take away because s/he owns or controls the resources necessary for the "realization of labour" (Marx, 1973: 471). When a pulp and paper mill closes down, or an insurance company or university buys some fancy new machines, people are thrown out of work and back onto the labour market. Understanding the unity of labour and capital is crucial for understanding feudal society, its particular form of the family/household, and how it differed from our own.

The implications of these arrangements can be best be understood by comparing them with what came later, with what we ourselves are familiar. Production and consumption were not two radically separate processes. We must go twice into the labour market. First we sell our labour, as any other commodity would be sold, in order to acquire a wage. Then we must take this money back to the marketplace to purchase what we need, and can afford, to get us by until the next paycheque (Luxton, 1980: 124–28; Secombe, 1980: 71). In feudal society, however, work and home were coterminous. The distinction between "real" work and housework was meaningless. Perhaps most surprising for us, only the glimmerings of a split between public and private life had developed. Today we go to such lengths to protect our privacy. Our houses, for example, are divided into rooms clearly demarcating different kinds of activity. We believe that children should be protected from witnessing expressions of adult sexuality. Our feudal forebearers did not share these delicate inhibitions. Peasant hovels, like overcrowded slums today, did not provide the space for carefully constructed retreats — we call them bedrooms — away from children. Even kings and queens in palaces did not believe that their sexual activities should be beyond the gaze of others, as Philippe Ariès showed in his path-breaking book, *Centuries of Childhood.*

As social life became divided into producing commodities and buying them, into work and home, as labour was divided into wage labour and housework, and as society settled into public and private realms, it is striking that women became associated with the second of these pairs of concepts, and men with the first (Hamilton, 1978: 24–28). It is assumed that men produce things; women buy things. Hence women are extravagant: how many Dagwood and Blondie comics have been a poke at Blondie, the wacky spendthrift? How many jokes have you heard husbands make about wives spending all *their* money? (See Luxton, 1980: 168–73 for some very unfunny examples.) Also, men go to work; women stay home — or should stay home. These ideas persist even in the face of much contrary

evidence. Women are the staple of private life. They not only do the housework, they protect the private realm, family life, intimacy, personal feelings, even morality (Hamilton, 1978: 96).

We accept all these categories as providing accurate descriptions of our life. They seem natural. All these aspects of life, however, were embedded within the feudal household. The dependent interrelations between men and women, the production and reproduction to meet daily needs and the needs of the next generation, were part of the same web of life. Men and women were unified within the family, which encompassed a mutual set of obligations and privileges. This also held true for the wives of craftsmen and tradesmen who were partners in their husband's businesses, and for noblewomen who ran the large, multi-faceted manors (Clark, 1919; Charles and Duffin, 1985).

A second point also relates to this idea of embeddedness in the feudal family. The peasant households possessed but did not own their land. Their tenure of the land was well protected in law, until the bourgeoisie gained power after the English Revolution and began changing property laws to suit its own interests (Hill, 1969: 147; Manning, 1978; Neeson, 1984). Even in feudal times, however, tenure was not absolute. People were obliged to turn over a certain amount (an amount which varied historically) of money, goods or labour to the lord, to the church and, in some places, with the rise of absolutism, to the state (Goubert, 1973; Mousnier, 1979; Bloch, 1966; Hilton, 1986). The laws of the society, backed by military force, ensured that peasants, however reluctantly, handed over some of the fruits of their labour to others. This was how the dominant class, the nobility, siphoned off the surplus that the rest of the people produced; indeed, this is how the elite secured and sustained its dominance. This served to make the lord, priest or tax collector quite unpopular, as the long history of peasant resistance attests (Ladurie, 1974: 201; Brenner, 1986).

All ruling classes must have a means of appropriating the surplus produced by the majority, whether they be peasants or wage labourers. Without this appropriation they would cease to be a ruling class. In our society, for example, most people are paid a wage. For Marx this wage represented a subsistence which ensured that workers had enough to keep body and soul together in order that they could continue to work. The amount of subsistence varies historically and depends upon many factors: the ratio of labourers to jobs; the sex, education, and bargaining power of workers; the mobility and alternative investment opportunities for capital. What workers produce, but do not get paid for producing, is this surplus which goes to the owners as both overhead and profit. If students work at Burger King in the summer, the profits from all the hamburgers that they make but do not get paid for producing go to Mr. Burger King, so that he can add yet another Burger King to the blighted cityscape. This surplus then contributes to putting some little corner restaurant out of business (Reiter, 1986).

In capitalist society, surplus accumulates through economic, not legal coercion. The relationship with employers is purely contractual: workers agree to work and employers agree to pay them until they quit or are fired. Beyond the working contract they have no responsibilities or obligations to each other. If a woman goes into labour, her boss will not send his wife over to supervise the delivery as a feudal lord might have done. More likely, if a boss can get away with it, he will fire her as soon as he knows she is pregnant. On the other hand, if he needs some help in his garden he will not expect her to send her husband or son over at the weekend to help, as might have happened on a feudal manor. The relationship between peasant and lord, between household and lordship, was embedded in a set of shifting obligations and privileges. If peasants did not much like their lords, they could not go shopping for new ones, and if nobles did not like their peasants they could not select others. The nobles, however, had ways of bringing recalcitrant subjects to heel.

So the peasants were tied to their land, as the surest guarantee of subsistence, with the greatest risks to survival being bad harvests and rapacious landlords. Husband and wife were tied to each other through their mutual need for each other's labour. Peasant and lord were tied through sets of obligations which, in general, went from the bottom up, although lords might earn a bad name if they proved inhospitable or lacking in properly paternalistic behaviour. The exploitative relations between peasants and lords were interwoven into a complex network of interdependencies. Challenging the lords' right to a surplus could jeopardize an entire family's fragile package of survival strategies, including the right to shelter and land. Furthermore, members of each household worked their own plot of land. This isolating work experience — unlike work in a modern factory or office — did not provide the collective work experience that can bind together those in the same circumstances while, at the same time, separating them from those above.

Similarly, most men and most women found it impossible to survive without marriage and household. Certainly, the interdependence of husband and wife was crafted within a society that never doubted the inferiority of women. The laws of church, state, and manor sustained and counselled the subordination of women to men, and wives to husbands (Middleton, 1983; Rogers, 1966). Some women did challenge their husbands' authority, particularly when the latter violated community standards. The penalties for resistance, however, were high in a society that provided only one location for work and home, and no alternative ways to piece together a living. These feudal arrangements obviously did not provide fertile ground for either a labour movement or a women's movement. Their entrance onto the world stage awaited the development of capitalism, with its own particular form of patriarchy.

The Transition to Capitalism

A great deal has been written about how capitalist relations developed in the very heart of feudal society (Marx, 1973; Dobb, 1963; Hilton, 1976; Hill, 1969; Brenner, 1986). In simplest terms, however, people had to lose their means of subsistence, namely the land, before they could be free to sell their labour power in the marketplace. At the same time there had to be those who owned and controlled capital with which to purchase the newly freed labour power. Surplus capital and surplus labour, therefore, can be seen as two sides of the same coin. The gradually accumulating capital derived from the surplus produced by the workers. This surplus capital then was reinvested in further capitalist (at first primarily agrarian capitalist) development. This capital accumulation underwrote the Industrial Revolution and, in a more general sense, the availability of capital and labour provided the preconditions for the Industrial Revolution (George, 1971; Hamilton, 1978: 15–17). The spiralling growth of capital and labour involved a snowballing and mutually reinforcing set of processes.

In general, during the transition to capitalism, people were forced or persuaded to leave the land: common lands were enclosed, rents were raised, and the parliament that emerged after the half-finished English Revolution confirmed the process through abolishing feudal tenures and in-

stituting the contemporary system of buying and selling land. In this process some grew richer, but many more took to the roads, embarking upon new lives of vagabondage and crime. Many others went to work for their better-off neighbours (Hill, 1969: 147; McMullan, 1984).

This process created not only wage labourers, but also consumers (Appleby, 1978). For landless people have to buy everything they need (that is, what they can afford) in the marketplace. By the end of the seventeenth century expanding markets were being created, not just in England but in America (Davis, 1983; George, 1971). These markets helped to make the already rich even richer, while creating the newly rich. These expanding markets have reached an illogical zenith today. Capitalism requires the continuing creation of new needs. People must be persuaded to spend their money in new and spectacular ways, preferably on things requiring frequent replacement. The importance of the isolated nuclear family to capitalist expansion is clear. Every household needs to own everything: washing machines, stoves, cars, cottages, videos, microwaves, blenders, all of which lie idle most of the time (Zaretsky, 1976; Hayden, 1981; Cowan, 1983).

This transition to capitalism encompassed more than the origins of contemporary economic relations. Challenges to political relationships accompanied the shift to contractual relations in the economic sphere. Kings and nobles had been compared to fathers. Their subjects owed them obedience and deference. In return, rulers were expected, at least in theory, to look after their subjects, according to their station in life. The authority of kings and other rulers was held to be divinely inspired, natural and unlimited. When the feudal world came asunder and new classes and new relations between classes developed, so too did new political ideas expressing these new economic realities (Manning, 1978).

The rising class of bourgeois capitalists no longer depended upon the pleasure of the court or on traditional property arrangements for their livelihood. The ideology of the self-made man finds its origins here. Self-made men made their money from agriculture, trade and colonization, or through providing services to those who did. Thus we find an expanding professional class of doctors, lawyers, and bankers, who shared in the new interests and lifestyles of the bourgeoisie. These men hired others to work for them on a contractual basis. Ideas about the divine right of kings held little sway for the new "self-made" men. Radical ideas (i.e., rulers only ruled because of a contract between them and the ruled) gained adherents, and men of property began insisting upon parliaments that would protect their interests. The door to universal suffrage creaked open. At the same time, religious reformers insisted upon a personal, unmediated relationship between the individual and God. In lay hands the Bible proved a controversial document. If still believed to be divinely inspired, it was now being humanly interpreted in a myriad of ways. Contracts between ruler and ruled, individuals and God, and employers and employees became the order of the new day. But wait a minute! Not between husband and wife.

As much as the economic, political and religious theorists insisted upon contractual relationships in the public world they continued to build this new world upon the indissoluble unit of husband and wife. Marriage was a property relationship, and the wife was still clearly part of the husband's property. The relationships between ruler and ruled, employer and employee, even individual and God, were becoming questions of personal choice, requiring constant renewal, part of the world seen to be humanly wrought. The family remained part of the natural order of things, with the woman as its linchpin (Eisenstein, 1981).

Contraditions were already developing around the position of women in this new society. These contradictions were experienced in very deep and significant ways for many women. To understand them we must explore how the family/household itself was changing during this transition to capitalism, how the role of women and the relationship between husband and wife were transformed, and how these changes had very different implications for the emerging bourgeoisie and the burgeoning proletariat.

To begin, peasants were becoming wage-earners. The split between work and home meant that women no longer could perform their reproductive tasks of bearing and rearing children in the *same* location as their other work. They were confronted with the necessity of making a living for their families and at the same time ensuring that their children did not die of neglect. The conventional division of labour between husbands and wives cast men in the role of economic providers. But this was little more than a cruel joke because the wages a man could command (certainly in early capitalism) barely covered his own food and drink. The family wage was a fantasy. It still is, except for the highest paid union workers who, at times, have been able, through the collective bargaining process, to earn sufficient money to support a family (Secombe, 1986; Barrett and McIntosh, 1980, 1982; Armstrong, 1984). The economic interdependence between men and women broke down. Women and children became a burden — for many men an insupportable burden. This "Second Humble Address" from the Poor Weavers provides an example:

That the Poor's Rates are doubled and in some places trebled by the multitude of Poor Perishing and Starving Women and Children being come to the Parishes, while their

Husbands and Fathers not able to bear the cries which they could not relieve are fled into France . . . to seek their Bread (Quoted in Clark, 1919: 118).

The family as economic unit encountered some perilous days, which have grown into decades and centuries. The number of children today with sole-support and poverty-stricken mothers indicates that this was a long-term consequence of the development of capitalist relations.

In the growing bourgeoisie, women also lost their productive role. As the former busy, hospitable, and many-faceted manor gave way to private homes with separate spaces for servants, children, and parents, and as work took men more and more away from home, women were increasingly relegated to and immersed in the privatized, isolated world of the newly constituted nuclear family. At the same time as their husbands, fathers and sons were remaking the world in their masculine image, wives ceased to be business partners and became instead the "Angel in the House" (Rowbotham, 1972: 29). Mary Astell lamented this change. She pleaded, "Can you be in Love with servitude and folly? Can you dote on a mean, ignorant and ignoble Life?" (1701: 52).

A new ideology was in the making, however. First a few, but then many, began to argue that a life in this newly constituted family was the pinnacle to which women should aspire. The home of the "honest, upright Englishman" was described as the "sweetest and purest thing on earth" (Flynn, 1920: 75). In time it was realized that women's special qualities — purity, chastity, patience, gentleness — would be bruised in contact with the raucous world that capitalists were creating outside their doors. This world included a growing class of desperately poor women in many areas of the city, as well as servants occupying the least favoured parts of the bourgeois home. Many of these working-class women supplemented their meagre wages by sexually servicing the men of the bourgeoisie who found the homes they created with their pure and protected wives to be too confining. What struck many observers at that time was the presence of two classes of women: one poor, one affluent; one overworked, the other bored; one sexual, the other chaste; one independent by necessity, the other dependent in every sense on a husband or father.

The ideology, "the cult of true womanhood" (Reuther, 1973) proved enormously powerful. As sections of the working class organized and commanded better wages, the ideology that good husbands supported their wives, and good wives were full-time home-makers was also spreading, and would receive, much later, a properly academic stamp in the sociology of Talcott Parsons (1959). As the economic interdependence of husband and wife became unravelled, new ways — ideological, political and economic — emerged to tie women to the family. But it was a very different sort of family than in feudal times.

Perhaps the most effective of these new ways was the development of a most novel idea: that love and marriage not only went together, but indeed *had* to go together (Sarsby, 1983). As long as marriage had been primarily an economic arrangement, as it was throughout the feudal era, there was no special belief that husband and wife had to love each other — certainly not in our sense of falling in love with each other. Passions such as this were known to exist, but their instability was well recognized and, therefore, better left to less permanent liaisons than marriage. Furthermore, the Catholic Church in the Middle Ages revered celibacy as an adult life course.

The Protestant reformers thought no better of lust and sexual passion than did the clergy of the Church of Rome, but they rejected celibacy as a means to achieve personal holiness, and argued that a godly life could be pursued best by those in other stations and callings. They promoted marriage and believed that man and woman should love each other even as they loved God. Even conjugal sex was blessed, providing that passion was kept well in check (Hamilton, 1978: Ch. 3).

What the Protestants did not (and could not) know was that the world was changing. They had intended the marital partnership to be embedded in the feudal life of economic interdependence between husband and wife, each working with and for each other, and collectively for their children. That kind of life, as we have seen, was disappearing. The emerging bourgeois family, stripped of its economic functions, became the site of a married couple brought together by mutual love and admiration, enough — as it had to be — to last a lifetime. Protestants were as adamantly opposed to divorce as Catholics, and they even closed the annulment option. The ideology of romantic love had found a vacuum, and the early Protestants would have undoubtedly expressed horror by its elevation to the modern foundation of marriage.

The women of the bourgeoisie became almost totally dependent upon their husbands. Other than governessing, there were few jobs open to, and suitable for, women of the middle and upper-middle classes (Petersen, 1972). The legitimating ideology for this life of dependence is still familiar: ideas about romantic love, idealization of family life, separate spheres for women and men, and the needs of children.

The First Women's Movement

The main focus for feminists at the turn of the twentieth century was neither women's location in the family, nor the inequality and oppression their position produced. Given the dependence of most women and

their children upon husbands and fathers, a frontal critique of the family would have been individually and collectively impossible. For as Jeffrey Weeks (1981: 163) put it, "in the absence of alternative avenues for middle-class women, their actual survival often depended upon a secure legal marriage." A critique of the family awaited the new conditions of the 1960s that ushered in the contemporary women's movement. So what, then, was this first movement about?

Primarily, it challenged the limitations on women's activities in the public sphere. The men of the rising bourgeoisie had been challenging their own subordinate place in aristocratic order for some two centuries. This challenge constituted the small "l" liberal assault upon the aristocratic order. It was accomplished in the name of the rights of man, of individual worth, expression and achievement. It insisted that contracts between subject and rulers be negotiated through elections. This liberal attack included demands for the freedom of worship, freedom of speech, freedom of the press, and equality of opportunity.

As so often happens historically, when a particular group or class insists upon certain rights for itself, others, who hear the rhetoric which often is cast in universal terms, believe that it means them too. Men of property, for example, only intended the vote for men of property. Increasingly, however, working-class men insisted upon inclusion. They fought and struggled and won the right to vote (Thompson, 1984). Sooner or later women would insist upon these same rights for themselves. Mary Wollstonecraft in *A Vindication of the Rights of Women* had provided the argument in 1792. Women, she pointed out, also were rational beings. If they did not behave rationally, it was a result of limited upbringing and education, not innate "feminine" qualities.

As time passed, women challenged their enclosure in the limiting and limited private sphere. They took over rhetoric (never intended by men to apply to women), insisted upon their right to participate equally in public. They demanded the right to vote, to own property, to enter professions and to receive an education. These were radical demands. True to their liberal roots, they were demands for equality of opportunity. They did not address squarely questions about equality of condition, although women's unequal starting place in the race of life, created by their reproductive tasks and their place in the family, was sometimes perceived. Women challenged their denial of property rights and the legal power of husbands over wives and children; they insisted upon their legal right to child custody when marriages dissolved, and their right to divorce abusive husbands. Yet they did not question the validity and underpinnings of the family itself.

These women of the bourgeoisie railed against the double standard which permitted their husbands to have sexual relations with other women, women who might have been working full- or part-time as prostitutes to supplement meagre wages. From the vantage point of bourgeois women — some of whom did comprehend the double exploitation/oppression of their working class sisters — their husbands' sexual activities were threatening: certainly they feared venereal disease. They wanted the vote, among other things, to clean up the world, including their husbands' behaviour; they sought to impose a single standard of sexual behaviour on the sexes. As one famous slogan went, "Votes for Women! Chastity for Men!" Could it have been otherwise in a world without, for example, safe and trustworthy methods of birth control, antibiotics, opportunities for economic independence, or access to child support from state or husbands?

These feminists emphasized that they wanted the vote and education to become better mothers. They argued that women's special role in the family equipped them to play an important role in humanizing the brutal public world. That world, with the participation of women, could become as clean as their own kitchens. Perhaps, at times, they phrased their demands in these socially acceptable ways to ward off criticism, to try to alleviate the monumental anxieties their demands had unleashed. But most often they must have been sincere.

Today their demands form part of the conservative status quo (Eisenstein, 1981: Ch. 10). Even Phyllis Shlafly and R.E.A.L. Women do not argue that women should not have the right to vote. (Dubinsky, 1984; Eisenstein, 1981). Their quarrel is with feminists who have uncovered the limitations of equality in the public sphere, and the inadequacy of such demands given the unequal social locations of men and women.

For it was one thing for women, like men, to be free to make and break contracts in public arenas: to vote in elections, to change their minds and vote for others in the next election, to take and leave employment, to prepare for that employment. But as second-wave feminists began to point out, there were several catches for women. This time feminists occupied a better position to criticize the family, that institution so revered by their predecessors. The nuclear family — based as it was on monogamy and compulsory heterosexuality (Rich, 1980), on men's breadwinning role and women's domestic role, and on the institution of motherhood (all of this confirmed in law) — constituted the primary site for the constitution and perpetuation of male domination and female subordination. Or so in the 1970s, feminists began to argue (Mitchell, 1971; Chodorow, 1978; Dinnerstein, 1976; Maroney, 1986). This argument encompassed many aspects, and more appeared with each layer that was uncovered.

Before looking more closely at this developing perspective on the family, let us look at why these feminists were in a position, as no women before them, to place the family itself under critical scrutiny. The earlier struggles for education and entrance to professions, together with the enormous expansion of service industries and state bureaucracies, had brought hundreds of thousands of women into the labour force and, therefore, towards new possibilities for economic independence. A marriage licence was no longer the only meal ticket in town: now some women could earn enough money to support themselves and their children. In particular, however, young university-educated women, unmarried and childless, were in position to confront the assumptions and practices of the conventional nuclear family.

These new possibilities for economic independence also carried with them new possibilities for structured sex inequality. The development of poorly paid job ghettoes and the double day of labour provide two major examples. These new forms for perpetuating patriarchy encouraged the feminist critiques of the economic, political, legal, social and sexual assumptions underlying the monogamous, nuclear family. Private troubles — wife battery, marital rape, disproportionate poverty of women (especially sole support mothers and older women), incest, isolation, unwanted pregnancy — were transformed into public issues (Mills, 1959). In calling the so-called natural world of the family into question, feminists insisted that this institution was socially constructed, and like the rest of society, thoroughly structured by sexual inequality.

For the new wave of feminists, nothing remained sacred. Even romantic love was examined as an historical development, carrying with it a dark underside for women (Firestone, 1970: Ch. 7). Most people who married, both men and women, did so because they were in love. In the absence of economic interdependence, the ideology proclaimed that love should both provoke and maintain marriages. But falling in love was played out very differently by men and women. The poet who wrote

Man's love is of man's life a thing apart,
'Tis woman's whole existence (Lord Byron)

was still not far off the mark. It is women who still choose marriage over education and career, and put aside both to start a family. When marriages break up because one or both partners are no longer in love, women are left with half-finished educations and few marketable skills for supporting themselves and, usually, their children. Their departed husbands, with their superior education and wage-earning potential, can fall in love again, and begin anew. The disproportionate number of women-led families below the poverty line provides grim confirmation of what otherwise might appear as a cynical interpretation. Futhermore, what stands between most middle-class women and poverty is a husband's or ex-husband's salary, and how he chooses to use it.

The same set of capitalist social relations that provided the preconditions for the contemporary women's movement also gave rise to the unreciprocated economic dependence of women upon men, and in their absence, upon the state. How can this apparent contradiction be explained? This is a difficult puzzle to untangle, and there are no easy answers. But the contractual relations of capitalism release men and women, in theory, to sell their labour power in the marketplace. That "freedom" has produced a new kind of tyranny. Karl Polanyi (1944: 163–64) argued that

the individual in primitive society is not
threatened by starvation unless the
community as a whole is in a like predicament

. . . The principle of freedom from want was equally acknowledged under almost every and any type of social organization up to about the beginning of sixteenth-century Europe.

Polanyi's point is true to the extent that the relations between people had not been parcelled out into a set of contracts. However devastating this new freedom — the freedom to sell your labour power or to starve — has been for men, its consequences for women and their children have been far more devastating. Women's lives are simply not divided up as easily as men's. It is dehumanizing for men to be reduced to wage-earning machines, and to have their labour power reduced to a commodity which may or may not be marketable. But how are women to sell their labour power in the marketplace if they are pregnant, or nursing infants? Furthermore, one must explain why there have been so many acts of commission and ommission that make it even more difficult for women to organize their lives for waged work. Laws against birth control and abortion; the lack of maternity and paternity leave; the refusal to spend societal resources on daycare and nightcare: all this stands in the way of women entering into the "gender neutral" contracts of the capitalist marketplace.

Explaining the enormous societal resistance to making the capitalist marketplace a truly non-gendered marketplace, that is, an arena that thoroughly takes account of the exigencies of women's and men's lives, constitutes a tall order. The nature of capitalism, the social and psychological dynamics of patriarchal relations, and especially the intertwining of the two, must all be taken into account. The capitalist quest to maximize profit will never offer the resources required for women and men to enter its marketplace and its corridors of power on an equal footing. Only the struggle of women and men for new ways to allocate resources and make decisions can

alter that reality. Their joint struggle for the welfare state in its broad sense, a state that puts the welfare of its citizenry at the top of its agenda, reveals this clearly. Many of the existing priorities of the state in the social arena that have been struggled for and won (that women now risk losing) stand as confirmation that women and their needs are particularly ill-served in capitalist society. Women alone with children are over-represented on welfare rolls, while a great variety of social services attest to the particular dilemmas that confront women in an unreconstructed capitalist society.

Women have found themselves fighting alone on many issues, fighting not only the state, but most men, and many women as well. For the demands of feminists for a whole world that includes women produce great anxiety for many people. Men may not need women economically, but they have needed them as sources of emotional support, domestic labour, nurturing for themselves and their children, and for their sexual lives. Feminists have challenged the gendered division of labour which underwrites all of these needs. Feminists struggle for a world that maximizes the possibilities for the economic independence of women from men; a world that does not privilege one kind of sexual arrangement — monogamous heterosexuality — over others; a social and political environment that makes it possible for women to raise children alone, with other women, or, if they choose, with men; a vision that pushes us not always gently toward economic and psychological restructuring.

Paradoxically, the contractual relations of capitalism make possible the articulation of these alternatives while at the same time denying their full realization. It is not an historical accident that we live in the midst of the greatest mobilization of women that the world has witnessed. Women sense the possibilities of freedom that the contractual relations of capitalism reveal. They no longer are tied inescapably to households and husbands for their very survival and the survival of their children.

Some women with education, economic resources and well honed juggling skills have more choices than those in any generation before them. Yet much evidence shows that if room exists for token women in the bastions of male power, new ways for preventing their collective inclusion are in the making. Breaking down the misogynist practices and feelings of men, and women, may prove a very long, and not always edifying, historical task (Horowitz, 1977; Hamilton, 1986; Burstyn, 1983; Bashevkin, 1985; Kaufman, 1987).

Today there are right-wing conservative governments in England, the United States, and in some Canadian provinces, most notably British Columbia and Saskatchewan. The federal Conservatives tried to deindex old age pensions, promised to reintroduce capital punishment and have responded to the crying need for universal daycare with a half-baked proposal for direct payment to parents. Much of the success of right-wing governments, particularly in the United States, rests upon the way they have managed to exploit people's legitimate anxieties about growing unemployment, reduced state services, and the threat of global annihilation. Their call is for a return to a time when "mothers were mothers and fathers were fathers" (Eisenstein, 1984). In other words, they advocate reinforcing the patriarchal family with a breadwinner father and a mother at home. They paint a nostalgic and harmonious picture of family/household life in the past that has little to do with the experience of most of the people, as we see from the historical interpretation presented in this chapter. At times they insist that all of society's problems, from the threat of nuclear war through youth unemployment and drug use, could be solved if only women returned to their god-given role in the family.

In this scenario, working women, homosexuals, lesbians and feminists become the scapegoats for deep economic, political and social problems. At its worst, it has become a campaign of hate. Although the feminist movement has never had so many adherents and supporters, it has also never had so many virulent and outspoken opponents.

Historical study can help in challenging these powerful myths about the past. But it can also help us differentiate the real options before us from those which rest on little more than anxiety, fear and misogyny.

Women have always had to support their families. In feudal society they toiled without respite to support themselves and their children. In capitalist society they have had to supplement their husbands' incomes through work done at home, through seeking waged work and making whatever arrangements they could for their children, or by fighting for a subsistence income from the state. Because of death, sickness, desertion, or unemployment, many have been sole supporters of their children. The particular contingencies of women's lives today emerged on the world stage with the transition to capitalism three hundred years ago. That world was also a patriarchal world, and the relations of patriarchy took on their own special form in the new society.

It is very clear then that the road to women's emancipation does not lie in the re-creation of a non-existent past but in the struggle for a society that takes account of and tries to resolve the contradictions with which women are confronted in contemporary society. Juliet Mitchell undoubtedly spoke better than she knew when she first coined the phrase "the longest revolution" in 1966. At times it seems that it has just begun.

FAMILY LAW RESEARCH IN A DECADE OF CHANGE

C. James Richardson

This paper first of all draws upon the experience of a decade or more of direct and indirect involvement with research on family law in Canada. For the most part, my role has not been to identify the issues and problems and most certainly not to draft legislation or develop procedural changes. Rather, my task as a sociologist and evaluator has been to observe and to evaluate. I have been asked to develop and conduct research that in the parlance of evaluation has been structured around issues of process, outcome and social impact of legislative and program innovations. In short, is the program or legislative reform performing well, is it reaching its intended objectives and are there unintended or unanticipated consequences?

Second, as a recent contributor to a federal Task Force attempting to predict what are likely to be the family law issues during the 1990s, I was forced to think about the role and impact of family law research over this past decade. This was a period in which, on the one hand, there were substantive and procedural changes in family law and, on the other, new concerns and new issues as various groups — established and emerging — made known their concerns and responded to the demographic changes in marriage, family and divorce.

From a paper presented at CSAA on Law and Society Meetings on "Issues Surrounding Family-Related Policy." Victoria, 1990. Views are solely those of the author and not necessarily those of the Department of Justice, Canada. Reprinted with permission by author.

Family Ideologies and Family Law Reform

Much of the research undertaken by the Department of Justice in the past decade has, understandably, focused on various aspects of the divorce process in Canada. As I will be describing, the issues seen as pressing at the beginning of the 1980s, particularly with respect to divorce, were ones of *process* and were largely shaped by liberal and sometimes Utopian views of the family that had their roots in the 1960s and early 1970s. While these issues did not entirely disappear, feminist-based research has had the major impact of directing attention to the *outcomes* of the divorce process and to the unanticipated and possibly negative consequences of the innovations and changes that it was hoped would make the divorce regime more humane and less adversarial.

Complicating matters is that the 1980s was also a decade in which various fundamentalist groups and movements sought to protect and preserve the sanctity of their version of the family, one clearly at odds with both the liberal views of the 1960s and 1970s and all the versions of feminism. And there were newly formed fathers' rights groups also calling for their version of family law reform. It has, in other words, been a decade of intense debate about family and marriage and the role of law and policy with respect to these institutions (Berger and Berger, 1983). The roots of the debate, of course, go back much further.

As Roderic Beaujot (1988) has recently described, it is in the mid-1960s that we begin to see the kinds of social and cultural changes that gave the decade its particular historical significance. With respect to the family, it is in the years after 1965 that demographers began to observe dramatic structural changes, and sociologists, in turn, began to reformulate their research questions in light of the ideological changes that accompanied these changes. It was in the mid-1960s that fertility began quite abruptly to decline, that age at marriage began, for the first time in this century to increase, that divorce rather than death of a spouse began to be the major cause of marital dissolution and that the proportion of Canadians ever married began a downward trend. And in the wake of these changes is an aging Canadian population.

Many viewed these demographic changes as a shift in or an erosion of family values. A better sociological explanation is that these behavioral changes were people's (mainly women's) responses to the increasing availability of contraceptive technology, married women's increasing participation in the labour force as we moved into a service economy based on a low-paid and often part-time labour force and the general inability of capitalism to provide a family wage, particularly as expectations rose in the 1960s.

But, of course, the independent role of ideas in shaping and changing society cannot be discounted. Probably, there is a reciprocal relationship between culture and social structure. The cultural transformation that we now associate with the 1960s — the growth of women's liberation and later feminism, a more pervasive sense of individualism (the so-called "me generation") and, more generally, what might best be described as the "de-institutionalization" of the family, were, on the one hand, products of the structural changes but, on the other, producers of these changing social structures. The counter culture both accelerated and legitimated changes in the individual decisions about nuptiality and fertility, which, when aggregated, become the demographer's statistical data.

By the early 1970s family and marriage — institutions which to the generation before had seemed inviolate, sacred and often "God-given" — were diagnosed as in a state of crisis, as outmoded, as irrelevant and in need of "decent burials." The literature of the time called for "revitalizing," "restructuring," "reconstituting" or "renovating" the very institutions idealized and revered just a decade before.

Monogamous marriage was now seen as out of step with the realities of the sexual revolution and the desire for "self-actualization." The nuclear family was under attack because of the constraints it imposes, the madness it generates and its generally oppressive and patriarchal nature. The catchwords were "swinging," "group marriage," "open marriage," "creative divorce"; and those most committed to the 1960s ideology argued for creation of communal family structures as an alternative to the crisis-ridden nuclear family.

At a less polemical level was the "discovery" that the traditional nuclear family, for a time idealized as the most appropriate family structure, is more stereotype than statistical reality. It is questionable whether even in the 1950s this family form had been the statistical norm, though it most certainly had been the cultural ideal. By the 1970s it was arguably not the prevalent family structure but, rather, one among a number of family forms in contemporary society and may, in fact, have become the minority. It was consistent with the general climate of cultural relativism to argue that family policy should treat all existing familial groups — particularly single parent families — as viable alternatives rather than deviations from the norm or, in any way, problem families.

Given this generally bleak depiction of the nuclear family and family relations, it is hardly surprising that by the 1970s divorce was no longer viewed as a singular and disastrous event but as an integral and normative part of marriage and family life and as often being a creative and liberating solution rather than a problem (Ambert,

1980). As well, emerging concepts such as the "bi-nuclear family," the "blended family" and the "remarriage family" were clearly efforts to capture the notion of a wider and broader definition of family. As was frequently pointed out, where there are children, divorce does not end familial relationships, it changes and complicates them.

From the point of view of the 1990s, the family ideology of the counter-culture strikes most as naive and, in the era of AIDS, its emphasis on sexual liberation, dangerous. Moreover, as was soon to be recognized, the proposed alternatives to conventional family life failed to recognize either biological and psychological constraints or those specifically related to structured social inequality, and are unable to transcend middle-class and sometimes sexist assumptions and biases. Thus the free school movement did not address the needs of disadvantaged groups for whom credentialism is functional for individual upward mobility. Communes, perhaps because they developed in the context of the drug subculture, were generally ill-equipped to deal with the day-to-day realities of child care and socialization, and were seldom premised on sexual equality and an equal division of labour. More open and permissive sexual arrangements seemed primarily to benefit men (Ambert, 1976). Moreover, some family forms, such as the female-headed family, much celebrated in the literature of the time, usually emerge not out of choice but from poverty and the inability of men to find regular and reasonably paid work and are abandoned when economic conditions permit.

Nevertheless, our ways of thinking about marriage, family and divorce were irrevocably changed and, as I have argued elsewhere, criticisms of family law and the resulting proposals for a new philosophy and set of objectives in this area were firmly rooted in and influenced by the family ide-

ology and the new rhetoric of the 1960s and early 1970s (Richardson, 1983). From the point of view of the Department of Justice and, in turn, the newly formed Law Reform Commission, the central and most obvious issue in family law was divorce.

Divorce and Family Law Research

That divorce was central to family law is hardly surprising. Canada's first uniform divorce legislation had come into force in 1968, literally in the midst of the counter-culture. The rate of divorce, of course jumped dramatically; but to the surprise of most continued to climb upward over the 1970s and most of the 1980s. It was generally perceived as having reached epidemic proportions and as a pressing social issue in Canadian society. Augmenting this was the general agreement that the 1968 legislation was a compromise which was not forward looking and which did not reflect the changing realities and conceptions of family life either before or after marital dissolution. Finally, divorce is the one area of family law that quite unambiguously falls under federal jurisdiction and where initiatives could be undertaken.

During the early part of the 1980s, family law research and program initiatives were mainly concerned with addressing the criticisms of the Divorce Act, 1968. The issues were mainly ones of process and centred around the philosophical, legal and administrative shortcomings of the divorce regime as it had developed during the 1970s. These shortcomings had been identified and discussed in a number of working papers commissioned by the Law Reform Commission. These criticisms centred on the inappropriateness of the adversary approach in family law, the irrelevance, generally, of fault grounds, the futility and hardship of long waiting periods to demonstrate marriage breakdown and administrative and structural problems, notably, fragmented jurisdictions and lack of support services such as divorce mediation and enforcement services.

The Law Reform Commission advocated the reform of the divorce legislation and the establishment of unified family courts across Canada. While new divorce legislation was to lie somewhere in the future, the Department of Justice did, in the late 1970s, decide to test empirically the unified family court conceptual model. Following negotiations with four provinces, demonstration projects were established in St. John's, Fredericton, Hamilton-Wentworth and Saskatoon between 1977 and 1979. All were three-year projects funded jointly by the federal government and the participating provinces; and all were, through separate but collaborative evaluations, designed to generate data to determine whether the model proposed could be implemented more generally.

While the evaluations are generally positive about the unified family court model, and the initial courts are still in operation, it is only in New Brunswick that the concept has been extended province-wide. Still, this particular initiative is a good example of a rational problem-solving model: a set of issues were identified, alternative solutions were proposed, a model was developed, implemented (on an experimental basis), evaluated and the results fed back to those working in these and similar family courts.

As was described in the synthesis report, the evaluations had generally shown the superiority of unified family courts over the existing court system. However, it was also noted that, for both technical and financial reasons, it had not been possible for researchers to do much in the way of outcome evaluation. It had not, for example, been possible to show the long-term impact of the social arm (the conciliation counselling and later divorce mediation service) in re-

ducing the adversary process and in bringing about more amicable and responsible settlements, which would better protect the interests of the children of the marriage and maintain maximum access to both parents.

In the 1983 synthesis report, it was recommended that there was need for further knowledge-building and evaluation research on "conciliation counselling" as it was then called. In 1984, and probably quite independent of this recommendation, the then Minister of Justice announced a sizable budget, both to encourage and promote divorce mediation (as it was now called) and to undertake research on this intervention. This was announced in conjunction with proposals for divorce reform. While that particular set of proposals died on the order paper, funds for research on divorce mediation remained intact.

The main research initiative consisted of two longitudinal research projects on court-based divorce mediation in Canada. The first project, entitled the *Divorce and Family Mediation Study* (Richardson, 1988; 1989a) examined divorce mediation in St. John's, Montreal and Saskatoon; the second project focused on the Winnipeg court where there was mandatory divorce mediation in contested custody cases (Sloan and Greenaway, 1988).

The two research projects each took as their starting point to test the belief that children in divorce will suffer less if conflict is contained and contact with both parents remains ongoing (Wallerstein and Kelly, 1980; Richardson, 1987). More specifically, the research was an empirical testing of the claim of divorce mediation proponents that the objectives of reducing conflict and maximizing post-divorce parenting are better accomplished through this approach to dispute resolution than through a purely legal process. The research also examined whether, as claimed, settlements reached through divorce mediation are more long lasting and therefore less costly because they involve fewer returns to court for variation or enforcement of support and custody orders. An underlying assumption was that joint legal custody, or, as many prefer, shared parenting, is generally the preferred option and one indicator of a "successful" divorce. Divorce mediation was "the way to go" because, in contrast to the traditional adversary process, it offered promise that these and other goals could be more effectively and more cheaply achieved.

As I have tried to make clear, the major policy and research initiatives of the 1980s were, in their embryo stage, shaped by and driven by the family ideologies of the early 1970s and, to a large extent, were products of the work and research undertaken by the Law Reform Commission of Canada. However, in the early 1980s it was, quite clearly, groups concerned with the status of women in Canadian society who set most of the agenda with respect to the debate about the family and family law; it was their concerns that became quite central to the divorce mediation research and, more generally, virtually all of the federally funded research on family law.

The issues that emerged were two-fold. The first centred on the implications of assumptions in the new family law about sexual equality and gender neutrality (Weitzman, 1985). The result was a much greater emphasis on the unequal outcomes of separation and divorce for women compared to men, particularly where the former have custody of the children and find themselves now living in poverty.

The second, and related, concern has been about the unintended consequences of informal justice or alternative dispute resolution approaches, particularly divorce mediation. There is distrust among feminist scholars that these alternatives, introduced so enthusiastically by earlier critics of the divorce process, may, because of power imbalances between spouses and larger patterns of sexual inequality, be detrimental to women's interests and contribute to the feminization of poverty following separation and divorce (Bottomley, 1985; Bailey, 1990). Thus, the research also sought to investigate the criticisms of these feminist scholars: that there were negative consequences for women who eschewed a strong lawyer in favour of a mediated settlement of custody, access and financial matters.

These and other criticism and concerns about the detrimental effects of family law on women were sufficiently focused and so forcibly and persistently articulated as to have had a major impact on the drafting of the provisions of the proposed reform of Canada's divorce legislation in the mid-1980s. To a considerable extent, these overwhelmed the earlier concerns about family law and its administration, which had led to experiments with unified family courts and research on divorce mediation. In short, by the time the legislation had reached the discussion and consultation stage, new issues had emerged and had become more focused in the political agenda of various interest groups.

Indeed, by the time Bill C-47 (The Divorce Act, 1985) reached the Committee stage, many women's groups, religious groups of longstanding existence, and newly formed fathers' rights groups were anxious to make their concerns known and to press for amendments to the proposed legislation. The criticism by religious and fundamentalist groups, what Margrit Eichler (1989) refers to as the "patriarchal family movement", was diffuse. It was ultimately aimed at making divorce more difficult to obtain on the premise that more liberal divorce laws threaten the sanctity of the family. The concern of fathers' rights groups was focused mainly on the inclusion of a presumption of joint legal custody, though this was not very clearly defined.

Women's groups were also focused in their concerns. Much of their effort went to opposing a presumption of joint legal custody, which they felt should be an arrangement entered into voluntarily and never imposed as a means of reaching a settlement. They also wished to broaden the grounds for variation of spousal support orders to soften the economic impact of divorce on older women who had not been in the labour force. Here the concern was that the objective of promoting self-sufficiency, if interpreted too narrowly or taken too literally, would, for such women, simply attenuate the feminization of poverty following divorce. This was opposed by various lawyers' groups who wanted legislation that would allow for finality and greater certainty in advice given to their clients. As well, the recently formed association of Family Mediation Canada wished there to be a provision requiring a mandatory visit to divorce mediation where child custody is being contested. Finally, there were some who urged that the language of "custody" and "access" be abandoned in favour of terms such as "primary caregiver" and "secondary caregiver."

In sum, by the time the new divorce legislation was ready for passage, four major issues had emerged: a presumption of joint custody; mandatory mediation; factors and objectives of spousal support, especially potential abuse of the objective of self-sufficiency; and variations of support orders. The result was that some of the clarity of the objectives set out in the earlier Law Reform Commission recommendations had become muddied by the need to respond to the competing and conflicting demands and interests of feminists, fathers' rights groups and various fundamentalist religious groups.

As in 1968, the legislation was again an attempt by the government to find compromises that would meet these sometimes conflicting demands. An evaluation component was built in and funded prior to the legislation ever going before Parliament. It was therefore possible to join the first phase of the evaluation of the divorce legislation to one of the divorce mediation research projects and collect baseline information in at least a sample of Canadian research sites before the legislation came into force (Richardson, 1987). And the second phase of the evaluation was able to replicate the research design of Phase I about three years later (Richardson, 1990).

The Impact and Politics of Applied Research

There is inevitably a lag between identification of a problem and a response in the form of law reform. This is partly due to the length of time required to formulate, undertake and disseminate policy-oriented social research and, on the basis of the findings and conclusions, to draft the necessary legislation. However, the larger problem is that politicians are often reluctant to act until there is perceived to be consensus that the legislative reform is overdue and that there is, on balance, political gain from supporting the proposed initiative or legal reform.

New legislation is almost never the independent variable bringing about certain kinds of changes. Rather, new legislation is itself part of the changing objective and subjective realities and is to a large extent a dependent variable. The most obvious example is the sexual assault legislation, which is generally perceived as having simply brought the Criminal Code of Canada in line with prevailing attitudes, practices and philosophies with respect to how victims of sexual crimes should be treated. Similarly, the provisions in the new divorce legislation do not so much cause change as reflect the already existing shift in attitudes and practices, many of which had already been incorporated into provincial legislation.

In the period between the Law Reform Commission's studies, the federal initiatives and our research, many changes had occurred in family law. All provinces and territories had, by then, enacted legislation concerning division of matrimonial property, child custody and child and spousal support essentially modelled on the seminal Ontario legislation. It is apparent, too, that through less formal means many of the problems identified by the Law Reform Commission were being addressed. In terms of attitudes and practices, family law in the 1980s was no longer the same as the Law Reform Commission had depicted it in the 1970s. For example, alternatives to the adversarial approach, such as divorce mediation, which was seen as novel and controversial in the 1970s, had become institutionalized in at least some parts of Canada by the mid-1980s. And, while there no doubt remained some extremely litigious lawyers in the area of family law, we found that many were coming to believe that when custody and access are at issue, a better settlement results from negotiation rather than from litigation. Moreover, there now seemed to be few family court judges who believed that, in the matter of custody, the adversarial approach will "reveal the truth" of who is the better parent. Many were coming to rely much more — sometimes invariably — on custody assessments or investigations, or they were referring the disputing spouses to mediation (Richardson, 1988).

It is not surprising, then, that neither of the major research projects by the Department of Justice was able to show major differences either between mediated and adversarial settlements or between the period just before and three years after the new divorce legislation. What differences there were between mediated and non-mediated settlements tended to be subtle rather than dramatic and similar to what had been found elsewhere. The reports were, therefore, in general agreement with Kenneth Kressel (1985: 26–27), who, after a

careful review and analysis of the American research, concluded that "mediation is a vehicle of social influence which is not inherently superior to any other method of conflict resolution. Like the others, it has its own decided liabilities as well as assets."

It seems that both proponents and opponents of divorce mediation might have overstated their cases. The former dichotomized a world that is not dichotomous. As Sloan and Greenaway (1988: 7), authors of the Winnipeg study on divorce mediation, put it:

Researchers falsely conceive of mediation as branching from a "fork in the road." One branch is the "traditional adversarial approach"; the other is mediation. One is the side of reason and compromise; the other the side of irrational power plays. This view masks the complexity of dispute resolution and the extent to which modes of resolution are mixed together; it also underestimates the rationality of the court process as well as the irrational aspects of mediation.

This is further evidenced by the data from the evaluation of the Divorce Act, 1985, which suggests that even with the encouragement built into the legislation for people to mediate their disputes, the demand curve for this intervention — whatever the service delivery model — is quite flat: approximately three percent of divorcing couples use this approach. This figure has not changed in the past five years and is also remarkably similar to what has been reported in the United States, where there has been much greater emphasis on alternative dispute resolution than in Canada (Kressel, 1985). In short, the rhetoric of the early 1980s suggested that divorce mediation was a new but burgeoning field which promised a radically new and growing approach to resolving family law matters. For the divorce mediation community, the reality has been disappointing. But on the other hand the feminist case *against* divorce mediation was not supported empirically. Rather, it was found that even after controlling for level of family income, women generally fared better economically in mediation than through a purely legal process (Richardson, 1988).

Similarly, while there were not great differences found between the divorce processes prior to and following the evaluation of the Divorce Act, 1985, there is evidence that the new provisions had been successful in meeting many of the objectives sought from this legislative reform. This is especially so with respect to the first of the stated objectives, that of reducing the adversarial nature of the divorce process. While it is apparent tht many of the changes to a less adversarial approach to marriage breakdown had occurred previous to the legislation, philosophical and procedural changes in the present legislation have served to actualize and, perhaps, hasten these trends (Richardson, 1990).

Concerns expressed about the erosion of women's rights to custody of their children and the contrasting concerns of men who feel denied equality with respect to sole custody or to access to their children were generally not borne out by the data from either the divorce mediation research or the evaluation of the divorce legislation. While there are undoubtedly men who have been denied access to their children, they were not evident in the four-city sample of divorcing families at either of the time periods. Nor does it appear that men are now more likely to be awarded sole custody than they were in the past. Nor, finally, is it evident that the spousal support objectives contained in the new legislation have had the unintended consequence of worsening the situation of women, particularly those coming out of long-term marriages.

At the same time, the evaluation shows quite clearly that the legislation had no measurable impact on reducing the un-

equal economic consequences for women and children of divorce; and it remains the case that whereas only about 10 percent of divorced men have incomes below the poverty line after paying support, upwards of 60 percent of women with custody of the children have, including the support payments, incomes below the poverty lines for various family sizes. These findings did not take into account that women may have remarried and that men, far from living in one-person households, were quite likely to be remarried or repartnered and to have new dependent children. Nor, to turn it around, did this analysis consider the implications of noncompliance with support orders, that a sizeable proportion of men do not make their support payments or do not do so regularly and predictably.

At the conclusion of the research, the reports on the research findings about divorce mediation and the impact of new divorce legislation were quite widely distributed: there were oral presentations to a number of different audiences and a number of enquiries from journalists. Yet, in the aftermath of the research, it was apparent from questions raised at presentations and subsequent publications that for feminists, for fathers' rights groups and for many members of the divorce mediation community in Canada, the research findings had rather limited impact on prevailing views and wisdoms about divorce mediation particularly or the divorce process more generally. The following contentions or beliefs are illustrative rather than exhaustive.

1. **Custody of the children is one of the more contentious matters in divorce.**

   While contested custody disputes are certainly bitter and emotionally draining on judges, the available research suggests that in the four to five percent of contested divorces, custody is less often at issue than financial matters such as division of property and spousal and child support. And, most Canadian judges faced with a custody dispute will order a custody assessment.

2. **Men generally want more access to the children of the marriage than is granted by the courts or allowed by mothers with sole custody.**

Evidence from the DFMS and Phase II of the evaluation of the Divorce Act, 1985 suggests that the major problem is that men do not live up to the agreed upon access arrangements or do so irregularly and unpredictably. This is further borne out in the follow-up study of DFMS clients. Denial of access by the courts or later by the custodial parent is extremely rare.

3. **There is increasing pressure for joint legal custody from the courts, from mediators and from fathers.**

While the proportion of joint legal custody awards has moved upwards from about nine to 13 percent of all awards since the Divorce Act, 1985 came into force, it is evident that most divorcing individuals do not want or seriously consider this option. For those who do opt for joint legal custody, it is generally the first choice and one which most (men somewhat more than women) would choose again. There is a high degree of satisfaction with these arrangements (Irving et al., 1984; Morris, 1988; Richardson, 1988). There is no evidence, then, that joint custody is being imposed on couples who cannot agree about sole custody.

4. **Gender neutrality approaches in family law have led to Courts**

being more willing to grant sole custody to fathers than in the past; as a result, women may be forced to barter away their support rights in order to keep their children.

While analyses of reported case law provides some support for the first part of this assertion (Boyd, 1987), the latter assertion seems to be purely speculative, unsupported even by anecdotal evidence. Statistically the likelihood of men receiving sole custody has not changed in nearly two decades (10 to 11 percent of all cases). When men request sole custody it is granted in about 40 percent of cases, generally when the wife, for a variety of reasons, does not want sole custody. Under these circumstances joint legal custody and split legal custody are also more common (about 20 percent). It remains the case that when women specifically request sole custody, men are virtually excluded from the likelihood of receiving custody since in 97 percent of such cases custody is awarded to the mother.

5. **The traditional adversary system is still the prevalent mode of settlement of divorce cases and continues to be destructive to divorcing couples and their children.**

This view can still be found in various articles and presentations by proponents of divorce mediation. While it is true that few divorcing people use approaches such as divorce mediation, most are able to work out a settlement on their own or with the assistance of their lawyers, who may sometimes negotiate a settlement. As noted earlier, there is considerable reason to believe that even if earlier depictions of the adversary system were fundamentally correct, the evidence from the divorce mediation and divorce evaluation research indicates that there has been an important shift in both attitudes and practices particularly with respect to custody and access disputes to more humane, socially conscious and less litigious approaches.

6. **There are in most divorces sufficient resources so that more equitable settlements coupled with tougher and more efficient enforcement procedures could substantially reduce economic hardship of women and children following separation and divorce.**

There is considerable research which provides empirical support for this assertion; on *average*, most divorced men could afford to pay more in support than is now generally the case without themselves also ending up with incomes below the poverty line. However, most of the cases cited in policy discussions are based on contested cases where there is an atypically high level of affluence which is not the general picture for the divorcing population particularly in the more impoverished regions of Canada. Morover, such analyses do not take into account the high rate of remarriage and that many men will have obligations to a second family. It is clearly a policy and value question as to which set of children should be left impoverished.

It is inevitable and hardly surprising that the same objective statistics and research findings will be viewed quite differently by different groups, often with clashing interests and perspectives. Thus, some will see a glass half empty while others see a glass half full. But as I thought over the general reception to the conclusions to the research, it seemed to me that there was another level or dimension to the problem: there is, today, a growing disjuncture in modes of inquiry, discourse and what is considered fact; in other words, groups concerned with improving family law seem to be talking past one another.

At present, the dominant paradigm in most of the social sciences is quite clearly feminism. The long struggle to incorporate feminist perspectives into the social sciences and humanities, the law and social policy has been largely successful. This change has meant more than simply "bringing women in" or reformulating the language. Feminism also challenges the traditional methodologies of the social sciences: quantitative methods; various forms of survey research; use of census data; commitment to the metaphor of the classical experimental design; hypothesis testing and the like.

Such approaches are rejected by many feminist scholars and replaced by more qualitative approaches, which draw upon women's "lived" experiences and definitions of situation or, in the case of legal scholars, close analysis of reported family law cases. Such cases are viewed as important because they create precedence, which, in turn, guides family law practitioners in advising clients as to the likely outcome were they to contest the matter (cf.: Mnookin and Kornhauser, 1979). And perceptions about trends and problems in various aspects of family law are strongly influenced by this kind of research. It is these approaches that inform many publications in the family law journals and presentations at conferences on women and the law and which are likely to capture the attention of the media and the popular press (e.g.: Crean, 1990).

The difficulty is that reported cases make up a very tiny minority of divorce cases or even of contested cases and are, by definition, the unusual ones. They are unusual in the degree and nature of conflict but probably also in the level of affluence of the disputants. Thus, as Mossman (1986) has observed, there is a middle-class bias in much of the thinking about family law. Certainly what is learned from a random sample of the divorcing population or from analysis of data from the Central Divorce Registry provides a quite different picture of divorce than the one derived from these other methodologies. Such research does not reveal many cases of interest to legal scholars, and it does not interest the media or the popular press. Issues related to dual-career families, business assets, marital property and joint custody seem far removed from the reality of most divorcing people, many of whom have uncertain and poorly paying jobs rather than careers, little in the way of property to divide and custody is not at issue.

There remains then, a considerable gap between what research has been able to show empirically through sample survey research and Census data on divorce generated from the Central Divorce Registry forms and the prevailing concerns and wisdom about divorce and its outcomes among those writing about family and who draw upon other kinds of sources and methodologies.

It is easy enough to draw up a list of probable family law issues: the persisting economic consequences and inequalities between men and women following divorce; the meaning and practical application of the "best interests of the child" principle; the possible unintended consequences of various modes of informal justice; the issue of marital and family status and what, under law should be defined as a family from the point of view of state bene-fits and individual rights and obligations; the social and legal implications of the reproductive technologies; and the ongoing problem of family violence. It is much harder to suggest how these can be transformed into family law *research* issues which will have traditional credibility and, at the same time, incorporate the methodological approaches emerging out of feminist scholarship and research, and thereby have credibility among those directly concerned with influencing social policy.

An important contribution of the research funded by the Department of Justice in the 1980s has been the development of knowledge-building about the divorce process and divorce outcomes. At the same time, it will certainly be necessary to develop research designs that incorporate the methodologies emerging out of the feminist perspective. However, these will be no substitute for continuing collection and analysis of basic statistics on divorce, which can be derived from the Central Divorce Registry Data. In the 1980s these were augmented by more detailed studies of the Canadian divorce process in selected jurisdictions. Without necessarily focusing on a specific issue such as divorce mediation, efforts should be made to conduct further detailed studies on the divorce process and the post-divorce situation of families in other, and perhaps more representative, jurisdictions in Canada. It is, for example, quite possible that there is a lag between patterns and trends found in reported contested custody cases and what is occurring in the larger population of uncontested divorce cases. Continuing collection and analysis of national statistics and survey research informed by feminist perspectives has the potential to augment rather than compete with the methodological approaches likely to be more prominent in the 1990s.

"THE FAMILY" AS A POLITICAL ISSUE

Margrit Eichler

The Current Situation of Canadian Families

... families are in flux (as are many of our other social institutions). ... We can note, overall, the following trends.

There is an increasing diversity of family forms. In particular, the tie between marital and parental relationships has been loosened and continues to loosen. As a consequence, men are significantly less likely to share, on a full-time basis, a household with their biological children than are women. This is due to a number of factors. First, an increasing proportion of unmarried women are giving birth — in 1985, 17 percent of all births were to unmarried women. This means that 17 percent of the children born were not living with both their biological parents. If we wish to express this same fact in terms of households, we need to double the proportion to encompass those households in which children live with only one biological parent as well as the other half in which an adult does not live together with his (occasionally her) biological children. Second, the number and proportion of divorces continues to be high. ... About half of all divorces involve dependent children, which generates another form of discrepancy between marital and parental roles. Third, due to the high proportion of divorces, many marriages are second or later marriages for at least one of the spouses. In 1985, slightly more than 30 percent of all marriages involved a previously married partner.

While in older times, marital disruption was very high, this was due mostly to death and not to divorce or a high proportion of children born to unmarried mothers. Upon death of one spouse and parent, that parent obviously was no longer available to form an independent household. Children would have had step-parents or have grown up in single parent families, as a consequence, but they did not have membership in more than one family household.

Due to the more recent high discrepancy between marital and parental roles, we are confronted with a new phenomenon in which members of one household are not necessarily all members of the same family. In a household of, for instance, a mother with two dependent children whose father has since remarried, the mother and children constitute one household and a solo-mother family. At the same time, however, the children also belong, at least partially, to the household and family of their father, provided that significant contact between them has been maintained. The children, therefore, have dual family membership, while their respective parents have single family memberships which include the children.

This has, of course, policy consequences. With the high rate of divorce and remarriage, the standard of living of the first and second (and possibly subsequent) wife and children becomes an important problem. It is a problem for the wife, and not the husband, since after divorce the living standard of wives and children tends to decline, while that of the husband tends to remain stable or to improve.

There is another economic issue. The majority of Canadian wives and mothers are now in the paid labour force, and consequently, childcare has become a burning social issue, which in the mid-eighties became part of the political agenda. The high proportion of women in the labour force has also created another political issue;

namely, which type of family should the state favour (if any), for instance, on tax policies: the single income husband-wife family, the dual income husband-wife family, the solo-parent family? In the latter case, how should the obligations of the non-resident parent be enforced, and what exactly are these obligations? How should the state deal with the competing claims of first and subsequent families? Has one more right to support than the other? . . . The demands of single-earner and dual-earner husband-wife families are contradictory. By necessity, the claims of first and subsequent families are also in conflict, for what the one receives, the other forgoes.

With greater acceptance of the notion of sex equality *in principle* (not always in fact), the family laws have all been changed. Divorce has been made simpler and speedier, and the underlying premise of the various provincial family laws is the notion of sex equality (and therefore equality of rights and duties of husbands and wives, mothers and fathers) rather than sexual differentiation. Given that women are at present still at a significant economic disadvantage as compared to men, this does not necessarily work to the benefit of women or children, who tend to remain in women's care.

Looking at the information available on childcare and housework, a tiny increase at the aggregate level in the participation of men in housework can be detected. It is too small, however, to make a significant dent in the lopsided work distribution of wives and husbands. Given the increasing proportion of wives and mothers in the labour force, this signals, therefore, an *increasing* imbalance — *at the collective level* — of work load between women and men.

Overall, fertility has decreased while life expectancy has continued to rise, creating a different type of dependency ratio for the nation as a whole than we have ever had before. While in earlier times most of the economic dependents were minor children, the balance is shifting towards the elderly population becoming the major group of economic dependants. As a consequence, care for the aged continues to increase in importance as a social issue for individual families as well as for society as a whole.

Different family lifestyles have become socially more acceptable than they were before, probably due to the fact that there is already so much movement due to the above-mentioned factors. Cohabitation has become socially acceptable in many circles, and homosexual couples are slowly gaining some grudging acceptance as an alternate family form.

It is also possible to note a change in attitude concerning all forms of family violence. While until the late 1970s the existence of family violence was one of the best kept secrets, it is now widely acknowledged. (This is not a comment on *trends* in family violence: there is little reason to believe it has increased or decreased. It simply addresses the issue of *public awareness* and acceptability.) By the late 1980s, family violence has been more widely recognized not only to exist, but to constitute a significant *social* problem (rather than a private problem). Police are instructed in most provinces to intervene in "domestic disputes" and even to lay charges, rather than expecting the wife to lay charges against her husband. Sexual abuse of children has been studied in a federal commission, and legislation is currently being prepared to address this problem. The first case of a sexually abused child who laid charges as an adult against her father has concluded with the father being imprisoned in 1986. Some schools "streetproof" children (this may not be helpful when the abuser is a family member or friend, as is the case in the majority of abuse cases).

Finally, the new reproductive technologies which burst upon the scene since the late seventies have already redefined the meaning of motherhood and will profoundly reshape the social meaning of parenthood, for both father and mother, as well as change the meaning of pregnancy, unless legislation is passed to regulate these techniques. The status of the fetus is changing with as yet unforeseeable consequences for pregnant women.

Overall, then, we can note a number of continuous social trends which together have resulted in increasing diversity of familial units. This in no way signifies a decrease of the importance that is accorded by people to their families. A recent Canada-wide poll found that a vast majority of people in Canada find the family becoming *more* rather than *less* important for them. Of those respondents with children at home, a total of 92 percent.

said that the family is becoming more important to them, a view also expressed by 73 per cent of those whose children have moved away and by the same proportion of respondents over age 65. By contrast, fewer than eight per cent of all those polled said that family was becoming less important to them. Similarly, the 77 per cent of poll residents who ranked family ahead of either career or religion in their lives included large majorities in every region and in every age, social and economic grouping.

At the same time, statistics from a variety of sources reinforce the fact that for many Canadians family life has undergone a profound change in the past two decades: (Finlayson, 1987: 72).

Against this backdrop of large-scale change we need to locate another phenomenon that has become increasingly important in Canada (as well as in other countries): the emergence of a social movement which identifies itself as "pro-family" while branding anybody who does not subscribe to their particular version of "the family" as "anti-family." This has led to the family becoming a political issue, which serves as a focus for an entire philosophy of life, going beyond an endorsement of a particular type of family.

The Patriarchal Family Movement

In Canada, a movement for the restoration of the patriarchal family has become increasingly active and visible since the early 1980s. This movement is concerned with working for the pre-eminence of one particular family form — the patriarchal family — over other types of families, all of which form part of our contemporary reality, as we have seen.

Patriarchalists (people actively involved in or supporting the movement for the restoration of the patriarchal family) subscribe to a notion of the family that can be characterized as follows:

1. "The" family is a divinely sanctioned institution. Its appropriate form in Western society comes from the Judeo-Christian tradition (but other religiously sanctioned forms may be acceptable provided they match the Judeo-Christian model). As a divinely sanctioned institution, it should be maintained even if this requires sacrifices on the part of the people who make up a family. This form of the family deserves special support and protection from the state, whereas extending such support and protection to other forms of the family is seen as a direct threat to "the" family which must therefore be resisted.

2. Sexual activity is considered sinful unless it happens within the context of marriage without any use of contraceptive means.

3. Abortion is considered sinful under all circumstances.

4. Sex equality is seen as consisting in valuing the specific gifts of men and women. Men and women are seen as *different* in an essential way. It is therefore seen as misguided to

strive for social equality of the sexes such as equal pay for work of equal value and other such social reforms. The rhetoric of equality may be used to argue against it.

Most important in understanding the position of the patriarchalists is the fact that there is no acceptance on their part of a diversity in family styles as an acceptable — or even desirable — aspect of our social reality. Only *one* type of family — the patriarchal family — deserves to be called "the family." Indeed, terminology is instructive here.

. . . Here we have a social movement which is firmly wedded to a monolithic notion of the family, so much so that even using the plural ("families") is seen as a threat to "the family." When the United States held a "White House Conference on Families" in 1980, a fierce battle was waged around the title, whether it should read "family" or "families." Eventually, the plural won out over the singular, but only after a very heated and prolonged attempt on the part of patriarchalists to change the title (see McGraw, 1980).

The self-identification of the patriarchalists as "pro-family" and the derogation of anybody who does not share their particular vision of families is indicative of their monolithic approach. One patriarchalist author identified the struggle as a "civil war between the Judeo-Christian and humanist orthodoxies" (McGraw, 1980: 18). As she puts it,

Which side one comes down on depends on whether one believes that the family is rooted in the laws of nature and a divinely created moral order, or whether one sees the family as a self-defined artificial human construct to be manipulated for the well-being of the individual.

The pro-family position is acceptance and affirmation of the family as the natural, beneficial, indispensable, and irreplaceable institution for human development. As James Hitchcock has said,

the debate divides between those who love and accept the family, and those who reject it, hate it or wish to change its meaning.

It is noteworthy that those who reject "the" family, hate it or *wish to change its meaning* — merely by accepting what is contemporary reality — are put into the same hopper. If one does not accept "the family" as put forward by the self-styled "pro-family" groups as the only acceptable family form, one is automatically tagged as rejecting and hating the family, as being anti-family. Gwen Landoldt referred in a taped interview with Dr. James Dobson which was broadcast in 1986 (and the cassette of which is sold) to all those who do not share their viewpoint as "the godless people who take over."

Given the clear attempt to declare one family form as the only acceptable one for social policy purposes, McGraw may be right when she states that the struggle is one "between two radically distinct and diametrically opposed moral visions of humanity."

The central political question of the coming decade will be which of these two competing moral visions of the family and of humanity will prevail and become the official orthodoxy of our society through the power and authority of the American state.

The power struggle is between the Judeo-Christian ethic, based on God-given eternal law, and the secular humanist orthodoxy that rejects God and traditional values. In the secular humanist world view, man, individually and collectively, has the absolute power, based on purely human will and reason, to determine all choices that will fulfil his individual and collective well-being.

In this sense, the struggle for the family and its meaning goes far beyond partisan battles and demographic or geographical differences which have characterized the conflicts of American political life. The struggle for the family is at the profoundest level an undeclared civil war, whose outcome will determine how our society defines itself (McGraw, 1980: 17, emphasis added).

What is opposed, then, is one vision of the family against acceptance of a multiplicity of families; one dogma versus the acceptance of diversity of beliefs; a fundamentalist state versus a liberal-democratic state which accepts a division between state and church as one of its most important principles.

THE EMERGENCE OF THE PATRIARCHAL FAMILY MOVEMENT

In many ways, the patriarchal family movement is not new, but specific organizational forms emerge at specific times. The roots of the movement seem to stem from two separate but related sources: the anti-abortion movement and fundamentalist religion.

In Canada, the discussion in the early 1980s surrounding the Charter of Rights and Freedoms served as an organizing focus. For instance, an edition of the Christian Inquirer Special Report of March 1981 provides the following rousing call to action, printed in bold letters:

THE CHARTER OF RIGHTS MUST BE SCUTTLED! Millions of unborn can be saved from abortion — our nation saved from moral degradation — our children from falling prey to homosexuals — our godly freedoms preserved — IF WE ACT NOW.

Are you prepared to bear the responsibility for your own inaction if this evil Charter becomes law?

Around the same time, the United States was deciding on the Equal Rights Amendment, which was eventualy defeated. Well in the forefront of the battle against the ERA was Phyllis Schlafly, whose ideology has obviously inspired the Canadian patriarchal family movement.

In Canada, a variety of organizations adhere to the ideology of the patriarchalist movement. The movement is an outgrowth of the anti-abortion movement. It is virulently anti-feminist (see Eichler, 1985, for an analysis), and homophobic. When Ontario prepared to include sexual orientation as a prohibited ground for discrimination into its human rights code, patriarchalists mounted a concerted attack on the legislation ... The amendment was passed anyway in December 1986.

POLICY STANCES OF THE PATRIARCHAL FAMILY MOVEMENT

Over time, the following issues have surfaced as central: abortion, morality, sexuality, the status of full-time housewives, "easy divorce," day care, and sex equality. In the following, we shall briefly examine the patriarchalist stance on each of these central policy issues.

Abortion

As stated, the patriarchalist movement is an outgrowth of the anti-abortion (pro-fetus) movement. The patriarchalists oppose abortion for any reason. Their viewpoint is most clearly expressed on a flyer of the Alliance for Life, an anti-abortion umbrella group which was founded in 1968 and incorporated in 1973:

DOES THE ALLIANCE FOR LIFE OPPOSE ALL ABORTIONS?

Yes, except when necessary to save a woman's life. But today, thanks to modern medicine, abortion is practically never necessary. At times it may seem a more convenient way to save her than some other medical techniques, but mere convenience is no justification for killing an unborn child.

SHOULDN'T ABORTION BE LEGAL WHEN THE CHILD MIGHT BE DEFORMED?

No, because a deformed or disabled human being has the same right to life as anyone else. Many such people live happy and useful lives, and medical science is achieving spectacular success in correcting even extremely serious defects.

SHOULDN'T ABORTION BE LEGAL WHEN PREGNANCY RESULTS FROM RAPE?

No, because the unborn child is innocent of any crime. At the very least, therefore, it has as much right to live as the rapist, whom we never execute for this offense. Of course, we must help and support women in every positive, constructive way possible; but this does not *include destroying another human life.*

In other words, the patriarchalist movement rejects abortion for *all* women, whether or not they agree with this stance, regardless of whether the pregnancy has resulted from incest or rape, or even when they know that the fetus they carry is severly deformed. The issue, for the patriarchalist movement, is not only to try to convince women not to abort — their right in any democratic society — but to re-criminalize abortion and to further restrict access by either eliminating therapeutic abortion committees or taking them over so that these committees will not recommend any abortions.

Morality

Morality, God's will, God's law and the Judeo-Christian ethic are invoked frequently by the patriarchalists. There seems to be no doubt or question what God's will is: it is clearly identical with the programme of the patriarchalist movement. Its two most important components seem to be the complete rejection of abortion under all circumstances, and a rejection of "immoral lifestyles," defined in sexual terms. Sexuality will be examined in the next passage.

Sexuality

Sexuality is seen as morally acceptable in one and only one form: if it takes place within a marriage without any birth control means. In other words, all forms of non-procreational sex are seen as morally corrupt and against God's will. This conviction explains the movement's stance concerning sex education, contraception, the use of condoms because of AIDS, and particularly homosexuality.

Homosexuality constitutes the epitome of non-procreational sex, and as such it is singled out for attack by the patriarchalist movement. "Homosexuality has a harmful impact on society that can no longer be seriously ignored" (from "Laws Protecting Homosexuals" pamphlet, n.d.). Society must not condone homosexual activity, since this would undermine traditional moral standards and threaten the family. Instead, we should look at homosexuals as people suffering from a disorder of "psycho-sexual development" which can be cured through Christian counselling. "The idea that homosexuals cannot change is a myth like the popular view at the turn of the century that alcoholics could never change" (ibid.). Homosexuals are likened, among other groups, to "bikers such as Hell's Angels" (from a pamphlet entitled "Homosexuality — and Issues Concerning Family Life," p. 2).

In line with the movement's rejection of all forms of non-procreational sex, contraception is rejected (even for married people), as is sex education in schools, or the teaching of preventive measures, such as the use of condoms, to lessen the further spread of AIDS.

The solution to preventing unwanted pregnancies, therefore, would be celibacy or chastity, which is likewise seen as the solution for AIDS. The fact that many people do not share this viewpoint does not diminish the movement's conviction that it has the right to impose its moral standards on other people, since these standards are seen as divinely sanctioned.

The Status of Full-Time Housewives

Full-time housewives are presented as an embattled group whose status needs to be upgraded. Consequently, full-time homemakers should receive a tax credit (to replace the marriage exemption). The feminist movement is charged with denigrating the status of wives and mothers. A homemaker's pension is rejected." . . . any contributions to the plan would mean sacrifices from the family's necessities, such as food, clothing or shelter. In short, we are concerned that the reality is that in the vast majority of cases, the woman cannot afford the costs of a contribution towards the homemaker's pension . . ." (from a pamphlet entitled "What are the Stresses on the Canadian Family Today?").

Homemaking is presented as a career option. The assumption put forward is that many women would choose to remain at home if it were financially viable for them to do so. The problem with this position is that no distinction is made between socially useful services and privately useful services rendered in the home. I have long argued for paying women (or men!) who are looking after dependent children or sick or disabled adults in their home, and doing so in the form of a tax credit would be an efficient and convenient means. However, there is no justification for paying women with public monies if they only look after physically and mentally fit adults (a husband, adult children, or other adults). Although their work would still be worth money, this should be paid privately by those adults who enjoy the benefit of the services rendered, as is standard practice with respect to other services rendered by adults to adults.

Failing to make such a distinction between the social or private nature of services rendered in the home would result in a situation in which women and men who have paying jobs *and* have to do their housework would subsidize, with their tax money, other people who either render or receive services which are of benefit only to those people receiving the services.

"Easy Divorce"

The patriarchalist movement mounted a vigorous lobby campaign against the introduction of the new federal divorce law which came into force in 1986. A 1985 booklet entitled "Easy Divorce: Trendy or De-

structive Legislation?" argues as its central point that "There is nothing new about unhappy marriages, only about people's unwillingness to put up with them. Easy divorce will not ease the pain of marriage conflict but only add to it in the long term" (ibid., p. 8, emphasized in the original). The thrust of the argument is to prevent marriage breakdown, primarily through counselling services, rather than shorten the waiting period needed before a divorce can be obtained in the case of marriage breakdown.

This stance becomes understandable when going back to the definition of the patriarchalist view offered above; the family is considered a divinely sanctioned institution. In order to maintain it, people making up individual families should make sacrifices. In other words the institution does not exist to serve people; people exist to serve the institution.

Day Care

The patriarchalists vigorously oppose the concept of universal day care. Mother care is elevated above all other forms of childcare. "To become secure, competent adults, infants require a close continuous nurturing relationship with a single caretaker, preferably a mother. Without this foundation of love and trust, the victims of maternal deprivation might be gravely damaged for life, pathologically suspicious and detached" (from a pamphlet entitled "Child Care," p. 1).

Correspondingly, universal day care is strongly rejected. "Public day care should be available according to NEED, not WANT" (from a pamphlet entitled "Universal Day Care"). It is an interesting but unanswered question as to *who* would define "need" and "want" for *whom* if this was official government policy. Could some official body decide who truly "needs" rather than just "wants" day care for their children? Presumably, if a woman was married and had a husband who earned enough to support her and the children, even if just barely, this woman would not "need" day care, even if she strongly felt herself that she wanted to continue her studies on a full-time basis or wanted to hold a paid job.

Other arguments made against day care in principle include that it is not of benefit to the child and that opportunities for individual learning and emotional development are superior in the home than in day care (ibid.). Neither of these contentions are true. Two other points are more interesting. Day care centres *do* need to impose schedules, and the cost of universal day care would be very high. However, costs need to be assessed against the cost of *not* having universal day care, given the high labour force participation of mothers and fathers. As far as individualized attention is concerned, this is a function of the number and quality of staff, their working conditions, and the philosophy of particular centres. These are important issues which require careful policy development and infusion of public funds to raise the status and *pay* of day care workers, as well as to improve their working conditions in general.

Sex Equality

Rhetoric is important in all the policy issues discussed so far, but it becomes paramount in this issue. The patriarchalists confess commitment to the notion of sex equality, but subscribe, at the same time, to a modified version of the "separate spheres" doctrine for the sexes: that the proper sphere for men is in the public realm, while the proper sphere for women is in the private realm. Equality, then, consists of valuing each sphere equally.

The doctrine is modified in that the voices we can hear from the patriarchalist movement on this issue range from strict separation of spheres to partial overlap. Strict separationists will ardently defend a very strict separation of tasks between husbands and wives, with wives being responsible for everything associated with childcare and housework, and husbands being responsible for breadwinning. They accept a strict hierarchical order of family relationships: at the top is God who has authority over the husband. The husband, in turn, has authority over his wife, and both he and his wife have authority over their children. "Women should kneel for peace" said one of the speakers at the first conference of REALWomen.

More moderate separationists, on the other hand, will accept helping on the part of the husband in childcare and housework as a positive feature, and accept either part-time work for pay on the part of the wife while the children are small or full-time work after they are grown or at any time in the case of "need." They are separationists insofar as they give *primacy* to the family functions of the wife over those of the husband and the economic functions of the husband over those of the wife, but the separation is not watertight.

The *effect* of this approach is that the movement explicitly rejects measures which would increase the equality of women in the public realm, and that it spends little effort on increasing the involvement of men in family life (other than through the economic provider function). In the past, this has included, as stated, campaigns against the equality clause in the Charter of Rights, a lot of agitation against the concept of equal pay for work of equal value, and all forms of employment equity as proposed in the Abella Commission Report (Abella, 1984). For instance, when the Ontario government tabled a bill on equal pay for work of equal value, the patriarchalist movement mounted a strenuous campaign against the bill. In particular, the National Citizen's Coalition submitted a brief entitled "Pay Discrimination" (to describe the introduction of equal pay for work of equal value) which promised on the title page to explain "How It Will Demean Women, Help Break Down The Traditional Family And The Free Market System" (National Citizen's Coalition, 1986).

The movement further vigorously opposes all feminist activities which are geared towards improving sex equality in Canada, and has singled out for attention the National Action Committee, which lobbies for sex equality (see Eichler, 1985) as well as the Women's Program, Secretary of State, which funds many of these efforts oriented towards increasing sex equality.

OVERALL ASSESSMENT OF THE PATRIARCHAL FAMILY MOVEMENT

The patriarchal family movement has organized itself at a time in which the notion of sex equality has gained broader acceptance in Canada. While it focusses on "the" family, this constitutes merely a focus for a broader perspective which constitutes a philosophy of life which tries to turn society backwards, towards an ideal state (which, incidentally, never was reality).

Important aspects are its explicit anti-feminism and its sophisticated use of rhetoric. The movement is self-consciously anti-feminist and in the process engages in severe misrepresentation of the feminist movement (see Eichler, 1985). In particular, the feminist movement is depicted as anti-family. This issue will be briefly addressed in the next section.

As to its use of rhetoric, the movement employs one of equality to argue for inequality, and one of choice to argue for the reduction of choices. So, for instance, "reproductive choice" is identified with abstaining from sex (from a position paper of REALWomen). Full-time homemaking is stressed as a career *choice*. In effect, however, the movement asks for privileged treatment of full-time homemakers. Pay equity is identified as "pay discrimination." "Pro-family" means fighting for the supremacy of one family form (the patriarchal family) at the expense of all others.

The Feminist Orientation Towards Families

The feminist orientation towards families can be described as multivalent. On the one hand, the feminist movement has been one of the sharpest critics of the patriarchal family and its effect on all its members, but particularly women. A fair amount of attention has been turned by feminists towards the abuses which happen in families: violence, physical and sexual abuse, enforced dependancy of wives on husbands, etc.

On the other hand, the feminist movement has a very good track record in trying to improve the situation of wives and mothers. In Canada, it has fought for legal reforms which have improved the status of wives and mothers; for maternity, paternity, pregnancy, and adoption benefits; for improving maintenance and custody orders; for pension reform for all women but particularly for housewives; for facilitating access to paid work by improving the conditions of part-time workers; for universal day care to meet the need of the majority of mothers and their children; and in general for recognizing childcare as a responsibility which should be shared between mothers, fathers, and society (cf. Eichler, 1985).

The feminist perspective, then, accepts that families come in different forms. No particular form is seen as superior to another. Judgments on the desirability of families are made in terms of their effects on their members, not in terms of their structure.

The Future of Families

It is a risky business to try to make predictions about the future. Often, they may come back to haunt one. Nevertheless, some predictions seem fairly safe to make. One of these is that family relationships will continue to remain very important to the vast majority of people. Family relationships have always been important, they are important now, and there is no reason to suspect that they will be any less important in times to come.

However, what qualifies as a family relationship is subject to change, and clearly open to debate, as we have seen above. On the one hand, we are currently faced with a major social movement that is centred on putting forward one particular definition of the family as the sole legitimate family form. On the other hand, we find an increasing diversity of actual family forms in Canada, and it can be assumed that this diversity will continue to exist and probably to increase. It includes families which consist of first marriages for both spouses who are legally married to each other and raise their own biological children. It includes an increasing proportion of solo-parent (usually solo-mother) families. It further includes an increasing proportion of families in which at least one spouse was previously married. Children residing with adults are increasingly less likely to live with both their biological father and mother in one household. Many children will have at least one step-parent, and many adults will be involved in raising step-children. Couples will continue to cohabit, and some of them may eventually marry; others continue to live common-law, and yet others separate. The category of cohabiting couples will continue to include some homosexual couples, some of whom will have children. None of these family forms are new; what is new are merely the shifting proportions and the way in which we regard this diversity.

The true innovation lies in the area of reproductive technologies, and in the legal and policy innovations which may follow in the wake of these technological innovations. . . . motherhood has already been irrevocably redefined. If it were to become Canadian law that pre-conception contracts for the production of children became legally enforceable, we would have taken an extremely serious step towards making parenthood a contractual and commercial relationship rather than a social-biological one.

Families have always been fundamentally affected by events taking place in the larger society. When there have been wars, in the past young men have been killed, wounded, or at least were absent for prolonged periods of time. Family formations consequently were delayed, fertility patterns affected, and so on. With changes in the economy, income generation patterns within families change, in their turn changing interaction patterns.

The development of more effective contraceptive means has had an effect on fertility patterns, which structure the nature of family relationships.

Such interaction between micro- and macro-level changes has always existed. However, at present we are hovering at a threshold of unprecedented significance for families. The new forms of genetic manipulation, generated in laboratories by a small group of medical researchers, may result in new forms of human beings, created not through sexual intercourse between a woman and a man, but by the fusion of an egg and sperm which may have been manipulated for "improvement." In the case of cloning, two cells may be merged to generate a human with only one biological parent. The genetic makeup of a human being would, with the use of such techniques, be the result of deliberate intervention by people other than the biological parent(s).

This would centralize decision-making power affecting the procreation of people in the hands of medical experts rather than leaving it dispersed throughout the entire population, as is the case at present. Such power has never been held by any group of humans over other humans, because the technological base for it did not exist. We are therefore dealing with a new phenomenon, which demands new legal, and social policy responses. It is to be expected that family forms and forms of procreation will remain in the public focus for a while to come.

Summary and Conclusion

. . . Families have never been monolithic structures, and they certainly cannot be pressed into one uniform structure today. And yet we are presently witnessing the parallel march of two opposing social forces: a movement that tries to impose one family form on the entire society, and another movement that is currently revolutionizing our reproductive processes. However, these two movements have so far not collided in a serious manner.

This seems incomprehensible until we realize that both movements *do* share some similar ideas about the *structure* of the family. While utterly altering the relationship between parents and their children and between the couple as a procreative unit, the new reproductive technologies and arrangements nevertheless are oriented towards a monolithic vision of the family in terms of its structure and composition.

As Judge Sorkow, of the Baby M case argued, when addressing the question whether pre-conception contracts for the production of children undermine the traditional notions of family:

How can that be when the childless husband and wife so very much want a child? They seek to make a family. They intend to have a family. The surrogate mother could not make a valid contract without her husband's consent. This statement should not be construed anti-feminist. It means that if the surrogate is married, her husband will, in all probability, have to sign the contract to establish his non-paternity pursuant to the New Jersey Parentage law. Both sides of the equation must agree.

In order to establish whether or not pre-conception contracts undermine traditional notions of the family, he addresses himself to the question of consent of the husband of the uterine-genetic mother and the fact that another husband and wife want a child. As long as the consent is provided and the baby goes to a couple, his criterion for maintaining a traditional family structure is satisfied. He does *not* address himself to the question of having a contractual relationship supersede a biological-social one, and of the intrusion of commercial relations into parental ones.

Similarly, medical bodies argue that it is preferable to have a child by artificial insemination by donor rather than through adultery, in spite of the fact that there is no *medical* need for medical involvement, only a social desire for medical legitimacy. In other words, as long as the *fiction* of a traditional family is maintained — namely that the end result of the medical, commercial, or legal intervention will be a family consisting of a wife, husband, and child that is socially constructed as their joint child although, in fact, it is genetically related to only one of them — as long as this fiction is maintained and accepted by those involved, a collision has been averted.

This approach, however, leaves unsolved the issue what these reproductive arrangements and techniques mean to the children thus produced, what effect they are going to have on women and men as groups, and on society at large. The patterns of thought underlying this approach are similar to those underlying arguments concerning the "death of the family." . . . By focussing on the structure and composition of families while ignoring the processes that result in these structures, the real changes slide out of the picture. We have thus come full circle.

$$\vdots$$

chapter

7

Deviance, Control, and Change

In one way or another, all of the selections in this chapter challenge the conventional definition of deviance as norm violation, as rule breaking. The first selection, by Rhonda Lenton of McMaster University, argues that even when discussing homicide we must recognize that there are different social definitions and that various groups in society have different amounts of power to make their definitions stick. Her examination of perceptions and causes of homicide suggest that we will only understand crime if we understand inequality and the distribution of power.

The second selection, by Leslie Miller of the University of Calgary, explores the evolving role of women as moral entrepeneurs who define crime and deviance. Increasingly, sociologists have recognized that what becomes criminal or deviant in

any society is the result of conflict of interest. The rich have defined deviance for the poor, adults for children, men for women, etc. Miller suggests that as women are showing greater influence in shaping what is thought of as crime, for example in the area of pornography, they are experiencing some ambivalence and role conflict.

The final two selections, by Paul Brantingham of Simon Fraser University and by Anthony Doob of the Centre for Criminology, University of Toronto, offer sociological perspectives of violence. Both challenge conventional wisdom. Brantingham demonstrates that we must examine the experience of violence rather than superficial accounts of supposed increased rates of violence. He illustrates some of the changes in public perceptions of and tolerance for various kinds of violence. Doob also warns against a simplistic view of violence. He discusses how the media have contributed to such a simplistic view, and to public expectations that the solutions are equally simple.

RELATED READINGS

Elliott Leyton: "The Modern Multiple Murderer" (Chapter 4)
Peter Clark and Anthony Davis: "The Power of Dirt: An Exploration of Secular Defilement in Anglo-Canadian Culture" (Chapter 4)

HOMICIDE IN CANADA AND THE U.S.A.: A CRITIQUE OF THE HAGAN THESIS

Rhonda L. Lenton

Culture and Homicide in Canada and the U.S.A.

One of the most striking and well known differences between Canada and the United States concerns their crime rates. Americans are roughly four times more likely than Canadians to commit homicide and rape, two and one-half times more likely to commit robbery and one and one-quarter times more likely to commit burglary. While some of these differences may result partly from crossnational variations in legal definitions of crime, methods of counting crime and levels of police surveillance, it is generally agreed that for the most violent crimes — homicide in particular — official crime rates reflect real

From "Homicide in Canada and the U.S.A.: A Critique of the Hagan Thesis" by Rhonda L. Lenton. Appearing in *The Canadian Journal of Sociology* Volume 14(2), 1989. By permission of the publisher.

behavioural differences between the two countries (Hagan, 1984 [1977]: 48–55).

John Hagan refers to the most serious forms of deviance as "consensus crimes." In his judgement members of society broadly agree that the most violent crimes are the most serious crimes, and that their perpetrators deserve the most severe forms of punishment. Violent crime involves avoiding, neutralizing and rejecting deeply and widely held societal norms and values. The rate of violent crimes therefore hinges on the ability of a culture to define achievable goals, impose constraints on behaviour, and prevent both the neutralization of community standards and the creation of subcultures that oppose the dominant value system (Hagan, 1984 [1977]: 80–120).

In explaining Canadian-American differences in homicide rates, Hagan follows this cultural approach. Borrowing from the work of S.D. Clark (1976), Seymour Martin Lipset (1986) and others, Hagan argues that two sets of historical forces created Canadian and American value systems that differ in important respects and that account for the lower rate of homicide in Canada. First, in the early years of North American economic development, Canada's frontier was "harder" than that of the United States. That is, Canada was a vast and inhospitable country compared to the U.S., and its natural resources were less accessible. While the development of the American frontier could therefore be left to the initiative of the lone, relatively lawless entrepreneur, the exploitation of the Canadian frontier required the assistance of state-supported armies, police forces, and other social organizations such as the established Roman Catholic and Anglican Churches. The "wild West" shaped American attitudes towards authority, the state, and law and order quite differently from the way the harmonious development of the Canadian frontier influenced Canadians' attitudes: Canadians became more respectful of authority and less inclined to break the law.

According to Hagan, the second main historical force that produced lower Canadian rates of violent crime was the tenacity of Canada's ties to elitist and conservative Britain. Presumably, those ties were reinforced during the American Revolution, when loyalist tories migrated northward, and persisted well into the twentieth century. Canadians' characteristic deference to authority supposedly derived in part from the British connection. In contrast, the American Revolution severed the American bond to Britain and institutionalized a deep and abiding anti-authoritarianism in the American psyche. Presumably, that attitude is reflected in the greater propensity of Americans to commit violent crimes.

My purpose in this paper is not to dispute the accuracy of the violent crime statistics, historical interpretations, or attitudinal differences discussed by Hagan. Other analysts have already raised serious questions about the precision of some of the "facts" he uncritically accepts. For example, there is a considerable body of historical scholarship contesting the old view, endorsed by Hagan, that the Loyalists were tories. Similarly, an analysis of recent sample survey data indicates that the purported Canadian-American value differences either do not exist or are in the opposite direction from that predicted by Hagan (and Clark and Lipset before him). According to Baer, Grabb, and Johnston (1989), Canadians are *less* respectful of government leaders and institutions than are Americans, and *less* traditional than Americans about the need for crime control.

Whether or not the predicted Canadian-American value differences actually exist, my aim in this paper is to demonstrate that variation in homicide rates is better explained by structural factors. I argue that the relationship posited by Hagan between some measured value differences and homicide rates may be largely an artifact of his choice of data. Hagan bases his argument mainly on a comparison of only two cases over a relatively short period of time. By increasing the cross-sectional and longitudinal variation in his independent and dependent variables, however, I cast doubt on the accuracy of Hagan's generalizations.

I also suggest an alternative explanation of Canadian-American differences in homicide rates. I argue that certain features of American and Canadian social structure account for Canadian-American differences in homicide rates better than do alleged cultural differences. Specifically, variations in the racial composition of the two countries and in the level of income inequality stand out as the two most important determinants of crossnational differences in my analysis. In general, I agree with Ian Taylor's view that "[t]here is a clear need to examine the *structure* of ... society (its demography, political economy and social institutions) and to relate these to ... pathological social interactions like homicide" (Taylor, 1983: 97; emphasis in the original). Apart from criticizing Hagan's thesis, then, my paper adds modest empirical substance to Taylor's assertion....

Variation Over Time

A key argument in Hagan's thesis is that the ratio of American to Canadian homicide rates has remained about the same or increased over time. A relatively constant or increasing ratio suggests that values first crystallized 100 to 200 years ago remain obdurate and that cultural differences between the two North American countries exert an enduring influence on criminal behaviour despite vast economic, political, and legal changes. A widely fluctuating or declining ratio of American to Canadian homicide rates, in contrast, would suggest that the values discussed by Hagan have no persistent effect on criminal behaviour.

Table 1
HOMICIDE RATES (PER 100,000 POPULATION), CANADA AND U.S.A., 1954–86.

	CANADA	U.S.A.	U.S.A./CANADA RATIO
1954	1.2	4.8	4.0
1955	1.2	4.5	3.8
1956	1.3	4.6	3.5
1957	1.2	4.5	3.8
1958	1.4	4.5	3.1
1959	1.2	4.5	3.8
1960	.9	5.1	5.7
1961	1.2	4.8	4.0
1962	1.4	4.5	3.3
1963	1.3	4.6	3.5
1964	1.3	4.9	3.8
1965	1.4	5.1	3.6
1966	1.2	5.6	4.7
1967	1.7	6.2	3.7
1968	1.8	6.9	3.8
1969	1.8	7.3	4.1
1970	2.2	7.9	3.6
1971	2.2	8.6	3.9
1972	2.4	9.0	3.8
1973	2.5	9.4	3.8
1974	2.7	9.8	3.6
1975	3.1	9.6	3.1
1976	2.9	8.8	3.0
1977	3.0	8.8	2.9
1978	2.8	9.0	3.2
1979	2.7	9.7	3.6
1980	2.5	10.2	4.1
1981	2.7	9.8	3.7
1982	2.7	9.1	3.4
1983	2.7	8.3	3.0
1984	2.7	7.9	3.0
1985	2.8	7.9	2.8
1986	2.2	8.6	3.9

When Hagan first made his case he compared American and Canadian homicide rates in 1957, 1960, 1967, 1968, and 1970. He concluded that the ratio of American to Canadian homicide rates is increasing over time (Hagan and Leon, 1978: 198–99). He later compared homicide rates for the years 1960–80 and concluded that the ratio has remained constant over time (Hagan, 1984 [1978]: 50).

It is unclear why Hagan selected these particular years for comparison. It does, however, seem that he based his conclusions on a simple visual inspection of the data. Table 1 assembles American and Canadian homicide rates from 1954 (the first year for which Canadian data are readily accessible from secondary sources) to 1986 (the last year for which data are currently available). Although the ratio of American to Canadian rates does not fluctuate widely from year to year, it appears to be very slowly *declining*. ... Rather than substantiating Hagan's thesis, these findings offer some support for Irving Louis Horowitz's contrary claim that homicide data reveal a tendency for the "cultural gap" between Canada and the United States to be closing over time. Horowitz asserts that this gap is narrowing due to the Americanization of Canada that is caused by such structural forces as increasing American economic and political influence (Horowitz, 1973).

Variation by Region

A second problem with Hagan's analysis is that he considers only two cases — Canada and the United States — and is consequently unable to determine whether the relationship he observes between homicide rates and culture patterns is fortuitous or generalizable. One way of getting around this problem is by comparing units of analysis smaller than countries, such as provinces or states. This seems sensible because there is more variation in homicide rates *within* both Canada and the United States than *between* the two countries. In 1986, the coefficient of variation (the standard deviation over the mean) of homicide rates within Canada was 1.534. Within the U.S. the coefficient of variation was .664, and between Canada and the U.S. it was only .593. . . . The range of homicide rates across the Canadian provinces was almost the same in 1986 (27) as the range of homicide rates across the American states (30). The ranges and coefficients of variation show that national comparisons mask wide regional variations within the two countries. This raises the question of whether it makes much sense to assume national homogeneity in values and homicidal behaviour, as does a simple comparison of national mean rates.

. . . In order to test the stability of correlations across time, [I calculated] zero-order correlations for 1986, 1981, 1976, and 1971. In order to test the robustness of correlations across groups of cases, [I used] all twelve cases. Next, the Northwest Territories, which has the highest homicide rate and the second smallest population of the twelve jurisdictions [was] removed and the

correlations recalculated. Then the Yukon, which generally has the second highest homicide rate and the smallest population of the twelve jurisdictions [was] removed and the correlations calculated for a third time. Finally, both the Northwest Territories and the Yukon are removed and the correlations calculated for a fourth time.

In Hagan's view, one correlate of homicide rates is the strength of the "Imperial connection." Presumably, an indicator of British influence is the proportion of British-origin people in each province or territory: it follows from Hagan's argument that the greater the proportion British-origin, the lower the homicide rate. In fact, out of the sixteen correlations between proportion British and the homicide rate only ten are in the predicted direction and statistically significant at the .05 level. Proportion British is in the predicted direction and statistically significant across time only if the two northern territories are omitted; and proportion British is in the predicted direction and statistically significant across groups of cases only in 1971 and 1981.

Hagan also suggests that Canadian values have been profoundly influenced by the predominance of the Anglican and Roman Catholic Churches, which provided Canada with "a set of hierarchical and traditionally rooted control mechanisms" that reinforced the effects of the hard frontier and the British connection. In contrast, Protestant sectarianism flourished in the U.S., thus reinforcing individualism and lack of respect for authority in that country. Yet of the thirty-two correlations between provincial and territorial homicide rates, on the one hand, and proportion Catholic and proportion Anglican, on the other, none is in the predicted direction and statistically significant. Combining proportion Catholic and proportion Anglican into one index . . . does not alter the conclusion that provinicial and territorial homicide rates do not increase with the greater numerical prevalence of Catholics and Anglicans.

Variation by Race and Economic Condition

The foregoing analysis generates only weak support for Hagan's thesis. The best that can be said for his argument is that proportion British predicts homicide rates well for the ten provinces. However, once the territories are included in the analysis proportion British fails to perform very well. And proportion Catholic and proportion Anglican systematically fail to predict homicide rates.

An alternative explanation of the Canadian-American difference in homicide rates can be derived from research on homicide conducted mainly in the U.S. over the past fifteen years. Perhaps the best substantiated finding of both ecological and individual-level analyses of homicide etiology in the U.S. is that poor, young, urban blacks and Hispanics are tremendously overrepresented among homicide offenders (e.g., Williams, 1984). In 1986, for example, blacks accounted for 48.0 percent and Hispanics for 15.7 percent of American murderers, yet they composed, respectively, only 12 percent and 6 percent of the American population. Significantly, Canadian homicide statistics for poor Native Canadians are equally startling. In 1986, for instance, Native Canadians accounted for 21 percent of Canadian murderers for whom race could be ascertained, yet Natives represented a mere 2 percent of the population. . . . There is a consistently strong and statistically significant association between homicide rates in the Canadian provinces and territories and the proportion of the population that is of Native origin: fifteen of the sixteen relevant correlations are in the predicted direction and statistically significant.

The racial skewedness of homicide in both Canada and the U.S., and the dissimilar racial compositions of the two countries, have important implications for Hagan's thesis. Consider, for instance, that the 1986 non-black, non-Hispanic American homicide rate was 3.1 (compared to 8.6 for the entire American population). The 1986 non-Native Canadian rate was 1.7 (compared to 2.2 for the entire Canadian population). If one compares American non-blacks and non-Hispanics with Canadian non-Natives, then the 1986 American-Canadian homicide ratio of 3.9 falls to a much less dramatic 1.8. Hagan virtually dismisses the significance of the racial composition of Canada and the U.S. in interpreting the two countries' different homicide rates. The fact is, however, that differences in racial composition account for over half the discrepancy that Hagan set out to explain.

Despite the fact that Hagan makes no mention of the higher level of poverty and inequality in the U.S. as compared to Canada, some portion of the remaining discrepancy is likely the result of the different distribution of economic advantages in the two countries (cf. Horowitz, 1973: 341). Consider the following:

1. We know from American research that measures of economic well-being, both at the aggregate and individual level, are associated with homicide rates. . . . To varying degrees in different studies, unemployment, poverty, levels of inequality, and so forth, have been reported to promote homicidal behaviour independent of the effects of race. While there has been some inconsistency in findings on the effects of economic variables, recent research suggests that that is because such effects are indirect and mediated by levels of family disruption (Sampson, 1987).

2. In Canada, too, economic condition appears to be associated with propensity to commit homicide. Thus, from 1961 to 1974, fully 56 percent of murder suspects had a primary education or less (compared to 35 percent of the population in 1971); and only 3 percent of murder suspects had a university education (compared to 10 percent of the population in 1971). In that same period, 61 percent of homicide suspects were blue-collar workers or self-employed workers in the primary sector compared to 36 percent of the population in those occupational categories in 1971.

3. Crossnational studies including Canada and the U.S. as cases have also found that homicide rates are positively associated with levels of inequality (Krahn, Hartnagel, and Gartrell, 1986; Messner, 1982). In this connection it is of interest that the level of income inequality in Canada is considerably lower than that in the U.S. In the mid-1970s the Gini index of income inequality was .33 in Canada and .41 in the U.S. and the gap between the two countries seems to have widened during the 1980s.

[I]nclude[d] are indices of structural poverty and family disruption. Structural poverty is operationalized as an index constructed from two items: the infant mortality rate and the proportion of households reporting no income. Scores on both these items were standardized and added together to create the index. Family disruption (cf. Sampson, 1987: 356) is operationalized as an index constructed from three items: the proportion of lone-parent families, the incidence of marital separation and the incidence of divorce. As with the structural poverty index, scores on these items were standardized and added together to create the index.

As a predictor of homicide, structural poverty performs nearly as well as percent Native, with thirteen of sixteen relevant correlations attaining statistical significance. The correlations between family disruption and homicide are much less robust and stable, with only four of the sixteen relevant correlations attaining statistical significance. I surmise that my family disruption index performs poorly in the Canadian context because it is derived from research on Black Americans and therefore fails to tap manifestations of family disruption among Native Canadians. Divorce, separation, and single-parent families are relatively common in American urban ghettos, but Native Canadians do not appear to be more prone to these forms of family breakdown than other Canadians. For Native Canadians, family violence and incest seem to be more valid indicators of family breakdown (Shkilnyk, 1985). Unfortunately, however, systematically collected national data on family violence and incest by ethnic group are unavailable.

In the light of these findings it is tempting to model my argument along the lines of Figure 1. I propose that structural poverty and racial discrimination are the two principle causes of homicide. Structural poverty exerts its impact both directly and indirectly through its effects on family disruption.

For two reasons, the proposed model cannot be tested without individual-level

---

Figure 1

A CAUSAL MODEL OF HOMICIDE ETIOLOGY IN CANADA

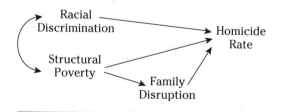

data. First, as a measure of racial discrimination, percent Native is highly correlated with structural poverty (e.g., in 1981, $r = .852$). . . . The second, related issue is that only individual-level measures of racial discrimination can enable one to unpack the cultural and structural effects that may be associated with race. Until ecological and individual-level data are analyzed for the Canadian case, the model in Figure 1 must be regarded as merely a more plausible and suggestive argument than Hagan's.

Discussion

If murder is the prototypical crime of passion, it seems evident that passion is much more likely to take such a violent course in particular types of communities. Cross-sectional data from both Canada and the U.S. suggest that when racial discrimination, endemic poverty, and family disruption cause hopelessness and rage, murder rates increase.

This social-structural interpretation is of course at variance with Hagan's argument, which borrows heavily from the "subculture of violence" thesis, until recently the dominant explanation of homicide in the U.S. (Wolfgang and Feracutti, 1967). Darnell Hawkins, a student of homicide among American blacks and a critic of the subculture of violence thesis, summarizes the thesis by noting that it

tends to identify the value system of a given subculture as the locus of crime causation. Emphasis is also placed on the role of social learning as the principal process by which aggressive behaviour is acquired. While there is some attention paid to the social, economic and political deprivation within subcultures, such deprivation is itself seldom seen as a direct cause of crime. That is, the impact of deprivation on crime is mediated by social values — in particular the existence of a positive attitude toward the use of violence. (Hawkins, 1986: 112)

In like fashion, Hagan tries to account for American-Canadian differences in homicide rates by examining value differences between the two countries and, in the process, ignoring differences in racial composition and the distribution of economic advantages.

The data assembled here do not unequivocally undermine the cultural thesis and support a structural interpretation of variation in homicide rates across Canadian regions and between Canada and the U.S. This is partly due to problems stemming from the highly aggregated nature of most of the data reviewed here and partly due to measurement problems. Although my inspection of individual-level contingency tables from Canadian government sources does suggest that my argument is not ecologically fallacious, I cannot be absolutely certain that the relationships discovered here hold at lower levels of aggregation or at the individual level because most of my data are highly aggregated. Moreover, partly because I use ecological data, my independent variables are highly correlated, thus preventing the construction of a multivariate model. On these grounds alone there is much room for additional research.

In addition, some of the measures used here — such as proportion British and proportion Native — are not unambiguously structural or cultural. Thus, it is unclear to what degree the prevalence of members of a given group indicates something about the value system of a particular region or about its social structure. Better measures are clearly needed. Until they are available one is obliged to note that there is apparently considerable variation in homicide rates across Native Canadian groups. . . . This casts doubt on the notion that there is some culturally uniform cause of homicide among Native Canadians.

All these qualifications notwithstanding, available evidence suggests that the conviction with which Hagan endorses the cultural theory of Canadian-American differences in homicide rates is unwarranted. The evidence supporting a structural theory is somewhat stronger, but considerably more research is needed before one can hope to call closure on the debate.

Conclusion

I noted at the beginning of this paper that homicide is considered by Hagan to be one variant of a broad class of "consensus" crimes, including murder, rape, incest, and kidnapping. According to Hagan, these are the most violent crimes and, as a result, members of society generally agree that they are the most serious crimes; their perpetrators receive the most severe forms of punishment; attitudes towards these crimes are weakly, if at all, related to status group membership; social and economic forces play a relatively small role in designating such acts as deviant; and these crimes are best explained by consensus theories, which focus on how cultures succeed or fail in imposing constraints on deviant behaviour. Hagan argues that, in contrast, crimes that do not match the criteria listed above are better explained by labelling, conflict, and Marxist theories, which emphasize the historical variability of crime and the manner in which dominant groups define and punish criminal behaviour.

My critique has questioned the applicability of a consensus theory to one of the most violent types of crime in two countries. But, more broadly, the foregoing analysis calls into question the utility of viewing the most violent crimes as consensus crimes. For in two senses — one concerning social definition, the other etiology — even homicide is a conflict crime. Consider, first, that some types of widespread killing are not socially defined as serious crimes because to do so would harm corporate interests; while homicide is "allowed" to be socially defined as a serious crime because it does not harm corporate interests. Thus, deaths that result from industrial pollution and the failure to implement more stringent worker safety legislation account for many more deaths per year than homicide. Yet these acts are not consensually defined as serious crimes, they are not subject to strict surveillance, they are often not detected and counted by authorities and their perpetrators are typically not punished severely when detected. Corporate influence is surely a major socio-economic force that prevents such killing from being classified as a crime on a par with homicide. As these examples illustrate, to the degree that there is consensus about what kind of killing is a serious crime, that consensus is not "given" by culture but is manufactured by the distribution of power in society. Crimes like homicide are *mala en sa* (wrong in themselves), but they are also *mala prohibita* (wrong by prohibition).

Homicide is also a conflict crime from an etiological point of view, as I have argued at some length in the body of this paper. The distribution of homicide by race, class, sex, age, and level of inequality indicates that most homicide is a manifestation of social conflict, a violent response to racial, class, and sexual antagonism. As Ian Taylor (1983: 84) writes, "antagonistic or competitive social relationships in patriarchal, capitalist societies tend to produce violent solutions to individuals' social, sexual or financial problems." Cultural interpretations of violent crime like Hagan's deflect our attention from the ways in which homicide and other violent crimes are, like all forms of deviance, socially constructed and socially caused. Such interpretations should therefore be treated with appropriate sociological skepticism.

UNEASY ALLIANCE: WOMEN AS AGENTS OF SOCIAL CONTROL

Leslie J. Miller

Introduction

This paper begins with the recognition that many women experience a real ambivalence about the desirability of the current war on "public immorality." (e.g. the war on pornography) and especially about the alliance with the forces of law and order that such a campaign seems to entail. The dilemma created by the clash of repressive and emancipatory interests appears in a whole host of contemporary issues. For example, as women move to defend themselves and their children against forms of public immorality such as pornography, they find this interest to be in direct contradiction with the emancipatory desire to defend the rights of other low-status or marginal groups in the society — the mentally ill, gays and lesbians, prostitutes, and advocates of artistic and sexual freedom. Can women both "Take Back The Night" (a clear law-and-order slogan calling for safer streets) and also fight for the rights of prostitutes or bath-house sub-cultures?

I propose to take this ambivalence as the occasion to examine the changing shape of women's involvement in social control. The paper which follows treats three related issues. First, we recognize that while history, feminist and otherwise, depicts women primarily as victims of social control, it is clear that they have also participated in the victimization of others, as agents or instruments. Section I, therefore, looks at this second less visible tradition.

From "Uneasy Alliance: Women As Agents of Social Control" by Leslie J. Miller. Appearing in *The Canadian Journal of Sociology*, Volume 12(4) 1987. By permission of *The Canadian Journal of Sociology*.

Here I consider women's historic role as "guardians of morality" for the society, in particular as members of bourgeois reform movements which regulated marginal groups under the banner of refinement and decency. Since the informal control of others through the regulation of manners was until the eighteenth century a man's preserve, I shall be asking what becomes of the role as it is reassigned to women. Section II looks at the credibility of women's claim to legitimately voice the morality of the social whole. In Section III, I focus more directly on the problem of ambivalence per se. If it *is* the case in fact that women have played the role of social control agents — society's "moral police" — why are many women reluctant to accept this skein in their history, and why are they uncomfortable wearing this mantle today? Here I suggest several structural supports for their ambivalence.

I. Women as Agents of Social Control

ORIGINS OF THE ROLE

The efforts of women to control the behaviour of others have long been associated with the "womanly" ideals of refinement, taste, and decency. The special role of women as "guardians of manners and morals" appears to have its historical point of origin at the moment when the emergence of the early modern family heralded the separation of life into public and private spheres. The rise of the modern state produced an analogous split in the institution of social control. In the modern world, the instrument of social control came to have two prongs; one, the shaping and enforcement of law; the other, the shaping of morality. The first is predominantly public, formal and male; the second domestic, informal and female.

For those readers unfamiliar with the recent renaissance in the social history of the family, I sketch below the main points which are relevant to the present discussion. Though there is considerable debate as to just what changed and why (see Anderson, 1980) the most influential of the social historians, Philippe Ariès, describes the emergence of the modern family as "a revolution in sentiment." His groundbreaking book *Centuries of Childhood* (1962) deals with changes in family life from the late Middle Ages until the end of the nineteenth century and focusses mainly on France. Ariès claims that until the late 1700s the family existed as a political and public body, a lineage or "house," with little or no private character. Gradually there emerged toward the middle of the eighteenth century a recognizable modern form of family, termed "intimate" or "domestic." This newly domestic family is characterized as a little nest of natural sentiment forged as a bulwark against the impersonal public arena.

In general, the vast body of data assembled by the early writers, including Ariès, documented on the one hand the gradual decline of so-called "public immorality" — a decrease in rowdy public festivals and drunkenness, in celebratory public torture and executions, in wandering bands of youths. It found, on the other hand, a new sense of the vulnerability of the child, the spread of the "little school" and of discipline, and a changed conjugal relationship marked by a new emphasis on the importance of sentiment, manners and hygiene. The outcome was a clear distinction for the first time between public and private spheres of life. With the concern for the protection of the child from the rough-and-tumble of the street, and a growing intimacy between spouses, the domestic family had seemingly emerged from a sea of brutality and had become an object of veneration.

The nature and progress of domesticity has become a topic of some disagreement.

Foucault and others have described it as the process of the rationalization of emotional life. Here, domesticity is understood as the means by which the barbaric life, the Hobbesian existence regulated only by force, is curbed by control, scrutiny and reason (Foucault, 1979). Others have described it as a process of embourgeoisement, according to which the standards of the new middle class family come to be defined as the *only* standard, are given moral weight, and are imposed gradually but inexorably upon the other strata of society. Still others have interpreted this body of data as the progress of social control over the family, and in particular as the increasing propensity of the state to regulate family life (Donzelot, 1979).

However the progress of domesticity is conceptualized, two things are beyond dispute: 1) that the newly domestic family came to be closely associated with refinement — "manners and morals" — and 2) that responsibility for the informal control of others through the imposition of standards of refinement was assigned to women. Therefore, when we say that modernity produced the separation between public and private spheres of social life, we refer not just to the separation between men's paid work and women's unpaid work which feminist sociologists have emphasized, but also to the split between a man's cultural world and a women's cultural world, between men's talk and women's talk, manly demeanour and ladylike demeanour. And whether or not women *forged* this separation, it is evident that women came to play the major role in *policing or enforcing* it.

The eminent German scholar Norbert Elias is one of the few sociologists to pay close attention to the history of manners before the "domestic revolution" and to relate changing standards of taste and comportment to social control. It is the gradual emergence of new standards of refinement and the ever-tightening restrictions upon displays of affect which Elias calls "the civilizing process" (Elias, 1978). In a sense we can think of Elias as unfolding the origins of the "revolution in sentiment" on which Ariès focusses.

Elias's project in *The History of Manners* is to trace the link between the social graces and social control: how and why the "implements of civilization," such as the fork, and handerchief and the nightdress and their attendant "proper" forms of behaviour, made their way gradually through Europe, usually from Italy, in the fourteenth, fifteenth and sixteenth centuries. With respect to the nightdress, for example, he notes that the sight of total nakedness was the everyday rule up until the sixteenth century. Sleeping had not yet been shifted behind the scenes of social life; as Ariès too notes, it was normal to receive visitors in rooms with beds, and opulent beds and bed clothes, well displayed for visitors, conferred prestige upon their owners.

Eventually, with the rise of the middle class, the unconcern with nakedness and bodily functions disappears; getting up and going to bed become "refined" or domesticated and are displaced from social life into the interior of the family. Finally, before World War I, the mere mention of sleeping and undressing are tabooed and these acts become surrounded with heavy prohibitions. Elias quotes one writer who had the freedom to complain somewhat later: "During the Genteel Era before the War, camping was the only way by which respectable writers might approach the subject of sleep. In those days ladies and gentlemen did not go to bed — they retired. How they did it was nobody's business. An author who thought differently would have found himself excluded from the circulating library." (Elias, 1978: 165).

Elias traces the changing structure of affect in the upper classes in society — the changing "shame frontier" — by examining documents such as manuals of etiquette from the Middle Ages to the 1800s. Under his analysis these documents are made to reveal not simply an evolution in taste —

When do spitting and defecating in public, for example, become unmannerly? — but also an evolution in the discourse of social control itself. From the 1200s to the 1500s counsels appear in the language of straightforward instruction and demonstrate a concern for harmonious social interaction ("If you share a bed with a stranger, it is not proper to lie so near that you disturb him; let your better choose which side of the bed he lies on"), but by the late 1700s their tone has become one of moral injunction, one which controls indirectly by flagging areas of social life with euphemism or with conspicuous omission. It is the shift from a tone of care and seriousness which invites public discussion to one which suggests privacy and strict prohibition which signals the advancing frontier of shame and delicacy and the march of civility.

What is the root of these changing forms of ritual and regulation? For Elias, they reflect the rise of new forms of social and economic organization. The feudal environment was warlike, but it also isolated rural estates from one another; when men came together, it was often to fight (e.g. the crusades) and pertinent social distinctions, such as where one came from or whose banner one flew, were distinct, clearly understood and easily observed. With the move of the landed aristocracy away from the feudal estates and into the life around the court and into the growing cities, "old social ties were loosened or broken" and individuals of different social origins were thrown together in new ways. In consequence, there is a higher danger of social conflict and the code of behaviour becomes stricter — "the social imperative not to offend others becomes more binding" (Elias, 1978: 79–80).

As authority shifts from a dispersed feudal form to a more centralized one, then, the rituals which once served to defend life and property in the isolation of the feudal estate now serve, as Goffman would say, to "manage social interaction" in close quarters. In these closer quarters, ritual begins to reflect the social hierarchy in new ways, as specific forms of address and apparel become firmly attached to social rank. Only the nobility, for example, will be allowed to wear certain colours and fabrics. The concern to declare social rank extends to other social practices: before servants, for example, there is no need to cover one's nakedness or to hide bodily functions; because they are below you in the hierarchy, and you need not worry about giving offense. At the same time, in order to minimize the possibility of conflict, displays of affect (e.g. aggressiveness) become the province of specialized groups and take on a purely ritual form, e.g. jousting, boxing as "sport," and wrestling in the highly theatrical form we still see today. Finally, says Elias, in the 1700s the rituals lose their purely social function and become internalized as psychological prohibitions which every adult observes. And the more integrated society becomes, the more these potential dangers must be regulated.

Thus, for Elias, the new sensibility in manners and family life develops in tandem with the move toward an integrated social milieu and a centralized form of state authority; manners/rituals are strategies for the management of interaction and their different forms are reflective of different social contexts.

THE ROLE IS FEMINIZED

What groups in the society set and police the shifting standards of civility? In *The History of Manners* Elias himself pays little direct attention to gender. But by carefully inspecting his materials we can tease out the following points.

1. The concern with manners in earlier centuries is tied to courtly life, and the individuals who best exemplify and enforce the new standard of refinement are male. Thus it is the court gentlemen who are the paragons of taste and fashion — in elegant costume, in song and dance, in brilliant social repartee — and it is Castiglione (*The Courtier*) and Erasmus (*De civilitate morum puerilium*) and Caxton (*Book of Curtesye*), all men, who codify their ways.

2. As the "revolution in sentiment" unfolds and the newly modern family form emerges, this role is *reassigned to women*. From the late 1700s forward the exemplars, enforcers, and codifiers are female. Mr. Manners is now Miss Manners and Erasmus has become (in this regard at least) Emily Post. Moreover, the "nursery of refined conduct" is no longer the court, as it was in Erasmus's time; that nursery is now the newly domestic family (Elias, 1978: 137). In short, both the sphere of regulation and the agents of social control have shifted.

It is worth examining in some detail the rise of the women to prominence in this newly feminized role. The most striking aspect of it is how recent it is, yet how swiftly and firmly it becomes lodged in the cultural stock of knowledge as a — perhaps *the* — defining characteristic of a "womanly nature." Before the separation of public and private spheres of life there is no real evidence to associate *women* with refinement and sensitivity; in fact, we can safely infer from Elias's account that women would not have been viewed as credible arbiters of "*courtoisie*" and "*civilité*" before this great shift occurs. Shortly after the role is reassigned to women it is reformulated as natural — the sign of its cultural centrality — and eventually invoked in order to rationalize the political division of social life, i.e. to affirm the rightness of women's participation in the home and their exclusion from the public realm, notably business, politics and war.

This leads directly to a second point: as men relinquish the role of guardian of manners and morals, the role suffers a loss in status. We can picture the decline as a demotion of this form of social control from the high-power institution of the courtly circle to the less powerful sphere of the newly formed domestic or bourgeois family. It is one of the curiosities of social history that the domestic family form upon its emergence is at once so venerated and yet so discrediting to all of the activities which fall within its domain. The prestige of the role under discussion is no exception: as it is feminized and reassigned to the private sphere it is accordingly trivialized. And it is just at this point in history that the cultural capital it possesses — the knowledge of correct deportment and the authority to enforce the latter — suffers a real loss in value.

The contemporary reader, long accustomed to assuming the low value of this form of social control, will have difficulty in appreciating the power of the role in the pre-modern world. Today "mere" mannerliness is seen as the province of women, girls, and little boys, and as such is thought to have little to do with the important activities of the public sphere. It is sometimes even portrayed as an obstacle to those who must make the transition to the (paid) workworld; thus "Miss Manners" reminds us that niceness or politeness properly belong in the home and are positive hindrances in the office ("Miss Manners," 1984: 50–3) and some scholars define the jettisoning of these polluting rituals as a necessary rite of passage in a boy's transition to manhood (in MacKie, 1983). These illustrations remind us that in the contemporary world, the possession of delicacy and refinement is understood as a detriment, not an increment, to one's power and prestige, based on the intimate association of these qualities with the discrediting sphere of women and the home.

Before the rise of the modern state, however, the power of the prince in his court and the need for *civilité* on the part of the nobles there were intimately interwoven: power was embodied and articulated in manners. In this milieu manners are the rituals through which the raw relations of super- and subordination are made livable. Their value as an accoutrement of power is reflected in the fact of their inclusion as an essential component of a gentleman's education and in the prestige accorded to the authors of manuals of etiquette, always men of respectable social class.

The emergence of the modern state appears to signal the declining importance of this form of social control. From the perspective of the history of regulation, one facet of the rise of the state is the bifurcation of the institution of social control into the two prongs mentioned earlier: one, the shaping and enforcement of law; the other, the shaping and enforcement of morality and taste.

This is a gendered division of labour. As the first prong gains in prestige and is stamped as a man's domain, the second is relinquished, sloughed off to women and the private sphere. We still tend to regard this division as "natural" today.

In the foregoing I have tried to sketch the place and power of the guardian of manners and morals before this split occurred — before men relinquished it and moved to consolidate their "real" power in the realm of formal or codified law. From this perspective the decline of manners as a form of social control (and the role of "guardian") is a small vignette in the larger story of the emergence and discrediting of the private or domestic sphere.

Some important points follow from this brief account. First and most obvious is the recognition that the concern for refinement and delicacy does not originate with women, as we so often assume. It began as a prestigious male role some centuries prior to the emergence of the domestic family, and was feminized — installed as the centrepiece in the cult of "true womanhood" — much later.

Second, those among us today who regard the arbiter of manners and morals as having no "real" (i.e., no formal or legal) power appear to have accepted and internalized the relatively recent androcentric picture of social life which denies real status to most domestic activities (notably housework). Despite this androcentric view, it is clear that women as arbiters and exemplars of manners have been engaged in an important and legitimate form of social control, just as they have been engaged in legitimate teaching (child-rearing) and legitimate, albeit unpaid, work. I mean to say here that women have, and have had, power, despite the social invisibility conferred upon these activities by that androcentric depiction. This is so, quite apart from whether we today approve or deplore the content of the standards of refinement and civility which women have enforced. The effort to restore visibility and credibility to women as agents of (informal) social control is directly analogous to the effort to restore visibility to house- and reproductive work as "real" work. From this perspective women who deny that other women have been or are presently acting as social control agents — in the family, or in the street — make the same claim as those who deny housework the status of real work. Both claims attest only to the veil which conventional history has dropped, until recently, over domestic life.

A third implication of this historical discussion concerns the credibility of the role since its "fall" into the domestic sphere. Having grasped the process of trivialization which accompanied the reassignment of this role to women, we are better able to understand the lack of credibility which the

civilizing interest encountered when women first attempted to extend it from the household into the street.

The attempt to civilize the street begins in the eighteenth century and builds into the characteristic project of the nineteenth century. Not long after the emergence of the "cult of domesticity" in the private sphere we see the redefinition of the public sphere — the street and the stranger — as corrupting influences which now must be cleaned up and refined. These new views are reflected in the appearance of fledgling organizations specifically geared to purifying or "civilizing" the street — to reducing the incidence of "public immorality" (drunkenness, brawling, "licentiousness," "indecency") and of religious festivals and spectacles which were thought to be the breeding ground of the former (Ariès, 1962).

Insofar as these campaigns were seen as "women's movements" and "women's issues," they suffered a credibility problem. Civilizing the streets was regarded in the same light as the ladylike concern to civilize the home and the child — laudable enough in its proper place, but not to be confused with issues of real public consequence. This legacy of trivialization continues to affect the perception of women's issues and projects of all sorts. Because of it, women's groups would eventually resort to borrowing credibility from the major privileged discourse of the modern era — scientific expertise. I shall return to this point later in the paper.

Despite efforts to trivialize the guardian of manners and morals, the movements which sprang up in the nineteenth century to clean up the streets achieved a certain impact. The history of such movements forms a long but direct line from groups like the Society for the Formation of Manners in the 1700s which targeted homosexuals, to the Society for the Reformation of Juvenile

Delinquents in the early 1800s, to the Prohibition movement of the early 1900s, to the recent campaigns to "Take Back the Night."

These movements sometimes included men, but were spearheaded by women, marched under the women's banner of bourgeois refinement, and, indeed, proved to be a useful early springboard for women into a place of some influence in the public sphere. But however much these movements gave women a voice outside the household, we must recognize that they helped to legitimate the rise of the great nineteenth-century bureaucratic institutions of social control — the prison, the workhouse, the asylum, the police and the army.

Whether there was, in fact, an objectively measurable increase in the level of street violence after the late eighteenth century is a question beyond the scope of this paper. What can be demonstrated conclusively, however, is the spread of the new sensibility, the concern for manners and morals against which the unruly tone of street life now offended. This standard is ever more broadly disseminated, and the agents of dissemination are women.

The alleged corrupting influence of the workplace, of streets and fields, and of the informal sociability of strangers (ethnic and class "undesirables") finally crystallized out as the characteristic social problem of the early modern era. The effort to re-form the public sphere in the image of a war on street violence and vice was launched by early women's groups referred to as "purity coalitions" by social historians like Barbara Finkelstein (1985) and Ronald Cohen (1985). This war is carried forward today in largely woman-sponsored programs such as the war on pornography, the campaign to "Take Back the Night," and even those like Block Parent and Neighbourhood Watch, which might be accused of confusing the best community with the most highly controlled one.

Of course, the early participation of women in the public sphere was not limited to social control; women also led or threw their support behind emancipatory movements. In the service of causes like abolition, civil rights, and disarmament "women struggled against injustice to others, then to themselves." My interest here is not to deny this skein in the tradition. Rather, I want to point out the tension between these two contradictory interests — one repressive, one emancipatory — and to note that conventional readings of history emphasize the second at the expense of the first. That is, received versions of history (including recent feminist versions) identify women largely as the underdog — either as the dog itself, or as the spokesperson for other underdog groups. My immediate purpose here is to restore visibility to the role of women as agents, not victims, of social control. In any debate over the question "Which side are we on?" women must recognize that they have in fact been on both sides — controlling and controlled — for some time now. The tension feminists feel today between the forces of emancipation and repression is not new. It is real and it has a considerable — though sometimes shadowy — tradition behind it.

If women and men today are to evaluate recent movements such as the antipornography one, they must be prepared to recognize straightforwardly that such movements are the offspring of the early repressive purity coalitions. This is so, no matter how unrefined or crude such an assertion sounds in the contemporary ear. The androcentric attempt to trivialize the "feminine" concern for refinement and decency must not cloud over our view of the sometimes repressive goals and social consequences of these early campaigns. As offspring of this tradition, recent programs are left open to the same charge which has been levelled at those early movements, i.e., that they have given women a voice in the community, but a voice which has often recommended the increased social control of other low-power groups or flotsam and jetsam in the society. A firmer grasp on the history of women's double-sided involvement in the institution of social control will help to transform private doubts about such campaigns into public issues.

II. From Disreputable to Dangerous: The Changing Rationale for Social Control

It might be objected that the kinds of campaigns mentioned in this paper (Take Back the Night, the war on pornography) are concerned not with refinement and manners but with real issues of violence and safety. This observation points up the fact that women's involvement in social control has not remained static since the rise of the domestic family.

Targets of social control campaigns have changed, as I shall show, but more importantly the *rationale for intervention* — how women understand and justify their efforts to regulate the behaviour of others — has shifted. Women now ground programs of intervention in an instrumental claim ("Do not do X because it causes harm to others") rather than a moral one ("Do not do X because it is wrong").

The recent anti-pornography campaign is a case in point. Those who would control pornography now generally argue that it should be excluded not for its offensiveness per se but for the "third person harm" it causes (i.e. the dangerous effect it has on behaviour). The slogan "pornography is the theory; rape is the practice" says, in effect, that pornography must be controlled not (only) for the harm it does to our sense of decency, but for the eventual harm

it does to our persons. This claim attempts to persuade society that pornography is *not* a victimless crime, as it might first appear, but rather leads to "third person harm." In hitching theory to practice, the anti-pornography movement hopes to achieve a redefinition of pornography from the "merely" morally disreputable to the dangerous. In so doing, the movement tacitly recognizes that any program which recommends the repression of the merely disreputable or offensive will find little support among liberals in the society.

By choosing to regard contemporary movements such as the war on pornography and Take Back the Night as guided by the concern for personal safety and not public morality, women are saying that they have lost, or wish to abandon, the high moral ground and their "traditional" role as the voice of moral rectitude. The shift away from a morality-based rationale for social control is conventionally described in ungendered political terms as the move from conservative to liberal positions (Canada, 1985). But it has special implications for women and it is these I want to touch on below.

The early modern era, especially the last half of the nineteenth century, was the heyday of the woman as the specifically *moral* guardian of society. Before this time — before the emergence of a genuine ethos of domesticity — the regulation of manners, still a man's role, had not yet taken on a genuinely moral tone. Looking again at the counsels of Erasmus, Caxton, Castiglione and the others, we can see that manners are deemed to be socially and politically necessary for those in or aspiring to elite circles. "Do not put your hand in the bowl for you will offend your betters" — here the tone is one of social rather than moral injunction. The importance of manners to social rather than moral standing in the premodern era is evidenced by the recognition, earlier noted, that there were some groups before whom *courtoisie* was unnecessary. In these manuals the arbiter speaks to a particular segment of society and makes no claim, yet, to voice (or to know) what is for the moral good of all.

The new and striking tone of specifically *moral* injunction whose emergence Elias so carefully traces — "If you are forced to share a bed . . . you should maintain a strict and vigilant modesty" — is a much more recent phenomenon. It and the role of the moral guardian arise in conjunction with the "new sensibility" attendant on the separation of public and private life, and especially the veneration of the latter as the "cult of domesticity." In short, it comes about as the role is feminized.

An important aspect of the veneration of domesticity is the cultural depiction of woman as endowed by nature with a special moral sense. The special moral sense was an important facet of what has been called the "cult of true domestic womanhood" (Anderson, 1980: 47). Such a view of women, though it served to exclude them from most public-sphere involvement, at the same time gave their voices a *distinctive* authority, so that when they moved to regulate manners (conduct, deportment) in the home, and later in the street, they were seen to be voicing the morality of the whole society, rather than merely defending the prudish interests of one of its parts. It is from just this period, when women's participation in campaigns to regulate licentious or "indecent" conduct lent those campaigns a *moral* weight, that we learned to say "manners and morals" in the same breath.

The targets of women's morality campaigns changed considerably from the eighteenth to the early twentieth century, but the tone of moral injunction was not relinquished. The earliest targets seem to have been the public tortures and executions which comprised the entertainments of the ordinary citizen in past centuries —

think of *A Tale of Two Cities* here — as well as ancient popular ceremonies like the cat-burnings with which townspeople celebrated the arrival of important visitors. Later targets were those which transgressed what Elias called the "shame frontier": drunken licentiousness, exhibitionism or "lewdness," homosexuality. Though these targets shifted as the "march of civility" progressed, at any given point a particular act was presented as offending against the sensibilities of all, i.e., as threatening the morality of the whole and not simply the safety of some. Even when women chose to articulate the moral cry through the image of the innocent child, that child was viewed not as a member of a group whose bodily safety and rights had to be protected, but rather as the symbol of the endangered moral health of the whole.

The extremes of prudishness which mark late nineteenth century women's morality campaigns ("purity" campaigns) as they vigilantly policed the shame frontier tends today to obscure the fact that women's specifically moral authority was then at its highest. For it was out of the special moral sense with which the era endowed them *as women* that women's groups were able to engage in social control campaigns with any credibility at all, whether the policing of "indecent" behaviour, or the championing of the oppressed.

One sign of this authority can be found in the fact that early (male) professional groups, notably medical doctors, sought out alliances with women in order to give programs of state intervention (e.g. early social welfare programs) an air of moral sanctity, without which they were deemed likely to fail (Donzelot, 1979). In short, in the era when women were still able to command the high moral ground, professional expertise needed *them* to bolster *its* credibility, a situation conspicuously reversed today.

The decline of a morality-based rationale for social intervention has proceeded apace through the twentieth century. With some exceptions (Gilligan, 1982; O'Brien, 1981) women no longer claim to have, nor are customarily regarded as having, a distinctive moral sense — not a special ear for what is right, nor the special authority to give voice to the morality of the whole. If we pause to consider the implications of this shift, we begin to see that relinquishing (or losing) the moral claim is not without its costs.

First, the issue of *credibility* will be affected. For the most part, a morality based program of intervention rests its credibility on the (supposedly) self-evident credibility of its authors or proponents i.e. on the readiness of the society to accept them as the legitimate voice of the whole. Thus, when nineteenth-century women drew themselves up to their full moral stature and inveighed mightily against the evils of drink, or of war, or poverty, claiming that the mere presence of these excrescences was an offence, we either accepted this claim or rejected it; we did not ask for proof. Then, "respectable" women were thought to speak for morality as priests spoke for God, and to have to offer proof was already to have lost the battle. In short, the credibility of the morality-based claim is *intrinsic.* Its form is: "This act must be forbidden because it is (i.e. we know it to be) evil."

By contrast, the claim which is based on an instrumental concern for personal safety is forced to rely on *extrinsic* authority for its credibility. The recent war on pornography, for example, depends (unlike the morality-based claim) on empirical support for the link between pornography and sexual assault to secure its legitimacy. Only by establishing "third person harm" can pornography be made a justifiable target for regulation. And on the matter of the link between pornography and assault the evidence continues to pour in, but we face

at this time a very mixed bag of findings (Canada, 1985: 99).

Once women relinquish a morality-based claim, then, they are faced with the rhetorical necessity of asserting — if not proving — such a linkage if a campaign of social control is to be credible to a liberal audience (here, an audience which no longer ascribes to them, or to any other group, a special capacity to transcend their particular interests and speak with moral authority for the whole).

In practical terms, this rhetorical necessity means that every campaign must assert the existence of a *victim* to whom harm is done. Thus, for example, it must be claimed that racist novels, violent fairy tales, lesbianism, exhibitionism and sexist language are not just offensive, as was once supposed; on the contrary, "studies have shown" that reading Huck Finn will lead to racist attacks, that Little Red Riding Hood will make children violent, that sexist language results in real inequality in the workplace, or assaults on women, and so forth. Each previously victimless act will be endowed with its victim; this will be the rhetorical strategy for turning morally offensive or indecent acts into dangerous ones that cry out for repressive intervention.

I do not wish to suggest here that women have frivolously abandoned a morality-based rationale, nor that they could easily have done otherwise. The two conditions which render moral crusades credible — 1) the existence in the society of a shared standard, a *moral consensus* against which a given act can be seen to offend and 2) a *cultural consensus* which endows a particular group in the society (here, women) with the "natural" ability to discern and voice that standard — appear to be lacking today.

The first condition is undermined by secularism and pluralism. The second (the cultural readiness to see women as moral guardians) was bound into the nineteenth-century "cult of true womanhood," and seems to have been a trade-off in return for women's exclusion from full public-sphere participation. Clearly, as this view of femininity is rejected, and as women press their claim as a special interest group with a particular set of rights, their credibility as the voice of the whole is jeopardized. Feminism is nothing if it is not this very claim.

Like other groups wishing to be heard, women have responded to these broad socio-cultural changes by changing the rhetorical structure of their social control campaigns (the way they must be framed to be heard as credible). But as those campaigns evolve from morality-based to instrumental, whatever distinctive power might have accrued to women's voices based on their "specificity" or special moral authority must be foregone. As women relinquish that claim, they become just another special interest group clamoring for the public ear by leaning on the authority of science.

III. The Structure of Ambivalence

So far I have examined the traditional role of women as agents of social control and considered the erosion of the allegedly natural moral authority which once grounded their campaigns to "refine" behaviour in the home and on the street. Yet despite the abundant evidence of women's considerable involvement in social life in this capacity, there are many who flinch at its mention, and others who would deny it outright. This reaction is not tied strictly to particular campaigns and targets (e.g. pornography) but to the *idea* of social control more generally. I now want to ask: regardless of the target, why are women ambivalent about participating in social control campaigns at all? Why is the alliance between women and social control *itself* an uneasy one?

We can begin by recognizing that ambivalence, especially if it is widespread, is better regarded as structurally rather than psychologically created. At the individual level, women may feel that the policing of others is offensive, immoral, uncivilized — in a sense, not nice. But from a structural perspective, women's ambivalence toward the social control role can be seen to stem, in part, from a shared belief that such a role is a culturally inappropriate one for women to play.

Our cultural heritage prescribes clear gender norms which govern, among other things, appropriate and inappropriate ways of exercising influence in the community. Women who feel ambivalence, I suggest, are responding to a recognition that they have violated the gender norm which says that women should exercise influence in indirect persuasive ways rather than in direct or coercive ones. This norm is itself a legacy of "sweet domesticity," and though it is weakening, its effects persist in subtle forms, and encourage women to exclude themselves from direct regulatory (i.e. "masculine") intervention in the public sphere.

In addition, the strongly militaristic language in which the exercise of influence is couched — a language I have consciously employed throughout the paper — is calculated to heighten that reluctance. The whole militaristic grammar — of "wars," "campaigns," "banners," "victims," and "policing" — represents the capture (to continue in the same vein) of a potent traditional male metaphor, and for that reason alone is bound to sound provocative to men and offensive to at least some women. Lipman-Blumen has remarked that "at times, domains previously under the exclusive control of one group have become the object of another's poaching" (1984: 38). The domains she is referring to are domains in the labour force. We can extend her insight by recognizing that linguistic domains are important symbolic sites of power struggles: metaphors, like occupations, can be poached, defended, surrendered. This metaphor, so long associated with a male preserve, carries the emotional and political force of a "Keep Out" sign, one which women recognize and document by the displays of reluctance and uncertainty which identify intruders and interlopers.

There is yet a third factor which weakens women's willingness to ally themselves with the social control role. In his book *Labelling Women Deviant* Edwin Schur observes that deviance, as well as conformity, is a gendered phenomenon. Schur states:

Among the various "standard" norm violations — that is, violations of widely agreed-upon norms which in theory apply to men and women — some more than others are treated as being "appropriate offenses" for females. These perceptions tend to reflect stereotypical assumptions regarding women's "nature" (Schur, 1984; 65)

Schur goes on to say that "passive" or "submissive" offenses are thought of as being "appropriately female." In the context of the present discussion Schur's insight means that the role of *victim*, not *victimizer* is the culturally appropriate deviant role for women.

Such gendered norms are likely to affect the kinds of constructions or interpretations women place on their own involvement in social life. With respect to past activities, it can readily be demonstrated that the image of woman as victim is the favoured historical one — the victimizer role being relatively less visible (because less appropriate). From the standpoint of cultural norms, then, this means that if women (women's groups) are going to be deviant, better they be deviant victims (i.e. displaying an excess of powerlessness) than deviant police (displaying an excessive abuse of power). Put briefly, women are culturally more acceptable, to themselves and to others, when they portray themselves as punching bags and doormats than as tyrants (Duffy, 1986).

Together, these considerations help to explain why it is that women find it easier (i.e. more appropriate) to see themselves as allied with society's powerless underdogs than with society's power-brokers, regardless of the real nature of their involvement. They will find it easier, for example to see abortion as "about" the freeing of women rather than the repression of the unborn child, or pornography as "about" the increased rights of the child rather than the lost rights of the pedophile or the artist. What is at issue, therefore, is not the event per se, but the normatively structured *interpretation* of it — and, indeed, the cultural and political acceptability of some interpretations over others.

The point of our brief historical exploration is to point out the fact that women have had their share over the past two centuries in the policing of others. But women remain reluctanct to accept this and continue to cast about for ways to couch the act of regulation so that it will sit more comfortably with traditional gender roles. The time may well have come for women to throw this burdensome interpretive task overboard. Once the discrediting grammar of militarism and coercion is stripped away, social control appears simply as one facet of the exercise of influence in the public sphere and there is no good reason for women to want to limit their voice in that sphere to fighting for the rights of the underdog. Authority always has two faces; it is the nurturing of some interests and the suppressing of others. A full participation in the public sphere will always entail controlling (limiting, curtailing) someone's rights. The real challenge for women is in the end the same as for others: how to preserve the distinction between a *principled* influence in the community and the *gratuitous* exercise of social control. Once women have faced up to the fact that they have been regulating others for some time now, it will become clearer that the real issue is not "Why regulation?" but "Regulation for *what?*"

VIOLENT CRIME IN CANADA, THE U.S., AND EUROPE

Paul Brantingham

When we view current situations in the world perspectives as well as in the historical perspective, the contemporary Canadian violent situation is not so bad. By whatever means we use to measure it, we have come through in the last quarter century with a massive rise in crime not only in Canada but throughout the Atlantic community and possibly in the rest of the world.

The levels of crime we put up with now are significantly greater than the levels of crime we put up with in the 1950s and the 1940s, but they are not substantially higher than the levels of crime that people had put up with in the 1920s or in the 1890s. They are substantially lower particularly in terms of violence than the levels of crime that people have historically put up with. Similarly, the levels of violent crime that we experience in Canadian society are relatively low on the world scale. We have a minor violent crime problem when we look to the world situation.

In 1984 and 1985, officially recognized violent crimes accounted for about nine per cent of the criminal code offenses in Canada. That number has remained stable for relatively long periods in recent times. That proportion puts us relatively close to the

United States where about 10% of their uniform crime report offenses are for serious violent crimes. It also puts us a bit over the English pattern where approximately 6% of their known offenses are for the kinds of violent offenses we report in our criminal statistics.

We criminologists spend a good deal of time pointing out to the world and particularly to undergraduate students and professional audiences that there are problems with criminal statistics. In fact, it turns out that criminal statistics are relatively robust measures of trends, distributions and patterns in the stuff they record and report. It turns out that Interpol data correlate reasonably well with national data. It turns out that all the different criminal justice measures of crime correlate well with one another. It also happens to be the case that, as we probe deeper into our alternative measures using victimization techniques and self-report studies, the correlations, the relationships, the ability of each of those measures to give you a solid prediction of what the other measures will tell you is on a very high order.

There is some reason now to believe that you can use criminal justice statistics to tell what has gone on and what is going on. Using Interpol statistics you can look at the Atlantic community and, using a robust figure like homicide, begin to get a feel for what the distributions are.

In 1982, the most recent year that the Solicitor General's Library had some Interpol statistics available, Northern Ireland led the rest of the Atlantic community with a homicide rate of about 24 per 100,000 population.

Surprisingly enough the United States was not second. It came third after the Netherlands. Canada falls into a broad middle ground of countries along with Italy, Belgium, Portugal and Austria with homicide rates in the vicinity of two to three per 100,000.

"Violent Crime in Canada, the U.S., and Europe" by Paul Brantingham in *Insights into Violence in Contemporary Canadian Society* 1987 edited by James M. Maclatchie. Reprinted with permission of the John Howard Society of Canada.

England has a much lower rate, below two, and Ireland reports the lowest homicide rate among the Atlantic communities. It is even more interesting if you look on a broader perspective which is much harder to do. For a variety of political reasons, various countries do not report their crime rates to Interpol, and the closest we have come to getting some kind of world picture of what crime is like is a survey conducted in the mid-1970s by the United Nations. They sent out carefully constructed de-politicized questionnaires to all member states and received a good response. A few places such as Soviet Union, China, India, and South Africa that we would like to know about declined. Most member states participated, and out of that we get striking comparative figures if our interest is violence.

On a map constructed of world homicide regions, using the United Nations data from the mid-1970s, we see that the communities of both Australia and New Zealand have a relatively low homicide rate on the world scale. The North American and European homicide rates are about one-third the world average rate. The Latin American regional rate is 20 times the world average rate.

Some African states that report to Interpol give us numbers that look absolutely horrifying. In 1976 Nigeria reported a rate of 81 homicides per 100,000 population, and one country reported a homicide rate of 137 per 100,000 population compared to our 2.7. You could now make similar observations with the United Nations data and the Interpol data. That tells us that in other categories of violent crime we look relatively good as well. In the United Nations survey, the North American and European assault rates were less than half the world average. The sex crime rate was about half the world average. The robbery rates were less than a third the world average, and the kidnapping rate was less than a tenth the

world average. Comparisons that go much beyond that begin to break down because of all of the things that criminologists like to tell us about statistics. But at this level they give us a robust measure of what our position is in the world pattern. We have the advantage of dealing with a violent crime problem that is sufficiently contained, and we can think about our options and explore new questions of violence that we have not looked at before and decide whether they need to be dealt with in criminal law.

On a map of the world theft pattern, we find that North America and Europe lead all the rest of the world in theft and fraud. If we have a problem in terms of the quantity rather than the quality of the offenses we deal with, it lies in theft and property crime and fraud, and not in violence measured on the world scale.

I would like to discuss the historical perspective. How are things now compared to the way they were? They are a lot worse now than they were in 1950.

Over the past decade or so crime has become a major issue for historians. Out of the historical research that has been done, much of it in Canada, we can begin to build a general picture of crime in England, Canada and the United States and, to a lesser extent, in some of the European countries over the last 800 years or so. One of the things we can say is that there has been a general decline in the level of violence experienced by European-based societies over the last 700 or 800 years. We have reliable measures that range from the 13th century to the present in England and consistent measures of that time span from other places that tell us the rate of violent crime is down.

We are very confident about measures of homicide because dead bodies turn out to be very difficult to explain, hide or dispose of. English homicide rates have declined steadily from the 13th century to the beginning of the 19th century. What is the magnitude of the drop? It has declined from about 20 per 100,000 population to something on the order of one per 100,000.

I have a rough comparison which tells us something about the pattern of crime and violence in 14th century England just before the Black Death decimated medieval society and 1977 which happened to be a handy year. What you see is a major shift in the relative proportion of the violent crimes. In the mid-14th century, homicide, robbery, arson and rape together accounted for about 30% of all the indictable offenses. If we take a comparable set of criminal offenses in 1977 and manipulate the figures into comparability, we see that that set of offenses accounted for 10% of the violent crimes instead of 30% of the offenses. That kind of shift in the crime mix has occurred probably most markedly in the last 100 years. In Canada it has occurred since 1886.

The shift in the relative proportion of violent crimes is striking. In 1886 violent crimes accounted for 21% of known offenses; now they account for about nine per cent and have done so for about the last 25 years. So we are looking at a crime situation in which we have relatively less of a problem with the traditional violent crimes against a person and more with other things. I can also say that many of the social and demographic characteristics of violent crime appear to be persistent and appear to have lasted in an essentially consistent form over such a long period of time that we can begin to think of them as constant.

One of them is the sex of violent offenders and victims. Violent crime is essentially a male activity, and this is particularly true of homicide. In the 14th century, in the 18th century and today, there are approximately nine male offenders for every female offender, and there are approximately nine known male victims for each female victim. Violent crime is also an enterprise of a somewhat older population as opposed to

the children who commit burglaries. The demographics are slightly higher. It is still characteristic of young adults rather than aging adolescents. The shift is somewhat higher.

There is also a link to violence. There is the link of alcohol to violence that we see today. In the 13th and 14th centuries and in the 17th and 18th centuries, all the accumulated data tells us that violent crime revolves around pubs, whiskey, beer and the social interactions that come out of that in a very large way.

There is one thing demographically that has changed. In the 14th century, clergymen, priests and real world equivalents of Robin Hood's jolly Friar Tuck were the major perpetrators, the biggest single occupational group known to commit violent offenses. In fact, much of the battle between Henry II and Thomas of Beckett was triggered over whether or not Henry could drive criminally-oriented priests and violent priests before the royal courts of justice. That has changed.

Contemporary data suggests that the clergy are now major opponents of the violent occupational group. That is a change for the better. There has also been a demonstrable change in our general social attitude towards crime. We tolerate it less. Violence is less tolerated, more frequently reported and more frequently prosecuted than it was before. We perceive forms of violence that we were blind to in the past now as appropriately criminal.

The growth of concern with wife-beating and child abuse is a good example of that. In the first half of the 18th century, wife-beating was not considered a crime at all. Although technically there was a way that you could perhaps bring it under the category of assault, people were as blind to that question as we are contemporaneously blind to the question of all the assaults that ought to come off a hockey brawl. We become very surprised if a crown prosecutor lays charges against the Flames or Canadiens. People were equally astounded.

Another recent change is the change in rape laws. Rape, historically, was sexual knowledge by force or threat to a woman other than the perpetrator's wife. A wife had no right to resist. The fact that an enormous amount of violence was used on a particular occasion was seen as acceptable under the law. We do not accept that anymore. We modified that law. We have gone to a sexual battery statute. If enforcement is not always the way everyone would like it to be, it takes time for the criminal law to move. But like a glacier, it does move. So we have begun to remove archaic limitations to the criminal law.

On the subject of crime waves in the future, one of the characteristics of the historical research has been to establish that there are two kinds of crime waves. One of them is the kind produced by the media when an editor says, "Things are slow . . . let's find some crime and write it up." And we have a long history of social scientists documenting that happening in locales. The other kind is real. There is a long-term cycle in crime that can be traced for 700 years. It has a roughly measured amplitude, and that varies about 100 years between peaks and valleys.

The English happen to have approximately 150 years of data readily available. Essentially there was a massive peak in crime in England sometime just before 1850. It had been building from sometime in the middle of the 18th century. There was a massive decline in crime which all involved historians and social scientists now believe was quite real. That took place from around 1850 until around 1920, and then there was a rise that began slowly and a massive rise that we have lived through in the last 25 years. That cycle can be projected backwards quite nicely through the data.

It is not very clear what drives it. Demographics fit into it. Changes in the size and rate of growth of population seem to change it and drive it. Major changes in the structure of the economy seem to drive it, and major changes in the structure of the criminal justice system seem to drive it. The 1850 peak corresponds to a massive modification in the structure of criminal justice systems in Europe and North America with the invention of police and the institutionalization of prisons for the first time.

It also corresponds to the beginning of a massive change in the structure of industrial life, and it also corresponds to some demographic changes. The general long-term crime pattern in the second half of the 19th century and beginning of the 20th century in the United State resembles that of the English and of the French as well as everywhere else where the data has been looked at in a serious way. The exception is perhaps with Canada.

With murder in the United States, there was a peak around 1890, one around 1930 and one recently. There may be a reason for thinking that the homicide cycle travels somewhat differently than the long-term major cycle, and there may be about 40 years duration between peaks. Does any of this mean anything other than it is great stuff to examine undergraduates on? Some of the demographic movements include the baby boomers who have moved into their forties, who are slowing down, who are not hanging out in bars at the same rate and who are not getting into fights in the market. There is a much smaller population doing that.

That structural change in society suggests that violence rates, and crime rates in general, should begin to drop and should drop for the next 20 or 30 years. I think it might not happen. There is a countervailing pressure, and it comes from what may be an industrial revolution going on now. We see it in British Columbia at the moment. We have very high unemployment and very real problems in the forest industries. The forest companies have never shipped more lumber.

It is not bad times for the forest companies. In order to compete against the Swedes, the Russians and the American South over the last five years, the forest companies have shaken up their operations and modernized their plants. They can cut more timber with fewer people. There are highly skilled forest workers who are never going to be re-employed in the forest industry no matter how good times get. They become structurally unemployed because they have been replaced by machines and better ways of doing things. The next place it is going to hit is Oshawa. In order to convince us to buy something built in Oshawa rather than something built in Yokohama, the car companies are going to robots and computers. A large number of workers are going to find themselves structurally unemployed. If we cannot re-absorb them, we have a genuine potential to create a situational opportunity to re-establish the kind of conditions that existed in London before the onset of the industrial revolution. This comes about with a large floating populace of unemployed and unemployable people who are not starving, who receive enough from the productivity of our economy to be able to afford food or whiskey, and they can take their choice. They also have more leisure time to get themselves into trouble. For them, disciplined behaviour, according to the requirements of the law, no longer pays off because they are not going to be employed and earn above minimum wage. If that scenario is correct, we may have a real problem coming from a very different kind of base, a problem that has been experienced in North American or European society for perhaps 150 years.

We therefore have a genuine challenge if that scenario is correct.

PORTRAYALS OF VIOLENCE IN THE MASS MEDIA
Anthony Doob

It is worth asking ourselves why we are talking about portrayals of violence in the mass media. Why is that such a concern for us? The concern is that fear, justified or not, rather than reality will form policy. Policy decisions will be driven more by myths than by what is actually happening in the world. Policy decisions should be made according to more information rather than according to the perceptions that many of us have.

Most of us, even criminologists, gain information about crime from the mass media. Approximately 95% of the public mention media as a prime source of information. Television, interestingly enough, is mentioned most often as a source of information about sentencing.

This is a problem when you consider the role of the media and the appropriate concerns. It is nice to say that the media's main concern is educational, but that ignores the fact that to a large extent it is an organization with interests other than educating. It is interested in selling products and maintaining its audience.

This leads inevitably to a pitfall, simplicity. If the public is informed about something in a 37-second news story, it has to look to simple solutions for complex problems.

When the efficiency of the media is questioned, that question has two different answers depending on whether we are involved in the media or trying to concern ourselves with an informed public. If we are interested in the media, criteria for a suc-

"Portrayals of Violence in the Mass Media" by Anthony Doob in *Insights into Violence in Contemporary Canadian Society* 1987 edited by James M. Maclatchie. Reprinted with permission of the John Howard Society of Canada.

cessful broadcast may well be in terms of something being interesting, understandable and simple.

There is no simple solution to a problem. There are quite different and important ways of evaluating a question. In some of my research I have shown for example that newspaper accounts of sentence hearings influence the public. The public conclusions could be quite different from the conclusions they would otherwise make. We compared people who had actually seen court documents or transcripts of court hearings to those who had read newspaper accounts and found that the response was quite different.

This is not necessarily a concern of the public. One reporter's response to this was that the reader would be discouraged by technicalities and an editor would cut them out anyway. He is probably correct.

We have to understand these constraints when we are trying to understand why the public believes what it does. The interesting thing is that the public, although it may hold initially a very simple view of issues, can quickly understand and appreciate the complexities of the issues. When the public is asked about the causes and solutions of violent crime, it often does not look initially to the criminal justice system. The public understands that crime is an integral part of society. Looking at violence is really looking at people rather than simply at the criminal justice system. We would like the public to put crime and violence into some kind of perspective.

When we look at what is informing the public, we understand why the public concerns sometimes do not make sense to us. If we look at newspaper accounts of crime, we find that half are violent. Half of that involves some form of homicide. There is very little about victims' independent relationships or corporate actions which threaten lives or well-being. It is not surprising to find that the public equates vio-

lence with crime. Only about 9% of reported crime in Canada involves violence. The public seriously overestimates the amount of violent crime. The public believes not only that violence is increasing, but also that violence is involved substantially in those millions of crimes reported each day.

People tend to view sentences as too lenient. When they think about what they mean by too lenient, they think about things involving violence. Yet the public says to the politicians, "You are being too lenient on criminals."

They are thinking about only 9% of those cases. The source of this in the media is clear to anyone who has looked systematically at reporting of individual crimes in the newspaper, radio or television. The kinds of things that one sees leads to the belief that if one wants to be informed about crime, the best thing to do is to stop reading about it.

What is important to remember is that it is not a matter of simply taking a larger sample. The more you read about crime, the more you are going to be informed about it. Because what I am talking about is a population of stories. If we sample them in larger degrees, we are going to become systematically less informed about the underlying social problem or social issue.

The problem is more serious than just the over-reporting of violence. There is some evidence to suggest that the media tends to pick the more serious instances of specific offences. The typical robbery reported in a newspaper, on television or on radio is going to be much more interesting and much more dramatic than an average robbery reported even to the police.

The same thing occurs if one looks at the reporting of manslaughter. What we find is that the most dramatic, disturbing events are reported. It is interesting to note that a substantial number of reports of manslaughter seem to talk about the crime as if it were not manslaughter, but murder.

There also exists a tendency of the media to pick themes and develop them. Examples of this include the muggings in Britain in the 1970s and at the same time in New York with crimes against the elderly. Since the Young Offenders Act was passed a couple of years ago, there has been a disproportionate amount of reporting of youth crime. What this suggests is that these issues can become public issues without any necessary reality behind them. They lead to false information and false allocation of time and resources.

The difficulty occurs when we pick up information and urge those who form policy to use it in informing. Violence is easy to report. It is easy to make stories about it. It is easy to entertain people with it.

There is a constant parade of horrible incidents which can be picked out in a society as large as Canada. We have to be careful how we respond. The issue of missing children has the potential of being one where we can be driven in the wrong direction. The concern most people have with missing children is abduction by a stranger and is the least common cause of missing children.

Does the media necessarily pick up this image or this information? Sometimes it does. The problem of missing children is a much more interesting issue if we are talking about abductions by strangers. It is a much more interesting topic than runaways or abductions by parents where there is an issue of custody. If we look systematically at the news coverage of missing children's day in May, we find a mix. Only some stories put the nature of missing children into context.

One radio broadcast discussed the release of 3,500 balloons with pictures of missing children without any mention of what we know about them. A newspaper story contained a long feature about a child taken away from his mother. Only towards the end of the story did it become clear that the father had abducted the child. That does not necessarily improve matters, but it changes the tone of the story and makes the kinds of solutions that you look for quite different.

The problem of understanding violence becomes serious as soon as we get into looking at solutions. The problem is that we have, as has mass media, linked violence to other kinds of phenomena. We have linked violence in many ways to mental illness. We have linked violence to other issues related to the criminal justice system such as parole, mandatory supervision and release on bail. We have linked violence to recidivists. All of these are missing the point. The problem with recidivism is that most people, or roughly half the people before the courts, are there for the first time. In dealing with recidivists we are therefore talking about at least half the people before the courts. We also have to remember that most people who do come before the courts for the first time never reappear.

Eighty per cent of first-time offenders will never come back into the criminal justice system. We have to keep this in context when forming policy. The difficulty is that the usual kinds of statistics or realities are not persuasive enough against the single salient incident. Those kinds of things stick in our minds. Unfortunately, those are the kinds of things which we listen to when we are trying to figure out solutions. So how do we approach the problem of violence? It has been suggested that the criminal justice system be used as a last resort in dealing with certain kinds of crimes. The criminal justice system is not the last resort of solutions. I suggest that the criminal justice system has almost nothing to do with solutions to the problem of violence. Looking at comparisons across countries, we find that the situations have not changed for some time. There have been historical changes, but to some extent those historical changes seem to be parallel ones. The criminal justice system is really a punishment system. It selects who needs to be punished and by how much.

That has relatively little to do with the problem of dealing with violence. It does not mean that we should ignore it. I do not see the criminal justice system as a last resort. It deals with a problem different from violence. It deals with the punishment of people who have perpetrated violence. If we evaluate solutions by criminal justice penalties, I think we miss the point. I would be concerned, for example, if we evaluated our system of dealing with pollution, occupational health and safety or fraud and theft according to the penalties that are given out. What we want to evaluate is whether or not change is necessary. That is much more important than the question as to whether somebody was penalized or brought before the criminal justice system. Dealing with the problem is more important than merely punishing.

We do not look to the criminal justice system for solutions, and I suggest three pitfalls to avoid. First, we should not think of crime as violence. Violence is an unusual part of crime and is quite varied. Second, we should not look to the criminal justice system for solutions to violence. We must look beyond to the process which leads to distasteful events. Third, we should not think of solutions to violence per se. We should look for solutions to specific problems and not categorize.

On a flow-chart, drinking and driving merge to create an impaired driver. Impaired drivers are more likely to make errors. With errors come accidents. With accidents come injuries and deaths.

There are therefore six different categories where we can intervene. We can intervene at the drinking level, but we can also intervene in driving by trying to provide alternatives to cutting down on the frequency. We can only intervene with the impaired driver within limits of the criminal justice system. We can intervene in trying to reduce the number of errors people make. For example, a relatively simple way of reducing wandering drivers is to put a white line down the edge of the road. People apparently find it easier to drive between two lines.

There are a variety of things that we can do in designing both cars and roads. Going beyond mere accidents, we know a variety of ways to avoid deaths such as with the use of seat belts or air bags. If we concentrate on the criminal justice system, we are concentrating only on one part of that whole process. We are concentrating on the driver after he has become impaired.

Looking at violence today we must deal with the structure of the specific kind of problem, not with violence per se. We cannot rely solely on the criminal justice system because it has a very limited role in controlling people's behavior. We must look at the troublesome problem itself. If we do that, we may be able to at least move in a useful direction.

3

PERSPECTIVES on CANADA

In the first half of the book we have tried to develop and illustrate some of the basic concepts and concerns of sociology. In this half we are attempting to use these concepts to understand a total society, Canadian society. For many of the classic sociologists, this has been the *raison d'etre* of their enterprise: to determine the nature and fate of their own society. But this has never been an easy task, especially given the complexity of Western industrial societies.

Indeed, so immense has this task seemed that many sociologists, particularly American ones, have been content simply to study aspects of their society, particular institutions — an approach of the middle range. This has had some unfortunate consequences for the development of Canadian sociology. Rather than attempting to develop a *holistic* approach, we have, by and large, inherited the more piecemeal strategy typical of American sociology. And too often we have seemed prepared to assume that the conclusions of American sociologists about, say the American family, could easily be applied to the Canadian case.

In these chapters, then, we are concerned with capturing what may be unique about Canada and what it shares with other Western industrial and capitalist societies. We shall also present a number of attempts by Canadians to develop a perspective that takes into account Canada's unique history, ideology, social structure and place in world capitalism.

POPULATION AND DEMOGRAPHY

Perhaps the most straightforward way to analyze any society is in terms of its demography — the systematic analysis of population phenomena. Though their measures are often complicated and sophisticated, demographers are essentially concerned with collecting very basic information about a population: births, deaths, movements of people, the distribution of the population and social characteristics of individuals and families.

Demographic data provide a good starting point for a study of society for several reasons. First, most of the information is collected by governments on a regular basis and comes closer than any other research to a complete and relatively accurate coverage of the population. Second, demographic data are about vital processes, literally life and death matters. Finally, these vital processes, what is happening to our population, set many of the parameters to social action and social change.

There is also something rather comforting and reassuring about the kind of work demographers do. At first glance it may seem to you objective and factual, happily removed and different from the uncertainties and confusion of the theoretical and ideological debates that seem to characterize so much of sociology. Don't feel too comfortable. Data about population distribution and change, about birth rates, death rates, migration, immigration and emigration, all have as their base just such complex theoretical and ideological concerns and certainly dramatic social and political consequences.

These statistics originate not only from the decisions people make (to marry, to have children, and so on) but also from the decisions made "for" them (in the form of immigration policies, health and welfare policies, and perhaps even deliberate underdevelopment of hinterlands). Moreover, these kinds of data are open to different interpretations as to their implications, depending on one's ideological position. Should we be alarmed by the projected growth of the Canadian population, by the decline in birth rate in Quebec, or by the increasing concentration of people in a few Canadian cities? Or should we feel optimistic?

Finally, these data reveal some of the real environmental constraints and obstacles that Canadians must confront and somehow resolve. For example, as Lorna Marsden (1975) put it, "Canada is not a huge uninhabited country, it is a small habitable country (about seven percent of the area surrounded by uninhabitable land, which provides many of its raw resources)." This means, for example, that there is competition for the most valued living space and rather unique forms of community for those who must live and work in the remaining ninety-three percent of the country.

In short, demography is important because its techniques offer us the possibility of drawing the outlines of Canadian society and the problems it confronts, and making projections of the problems it will confront. But as the above should suggest to you, things are never quite that simple. Which problems we define as important, how we define them and how we look for solutions are as much the product of ideology as of science. As we have described in our discussion of political culture in Part 2, in Canada, as in other societies, there is not one but several ways of thinking about our society, about what constitutes a problem and what constitutes a solution. Therefore, an even more important step in theorizing about our society requires that we analyze its political culture, the ideologies that comprise the common stock of knowledge Canadians, including its sociologists, use to understand themselves and their society.

CANADIAN SOCIOLOGY

How have Canadian social scientists tried to understand their society? As we pointed out at the beginning of this chapter, one approach has simply been to avoid the issue by concentrating on a single institution, such as the educational system or the family, or a specific social process, such as social mobility or ethnic relations. For the most part, the problem of placing such research in the wider context of Canadian society was ignored or avoided.

Inevitably, thinking about Canadian society and its problems was strongly influenced by American liberalism, particularly structural functionalism. But there have always been some sociologists who have felt uncomfortable that the kinds of questions this ideology and perspective lead us to ask miss most of what is unique and important about Canadian society. For instance, S. D. Clark, one of Canada's best known sociologists, argued that American sociology — structural functionalism — is inappropriate in the Canadian context. Clark has long held that to understand Canada one must understand its history and its particular geographical constraints, its harsh climate and terrain and the fact that it shares a border with the most powerful country in the capitalist world.

While in his work he concentrated on social rather than economic problems, Clark was heavily influenced by Harold Innis, an economic historian. Innis developed what he called a *staples approach*; that is, he shows how the Canadian economy was retarded or hampered in its development because its base was not manufacturing but the export of raw materials to a series of "mother" countries: France, Britain and now the United States.

More recent theorists have drawn upon Innis's and Clark's insights. But because these recent theorists have also been strongly influenced by Marx's insights, what we have called a *conflict perspective*, they have simultaneously tried to move beyond the world view liberalism provides us to develop a critical Canadian sociology. One such approach, usually called *dependency theory*, is grounded in our particular historical development as first a colony and then a nation in the shadow of a powerful empire.

One aspect of dependency theory is captured by the distinction between *metropolis* and *hinterland*. Hinterland refers to relatively undeveloped or colonial areas that provide raw materials, semiprocessed goods and people to the more developed centre of political and economic control. In Canada, this has meant that the rest of the country is a hinterland to Ontario, particularly Toronto. In larger terms, Canada can be seen as a hinterland to the United States. This position falls squarely within the conflict perspective because of the emphasis on the exploitation of the hinterland by the metropolis and the recognition of the perpetual potential for conflict.

In the 1970s Marxist social scientists extended the conflict perspective and examined its implication for Canadian economic and, in turn, cultural development. They argued that we can only understand Canada's underdevelopment and cultural malaise as we examine Canada's relationship to imperialist powers, particularly Britain and the United States. As Robert Laxer (1973: 6) put it, "Canada is a dependency moving towards colonial status in the American empire."

The issues these theorists raise are crucial. More recently, however, some sociologists have been critical of dependency theory. They have argued that as it developed in the 1970s, Canadian sociology was perhaps too parochial and nationalistic, and gave too much emphasis to the economic determinants shaping Canadian society. More careful historical analyses and research of a more comparative nature has led to the conclusion that looking at Canada solely in terms of its dependency may lead us to ignore its full place in world capitalism, as well as the fact that it is a capitalist society that has many features in common with other such societies. For these sociologists, then, the image of Canada as a passive victim of American or British exploitation, though comforting, is simplistic and misleading: Canadians are part of a world system of capitalism and Canadian capitalists operate very much as their counterparts in other Western industrial societies.

While the debate about dependency theory continues, the most fundamental challenge to Canadian sociology, indeed sociology generally, has undoubtedly come from the development of feminist theory and feminist research. Feminist perspectives have made clear the extent to which sociology has presented a distorted picture of the social world because it was written mainly by men and about men. Countering the sexist bias of what has sometimes been called "malestream" sociology has meant more than simply doing more research on women or "bringing them back in" to sociological research, though both of these aspects are important. Nor is feminism simply about documenting and seeking explanations of gender inequality in the workplace and in the home, though, again, these have been important contributions. Rather, the more fundamental contribution has been to show how our institutions and laws are shaped by patriarchy and have, among other things, had the consequence of oppressing women. Thus feminism has forced us to rethink and reconceptualize such acts as rape, incest, sexual harrasment and wife battering and to consider the implications of pornography. And, in the process of developing a feminist perspective and doing research within that perspective, the traditional ways of doing sociological research have been challenged. Feminist theory and research has brought about a radical transformation of sociology and of what are considered to be social problems and social issues.

ECONOMIC PERSPECTIVES

Should someone ask you what Canada is like, you are most likely to focus on its physical and demographic characteristics, or perhaps some aspects of its culture, the ideas Canadians hold, their arts and artifacts and, perhaps too, its political system as you understand it — its parties, the democratic parliamentary process. Far less likely are you to consider Canada's historical development and its material or economic base. In simple terms, if someone asked you to describe Canada, you would be very unlikely to use the words monopoly, capitalism, exploitation. But these are crucial words, and in recent years sociologists have become increasingly concerned with understanding how our particular brand of capitalism in Canada has evolved and how it shapes our culture and our lives. We say that these are important words; but they are not mere words. Rather, they are ways of viewing Canada that, when you come to understand them, may often be unsettling: that Canada is a capitalist society of a particular sort and this has consequences for what we do and how we think; that some people own or control and others do not, and this shapes the nature of our relationships, the quality of our lives and, most graphically, the nature and quality of our work.

This way of viewing Canadian society is in marked contrast to the approach of structural functionalists who were concerned mainly with industrial as opposed to capitalist society. For such theorists, capitalism, the particular mode of production, was simply seen as one way systems have adapted to the process of industrialization or, more generally, modernization. However, with the renewed interest in Karl Marx, capitalism has become the focus for most theorists. Increasingly, these theorists have been concerned with how the historical development of capitalism has shaped these processes of industrialization and how, in turn, it has shaped capitalism.

For Marx, industrialization was an impressive creation of a new class of people who emerged out of feudalism and who, in pursuing their own interests, fashioned a new social order based in a new mode of production and technology. Marx's sociology of capitalism, among other things, revealed to us that modernization was not a unitary phenomenon but rather was experienced differently by different groups in society and had different consequences for them. For Marx, industrialization, as the central aspect of modernization, was the child of capitalism. The fundamental changes it brought were new layers of inequality and a relatively new phenomenon: layers of vulnerability, as the constraining, but also relatively secure, ties of feudalism gave way to the more precarious relations of the urban-based marketplace. In providing us with a sociology of capitalism, Marx also provides us with a way of understanding modernization not as a mystical force independent of human actions but as a human product. For example, while technological change may often seem inexorable and beyond our control, Marx's insights allow us to see that certain groups do in fact control technology and direct it in ways they believe will benefit, be more profitable, to them. He also provides us with an image of a future when we, through ending structured inequality and vulnerability, would gain control of technology to reshape it to suit our human needs and, in the process, reshape our natures.

As some of the readings in this half of the book will show, Marx's insights into capitalism lead to what are often complex political and economic analyses of the world in which we live. However, for now, let us just describe capitalism as a system based on profits which necessitates capital accumulation. It is a system which requires that capitalists — who Marx referred to as the *bourgeoisie* — amass great wealth through the ownership of the means of production, while workers — who Marx referred to as the *proletariat* — have only their labour to sell.

The feature of capitalism which most intrigued Marx was that it seemed to be a system in which capitalists were able to get more out than they put in; they must, in other words, make a profit. Where does this profit come from? Marx concluded that in selling their labour to the capitalist, workers are exploited because they receive a wage that is less than the full value of their work. Simply, workers using the technologies of mass production are able to produce more in a day than they need to live. The capitalists, in expropriating this *surplus value*, are able not only to finance the costs of running the business but are able to accumulate wealth for their own needs and to expand their businesses.

The history of capitalism is in many ways, then, the history of the transformation and progressive alienation of work. In the first stages of industrial capitalism the most obvious change in how and where people work was the shift from agriculture to urban-based occupations and the gradual replacement of cottage or craft industries by factories. A second transformation of work is what Harry Braverman (1974) calls the "degradation of labour." Capitalists, in their need to increase profits and to maintain control of the workplace, attempted wherever possible to de-skill their labour force, to break the skilled labour of craftsmen down to a series of discrete tasks that could be carried out by low-paid unskilled workers and increasingly by machines. Not only was this more profitable, it also reduced the power and autonomy of skilled artisans.

A third transformation of the work world has been the growth of what is usually called the *service sector*. As capitalists tried to free themselves from wage labour demands through increased mechanization and de-skilling, certain types of work became obsolete. But gradually, as the traditional capitalism of the nineteenth century was replaced by the monopoly capitalism of the twentieth century, the search for profits led to the creation of a host of new occupations. Whereas the traditional capitalist could both own and manage the enterprise, occupations concerned with the managerial, technical, marketing, financial and research needs of the modern, multinational corporation have sprung into being.

Further, as the state is required to play an ever-expanding role in maintaining, developing and legitimating the capitalist system and in responding to the demands of the welfare state, there has been a dramatic expansion of the labour force in the public sector. In short, accompanying the development of monopoly capitalism has been a fundamental shift in the nature of work. Canada, like other capitalist societies, has been part of the rapid shift from primary industry to secondary industry to tertiary industry; from a producer of raw materials to manufacturing to a postindustrial society, a service economy. Manufacturing, though still a crucial component of capitalist economies, has been overwhelmed by the more elusive and invisible industry of symbol manipulation, the use in both private and public sectors of specialized skills, knowledge and professionalism.

Living as he was during the period of "high capitalism," the most obviously brutal period of industrialism and capitalism, Marx could hardly forsee all of these transformations of work. What he did perceive, however, was that work was becoming progressively dehumanized under capitalism; what he viewed as a central life activity was being transformed into *alienated labour.*

Alienation of labour means several things. At the simplest level it means that the work most people are compelled to do is boring, monotonous, routine and unsatisfying. At another level, we understand that when production is broken down to its component parts and each worker is performing only his or her small component activity people are alienated from the products of their labour. Not only do such workers not see the final product, they may not even know what it is they are producing. They are no longer able to say, "I made this thing, and its virtues and its weaknesses are my responsibility." Nor, as Marx recognized, do workers enjoy the full fruits of their labour, since what they produce in a given day comes back to them as a wage that is not the full result of their hours in the factory or the mine. At the most profound level, alienation meant for Marx that what should be an expression of self and a source of fulfillment comes to involve a loss of respect for self and a source of discontentment. Yet, in the final analysis, part of what Marx tried to capture by alienation is hidden or buried under the very language of capitalism, a language that allows us to view others as means. In viewing others as means, we come together in social ties of exploitation rather than cooperation. Finally, people themselves are "split up," a means, parts of a larger machine. People no longer use tools but become tools and, therefore, lose all freedom.

Contained within Marx's theory of alienation is, then, a powerful indictment of the capitalist system. However, to think about alienation is to imply that alienation can be overcome, that things could be different. As we have stressed, Marx has provided us with theory and concepts that in our view most adequately allow us to analyze our society — capitalist society — in its entirety. But, throughout his work and especially in his theory of alienation are constant reminders that sociology is and should be a humanistic discipline. Marx's philosophy, his concept of humankind, is a strong counter to the conservative argument that there is something in human nature that makes acquisitiveness and exploitation of others inevitable features of all societies. In contrast, there is in his work optimism that through our own efforts and intellect we can both imagine and, perhaps, fashion a new social order.

chapter

8

Demographic Perspectives

The selections in this chapter are intended to provide you with some basic information about Canada's demographic structure and the future of Canada's population. This information should provide you with a context in which to place many of the readings in the rest of the book. While demographers are, of course, concerned with quantification, accurate measurement and development of models from which to develop future projections, the best of them go beyond mere compiling of statistics to consider the economic, social and political consequences of demographic changes and the implications of these changes for us in our everyday lives.

The benefits of combining sociology and demography are vividly illustrated in the first selection, by Roderic Beaujot. He deftly summarizes the major changes in marriage patterns, fertility and divorce since the mid-1960s and offers a sociological explanation as to why these changes began to occur at that particular time, and why they are not limited to any one industrial society. And, in seeking to answer the question of the title of his brief article, he forces us to ask: "A crisis for whom?"

In the second selection, an excerpt from her book, *Canada's Aging Population*, Susan McDaniel, who is, like Beaujot, both a sociologist and a demographer, introduces you to the usefulness of population pyramids as a graphic method of illustrating the likely demographic consequences for Canada's age-sex structure of declining fertility, a relatively high life expectancy and more or less constant levels of immigration and emigration to and from Canada. And, second, she briefly contemplates the social and policy challenges generated by an aging population. While the concept of demographic aging may seem remote and academic to you at this point in your life, it can be made more personally relevant if you consider how different Canada's population will be as you reach your 30s and 40s and, eventually, as you reach your proverbial three scores and ten.

At the time of writing, the major internal challenge to Canadian society is the obvious desire of Quebec society to forge a new and different relationship with English Canada. The quest for Quebec sovereignty is partly cultural, partly political and partly economic. But, as Gary Caldwell and Daniel Fournier show in the third selection of this chapter, underlying all of these forces is the demographic structure and future of Quebec. As they point out, Quebec society has shared the same demographic trends outlined by Susan McDaniel for Canada as a whole but most of these changes have been more dramatic than in any other Western industrial society. In short, without understanding the demographic fragility of Quebec, it is impossible to understand the perceived need for language legislation within the province as well as broader political developments that currently threaten to split the nation into two sovereign states.

RELATED READINGS

Bali Ram and A. Romaniuc: "New Trends in the Family" (Chapter 6)

THE FAMILY IN CRISIS?
Roderic Beaujot

Family trends have changed rather extensively in the past twenty years: greater propensities to cohabit, lower marriage rates, older ages at first marriage, higher divorce rates, and lower levels of childbearing. These changes are highly interrelated and they have brought us to a "demographic turning-point" involving markedly lower population growth and significant population aging.

These are among the observations made at a November 1986 meeting of the Federation of Canadian Demographers, co-sponsored by the Royal Society of Canada. This conference brought together some 150 people on the theme "The family in crisis: a population crisis?" The meeting was centred around recently released data from two surveys taken in 1984: the Canadian Fertility Study and the Family History Survey.

Participants at the meeting disagreed on the nature of the "crisis in the family" and even as to whether there really was a crisis. They did agree that there was a crisis in the sense of a "sudden and profound change." Since the mid-1960s a series of demographic indicators have changed, in the entire set of countries of European civilization, both in the market economies of the West and in the state economics of Eastern Europe. Like the earlier demographic transition that brought markedly lower levels of mortality and fertility to this same cultural region, these more recent demographic changes are deeply rooted in the institutional and cultural make-up of these societies, and they have profound effects on us all.

"The Family in Crisis?" by Roderic Beaujot. Appearing in *The Canadian Journal of Sociology* 13(3) 1988. By permission of *The Canadian Journal of Sociology*.

Before treating the causes and consequences, let us briefly document these recent family-based demographic changes (see also Table 1). The best known change relates to divorce. Of the marital dissolutions that occurred in 1965, only 11 percent were due to divorce; the remaining 89 percent involved the death of a spouse. Just twenty years later, in 1985, a full 42 percent of dissolutions were due to divorce and 58 percent involved the death of a spouse.

It is, in fact, difficult to accurately estimate the level of divorce. According to the Family History Survey, the highest rates of divorce thus far have occurred in the cohort of persons who were 40–49 in 1984. Of the persons who ever married, some 15 percent had ever divorced and an additional 4 percent had ever separated by 1984. On the other hand, Owen Adams and Dhruva Nagnur of Statistics Canada reported that if we project the 1983–84 rates of divorce by age group over the entire marital life cycle, it would suggest that 28 percent of marriages will end in divorce.

This is the difference between a "cohort approach" and a "period approach" to the measurement of demographic rates. The cohort approach has the advantage of better representing the underlying reality, but the measurement is incomplete until the cohort has all died out. The period approach has the advantage of appearing more current, but it may misrepresent the underlying reality. For instance, if people become less likely to divorce in the future, the projections of the period approach would be misleading. However, in general, the changes have been so profound as to be visible regardless of the measurement used.

The changes in nuptiality have been equally extensive. Over the first six or seven decades of this century, marriages were occurring earlier and higher proportions were getting married. Suddenly, around the mid-1960s the trends reversed. In 1965 the median age at first marriage was 21.2 for brides and 23.7 for grooms, but by 1985 it has risen by 2.5 years for brides and

Table 1
INDICATORS OF FAMILY-RELATED DEMOGRAPHIC CHANGES,
CANADA, 1965 and 1985

	1965	1985
DIVORCE		
Percent of marital dissolutions due to		
— divorce	11	42
— death of a spouse	89	58
NUPTIALITY		
Median age at first marriage		
— women	21.2	23.7
— men	23.7	25.6
Proportion of adults expected to marry	95	86
Percent of 18–29 who have ever been in common-law unions		23*
FERTILITY		
Total fertility rate (average births per woman)	3.1	1.7
Median age of women at first birth	22.9	25.4

* 1984

1.9 years for grooms. The combined 1965 age-specific marriage rates would imply that 95 percent of adults could be expected to marry at some point in their lives. By 1984 this figure was down to 86 percent. Thus, not only was there a greater likelihood of leaving marriage, there was also a lower likelihood of entering it. The propensity of re-marriage has also declined for the divorced and widowed so that by now a higher proportion are living in a post-marital single state.

Cohabitation, of course, was not even measured in 1965. In 1984, some 8.7 percent of persons aged 18–29 were in common-law unions and a total of 23 percent had ever been in such unions.

Rates of childbearing are also radically different. In 1965 the age-specific fertility rates implied an average of 3.1 children per woman. Stated differently, the generation of children was 48 percent larger than the generation of their parents. In 1972 the rates moved below the figure of 2.1 needed for population replacement, and by 1985 it was 1.7 births per woman, representing a decline of 45 percent in twenty years.

This does not imply that the population is no longer growing. Births continue to outnumber deaths because the large cohorts born in the period 1945 to 1965 are now at childbearing ages. Even though they are having small families, the fact that they are so numerous, along with net migration, ensures continuous population growth for the time being.

The difficulty of interpreting below-replacement fertility is that it takes a whole generation before its implications are felt in terms of population decline. Also, this again is a period measure. It could be that the rate is low because the births that people will eventually have are currently being postponed. However, there is a limit to the possibilities of postponement.

If we take seriously the figure of 1.7, and it cannot be too far off the mark, it means that the generation of children will be 20 percent smaller than that of their parents. Unless immigration is particularly high, this obviously implies an eventual decrease in population. It also implies a significant aging of the population.

As Karol Krótki of the University of Alberta observed, compared to what we are used to as a people, "continuing below replacement fertility is a world-shattering experience." We have always experienced population growth in our past, in fact relatively rapid growth in the range of 1–3 percent per year. Population decline is an unkown for us. Besides, there is a negative "population momentum" to negative natural increase. That is, low fertility produces an older population and an older population has fewer children even if fertility rates increase.

Thus we have seen a number of changes in key demographic indicators over the past twenty years. What is interesting is that these changes have occurred over all the countries of European civilization. In the course of human events, these changes are also rather sudden. The changes overtook a number of generations at one time. It is not only young people, but also older ones who suddenly became less likely to marry and more likely to divorce and to live in common-law unions. It is not only younger couples who were having fewer children, but the family size intentions of somewhat older couples were also being revised downward.

No one would have predicted these changes two decades ago. It was suggested at the conference that a demographer who had died in 1965, but been allowed a special dispensation to visit this conference, would have been so shocked as to suffer another heart attack on the spot.

Why would so many behaviours change so suddenly and so radically across such a range of countries? The most complete statement on this question came from Louis

Roussel of France's *Institut National d'Etudes Demographiques.* He noted that these changes were certainly not produced by an economic crisis or a war that can sometimes produce profound social changes. We obviously must look elsewhere for an interpretation. Roussel first suggested three factors that were probably important. Fertility became rather completely under control, and by women in particular. As Anatole Romaniuc of Statistics Canada said, "coitus-independent birth control is more than a method of contraception, it can erode traditional family values." A second factor involves the greater participation of women in the paid labour force, which, among other things, changes the relations between women and men, and makes divorce a more feasible alternative for women. Finally, legislative changes made divorces easier, signifying also a greater acceptability of alternative sexual and marital arrangements.

While these three factors are no doubt relevant, the explanation remains incomplete. For instance, why would these changes have all started to occur together, around the specific period of the mid-1960s? Roussel suggested that the more fundamental issue involved a cultural change wherein people become less interested in living up to external norms and more interested in living up to what they themselves wanted. We can call it de-institutionalization in the sense that there are fewer constraints on family-type behaviour. Others have referred to increasing individualism or to the "me generation." In any case, there has been a fundamental change in the very "logic of family life" brought about since the mid-1960s.

In other words, people are committed to their relationships only to the extent that these remain gratifying. But having children involves a long-term commitment, at least to the parent-child relationship, which stays with you forever. Thus people may be having fewer children in order to avoid commitment to relationships that may not last a lifetime.

Others would disagree with this interpretation. Kevin McQuillan of the University of Western Ontario argued that the fundamental factors involve economic structures, especially the greater importance of the service sector. This has radically changed the economic opportunity structure of women in particular. Certainly, the radically increasing levels of living brought about in the post-war era have made alternatives like pre-marital cohabitation and divorce much more feasible.

One could argue that until the mid-1960s the division of labour encouraged a reciprocal state of dependency between the sexes. Economic and policy structures discouraged women from participation in the labour force, and thus the family was based on a "breadwinner" model where wives were dependent on their husbands' incomes and husbands were dependent on wives for the care of home and children. The possibility for some women to become self-sufficient broke this state of dependency. The greater involvement in work outside the home has obviously cut heavily into the time available for childrearing, a very labour-intensive activity.

Thus there are disagreements with regard to interpreting the causes of the change. One might include both perspectives and argue that the roots of the change involved both economic structures (changing the relations between women and men) and cultural norms (permitting more freedom of choice in family-related matters).

What about the consequences of these radical changes on the family? Are they sufficiently serious as to justify the term "crisis" in its negative sense? While some may regret the erosion of "traditional family values," others can see these changes as liberating. Why should we decry an evolution that allows for more freedom of choice? As Alan Simmons of York University said, "living common law is not a problem, except possibly for old-fashioned parents, divorce is often a solution to a poor marriage, and lower fertility is liberating for women in particular."

Susan McDaniel of the University of Waterloo noted that in times past a family crisis especially involved the premature death of a spouse. She suggested that the more serious family crises today still involve factors like unemployment and economic incapacity on the part of family members. She also argued that these other changes in the family may be a crisis from the point of view of persons who want to defend the traditional family, but feminists would not see higher divorce, lower marriage, and lower childbearing as a crisis.

Some argued that children themselves may be suffering from the new patterns of family behaviour. Nicole Marcil-Gratton of the University of Montreal noted that smaller family sizes have important consequences on the typical experiences of children. In the average case, children would have parents who are younger and less experienced at childbearing. Children are also less likely to have a brother or sister who is five or more years older and who might give them guidance in life.

Obviously, more divorce means more female lone-parent families who are worse off economically. From the point of view of children, the term step-parent, like the associated terminology of broken marriage remains linked with negative connotations. Using data from Quebec, Louis Duchesne of the Quebec Bureau of Statistics noted a doubling in the proportion of children living with only one parent, from 6 percent in 1966 to 13 percent in 1981. Almost all of the changes follow an increase in the proportion of children living with their mothers only. The proportion living with only their fathers is 2 percent. While we speak of an increasing involvement of fathers in child-rearing, on this crucial dimension they have become less involved. If men are becoming less responsible fathers, it is hard for women to become less responsible mothers.

While these changes are significant, they probably cannot be called a crisis. If there is a crisis, I would suggest, it may be between the interests of women on the one hand and the interest in sustaining the reproduction of the society on the other hand. Anatole Romaniuc noted that fewer people are "enjoying the optimum conditions for procreation," that is, stable and lasting marriages. However, the term optimum in this context is not value free; it is premised on a traditional view of desirable family forms. Standards of optimality are being challenged by feminists and others who argue that the traditional family is not necessarily an ideal environment for all concerned.

Leaving aside complex psychological issues, the gender-based unequal costs of the traditional family can be assessed in more economic terms. Patricia Robinson of the University of Western Ontario presented data showing that marriage is costly to women. For instance, married women are more likely to suffer job interruptions. That does not apply to men since they are less likely to have job interruptions if they are married. As Robinson noted, the differentials are accentuated by the fact that on average marriage involves a wife who is two years younger than the husband. In terms of optimizing family income, if one spouse has to withdraw from the labour force it makes sense to sacrifice the lower salary. In part, wives have lower salaries simply because they are younger.

Other evidence also suggests that men and women have different stakes in marriage. A recent article by Frances Kobrin and Linda Waite finds that in the United States, men are more likely to get married when they have a secure economic status.

In contrast, women are more likely to use a higher personal income to "buy out of marriage." That is, when women have a choice, which still involves a minority of women given current wage levels, they are more likely to see marriage and childbearing as a cost that might best be avoided.

Thus men and women have different stakes in these changes. To the extent that women are interested in optimizing their personal opportunities in the paid labour force, marriage and children represent costs. Marriage may not be that costly as long as children are not part of the picture, and that is surely the important factor behind the increase in childlessness. Children infringe more on women, bringing a more traditional division of labour even to marriages that started out on a relatively equal footing.

If sustaining fertility is important, and on this not everyone would agree, it should not be promoted at the expense of the gains that women have made in the last two decades. It is the roles of men that need to change, as they have started to do, in order that they bear more of the costs of children.

The supportiveness of the surrounding society could also be more favourable to childbearing. This support is not particularly forthcoming, as we see from the lack of public initiatives in the area of early child care and for that matter from the constraint on educational budgets. An interesting case in point, as Karol Krótki observed, involved the 1985 federal budget which had first proposed a slight deterioration both of pension income and of family allowance/child tax-credit type revenues *vis-à-vis* the increase in the cost of living. While the former provoked such an outcry that it was reversed, hardly a word was said about the situation of young families with children. In the short term, we can pay for higher pensions with higher taxes, but in the long term only if young families have children will it be possible to pay for the inevitable costs of population aging. The conflict between the young and the old is a serious one. Transfers from the working-age population to the elderly are also transfers from children, since it is people at working ages who have or might have children.

Population aging itself is a consequence of the evolving family patterns because fewer young people means an older population. Here the costs largely result from the fact that health and pension expenses are greater than educational ones. Given that public expenditures on these social security programs are on a pay-as-you-go basis, these expenditures are strongly affected by the age distribution. For instance, in 1981 there are six persons aged 20–64 for every person aged 65 and over, in 2000 there will still be 4.5. Extending current levels of fertility, by 2030 there would only be 2.3 persons of labour-force age for every person at retirement age. At the family level, children are no longer needed as a means of old-age security. But at the level of the society, there is no escaping the need for younger generations to take care of the aged.

When these family changes were gaining momentum, Pierre Trudeau became popular with his justly famous "the state has no business in the bedrooms of the nation." In one sense this is a liberating idea, permitting more freedom. In another sense, the state does have a fundamental interest in the reproduction of the society. In the extreme case, if there is no population, obviously there is no state. More realistically, might it not be in the society's interest to ensure population growth, or at least to avoid population decline? If so, there is a crisis.

THE FUTURE AND IMPLICATIONS OF DEMOGRAPHIC AGING

Susan A. McDaniel

Population aging is a process that has been under way since before Canada came into existence as a country. It has accelerated over the past two decades as a result of the precipitous decline in the birth rate. Despite the wishful talk of some policymakers and a few hopeful social scientists, it is unlikely that the present-day trend toward an older population will be turned around. The birth rate is low in Canada now because people prefer to have smaller families. Even if there were an increase in the birth rate as the women of the baby boom generation approached the end of their reproductive lives, this increase would likely be a temporary phenomenon. The overall effect on the inexorable process of demographic aging of such an echo boom or a boomlet, as this upturn in fertility is often termed, would be minimal. It is similarly unlikely, for a variety of reasons (some of them political and economic), that Canada would be willing to increase the annual number of immigrants to the degree necessary to offset the contemporary trend in demographic aging. For these reasons, demographic aging in Canada is here to stay....

Since people who immigrate are often young adults, typically between 20 and 30 years old, the net immigration of the 1950s was sufficiently high to make an impact on the ranks of today's retired population. Those immigrating to Canada in the 1950s would have been born in the 1920s and

From "Canada's Aging Population" by Susan A. McDaniel. By permission of Butterworths and Susan A. McDaniel, Professor of Sociology, University of Alberta.

1930s. Thus, the oldest group of these immigrants would turn 65 in 1985–86, with the youngest group retiring in the early part of the next century. On the other hand, at the time they arrived in Canada, these 1950s immigrants contributed to the relative youthfulness of the population, and added further to this youthfulness by having children....

Canada's Age Structure in the Future

The fluctuating trends of fertility, mortality and immigration, past and present, leave an inexorable pattern on the shape of a population, just as footprints left in wet cement remain long after the cement dries. The pattern thus formed is the population's age-sex structure.... Canada's present age-sex structure is examined and analyzed as to its implications for demographic aging. The present structure is then projected into the future to allow an analysis of the dimensions of demographic aging that lie ahead for Canada.

IMPLICATIONS OF CANADA'S PRESENT AGE-SEX STRUCTURE

The age-sex structure of a population at a given point in time is typically depicted by a population pyramid, a back-to-back bar graph showing males and females separately. The bars usually represent five-year age groups, but can be single years. These graphs provide, in one glance, a history of the population's demographic experience. A broad stubby pyramid manifests a large birth rate and high death rate with low life expectancy. A country that has experienced enormous losses of men due to a war, as did the U.S.S.R. during World War II, will have a visible indentation on the male side of the pyramid at the crucial ages. Similarly, a country that has experienced net gains due to immigration, as did Canada particularly in the 1901–11 and 1951–61 periods, will show bumps in the age pyramid for the relevant age groups of immigrants.

Canada's 1981 age-sex structure, as shown in the top pyramid in Figure 6.1, clearly attests to the country's past experiences with fertility, mortality and immigration. Most striking in the 1981 population pyramid is the rapid transition from baby boom to baby bust. People aged 15–39 in 1981 form the bulge of the pyramid. Their presence in schools in 1968 caused enrolments to peak. By 1976, school enrolments had dropped by 22 percent. Similar enrolment drops are on the immediate horizon for postsecondary educational institutions, as the baby boom generation moves out of university.

The baby bust period, begun 10–15 years prior to 1981, shows in the age-sex pyramid as a shrunken generation. A tiny group of people seems to lie in the shadow of the largest generation the world ever experienced. Although Canadian fertility has now hit an historic low, the indented bottom of the population pyramid in 1981 is characteristic of many modern industrial societies. As a population experiences lowered birth rates for a prolonged period, the pattern of demographic aging manifests itself in a *rectangularization* of the population pyramid.

Even though Canada's 1981 population pyramid in no way resembles a rectangle, its classic, pyramidal shape is changing. No longer is it characterized by the wide base and gently sloping sides of a young population. As a population ages, it seems to gain a "spare tire" around the middle (a pattern not unknown to many aging individuals).

The economic and social significance of the sudden, sharp and prolonged decline in the birth rate in Canada in the 1970s and 1980s may become most apparent in the 2020s and 2030s, when the baby boom generation hits retirement and old age. At this time, the small baby bust generation will be called upon for support. Given this imbalance in size between the work force and the older population, there might be a strain. Alternatively, it might be that patterns of work and retirement would be sufficiently transformed so that many baby boom generation people would, in fact, support other baby boomers in their retirement.

It is clear that the rate of population growth has begun to decline, with the end of the baby boom era. This decline in population growth rate has concerned many analysts, who associate it with a decline in economic growth rates. Close examination of the 1981 Canadian population pyramid, however, shows that the long-term rate of decline in population growth may be falsely inflated to some extent. The period of the baby boom was also marked by a particularly healthy rate of net immigration during the 1950s, hence the rapid growth rate in Canada. It seems almost inevitable that this very high rate of growth would even out eventually. The surprise was that it turned around so very quickly, and gave way to the lowest birth rate level in Canada's history.

Looking only at short-run trends in the birth rate might lead to the conclusion that Canada is experiencing a precipitous drop in population growth. However, if the baby boom period is defined not as the standard of population growth, but as a somewhat anomalous period, then the drop in the rate of population growth may be viewed as less precipitous and may cause less concern.

There is one aspect of the relationship between the baby boom and baby bust generations, even in 1981, that some analysts believe might offset their predictions of zero population growth and accelerated population aging in the future. The women of the baby boom generation are now beginning to arrive at their last years of re-

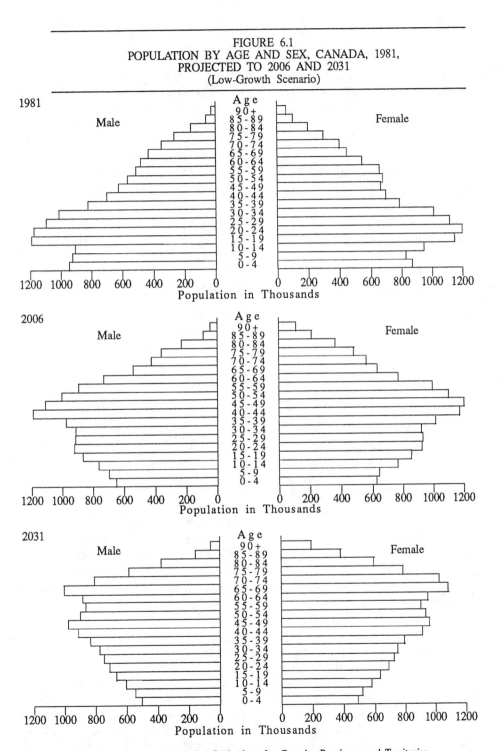

FIGURE 6.1
POPULATION BY AGE AND SEX, CANADA, 1981,
PROJECTED TO 2006 AND 2031
(Low-Growth Scenario)

Source: Statistics Canada, *Population Projections for Canada, Provinces and Territories,*
1984-2006 (Catalogue No. 91-520). p. 49 (Ottawa: Minister of Supply and Services, 1985).

production. Some of them may be late childbearers, since the birth rate among women over 30 is increasing (Statistics Canada, 1984: 27). Researchers, however, note only a slight, largely negligible adjustment in the fertility rate of women over 30 (Grindstaff, 1984).

Additionally, there are so many baby boom women of childbearing age that, even if they maintain a low birth rate and small family sizes, the actual numbers of children in the population can increase. This is known as population growth momentum. The population continues to grow despite much lowered birth rates because of the momentum built into the age structure. There was evidence in 1983 that this is already occurring. The steady downward decline in the birth *rate* has masked the slight increase in the actual *number* of children, particularly pre-school age children. Since 1976, when the last group of baby boom generation women began having children, the numbers of children aged 0–5 have been increasing. This in no way signals a reversal in the fertility trend but is due to the age structure, i.e. because of the size of the generation of potential mothers, the growth in numbers of pre-school children at present partially offsets the decline in school-age population. This large group of 1981 pre-schoolers may also be important in the future as supporters of the retired baby boomers.

The merit of the population pyramid lies in its capacity to reveal at a glance the past and the future of population aging. The future of population aging in Canadian society will not be entirely surprising, since it is revealed in the population pyramid of 1981. The older people of Canada's tomorrow are the young and middle-aged people of today. Given present levels of mortality and high levels of life expectancy, these people are not likely to disappear, nor, given Canada's past experience, are they likely to emigrate in large numbers.

CANADA'S FUTURE AGE-SEX STRUCTURE

The age-sex structure of the future will depend on the future course of the basic demographic forces — fertility, mortality and immigration. . . . all three forces are the complex products of multiple social and economic trends, and thus subject to change. As a result, predicting their future course with a high degree of certainty is difficult. On the other hand, certain aspects of fertility, mortality and immigration have been analyzed and are well understood. This allows for prediction within a relatively narrow range. The projections we will discuss here are based on methods of projection devised and carried out by some of the best demographers in Canada (who have access to sophisticated trend analysis of the three basic variables, as well as to the most recent data). It should be remembered, however, that demographers' predictions in the past have been wrong. The baby boom was not anticipated, nor was the recent sharp decline in fertility.

The future age structure of any population depends, to a large degree, on the future course of fertility. (The patterns of mortality and immigration also matter, but to a much lesser degree.) The challenge is that fertility is the least amenable to prediction of the three variables. If errors are made in projecting the future age-sex structure of Canada, or the *degree* of demographic aging to be expected, these errors would probably be due to incorrect fertility projection. Given this, and the fact that there has been much speculation about what will happen to Canada's fertility rate in the future, most projections allow for at least three possible ranges of fertility — a high, a medium and a low range. The most recent Statistics Canada projections, from which much of our data here are drawn, are based on the most likely future scenario — an assumption of continued low fertility.

When the future age structure is referred to, it is generally taken to mean the entire age structure as represented by the population pyramid. The numbers of those who will be 65 in, say, 20 years' time are known now, barring any enormous change in current patterns of either mortality or immigration. The proportion that will be constituted by the population over the age of 65 cannot be known with full certainty, because of possible future influences on the birth rate. The further we project into the future, the greater the uncertainty of the projections. . . .

Keeping all these precautions in mind, let us examine what the future may hold for Canada in terms of age-sex structure. Figure 6.1 . . . shows a 1981 age-sex pyramid and projected pyramids for 2006 and 2031. These projections are based on the following assumptions made by Statistics Canada: (1) the total fertility rate (number of children per woman at the end of reproduction) will continue to decline from 1.7 in 1981 to a low of 1.4 by 1996 and will remain constant thereafter; (2) the total level of immigration will stabilize at 50,000 net gain in immigrants a year and will remain constant at that level; (3) future changes in life expectancy will be lower in future than those observed for 1976–81; (4) the male-female difference will narrow; (5) the similarity between mortality levels of males and females at very young and very old ages will continue. These assumptions underlie the low-growth scenario projection by Statistics Canada.

From the pyramids presented in Figure 6.1, it is apparent that, if these assumptions hold, Canadian society in the future will be substantially different than it is today. The aging process, begun in the nineteenth century, will continue and accelerate. For example, the median age of the Canadian population will rise from 30 years in 1983 to 41 years in 2006 and reach 48 years by 2031. This change is illustrated in the dramatic shift that is seen to occur in the shape of the age pyramid over the 50 years portrayed in Figure 6.1. The pyramid changes from being relatively bottom-heavy to being top-heavy. Among electors, for example, 14 percent in 1981 are above the age of 65. By 2006, the comparable proportion will be 18 percent and by 2031, it will be 31 percent. A slowdown in the rate of population growth is also apparent over the projection period, reaching zero around 2006 and declining thereafter. Among the most dramatic shifts portrayed in the low-growth scenario of Figure 6.1 is the growth in the proportion of the population over the age of 65. . . .

A second large change in the age structure of Canada's future population occurs with the working age population. Under the low-growth scenario, portrayed in the population pyramids (Figure 6.1) it is clear that the working age population will constitute a larger percentage of the total population as the fertility rate declines, at least in the short run. This is particularly evident in the 2006 pyramid. By 2031, however, as the proportion of older persons exceeds the proportion of younger persons, it seems from the pyramid that the working age population might constitute about the same proportion as it does in 1981. . . .

A close examination of the projected population pyramids in Figure 6.1 reveals a fairly dramatic change in the age and sex composition of the older population. At older ages, the bars get longer on the female side of the pyramid. As well, the very old population grows, relative to the younger old population. . . . the proportion of the population 80 years and over has grown even more dramatically than the proportion 65 years and over. In future, this oldest group is expected to grow even more. . . . both the future growth of the proportion 65 and over and the fluctuation and ultimate growth of the preretirement age group, 55–64, are apparent. . . . In the mid-twentieth century, males slightly outnumbered females in Canada. By 1971, the sex ratio was in balance for Canadians of all ages. Among the older groups, women have always predominated. What is striking is the degree to which women, particularly women over 80, will predominate in the future. The future of demographic aging in Canada, as in most demographically older countries, has a female face. . . .

It is clear from this brief look at the relationships among age groups in the future that changes are on the horizon in Canada. The peculiar pattern of a baby boom followed by a baby bust has created a situation in Canada, as in many other places in the industrialized Western world, in which the transition from a youthful society to an older society can be made gracefully. In fact, if we consider that total dependency is projected to reach an all-time historic low in Canada in 2011 or 2016, it seems as if a period of grace has been built into the Canadian age structure. This period can be used as a time of transition, planning and innovation, during which economic and social resources can be gathered in order to provide less to the young, whose diminishing numbers will place less of a burden on society, and more to the old, whose numbers will increase. . . .

Implications of Demographic Aging for Canada

There is no doubt that aging of the Canadian population will create new challenges for policy-makers. It is also clear that the capacity exists to meet these challenges. A panic reaction to an alleged crisis of population aging seems unwarranted and ill-advised. Good decisions can seldom be made in a crisis mode. Realistically, however, it is apparent that some policy-makers will be forced to react to the situation as it develops, rather than with the long-term planning required by demographic aging. This

is unfortunate because planning for the shifting needs and requirements of an aging population requires a long-term vision of the future. There is a need now for flexible and rational social planning and problem solving.

Planning, ideally, should entail not simply meeting the growing needs of the older population (although this must be done), but holistic planning for a society experiencing demographic aging. There will no doubt be some who hark back to the "good old days" of high fertility and population growth. There will even be those who will argue that the solution to the demographic "problem" of an aging population rests with increasing the birth rate or levels of immigration or both. Even if these demographic approaches are tried, and even if they work to some extent, the challenges of an aging Canada will still require realistic social planning. The ultimate solutions will not be demographic, but economic and social. Canada's capacity to meet these challenges depends on our willingness to anticipate the future and plan accordingly.

A central issue of the future in an aging society is redistribution of wealth on a relatively small scale. This, no doubt, will not come easily, but neither is it impossible. It could entail a streamlining of the cumbersome and expensive health care system to better meet people's needs and also to reduce costs. It could involve increased taxation to pay for pensions. (This money, however, might be seen as money that would otherwise have been spent on a never-born third child.) There will be transfers of funds from public education to health and social insurance budgets. The blessing of an aging population is that there will actually be fewer people, given a zero or negative population growth rate, and there will be more collective income than in a population composed largely of dependent children.

Unanswered Questions

A great deal is known about demographic aging, yet many questions remain to be answered. . . . Although much is known about the process, dimensions and dynamics of population aging itself, far less is known about the *links* between demographic aging and socio-economic institutions, structures and systems. In a broad sense, this linkage is an important area of future research on demographic aging. All the specific questions mentioned below essentially fall in this general area.

One unanswered research question is not new at all, but remains to be explored satisfactorily: this is the relationship between personal experience and wider social forces. We are all products of the times in which we live. These times are shaped, among other things, by age structure. This question was addressed by C. Wright Mills' *Sociological Imagination.* It is the crux of what constitutes sociology. Yet it still eludes understanding. With respect to demographic aging, research into intergenerational differences in experience with aging, if framed by the age structures that exist at the different points in time, might provide answers to how personal experience is shaped to some degree by wider forces. For example, research might compare the Depression generation's experiences of retirement with those of the World War II generation. The experiences of the baby boom generation might be contrasted with those of the baby bust generation. This type of research could, if done well, bring together the interactions of generational effects with cohort flow through time.

Another area of potential research would be the changing meaning of old age over time. Demographic research, of course, is predicated on assumptions about when old age begins, as well as assumptions about the social meanings attributed to being in a certain age group. At present, old age is thought to begin at age 65. Should mandatory retirement at age 65 be abolished, this assumption might be called into question. As older people change and become more diversified, it might be that demographers' definitions of dependency would require alteration and increased specificity.

A third unanswered question is actually a cluster of questions, related to the effects of planning. With modern computers it is possible to project many things, including the future effects of alternative plans and policies. For example, what would be the economic and demographic consequences of a rationalized health care system? A projection could be made by anticipating the effects of improved home care, less use of acute care facilities by chronic care patients, less reliance on acute medical intervention where it is not likely to be effective, etc. The relative effects of rationalizing the health care system compared to improved pensions might be assessed. This exercise, of course, would not be straightforward but would involve multiple assumptions about both the present and the future.

Many unanswered questions surround the actual economic needs and activities (consumerism, savings, investments, etc.) of older people. In anticipating the economic consequences of an aging population, many researchers engage in rather sweeping generalizations about the behaviour of older people. For example, economic dependency is often assumed, as is reduced consumer activity. These assumptions need to be backed up by research evidence, rather than taken as given. It may be that the economic activity patterns of older people are very different than we have assumed and will become more so, as you and I arrive at that stage in life. One clue might be derived from the examination of the consumption patterns of the present cohorts of middle-aged Canadians, compared to earlier cohorts.

There is also a need for research to explore the relationship between older people's political power and the demographic definitions of dependency. Dependency suggests helplessness. Older people who are increasingly politically active may be anything but helpless or dependent. The manner in which Canadian pensioners organized to protest the proposal to de-index their pensions in the spring and summer of 1985 provides testimony to their political power. This may be particularly true for women, who tend to outlive men and who also tend to become increasingly politically active as they age.

Finally, there is a need for research to examine the demographic, social and economic implications of abolishing mandatory retirement. It is important, before taking action on mandatory retirement, to understand how this major policy change would affect the various age groups (not only the old), directly or indirectly. This area of research could show the relationships that exist between economic and age structure. It could also address the interactive effects of actions meant to protect the interests of one group in society. . . .

THE QUEBEC QUESTION: A MATTER OF POPULATION

Gary Caldwell
Daniel Fournier

Introduction

For as long as there has been a Quebec the overriding issue has been one, not, as in the case of Poland (another "impossible" society), of political independence, but of

From "The Quebec Question: A Matter of Population" by Gary Caldwell and Daniel Fournier. Appearing in *The Canadian Journal of Sociology*, Volume 12(12) 1987. By permission of *The Canadian Journal of Sociology*.

population. Indeed, the question was put as early as the seventeenth century. At that time it took the form of getting population numbers up to a critical level sufficient to assure the simple biological perpetuation of the resident population. Until the native-born population, which was adapted to the new environment, was sufficiently numerous that it outnumbered the more volatile immigrant population, French colonial administrators continued to be concerned. In the subsequent race with the English for control of the continent that had been largely discovered and explored by the French, the insufficient size of the French population has been judged to be the decisive factor in the defeat.

After the final military defeat in 1759 and the containment of French North America to, essentially, Lower Canada (the Quebec and Constitutional Acts) the issue became one of establishing a French demographic hegemony in Lower Canada at a period when the St. Lawrence River had become a funnel for English and Irish immigration to British North America. As a result of this both Quebec City and Montreal became English cities as French society ruralified in a retreat to the land. Soon after, at the time of the controversy over the creation of the Union in 1840, the demographic gauntlet was thrown down again as French Quebec was faced with the prospect of minorization in a united Canada. Subsequent failure of the union and the advent of Confederation in 1867 provided a certain respite. The French population was by then firmly established as the majority in Lower Canada which was to become the new province of Quebec. It was at this time (the mid-eighteenth century) that Quebec managed a period of super-fertility — relative to the surrounding population — that lasted a century. This period constituted a demographic investment that alone ensured the survival of French society in geographical Quebec as we know it today, despite political and economic subjugation.

But demographic superiority was only a limited consolation as this Quebec was indeed part of a larger political entity, the new Dominion of Canada which was expanding to the west. The race for the west was on and the dream of Quebec nationalists at the time (Henri Bourassa) was to establish its land-hungry progeny on the fertile plains of the new frontier. Debates on who would people the west constituted a major public issue of the day. As fate — or rather politics — would have it, the battle for the settlement of the west was lost by Quebec as her sons and daughters (for whom the cost of going west was higher than it was for east European immigrants) poured over the close-by international border into the demographic vortex of the new republic, never to be seen again as a distinct national group. From this point on, any hope of influencing the Canadian demo-linguistic equilibrium in favour of French was lost. Had it not been for the dividends reaped in the early half of the twentieth century from the great demographic investment of the nineteenth, as well as massive emigration from Western Canada to the United States, the one-third/two-thirds linguistic balance would not have held as it did for a century.

However, the post-World War II economic boom, the consummation of the industrialization of Canadian society, massive immigration from Europe, and the modernization of Quebec society opened up two cracks in this precarious equilibrium. First of all, it became apparent that the French-speaking population outside of Quebec was destined to melt away under the hot sun of language assimilation. Quebec nationalists finally abandoned the dream of a Canada of two nations from coast to coast. The *Report on Bilingualism and Biculturalism* was the last gasp. The French nation was, ineluctably, fading away outside of Quebec, except perhaps in northwestern New Brunswick. Indeed, even in the part of the bilingual belt which

is in Quebec, the outcome appeared dubious.

Hence, the "French-Canadian" question had become, for French-speakers, the "Quebec" question and French-speaking non-Quebecers were abandoned to their fate. However, as soon as these losses had been cut — ideologically speaking — and a new line drawn (the provincial political boundary), it was discovered in the sixties that within bastion Quebec was a demographic Trojan horse. Differential linguistic assimilation of immigrants into the English sector was such in Montreal, that had trends then current continued uninterrupted there would have been more students in English than in French schools today. Differential linguistic assimilation to English was not new: what was new was francophone out-migration and falling francophone fertility which, combined, left the French population exposed to the consequence of language assimilation.

Incidentally, it is now *de bon ton* in English-Canadian journalistic and academic circles to show that this perception of a threat to the demographic predominance of French in the Quebec metropolis was an alarmist scare which did not come to pass. This is an error: the facts of the situation as they existed in the sixties have not changed. What did change was the political context which in turn acted on reality to reverse certain trends. We repeat, there has been no systematic demographic demonstration that, in the light of conditions prevailing at the time, the analysis of the sixties was in error. Indeed, as a consequence of political action stemming from an ideological *prise de conscience* with regard to the demographic threat, a lowered level of immigration, increased out-migration of anglophones from Quebec, as well as the constraint of language laws, have averted the feared outcome.

But to little avail, because Quebec is again faced with the issue of the early seventeenth century: that of a level of fertility insufficient to assure the biological per-petuation of its existing population base. For over a decade now Quebecers, as a population, have not been reproducing themselves: with the lowest fertility rate in the industrialized world, with the exception of Denmark and West Germany, the pros-pect of a declining population within fifteen years now faces Quebec. Once again, in its simplest form, the Quebec question has be-come one of numbers. Having put into place a quasi-state, which assured the role of French in public life and insured itself from being swamped by immigrants, the inhabitants thus protected are fading away.

The importance of demographics as the dialectic of the Quebec question is also re-flected in the importance of the discipline of demography in contemporary Quebec. The "Association des demographes du Québec" has almost two hundred members and these members have probably been more effective in reading, empirically, the changing social reality of Quebec society than have been all the other social scien-tists put together. It is the demographers, and the demographic writers who were their precursors, who have defined the Quebec issue for over a quarter of a century now. The vitality and productiveness of the discipline is reflected in the fact that Quebec demography is the only Quebec social science that has attracted interna-tional recognition for its scientific production.

Furthermore, although individual histo-rians and sociologists may have played a role in shaping a national consciousness in contemporary Quebec, only demography has directly inspired political action. This happened in the late sixties and early sev-enties when concern over the consequence of language assimilation of both immi-grants and francophones led to language legislation, particularly Bill 101. The latter created a situation of reduced immigration, of increased out-migration of anglophones, and the channeling of immigrant children into French schools, which indeed changed the course of events in as much as the linguistic composition of Quebec so-ciety is concerned.

Why is it that demographic issues have been so critical throughout the history of Quebec? Before attempting to address this question, a preliminary remark is in order: although there is a very developed demo-graphic tradition of a descriptive nature on such issues as immigration, language as-similation, fertility, and ethnic studies, there is in fact a very limited contemporary literature on the role of demographic fac-tors as a causal variable in the long-term determination of the nature of Quebec so-ciety. Cultural or economic factors are more likely to be cast as the key to Quebec's survival. Indeed, the classical thesis is that if there continues to exist a Quebec cultural consciousness and economic expansion, Quebec will retain and expand its popula-tion and thus persevere.

Our contention is that, in the case of Quebec this has not been adequately dem-onstrated, despite the conventional wisdom in this regard; but rather, on the contrary, both the longer view of Quebec history and a more detailed analysis of the post-war period would suggest that eco-nomic growth in Quebec is a consequence of demographic expansion. In other words, in Quebec history the most successful so-cietal investments have been demographic rather than economic. The obverse demon-stration of this is the economic conse-quences of the contemporary demographic disinvestment.

However, such a thesis — growth in Quebec is population driven — has neither been convincingly laid out in the social sci-ence literature, nor is it the object of a con-sensus of opinion, to say the least! However, were it to be the case — as one of us has suggested — why might such be so?

Quebec society is, and has been histor-ically, subject to at least three conditions or geo-political constraints that limit its ability to use either the state or the economy as levers of development. First, Quebec is, and always has been, a truncated political entity; second, it is, and always has been an integral part of a metropolitan economy (French, English, and now American) that it responds to but does not determine; and finally, Quebec has, and always has had (albeit for different reasons) an open boundary for those wishing to leave. These three geo-political constraints combined — political truncation, economic dependence and unrestricted emigration — result conceivably, in the fact that the only effective lever Quebec possesses to make its influence felt is sheer numbers, and that from numbers all else follows. Let us now look at the contemporary numbers and how they are evolving; after which we will consider briefly the political, economic, and social consequences of these numbers.

Contemporary Evolution of the Population

In terms of the volume of its population and its rate of growth, Quebec, like the rest of Canada, has experienced a declining growth rate since the fifties. Quebec has, however, distinguished itself since the sixties with a growth rate that has been declining faster than that of the rest of Canada. Relative to the period between the two wars (1921 to 1941) when Quebec was growing faster than the rest of Canada, the tables have been turned.

At the beginning of the sixty-year period . . ., Quebec was growing considerably faster than Canada as a whole. Half-way through the period the rates were equal, whereas by the end Quebec was growing at a rate half that of (or twice as slow as) Canada as a whole.

Looking more closely at the second half (1951–1981) of the more than half century under consideration . . ., we can see that the turning point was indeed the middle six-

ties. Up until that time Quebec's growth rate, for whatever reasons, was essentially equal to Canada's; although already less than Ontario's. Rather suddenly in the five-year period 1966 to 1971 Quebec's growth rate weakened dramatically and fell to half that of Ontario's and 45 percent of Canada's. Despite the fact that Canada's and Ontario's growth rates have continued to decline, Quebec's has remained lower.

MIGRATORY MOVEMENTS

However, the single most important factor in the relative (to the rest of Canada) deterioration in the growth rate of Quebec's population between 1951 and 1981 was not, as is often assumed, the relative decline in natural increase. Although the natural growth rate in Quebec declined more in the fifties and early sixties than in Ontario, since the mid-sixties . . . the rate of natural increase in Quebec and Ontario have been almost identical. Consequently, the cause of the relative deterioration of the Quebec growth rate is to be found elsewhere: the answer lies in the nature of migratory movement. . . .

Again, it is the late sixties, the period 1966–1971, that was the turning point . . .: it was from this period on that the migratory balance (obtained by subtracting natural increase from actual increase) became negative. The loss reached a peak of almost seventy thousand for the five-year period 1976 to 1981. However, according to a recent estimation of Statistics Canada . . ., Quebec's migratory balance began to improve in the early eighties and in 1985 became positive once more.

. . . the evolution in migratory currents is very instructive as it allows us to draw a number of conclusions. First, it is apparent that the negative migratory balances experienced by Quebec during the sixties and seventies were a consequence of its disproportionate net losses to the other provinces, losses constantly higher in volume than the net international migratory gain. Second, since 1983 the hemorrhage has been stemmed and, furthermore, it appears that since 1985 Quebec has been experiencing a positive net-migratory balance. Third, and a consequence of our first conclusion above, this turnaround is due to a decline in out-migration to other provinces. And fourth, notwithstanding the decline in inter-provincial out-migration, there has also been a marked decline in international immigration to Quebec.

At this point in our description of the contemporary evolution of Quebec's population we can characterize what has happened to Quebec demographically thus: as in the case of most Western societies, the growth rate of Quebec's population has slowed since the fifties. As has generally been the case in industrialized societies, in Quebec the origin of this population growth slow-down has been a decline in natural increase. But in Quebec's case, the decline has been more marked than in the rest of Canada, especially when compared with the neighbouring province of Ontario which shares a similar geographic and industrialization history. It was more precisely in the mid-sixties that Quebec began to lag seriously with respect to the other provinces; and, it is precisely at this time that Quebec's net-migratory balance became negative, owing largely to heavy net losses to the other provinces. These two tendencies, dramatic decline in natural increase compounded by negative net migratory balances led to a reduction of Quebec's relative demographic weight within the Canadian confederation.

Linguistic Composition of the Population

One of the outcomes of the recent demographic evolution of Quebec has been — all the recent consciousness of immigrant communities notwithstanding — an incip-

ient homogenization of the population around the French linguistic pole. Although the proportion of those whose mother tongue is French declined from 81.2 percent to 80.7 percent between 1961 and 1971, the proportion climbed back up to 81.1 percent in 1976 and to 82.4 percent by 1981. Meanwhile, the size of the English mother-tongue population had been declining in relative terms since 1961, from 13.3 to 12.8 percent in 1976. In the course of the five-year period 1976–81 the decline accelerated with the result that by 1981 the English mother-tongue population constituted only 11.0 percent of the total Quebec population. We have here, as far as the English mother-tongue population is concerned, not only a relative but (between 1976 and 1981) an absolute decline.

The beginning of the period of absolute decline of the English mother-tongue population coincides, as history would have it, with the ascension to political power of the Parti Québécois; which coincidence allows us to speculate on the demographic effect of this exceptional political event. To put the change at issue — the reversal of English demographic fortunes — into relief it is sufficient to say that while the English mother-tongue population grew by 1 percent between 1971 and 1976, it declined by a full 11 percent in the succeeding five years. It would appear then that the péquiste victory had an important impact on the out-migration of anglophones.

Yet, in historical terms, the heavy out-migration of anglophones in the period 1976 to 1981 was rather an amplification, albeit intense, of a long-term trend of disproportionate anglophone out-migration from Quebec: even in contemporary times this trend has been distinctly evident. . . .

Hence, in the period 1966 to 1971, the interprovincial migratory balance of the English mother-tongue population of Quebec already amounted to a deficit of 52,000 persons; which represents, in absolute terms, 4 times the French mother-tongue deficit, and 23 times in relative terms taking into account the proportionate size of each language group in the Quebec population. In the subsequent five-year period, 1971 to 1976, the English losses remained at the same level while the French and Other mother-tongue losses declined considerably. Then between 1976 to 1981 — the péquiste period — the English losses doubled compared to the two pre-ceeding five-year periods; as however did the losses to the Other mother-tongue population. The French losses to the other provinces also rose substantially.

Indeed, at least in so far as interprovincial population movements are concerned, the net-migratory deficit of Quebec, since 1966, has been largely at the expense of the English population of Quebec. This trend, already evident — in fact, dating back to Confederation — was amplified by the political events of the seventies. On the other hand, the Other mother-tongue population, thanks to important gains from immigration, experienced positive balances. (Here reference should be made to the ephemeral nature of immigration currents: for example, there is reason to believe that more Greeks are now leaving Quebec than are arriving.) As for the French mother-tongue population, it appears that an equilibrium has been reached between out and in migration. Such was indeed the case for the decade 1971 to 1981. Even English out-migration appears to have moderated considerably.

The increasingly francophone character of immigration to Quebec has, as we shall now see, contributed to this situation. This becomes apparent when one examines the complex of population movements that produced the 1971 to 1981 migratory balance equilibrium. Effectively, the variation in the size of the French mother-tongue population of Quebec corresponds to what would have been expected from the effect of natural increase alone. Put rather simply, for the ten years 1971 to 1981, 85 percent of

the natural increase of the Quebec population has been French mother-tongue: more precisely, 441,000 of a total of 519,000. As it happens, this 441,000 added to the 1971 French mother-tongue population of 4,866,000 gives us 5,307,000 exactly the 1981 French mother-tongue census population.

Yet . . ., on balance, more francophones (4,100 between 1971–76 and 18,000 between 1976–81) left Quebec for the other provinces than arrived from the same provinces. . . . But during the same ten-year period between 35,000 and 40,000 French mother-tongue immigrants came to Quebec, notably 22,000 Haitians and a further 10,000 from France. These facts allow us to conjecture that between 13,000 and 18,000 French mother-tongue Quebecers left Canada: more than 1,000 a year but less than 2,000 — rather few given that the size of the French mother-tongue population is over 5,000,000.

Given the above we can conclude that the recent relative decline in the demographic growth of Quebec — relative to the rest of Canada — is, above all, attributable to a movement of departures among the English element of the population.

LANGUAGE ASSIMILATION

Up to this point in the discussion, we have touched on the evolution of population size and of natural increase and migration as factors determining this same evolution, and what is crucial in the Quebec context, the ethnic composition (using mother-tongue as a surrogate for ethnicity) of this same population. What we have not touched on is the question of language use, as opposed to mother tongue.

The issue of language use and change in language use — language assimilation — provoked a heated debate, leading, as we mentioned in the introduction, to political action. Language assimilation became an issue fifteen years ago when it became generally appreciated that the number of people using English in their homes was substantially greater than those whose mother tongue was English. And as, on the other hand, the number using French was only marginally greater than the number of those whose mother tongue was French, the issue was posed in terms of the relative power of attraction of the two languages and what was seen as, inevitably, a long-term deterioration of the status of the French language. How many francophones were assimilating to English, and of even more import, would allophones continue to opt massively for English. . . .

. . . English still has a superior power of attraction, having attracted 33,000 net from French; and the breakdown by age group indicates no let-up in this superiority, rather than the contrary. However, the accumulated total of those having assimilated from French to English is relatively small, 1.4 percent of the present French mother-tongue population; whereas those who assimilated from English to French represent 6.5 percent of the present English mother-tongue population of Quebec. As for the Other mother-tongue population, English has attracted almost three times more individuals than has French. In round figures, English has gained 108,000, French has lost 9,000 and the Other mother-tongue population has lost 100,000.

Most of the gains to English are from the Other mother-tongue population rather than from French. As we pointed out earlier, three times as many Other mother-tongue language transfers are to English as opposed to French. Obviously, there are reasons, arising from the North American cultural and economic context, for this language behaviour. This is not the place to elaborate on or to try to fathom these reasons: suffice it to say that such a phenomenon is of great demographic consequence for Quebec society. Bill 101, with its measures for the francization of the work place and French-language schooling for immigrant children has been imple-

mented precisely with this phenomenon in mind. The question now becomes whether or not Bill 101 has in fact been successful in terms of the issue it addressed.

Bill 101 did result in making French the predominant language of work in Quebec as well as creating a situation whereby the children of new immigrants found themselves in French-language schools. As a result of these two developments, by the early eighties there began to emerge what might be called a French-language public culture. Nevertheless, subsequent developments — the referendum defeat, the triumph of a neo-conservatism, the effects of the recession and stagnating population growth have created a climate in which the French-language public culture has become extremely fragile. Indeed, the speed with which the population at large, French and English, are reverting to pre-Bill 101 patterns of linguistic behaviour is disconcerting. The moroseness that has overcome the nationalist movement in Quebec and the victory of the liberal party in December 1985 have both contributed to this new climate.

Returning to Bill 101 itself, as well as the intended legal coercive effects of the law, there were unintended effects which also contributed to the emergence of a French-language public culture. One was the selective nature of out-migration from Quebec in the late seventies. As already mentioned, considerable numbers of anglophones chose to leave Quebec. Another effect made itself felt in both the volume and the linguistic composition of immigration. The negative, and largely undeserved, publicity Bill 101 gave Quebec in the other provinces and internationally resulted in a decline in immigration; and of those who did come, a higher proportion than in the past were francophone. . . .

PROCREATION

Despite the changes that have taken place in Quebec's demographic history with regard to migration, domestic and international, the most fundamental changes have been at the level of procreation. Moreover, it is changes at this level — reflecting themselves in a lowered natural increase — that put the problem of out-migration and language assimilation into relief, making issues out of phenomena that were not at all new. We will review the procreation revolution in terms of changes in nuptiality and fertility, beginning with the former.

Like other industrialized populations in the Western world, Quebec has recently experienced a new pluralism with regard to the marital status of the adult population. The most sensitive indicators of this, that of the number of marriages per thousand population . . ., reveals a continuing decline since the middle of the seventies. Yet, the rate of total nuptiality of the ever-married, that is, the cumulative marriage rate of all age-groups under fifty, reveals an even more precipitous decline. In the case of men it passed from 906 per thousand in 1971, to 571 in 1981, to 493 in 1984; whereas in the case of women the rate for the same dates are 863, 579 and 514 respectively. This means, quite simply, that if present trends continue to prevail, one in two Quebecers will not marry. . . . this is, in Western terms, a rather exceptional performance.

The transition to this new state of affairs was a steady progression, without any remarkable discontinuities, during the period 1971 to 1983. However, the decline in nuptiality was arrested — for the first time in twelve years — in 1984 as the combined male and female rate bounced back from the floor of 500 per thousand population, moving up from 493 to 514. But it is too early to tell if the trend of the last twelve years has been reversed. As for the divorces of those who do marry, their number has varied considerably over the last fifteen years. Following the liberalization of the divorce law in 1968, the number rose from 2,947 in 1969 to 15,186 in 1976, falling back to 13,899

in 1980 only to climb again in 19,931 in 1981 (a gain of 38 percent in one year), levelling off at 16,845 in 1984 (Quebec, 1985). Quebec is close to a situation whereby only half of the population marries, and of that half, between a quarter and a half divorces.

It is widely believed in Quebec that one consequence of this state of affairs has been a spectacular increase in the number of common-law unions. Yet the census figures do not bear this out. In 1981, well after the change in marriage behaviour described above was well underway, only 4.8 percent of the Quebec population fifteen and over admitted to living common-law, as opposed to 30.2 percent who were single, 56.5 percent married, 5.8 percent widowed and 2.6 percent divorced. Nonetheless, this was five years ago and the proportion of the population living common-law or divorced has certainly increased. As for the tendency of the divorced to re-marry, it has declined from 603 per thousand divorced in the case of men and 521 in the case of women to 325 and 282 respectively in 1983. What is in fact happening is that an increasingly important part of the population is living alone, which state is reflected in the ever declining average size of households, 2.8 persons in 1984 as compared to 4.6 in 1953.

Yet the dramatic decline in nuptiality notwithstanding, the precipitous drop in the fertility rate constitutes the most remarkable demographic development in Quebec since the great out-migration of the turn of the century, 1850 to 1920. In the late fifties (1955 to 1960) Quebec still had one of the highest fertility rates in the industrialized world. Today she finds herself at the bottom of the list with a rate similar to or lower than that of the Germanic and Scandinavian countries.

The phenomenon of fertility decline began to make itself felt in the late fifties. It accelerated shortly thereafter and became vertiginous in the late sixties, a fall of 28 percent in the three years 1964 to 1967. A slippage in the fertility rate of this amplitude is rather extraordinary, however it coincides with what is recognized as the watershed years — in terms of fertility decline in Western Europe and North America generally. By 1969–1970, the total fertility rate fell under the critical 2.1 children per woman level required for replacement. Thereafter, it appeared to stabilize at around 1.8 between 1977 and 1979, which level (well below replacement) provoked much concern at the time. Yet after 1979 the rate began to decline again, heading for a new floor just under 1.5 (1.454 in 1983 and 1.447 in 1984). Preliminary 1985 figures indicate a stabilization at just under 1.5, a far cry from the 4.0 of 1954.

However, the birth rate (births per thousand population . . .) itself did not decline as rapidly in the seventies as did the total fertility rate. What happened was that the arrival of the baby-boom generation at the age of maximum procreation (25 to 34 years) temporarily compensated for the decline in the number of births per woman. This effect was such that the birth-rate which was 14.6 in 1972 rose to 15.8 in 1979. Subsequently, however, the collapse of fertility was such that even this favourable evolution in the age-structure of the female population was insufficient to compensate for the missing births per woman. Consequently, in 1984–1985, the birth rate was in the 13 to 14 per thousand range. What does the future hold in terms of the natural increase of the Quebec population? After 1986 the age structure of the female population will cease to favour more births, in fact, it will begin to play in the opposite direction. As for mortality, the rate has been vacillating between 6.7 and 7.0 per thousand population since 1960 but will begin to rise soon as the population ages, as we shall see in the next section. Inexorably, given present trends, natural increase in Quebec will be negative by the turn of the century — only fourteen years away!

THE AGE STRUCTURE

As a consequence of the fertility decline, the population of Quebec is experiencing an aging process which will be more accelerated than elsewhere in the industrialized world, although the imminence of this reality is being temporarily camouflaged by the baby-boom echo (births to baby-boomers). Recently the Quebec Bureau of Statistics published a series of three population projections based on three different migration and fertility scenarios. These projections cast some light on future consequences in terms of the age-structure of the population. . . .

The aging process is already well under way as the 0 to 14 years-old group indicates, having passed from a total of 35 percent of the population in 1961 to 22 percent in 1981. However, the aging process has yet to strike the active population, but will do so in the next twenty years. The age-groups of those over 50 and those over 60, have, however, represented a steadily increasing proportion of the population since 1961. By the end of the period envisaged here, the year 2041, the proportion in these four age groups will stabilize, by ascending age-order, at 15, 17, 42 and 29 percent respectively. In other words, half the population will be over forty-five! . . .

Overall, the contemporary demography of Quebec is singular, not by virtue of the trends that have manifested themselves — trends in fact common to other industrial countries — but rather by the amplitude of these same trends which in Quebec have attained extremes unknown except in very rare instances in the most "modern" industrial democracies. The fact that this extreme evolution has occurred with respect to several demographic phenomena points to something more than a chance or ephemeral circumstance. From the highest to the lowest fertility, from a traditional extended family-based society to a state of extreme fragility of marriage itself, low nuptiality and high divorce rates; the accompanying changes in values reflect, directly, what has been a rather surprising ideological, electoral, and economic volatility of this same population: since the fifties the most revealing aspect of change has been the velocity of these same changes. A dramatic manifestation of this "velocity" is the rapidity of recourse to female sterilization by tubal ligation in the early seventies: in the short space of *two* years the annual rate of sterilization by tubal ligation of women of child-bearing age quadrupled, progressing from 4.2 percent in 1971 to 17.1 percent in 1973.

A contributing, but not sufficient factor, in generating this velocity has been, we submit, the small scale of Quebec population, constituted in the main, of five and a half million francophones in an anglophone continent. In the small states of Europe such as Switzerland, the Scandinavian countries, Holland and Belgium — and for the same reasons — one finds the same tendencies. Although there are, no doubt, other and perhaps more important factors behind the amplitude and velocity of the changes, the consequence of size alone merits consideration.

Returning to the very concrete and very present consequences of current demographic trends upon the fabric of Quebec society, the decisive rupture — the beginning of the fertility collapse — took place at the beginning of the Quiet Revolution. Whereas it was fifteen years later, at a time when the fall in fertility appeared to have been arrested between 1973 and 1979, that the marriage and divorce graphics began to take a strange turn. These changes are, of course, interdependent — the fading of children from the social stage and marriage instability — resulting in a decline in procreation that constitutes a world record. No sooner had Quebecers come to grips with the fact that their society was no longer

biologically perpetuating itself than they found coming, on a not-too-distant horizon, the spectre of a rather brutal aging of the whole society.

Political, Economic and Social Consequences

In the previous section, where we sketched the outlines of the contemporary demographic evolution of Quebec society, we found a population that is about to stop growing and is aging rapidly. Moreover, this population which threatens to become more, rather than less, ethnically homogenous, is at the same time undergoing a process of atomization which is reflected in the ever-smaller families and average household size. Paradoxically, the same population, in terms of the people making it up, is more stable than it has been for a long time: fewer and fewer people are leaving Quebec and fewer and fewer are arriving. Incidentally, we also suspect that, despite the available figures on population distribution that Quebec is experiencing an increasing concentration of an almost constant population around the existing urban poles; with the result that the density is falling in the rest of the inhabited territory. What then are the political, economic and social consequences of these changes.

POLITICAL AND ECONOMIC

Geo-politically, the most obvious consequences of the present situation is a weakening of Quebec's political weight within the Canadian federation. As we pointed out earlier, Quebec has — for varying demographic reasons — been able to maintain its three-tenths position in the Canadian demographic balance for over a century and a quarter now. This remarkable demolinguistic equilibrium is now seriously threatened with the importance of the Quebec population in the federation down to 28 percent in 1981, and even lower in 1986.

A second less obvious geo-political consequence is internal to Quebec's own territory: it is the potential threat to cultural, and eventually political, sovereignty represented by a failure to occupy adequately her territory. This potential problem presents itself in the peripheral areas, many of which are contiguous with other more demographically dynamic jurisdictions, as for instance Ontario and a number of American states. The prospect of almost unoccupied territory in the Eastern Townships, the upper Ottawa valley and the lower Gaspé regions may prove an irresistible temptation to those for whom the "open" border may seem a temporary obstacle.

The decline in the population of municipalities outside of the shadow of the three metropolitan areas (Montreal, Quebec, and Hull) and the dozen or so regional urban centers will have the further political consequence of reinforcing the centralization process already underway, despite a rhetoric to the contrary. Communities facing population decline, onerous debts and a scarcity of available talent will not have the means or the will to oppose the logic of efficiency which presages further centralization.

Economically, the major consequences of the present demographic state of Quebec society are the eventual burden of an aging population and increased costs per person of the social infra-structure. As for the consequence, that of aging, George Mathews has dramatized it in his book *Le choc demographique* (1984). He points out that the short-term and immediate social-cost relief of the fertility decline is inversely related to the weight of the burden which will be occasioned by the implacable outcome of lowered fertility — an aged population.

As for the second consequence, increased costs per person of the social infra-

structure, this is already upon us. Part of the legacy of the Quiet Revolution was an infra-structure built on the premise of a growing population, and the debt that goes with it. Population growth has since declined from 2.5 percent annually to 0.5 percent or less, whereas the accompanying debt has continued to grow (10 percent in the last year).

In fact, as the "French" Commission pointed out, Quebec is facing the prospect of a reverse investment dynamic. When investors and government foresee growth they undertake capital expenditures — production plant, housing, highways, hospitals, schools, etc. — to be paid for by a greater number of consumers or users in the future. The economic activity generated by these capital expenditures itself contributes to stimulating the banked-upon growth. When non-growth is foreseen, the opposite happens, no investments are made; and in some cases even already existing investments are not maintained or replaced, which amounts to disinvestment. Such a process of decapitalization has clearly taken place in, for instance, Quebec's health services sector where hospitals and equipment are not being capitalized at a rate sufficient to maintain or replace them.

Although there is presently a flurry of construction activity in Quebec in residential and commercial facilities such as shopping centers and office buildings, there is no corresponding investment in industrial or social infra-structure. In fact, the consumer-oriented investment — housing, shopping centers and office space for service-oriented companies — now taking place is being fueled by the arrival in the market of the baby-boomers, the "groundswell" cohort born between 1953 and 1964 of which we spoke earlier. However, behind them there is no follow-up and in a decade housing and commercial capacity will be so plentiful that there will be little need to even replace existing but obsolete facilities; hence, disinvestment in the consumer-oriented sector is also likely. Should such come to pass, as it will unless present demographic trends change, there will be (as Mathews points out) few jobs in construction, the activity that has been the mainstay of the Quebec economy since the war.

A striking example of over-capitalization relative to the effective market demand, and the subsequent de-capitalization and the havoc such a situation creates in terms of those stuck with the debts, is Quebec agriculture. Having increased, in real terms, capitalization by two and a half times in the ten-year period 1971 to 1981, and now faced with declining demand, a productive capacity premised on growth has become superflous. As a result, the numbers of farmers in Quebec will probably decline by half in the last twenty years of the century as those saddled with too much debt abandon land and equipment at fire-sale prices to the high equity-to-debt ratio farmers who can afford to weather the crisis. Those who leave the land will go to the regional urban poles, or in some cases, to Ontario or to the United States.

We conclude these brief remarks on the economic consequences of the contemporary demographic evolution of Quebec by remarking that the processes invoked here are the obverse confirmation of the thesis that in Quebec economic expansion is population-fueled, and not vice versa as conventional wisdom would have it. In answer to those who point out that income per capita in Quebec has been maintained or even improved relative to Ontario, we recall that in 1950 the Quebec population was 89 percent of Ontario's and today it is less than three-quarters (74 percent).

SOCIAL

The difficulties faced in maintaining a social capital put into place in an investment perspective is an instance of the social consequences of Quebec's present demographic state. This stagnation, even decline, in the social infra-structure reflects itself in the personnel of the public administration establishment — which, when one includes all levels of government, includes over 40 percent of all employment — in which there is no expansion. No expansion — contraction is rather the rule — results in few openings and few promotions. Were the same situation to prevail in the private sector, one would get what Lise Bissonnette calls *une société bloquée.* Those who are securely installed in the bureaucratic apparatus, public or private, hesitate to venture elsewhere, knowing that the opportunities are limited and that there is no coming back. Everyone stays put and new talent does not get beyond the door. A striking example of this is the CEGEP (Junior College) establishment where, of ten thousand teachers, half would like to get out but do not dare.

In a blocked society which is tending towards greater ethnic homogeneity, the objectives of democratization and pluralism become more difficult to achieve. Democratization is easiest when "system" social mobility is possible, that is, when everyone moves up in terms of socio-economic status because the system itself is expanding. This in fact happened in Quebec in the fifties and sixties. An expanding population, an expanding economy, and more particularly in the case of Quebec's francophone population, an expanding public sector meant better jobs for all and inter-generational mobility was high. But there was also a political will to ensure democratization, particularly in health services and by providing for equality of opportunity through an enlargement of the educational establishment.

In a context of system expansion, democratization as a political *leitmotif* was in everyone's interest. In a context of non-expansion it is a different story. Every social formation, class or otherwise, looks after its own — if it did not it would cease to be an effective social force. In Quebec the rough waters being encountered by democratization (the ideological and institutional bases for which the society committed so much energy and financial resources in the sixties and seventies) are reflected in the flight from the public school. The private school sector in Quebec is the fastest growing private educational sector in Canada, having doubled its enrollment in a period in which public school enrollments actually fell. The institutionalization of the "pure science" route in high school and CEGEP as the elite corridor is another instance. Effectively, the pure-science option, beginning with the third year of high school, has replaced Greek and Latin as an elite screening process to the extent that it has become the best entree to even non-science fields. Indeed, any middle-class child who can manage it would have to be very much of a maverick not to take the pure-science option.

Pluralism and democratization are interdependent, the latter facilitating the former. Ideologically, Quebec society has, in the last twenty years, committed itself heavily to pluralism. Yet a blocked society (in at least as far as the public sector is concerned) and the decline of immigration mean a different reality. A rather dramatic instance of this was the fate reserved for the Quebec government's announced objective of increasing the presence of ethnic minorities in the public service: instead of rising from 5 to 9 percent between 1976 and 1985, the percentage actually declined. We have here an example of how corporate self-interest — the Quebec francophone civil service — in a period of contraction produces defensive postures that do not augur well for pluralism, be it ethnic or otherwise. In a small society, particularly in

a period of contraction, it is difficult to countenance the same degree of value plurality that is possible in a larger society.

Indeed, the relationship that exists between size of a society and its potential for pluralism is a crucial one. In as much as pluralism is one of the conditions of and motors of the dynamism of a modern society, the demographic stagnation of Quebec is a threat to its continued existence. The rapid evolution of Western civilization in the last twenty years has led to a splitting apart of populations into heterogenous cultural fragments, distinguished by increasingly subtle criteria of taste, lifestyle, and economic priorities. This centrifugal process is underway in Quebec as elsewhere, albeit temporarily masked by the ephemeral preeminence of certain culturally innovative groups (yesterday the technocrats of the public sector, today the "Yuppies"). The process is not endogenous, but is accelerated by the confluence in Montreal of two poles of cultural diffusion, that of the United States and France.

The risk to a small society in such a context is that none of the new cultural groups, emerging from an already limited population base, will attain the threshold at which the number of adepts will be sufficient to generate a subculture rich and dense enough to play an integrating and innovative role. Failing to attain the critical threshold, a subcultural group runs the risk of being still-born, its members overcome by social atomization and psychic depression. The diversification of cultural affinities, implacable corollary of modernism, leads in a population of limited size to disintegration.

Quebec is then, we advance, condemned to confronting the following dilemma: either arrest cultural dispersion by putting up barriers to foreign cultural influences; or expand its population, especially in as far as the younger half of the age pyramid is concerned. This dilemma is all the more cruel as regards Quebec in that it is precisely the essence of modernity — the cultural force of our time emanating from New York — that leads to a fall in fertility undermining the demographic rampart of peripheral societies. The ideological plurality, ethnic and cultural, of the great metropolitan centers which is the manifest sign of their vigour, constitutes thusly a mortal threat for the unsuspecting hinterland. Or, allegorically, the fire from the center illuminates the hearth but it scorches the forest, destroying thus by its very vigour the exterior and ultimate sources of its own regeneration. When the process is complete there are no more Jack Kirouacs to wander America, sparking a beat culture and a cultural revolution while haunted until his death by his French-Canadian origins. He did not speak English until he was fourteen.

The drama of contemporary Quebec is that in achieving the so much sought after modernism she has effectively liquidated the essential spring of her survival as a society, her demographic dynamism. Worse yet, the comforting thought that by economic development she may regain the vitality necessary to survive in a modern world will prove to have been a cruel illusion when the present consumer-oriented mini-boom dries up for want of consumers; and because of a crippling debt burden on the shoulders of a constant or declining population, public sector or government stimulated investment in construction projects ("mega" or "mini") will no longer be possible. Such an outcome might have been averted had the tertiarization of the Quebec economy been turned around by the state-as-lever economics of the Quiet Revolution, but such was not to be for reasons too complex to be invoked here. The only lever that remains — having used up the collective financial credit — is, as has always been the case, demographic; and in the short term this can only mean more

(not less) immigration. Such a prospect is not very likely given the present rather defensive and corporatist posture. Rather a shame in the light of the economic sense inherent in being able to capitalize on an over-developed infra-structure and surplus human capital in the social services, health and educational sectors; as well as the existence of better-than-ever protective cultural legislation.

Unfortunately, there is no looking back from modernism, as George Grant (1965) in his *Lament for a Nation* (in which he foresees the inevitable modernization and subsequent demise of Quebec society) so eloquently pointed out. Yet, there lies in another of the essential springs of Quebec society, its capacity for collective mobilization (itself a heritage of its pre-modern social structure and which, if the velocity and monolithic character of recent demographic change is any indication, still persists) the key to averting the inevitable.

9

Canadian Sociological Perspectives

The selections in this chapter do not so much tell you *about* Canadian society as how recent sociologists have *thought about* Canadian society. As we pointed out in the Introduction to this Part of the book, central to the scientific method is that initial theories and research findings are, through further research and thinking inevitably challenged and perhaps refined or modified. We have also described how the dominant paradigm in Canadian sociology during the 1970s emerged out of a combination of the earlier political economy perspective and a renewed interest in the theory of Karl Marx. Yet, as we might expect, many of the findings and specific theories that were part of this initial attempt to develop a distinctive Canadian sociology were, during the 1980s, subject to further examination and thinking. At the same time as there was

a rethinking of dependency theory so, more generally, was there a much broader rethinking of what came to be called "malestream" sociology. Certainly the 1980s has been a decade in which the major challenge to sociology and social science generally has come from feminist theory and research. The selections in this chapter provide you with both a critique of anglophone Canadian sociology and various indications of what may be the future direction of sociological theory and research in Canada.

In 1980, the year after his death, the Canadian Sociology and Anthropology Association established The John Porter Award to honour outstanding Canadian books in "the John Porter tradition." The 1988 recipient was William Carroll of the University of Victoria for his *Corporate Power and Cana-*

dian Capitalism. The selection in this chapter is an abridged version of the first chapter of his book. Here, in describing the development of the political economy perspective in the 1960s and 1970s, he is setting the stage for his subsequent critique of many aspects of that perspective. His central argument in the book is that these earlier dependency theorists did not adequately take into account the complexities and changing nature of world capitalism and Canada's position in that system. His subsequent argument is complex and largely beyond the scope of an introductory sociology course. What you should take away from reading the selection is some sense of how and why dependency theory developed in the late 1960s and early 1970s and its appeal to nationalistic young Canadian academics.

The second and third selections, by Gordon Laxer and Robert Brym, are reflective pieces based on their own attempts to understand Canadian society and to assess the adequacy of the earlier attempts to do so by the first wave of dependency theorists. Like William Carroll, both received their graduate training during the period Carroll has just described as so seminal in the development of Canadian sociology. In rejecting American functionalism of the 1950s and 1960s, dependency theorists were also rejecting the quest for universal sociological laws that would be independent of time and place. In the view of many Canadian sociologists, the task was to develop a distinctive Canadian sociology that reflected both our particular history and our present relationships, particularly to the United States. In somewhat different ways both Brym and Laxer are concerned with the issue of whether sociological theory and research should be able to produce, if not exactly laws, at least generalizations that are general rather than culturally and historically specific. The debate is whether it is more productive to search for

broad and, perhaps, universal laws — nomothetic explanations — or explanations of more culturally and historically unique events — idiographic explanations. In different but complementary ways, both conclude that sociology in Canada and our knowledge of Canadian society will be strengthened and enhanced when we are able to strike some balance between these competing objectives. For Brym, the way out of the "Great Identity Trap" lies in the greater use of comparative studies, which will then allow us to determine what is unique about Canada and what Canadian society and Canadian capitalism have in common with other capitalist societies. In turn, Laxer suggests that along with comparative studies is the need to use theory to explain history rather than drawing selectively upon history to confirm particular theoretical perspectives and prejudices.

The final selection by Margrit Eichler, of the Ontario Institute for Studies in Education, is a slightly abridged version of her contribution to a special issue of the *Canadian Review of Sociology and Anthropology.* This issue focused on the "the state of the art and new directions" in anglophone Canadian sociology. As we noted above, in the 1980s the major growth area in sociology has been in feminist-based theory and research. Eichler both provides you with something of the historical development of feminist approaches and assesses the contribution of feminist analyses to sociology generally. This selection is from a prolific and influential writer. In other works she has described what it is that makes a social science sexist and concludes that the ultimate goal is not a feminist-based sociology but a sociology that is nonsexist. Her conclusion in this selection is that, to date, the impact of feminism on sociology has been uneven and that the goal of a nonsexist sociology still lies in the future; hence the title of her article, "the work never ends."

The selections in this chapter are intended to introduce you to some aspects of Canadian sociology. However, as you read the selections in the following two chapters, it should be apparent to you that what you have read here has relevance both to issues of "industrialism and capitalism" and "social inequality." And, turning it round, you should try to keep in mind what the later selections tell you about Canadian society and the direction of Canadian sociology.

RELATED READINGS

S.M. Lipset: "Historical Traditions and National Characteristics: A Comparative Analysis of Canada and the United States" (Chapter 3)
Wallace Clement: "Does Class Matter? Accounting for the Direction of Canadian Society" (Chapter 11)

THE THESIS OF CANADIAN DEPENDENCY

William K. Carroll

The image of Canada as a resource hinterland dominated by powerful foreign interests in concert with a local elite of commercial capitalists is a familiar one among Canadian social scientists. Its intellectual roots can be traced to the historical studies of Harold Innis and Donald Creighton and to their basic notions of staple production at the margin of western civilization (Innis, 1970: 385) and the commercial empire of the St. Lawrence

(Creighton, 1970; see also Naylor, 1972: 1). It was not, however, until the appearance of Kari Levitt's *Silent Surrender*, (published as a monograph in 1968 and expanded to a book in 1970) that a "thesis of Canadian dependency" found its first fully articulated expression.

In *Silent Surrender*, Levitt builds on Innis's (1956, 1970) conception of the Canadian economy as a staple-producing hinterland. But Levitt also incorporates the dependency theorists' claims about the connection between foreign direct investment and underdevlopment . . . along with a Schumpeterian notion of capitalist enterprise as "entrepreneurship." A key metaphor uniting each of these ideas is that of the "new mercantilism," which Levitt associates with multinational corporations:

The central thesis of our argument is that the subsidiaries and branch plants of large American-based multinational corporations have replaced the operations of the earlier European-based mercantile venture companies in extracting the staple and organizing the supply of manufactured goods. In the new mercantilism, as in the old, the corporation based in the metropole directly exercises the entrepreneurial function and collects a "venture profit" from its investments. It organizes the collection or extraction of the raw material staple required in the metropolis and supplies the hinterland with manufactured goods, whether produced at home or "on site" in the host country (1970: 24–25).

As an external force acting on the penetrated society, the new mercantilism breaks down national ties which integrate economic and cultural life, leaving in its wake a politically balkanized and culturally homogenized hinterland, increasingly dependent on the metropole. The process embraces both the older peripheral countries like Canada, which gradually regress toward underdevelopment, and the new ones, which gain political independence but "cannot easily escape from their colonial status of economic satellites" (ibid.: 25). In the former case, Levitt recognizes three historical periods:

Canada was discovered, explored and developed as part of the French, and later the British mercantile system. It grew to independence and nationhood in a brief historical era in which goods, capital and people moved in response to forces operating in relatively free, competitive international markets. Present-day Canada may be described as the world's richest underdeveloped country (ibid.).

Levitt concentrates on an unravelling of the specific manner in which Canada has been recolonized.

Levitt ascribes a particularly important role to the changing character of foreign investment, which has always played a key role in the financing of Canadian enterprise. Financing from foreign sources may take the form of portfolio investment: that is, the selling of bonds or other credit instruments on foreign money markets, usually entitling the creditor to a fixed rate of interest over a long time period but denying the creditor any direct control over the financed enterprise. This internationalization of loan capital is the classical form of foreign investment. In combination with domestic savings, it was used to good advantage in the late nineteenth century by Canadian entrepreneurs in building a national economy on the basis of railroads, western wheat, and associated manufacturing (Levitt, 1970: 60–62).

According to Levitt, the developmental implications of the second form of foreign financing, foreign direct investment, are quite different. In this case the investor is not a money capitalist but a multinational corporation intent on controlling the production process (and of course the profits) in the "branch plants" that it establishes or takes over in hinterland countries. This form of foreign investment has become predominant in the twentieth century, particularly since the First World War. Thus, Canada's brief respite from colonial domination ended, as the United States gained power, Great Britain declined, and direct investment replaced portfolio investment in international capital flows. Levitt describes the "silent surrender" of indigenous capital which culminated in the postwar incorporation of the Canadian economy into the American empire:

In Canada economic resources are allocated primarily to suit the requirements of large scale private corporations, and the majority of these are under United States control. The constellation of the east-west economy and strong central government has largely been destroyed by the economic forces of corporate centralization and corresponding regional political fragmentation. The Canadian entrepreneurs of yesterday are the coupon clippers and hired vice-presidents of branch plants of today. They have quite literally sold out the country (ibid.: 39–40).

The data from which Levitt infers this "sell-out" are official statistics on foreign control of Canadian industry, which show dramatic increases between 1948 and 1963. Moreover, the specific industries in which foreign, mainly American, control predominates are the strategic sectors "in which metropolitan taste-formation and technological and product innovation are crucial" (ibid.: 121): automobiles, rubber, chemicals, electrical products, aircraft. Canadian-controlled industries, in contrast, "are characterized by either small production units, such as sawmills, construction concerns or certain food-processing industries or, as in the case of textiles, by thoroughly dim prospects" (ibid.: 123). Hence, in the distribution of indigenous industrial assets there is little basis for domestic control of the portion not yet committed to branch plants. Rather, foreign direct investment produces a peculiar economic structure in which Canada serves the United States both as a hinterland for raw materials and as a market for American manufactured goods (ibid.: 60).

The coming of branch-plant capitalism carries with it a transformation of the hinterland bourgeoisie. The pervasively dependent character of Canadian capitalism is reflected in a business elite that retains the trappings of economic dominance without any semblance of effective power. This is because:

The executives of branch plants are managers, not entrepreneurs. They dispose of funds, equipment and personnel within the means allocated to them. They do not formulate policy, they administer it. . . . An economy composed of branch-plant industry must of necessity lack the self-generating force which characterizes successful entrepreneurship. To the degree that Canadian business has opted to exchange its entrepreneurial role for a managerial and rentier status, Canada has regressed to a rich hinterland with an emasculated, if comfortable, business elite (ibid.: 77).

The regression, furthermore, is cumulative. Lacking its own indigenous entrepreneurship, the branch-plant economy depends increasingly on imported technology: less and less research and development are carried out in Canada. By the same token, the predominance of foreign-owned industry "chokes the development of local capitalists and inhibits the development of a local capital market" (ibid.: 109). As was mentioned earlier, branch plants tend to locate in the most dynamic sectors, diminishing opportunities for local capitalists to develop these industries. The domestic capital market is likewise crippled since control of branch-plant profits rests with the parent firm. Even where profits are reinvested in the hinterland they function merely as an extension of the metropolitan economy: the appropriated domestic savings of the hinterland. As Levitt notes, "the structure of ownership and control is such

that there are barriers to the flow of Canadian savings to finance new Canadian enterprises" (ibid.: 119).

When she turns her attention to the issue of Canada's position in world economy, Levitt grants that there are more extreme cases of dependency and underdevelopment. Some other countries actually serve as hinterlands of Canada. With this analysis, she anticipates Wallerstein's (1974) notion of a world capitalist system composed of core, peripheral, and semi-peripheral economies, as well as Galtung's (1971) concept of "go-between" powers in a structure of global imperialism, characterizing the world economic order as

a system of corporate empires, most of them centred in the United States. They extend into hinterland countries through branch plants and subsidiaries. Where the subsidiaries and affiliates are located in countries which are not themselves in a relation of metropolis to other countries, there is extreme technological, financial and organizational dependence. But there exists a range of intermediate situations where a country stands, at one and the same time, in a metropolitan relation to some countries and in a hinterland relation to others. Canada falls into this category. Both her resource and her manufacturing industries are dominated by foreign-controlled concerns. At the same time, her financial institutions, which have always been highly concentrated and powerful, have extended to the Caribbean and other countries through affiliated branches. So have some of her resource industries, such as the aluminum industry (ibid.: 103).

In the context of world economy, then, Canada is both advantaged and dependent. But for Levitt it is clearly the latter attribute that has been ascendant since the Second World War. In her analysis, Levitt describes a range of tendencies that portend increased dependence over time. The domination of domestic industry by foreign interests, the economic, political, and cultural dependence that foreign control engenders, the continued emphasis on staple production for export, the prospects of economic stagnation as indigenous entrepreneurship disappears while branch-plant profits are remitted to parent corporations are phenomena that dependency theorists have associated with the so-called Third World.

Levitt's documentation of these features in Canada was both intellectually intriguing and politically momentous. There was a definite radical edge to the identification of Canada as "the world's richest under-developed country." This radicalism, however, was based not on a concept of class exploitation but of national oppression. As such, Levitt's analysis played an important part in providing a coherent theoretical framework for the Waffle, a left-wing movement that formed within the New Democratic Party in 1969, emphasizing the need to combine the struggle for socialism with the struggle for Canadian independence from American imperialism. As Penner suggests, "there is no doubt that by the time the Waffle Manifesto was drawn up, most of the signatories, and certainly all of the authors of that Manifesto, were fully acquainted with Levitt's study, and were enormously influenced by it" (1977: 240).

In a more academic vein, *Silent Surrender* was equally influential, setting the terms of reference for a considerable volume of critical scholarship on Canadian political economy that emerged in the ensuing decade. Indeed, in introducing the thesis of Canadian dependency I have focused directly on Levitt's essay precisely because it has been paradigmatic to the formation of "a Canadian Marxist school of political economy" (Drache, 1977: 26), whose major strength has been described as "its ability to situate Canada's dependency within the world system and the power of this to account for internal development" (Clement, 1983: 142).

Contributing in no small measure to this ability was the more general dependentist approach to world political economy which formed a major current in critical western scholarship in the late 1960's and throughout the 1970's. "Dependency theory" — an eclectic combination of models converging around the concepts of dependency and underdevelopment — sought to present a comprehensive critique of foreign capitalist domination in less developed countries and colonies. The theory had its origins in two sources: (1) the radical structuralism of Prebisch (1950) and ECLA (the United Nation's Economic Commission for Latin America), cited by Levitt in *Silent Surrender*, and (2) Paul Baran's (1957) neo-Marxist analysis of the political economy of backwardness, which Andre Gunder Frank (1966) drew heavily upon in his seminal essay on the "development of underdevelopment." This second stream of dependency analysis proved particularly influential in the Canadian literature subsequent to Levitt and therefore merits closer examination.

In Frank's (1967: 30–38) original formulation, underdevelopment on the periphery was attributed to three contraditions of capitalism: (1) the hierarchical chain of metropolis-satellite relations, (2) the extraction of surplus from satellite to metropolis, and (3) historical continuity in change, conserving basic structures of dependency in spite of such apparent transformations as political independence. In later accounts Frank injected a class element into his analysis with the claim that the metropolis-satellite relation transforms the class structure of the periphery, creating a close alliance between the metropolitan power (such as the colonial administration, transnational corporations) and the local reactionary interests (composed of merchants and landowners, [1972, 1979]). Thus, for Frank, as for Baran (1957), the peripheral bourgeoisie is essentially dependent on external forces and therefore is unable to play a progressive role in national development (Angotti, 1981: 127).

In the 1970's, this notion of a sustained metropolis-hinterland alliance of ruling classes became a pivotal element in the emerging Canadian dependency school. At that time, analyses moved away from Levitt's descriptive periodization of Canadian economic history into colonial, national-developmental, and neocolonial eras, toward a stronger claim that the capitalist class in Canada has had a "colonial character" throughout its history. The works of Drache (1970, 1977), Naylor (1972, 1975), Clement (1975, 1977) and Marchak (1979) developed this theme at some length.

In "The Canadian Bourgeoisie and its National Consciousness" (1970) Daniel Drache asserted that the roots of Canadian dependence are very deep indeed, ultimately devolving to the historically comprador mission of the Canadian bourgeoisie as a mediating agent of foreign colonial powers:

The disintegration of the country cannot be seen and studied in isolation from the historic mandate of the bourgeoisie to rule Canada. . . . The bourgeoisie are in the process of dismantling the Canadian state economically, socially and culturally. By this process, Canadian history has come full circle — from a colony to a colonial dependency (1970: 4–5).

Buttressing his argument with citations of Innis, Creighton, Levitt, and Watkins, Drache argued that the Canadian bourgeoisie is different from that of Britain or the United States. Instead of aggressively searching after world markets and imperial domination, the Canadian capitalist class in the nineteenth and twentieth centuries consistently pursued as its national goal

"protection, preference, entry and accessibility into imperial markets" (1970: 9), forgoing indigenous industrialization for the safety of colonial status (ibid.). According to Drache, this form of "nationalism" is consistent with the description of the "colonial bourgeoisie" offered by Franz Fanon (1965), a bourgeoisie devoted to pacification of a subject people in the service of draining economic surplus from colony to imperial centres (Drache, 1970: 20).

A more detailed historical account consistent with this interpretation was given by Tom Naylor (1972), who followed Creighton (1937) in depicting Canadian economic history as the rise and fall of three "commercial empires." The first coincided with the era of French colonialism and ended with the British conquest of New France. The second spanned the period of direct British control, from 1760 to 1846, during which the British merchant class gained and maintained control of the land, the staple trade in fur and timber, and the emerging financial institutions. The mercantile character of this class inhibited industrial development by focusing on primary staple extraction, which maximized the surplus appropriated by Britain while minimizing local capital formation (Naylor, 1972: 6).

For Naylor, Confederation and the National Policy were merely political devices to effect the third era, one of dependent alliance with the emerging American metropole:

Far from being the response of a rising industrial capitalism striving to break down intercolonial tariff walls, Confederation and the national policy was the work of the descendents of the mercantile class which had aligned itself with the Colonial Office in 1837 to crush the indigenous petite bourgeoisie and nascent industrialists. As we indicated earlier, the direct line of descent runs from merchant capital, not to industrial capital but to banking and finance, railways, utilities, and speculation, and so on (ibid.: 16).

The linchpin of the new dependency was the tariff, whose purpose was not to protect existing industry but to expand the scale of the economy and thus the volume of commercial activity (ibid.: 20). Following Bliss (1970), Naylor claimed that what the tariff actually accomplished was an interiorization of the mercantile nexus. Instead of American-produced goods being mediated by Canadian merchants via the St. Lawrence, the new intermediation would be internal. The branch plants merely shifted the locus of metropolitan production inside the border. Produced commodities, as before, were circulated within the mercantile system "by the same merchant class in a slightly new guise" (ibid.: 21).

Throughout the twentieth century this continental system of U.S. industrial capital and Canadian commercial capital has developed, in step with the decline of Britain as a metropolitan centre. Canadian capitalists' commercial predilections led them to reproduce their wealth in the form of merchant and financial capital, while joining with American monopolies offering safe investments. Canadian investments abroad have taken on a character of "branch plant quasi-imperialism," centred around the same nonindustrial sectors that the Canadian bourgeoisie retains under its control: banking, life insurance, transportation and utilities (ibid.: 34).

Naylor's general conclusions were similar to Levitt's and were wholly pessimistic regarding the future of the Canadian bourgeoisie. The advance of branch-plant industry engenders more and more north-south linkages, decimating the east-west axis of national development by fragmenting national markets and balkanizing the state structure. Ultimately, "a Canadian capitalist state cannot survive because it has neither the material base nor the will to

survive, the former contributing substantially to the latter" (ibid.: 36).

This, then, is the final implication of Naylor's thesis. His account of Canadian political economy integrates Levitt's more descriptive analysis of "silent surrender" to the new mercantilism with a dependentist interpretation of the Canadian bourgeoisie as an essentially mercantile class, inherently receptive to, and even dependent on, such foreign domination for its own wealth.

Three years after the appearance of his seminal essay on the "Third Commercial Empire," Naylor published a copiously documented two-volume study whose main purpose was to elucidate "the roots of contemporary economic structures" in Canada through investigation of Canadian business in the period of the National Policy (Naylor, 1975: I, p. xvi). In this densely empirical work Naylor attempted to lay bare what he termed the "logic of Canadian development strategy": a history of colonialism and mercantilism whose legacy is dependent integration within the American economy. Using official statistics and a plethora of sources in the contemporary business press, Naylor characterized the era as one of "industrialization by invitation," as patent regulations and tariffs closed the border to commodity flows while keeping it open to the influx of "factors of production": first American entrepreneurs and pirated patents, later, and increasingly, direct investment (ibid.: II, p. 276).

Meanwhile, Canadian capitalists busied themselves with the financing, transportation and trade of staples such as wheat and forest products. The enormous works of infrastructure necessary to the commercial economy — canals and railways — were funded mainly by long term foreign debt, while Canadian capital flowed into short term investments in commerce and staple transport, a pattern that would persist thereafter (Naylor, 1975: I, pp. 21, 68). In the "commercial" sectors of railways, utilities, commercial banking and finance, Canadian entrepreneurs were quite successful in consolidating control and even exporting capital in the same form to the United States, West Indies, and Latin America. Yet,

this strength was not matched by industrial efforts. Rather the strength of the commercial sector went hand-in-hand with industrial weakness, by virtue of the absence of funds due to the twisting of the capital market so that funds flowed freely into commerce and staple movements, and away from industry, and because of the absence of independent innovative capacity (1975: II. pp. 282–83).

In this work, Naylor assigned less importance to the conscious metropolitan-hinterland alliance of ruling classes than to the complementary division of Canadian and American investment interests (Ryerson, 1976). However, the thrust of the study was consistent with earlier Canadian dependency analysis. The themes were familiar: the hinterland economy, specialized in staple production, the hegemony of commercial capital; and the emphasis on "industrialization by invitation" instead of the accumulation of industrial capital under domestic control. Further, they are structural features that, within the confines of Naylor's conceptual framework, would seem to have determined Canada's pattern of development throughout the twentieth century.

In *The Canadian Corporate Elite* (1975) Wallace Clement investigated the consequences of this pattern of development in the post-Second World War period, as reflected in the composition and structure of dominant Canadian corporations and their directors. Clement's work is of particular importance because of its novel synthesis of two traditions in social inquiry. On the one hand, *The Canadian Corporate Elite* replicated Porter's (1965) study of the di-

rectors of 183 dominant corporations in the early postwar period, focusing on elite social backgrounds, recruitment patterns, and interlocking directorships among 113 dominant corporations. On the other hand, Clement's systematic analysis of corporate directors was influenced by the concepts and concerns of the Canadian dependency school.

For Clement, the legacy of the new mercantilism is visible in Canada's social structure: "Primarily using the multinational corporation, U.S. economic elites have penetrated the Canadian power structure and created a distorted elite formation at the top of the economic hierarchy" (1975: 117). The formation is distorted in the sense that foreign-owned corporations are directed not by citizens and residents of Canada but by a "comprador elite" made up of their senior management and directors. The companies are ultimately controlled by a "parasitic elite": the directors and executives of foreign parent firms. Thus, on the level of the economic elite, the massive influx of U.S. direct investment has brought "compradorization," creating a situation "where capital, entrepreneurial talent and investment potentials are eliminated from the 'host' country with the effect of decreasing, rather than increasing, autonomy with development" (ibid.: 119). Ordinarily, one might expect conflict between an indigenous economic elite and a growing comprador elite, as the former attempts to defend its home market from foreign penetration. Yet in Canada,

the position of the traditional indigenous elite is reinforced by the industrial development occurring with U.S. direct investment. It is the smaller entrepreneurs based in industries which have not established themselves as dominant who feel the squeeze of U.S. penetration (ibid.: 121).

This congenial relationship between the two dominant elite fractions results from their specialization in different spheres of economic activity, the indigenous elite in circulation, the comprador in production. Clement echoed Naylor in claiming that the indigenous elite's specialization in unproductive pursuits such as finance, transportation and mass media

has stifled the development of indigenous social forces in most manufacturing and resource activities — the sectors which are actually engaged in the creation of surplus within a capitalist society. In the process, [the indigenous elite] has become allied with foreign capitalists in these surplus-creating sectors. . . . This rather unique development of elite configurations makes the Canadian corporate elite atypical compared to other industrialized liberal-democracies. . . . [T]he Canadian bourgeoisie is primarily a commercial one, engaged in circulation rather than production while in other nations the bourgeoisie is typically both industrial and financial (ibid.: 355).

Clement elaborated on his thesis about the uniqueness of Canada's corporate elite in his comparative study of the American and Canadian political economies. As a major hypothesis, Clement suggested that:

What has been forged over the past century is an alliance between the leading elements of Canadian and U.S. capital that reinforces mutually the power and advantage of each. The particular type of economic development Canada has experienced has occurred in the context of two overriding factors: the dominant place of financial capitalists in Canada and the presence of the world's largest industrial giant immediately adjacent (1977: 6).

Clement endeavored to document the emergence of this continental alliance through parallel accounts of Canadian and American economic histories.

The dominance in Canada of a financial elite and the concomitant "underdevelopment" of industrial and resource entrepreneurs were presented in stark contrast to more balanced and diversified patterns of American economic development (ibid.: 8). Arising in the early mercantile period, the indigenous capitalist class in Canada comprised a commercial elite whose mission was to intermediate in the staples trade. With further development of world commerce, and with the decline of mercantilism, Canada's leading capitalists moved into both financial institutions, and the transportation of goods (canals and railways). Their strategy for industrialization, however, was quite different. Following Naylor, Clement suggested that the commercial elite "sought out and found foreign capitalists willing and able to enter the sphere of production in Canada" (ibid.: 17), laying the framework for the development of a continental economy.

In the United States, industrialization occurred from within, and its hallmarks — the introduction of technological innovations particularly in expanding industries and the concentration and centralization of capital — were evidenced earlier. American capitalists were not encumbered by a colonial, commercial status, so the coming of the railways greatly encouraged indigenous industry by spurring production of primary metals, locomotives, and so forth, and by opening markets, particularly in the northeastern and northcentral areas (ibid.: 45). As these industries arose, financial capitalists such as J.P. Morgan became interested in them, and a tightly knit structure of interlocking directorates emerged between financial, railway, and manufacturing companies (ibid.: 46). In contrast to Canada, where a commercial elite "stultified indigenous entrepreneurs by dominating them" (Clement, 1975: 93), major financial and industrial interests in the United States effectively merged with the development of railways and heavy industry.

Although the structure of foreign ownership was already largely in place by the early 1900's, Clement followed Levitt in viewing the Second World War period as a watershed for Canadian development. During the war, the economy experienced rapid industrialization with the assistance of state aid, only to have most of the new means of production sold to U.S. industrialists at the war's end (Clement, 1977: 18). American penetration of Canadian industry intensified in the early postwar years. In 1946, 35 per cent of Canadian manufacturing and 38 per cent of mining and smelting were foreign-controlled; by 1957, 56 per cent and 70 per cent of these industries were under foreign control (ibid.: 80).

According to Clement, American ownership of Canadian industry, together with strong trade relations, provides the economic basis for a continental alliance of Canada's leading commercial capitalists and the major financial-industrial interests in the United States. But the alliance is also discernable, and is cemented, through interlocking corporate directorships:

Since the Canadian elite has overdeveloped the sphere of circulation and allowed the sphere of production to become U.S. dominated, it has put itself in the position of having to find outlets for its capital and services. This is done in part through joint directorships, and it is clear that a good many of the indigenous members have been successful in forging these relations (ibid.: 287–88).

Clement examined the extent of corporate interlocking among dominant Canadian corporations, dominant American corporations, and between the two sets of firms. He compared the density of interlocking within and between major economic sectors in each country, and found the financial sector to be densely connected to other sectors in both countries. In the U.S., the manufacturing sector is equally integrated with other sectors while in Canada the transportation-utilities sector is especially well integrated. Clement also found greater interlocking within the financial sector in Canada than in the U.S.,

and greater interlocking within U.S. manufacturing than within Canadian manufacturing. From these results he concluded that

in Canada, elite members in the sphere of circulation are thoroughly integrated with each other but have tenuous connections with the sphere of production, which is foreign controlled. They have consolidated their position only in circulation, while members of the U.S. economic elite have effectively maintained control of all economic activities in their society (ibid.: 167).

Moreover, within the Canadian elite, Clement reported that "many of those who hold indigenous positions simultaneously hold comprador positions," suggesting that "a high degree of interconnection exists in Canada between indigenous and comprador fractions of the elite" (ibid.: 287).

Finally, the pattern of interlocking between dominant American and Canadian companies showed two kinds of ties: (1) those between U.S. parents and Canadian subsidiaries and (2) those between firms controlled in Canada and firms controlled in the U.S., many of which lead from Canadian financial institutions or lead to U.S. manufacturers. These interlocks were seen as manifestations of a "continental elite" in which "the exchanges, because of the particular historical development of each nation, occur in such a way that they are mainly from Canadian finance to U.S. manufacturing and from U.S. manufacturing to Canadian finance — from strength to strength" (ibid.: 179). Clement was led by these observations to an interesting conclusion which will be contested in this study. The dependent, commercial orientation of Canada's elite, in continental alliance with the autonomous corporate interests in the United States, has produced a peculiar situation in which "the financial-industrial axis is continental for Canada but national within the United States" (ibid.).

To be sure, Naylor's and Clement's detailed investigations of the capitalist class present the most compelling empirical evidence for the thesis of Canadian dependency. Together they evoke an image of remarkable consistency in the character of the Canadian bourgeoisie, reaching from the period of the emergence of capitalism in Canada to the present day. The key element that has steered Canadian development along its exceptional path is the mercantile or commercial nature of the country's dominant capitalist fraction, itself a product of prolonged colonial status.

Other contributions to the study of Canadian dependency also adopt this line of argumentation in one form or another.... Still, several recent works have de-emphasized the role of ruling class alliances and agency in favour of structural features which have limited or distorted Canadian development, such as the "externalities" surrounding the social and economic relations of colonialism (Drache, 1983: 34) and the stultifying dependence on American technology.... In general, however, the claim that Canada occupies an unusual location in the world capitalist system, in large part owing to the commercial proclivities of its ruling class, retains considerable popularity in academe.

More than exceptional, however, dependency analysts consider Canada's position in world capitalism to be unviable. The cumulative, long-range effects of dependency bring a host of distortions and deficiencies to the Canadian economic and social structure. Instead of a balanced, diversified industrial structure, the economy is comprised of a truncated, branch-plant manufacturing sector — whose concentration in the golden triangle of southwestern Ontario exacerbates regional disparities — and an overextended raw materials sector precariously based in non-renewable resources and vulnerable to fluctuations in world markets.... The leakage of capital in the form of patriated dividends, the lack of domestic research and development, and the tendency for the employment priorities of U.S. multinationals to favour American workers lead to flagging international competitiveness, economic stagnation, and even deindustrialization.... The economic costs of dependency are great, but the social price may be even steeper: political balkanization, cultural homogenization toward metropolitan values and tastes, and the regression of the Canadian state to "a relatively dependent position within the system of U.S. hegemony" (Clement 1983, 84).....

To summarize this thesis of Canadian dependency: (1) the "new mercantilism," whereby Canada supplies the American metropole with raw material for its industries and provides a market for manufactured goods from the metropole or its branch plants is said to have emerged on the basis of a peculiar bourgeois class formation, and to have the effect of reinforcing that formation. (2) The Canadian bourgeoisie, or more properly its dominant fraction, is claimed to have been overwhelmingly commercial in its orientation, eschewing an interest in domestic industry. (3) By implication, an essential element in Canada's dependency is the deeply rooted disarticulation of indigenous financial and industrial capital, which has engendered an uneven pattern of capitalist accumulation by "overdeveloping" the financial and service sectors in tandem with the underdevelopment of domestic industry. (4) Concomitantly, the dominant commercial fraction has allied with foreign industrial interests, represented by the "comprador fraction," and has become dependent for its own wealth on these surplus-producing clients. Finally, (5) Canada's branch-plant economy may well contain the seeds of economic stagnation and politico-cultural decay: a bitter "harvest of lengthening dependency" (Levitt, 1970).

The task of this study is not to evaluate all of these claims. Rather, our empirical analysis focuses on the basic issues of class and capital accumulation. I will attempt to refute the claims of Naylor, Clement and others about the commercial character of the dominant bourgeois fraction, its disarticulation from indigenous industrial capital, and its dependent alliance with American interests in the period since the Second World War.

But a strictly empirical critique of so wide-ranging a thesis is clearly insufficient. Indeed, the Canadian dependency school has already provoked numerous critiques that question the particular relevance of dependency analysis to Canada. . . . In these works, however, the copious international literature which questions the validity of dependency as a general theoretical construct has not been systematically brought to bear on the Canadian case, nor has much attention been devoted to the articulation of a theoretical alternative capable of integrating the patterns of Canadian capitalist development within a qualitatively different perspective on world capitalism. To understand the problems of the Canadian dependency interpretation and to formulate a more adequate account, we must widen the scope of our analysis beyond the North Atlantic Triangle that has formed the focus of Canadian dependency analyses. We must, in short, situate the Canadian political economy within a framework that faithfully reflects the general dynamics of world capitalist development.

THE GREAT CANADIAN IDENTITY TRAP: IMPLICATIONS FOR THE COMPARATIVE STUDY OF CLASS AND POWER

Robert J. Brym

The Great Canadian Identity Trap is a compelling puzzle that pervades Canadian intellectual life. It originated in the unease many Canadians felt about the U.S. when plans were devised back in 1775 to push the American Revolution northward. Its influence is felt most sharply today in reactions to the Canada-U.S. free trade agreement, which many Canadians regard as a belated American victory by other means. It consists of a thesis and an antithesis that are equally appealing to most Canadians. The thesis is that English-Canadians are just like Americans. The antithesis is that English-Canadians are fundamentally different from Americans. A surprisingly large part of Canadian intellectual life consists of defending the thesis, defending the antithesis or oscillating back and forth depending on your opponent's opinion. For example, the Great Canadian Identity Trap has helped shape the contours of Canadian research on stratification and power — and not necessarily with uniformly positive results, as my use of the word "trap" suggests.

In Canadian stratification and power research, The Great Canadian Identity Trap has operated in two successive phases: the first liberal, the second Marxist. The publication of John Porter's *The Vertical Mosaic* in 1965 signalled the start of the

"The Great Canadian Identity Trap: Implications for the Comparative Study of Class and Power" by Robert J. Brym appearing in *The Canadian Journal of Sociology*, Volume 14(4), 1989. By permission of *The Canadian Journal of Sociology*.

liberal phase. Porter borrowed theoretically from mainstream American sociology of the 1950s and 1960s. He agreed with Parsons, Lipset, and others that patterns and rates of mobility derive from the way core societal values interact with individuals' achieved characteristics. Substantively, he concurred that the U.S. is an achievement-oriented society in which people's talents are translated into rewards through the operation of a highly accessible education system and a free market in labour. But, Porter held, Canada falls short of that American ideal. The reason: Canada's more conservative value system allows ascriptive characteristics to exert greater influence on status attainment. In Porter's opinion, Canada is less egalitarian than the U.S., as is evident from the social composition of Canadian elites, the country's comparatively low rate of net upward mobility, and the strong and persistent relationship in Canada between socio-economic location and ethnic origin.

Porter's work greatly stimulated the Canadian study of elites and social mobility. But for the better part of a decade after the publication of *The Vertical Mosaic* many researchers succeeded in demonstrating that in certain respects emphasized by Porter, Canadians are not in fact all that different from Americans. For example, the National Mobility Study, essentially a replication of the Blau and Duncan mobility model, was undertaken by a team of southern Ontario researchers in the early 1970s (Boyd et al., 1985). Two of their most noteworthy findings are that the rate of net upward mobility in Canada is actually about the same as or higher than that in the U.S.; and that ethnicity is not a significant predictor of intergenerational mobility net of other causes. Other reseachers produced similar results or found that Canadian elites are considerably more permeable than Porter thought.

Just as proponents of the view that Canadians are similar to Americans appeared to be a position to declare victory, however, a sea-change in the study of inequality and power took place. As in the U.S. and elsewhere, the mid-1970s witnessed a series of empirical and theoretical assaults on the liberal assumptions of earlier research traditions. For example, the status attainment model was scored for ignoring the structural constraints imposed on mobility by class, gender, race, and segmented labour markets. Those structural constraints were eventually shown to explain more of the variation in income and status attainment than do years of education, father's occupation, and the like (Ornstein, 1983). The debate familiar to those ensnared in the Great Canadian Identity Trap thus continued — but in new, Marxist guise.

The reorientation of stratification and power research in Canada towards the study of structured social inequality was entrenched by the publication in 1975 of Wallace Clement's *The Canadian Corporate Elite.* Clement and his colleagues held that vastly powerful American businesses had established controlling interest in many Canadian resource and manufacturing enterprises in order to secure a source of raw materials and a market for manufactured goods. The Canadian economy therefore exhibits an extraordinarily high level of foreign control; substantial natural wealth and profit is being drained out of the country; and the growth of the Canadian economy is sharply limited. What is more, Canadian financial capitalists are lending money to American multinationals and influencing Canadian state policy for their benefit, thereby helping to weaken Canadian capitalism. In this "left nationalist" schema, as it came to be known, Canadian financiers were well situated for influencing government: allegedly, a striking peculiarity of the members of the Canadian capitalist class is their very close personal ties to state personnel. These close ties presumably help account for the relatively undeveloped nature of the Canadian welfare state and its weak redistributive role (Panitch, 1977b).

The left nationalists thus characterized Canada not merely as different from the U.S. but as a unique historical entity — a "rich dependency." However, by the late 1970s and early 1980s a group of Marxist "internationalists" began publishing research findings that seriously challenged this interpretation. The internationalists regarded Canada as merely one more advanced capitalist country, evolving, like the U.S. according to certain universal principles of social development. In this manner, just as liberal sociologists had earlier fallen into the Great Canadian Identity Trap, so did the Marxists.

The internationalists (see especially Carroll, 1986) pointed out that during the 1970s the level of foreign ownership of the Canadian economy declined substantially while the level of foreign investment by Canadian-controlled companies rose markedly. In their judgement, the Canadian experience thus demonstrates how government action and the multiplier effects of foreign direct investment enable less developed countries to *reduce* dependency and experience vigorous capitalist growth, particularly if the dominant capitalist power finds itself weakened, as the United States did from the 1970s on. On the basis of this observation and their analyses of directorship interlocks the internationalists concluded that many Canadian entrepreneurs are independent, medium-scale players in global capitalism whose rise to maturity has been assisted by the Canadian state. Supposedly, the capitalist system imbues the state with certain functional imperatives, so that it helps legitimize capitalism, ensure capital accumulation and, if necessary, employ coercion to control protest.

This line of argument did not, of course, go unchallenged. But rather than reciting a list of criticisms of structuralism and the supposed logic of capitalism, I want to end my caricature here, circa 1985, and reflect a little on what the liberal and Marxist phases of Canadian stratification and power research tell us about the virtues and limitations of the Great Canadian Identity Trap. Its great virtue, I think, is that by posing questions about the nature of national identity and the conditions of national survival it has prompted students of inequality and power, whether liberal or Marxist, to research macro-sociological processes of development and make them mainstream concerns. In a discipline that still knows well the problems associated with grand theory and abstracted empiricism, that is no small accomplishment. But the Great Canadian Identity Trap nonetheless remains a trap insofar as it pulls researchers towards one of two extremes — towards ideographic particularism or nomothetic universalism (Laxer, 1989b). The particularists stress Canada's unique features, and the explanations they proffer therefore have little currency outside the Canadian case. The universalists stress Canada's commonality with other countries, especially the U.S., and the explanations they proffer therefore fail to capture important cross-national differences in a whole range of phenomena associated with stratification and power. Another way of stating this problem is that the ideographic and nomothetic extremes severely truncate not only the sorts of answers that can be given but also the kinds of questions that can be asked about stratification and power in Canada.

In my judgement there are exactly two methods of getting out of the Great Canadian Identity Trap. The first involves detailed historical comparisons of a few cases chosen for their theoretical relevance. The second involves comparisons within entire populations of theoretically relevant countries. Let me now illustrate these two methods by referring to the work of some Canadian sociologists who have begun to move beyond the confines of the Great Canadian Identity Trap.

A good example of the first, historical approach is Gordon Laxer's (1989a) recent attempt to explain the roots of foreign ownership in Canada. He reasons that Canada, a late industrializer, should be compared with other late industrializers that managed to avoid the pitfalls of high levels of foreign ownership and a weak manufacturing base — countries like Sweden and Japan. According to Laxer, nineteenth-century Sweden and Japan had strong, ethnically homogeneous agrarian classes that exerted unintended but beneficial effects on industrialization. For example, in Sweden and Japan agrarian "land hunger" encouraged military expansionism. In consequence, the state took an interventionist role in the economy and became directly involved in the manufacture of military wares. Out of the countryside there also issued a demand for the breakup of old commercial banking systems, oriented towards short-term loans, and the creation of investment banks, oriented towards long-term loans. This had the unintended consequence of making domestic capital more readily available for industrial investment. In Canada, by contrast, farmers were ethnically disunited and politically weak. The French-English conflict so completely overshadowed class-based politics at the turn of this century that the farmers had relatively little influence on public policy. State intervention in the economy was thus minimal while domestic, long-term investment capital was scarce so that foreigners — mainly British at first, then Americans — made up the shortage.

What is striking about Laxer's book is that, although his *Problemstellung* is clearly borrowed from the left nationalists,

he takes the heretical step of comparing Canada with countries other than the U.S. He chooses cases for comparison because of their theoretical relevance, not because of the basically ideological dictates of the Great Canadian Identity Trap. This has at least three advantages over comparisons made for essentially ideological reasons. First, it enables him to propose a novel and compelling answer to the question of why Canada has a weak, largely foreign-controlled manufacturing sector. Second, it allows him to reject the view, shared by both left nationalists and internationalists, that Canadian history is largely made elsewhere, that it derives either from the demands of an imperial centre or the imperatives of global capitalism. Instead, Laxer shows how *domestic* class forces contributed substantially to the pattern of Canadian economic growth. Third, Laxer's approach has the advantage of demonstrating that Canadian history is not rigidly determined by these outside forces but is shaped in the political arena by the interaction of human choice with social context (cf. Myles, 1988). The Great Canadian Identity Trap demands that one compare Canada with the U.S. whether for purposes of stressing Canada's differences or similarities; but the benefits just listed all derive, I repeat, from Laxer's decision to ignore this demand and make theoretically appropriate comparisons.

Laxer's methodology is essentially Weberian: by comparing in depth a few carefully chosen countries that have similar starting points and dissimilar end points he is able to isolate a set of plausible reasons for their different trajectories. The limits of his method become apparent, however, if one wants to generalize beyond his few cases. Obviously, there are late-industrializing countries with solid, indigenously controlled manufacturing bases that never had strong agrarian classes in Laxer's sense. Examples include Israel and

Hong Kong. If one were interested in developing a general explanation for successful late industrialization, one would clearly have to examine the entire population of late-industrializing countries.

That is the second way out of the Great Canadian Identity Trap: analyzing entire populations of theoretically relevant countries in order to formulate and test generalizations. The method is well illustrated by the work of John Myles, one of Canada's leading comparativists. In his well-known study of public pension systems in fifteen capitalist democracies, Myles (1984) shows that where working classes are comparatively powerful, welfare spending is relatively high. If Canada ranks near the bottom of OECD countries in level of welfare spending, that is partly because of the country's low levels of working-class unionization and working-class representation in federal cabinets. In contrast, as other researchers have shown, the Canadian capitalist class is relatively powerful: by international standards, the economy is fairly highly oligopolized and, as Michael Ornstein demonstrates in his recent eleven-nation network analysis of corporate boards of directors, interlocking among top capitalists is relatively dense (Ornstein, 1989). The high capitalist-to-labour power ratio has so far capped popular support for Canada's social democratic party at about a fifth of the electorate (Brym, 1986; 1989; Brym, Gillespie, and Lenton, 1989). This prevents the state from acting decisively to more equitably redistribute benefits; and such state action is further constrained by the country's decentralized federal structure, which limits tripartite societal-level bargaining (O'Connor and Brym, 1988). Seen in this comparative light, the Canadian state is neither strikingly peculiar, as the left nationalists claim, nor is it just like every other capitalist state, as the internationalists maintain. Myles and others have demonstrated

that its redistributive impact is about what we should expect it to be given the contemporary and historical distribution of class power in Canada.

Refinements are clearly needed in the methodology employed by Myles and other comparativists. In particular, researchers who want to make generalizing comparisons must come to grips with the fact that they often — and problematically — compare *cross-nationally* in order to make *historical* arguments. It nonetheless seems reasonable to state the main lesson of the past twenty-five years of comparative stratification and power research in Canada as follows: We will learn most about Canada if we make comparisons either in order to isolate important causal variables, as illustrated by Laxer, or in order to generalize and specify the limits of causal arguments, as illustrated by Myles. On the other hand, we will be in trouble if the Great Canadian Identity Trap holds sway, if Canadian students of stratification and power are ideologically compelled to do research whose stated or unstated purpose is to stress either Canada's uniqueness or its similarity to other countries. In the latter case our knowledge is likely to advance very slowly indeed, because the Great Canadian Identity Trap inhibits the choice of theoretically appropriate comparisons and the formulation of sound and broad generalizations about variations in the way class and power interact across nations and over time.

THE SCHIZOPHRENIC CHARACTER OF CANADIAN POLITICAL ECONOMY

Gordon Laxer

In the 19th century, orthodox liberal economics was called the "dismal" science while the revolutionary doctrines of Marx were full of hope about the coming triumph of a new, better social order. In the late 20th century the roles have been reversed. Neoconservative economists exude an optimism that society will be transformed to a pure, market-driven capitalism. In the 1980s, business has become "sexy." Radical political economists on the other hand are full of pessimism. Mostly they demonstrate that whatever the working class does, it always loses.

Canadian political economy shares the pessimism of Western Marxism in the late 20th century, but its cheerlessness is also derived from a homegrown perspective, known as the staples approach. Some scholars, the "new political economists," have combined the staples approach with what they conceive of as Marxism, to produce a Canadian version of dependency theory. This approach is pessimistic too. Instead of detailing how the workers always lose, they show how Canada is stuck in a perpetual trap of resource-exporting, foreign ownership, and economic and political dependence.

Canadian political economy may appear to be a coherent, unified perspective with its focus on such issues as the role of the state, capitalist co-ordination and conflict, the welfare state and the role of unions, class culture and the nature of economic

development. The language of discourse is Marxist. But beneath the surface are two basic perspectives, developed in the 1970s and in their basic assumptions still to a large extent stuck in the 1970s. They are the perspectives of the new political economists and of those who consider themselves pure Marxists — whether they come from the instrumentalist, structuralist or critical tendencies. (Some political economists, often the most creative ones, go beyond the confines of these perspectives). The two perspectives share few common assumptions. For many Marxists, Canada is largely a place in which to demonstrate the workings of general Marxist laws. They are the nomothetic "internationalist" theorists. On the other side, the new political economists start from nationalist and historical assumptions and emphasize the uniqueness of Canadian political and economic structures. Issues are explained by external influences and factors which are peculiar to Canada. They are the idiographic historians. Instead of learning from each other, debates within Canadian political economy have tended to encapsulate each side in methodological extremism. Much of the work is directed toward using history to validate theories rather than trying to understand and explain history. The debates often seem to be a dialogue of the deaf.

In this paper I examine the one-sided natures of the explanations of both the "pure" Marxist and the new political economy approaches. This is not a major review article or survey of the work of Canadian political economists. My aim is more modest — to comment in an editorial way on Canadian political economy's basic approaches and assumptions. In attempting to clearly differentiate the two basic perspectives, I create ideal types. All such endeavours are open to the charge of drawing caricatures to which individual scholars do not conform precisely. I plead guilty at the

From "The Schizophrenic Character of Canadian Political Economy" by Gordon Laxer. Published in *The Canadian Review of Sociology and Anthropology* Volume 26: 1, February 1989. By permission of *The Canadian Review of Sociology and Anthropology*.

outset. My defence is that the exercise aids clarification.

The new political economy perspective emerged in the late 1960s and early 1970s amidst an intellectual and political climate conducive to an acceptance of its main tenets. Those were the days of popular disaffection with American society, ranging from issues of the Vietnam War to the role of multi-national corporations. The world had witnessed a decade of anti-colonial struggles against western empires. In Canada, national and regional movements to some extent mirrored these international events as Quebec nationalism, English-Canadian nationalism and western and Newfoundland regionalism reacted against and inflamed each other. Young political economists in English-speaking Canada absorbed currents from Marxism, radical liberalism and dependency approaches.

Like many of their counterparts in the Third World, new political economists in Canada rejected orthodox western Marxism whose theories were derived largely from historical experiences in the centre of the developed capitalist world. The assumption, common amongst American and Western European Marxists, that capitalist economies were all moving in the same unilinear direction, did not seem to apply to Canada in important respects. Canada was not progressing away from a primary commodities economy; foreign ownership was at the highest of the levels in the Third World and an indigenous bourgeoisie with a distinct national consciousness was not in evidence. As well, nationalism, of an anti-imperialist kind along the lines of national liberation movements in the Third World, appeared to many Canadians to have progressive rather than reactionary potential.

In this context it is not surprising that some political economists (in English Canada) rediscovered an earlier, non-Marxist intellectual tradition in Canada that addressed the issues of Canadian pecularities and dependence described above (Drache,

1978). This was the staples approach of Harold Innis, W.A. Mackintosh and others. Begun in the 1920s, the staples approach or "old political economy" was an establishment movement that became dominant in the discipline of economics. Adherents had close connections with private research foundations and governments of the day, acting as advisors and teachers of civil servants (Creighton, 1957; Berger, 1976).

The old political economy was guided by several questions, all of which grew out of nationalist concerns. First, why did resource exports continue to shape the Canadian economy or, in other words, why had Canada not yet matured economically? Second, why were so many of the decisions about the Canadian economy regarding capital, technology, management and demand, made outside Canadian borders? Third, did Canada make sense as a geographic entity and under what conditions did the regions become economically united or fractured (Innis, 1973: 209)? In attempting to answer these questions, the old political economy adopted what would now be considered an interdisciplinary approach.

The old political economy had four main assumptions:

1. Canadian history could be understood best by Canada's persistent search for staple products with ready markets in more advanced countries. This was an emphasis on the external determination of much that happened in Canada. Canada should not be studied, it was thought, as a self-contained economy using Ricardian assumptions of international trade, namely that capital and labour were relatively immobile. Staple-exporting sectors were analysed in their global contexts. Canada was an "open economy."

2. The role of elites was emphasized, reflecting the political dominance of "Toryism" in Canada (in reality Whiggism) in the 19th and early 20th centuries (Whitaker, 1977). Canadian business elites were generally not portrayed as independent actors but rather as working in close connection with foreign business interests. Bankers, merchants and resource capitalists were seen to be more powerful than industrialists. The state acted as "capital equipment" (Innis, 1973: 260).

3. History was thought to be the key to understanding Canada. Historical study was a way to escape from the assumptions of orthodox economics which had developed in the context of the old world of Western Europe. "A new country presents certain definite problems which appear to be more or less insoluble from the standpoint of the application of economic theory as worked out in the older highly industrialized countries," wrote Innis early in his career, thus mapping out his life's ambition to create a new approach to the study of new world societies. "Economic history consequently becomes more important as a tool by which the economic theory of the old countries can be amended" (Innis, 1973: 3). Innis' view that the new world had unique characteristics, making comparison with the old world of Europe less than fruitful, was widely shared. The idea that America was different, was a classless utopia, was the future, dates back to early colonial days. Innis took up the theme of new world exceptionalism and gave it a different content.

4. The important explanatory factors were geographic, with great emphasis on waterways, economic in the neo-classical sense and technological. Cultural factors were included but were usually conceived narrowly as consumer taste, technique and the centralized character of government and business institutions. Internal political and social events, though often discussed, were hardly ever considered causal factors. Innis' "history, as history, was dehumanized" (Berger, 1976: 98).

The old political economy went into eclipse in the 1950s, a victim of the shift in western economics towards econometrics. Mathematics and deduction replaced historical inquiry into such matters as changes in technology and institutions (Kuttner, 1985), the objects of study of the old political economy.

When the new political economy emerged a decade or more later, it had a very different look. Gone were the department chairmen and other pillars of the academic establishment who had led the old political economy in the 1930s to 1950s. In their place were radical academics, most of them young, who struggled against the mainstream of their disciplines. Glen Williams (1988) has pointed to basic differences from the old political economy. Whereas Innis had conceived of Canada as being on the margin of western civilization, the new political economy saw Canada on the periphery (i.e., Third World) of international capitalism. Innis' constraints against economic diversification became more rigid blockages to development in the new political economy. Instead of the Canadian state acting positively to adapt to international fluctuations, it was seen to be a puppet of foreign capital (Williams, 1988: 122).

The new political economy was influenced by elite theory as interpreted by C. Wright Mills (1956) and John Porter (1965) and mixed with a crude version of Ralph Miliband's approach to the state (1969). It spoke in Marxist and anti-imperialist tones.

Looks can be deceiving, however. The aura of dissent was there, but the epistemology was much the same. If the new political economy was more rigid and closer to dependency theory, it still shared the old political economy's assumptions about the important causal factors in history:

1. External control of Canadian life. The sources of foreign influence were seen to be multinational corporations, imperial states and metropolitan centres of finance.
2. The emphasis on elite power was still there. Capitalists of various sorts were portrayed as dominant while popular influence was thought to be nearly non-existent. The contest between internal Canadian classes was unimportant (Naylor, 1972: 2). The Canadian state was seen as a spokesman for external and internal capitalists, with little independent input on its own (Watkins, 1977).
3. Historical analysis was crucial, not for Innis' purpose of developing a new theory for the understanding of new world societies, but because it was thought that Canada occupied a unique place in the world. Canada was a western advanced country, yet it shared many features with the Third World. Canada was exceptional because it was so overwhelmed economically, politically and culturally by the American Empire. But for all the emphasis on Canadian history, the new political economy assumed that whatever happened in Canada had an external cause. Canadian uniqueness stemmed from its distinct relation to the United States. Canada's history was the history of a victim.
4. Despite its Marxist language, the new political economy attributed continuity and change to the same factors as the old political economy: technological dependence on multinational corporations (Naylor, 1975: 38–64), geography — especially proximity to the U.S., economics as the power of capital to determine events and culture in the limited sense of the culture of corporate capitalism. Again, except for the role of Canadian elites, internal social and political factors were largely ignored. Victims do not make their own history. The old and new political economies also shared a mood: determinism and pessimism.

We can now return to our earlier discussion comparing structural-functional Marxism in English Canada with the new and old political economies. Assumptions about the causal factors are virtually the mirror image of those of the new and old political economies. Furthermore the whole object of inquiry is different. Rather than attempt to explain Canada's economic development and its place in the international political economy, the structural-functional Marxists are concerned primarily with the social order/revolution question. The latter's assumptions about the causal factors in history are:

1. While it is assumed that Canada is part of an international capitalist order, the business class and state are seen as largely autochtonous or indigenous, as in other advanced capitalist countries. This view contrasts with the dependent or colonial characterization of the Canadian bourgeoisie in the new political economy.
2. Rather than focussing exclusively on the capitalists, there is a healthy

examination of other classes and of class relations.

3. While there has been a lot of historical analysis, much of it begins with the ahistorical goal of confirming Marxist theory. Recently there has been a move away from such an ideologically-bound starting point.

4. Rather than emphasize geography, technology and economics in the narrow sense, Marxists concentrate on class relations, politics, ideology and economics as it relates to class struggle.

The new political economy and the dominant tendency in English Canadian Marxism, that of structural-functionalism, tend to methodological extremism. The former emphasizes the unique aspects of Canada while the latter tends to view Canada as only a place in which Marxist laws unfold. These are the two ends of the pole of idiographic and nomothetic inquiry. Each extreme leads to arid studies since a proper balance is not achieved. (Some studies in each camp have been fruitful in spite of themselves because in practice they have deviated from their theoretical assumptions.) This paper has been written to suggest ways to reach that balance.

The new political economy has achieved little in the 1980s and some of the early adherents have moved on to other things. This was the fate of the old political economy too, as some of the leading staples scholars moved away from Canadian inquiries.

This is a natural tendency for idiographic studies, as the best scholars pursue the connection between patterns observed in Canada and those occurring elsewhere.

To renew itself, the new political economy needs to modify several assumptions which have more to do with belief than with the reality of Canada's international posi-

tion. The idea of external control of Canadian life is too rigidly held. It is easy to blame others. George Grant (1965: 43) understood the internal basis of foreign capital's power in Canada: "foreign capital is able to determine possible governments by incarnating itself as an indigenous ruling class." The danger to Canadian independence lies largely within Canada itself.

The emphasis on elite control is also overly determinist. While popular forces have as yet failed to coalesce at the federal level because of regional and national divisions, their impact can be seen in the consistent level of support for the social service state and the extent of opposition to the 1988 Canada U.S. trade deal.

The range of causal factors in the new political economy must be broadened beyond those of traditional economic history to include politics as a more independent factor, social movements and culture broadly conceived. The new political economy's historical emphasis is its saving grace.

The structural-functional Marxists also need to make some changes. The first thing to do is to discover the proper use of history. The object of scholarly inquiry is to understand and explain history, not to confirm theory. Theory is a guide to understanding history and remains useful only as long as it does this. If, on the contrary, history is used to confirm theory, it is a retreat into belief or religion and stands in the way of genuine understanding. Happily, an increasing number of Canadian Marxists are "doing" good history.

In discovering history, the pursuit of developing a theory of the state should be abandoned as a wrong-headed goal. It is like pursuing a theory of history. "Doing" good history usually results in better theory than "doing" theory because historical interpretations and assumptions are not formed before finding out what was actually going on (Stinchcombe, 1978: 4, 17). I am not advocating the opposite extreme of abandoning theory. Theory, however, should be seen as relative, limited in its scope and modifiable.

The state cannot be understood in isolation from class formation and class consciousness. E.P. Thompson (1968: 10) has argued the impossibility of developing a law about class consciousness:

The class experience is largely determined by the productive relations into which men are born — or enter involuntarily. Class consciousness is the way in which these experiences are handled in cultural terms: embodied in traditions, value-systems, ideas, and institutional forms. If the experience appears as determined, class-consciousness does not. We can see a logic in the responses of similar occupational groups undergoing similar experiences, but we cannot predicate any law. Consciousness of class arises in the same way in different times and place, but never in just the same way.

If Thompson is right about classes and class consciousness, then we cannot develop a law about the state. States must be understood historically.

Structural-functional Marxists should also modify their almost exclusive focus on the social order/revolution question. It was this fixation which led them to adopt the same epistemology as Talcott Parsons and other conservative functionalists who were also mesmerized by social order because they worried about threats to capitalist society. Many aspects of political economy, including Canada's place in the international community, cannot be understood well by reference to social order/revolution questions.

There are ways to bridge the bifurcation of the uniqueness versus general laws approaches in Canadian political economy. The comparative-historical method is a promising approach. Instead of assuming that either everything in Canada is unique or else that nothing in Canada is unique, we can do comparative work on a whole range of questions to see in what ways events and patterns in Canada are similar to and different from those in other countries. One group of Canadian Marxists, the labour studies group around *Labour/Le Travail* already adopt this approach, at least implicity. Outside Canada, the historicist school of writers such as Skocpol et al. (1985) and the democratic socialist school, centred in Sweden, are using comparative studies creatively.

Comparative studies must be approached with sensitivity to be fruitful. To think of Canada as a Third World country is absurd. But to go to the other extreme and consider Canada as just another relatively independent, advanced capitalist power may also be wrong, at least for certain questions. The country or countries with which Canada can best be compared will vary from question to question. For certain political questions, the "white dominions" may be best, while for economic development questions, perhaps the 'late follower' countries are best (Laxer, 1985).

Another way to cure the schizophrenic character of Canadian political economy is to end the ideologically-motivated studies. The first step to mental liberation is to forget trying to prove that Marx or Innis or any other intellectual icon was right or wrong. As Max Weber (1949: 103) wrote:

All specifically Marxian "laws" and developmental constructs — insofar as they are theoretically sound — are ideal types. The eminent, indeed unique, heuristic significance of these ideal types when they are used for the assessment of reality is known to everyone who has ever employed Marxian concepts and hypotheses. Similarly, their perniciousness, as soon as they are thought of as empirically valid or as real (i.e., truly metaphysical) "effective forces," "tendencies," etc. is likewise known to those who have used them.

The way out for Canadian political economy is for scholars to read history closely, armed with a range of theoretical questions. We should not be afraid to abandon preconceived notions that do not stand the test of history. Perhaps in this way Canadian political economy will abandon its pessimistic mood.

AND THE WORK NEVER ENDS: FEMINIST CONTRIBUTIONS

Margrit Eichler*

This paper briefly describes the historical development of feminist approaches to anglophone sociology within the overall context of feminist scholarship by identifying four distinct but overlapping stages of development. Salient issues in feminist analyses and contributions of feminist theory to various sub-areas of sociology and to sociology in general are noted. Finally, some current epistemological considerations in feminist scholarship are briefly discussed.

Historical Development of the Field

In discussing feminist studies as having gained some modest legitimacy within the university system, we consider quite a re-

From "And the Work Never Ends: Feminist Contributions" by Margrit Eichler. Published in *The Canadian Review of Sociology and Anthropology*, Volume 22: 5, 1985. By permission of *The Canadian Review of Sociology and Anthropology*.

* I would like to thank Linda Williams who has acted as research assistant for this article, and I would like to thank the following people for reading and commenting on a version of this paper: Frieda Forman, Jane Gaskell, Rhonda Lenton, Meg Luxton, Thelma McCormack, Mary O'Brien, Dorothy Smith, Marylee Stephenson, and Jill Vickers.

cent phenomenon. If, by contrast, we consider feminist studies as the struggle of individual women questioning central assumptions of male-generated, -oriented and -dominated theories and creating alternative approaches to social reality, we discuss not a new phenomenon but one with a long history. . . . This history is certainly of longer standing and greater depth than we can currently appreciate, since most of it has probably not yet been reclaimed from silence and some may be irretrievably lost.

In Canada, modern feminist approaches to scholarship can be dated to the beginning of the 1970s. As in the U.S. and elsewhere, they were an outgrowth of the women's liberation movement which had reemerged in the late 1960s in North America. The women's liberation movement identified women as an oppressed group, demanded equality for women in all social, economic, cultural, judicial, and sexual matters, and looked critically at scientific and other theories to examine to what degree they bolstered and maintained patriarchy while at the same time often claiming to be value-free and neutral.

Considering that we deal with a relatively short period of time during which feminist scholarship emerged as an academic perspective (less than a decade and a half at this writing) and given that feminist approaches continue to evolve, it is somewhat risky to attempt any periodicization. The following periodicization is only preliminary, developed midstream in time rather than at the end of time's course.

Roughly, we can distinguish four stages in feminist approaches, which, although overlapping and not always clearly separable, do identify shifting emphases at the *collective* level, if *not* necessarily at the level of the individual scholar. The four stages can be identified as: 1) a focus on women; 2) a focus on sex roles (gender roles, gender relations); 3) the development of a feminist approach; and 4) a focus on epistemological concerns. These foci are not mutually exclusive and continue to co-exist. Furthermore, two continuous threads crosscut the four stages: one is a critical attitude towards sexism in sociology itself, and an effort to expose and overcome this bias by tranforming the discipline itself. The other is to assume an intentionally Canadian focus which derives from the need to collect new and pertinent data. This second tendency has greatly enriched Canadian studies since the very beginning of feminist studies in Canada.

THE FIRST STAGE: A FOCUS ON WOMEN

On 28 September 1970, the Report of the Royal Commission on the Status of Women was officially released. This report constitutes the first comprehensive look at the status of women in Canada. Its policy analyses and recommendations remain important and relevant to Canadians today. Subsequent to the report itself, a number of background studies were published which in their totality must be seen as the beginning of a scholarship which is concerned with understanding women's situation in Canada. . . .

The first credit courses at the university level which focussed on women (or alternatively, on sex roles, see next section) were probably offered in 1971.

At the time, besides the Report of the Royal Commission and some other government reports and a popular book on women and the law (Zuker and Callwood, 1971) there were virtually no other materials available on Canadian women. Academic scholarship on women in Canada was effectively non-existent until only recently.

Problems experienced by faculty teaching courses on women included an extreme lack of Canadian materials, the need to construct reading lists with literature from other cultures, lack of systematically structured access to even these scarce sources

(the first bibliographies were just being prepared at that moment), and lack of models around which courses could be structured. Typically, faculty (usually female and often junior in rank) who developed courses on women were quite isolated. More often than not they received little or no institutional support and sometimes had to face concerted administrative resistance and trivialization by colleagues.

Coupled with the two other problems generally experienced by faculty in Canada at the time, namely the geographic and social isolation of one Canadian university from the other (sometimes described as an intellectual North-South orientation in lieu of an East-West orientation) and a general lack of Canadian materials in the social sciences, the few who tried to collect and create knowledge about the position of women in Canada almost inevitably worked in a non-cumulative manner.

In order to minimize duplication of work and provide a means of communication for feminist scholars, Eichler and Stephenson founded the *Canadian Newsletter of Research on Women* in 1972. (The newsletter continues to exist and to serve this function under the name of *Resources for Feminist Research*.) In 1972, the first session on women was held at the annual meeting of Canadian Sociology and Anthropology Association, and in 1973 the first two academic books on women in Canada appeared (Stephenson, 1973; Henshel, 1973).

THE SECOND STAGE: A FOCUS ON SEX ROLES (GENDER ROLES)

While the first feminist approach clearly centred on women as a subject group, arising from a concern with the lack of the most basic sociological information on women in Canada, the second stage, which followed closely on the heels of the first, was characterized by the need to place women in a larger sociologial context — a context constructed around the concept of sex roles. Two problems with this approach soon became evident: a problem with the concept of "roles": and a problem with the concept of "sex." A focus on roles does not permit a serious discussion of systemic problems encountered by women, such as economic discrimination, violence against women, etc. In other words, male power over women cannot be adequately dealt with under the heading of sex roles, just as race relations cannot be understood as "race roles," since the important issue is not one of behaviour expectations, but of systemic variables which keep women in subordinate positions.

The problem with the first word of the conceptual pair, "sex," is at the very core of accepting sociology as a way of understanding social life. Sex is a biological variable, not a social variable. In order to distinguish between biological sex differences (i.e., primary and secondary sex differences) and attendant behaviours (e.g., the capacity to lactate results in many women breastfeeding) and behaviours which are associated with sex but *not* dependent on it (e.g., rearing children, which is a social activity, vs. bearing children, which is a biologically determined activity) a distinction was introduced between sex and gender, and it was and continues to be widely used.

Gender was meant to denote socially determined aspects of behaviour patterns differentially associated with the sexes, while sex was reserved for the biologically determined aspects. There is, however, a serious problem with this intended distinction. Since no human activity exists that is not mediated through culture, there is also no female or male activity that is not mediated through culture, i.e., there are always aspects of gender in sex, if we use this language. In principle, therefore, the distinction cannot be clear. In fact, even a quick scan of the relevant literature reveals that sex and gender (in spite of occasional careful definitions distinguishing between the two) are used interchangeably. If pushed to an extreme, the distinction between gender and sex, especially if combined with the concept of roles, can inadvertently lead to a form of biological determinism. Distinguishing between sex and gender roles suggests that some social differences between the sexes can be explained by a biological variable (sex) rather than through cultural variables associated with this biological variable.

A truly sociological approach treats sex as a residual variable, and tries to explain social sex differences with social variables. This makes it unnecessary to distinguish between sex and gender, since sex is only used as a *descriptive variable*, not as an *explanatory variable*. . . .

THE THIRD STAGE: THE DEVELOPMENT OF A FEMINIST APPROACH

A focus on women suggests a subject area: women. A focus on sex or gender roles suggests a particular theoretical approach within a previously defined area. Both these approaches are therefore limited in terms of their subject matter. By contrast, a feminist approach is much broader — most social matters can fall under its purview, including male behaviours, not only towards females but also towards other males. It is therefore characterized not so much by subject matter, as by a set of assumptions. It is difficult to codify these assumptions at the present time, but they would certainly include the following:

1. Women (as well as men) are both historical actors as well as the acted upon, subjects as well as objects. Societies cannot be understood if we fail to understand the female experience;
2. Contemporary Canadian society, as well as most other societies of today

and of the past, are characterized — whatever their differences — by being patriarchal. Patriarchy, in turn, consists of and reinforces the social, cultural, economic, and sexual oppression of women and girls;

3. All scholarship is by necessity value-oriented, whether this is admitted or not. Most non-feminist scholarship is sexist, insofar as it accepts the inferior social, economic, cultural, and sexual position of women as unproblematic and may even serve to actively maintain patriarchy.

By contrast, feminist scholarship is explicitly dedicated to the political goal of equality between the sexes. Since knowledge production and transmission are necessarily intertwined with the existing social power structure, feminist scholarship must work towards a new theory of knowledge, premised on the notion of equality of the sexes rather than inequality.

The development of a specifically feminist approach has been greatly facilitated by a feminist network developed since the early 1970s. This includes feminist publications, the emergence of feminist publishing houses, and a multitude of conferences across the country, usually of a cross-disciplinary nature, as well as organizations specifically oriented towards fostering feminist research and teaching. In 1984, the liberal government announced the creation of five endowed chairs in women's studies, one in each of Canada's regions.

The development of a feminist approach within anglophone sociology has not only been informed by feminism, but also by already existing theoretical orientations within sociology. The two most important ones are ethnomethodology and Marxism.

Ethnomethodology, or some version thereof, with its focus on the meaning of social facts for individual actors, has been seen by various scholars as a means to engage in feminist scholarship while remaining within an already existing theoretical framework. Proponents argue that such an approach is most appropriate for understanding the position of women, since it allows women to speak for themselves. An important starting point is "the essential validity of personal experience" (Stanley and Wise, 1985: 53) which derives from the feminist conviction that

the personal is political . . . the essence of feminism, for us, is its ideas about the personal, its insistence on the validity of women's experiences, and its argument that an understanding of women's oppression can be gained only through understanding and analysing everyday life, where oppression as well as everything else is grounded (Stanley and Wise, 1985: 135).

There is little doubt that an experientially grounded approach can be most instructive in illuminating the situation of women, but by no means would all feminist researchers subscribe to the notion that it is the *only* appropriate approach rather than *one* appropriate approach among others. Rather than arguing for the suitability of the ethnomethodological approach in studying women, it might be seen as particularly suited to areas in which, as yet, little is known. This view recognizes the contributions such an approach can make to feminist studies without divesting ourselves of other, potentially very powerful, tools.

Marxism is the other (and in many ways the first) already existing framework for feminist analysis. The relationship between Marxist and feminist scholarship can perhaps best be described as one of creative tension. On the one hand, some of the earliest feminist analyses were conducted within a broadly Marxist framework . . ., and analyses within the Marxist framework continue to generate creative and valuable research. . . .

On the other hand, scholars using this framework have criticized Marxism for its male orientation. Smith (1979) has identified a "'line of fault' in the social consciousness separating women's experience from the social forms of thought available in which to express it and make it actionable" (Smith, 1979: 181). O'Brien (1981), while acknowledging a debt to Marx and Hegel, identifies her work as

not a "Marxist" analysis in the orthodox sense, for I want to suggest that Marx's metatheory cannot make sense of the oppression of women, which clearly transcends class even though the theory did appear to make sense within the historical boundaries. . . .

There is an ongoing debate whether capitalism and patriarchy should be seen as two parallel and equally important forces in history, or whether the process of commodity production has primacy. Hartmann argues that

The present status of women in the labor market and the current arrangement of sex-segregated jobs is the result of a long process of interaction between patriarchy and capitalism. . . . Capitalism grew on top of patriarchy; patriarchal capitalism is stratified society par excellence. (1976: 167–8).

By contrast, Armstrong and Armstrong distance themselves "from those who advocate a dual systems approach, with structures of patriarchy assuming a weight equal to, or at least independent from, those of capitalism" (1983: 10). For them "Patriarchy and capitalisms are not autonomous, nor even interconnected systems, but the same system" (1983: 29).

The struggle with established theoretical perspectives, be they positivism, Marxism, ethnomethodology, or the relevance of quantitative methods for feminist research eventually leads to questions about the underlying theory of knowledge itself. These questions have now been raised by a number of feminist scholars.

THE FOURTH STAGE: TOWARDS A NEW EPISTEMOLOGY

Several researchers have raised, in different contexts, the issue of the need for a new epistemology. While some of these points have been raised before, a serious debate concerning this issue has started only in the 1980s. Several disciplines debate the issue from a variety of perspectives, but it involves relatively few researchers, who must necessarily crosscut disciplines as well as national boundaries. This debate will be discussed in this paper's final section.

Feminist Approaches to Various Areas in Sociology

At the most fundamental level, feminist scholarship is committed to understanding and improving the situation of women. It starts from the premise that all scholarship is necessarily value-oriented and that more often than not a lack of feminist consciousness results in sexist theories and descriptions. Identifying and criticizing sexist elements in the existing literature is therefore an important aspect of feminist work. Once a critique has been achieved, and basic data have been collected, new concepts and models are created, either to express female experiences, or to encompass the experiences of both sexes. The latter can only be achieved after the former has at least been partially done. In either case, feminist work eventually gropes towards for a new epistemology which allows for the adequate understanding of both female and male life.

This paper was assigned the task to assess the contributions of feminist approaches to existing substantive areas within anglophone sociology. This is difficult in that the components of feminist research as outlined above necessarily involve a blurring of current disciplinary and sub-disciplinary boundaries. Typically, feminist research is issue oriented. In investigating an issue, disciplinary and sub-disciplinary boundaries are usually considered irrelevant. Therefore, the discussion around several critical issues *eventually* influenced various sub-disciplines of sociology, although typically they did *not* generate within the sub-discipline. The following discussion will attempt to be faithful to this process by first discussing the major issues and then evaluating their impact on several areas within sociology.

CENTRAL ISSUES IN FEMINIST ANALYSIS

One of the earliest concerns of feminist research focussed on *housework*. At that time (late 1960s to early 1970s) most Canadian women worked full-time as housewives. (As of the early 1980s, most Canadian wives have a paid job, meaning that they do housework only on a part-time basis.)

One concern was to understand the nature of housework as real work, albeit unpaid. . . . This analysis was located within the context of an overall capitalist society. There was a debate about whether housework produced use-value, or exhange-value. Its contribution to reproducing the labour force in a double sense — by producing a new generation of workers (through birth, child rearing, and socialization) as well as by providing the adult worker with the necessary care and sustenance to be able to continue to sell his (occasionally her) labour power on the labour market — continues to be explored. The connection between housework, family structure, and corporate capitalism, in which housework is seen as largely organized around the interests of capital, shattered the conception of housework as only a privately organized activity.

Empirical studies have focussed on the historical role of domestic servants, the prestige of the occupation of housewife, the domestic division of labour between husbands and wives, housewives as role performers, the value of unpaid work in terms of standard economic measures of value, various methods of recompensing housewives for their work, immigrant housewives, and class differences in the performance of family work.

The nature of the interaction between paid and unpaid labour has been examined from various perspectives. Changes in the nature of housework (influx of technology into households as well as purchasability on the market of all goods and services provided within households) has facilitated the entry of women into the paid labour force, while women's family position (and their attendant work) facilitates their treatment as a reserve army of labour by employers.

A second issue which was seen as being extremely important early on was the issue of rape and the way it was conceptualized. Rather than seeing it as a sexual offense, rape was reconceptualized as a violent offense. The old legal definitions (since that time changed) were grounded in property law, with the woman being considered the property of her husband or father, rather than the person against whom the aggression was directed. "Rape is simply theft of sexual property under the ownership of someone other than the rapist." (Clark and Lewis, 1977: 116). This reconceptualization led, in practical political terms, to the establishment of rape crisis shelters and to intensive lobbying for a more adequate legal approach. This is a particularly clear example of the interconnection between innovative theoretical and empirical work and political work towards social change.

The new understanding of rape includes marital rape. No major study on this issue has yet been published in Canada, but an

American study by Russell (1982) is applicable in its methods and conclusions to Canada.

The concern with rape broadened into a concern, on the one hand, with *sexual assaults* against females of all ages, especially *incest*, and on the other hand, with violence against women in all forms, but particularly *wife beating* and lately *pornography* as well as *prostitution* and *sexuality* in general.

Pornography is currently being hotly debated, in print as well as in other forums. Virtually all feminists agree that pornography is an immportant issue, and that it represents a social evil. However, there is no agreement as to what should properly be considered pornographic and what should be done about it. Some writers include so-called "soft porn" in their definition of pornography . . ., while others restrict its definition to hard-core porn. . . . Some feminist writers argue strongly for censorship, in what their opponents call sometimes "an unholy alliance with the new right," while other feminists argue that although the danger posed by pornography is real, the danger that derives from seeking protection from the state is even greater than the danger posed by pornography itself. . . . A way out of this impasse might be to separate the issues of violence, incitement to hate, and sex altogether, and to censor violence (whether or not it is linked with sex) and incitement to hate, while combatting with other means the depiction of females as a marketable sex-commodity for the benefit of some men. Hughes (1985) has discussed a number of strategies for dealing with pornography to widen the scope beyond censorship vs. non-censorship.

As far as *incest* is concerned, very little research has been done until quite recently. The most comprehensive look at the problem is contained in the Report of the Committee on Sexual Offenses Against Children and Youths (1984). The report estimates the incidence of the most serious forms of assault (whether anyone had ever tried to have sex with the victims or had sexually assaulted them) at 22.1 per cent for the women and 10.6 per cent for the men. In the committee's estimation, such incidence does not represent a significant change from previous levels. The major change has been in the awareness of people that such problems exist.

Wife beating, as well, has not been comprehensively studied in Canada, but a number of limited studies are available on the topic. It is now recognized as a social problem of major proportions, which can be found in all social strata. The currently used estimate is that about 10 per cent of all Canadian wives are being battered by their husbands.

Such focus on women as victims of male sexual aggression has recently led to the emergence of a *sex-positive approach*, which calls for a recognition of a multiplicity of sexualities — a sexual pluralism — instead of the silencing of prescriptivism, and a recognition of female empowerment, not simply a dangerous and distorted focus on female victimization.

Another area of significant reconceptualization concerns the *reproductive functions of men and women*. Mary O'Brien has built an entire theory around this issue, concluding that patriarchy can be understood as a male reaction to the insecurity of their contributions to the reproductive process. "The isolation of the moment of sexuality from reproductive process in general is as old as male dominance, and is, indeed, a material base of that dominance" (O'Brien, 1981: 191). This stance leads to a reconceptualization of the culture/nature distinction as it relates to technology and its effect on the birthing process.

As far as work is concerned, an important feminist reconceptualization already discussed concerns the reconceptualization of housework as work (which previously had been explicitly excluded as work . . .).

Beyond that, it has been shown that *paid and unpaid labour* are inextricably linked, in particular as they collide in the need to provide care for people unable to care for themselves, especially (but not only) dependent children, and the achievement of equality for women on the *labour market.* This link was already explicitly recognized in the Report of the Royal Commission on the Status of Women (1978) and has been strongly reiterated in the Report of the Royal Commission on Equality in Employment (1984).

As far as the labour market itself is concerned, the sex segregation of occupations has been repeatedly documented. Similarly, the continuing wage differential is well documented as is the increasing tendency of women to work part-time. Special problems of women on the labour market such as sexual harassment, the attitude of and towards unions, the connection between childcare and labour force participation and the effect of technology on women's jobs have also been examined.

The various findings have led to strong criticisms of neo-classical and human capital theories of economic development and the status attainment theory . . . as being in principle incapable of explaining existing economic sex differences.

Socialization into sex roles is another major area which has received attention. One of the earliest contributions was to show the variability of sex roles across different cultures. This deprives them of any claim to universal validity that could be biologically explained, although the fact of the existence of some sex role differentiation is almost universal. Feminist scholars have moved the understanding of sex role socialization from that of socialization into *appropriate* sex roles to that of sex role socialization as limiting female development and, increasingly, male development as well. The role of the school system in producing young people with gender-differentiated skills and self-conceptions involves rethinking schools' links to the labour market, to families, and to the social production of knowledge.

A consequence of this critical approach to sex role socialization is a reconsideration of the concept of *androgyny.* By and large, androgyny is now seen as neither an adequate concept, nor a desirable social goal, since it remains antithetically tied to conceptions of appropriate feminine and masculine identities and behaviours.

Another central aspect of feminist research focuses on the concept of *sex stratification.* One of the earliest concerns of feminist scholarship was to analyze how conventional approaches to social stratification not only cannot deal satisfactorily with sex stratification, but to some degree even hide the stratification between the sexes. Early critiques in the U.S. (Acker, 1973) and in Canada (Eichler, 1973) pointed out that the assumption of the family as the major unit of analysis made it impossible to properly identify and analyze the different positions of wives and husbands. Only an unmarried adult woman who lived on her own or with dependent children could be treated like a man. Wives presented a double dilemma: if they were not earning income, there was no satisfactory way to independently assess their social position. If they were earning an income, there was no satisfactory model to adequately assess the independent status of both husband and wife as well as their joint status.

To this dilemma we may add the problem in analyzing the position of children due to the currently changing family forms, specifically the high proportion of divorces and remarriages. There is, as yet, no satisfactory way to measure the social position of children who have parents in two households both of whom may contribute, financially as well as in social ways, to the social status and placement of the children.

This problem remains with us today, in spite of attempts to integrate women into existing socioeconomic indices and in spite of attempts to consider prestige differentials between the sexes.

Another topic which has received some attention is the *women's movement* as a social movement. While up to the 1970s there was only one major work on the early feminist movement in Canada there are now several works which deal with both the old feminist movement and the new feminist movement. This concern is closely related to a critique of current models of *political participation* as insufficient for understanding the political participation of women. Movement politics must be seen as a logical route of political participation when pathways to higher levels of traditional forms of participation are effectively blocked. We must furthermore examine the political culture in order to understand behaviours such as political participation.

Assuming the existence of a female and a male political culture has significant implications for a large range of issues, among them a reconceptualization of the interplay between politics and culture. McCormack (1984) has suggested five propositions concerning *the media and feminism* which link media economics with the sexual division of labour, dual male/female political culture, and censorship.

This is not a complete discussion of important sociological contributions by feminist researchers, but rather a selection of issues considered particularly important where work has been done by a number of Canadian scholars. Issues neglected here but having had some significant work include the sociology of sport, urban sociology, women and development and the sociology of mental health. Contributions to the sociology of knowledge will be discussed below.

FEMINIST CONTRIBUTIONS TO MAINSTREAM SOCIOLOGY

The area most marked by the impact of feminist thought is the *sociology of the family*. Several topics as well as underlying assumptions have been newly introduced. In particular, family violence in all its forms is now seen as an important issue, the division of labour between husband and wife is no longer seen in functionalist terms as "appropriate" but as culturally determined and currently shifting, and the notion of the need to examine marriage, or a dyadic relationship in general, from the perspective of both participants has found some acceptance. (This notion stems from Jessie Bernard's (1973) work on "his" and "her" marriage.) The relationship between family and work has been problematized not only for women, but also for men, and housework is seen as important to an understanding of the workings of a family. Reproductive technology, clearly one of the most important emergent issues, has so far received little attention in Canada, in contrast to the work done elsewhere. . . .

One of the consequences of the notion that the situation of women cannot be examined appropriately by subsuming it under the family is an emergent literature on *social policy*. While the topics covered (and the solutions proposed, where applicable) vary considerably, these analyses are concerned with examining policies with respect to how they affect women, not some presumably "larger" group, or some presumably "superordinate" issue. . . . Nevertheless, few studies examine major economic and social policies with respect to their effects on women.

Sociology of education has been greatly enriched as well as altered by feminist scholarship; "the process of dismantling the pedagogy of patriarchy," to use Madeleine Grumet's felicitous phrase (1981: 165–84) has created "new frontiers in

teaching, research and epistemology"
(O'Brien, 1983: 6).

Those areas of sociology concerned with
the labour market — i.e., *sociology of work,
sociology of industrialization, urban sociology, sociology of modernization, theories concerning the social division of labour* — should no longer be able to treat
the existing division of labour (inside and
outside of the home) as natural or unproblematic or functionally adaptive, but
as a socially constructed (and therefore
potentially remediable) systemic problem.

As far as *stratification theory* is concerned, the effect of feminist critiques has
been rather modest, probably because
there has been better success in identifying
the problems than in developing solutions.

Overall, feminist approaches have had a
more *generalized impact on sociology* than
that on specifically shaping particular sub-
disciplines. The following new viewpoints
have been introduced:

1. Statements made with a male
   population in mind cannot
   necessarily be extended to a female
   population. In other words, sex is a
   socially significant variable until
   proven otherwise. This is the exact
   reversal of previous approaches
   which by and large saw sex as a
   socially insignificant variable until
   proven otherwise, *not* by explicitly
   stating this assumption (indeed,
   most researchers might have
   disagreed with it even fifteen years
   ago if stated as baldly as has been
   done here) but by implicitly
   practising it. It was assumed that the
   male provided the norm for social
   behaviour, and women were treated
   as the exception to the rule,
   provided such exception had
   previously been established. From
   this derives the practise, commented
   upon by Maccoby and Jacklin
   (1974), that it is hard to publish

findings of "no sex difference," since
such findings tend to be seen as
"insignificant," while findings of sex
differences tend to be seen as
significant.

2. A corollary, but not identical,
   viewpoint is the recognition of male
   and female perspectives on social
   phenomena.

3. A third recognition is the realization
   that one cannot merely ask one sex
   about the other when trying to
   discover the other's viewpoint;
   rather, one must ask both sexes
   about themselves and, if opinions
   are desired, about their opinion of
   the other sex, without treating such
   opinions as statements of fact.

The most overarching contribution of
feminist approaches, then, has been in the
sociology of knowledge, and in the general
importance accorded women (females) in
sociology, rather than in specific sub-
disciplines.

Towards a New Epistemology

It is difficult, and arguably impossible, to
deal with such a complex issue in the
amount of space available. The following
discussion must therefore be read with the
caveat in mind that it is extraordinarily ab-
breviated (hopefully not beyond recognition). No attempt is made to argue points,
instead, they are simply stated.

Feminist scholarship accepts, and extends, four central conceptions of sociology of knowledge:

1. that all knowledge is socially
   constructed;

2. that what is accepted as a dominant
   ideology is the ideology of the ruling
   group;

3. that there cannot be such a thing as
   a value-free science (and it is
   debated what constitutes objective

science in contradistinction to value-free science); and

4. that the perspective of people, including their insight into the workings of society, varies systematically with their position within that society.

To turn this into specifically feminist propositions:

1. knowledge has been, so far, constructed by some men for the benefit of men;

2. the dominant ideology, including the dominant approaches to sociology, bolster and maintain patriarchy;

3. social science in general has so far largely been the handmaiden of sexism;

4. women and men have a different perspective on society stemming from their different positions within that society and which will continue to be crucially significant for as long as a sex structure continues to be crucially important to a society. Women, therefore, have their own perspective which is of at least equal value — and arguably of more value — than the corresponding male perspective on the same issue. This is so because those in an inferior position tend to have keener insight into society's workings than those in a superior position, as has been argued for the working class in the Marxist tradition.

KNOWLEDGE HAS BEEN CONSTRUCTED BY SOME MEN FOR THE BENEFIT OF MEN

This proposition includes female scholars who have been educated in a male-dominated educational system and have adopted questions, methods, procedures, concepts, priorities, and answers gener-

ated by male scholars. One of the major ways in which this phenomenon shows itself is in omission and silencing, what Dorothy Smith (1978) has called a "peculiar eclipsing." Issues of importance to women have traditionally been trivialized. The male was considered the norm; the female, when studied at all and found not to conform to this norm, was seen as the deviation.

Inherent in this proposition is a distinction of knowledge *about* vs. knowledge *for*. Studies may be about women, but are women served by this knowledge? Does it serve to empower them or to better control them? According to this proposition, non-feminist studies *about* women have tended to be directed by male interests, without serving to empower women in confronting the world.

Related to this proposition is an underlying assumption that much present and almost all past sociology is sexist. This sexism may often be unconscious. It is deeply ingrained in the structure of our thoughts and procedures, and extremely difficult, for that reason, to detect. Once it has been pointed out, it becomes easier to recognize, but the initial analysis is extraordinarily difficult and involves a creative leap out of established patterns of thought.

Analyses with respect to sexim in sociology include the identification of overgeneralizations, the existence of an androcentric perspective, sexist language, one-sided, asymmetrical or differentially value-laden concepts, interpretations of data which either ignore sex as a social variable or use a double standard in interpreting findings for females and males, and a pervasive dichotomization which associates certain traits or behaviours with women and others with men, such as is implied in the notion of "sex appropriate roles." . . .

There is a direct relationship between the social construction of knowledge (as referred to in this first proposition) and the effect of such knowledge on the social structure per se, addressed in the next proposition.

Examples of this include omissions as well as particular ways of presenting materials. Women's contributions to public life have, for a long time in western thought, been dismissed as unimportant, thus denying a history to women and requiring the continuing repetition of thought which is largely non-cumulative. It is a shocking discovery to find older writings by women which display some of the same insights of modern feminists. This process of exclusion continues even today, with gate-keepers of major scientific publication outlets preventing feminist research from being published in mainstream journals. . . .

SOCIAL SCIENCE MAINTAINS PATRIARCHY

Beyond silencing women and distorting their contributions to society (and by implication, overestimating those of men), social science has actively contributed to justifying the inferior position of women by largely equating them with the private realm, and by equating men with the public realm. A double standard was thus created which measured the same activities, depending on their performance by a male or female person, with two different rods. A primary example of this double standard can be found in the assumption of a natural differentiation with respect to the tasks of women and men. A contemporary example of this is sociobiology, with its assumption of a natural double standard, and its rapid acceptance as a major new approach by the public.

SOCIAL SCIENCE HAS NEVER BEEN OBJECTIVE ABOUT WOMEN

The old debate about whether there can be a value-free science has been clearly an-

swered: it is not possible. However, there nevertheless continues to be a tendency of non-feminist scholars to see feminist scholarship as value-laden, without the concomitant recognition that sexist science is just as value-laden if unaware of that fact. Unconsciously held values are more problematic than acknowledged ones. The debate on this issue has not been helped by the terminology used. Mary O'Brien's dictum that feminist science must be biased because sexist science is biased expresses the dilemma admirably (O'Brien, 1981: 12), but perhaps a clearer statement is that all science is value-laden with feminist science being no exception.

WOMEN'S PERSPECTIVE IS AT LEAST AS IMPORTANT AS MEN'S PERSPECTIVE

Dorothy Smith has defined the women's standpoint 'as a determinate position from which society may be known' (Smith, 1979: 182).

Beginning from the standpoint of women locates a subject who begins in a material and local world. It shows the provinces of meaning described by Schutz . . . not as alternatives — a paramount reality on the one hand and the scientific domain on the other — but rather as a bifurcation of consciousness, with a world directly experienced from oneself as center (in the body) on the one hand and a world organized in the abstracted conceptual mode, external to the local and particular places of one's bodily existence (Smith, 1979: 169).

She therefore argues that our inquiries must begin with the everyday world as problematic. Other researchers. . . . have criticized the notion of objectivity.

Starting from the assumption of male and female standpoints, two issues have emerged within the feminist research community: first, whether particular methods exist which are more appropriate to the study of women than others; and second, whether the task of feminist scholarship is to develop the woman's standpoint, or to move into a non-sexist direction equally applicable to all researchers.

With respect to the first issue, one tradition argues that in principle qualitative methods are more appropriate than quantative approaches in studying women. Perhaps the most influential formulation of this choice was proposed by Bernard (1973) who used the dichotomy of research into "agency" and "communion."

Agency has to do with separation, repression, conquest, and contract; communion with fusion, expression, acceptance, noncontractual cooperation. Agency operated by way of mastery and control; communion with naturalistic observation, sensitivity to qualitative patterning, and greater personal participation by the investigator . . . (Bernard, 1973: 22–3).

The most creative outcome of struggling for appropriate methods is a renewed focus on action research, which couples research with concrete social action. . . . In Canada, francophone feminists in particular have developed this important approach. . . .

On the other hand, equally strong and compelling arguments can (and have) been made for the use of particular quantitive methods such as simulations in overcoming sexist limitations, or which argue that all methods can be used in a sexist or non-sexist manner. The latter view suggests that no method should be dismissed in principle as inappropriate for studying women but that all must be revised.

This apparent contradiction can be understood to derive from a stage in development rather than a contradiction in principle. When little is known about a subject matter, qualitative methods are generally more appropriate than quantitative matters. Since so many issues have not yet been explored with women being central, qualitative methods will often be more appropriate than quantitative methods.

However, once initial knowledge has been generated, other methods may constitute powerful tools of analysis to be abandoned only at the risk of contributing to the maintenance of inappropriate (sexist) ways of understanding the world.

With respect to the second issue, whether the primary task of feminist scholarship is to develop the women's standpoint or to work towards a non-sexist scholarship, the contradiction is also more apparent than real. At the *individual* level, real choices may have to be made concerning the attempt to understand a particular issue from the woman's point of view or from that of both sexes. If taken as a program, the first approach would lead to a new discipline focusing on women, while the second would lead to a reform of all existing scholarship, irrespective of discipline, methods used, researcher(s) involved (whether male or female) or subject matter.

In general, the development of principles for non-sexist scholarship is clearly important to feminism and it is to be hoped that such principles will go beyond the feminist research community to become part of the accepted canon of scientific inquiry. In Canada, we have started to move in this direction. With the release of the booklet "On the Treatment of the Sexes in Research" the Social Sciences and Humanities Research Council has gone on record as stating that research cannot — by definition — be good research if it is sexist. (It can, however, be non-sexist and nevertheless bad research!) In other words, avoiding sexism in research in all its various forms is necessary, but not sufficient for producing good research. The Canadian Sociology and Anthropology Association made a similar statement and commitment to change at its 1984 Annual Meeting in Guelph when the general assembly passed a motion to the effect that all official publications of the association must henceforth be non-sexist in language and *content*. . . . The Canadian Psychological Association has officially adopted a set of principles for the conduct of research which declares research influenced by largely unconscious sexism as unscientific.

However, a truly non-sexist scholarship cannot be developed unless we also have a body of work which treats women's experiences and views with the same respect as it treats those of men. In order to move towards a non-sexist scholarship, we must struggle to develop the women's standpoint.

Conclusion

Overall, then, feminist scholarship has matured rather rapidly, and the body of knowledge produced is impressive. However, there are some distinct lacunae: At the most general level, only a few books which claim general theoretical relevance deal adequately with women. In other words, by and large mainstream sociology remains sexist. In particular, very few studies look at general economic and social policies (in distinction to family-oriented policies) in terms of their impact on women. For instance, analyses of budgets of federal and provincial governments, or assessments of the effect of major policy programs (e.g., Unemployment Insurance) on women are largely missing.

In general, the impact of feminist approaches on sub-disciplines has not been impressive. This is, however, not the fault of feminist scholars. Feminist scholarship *has* demonstrated that by and large sociology in Canada (as elsewhere) has been sexist. It has identified the problem, and has started to develop the tools to move beyond this stage to a non-sexist sociology.

This task is by no means complete. At a minimum, new standards have been set, although their achievement lies in the future. Nor has the work been completed which would allow us to recognize and overcome sexism in all its various forms. There is a large gap between the recognition and overcoming which can only be filled by hard, sustained, and creative work. Recognizing a problem and providing a solution do not necessarily go hand in hand.

With non-sexist scholarship's acceptance by the general research community rather than the small community of feminist scholars (as indicated by the actions of the CSAA, the CPA and SSHRC, and the establishment of women's studies chairs), we are at the threshold of a new stage for feminist scholarship, coinciding with a new phase of development for sociology in Canada — the move towards a non-sexist scholarship. This involves a vast re-thinking of old premises, and if it is to succeed, it will need the active cooperation of the majority of Canadian sociologists.

chapter

10

Economic Perspectives

In the preceding chapter, three of the selections you were asked to read introduced you to the debate about Canadian capitalism and Canada's position within the system of world capitalism. Whatever the outcome of that debate, no one denies that Canadians live in a capitalist society that shares many features in common with other capitalist and industrial societies. Rather than choose articles which deal specifically with the nature of Canadian capitalism, we have chosen ones which take as their starting point that the development of industrial capitalism has shaped and transformed the way in which we work and our social interactions within and without the world of work.

The first selection consists of two excerpts from R.E. Pahl's book *Divisions of Labour*. Pahl, a British sociologist, explores the manifold meanings of the concept of work and how the meaning of work has changed as we moved from household economies to a market economy and eventually to industrial capitalism. In the process, he also shows how the related concepts of "employment" and "unemployment," terms which had no meaning prior to the development of industrial capitalism, have changed our notions of what is and is not work. As you read what Pahl has to say about the changing nature of work, as well as the following selection by James Rinehart, think back to the selections in Chapter 6 "The Changing Family" by Emily Nett and by Roberta Hamilton and what they had to say about the implications for women, children and men of the separation of the world of work from the world of the home and the household.

The second selection is taken from James Rinehart's book *The Tyranny of Work.* As we noted in the introduction to this Part of the Reader, for Karl Marx the history and development of capitalism is, in large part, the history of the progressive degradation and alienation of labour. In his empirical work, Marx was, of course, focusing largely upon Europe and particularly on Britain, where he spent much of his life. Rinehart, a sociologist at the University of Western Ontario, shows in this selection how the same processes identified by Marx more than a century ago worked themselves out in nineteenth- and early twentieth-century Canada. In tracing the development of industrial capitalism and its drastic effects on the nature of work, Rinehart draws upon the now rich body of work by Canadian labour historians and interprets this research for you through the lens of British Marxist theory and Marxist-based research. As well as learning something of how industrial capitalism developed in Canada, you should take away from reading this article an appreciation that the transformation of work into its present-day alienated and degraded forms was not generally an inevitable result of new technologies and of industrialization but was, rather, what transpired as earlier capitalists sought both to maximize profits and to control their work force. And, as Rinehart documents, workers were not always passive agents in this sometimes brutal transformation of their work and livelihood; they joined or formed social and political movements, which offered alternative ways to organize the economy, and formed unions in order to do battle with the harsh conditions in specific work settings and industries.

The third selection, by Marilyn Porter of Memorial University of Newfoundland, could easily have been included in Chapter 6, "The Changing Canadian Family." We include it here in a chapter on industrialism and capitalism because, in our view, it nicely compliments R.E. Pahl's more general discussion of the nature of work, and it does so by providing a Canadian empirical example of some of Pahl's themes. Moreover, Porter is examining a traditional resource-based economy, one which at least initially escaped the kinds of transformations of work Rinehart describes as occurring much earlier in the industrial heartland of Canada. Porter is both a feminist and a Marxist, and it is in this context that she examines the changing nature of gender relationships as women, men and families, generally, try both to cling to a traditional economy and to adapt to capitalism and the consumerism engendered by that capitalism.

The fourth and final selection in this chapter is by John Myles, a sociologist at Carleton University. In this article he presents a fairly sophisticated test of a rather complex debate: has present-day capitalism created new and technically sophisticated jobs or mainly more unskilled, dead-end and low-paid jobs — the "knowledge society" or the "hamburger economy"? As you will learn, the answer is that capitalism produces both and has led to a dichotomized work world. In editing the article for this chapter, we have left out most of his statistical data and methodology and have tried to present you with the overall argument and his conclusions. There are two reasons why we felt that this article should be of interest to you. The first is that it does address a very important question about the nature of work in modern Canadian society. That is, as we near the end of the twentieth century, will most people be largely engaged in challenging, demanding and fulfilling work, or will most be destined to work in alienating and degrading jobs. If the latter, are there policy changes that might improve the lot of those who would form a kind of underclass in Canadian society? The second reason is that many of you who are reading this book are in the somewhat schizophrenic situation of working part time in the "hamburger economy" to pay for an education that you hope will transport you into the "knowledge society." As you read this article and the ones that follow in the next chapter, you may want to consider the lot of those who have little option but to live out their work-lives as part of the working poor.

RELATED READINGS

Karl Marx: "The Materialist Conception of History" (Chapter 1)
Roberta Hamilton: "Women, Wives and Mothers" (Chapter 6)
William Carroll: "The Thesis of Canadian Dependency" (Chapter 9)

DIVISIONS OF LABOUR
R.E. Pahl

Words take their meanings in social contexts: when a word loses its precise meaning it loses something of its currency. It is deeply significant that, as we come to the final years of the twentieth century, "work," an apparently fundamental and unambiguous word, has come to lack precision. Part of the difficulty may be simply that the word is being asked to do too much. From voluntary work through doing the washing up to being a brain surgeon, a vast range of activities is encompassed in the term "work." Whatever the reason, a society that falters when referring to something apparently so basic to human existence is likely to be changing in a fundamental way. The resounding confidence of the

From *Divisions of Labour* by Ray E. Pahl, 1984. By permission of Blackwell Publishers, London, and the author.

mid-century slogan in the United Nations Charter — "the right to work" — should now, perhaps, be formulated more cautiously as the right to some minimum level of subsistence. Some societies are now recognizing that it is economically (if not socially) better sense to pay people a modest income directly, rather than to burden employers with workers they do not want to pay, simply because they are able to get higher profits without them. The situation in which one society — say an oil-rich Middle Eastern sheikdom — gets members of another society or other societies to do most of its work for it is no different in principle from what happened in the households of English gentlemen in the eighteenth century. Societies well-endowed with energy, technology and capital are unlikely to generate the same slogans as those more plentifully supplied with labour but rather short on the other factors of production. The workers of the world are manifestly not uniting.

The same word, "work," generates equal confusion and often, indeed, conflict within the household. It is now less easy and less likely for men to return home from employment to a wife who is "not working." The woman's work may or may not be paid, but few would argue that the question of payment is the sole determining factor in deciding whether her activity can be appropriately described as work. Whether prompted by the high levels of unemployment in the advanced industrial societies and the gloomy forecasts of most economists, or by the tensions generated by the uneven distribution of paid employment within and between households, the confusions surrounding the word "work" are now widespread.

As with most things, these current confusions are not without historical precedents. M. Godelier has reminded us that the words "work," "to work" and "worker" took on their meanings in our language at a certain period and it was not until the development of political science in the nineteenth century that the idea of work became a central concept:

According to Lucien Febvre, it was in the sixteenth century that the word "to work" (travailler) *entered the French vocabulary, replacing, in part, two earlier words,* labourer *(now meaning to plough) and* oeuvrer *(no longer in use as a verb; as a noun it means a work of art).* Travaillier *(to work) came from the latin which means torturing with a* tripalium, *an instrument made of three stakes. Before that in about 1120,* labeur *(now meaning toil), from the Latin* labor, *became common usage for agricultural activity; also in the 12th Century* ouvrier *(worker) made its first appearance, derived from the Latin* operarius *(man of pain or affliction), a term which itself went back to two words,* opus *(an action or piece of work) and* operae, *the tasks or obligations which had to be performed in respect of someone else, as for example, those of a liberated serf towards his old master, or those of the artisan in respect of the customer with whom he had a contract. But even before these words had appeared,* travailler *meant to torture an offender on a tripalium and* travailleur *in this case was not the victim but the torturer (Godelier, 1980: 165).*

We cannot, of course, understand what these distinctions of meaning implied for the contemporary experience of the people involved. Presumably, they implied some changes in social relations; but it is not possible to infer simply from etymological evidence the exact nature and timing of these. Godelier suggests that these new ideas and new meanings emerged at different and distinct historical periods: at the height of the feudal era in the twelfth and thirteenth centuries, when towns and domestic manufacture first emerged, and then, later, at the end of the fifteenth and beginning of the sixteenth century, with the rise of international trade, the colonial system, banking and state and private manufacture. The final period was at the end of the eighteenth century, when the contemporary meanings of worker and wage earner appeared. It may be that the last two decades of the twentieth century will see yet a further redefinition of work.

Much of the current debate about the future of work begins from assumptions that should initially be questioned. The fact that "work" can apply to all kinds of activity, much of which is not paid, but that "employment" refers more precisely to activity that is paid is evidently of crucial importance now. It is likely that the "right to work" in the late 1940s then meant "the right to employment for a reasonable wage, primarily for males in households with dependent women and children." Yet by 1980 about a third of all households were married couples with dependent children and, of that third, half of the wives were in full or part-time employment. So, in less than forty years, implicit meanings have substantially changed. Households with more than one adult supported by a single earner are now a special category, not the norm. Women now doing unwaged work in their dwellings are unlikely to claim that this is fulfilling their right to work.

A problem with many of the scholarly discussions of work, certainly since the time of Adam Smith and Karl Marx, is that too much emphasis has been given to that work narrowly perceived to be connected with a specific conception of production and too little to the other productive work connected with reproduction and consumption. A recent book entitled *The Ideology of Work* (Anthony, 1977) is almost entirely about employment — that is, waged work for an employer. Self-employment and unwaged work are largely ignored. Implicitly, that was the common view of work that held sway until very recently. Antecedents of the conventional view have a long pedigree: God cursed Adam, according to the Judaic myth, in a very thorough-going way. First, He imposed a gender-based conflict ("enmity between thee and the woman"); second, biological reproduction was to be painful ("in sorrow shalt thou bring forth children"); third, patriarchal relations were to be formally established ("thy desire shall be to thy husband and he shall rule over thee"); and, finally, production, implicitly a male activity, was to be made difficult ("cursed is the ground . . . thorns also and thistles shall it bring forth") and tiring ("in the sweat of thy face shalt thou eat bread"). Thus were the social relations of a pastoral tribe confirmed and supported. Happily, conditions are not as tiring and painful now as that particularly myth predicted. Some women may choose to bear children even when they are not economically necessary for the survival of the household; some men and women may also choose to engage in employment, seeing it as more liberating than constraining.

Until very recently, in European societies certainly, the notion that work was the prerogative of one gender more the other would not have been understood. Work was done by members of *households* for the collective well-being of household members. The analytical distinction that can arguably be made between work for production and work for reproduction could also have been made in the past but was not very important. Individuals were largely obliged to be members of households, and they had to get a livelihood, had to get by, and would have seen little need to philosophize about whether or not the roof should be repaired or the cow milked. In practice, households in pre-industrial England, as elsewhere, had to be based on an economic partnership between men and women and other household members. A *household work strategy* developed which made the best use of resources for getting by under given social and economic conditions. It is one of the central concerns of this book to demonstrate that this emphasis on the household rather than the individual as the basic economic unit is a more fruitful way to approach the work of production, reproduction and consumption. This focus makes no *a priori* assumptions about either internal conflict or consensus within the household and none about the necessity for identifying putative household heads. Households are simply units for getting various kinds of work done. They were not, of course, isolated units: households were bound to each other in many complex ways and the boundaries between them were often very fluid, as members moved back and forth at different stages of the life cycle. Certainly, in the past the Church and more recently the State have imposed gender ideologies and hierarchies within the household — the former as a reflection of the development of hierarchy and organization with the Church (Reeves Sanday, 1981) and the latter as a convenient way of gathering taxes. . . .

Household Work Practices in Pre-industrial England

Reconstructing past household work strategies is inevitably complex and difficult. Records are scanty and, in so far as they refer to specific types of work, they generally do so only selectively. It would be wrong therefore to infer, if a given task is not mentioned, either that it was done or that it was not done. Thus, we may learn that a given woman bears a child, but we cannot infer that she then has the task of caring for it, nor can we be sure that we know what the task of caring comprises; similarly, if a man buys a cow at market, it certainly does not follow that he will milk it or look after the calves. However, if a child of the same name remains in the household or if later calves are sold at market, we know that *somebody* has looked after the child or cared for the cow. Yet even here there are pitfalls. The degree of co-operation and collectivity in the way work is done *between* households is also open to question and discussion. The divisions of labour both within and between households can be revealed only after very careful analysis, and historians have only recently turned their attention to this. . . .

Exploring the Social Relations of Employment

Employment is the form of work that appears the easiest to understand: in very simple terms, a worker brings his or her skills and strength to an employer and in return receives a wage or salary for the time spent or the task achieved. However, it is not always quite as simple as that, since it would be wrong to see all workers as equally well-placed. Some have conditions of service agreements which give them almost complete security of tenure (such as dockworkers); others, such as contract research workers in universities and elsewhere, have no security and are obliged to waive their redundancy rights. Some employees work for large multi-national corporations, whose policy is to provide security and substantial fringe benefits; others work for companies with very uncertain futures, whose concern is to get the maximum return from labour at the minimum cost. Some employees are full-time, some part-time; some have facilities provided at formal workplaces — factories and offices — whereas others are employed on a piecework basis in their own homes.

The state intervenes to a greater or lesser degree to regulate the employer-employee relationship: health and safety regulations, obligatory national insurance contributions, statutory paid maternity leave and so forth. However, there is a wide diversity of practice across the range of employment situations; employers may legally or illegally change the conditions of employment for their own or their employees' benefit. In the case of the former, they may shift from employing male full-time skilled workers to employing part-time semi-skilled married women workers. This strategy may produce a more docile, flexible and cheaper workforce, putting second incomes into some households and reducing some households to having no earners at all. Certain formal employment protection legislation, devised by the state for the protection of the assumed "normal" male full-time worker, may be avoided. This must be seen as the "informalization" of formal contractual systems. Whether the employee is male or female will substantially determine levels of pay and conditions of service, irrespective of skill or capacity. This is particularly likely when formalized grading systems are not in operation. In a study of a wide range of companies and industries designed to understand the determinants of women's pay and employment position, the authors concluded:

Most of the small firms in the survey used relatively informal systems either ad hoc individual systems or mainly flat-rate payment systems with little reward for skill, experience or differences in job content. The ad hoc systems were often described as merit-based systems, but in practice pay levels more often reflected the wage at which workers were recruited than an assessment of their current worth (Craig et al, 1983: 146)

The desire for informal employment practices is well illustrated in Scase and Goffee's study of small firms in the building industry, where there appears to be a constant battle to avoid the government's regulatory legislation.

Sometimes employers will informalize the relations between them and their workers to the advantage of the employees. Thus, a minimally low "declared" wage is provided and the remainder is paid in cash, thereby providing the employee with a tax-free bonus up to the level of the informally agreed wage. The employer also gains, since he pays less, but it depends on his having cash off the books. Some employers can, as it were, employ no one. All their wages are paid in cash: they can even do this legally if their payments are small enough. Many employers prefer to employ pensioners on a part-time basis for this reason.

There is no need to elaborate the point that the same kind of work — employment for a wage — can range from the stable, protected employment in a large organization to the unstable, informal employment practices of small organizations. Clearly, the social conditions of employment vary substantially, but so long as there is an employer and employee the social relations remain the same. However, the social relations of the self-employed are different.

According to Scase and Goffee (1980), many of those starting an independent business do so as an explicit *rejection* of the capitalistic ethic. It "enables a person to escape from the contraints of authority, the wage-profit relationship and other features of being an employee." Some can, of course, combine wage labour with self-employment, and this is particularly likely in the building and allied trades. It should be recognized that under certain circumstances informal ties of mutual trust and obligation can bind an employer to an employee far more effectively than formal statutory legislation. However, there is generally a price to be paid in informal sanctions, which of course can work both ways, and the shift from status to contract, from *Gemeinschaft* to *Gesellschaft*, is generally held to be a progressive one.

There is, of course, a range of work where the social relations of the market and of capital do not apply so directly, where transactions take place partly or wholly on the basis of other imperatives such as the need to maintain social solidarity and to confirm the norm of reciprocity. There are many other kinds of work than simply selling labour power to an employer. . . .

The Social Relations of Work Outside Employment

Let us, by way of illustration, take some relatively simple task — a woman ironing a garment in a domestic dwelling. Viewing that activity on its own, without knowing the social relations in which it is embedded and which to a degree create it, is an inadequate basis for determining the precise nature of the work involved. The various possibilities will be systematically reviewed, providing an alternative typology of work.

The woman could be completing a task for which she is employed as an outworker for a garment manufacturer. This work would be unequivocally *wage labour*. If, on the other hand, the woman was proposing to sell the garment she has just made in her own boutique or market stall, she would be engaged in *petty commodity production* as a self-employed worker, since she would be producing for herself and not for her employer. Both of these forms of work could be undertaken without informing the controlling agencies of the state, which may be referred to then as *shadow wage labour* or *shadow petty commodity production*: the social relations might remain the same, but the system of national accounting would certainly be affected.

The woman could, on the other hand, be ironing a garment for which she received no direct monetary reward. If she is ironing her own blouse in preparation for her next day's wage labour, then she could be said to be engaged in *individual reproduction*. All wage labourers have to be, as it were, reproduced from day to day. Some have much of this activity done for them by others: young wage labourers get the support of their parents; men frequently get the support of their unpaid wives. This work, called *social reproduction*, is to do with the maintenance of existing workers or the reproduction of new ones and is typically done by women: it may be said to be structured by the social relations based on patriarchy, as wage labour is structured by the social relations of capitalism. In both cases, patterns of domination and subordination structure the social relations of the work. However, in the case of social reproduction, while the ironing of the shirt may be described as patriarchally structured social reproduction work, it could also be shared wage labour (the wife is preparing herself for business entertaining on behalf of her husband, for which she gets paid) or shared social reproductive work (tomorrow the husband does the ironing) or undominated subsistence work (the tasks have been equitably divided between all members of the household, none of whom is a wage labourer or self-employed worker, and the woman has agreed to do the ironing as part of her overall contribution).

It would be wrong to assume that all women ironing a garment for another person are constrained to do so by patriarchal values. If the woman were ironing the garment for colleagues in a local dramatic society, it would make a difference if they way the work had been allocated involved a degree of "friendly coercion" or had been given without question because she was a woman. If, on the contrary, she had *offered* to do this work for her colleagues in the society, or for a neighbour who was sick, then she would be doing what may be described as *social solidarity work*. Such work, based on generalized or specific reciprocity, reflects the social constraints of sharing the same dwelling or locality and is essential if people are to live together reasonably amicably. This is distinct from *voluntary work*, which may be done anonymously and is not based on the constraints of interpersonal interaction or related to any reciprocal recompense.

In all these descriptions of a given task being done, the type of work may be understood by exposing the pattern of social relations in which it is embedded. It is these social relations of work that produce exploitation. The circumstances under which the ironing was agreed to be done and the relative balance of power between the woman doing the ironing and her significant others would need to be known and understood before the particular work task could be appropriately categorized. Such might be an advance in sociological conceptualization, but this intellectual exercise is not self-evidently of any more general significance.

Is All Social Activity or Social Behaviour "Work"?

The attempt to set out systematically a preliminary typology of work (see Figure 5.2) shows that most types of work can be illustrated through the example of ironing, but this possibly supports the position rather too neatly. Some tasks cannot be so easily manipulated in and out of different categories of social relations, yet there are, perhaps, many more tasks in industrial society that could shift out of one category into another. Nevertheless, a valid criticism is that the typology, by attempting to be comprehensive, weakens the distinctive meaning of the word "work" so that it becomes synonymous with "activity," or "task," or simply "social behaviour." Since, it may be argued, we live in a capitalist social formation, *all* activities are concerned with the production and reproduction of that system. According to such an extreme position, productive work is seen as central and all other activities as secondary and sub-

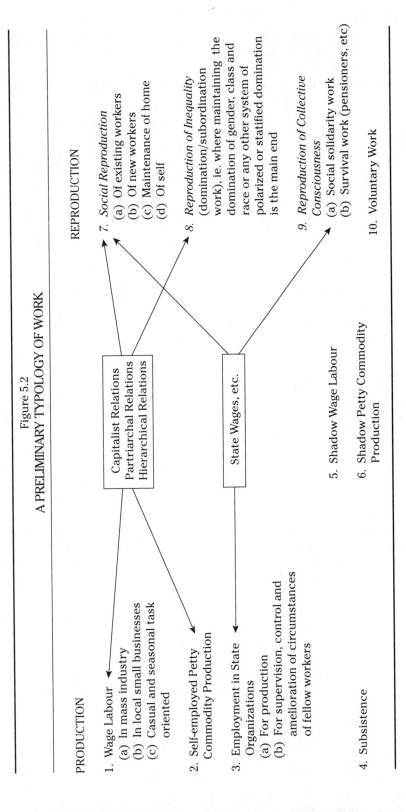

Figure 5.2
A PRELIMINARY TYPOLOGY OF WORK

servient to it. Thus, people's leisure, free time or play can be seen as recreating the energy and momentum to return to productive work, and, somewhat humourlessly, *re*productive work is seen as serving the function of reproducing the labour power and social relations of the social formation.

Again, those who are in receipt of state benefits because they are physically or mentally disabled or are over the official age of retirement are paid to survive — not because a capitalist social formation gets material benefit from dispensing such minimal largesse, but because the alternative would disrupt social stability. To make the point rather sharply, if those who, for whatever reason, are incapable of doing productive work (and here we include reproductive work as productive work) were obliged to take a painless death, nakedness of the system of expropriation would be apparent and hence the system would be unsustainable. Paying out state benefits to people whose main work then becomes largely one of survival is, in this bleak perspective, a way of maintaining social stability and cohesion. From this point of view, neighbourly exchanges which promote social solidarity can also be seen as helping to create social cohesion and so may be functional for the stability of a capitalist social formation. Even the social relations based upon patriarchy can be seen as functional for the maintenance of capitalism, but they apparently seem to be functional for all other social formations as well.

Such an obsessive and misguided radical functionalism is able to describe most of the processes and practices of social life as necessary to the maintenance of the present system. It is also necessary and in the interests of capital to mystify the workings of this self-sustaining exploitative system. All work — including even revolutionary sabotage — then becomes one kind of work: that necessary to perpetuate the system. (The saboteurs provoke a "defensive"

response which can then be legitimated by the state as necessary for the maintenance of peace and the control of violence. This response may be in the form of a secret police, an armed police, the armed forces used for civilian control and so on.) True subsistence work, which appears in the typology, is not therefore possible in capitalist society according to this perspective, except in very isolated and special circumstances. Certainly, it is difficult to escape from the exigencies of the money economy completely, although with determination and some privation a modest degree of self-sufficiency is possible, even in highly developed capitalist societies.

How then can one escape from this intellectual impasse? A number of points need to be made. First, it is clear that domination/subordination-determined social relations occurred in pre-capitalist societies; and, while it may be argued that patriarchal attitudes have been incorporated and "used" by capitalism, this does not deny that the social relations of, for example, domestic labour or social reproduction pre-date capitalism and are qualitatively different from the class domination associated with capitalist relations of production. Second, all societies require work to maintain the collective conscience, in a Durkheimian sense, and social solidarity has universal significance and importance in a way that cannot be reduced, perhaps over-simply, to another of the "needs of capitalism." Third, and perhaps most important, people themselves recognize that work can be qualitatively different and that "work" for a neighbour, "work" for oneself or one's spouse and "work" for an employer are different activities, even though, as shown in the example of ironing, they may involve the same task. Those who wish to reduce the types of work available to a person to simple dichotomies, as being either productive or non-productive, money-generating or non-money-generating, producing either exchange value or use value, do violence to people's experience and make the unwarranted assumption that the social relations of capitalism have become dominatingly all-pervasive. According to this view, principles of social reciprocity have become corrupted by ideas based on market principles, so that the metaphors of exchange infiltrate into personal relationships, with careful calculations of the costs and benefits of various courses of action.

We are now in a better position to answer the question of whether all social activity is "work." Quite evidently it is not. But, equally, work cannot be narrowly defined by constraining definitions, which limit it either to employment, or as a result of abstract philosophizing on the nature of "productive" labour. Work can be understood only in relation to the specific social relations in which it is embedded. Specific people in specific circumstances in specific sets of social relations and social relationships can be described precisely in terms of whether they are engaged in work or play. The word "work" cannot be defined out of context: that, indeed, is the conclusion and answer to the question. . . .

ALIENATION AND THE DEVELOPMENT OF INDUSTRIAL CAPITALISM IN CANADA

James W. Rinehart

Over the past one hundred years or so Western societies have undergone massive social changes that have fundamentally altered the way people work. While the . . .

From "Alienation and the Development of Industrial Capitalism in Canada" from the book *The Tyranny of Work*, 2/e by James W. Rinehart, 1987. By permission of HBJ-Holt Canada. (Harcourt Brace Jovanovich, Canada)

sources of alienation . . ., when taken together, are almost synonymous with what we mean by the term industrial capitalism, they have followed unique developmental paths in different societies. Consequently, to understand how these factors have affected work in Canada requires an examination of Canadian history. The sections which follow trace the rise and development of industrial capitalism in Canada and its impact on work patterns. Special emphasis is placed on the manner in which changes in ownership, markets, and the division of labour have contributed to the intensification of alienation.

The Pre-industrial Setting

Prior to 1840 there were but few signs of the future industrial society. As a colony first of France and later of Great Britain, Canada was built up around the exploitation and export of natural resources. This economic emphasis persisted long into the nineteenth century. Although the dominant industries were trade in lumber, timber, and grain (the fur business was in a state of decline), the lives of the majority of nineteenth century Canadians were relatively untouched by the international trade in staples. The majority of the populace was engaged in agrarian pursuits; the family farm was the unit of production upon which a sizable proportion of inhabitants depended for a livelihood. The nexus of economic activity was the small rural village, which was virtually a self-contained economic unit. As late as the 1860s, Harris and Warkenton (1974) observe, pre-industrial methods of production and distribution made rural areas self-sufficient in most of the necessities of household and farm.

The average farmer was only a marginally linked to markets in agricultural produce. Wheat was grown as a cash crop, but between 1815 and 1850 it proved to be a highly unreliable source of income. Market ties were also attenuated by the fact that most farmers were unable to generate much of a surplus for sale. Many household essentials were produced domestically. Farm families prepared their own soap, candles, and sugar, turned out clothing on handlooms, and fashioned their own ploughs and harrows. Needs that could not be provided by domestic production were supplied by local artisans and tradesmen. The rural economy also had saw, grist, and fulling mills, breweries and distilleries, and small village workshops or *manufactories* where artisans, working with hand tools rather than machines, set their talents to the production of needed goods. The economy of the period was rounded out by itinerant peddlers and craftsmen such as tailors and shoemakers. Barter was the prevalent mode of exchange in this local economy; articles produced or processed in village shops and mills typically were exchanged for payment in kind rather than for money.

The stability and harmony often attributed to rural life in pre-industrial communities were upset in Canada by the presence of capitalist institutions. Pre-industrial capitalist formations created insecurity, dependency, and impoverishment in what was essentially a *petit bourgeois* society of small, independent producers. One major source of instability was the pattern of land ownership. Land was concentrated in the hands of a few persons who amassed fortunes through market speculation. As a result of land monopolies and land markets, large numbers of nineteenth century immigrants, who arrived in Canada virtually penniless, were prevented from purchasing land and establishing their independence. A second cause of instability was the political and economic dominance of a mercantile capitalist class. As the nineteenth century progressed, more and more farmers who relied

on the adverse terms of credit advanced by merchants were reduced to indebtedness. Many were ultimately forced to sell their land. The hegemony of large land owners and mercantile capitalists drove or kept many individuals from ownership of the means of production. By the 1840s thousands of landless people were forced into dependent employment as farm labourers or workers on the construction of roads, canals, and railways. That many individuals were unsuccessful in the pursuit of land or jobs is evidenced by the high rate of transiency within Canada and by the large scale emigrations to the United States.

Despite the fact that capitalist institutions affected the lives of Canadians in the pre-industrial era, priorities of work and life were not ordered strictly in terms of economic criteria. Prices and profits were not the sole or decisive determinants of the means and ends of productive activity. The cultivation of the soil and the production of goods and services were guided by considerations of what was useful as well as by what could be exchanged on a profitable basis. Certainly, cultural factors influenced individuals' orientations to work and the market. Upper Canadians, with backgrounds predominantly in the British Isles, had been exposed in their native lands to the Protestant ethic and its positive enjoinment of hard work, frugality, and commercial success. Because of their exposure to these religious tenets, it is probably true that the relaxed and sporadic work patterns characteristic of other pre-industrial peoples found no strict parallel in Upper Canada. Nevertheless, the structure of the pre-industrial economy dictated a rather casual adherence to the principle of economic rationality and the maximization of pecuniary gains. Local markets, lack of agricultural surpluses, domestic production, a barter system, and workshop and artisanal production geared to personal orders — all combined to form a matrix which inhibited the development of "economic man."

The undeveloped state of the market was accompanied by a rudimentary division of labour that was manifest in the limited number of occupational specialties and in the diversity of tasks performed by individual workers. The distinction between persons who worked with their hands and those who worked with their minds was not a sharp one. Moreover, work often allowed for a relatively broad use of talents and skills and required initiative and responsibility from the worker. Certainly, there were differences in the functions and duties of shop owners and clerks, craftsmen and apprentices, farm owners and farm workers. But in comparison to the intense specialization that accompanied the rise of industrial technology, the pre-industrial division of labour was much less detailed. . . .

Artisans . . . were free from the constraints imposed by a complex division of labour. As late as Confederation, "blacksmiths, coopers, wheelwrights, tinsmiths, and many other artisans practised their trades much as they had been practised for centuries. . ." (Harris and Warkenton, 1974) They established their own production goals (Harris and Warkenton, 1974) and patterns of labour. The finished product initially took shape in the minds of artisans, and it was they who were responsible for executing the operations necessary to complete the project. In discussing the nineteenth century craftsman, Rocher (1970) says, "this is a stage where the division of labour still does not exist and where the maker or manufacturer carries out himself the entire labour for the object from which he derives his name." Of course, the growing number of craftsmen who worked for wages in manufactories had less control over the labour process than their independent counterparts. Employers began to subdivide the labour process and assign specialized jobs to individual workers. Nevertheless, specialization in these transitional production units rarely advanced beyond a primitive stage, because handicraft technology did not lend itself to a detailed division of labour.

Our final concern is with pre-industrial patterns of control of the means of production and their impact on the labour process. As we mentioned above, from an early date the political economy of Canada was ruled by a loose coalition of political office holders, merchant traders, and large land owners. The broad economic contours of the nation were shaped by its colonial status and by the activities of this mercantile ruling class. Native peoples and settlers alike were forced to accommodate themselves in one way or another to these forces. Nevertheless, the continued hegemony of the mercantile class derived mostly from activities connected with the staples trade, land speculation, and control over the credit market, rather than from appropriation of a surplus (and capital) through ownership of the means of production and regulation of the labour process.

This was a society of small producers. Independent artisans set the pace of work in accordance with their own inclinations. Farmers too could control the flow of work, subject, of course, to such exigencies as climate and seasons. Because of their independent status and the undeveloped market, such persons were likely to be task-oriented rather than time-oriented. Labour was not geared to the clock. There was a certain irregularity and lack of precise scheduling of work. Activities were carried out with an eye to accomplishing what was an absolute necessity, and people often alternated between toiling steadily for several days and enjoying extended periods of idleness and leisure.

A casual approach to work is found in the fusion of work, sociability, and play charateristic of the activities of many nineteenth century farm families. During this period, Lower (1958) writes, people worked together, played together, lived together. One prevalent pattern of labour was the "bee" — a gathering of neighbours who collectively assisted with necessary chores. Bees were occasions for entertainment and sociability as well as plain hard work. Guillet gives the following description of bees in Upper Canada: "Besides large quantities of food and drink, it was customary to provide a dance or a 'hoe-down' as the main amusement, while those who chose not to dance engaged in sports, games, and conversation." A tradition of co-operation also permeated the lives of habitants in Lower Canada. Deffontaines says that work bees, whether they were for moving, wood cutting, land clearing, wool spinning or husking, were frequently organized for mutual aid. . . .

The main argument of the above discussion is this: The undeveloped state of the division of labour, the virtual absence of advanced markets in commodities and labour, and the relatively widespread ownership of the means of production meant that a greater proportion of people in pre-industrial Canada exercised control over the means and ends of production than is the case in modern society. The way people worked and the way they defined work were quite different from what now prevails. The consequence of this set of circumstances was that there was less alienation from work than there is in Canadian society today.

The Setting at Mid-century

After 1840 the self-contained rural economy was gradually transformed into a more sophisticated system of production and exchange. By mid-century the basis for the emergence of industrial capitalism had been laid by the construction of railways and canals. These transportation arteries stimulated the growth of cities and linked the scattered rural villages, integrating them into a national market.

By 1850 there were over 3000 manufactories in Upper Canada, and in the next two decades the number of skilled tradesmen — carpenters, bricklayers, coopers, iron-founders, and tailors — grew rapidly throughout the country. The economic crisis of the late 1850s eroded the dominant position of merchant capitalists and simultaneously hastened the decline of small-scale craft producers, who often depended on merchants' credit. At the same time a new trend was emerging: steam-powered shops increased twofold, and mechanization was introduced into the iron, wool, and wood industries. That the new society was growing up in the midst of the old one was clear in a city like Hamilton where small stores, offices, artisan shops, and manufactories were still very much in evidence. In such enterprises, relationships between employers and employees were often personal, and their duties and functions did not differ greatly. Production was still largely shaped by direct orders from customers (Katz, 1972a). Appearing alongside these pre-industrial institutions were larger, more capital-intensive enterprises. "Before the end of the fifties, Hamilton, besides its locomotives and railroad cars and foundry products, was turning out ready-made clothing, tobacco products, and sewing machines. The expansion was geared to investment in labour-saving machinery, involving growth of the cities at the expense of village handicraft" (Pentland, 1959). Between 1851 and 1871, the number of machinists in Hamilton increased by 800 percent. During this same period the percentage of the city's labour force working in firms employing ten or more persons rose from 24% to 83%.

But overall, the process of change was slow and uneven. At the time of Confederation, Canada remained a basically rural nation (50 percent of the labour force was engaged in agricultural pursuits). The future shape of the Canadian economy was most clearly visible in the presence of factories located in metropolises like Hamilton and Toronto, and particularly Montreal, which, by the 1870s, accounted for approximately three-quarters of all production in the nation. (Palmer, 1983) A set of forces were actively at work in these urban centres rendering craft skills redundant by the substitution of factories for the craftsman's shop and the small manufactory. We can regard the decades of the fifties and sixties, then, as the prelude to the industrial revolution in Canada. And while the take-off point for industrialization had not yet arrived, this period was important, for during it the village economy was slowly being eroded. Ryerson emphasizes the significance of the gradual dissolution of the local economy:

The "division of labour" between owner and non-owner, between industrialist and factory hand, became possible only with the break-up of the old, self-sufficient, "natural economy" and with the spread of trade, the universalizing of commodity production to embrace labour power itself as a marketable item (Ryerson, 1973: 36).

The Emergence of Industrial Capitalism

Although the date is an arbitrary one, 1870 can be considered as the year when large scale production first began to dominate productive activity in Canada. Between 1870 and 1890, stimulated by a protective tariff, investment in machines increased, and more and larger factories emerged. In 1870 there were about 38 000 manufacturing units in Canada. By 1890 the figure had swollen to 70 000. And during these two decades the number of firms with a capital of $50 000 or more nearly doubled. Manufacturing output increased rapidly, especially in agricultural equipment, furniture, foundry products, tobacco, wood products, and textiles. While the major cities of Ontario and Quebec were the locus of this growth, the Maritime provinces also enjoyed substantial industrial development.

THE FACTORY SYSTEM

Canadian industry arose in a competitive, market-oriented context under the aegis of capitalist ownership. Since the driving force of a capitalist economic system is the necessity to generate profits and accumulate capital, workers are treated as "costs" and it is to the competitive advantage of employers to keep costs at a minimum. Employers also seek to exercise maximum control over workers, for when workers regulate the labour process their activities reflect their own interests and inclinations, not those of employers. Before the factory system came to dominate production, Canadian skilled workers customarily regulated modes of wage payment, the methods, pace, scheduling, and allocation of work, and the recruitment and training of workers. Employers regarded these craft regulations as inimical to their drive for profits and sought to transfer power from the shop floor to the front office. To cheapen and subordinate labour, employers specialized and rationalized the work process, installing machines that replaced workers and reduced the need for skilled labour, and constructing a hierarchy of authority ranging from top executives to supervisors. These measures were used in varying degrees in all spheres of production, but the organization that epitomized the new order was the factory.

A factory is a large scale production unit that uses machinery and a central source of power, such as steam or electricity. Power-driven machinery offered multiple advantages to the capitalist. It reduced the production time per unit as well as the "value" of commodities. Machines with fixed motion paths or those whose speed could be regulated by management, intensified the pace of work and eroded workers' capacity to govern the labour process. In contrast to handicraft technology, machines generally required less skilled, more easily replaceable, and hence cheaper workers. As a result, the number of unskilled and semi-skilled workers — including women and children — grew rapidly. In fact, capitalist employers often preferred to hire women because they were viewed as docile, quick, sober and above all, cheap. An early twentieth century article in *Canadian Machinery* extolled the virtues of the machine which

can work the whole twenty-four hours without stopping, knows no distinctions between Sundays, holidays and any ordinary day, requires as its only lubricant a little oil, being in fact abstinent in all other matters, has no near relatives dying at awkard moments, has no athletic propensities, belongs to no labour organization, knows nothing about limitation of output, never thinks of wasting its owner's time in conversation with its fellow machines. Wars, rumours of war and baseball scores, have no interest for it and its only ambition in life is to do the best possible work in the greatest possible quantity. (Heron, 1980: 23)

While employers were keenly aware of these benefits, skill degradation via mechanization was a lengthy and uneven process. Some machines generated a demand for skilled workers, and some traditional crafts managed to escape the degrading impact of the new technology. For example, the slowness of technological innovation in the metal-working industry enabled Canadian iron moulders to retain a considerable degree of control over the work process and

conditions of employment until the 1920s. Printers also held on to craft prerogatives despite the introduction of the linotype machine, because their organizational strength compelled employers to use skilled workers to operate the new equipment. But the experience of coopers was more common: their inability to regulate the introduction of machine tenders led to the virtual extinction of the coopers' craft by the 1880s.

While we correctly associate the factory with machines and a central source of power, another of its prominent features involves techniques of human co-ordination, supervision, and discipline used by employers to shape the work process to their own ends (Kealey, 1976). A nineteenth century chronicler of the factory system in England, Andrew Ure (1835) recognized this fact, attributing the success of the factory to human rather than technical factors. Writing of Richard Arkwright, who was recognized as the first successful English industrialist, Ure says:

The main difficulty (faced by Arkwright) did not, to my apprehension, lie so much in the invention of a proper self-acting mechanism for drawing out and twisting cotton into a continuous thread, as in . . . training human beings to renounce their desultory habits of work, and to identify themselves with the unvarying regularity of the complex automation. To devise and administer a successful code of factory discipline, suited to the necessities of factory diligence, was the Herculean enterprise, the noble achievement of Arkwright (1835: 15).

Paul Mantoux (1961), in his classic work on the industrial revolution in England, provides a lucid description of conditions of early factory life, and one which could be applied equally well to the Canadian factory system over a century later.

Hard and fast rules replaced the freedom of the small workshops. Work started, meals were eaten and work stopped at fixed hours, notified by the ringing of a bell. Within the factory each had his allotted place and his strictly defined and invariable duty. Everyone had to work steadily and without stopping, under the vigilant eye of a foreman who secured obedience by means of fines or dismissals, and sometimes by more brutal forms of coercion (1961: 375).

Wherever it has occurred, the change from pre-industrial to industrial modes of work has been harsh, and the Canadian experience was no exception. We emphasized conditions of work in the factory because it was the prototypical organization of industrial capitalism. Labourers in construction camps and wage earners in the extractive industries — fishermen, loggers, and miners — were also exposed to miserable working and living conditions. Women, as well as being paid far less than men, experienced working environments as domestics, seamstresses, and laundresses that were at least equally oppressive. So intolerable were these "feminine" jobs that many women working at them preferred employment in factories. In some cases, for example, in the textiles and garment industries, the work forces were predominantly female (Cross, 1977).

In both the primary and secondary sectors of the Canadian economy workers were driven to toil diligently by a series of punitive measures, which were later supplemented by the more refined techniques of persuasion, manipulation, and economic incentives. Among the early measures were oppressive work rules forbidding talking, leaving one's work station, lateness, absenteeism, laxness, and spoilage. Rules were enforced through fines, dismissals, and physical coercion.

Spurred by unrest among the nascent working class, factory acts were repeatedly introduced at sessions of the Canadian Federal Parliament during the 1880s — though none were passed. In the latter years of the decade the federal government launched an investigation of working conditions faced by factory workers, longshoremen, miners, and construction hands. The inquiry documented the exploitation and brutality of the new system — child labour, long hours, appalling working conditions, authoritarian discipline, and low wages.

The testimony of those interviewed and the summary reports of the commissioners unmasked the full meaning of the industrial revolution in Canada. The chairman of the commission bemoaned the growth of the profit motive, which drove the new employers to hire and exploit women and children. Another member of the committee, criticized in labour circles for his anti-labour sentiments, could conclude from the hearings that:

Many children of tender age, some of them not more than nine years old, were employed in cotton, glass, tobacco and cigar factories . . . Some of them worked from six o'clock in the morning till six in the evening, with less than an hour for dinner, others worked from seven in the evening till six in the morning.

He then added:

The darkest pages in the testimony . . . are those recording the beating and imprisonment of children employed in factories. Your Commissioners earnestly hope that these barbarous practices may be removed, and such treatment made a penal offence, so that Canadians may no longer rest under the reproach that the lash and the dungeon are accompaniments of manufacturing industry in the Dominion.

REACTIONS TO THE INDUSTRIAL SYSTEM

We have seen how the new industrial order intensified structural alienation among Canadian workers. But was there a subjective counterpart to this structural powerlessness? And if working people were in fact psychologically estranged from their work, how can this be demonstrated?

Initial information on the extent to which structural alienation penetrated the consciousness of Canadian working people can be inferred from the known disparity of work styles typical of pre-industrial and industrial societies and the major adjustments in work habits and culture necessitated by the latter. Wherever it has arisen, industrial capitalism and its work requirements have clashed with pre-industrial cultural values and practices. E.P. Thompson informs us that "the transition to mature industial society entailed a severe restructuring of working habits — new disciplines, new incentives, and a new human nature upon which these incentives could bite effectively (Thompson, 1967: 5).

As in England and other societies that experienced an industrial revolution, early Canadian capitalists had to call on people from non-industrial backgrounds to form their work forces. The bankruptcy of small farms and the shrinkage of land available for settlement forced individuals with agricultural interests and work habits to search for jobs in industry. It takes no special imaginative powers to understand why these "men and women fresh from Canadian farms and Old World fields did not adjust easily to the new discipline of machines and factories" (Kealey, 1976). Tradesmen accustomed to the more irregular pace of work typical of small manufactories (which were being forced to close because of their inability to compete with larger, mechanized units) and independent artisans were also obliged to join the ranks of the industrial proletariat. With the exception of Irish labourers who worked as navvies in the construction of Canadian canals and railways, all the others who made up the new working class had been accustomed to patterns of work and life far different from what they were exposed to in industrial settings. Given the dramatic disruption of work patterns induced by the emergence of industrial capitalism, a solid *prima facie* case can be advanced for the presence of widespread and intense feelings of alienation among the early Canadian working class.

More direct evidence of alienated mental states can be inferred from behavioural expressions of discontent among Canadian workers. The most obvious of these were the formation of trade unions, strikes, picketing, demonstrations, and other easily recorded manifestations of unrest. These easily identified expressions of restiveness can be construed as efforts to reduce or overcome alienation by striking at its sources. Workers organized in various ways to challenge the power of employers to dictate the terms and conditions of work. Their efforts were also directed at regulating market forces, upon which wages as well as the right to work depended. Equally revealing of subjectively experienced alienation are activities that ordinarily elude public recognition. These largely unrecorded behaviours involve, in part, the *ad hoc* devices workers employ to resist on a day-to-day basis the organization of work. These behaviours range from individual acts of sabotage to various forms of insubordination and subversion, operating through the medium of cohesive groups of workers. Such actions can be interpreted not only as angry reactions to work but also as attempts to humanize work and to establish control over the production process.

Driven by the need to earn a living, the early proletariat adjusted in various ways to the industrial system. Some simply endured the hardships and deprivations. Others embarked on a lifelong series of job hunts, moving from town to town in search of a living wage and more tolerable working conditions. But the majority of workers never passively surrendered to the exploitative and alienating nature of industrial life. We can only piece together a vague, albeit revealing, picture of the *ad hoc* resistance among working people of this era.

Testimony given to the 1889 Royal Commission affords glimpses of workers' daily unwillingness to put up with industrial injustice and the strategies they used to protest against it. Expressions of discontent included spontaneous walkouts, work stoppages in the plant, restriction of output, industrial sabotage, insubordination, and simple refusals to show up at work on holidays and the day after payday. . . .

The Concentration of Production: 1890–1920

If the 1870s and 1880s witnessed the rise of the factory system, the period 1890 to 1920 was one of concentration of the means of production. The 70 000 manufacturing units of 1890 dwindled to 22 000 by 1920, a reduction which indicated more rather than less industrial activity. Through the formation of joint-stock companies (business organizations set up to amass large sums of capital), mergers (between 1900 and 1914, 73 mergers absorbed 345 firms), and internal growth, the manufacturing industry was becoming more concentrated, centralized and bureaucratized. This trend was also evident in the extractive industries, particularly in British Columbia and Nova Scoita.

As industrial units grew in size, business activity became more complicated, and the work process was further specialized and rationalized. This created a demand for administrators, managers, and clerks. In 1901 approximately 15 percent of the work force was employed in white-collar occupations. By 1921 one of every four members of the Canadian labour force wore a white collar, a proportion that would hold fairly constant until the middle of the century. The rationalization of production also stimulated the need for unskilled labourers. Old skills were now rapidly being built into machines and factory work was increasingly subdivided and simplified. By 1920 the factory system had virtually eliminated the manufactories and handicraft production.

Factory owners were not alone in their need for unskilled workers. The mechanization of the mining industry and the growth of railway construction also created demands for fresh labour supplies. Employers, unable to to satisfy their labour needs domestically, looked for help outside Canada. Immigrants, especially those unfamiliar with the English language, were regarded as eminently suitable recruits. Many Canadian businessmen "wanted hardy, malleable labourers whose salary requests would be 'reasonable,' who were not unionized, and who could not use the English-Canadian press to focus public attention on their grievances." Responding to the call of employers, the government initiated an "open-door" immigration policy. Between 1900 and 1920, huge waves of immigrants reached Canadian shores.

Immigrants were employed by factories, mines and construction camps to take on the heaviest, dirtiest, cheapest, and most dangerous jobs. Their presence also created a surplus of lowskilled labourers, which enabled employers to hold wages down and to impose strict discipline on those fortunate enough to have jobs. But new Canadians, counted on to serve as a cheap, docile labour force were not as enamoured of their circumstances as employers would have liked. Once they became accustomed to their conditions of work and life, immigrants enthusiastically supported unions, published radical foreign-language newspapers, and built their own militant organizations. . . .

The Transformation of Work and Society: Broad Trends

In a little over 100 years developments in the ownership of the means of production, the division of labour, and markets have combined to transform the nature and organization of work in Canadian society. From a rural society of small independent producers and shopkeepers in the middle of the nineteenth century, Canada has become a nation dominated by monopoly capital, giant enterprises, and government bureaucracies. Once numerically and politically dominant, the traditional *petite bourgeoisie* (self-employed persons in trade, business or the professions, like farmers, fishermen, independent artisans, or physicians) now constitutes about six percent of the Canadian labour force. If we add to the category of *petite bourgeoisie* small employers (about four percent) and major capitalists (no more than one percent), then approximately 89 percent of persons in the Canadian labour force are dependent employees who must sell their labour power for wages or salaries. This enormous growth of employment dependency has meant that the work of more and more individuals is defined and controlled by central authorities.

As the *petit bourgeois* mode of production was being replaced by large corporate and government organizations, labour was increasingly fragmented, first on the shop floor and later in offices. While this trend was facilitated by the introduction of ever more sophisticated technology, the elaborate division of labour did not flow inevitably from technical and mechanical innovations and their requirements. The vertical and horizontal extension of the division of labour was initiated, stimulated, and institutionalized by the employing class, who stood to benefit materially from such changes. In the 1870s the casual rhythms of toil and the comparatively rudimentary division of labour characteristic of the pre-industrial period were shattered by the rise of the factory system in which work was specialized, timed, and closely supervised. The compartmentalization and regimentation of work entailed in the factory system were heightened in the early twentieth century by the application of the principles of scientific management and the introduction and spread of mass production techniques. By chopping up work into minute tasks and divorcing the conception of work from its execution, these two innovations not only made the labour process more repetitive, stultifying, and meaningless; they also were responsible for substantially reducing workers' control over the production process.

Hand in hand with the trends described above, markets in labour and commodities grew and matured. In the middle of the nineteenth century markets were still local and undeveloped and only of marginal importance to the lives of many Canadians. With the construction of major transportation arteries and the emergence of capitalist production units, trade and commerce spread, and the self-sufficiency of the small village was destroyed. Increasingly, Canadian people were compelled to order their lives in terms of economic criteria. Human labour was converted into a commodity that was bought and sold. The overriding objective of business firms — to generate profits and amass capital — was often achieved at the expense of the needs and interests of workers and the community.

The developments delineated above extended and deepened structural alienation. And the alienation spawned by the new industrial order penetrated the consciousness of workers. Since its inception, industrial capitalism has been met by fierce resistance on the part of Canadian working people. While this resistance varied widely in substance and effect, it can be seen as an attempt by workers to deal with the causes and consequences of their inability to govern the process and products of labour.

"WOMEN AND OLD BOATS": THE SEXUAL DIVISION OF LABOUR IN A NEWFOUNDLAND OUTPORT

Marilyn Porter

Introduction

In this paper I want to explore the nature of the sexual division of labour and its relation to the subordination of women by examining how it operates in one, particularly clear, context. By the sexual division of labour I mean something altogether broader than "men's jobs" and "women's jobs," or how a married couple split the household chores. I mean all those things we say and do, how we say and do them, and what social consequences they have that are conditioned by our gender. We need, I think to return to our initial astonishment that so much human activity is gender specific.

Feminist attention has been focussed on societies, or groups within a society, that have demonstrated a more flexible sexual division of labour, or where women have constructed areas of autonomy or even power — where the mould of inevitability has been broken (e.g., Rowbotham, 1972; Caplan and Bujra, 1978; Croll, 1978). Behind this search lies the hope that such exceptions, like the swallow, will herald the summer.

We have long since exposed the myth of the "tokenism" at the individual level, but at the societal level we still cling to it — a habit that prevents our understanding how the struggles of the few can become the common sense of the many. In this paper, however, I want to take the opposite approach, and turn my attention to a situation in which the sexual division of labour appears to be especially rigid and intense. In this way I hope to get some purchase on the interlocking and overriding structures of male domination and capitalist exploitation. My focus is *labour*, rather than sexual divisions rooted in religion, forms of marriage, or other ideological structures. It therefore seemed appropriate to examine a society or community that was characterized by an entirely male occupation.

Maritime Communities

There are many occupations that are pursued principally by men. But fishing was isolated by Murdock and Provost (1973), along with hunting and herding large animals, as a task most often reserved entirely for men in most known human societies. Stereotypically, fishing is dangerous and requires great strength and stamina and long absences from home. Even so, there is, as Andersen (1979) says, "no clearly natural sexually based division of labour in fishing." Despite a number of women actively engaged in fishing around the world (e.g., in Japanese oyster fishing or in Russian freezer-trawlers), it continues to be identified as something that only men can or should engage in. Very occasionally, intrepid women have fished in Newfoundland but, by and large, the stereotype holds there too. From the time of the earliest settlements in the sixteenth century, the principal and very nearly the only occupation on the island was fishing. Eschewing the barren interior, the colonists set up tiny communities all along the 6000 miles of rugged coastline to exploit the bountiful supplies of cod offshore. Thus, each little "outport" is a microcosm of a wider community devoted to fishing. And only men

From Marilyn Porter "Women and Old Boats: The Sexual Divison of Labour in a Newfoundland Outport." From *The Public and the Private* edited by E. Gamarnikov et al., 1983. By permission of Marilyn Porter, Memorial University.

fish. James Faris (1972, 12), like many of the anthropologists who have described out-port culture, economy, and social structure, took it for granted that "in a fishing community one could reasonably expect a sharp division of labour along sexual lines." The title of this paper is taken from one of his informants in Cat Harbour who, accounting for why they called new boats "he" old boats "she," said "You can't count on women and old boats; they'll both leak after a few years." Indeed, Faris describes a sexual division bordering on hostility. Women, if not witches, are certainly strangers and "jinkers" who pollute the fishing so that they might not set foot in the the boat or go near the nets. Here we are not talking simply about "men's work," but about entire communities that are identified in terms of an activity that is, by definition, gender specific. In such communities women do not simply have unequal access to the means of production, as in pastoral communities; they are specifically excluded from fishing. But, as Andersen and Wadel (1972) point out, in Newfoundland women are (or were) undisputably part of the *fishery*. In the production of the traditional sun-dried cod, they made up most of the "shore-crowd," who split, salted, washed, and dried the fish on the "flakes," a process that was both skilled and added considerably to the value of the catch, (Brox, 1969: Antler, 1976).

Thus, in the traditional inshore fishery in Newfoundland, the sexual division of labour was drawn between the harvesting and processing sectors. With the changes in the inshore fishery to produce deep frozen cod products, this division has had to be renegotiated with crucial consequences for the sexual division of labour.

There were many technological changes in the Newfoundland fisheries from the 1960s to the early 1970s. However, the vast majority of the smaller outports are still characterized by the traditional inshore fishery, heavily concentrated on cod, using small (under thirty foot) open skiffs, operated by family-based crews, and employing a variety of strategies, e.g. jigging, gillnets, trolling, and lines — but with the cod-trap predominating. In contrast, the women's lives have been directly affected and fundamentally changed by the virtual elimination of the dried-salt cod industry and its replacement by frozen products. From the 1950s, the sun-dried lightly salted cod trade declined as frozen fish processing plants began to be established round the island until now the frozen fish products are dominant. There are fish-plants, or at least holding depots, in virtually all communities. Instead of going to the family stages and flakes for processing, fish now go directly from the boats to the fish plants. These plants employ a substantially female workforce, and any involvement the women have in the fishery is now as individual wage labourers in these local fish plants. Thus, while the catching sector remains virtually untouched, both the technical means and the social relations of production have been transformed in the *processing* sector. Under the old system, the men who "owned" the fish could appropriate women's surplus in accordance with the amount of fish caught. As this no longer happens women are free to redistribute their own labour and to control the wage they earn, by "choosing" to work in the plants.

The men are fishermen, but are the women fishermen's wives?

Women in Newfoundland

There is very little specific material on any aspect of women's lives in the Newfoundland outports, apart from a few descriptive accounts of "life in the old days" and a scatter of papers dealing with different aspects of outport life. But even among these there is evidence of an unexpectedly positive economic role for women (Antler, 1976; Szala, 1952; Davis, 1979 and 1980; Bradbrook, 1980).

For the rest, there is some implicit and covert material hidden in "general" studies, but a more important source are the anthropological monographs published by ISER. These are, coincidentally, all written by men who tend to be preoccupied with fishing, the composition of crews, land inheritance and other androcentric concerns. Women only appear momentarily as they scuttle 'round doing odd chores and not being very interesting, or as the "O's" in kinship diagrams. They are, as Lofland (1975: 144-5) has said "essential to the set, but largely irrelevant to the action. They are, simply, there." More importantly for the purposes of the present paper, male anthropologists usually talk to men, and their information is, therefore, often skewed.

Aquaforte

Aquaforte is a small maritime community dominated by traditional inshore fishery described above. The sun-dried fish gradually gave way to frozen fish after the Fermeuse plant was opened in 1952 and the smaller owner-managed plant at Aquaforte opened in 1972. The flakes and stages, which used to stand at the water's edge below each house, fell into disrepair and boats now gravitate to the community wharf by the fish plant. Forty men in fourteen crews are involved in fishing on a regular basis.

Aquaforte lies some sixty miles south of St. John's on the southern shore, with a total population of 203 in 56 households (1981). All the houses have electricity, and all but one have a telephone. Many of the younger couples have built larger modern bungalows with help from the Newfoundland & Labrador Housing Corporation. Most families have at least one car or

truck. There are three general stores, two garages, and the old school is used as a community hall. The (Catholic) parish church, three schools, doctor, clinic, post office, and government agents are situated in Ferryland, a larger community lying on the adjacent bay to the north. Ferryland and Fermeuse also provide a few jobs, some slightly larger general stores and the bars and other social meeting points. Branch meetings of most of the voluntary associations, the bingo evenings, and other social events take place in Ferryland, often in the Legion Hall. There is no bank anywhere on the shore and, for larger shops, hospitals, and most government offices, they must go to "town," St. John's, sixty miles away.

One of the important changes in recent years is the ease and frequency with which they can do this. The road was "made" in 1965, and paved in 1972. It is no longer an all day trek in a four-wheel drive vehicle, but an easy one-and-a half hour trip. Five women and one man commute daily, during the summer, and some through the winter as well.

In this respect, too, Aquaforte is typical of many small communities that were linked up by road in the last fifteen years, thus vastly increasing both mobility and a tendency to depend more heavily for jobs, goods, and services on the larger towns. This opportunity for employment outside the narrow confines of Aquaforte is especially important for the younger women, as we shall see later.

Aquaforte provided the context I needed — a small maritime community with a traditional inshore fishery. Here I should be able to observe a clear and visible sexual division of labour.

The method I used was ethnographically based. I went to live in Aquaforte, and though the stay was too brief for a real ethnography, I was able to collect most of the usual demographic, economic, and kinship data as well as conducting thirty-nine formal interviews. But most of the time I spent where the women were — visiting, shopping, in church, and at the Darts Club, Bingo, and the Women's Institute — watching to see what the sexual division of labour was, how it operated, and how it was interpreted. Most of the material that follows derives from this "watching." Let us first take, for example, two women — a widow, whose three sons fished together in their father's boat, and one of her young daughters-in-law.

TWO WOMEN: LIZZIE AND CHERYL

Cheryl was twenty-two years old. A few months before I met her she had married Russell (aged twenty-three years) whom she had dated since she was fifteen. When she left school she took a secretarial course at the Trades College in St. John's and then worked as a secretary in the College of Fisheries. All her six sisters are — or were — in clerical work and all six brothers fish in her home community of Renews.

Russell fishes with his two brothers, and Russell and Cheryl live in a modern bungalow he built with their help, a few hundred yards from his widowed mother's house. Lizzie (aged fifty-nine years) was widowed six years ago. Her three daughters are all in St. John's — one married with two children and the other two in clerical jobs. One of her sons, Steve, still lives with her and the other two are close by.

Cheryl "called by" as many as six times a day to see to her mother-in-law because "I get bored up there by myself." It didn't take long to clean their newly built bungalow (with a vacuum cleaner) or to cook for the two of them (in a modern oven). In the afternoon, like all the younger women and most of the older ones, she watched "The Story" on TV. When the truck was free, she drove across to visit her mother and about once a month she took her to St. John's.

When I first met her, Cheryl said she didn't want a job at the plant, "I wasn't trained for that," and she didn't fancy standing ankle deep in water all day for less money than she got as a secretary. But when a job did come up, she snatched it. At least it was something to do, and someone to talk to. She didn't belong to any association or club, but she was pressing Russell to join the Kinsmen so she would be eligible to join Kinettes and, as Lizzie said, "if she leans long enough, she'll get there."

Lizzie was always aware of Steve's departure at 4:30 a.m. though she didn't get up until it was time to cook his breakfast at 9:00 a.m. After that, her days were a whirl of activity. Both her other sons and daughters-in-law visited several time a day, and Steve wandered in and out constantly, all of which kept Lizzie supplied with information, which was traded to the stream of visitors, or on the phone "up and down the road." Lizzie knew all the ways with cod, salmon, herring, and caplin. There was frozen moose in the freezer and fresh eggs from her hens. But her real pride was her knitting and her bedspreads, some of which she had sold through craft outlets. A devout Catholic, she went to mass some weekday evenings, as well as on Sundays, and she took part in the church cleaning, flower arranging and other Women's Auxiliary activities. The church ran a bingo evening once a week, which she rarely missed, sitting with her friends at the same table. A recent past president of the local WI, she not only attended the meetings but was active in the works projects, craft displays, and fund raising, to say nothing of the outings they arranged. She had just triumphantly passed her post to a much younger woman, "it's so difficult to get the young ones in." With showers, weddings and funerals and going along to "support" the guides dinner, the 4H Achievement Day, and other gatherings, she was rarely at home in the evenings.

At weekends the two younger daughters came down from St. John's and Lizzie prepared even more enormous meals to sustain them through their hectic evenings at the bars and the dances in Ferryland and Fermeuse.

Although Lizzie had never been in a boat and knew little of the technology, she could store the figures of the catches in her head and watched her sons' progress intently and with pride. For her, it was part of a long and valuable tradition epitomized by her life with her husband. She liked talking about "the old days" and much of her effort in the WI was spent preserving the old "women's culture," and trying to pass it on to the relatively few young women members.

Lizzie was well aware of Cheryl's predicament, and worried about what would happen to her own younger daughters. One was courting a draggerman from Portugal Cove South, an even more remote outport beyond "the barrens." She could see clearly that for Selene to live there, away from her job, her friends, her svelte jeans, and her holidays, was a recipe for disaster, but Selene was impervious to her warnings. All Lizzie could hope for was that, when they married, Paul could get a job on the St. John's draggers and they would live there.

Lizzie's position of helpless concern typified the older women's desire to preserve what was left of their identity of "fishermen's wives" in an active present, coupled with the realization that the structural basis for that life no longer existed for her daughters.

PAST AND PRESENT

The past is a powerful influence in Aquaforte — less the historical past, than a collective, constructed memory, hypostatized to protect them from an unpredictable and wicked present day world.

For the men, this past is bound up less with the occupation of fishing than with the identity of "being fishermen." Even the twenty-three out of the seventy-three adult males who had other occupations (including four in fish plants) still acknowledged the primacy of fishing. Many of them fished in their spare time or intended to return to fishing when they could afford to. For the Aquaforte fishermen (in common with most of the other inshore fleets) could not live from what they caught. They, in the disparaging words of the local rural co-ordinator "fish for stamps." In other words, their catches during the summer are chiefly valuable because they qualify them to claim Unemployment Insurance Compensation for the rest of the year. Far from detracting from their status as fishermen, they, and everyone else, saw it as an advantage to have time to "go to the woods," "to be free," "to be your own man." In fact, on the basis of a relatively short season, the men won time to build and maintain their houses, their boats, and their gear, cut timber and hunt moose, caribou, turrs, and rabbits, and pursue any number of more individual activities. This combination of cash and subsistence ensured, for most of them, a reasonable standard of living, with comfortable houses, TVs, and cars. Their winter identity was just as much that of a fisherman as the actual fishing they did in the summer. "Fisherman" means that set of plural adaptations that enabled them to continue the traditional *lifestyle*.

Life in the outports has always demanded this kind of flexible response in order to survive in a harsh physical environment at the end of a harshly exploitative capitalist chain. What distinguishes the present set of adaptations is the way in which they have negotiated a space between capital, state, and subsistence that ensures both a much improved material standard of living and a degree of autonomy.

There is very little distinction in either ideas or practice between the older and younger men. The younger ones are slightly more inclined to try new methods, and they certainly drink more alcohol, but their sense of identity is the same.

Not so among the women, for whom there is a definite generation gap between the women of about fifty years and over who can remember life before Confederation in 1949, and the women of forty-five years and younger. The older women are guided by the past in much the same way as the men, and they too defer to the identity of "fishermen." The younger women have no such allegiance and most of them frankly dislike their husbands' role. Everyone agrees that "fishing is a gamble," but younger women are not prepared to tolerate such insecurity, and, believing that there are alternatives, they maintain only a reluctant loyalty to the status quo.

None of the women can actually live the traditional lifestyle the way the men do. Their role as fishermen's wives has vanished. Not only are there no fish to be dried on the flakes, but virtually all other aspects of their past lives have gone as well. In particular, women have stopped having large families. None of the younger women had more than three children, while the women in their sixties had brought up eight or nine or ten children — one had seventeen. Furthermore, they had done this before labour saving devices, convenience foods, or easy access to St. John's. Many of them had reared children before Confederation in 1949 had eased the crushing poverty in the outports. All the women over fifty could remember life as Hilda Murray described it: they could tell you where the fish flakes were, the variety of animals and poultry they kept, about the constant baking, cooking, and washing, the wood chopping and water drawing, the gardens and the berry picking, the bottling, pickling, and preserving — and the "times," the festivals and ceremonies. Now they were left with faint echoes. The older women still

baked bread two or three times a week, used traditional recipes and ingredients, knitted, kept hens, grew potatoes and cabbage, and went berry picking and trouting. But it was not like it was. The women under forty who couldn't remember pre-Confederation days showed little inclination to keep it alive. So whereas the past is still an active part of the young men's lives, for the younger women it has become mere idle tales.

This tension between older and younger women is intensified by exogamy. Men (aged about twenty-five) marry women (aged about twenty-three) from the other villages up and down the shore. Initially, they bring their wives into their parents' house and then, when means allow (fairly soon these days), they build a house close by. Thus, women are separated from their own mothers and thrust into a very close proximity with their mother-in-law. This they resist by keeping close contact with their own mothers, greatly aided by the telephone. Mothers and daughters in neighbouring outports ring each other at least once a day and, as local calls are free, the conversations can be lengthy. As most of the younger women also have access to a car, they can expect to visit their mothers at least once a week.

The older women's criticisms of their daughters' "modern" lifestyle were muted by their acute sense that they themselves have lost their own place as "fishermen's wives," and this was expressed in a grudging admission that, materially speaking, life was a lot better for the younger women. The women in their sixties admitted that "there was a lot of fate in those days." It was hard work, they were poor and there were no luxuries. This remembered reality meant that they didn't really expect their daughters to wash nappies by hand when they could get Pampers, or to use the local midwife when hospitals were available and so good, or have too large families when it would threaten their new (relative) affluence. How can they deny a "better" life for their daughters, when they can't assert, positively, as their husbands can, the benefits of the traditional lifestyle?

Ironically, the older women's eroded identity as fishermen's wives is reflected in their interest in the fishery and their fervent avowal of the fishermen's cause. Many provided details of the fish, the traps, the problems, and the politics. Many of the details were wrong because the older women had rarely been out in the boats and had no direct connection with the fishing. Nor did they go to the many meetings called to decide the trap-berths, to vote on the price of fish, or to protest at the depradations of the inshore draggers. But they were keenly interested and listened carefully when the men discussed such things in the kitchen. Some of them handled all the paperwork, most worried about getting the men up in the morning at 4:30 to go off. When the fishing season starts, the phones buzz with an efficient information network, so that within minutes of the boats returning, every house will have the details of sizes of catch and who caught how much and where.

Whenever I returned after a few days away, my landlady's opening remarks all had to do with the fishing, how many pounds her son had that morning, what it was like in Renews, or, if it was bad, "it's so quiet it's like a place in mourning." The younger women took part in the information network — especially in terms of relaying details of catches from other outports via their mothers — but they usually disclaimed all knowledge of the fishery and even resisted being drawn into the white hot debates of the day, for example, whether someone should lose his trapberth when he went to work on the oil rigs or how to stop the inshore draggers from trespassing inshore. On the other hand, they were less inhibited about actually

going in boats and quite a few enjoyed a Sunday's jigging, though this was never equated with fishing proper.

Let us now look more closely at these younger women.

AND THIS LITTLE PIGGY WENT TO MARKET . . .

More girls than boys continue in post-high school education. A few boys and girls go straight to work in the fish plants. A few boys go fishing, and a few girls babysit for the women working in the plants. A majority of girls who go to university become teachers and nurses, and they, like the male graduates from this town, will not return to Aquaforte, but will marry and settle elsewhere on the island, Labrador or the Mainland. However, the boys who go to Trades School will return as soon as they finish their courses, and will go directly into fishing if they can. If not, they will work on the roads, the forestry, or in garages, until they find a berth. For the girls, it is different. Usually, after a Trade School secretarial or clerical course, they will get jobs in St. John's, for there are no jobs in Aquaforte and precious few (e.g., as doctor's receptionist) in Fermeuse or Ferryland. Some of these girls may well commute up to St. John's daily, at least during the summer. The rest "come down on week-ends" specifically to go to the bars and the dances — to have a good time and look for husbands. In this they are usually successful. Very few of the young Aquaforte secretaries will marry "off the shore."

So within a few years of leaving school, men and women have opted for two contrasting worlds. The young men have returned to the ways of their fathers, but the young women are wholly absorbed in the modern, urban, sophisticated, and materialist life of the big city. In dress, manners, assumptions, and ambitions they are indistinguishable from millions of young North

American women. They enjoy their financial and social independence. They dress smartly and travel afar — to Florida for holidays or to Alberta to visit emigrant relatives. Yet unlike their sisters who are teachers and nurses, they remain firmly attached to the shore and, above all, they marry on the shore. When I talked to them at weekends, they accepted that they would, one day, have to give up their jobs, independence and lively social life because "there's no work down here."

AND THIS LITTLE PIGGY CRIED "WEE WEE" ALL THE WAY HOME

When it actually happens, it comes as an acute shock. Even if, at first, the young couple live in St. John's, they will be unable to afford a house there. And, inexorably, when the babies come, they return to their husband's outport. This is the point of maximum disillusionment. The young married women in Aquaforte were, of course from neighbouring outports. They confessed openly that they were bored, lonely, and frustrated.

Why, then, do they do it? Marriage and return to the shore are not inevitable, as the experience of their more qualified sisters shows. Yet, it had not occurred to any of the young women I spoke to that they would do otherwise. A combination of very expensive housing, acute unemployment, and low wages force the issue once the young couple marry, but it does not answer the question as to why the girls did not move to the mainland, or marry boys with good St. John's jobs, or even marry boys from one of the other towns with more clerical jobs.

It is not, of course, seen as choice. Such "choices" rarely appear as obvious as they do to watching sociologists.

In the social determinations of the young St. John's typists, the option not to marry is not appealing; nor, indeed, are the wages and prospects good enough to offer a long-term career. And through the rosy spectacles of romance there were clear prospects that offered some trade-off beyond the immediate disillusionment. They would secure a modern house, a car, and a decent material standard of living. They would all insist on acquiring all the material accessories they knew to be vital — the electrical gadgets, the luxurious furnishings, the large picture window. Nor were they blind to all the real advantages of outport life. They enjoyed the lack of traffic and the healthy environment for their children.

As the babies come, the young mothers see more of each other and dedicate themselves to building a reproduction Canadian suburban lifestyle. Soon, too, they are drawn into the energetic activities of the voluntary associations — Women's Institute, Kinettes, Darts Club, and the Legion to name but a few.

Most of the Voluntary Association activity was dominated by older women who saw in it not only some outlet for their own energies but also a way to involve younger women in the activities of the community.

Indeed, after the initial singles "hunting" sessions in the bars, the two sexes draw apart for the bulk of their social life, only coming together for the big banquets and garden parties and certain Church and Legion events. Apart from meeting about the fishing, men go out very little, especially during the fishing season. Thus, in the evenings you find the men in each other's kitchens, visiting and babysitting, while the women are more frequently out than not. In this, the older women's frustration at being deprived of their traditional role combines with the younger women's frustration at being deprived of their suburban Canadian role to create a defensive but effective "women's culture."

Men, Women and Power

The ideology of male dominance is strong in Newfoundland culture. A combination of the male culture of fishing (as exemplified in Faris, 1972), a strong Church presence, a kinship system that separates women from their own community, seems to ensure an ideological domination that reflects the male control of the technical means of production. But we have already noted that, while men controlled the gathering sector of the fishery it was women who commanded the *processing* sector. They also showed other signs of economic self-reliance and female solidarity (e.g., selling berries, taking jobs as telegraphists, selling bait to schooners, etc.) Ideological domination, indeed, did not seem to reflect the much more complex economic reality. If we look more carefully at the material on traditional outport life, it is clear that both sexes accepted the sexual division of labour; both men and women worked unremittingly hard and everybody was poor. Nobody had any *real* power, being helpless in the hands of the merchants and the "truck system." Family co-operation was a matter of necessity, and beyond that emerges an equality of respect. "Outport men can turn their hands to anything." "The woman was more than 50 percent." While a certain ideological authority was invested in the man by the outside world (Church and merchant), it had less reality in the practice of the family. For without the women, the men could not operate. They were manifestly dependent on the women not only for the usual "servicing" of cooking and caring, but to realize the value of their catch.

Returning to contemporary Aquaforte, we find evidence of some ideological skewing (though not as much as Faris reports). The Church was still powerful and both men and women accepted the place of fishing and fishermen at the apex of community esteem. But what does this mean in practice? Is ideological dominance reflected in real power? What, in other words, do the women lose by not fishing?

It is women who, by tradition, run the post office. They also run all three shops. Few women are active on the public politi-

cal stage, but two who are have gained places at the provincial level. Marriages are longlasting and, in conditions where the couple are in close physical proximity, there is little overt tension. Nor is there much deference. On the contrary women speak their minds, come to decisions jointly with their husbands, and lead independent social lives.

The sexual division of labour is strong but, while to an outsider (and to the men) fishing is valuable, exciting, and skilful, and men's activity is, therefore, evaluated as more significant than women's, it is hard to see that this assumption is justified by the correlation of economic with ideological dominance.

Conclusion

The mutuality of the relationship between men and women based on the traditional division of labour between fishermen and fishermen's wives has been broken. Men no longer depend on women to "make the fish." Yet the economic independence shown by women has been transferred to their new position as wage labourers in the fish plants. In many households, their wage is not just crucial to the family's survival, it may even be more than the men's contribution from fishing. What has altered, then, is that the women now have a direct relation with capital as individual workers.

Ever since Joseph Smallwood took Newfoundland into the Confederation in 1949, there have been disputes about how to support the scattered outports of the island, and the outcome has been a conflict within the capitalist structure that the inshore fishermen have been able to exploit. Fluent in the complex vagaries of UIC, licensing and quotas, they have carved a niche that is an amalgam of welfare state and subsistence. Despite the obvious disadvantages and drawbacks of outport life — high unemployment, low wages — the outport men have retained dignity and independence.

Their time is their own, and few would swap it for the dehumanized existence of a Hamilton assembly line or an Alberta oil rig. And, at the moment, they don't have to. But the younger women have rejected this package of plural adaption. Deprived of their substantive share in outport economic life, they now want the suburban lifestyle, and that means more money. They therefore put pressure on their husbands to "go to the rigs" or at least to get a job on one of the big draggers working out of St. John's or Trepassey. They also demand more services on the shore, not only for their convenience as consumers but also to provide them with the jobs they so desperately want. Yet would a transformation of the shore in this direction enable capital to redirect the fishermen into waged jobs and to withdraw the substantial subsidy to the inshore fishery and thus force the men into the waged jobs they so desperately *don't* want?

In other words, the thrust of the younger women's initiatives may be to sabotage the delicate accommodation the men have come to. The sexual division of labour in Aquaforte has been transformed by the intervention of the capitalist means of production in the processing sector. The men and women occupy wholly different positions in the relations of production. The sexual division of labour cannot be understood simply or even primarily as a matter of subordination; and without clarification of the role of the sexual division of labour, we are unable to understand this complex social formation. In this paper, I can only raise certain questions and indicate some possible consequences.

While the existence of the generation gap among the women and the consequent fracturing of the "women's culture" seem clear enough, it is by no means certain that the combination of a reasonable material standard of living and increased involvement in the culture of the voluntary associations will not, in time, erode the younger women's resentment. There is nothing inherently antagonistic about the new sexual division of labour.

Nor is it clear what would be the consequences of the pressure from the younger women for clerical jobs resulting in, for example, the establishment of a bank on the shore. On the one hand, clerical work pays better wages than the fish plants and could result in both a greater discrepancy between the women's economic contribution and the men's from fishing, and also between families with a wife so employed. On the other hand, a bank would certainly make life easier for the fishermen. Would it, at the same time, intensify the encroachments of capitalistic "rationality" on one of the last outposts of petty commodity production? There is no doubt that most of the women, if they had the choice, would take any clerical or service job in preference to work in the plants. Would they be replaced by male labour for which the companies have an undisguised preference, and would that drive the women even further from any involvement in the fishery?

Such questions point the way to further research. But such questions cannot even be raised until we take seriously the concept, and the complex reality, of the sexual division of labour. There is no inevitability about capitalist development. Class struggle can intervene in the process — but classes consist of men *and* women. The Aquaforte men cannot either resist or redirect the forces of capitalism without the active help of the women. They are still dependent on them: women are still "more than 50 percent." Nor can the women retain their economic independence and social autonomy without that space that the men have guarded so carefully. The fractured sexual division of labour has to be renegotiated to enable men and women to construct their own lives in conditions of their own choosing.

THE EXPANDING MIDDLE: SOME CANADIAN EVIDENCE ON THE DESKILLING DEBATE

John Myles

Since the mid-seventies, the debate over trends in the skill distribution of jobs has emerged in two contexts. The first, and most well-known, followed publication of Harry Braverman's *Labor and Monopoly Capital* (1974). More recently, it has surfaced in discussions of deindustrialization and the "declining middle," a debate initiated by Barry Bluestone and Bennett Harrison's *The Deindustrialization of America* (1982), and popularized by Bob Kuttner in *The Atlantic Monthly* (1983), and has now made its way into Canada (Shifrin, 1986; Steed, 1986; Economic Council of Canada, 1987).

Contrary to prevailing wisdom, Braverman argued that, under capitalism, employers introduce patterns of work organization and technological innovation in ways that rob workers of their skills. The reason for this is what economists refer to as the incomplete character of labour contracts. Employers buy labour for a specified time period, but of an unspecified intensity and content. The solution is deskilling: management appropriates the knowledge of workers to gain control over the labour process and the effort bargain. As a result, conception and execution in the labour process are separated giving modern economies their characteristic structure — a small elite of managers and knowledge workers standing over a mass of unskilled and semiskilled labourers. The new mass

From "The Expanding Middle: Some Canadian Evidence on the Deskilling Debate" by John Myles. Published in *The Canadian Review of Sociology and Anthropology*, Volume 25: 3, 1988. By permission of *The Canadian Review of Sociology and Anthropology*.

occupations of unskilled and semiskilled workers in manufacturing, sales, service and clerical jobs, according to Braverman, made up at least two thirds of the American labour force in 1970.

The issues raised by Braverman go well beyond concerns with the organization of work. As Panitch (1978) observes, Braverman's study was not just a book on the labour process. Its central purpose was to identify the class structure of the advanced capitalist economies. His critique, like Porter's (1965), was directed at the view that, with the decline of agriculture and the expansion of white collar work, the shape of modern economies could be described in terms of a large middle *mass* of skilled, mental workers resting on a small and shrinking working *class* of blue-collar manual workers. Instead, modern economies should be thought of as constructed on a base of both new and old "mass occupations" of unskilled and "semiskilled" proletarians — workers with nothing to sell but raw labour power. He was challenging claims concerning the composition of the working class on the one hand and the size, importance and likely evolution of the "new middle class," on the other. His conclusions concerning the new middle class were that its size had been exaggerated, its future expansion was intrinsically self-limiting, and that it too would slowly be subject to internal proletarianization. Moreover, the growth of new middle class professional and managerial occupations had come at the expense of the working class, i.e. by the appropriation of their skills and the erosion of craft autonomy.

It is useful to divide Braverman's thesis into two parts since in this paper I address only one of his claims. The first concerns the pattern of development that led up to the present period, his claim that the current "Taylorized" organization of production was preceded by a labour process in which most work was performed by skilled craftworkers. The second concerns where things will go from here, the likely pattern of development as we move into a "post-industrial" economy. My purpose in this paper is to evaluate the latter claims and, here, Braverman's thesis can be contrasted to Daniel Bell's (1973) classic statement on these matters.

For Bell (1973: 127ff.), the prototypical worker of the post-industrial period is the professional who provides the services — health, educational, recreational and social — and the technical knowledge that define a post-industrial economy. Braverman thinks otherwise. Anticipating the deindustrialization theorists, he argues that the main result of the sectoral shift into services is expansion of the new mass occupations of unskilled clerical, sales and service workers. The usual bias of capital towards low skill, low wage industries is exacerbated by the availability of surplus labour generated by the increasing productivity of machine-based industries (Braverman, 1974: 384) and previously untapped sources of paid labour such as women.

The deindustrialization theorists carry Braverman's account a step further but the concern is with wages not skills. The imagery invoked is not the replacement of skilled by unskilled workers but the replacement of well paid, unskilled, industrial workers by poorly paid, unskilled, service workers (Kuttner, 1983: 61). Like Braverman, however, they conclude that the direction of change is toward the unskilled sectors of the service economy. The shift from goods to services does not mean our children will become knowledge workers; the more likely prospect is a job in a fast-food outlet.

In this paper I address these claims with an analysis of changes in the skill distribution of jobs in the Canadian economy between 1961 and 1981 with estimates based on the census distribution of occupations ranked by skill level. I also compare these findings with self-reported skill requirements from the Canadian Class Structure Survey (Black and Myles, 1986) conducted in the winter of 1982–83. In general, the results support Braverman's conclusions concerning the shape of the skill distribution but not about trends. During this 20 year period, skilled jobs expanded at an accelerating rate. A significant part of this upgrading was a result of growth in new middle class professional and managerial occupations but there is no evidence that this occurred at the expense of (i.e. by deskilling) the working class.

Survey results based on self-reports do indicate a "polarized" skill distribution but not of the sort anticipated by Braverman. Rather than dividing managers and professionals from the "new mass occupations," the cleavage created by the skill distribution is *within* the working class. Neither Braverman's nor Bell's imagery of the emergent skill distribution describe this pattern adequately. A more appropriate model to guide future research, I argue, is found in the split or dual labour market metaphor of the segmentation theorists.

Data and Measurement Issues

One of Braverman's major contributions was to persuade a wide spectrum of social science opinion that conventional indicators of skill were seriously flawed (Allen, 1986; Porter, 1979). Traditionally, two sorts of evidence have been used as indicators of upgrading — changes in the educational qualifications of the labour force and changes in occupational composition. With respect to the first, Braverman identified the fallacy of equating the possession of human capital with its use — the debate is about the characteristics of jobs not their incumbents — and pointed to a growing body of evidence that questioned the relation between educational credentials and the way jobs are performed.

The second type of evidence from which upgrading has been inferred is change in occupational composition using what Spenner (1983: 828) calls the non-measurement strategy for studying job skills. Quite simply, an underlying skill distribution is *imputed* to broad occupational groups (white collar, blue collar) and conclusions are drawn accordingly. As Allen (1986: 94) observes, traditional evidence from occupational data has tended to reflect "the middle-class conceit that white collar work is better than blue-collar work whereas factory work is better than farm work." Braverman undermined this conceit by pointing out that the majority of jobs — including white collar jobs — could be mastered in a maximum of two to twelve weeks compared to the years of training required by traditional craft occupations.

The skill measures for this study reflect these concerns. The core of the analysis rests on distributions in which occupations are ranked on the basis of training time and skill requirements. The indicators are from the worker trait data used in compiling the *Canadian Classification and Dictionary of Occupations* or CCDO. Designed as a tool for employment counselling, the CCDO provides scores of the skills and training required for several thousand different occupational titles and refer to requirements of positions rather than to attributes of incumbents.

The data are samples from the 1961, 1971 and 1981 censuses for which detailed occupation (four digit) and industry (three digit) codes based on the 1971 standard were available for all three periods. The 1961 data are a special sample of approximately 134,000 observations recoded to the 1971 standard as part of a special project conducted by Statistics Canada in the 1970s. In the 1981 census, all observations

were coded to both the 1981 and 1971 standards. The recoded 1961 sample was a representative sample of the experienced labour force in Canada's ten provinces. The 1971 and 1981 samples were drawn from the same universe following the same method used to construct Statistics Canada's public use samples. . . .

General Trends

The distributions in Table I confirm Braverman's claims about the shape of the skill distribution. Occupations that could be learned in less than a year still accounted for almost two thirds of all jobs in 1981 and "skilled" occupations on the GED scale (level 4 or higher) represented less than a third of all jobs. The survey data examined later indicate the worker trait data may provide a low estimate of the number of skilled jobs but sustain the conclusion that the majority of jobs still have modest training or skill requirements.

In contrast, Braverman's claims about emergent trends are not supported. All four indicators show a monotonic increase in skill levels over time. And rather than slowing down, there was more upgrading during the seventies than during the sixties. These underlying trends were similar for both men and women (Table II). Young workers were the exception. They shared in the skill growth of the sixties but not the seventies despite rising educational credentials.

At this level of analysis, the deskilling thesis clearly does not do very well. However, any fair assessment of Braverman must do more than examine general trends. Ultimately what is at issue is not the trend line but the structure and processes underlying it. In the following sections I examine two of these. First, I consider Braverman's discussion of the occupational shifts that underlie changes in the skill distribution. Second, I take up the debate over

Table I
CHANGE IN THE SKILL DISTRIBUTION OF JOBS, EXPERIENCED NON-AGRICULTURAL
LABOUR FORCE, CANADA 1961–1981

1. Specific Vocational Preparation	⟨ 30 Days	1–3 Months	3–6 Months	6–12 Months	1–2 Years	⟩ 2 Years	Total
1961	20.6	21.8	15.0	14.9	11.1	17.6	100%
1971	18.2	19.8	16.6	14.7	11.2	19.9	100%
1981	12.0	17.2	17.8	18.9	11.1	23.1	100%
2. General Educational Development [a]	1	2	3	4	5–6		Total
1961	8.0	31.7	35.6	16.6	8.2		100%
1971	7.6	26.9	37.2	18.9	9.4		100%
1981	6.1	21.3	40.9	20.1	11.5		100%
3. Cognitive Complexity [a]	1	2	3	4	5		Total
1961	22.6	15.1	32.8	15.6	12.9		100%
1971	19.9	14.2	32.6	15.8	17.4		100%
1981	16.9	13.7	28.9	19.5	21.0		100%
4. Routine Activity [a]	1	2	3	4	5		Total
1961	28.1	19.3	23.8	15.7	13.6		100%
1971	24.5	19.4	24.6	16.5	15.1		100%
1981	17.4	19.2	28.4	17.8	17.2		100%

[a] Skill measures are ordered from low to high

the expected consequences of the transition to a post-industrial economy.

Occupation and Skill

Skill change can occur in two ways (Spenner, 1983: 826): through changes in the work *content* of occupations and through *compositional* shifts in the distribution of occupations. The skill mix in hospitals, for example, can be altered by changing the work done by nurses (a change in content), by changing the ratio of nurses to nurse assistants (a change in composition) or both. Moreover, the effects of one may offset those of the other. Engineers, for example, may be deskilled relative to some point in the past but their enormous growth and

high skill levels relative to other occupations has resulted in a net increase in skill levels for the economy as a whole. Indeed, as Wolff and Howell (1986: 4) suggest, deskilling in work content may well result in compositional upgrading: as the skill requirements of jobs decline (a change in content) it becomes feasible to phase them out altogether (a change in composition).

Part of the observed change in skill distributions is the result of the changes in occupational composition. . . . Over the 20 year period, there was significant expansion of the share of professional-managerial occupations, more modest expansion of mass white collar occupations and a decline in the share of blue collar occupations. These patterns are important since

Table II
CHANGE IN THE SKILL DISTRIBUTION OF JOBS, WOMEN, EXPERIENCED NON-
AGRICULTURAL LABOUR FORCE, CANADA 1961–1981

1. Specific Vocational Preparation	⟨ 30 Days	1–3 Months	3–6 Months	6–12 Months	1–2 Years	⟩ 2 Years	Total
1961	33.1	16.1	13.8	13.1	10.3	13.6	100%
1971	23.3	17.4	20.9	15.4	9.8	14.2	100%
1981	13.0	15.2	23.8	21.2	9.7	17.0	100%

2. General Educational Development [a]	1	2	3	4	5–6	Total
1961	3.9	36.8	35.4	20.1	3.8	100%
1971	4.5	27.3	45.2	18.6	4.4	100%
1981	3.9	17.7	51.3	20.2	6.9	100%

3. Cognitive Complexity [a]	1	2	3	4	5	Total
1961	26.6	7.0	34.5	18.9	13.1	100%
1971	21.1	7.6	38.5	19.7	13.2	100%
1981	17.3	7.4	33.1	24.7	17.5	100%

4. Routine Activity [a]	1	2	3	4	5	Total
1961	40.5	13.2	22.3	16.7	7.3	100%
1971	29.2	19.6	27.4	15.9	7.5	100%
1981	18.2	19.7	34.4	17.7	10.1	100%

[a] Skill measures are ordered from low to high

Braverman did not deny that professional and managerial jobs would expand. Rather, he argued that the growth of the new middle class of managers and professionals occurs *at the expense of* (i.e. by deskilling) the working class. The new middle class expands by appropriating the knowledge and skills of traditional craftworkers thus rendering them redundant.

Braverman (1974: 403–9) goes further and argues that in the long run there is a tendency to proletarianize the intermediate strata as well. This begins to occur as soon as the size of these professional and management occupations is large enough to warrant application of the forms of rationalization previously applied to craftworkers. An extensive literature on the "crisis" of the new middle class suggests the recession of the seventies exacerbated this trend.

The implication of all this is that the upgrading observed in Table I may well be the result of compositional shifts in the occupational structure (more managers, professionals and technical workers) that conceal the deskilling that has gone on within these broad categories. Inspection of the underlying skill by occupation distributions . . . provides only modest support for these claims. There has been no change in the skill composition of blue collar jobs and substantial upgrading of white collar jobs. There was also a significant shift from lower to higher levels of administrative work. Only among professional and tech-

Table VII
CHANGES IN THE COMPOSITION OF THE EXPERIENCED NON-AGRICULTURAL
LABOUR FORCE BY INDUSTRY, CANADA 1961–1981

	SHARE OF LABOUR FORCE (%)		
	1961	1971	1981
1. Industrial Sector			
— Extractive	4.3	3.1	3.1
— Manufacturing	25.3	22.8	20.1
— Construction	7.8	6.8	6.7
— Transport, Communication, Utilities	10.6	8.8	8.4
Total Industrial	47.9	41.5	38.2
2. Service Sector			
— Trade	18.3	17.6	18.1
— Business Services	6.2	7.9	10.2
— Social Services	9.9	15.1	15.1
— Consumer Services	9.6	9.8	10.7
— Public Administration	8.0	8.2	7.8
Total Services	52.1	58.5	61.8

nical workers is there some indication of "deskilling" and then only during the sixties.

In sum, there is little evidence that the new middle class has expanded at the expense of (i.e. by deskilling) the working class. Nor is there evidence of an ongoing decline within the middle class. On the contrary, the expansion of new middle class jobs, especially higher level managerial jobs, accelerated in the seventies. The implication would seem to be that Bell and the post-industrialists provide a more useful starting point for understanding emergent trends in class structure than Braverman and the deindustrialization theorists. In the following section I consider whether this is the case.

Bell, Braverman and the Post-Industrialism Thesis

Bell (1973: 126–7) and Braverman (1974: 425) agree in broad terms about the skill content and class structure of industrial so-

cieties. For both, the basic feature of an *industrial* economy is the polarization of skills between a small elite of managers and engineers, on the one hand, and a mass of unskilled and semi-skilled machine operatives on the other. The source of contention concerns where things are likely to go from here. . . .

Two features of the industrial skill mix stand out. First, the "industrial" sector of the economy has few skilled jobs. Second, the implications of the shift to a service economy are ambiguous because of the bifurcated character of the service sector. On the one hand, there are the highly skilled social services (the "welfare state" industries) and business services (the "information economy") and, on the other, the unskilled services associated with wholesale and retail trade and consumer services (where the fast food industry is located). Bell is betting expansion will occur in the former set of industries; Braverman and the deindustrialization theorists anticipate expansion in the latter.

The changes in industrial composition ... indicate that both were correct but that Bell was closer to the mark than Braverman. Wholesale and retail trade, the largest employer of unskilled service workers, was relatively stagnant during this period. Consumer services (and especially accommodation and food services), the least skilled sector of the economy, did expand but modestly. In contrast, both social and business services, the most skilled sectors of the service economy, increased their shares significantly, the former during the sixties and the latter during the seventies.

On balance, then, we would expect changes in industrial composition to have an upgrading effect on skill levels. What of the trends *within* industries? ... There is evidence of deskilling within a few selected industries during the sixties but the changes were small and reversed by larger positive changes during the seventies. A similar pattern for this time period using very different measures of "deskilling" has also been found in the United States. ...

... [T]here was modest upgrading of skills during the sixties and this was largely due to changes in industrial composition. In general, the industry shift effects are larger than the skill composition shifts during this decade. The more important conclusion, however, is that most of the change in skill levels occurred in the seventies and changes in industrial composition had little or nothing to do with these shifts. Virtually all of the change during the seventies was a result of the changing skill mix within industries. In sum, neither Bell nor Braverman provide a useful point of departure for understanding the shifts that occurred during this 20 year period. There is little of the deskilling anticipated by Braverman; and the upgrading observed was only marginally associated with the emergence of the service economy described by Bell.

The general conclusions to be drawn ... are that the years from 1961 to 1981 were a period not only of continued but accelerated expansion of new middle class jobs; that this "upgrading" did not occur by deskilling the working class; and the prevailing accounts derived from theories of post-industrialism are little help in explaining these trends. I return to this issue in the conclusion. ...

Discussion

These results and similar studies of changes in occupation and class composition in both Canada and the United States show that through the sixties, the relative increase in the number of "good jobs" in the economy was largely a result of changes in industrial composition. A major component of this was employment growth in the state sector — public administration during the fifties and the health, social and educational services associated with the modern "welfare state" during the sixties. By the seventies, however, this source of growth was exhausted. What accounts for the expansion of "good jobs" thereafter is a more speculative matter.

Foot and Meltz (1985) suggest changes in relative wage differences and technological factors as explanations. Wright and Martin (1987) propose changes both in technology and in the international division of labour. An account that directly incorporates the major economic turning point of the seventies, the economic "crisis" that became manifest after 1973, is that of Bowles, Gordon and Weisskopf (1983). They argue that the expansion of non-production workers in the American economy formed part of the "Great Repression," a concerted effort by employers to regain control of the workplace lost in the preceding decade. This is a plausible interpretation because of the well-known historical bias of the American economy towards greater reliance on managerialist solutions to problems of productivity and technical change. In sum, a traditional response of North American management to economic crisis and productivity slowdown is to throw more management at the problem. This bias continues to be evident in the structure of the contemporary American economy and also in the Canadian, especially in those sectors dominated by American branch plants (Black and Myles, 1986). This interpretation is also broadly consistent with trends in the Canadian economy during the seventies. During this period, the growth of managerial occupations accelerated while the reverse was true for professional occupations (Foot and Meltz, 1985: 17).

None of the results presented here, however, should be construed as providing direct or indirect evidence for this conclusion. By itself, the evidence is ambiguous. More managers and professionals may mean a greater effort to gain control over the "shop floor"; it may also be the result of eliminating less skilled jobs and a shift to a more complex labour process. Rather, my point is to underline the sort of explanation these data require and it is not one that can be deduced from general theory in the manner of Bell or Braverman. The "managerialist bias" identified by the economic historians was a distinctive feature of *American* capitalism, not of capitalism per se. Hence, it is a subject for historical-comparative class analysis, not something to be mechanically deduced from general theory.

Whatever the explanation, it is clear that at this point in history traditional dichotomies based on the "goods" to "services" distinction are no longer adequate for anticipating emergent trends in the skill distribution of jobs or class structure. The main reason for this is that most of the labour force is now part of the service economy. As a result, future changes will take place largely *within* the service sector. Over the postwar period, the service economy has had three major growth centres:

the state sector including social services and public administration, business services and consumer services. Each has had, and will continue to have, rather different effects in shaping both the supply of "good jobs" and the class structure. Of these, two developments warrant particular attention.

First, the threat of the "hamburger economy" portrayed by Kuttner and the deindustrialization theorists is quite real. Food and accommodation services made the list of the ten fastest growing industries in all three decades between 1951 and 1981. The effects of this growth were outweighed by expansion in the higher skilled industries but were not without consequence. The growth of consumer services in general has helped produce a bifurcated post-industrial labour market in Canada, especially in the commercial sector. Should these industries continue to experience disproportionate growth, this pattern will become even more pronounced. In the past, the effects of rapid growth in these industries were muted by their small share of the economy but this will not be the case in the future. One of the consequences of an increasing share of the economy is to magnify the effects of subsequent growth. Fortunately, this dual labour market for job skills is a contingent not a necessary feature of a post-industrial economy. Esping-Andersen (1987) has shown that the rapid expansion of what he calls the "food, fun and wine industries" is an American trend that is not replicated in either Sweden or Germany. But it is one that has spilled over into Canada.

There are a number of reasons for this including characteristics of the labour supply (a large number young workers) and the demand for such services (a large number of single-person households). But labour politics and public policy are also important. In Sweden, wage policies that systematically put low wage employers out of business combined with the "crowding out" effects of a large welfare state create an inhospitable environment for low wage, unskilled service industries (Esping-Andersen, 1987). Conversely, policies that encourage "flexible" labour markets at the bottom of the wage structure and government "restraint" in providing public services will tend to have the opposite effect.

Public policy is also related to a second important development observed here — the *relative* decline of the "public sector/welfare state" new middle class. Until the seventies, the growth of professional and managerial occupations was concentrated in the state sector — public administration in the fifties and social services in the sixties. In contrast, the seventies favoured the growth of a "commercial" new middle class. This change in the composition of the new middle class is most evident among its credentialed members (university graduates). In 1971, over 60 per cent of all graduates were employed in the public sector. By 1981, the figure had fallen to 54 per cent and among young workers (age 15–29) the change was even more striking — from 60 to 45 per cent. This shift was reflected in a political culture increasingly hostile to "big government" and distrustful of the "welfare state" as a solution to social problems. The new middle class formed in the fifties and sixties (civil servants, teachers, social and health care workers) became the target of this distrust. But the result — government restraint in health, education and welfare — is probably less indicative of a "crisis" of the new middle class than the emergence of a new political fault line within it. If so, the seventies may come to mark an important turning point for understanding emergent processes of class formation in Canada. At the level of class structure, however, the seventies not only continued but accelerated the postwar trend that has resulted in the "expanding middle."

PART

4

INEQUALITY in CANADA

SOCIAL INEQUALITY

It should be apparent to you by now that many of the readings and our discussions in this book have directly or indirectly touched upon questions of social inequality. Indeed, by this point, you may well have concluded that sociologists are obsessed by social inequality and its consequences. In this you would be mostly correct: sociology is, to a large extent, the study of social inequalities — their origins, their inevitability, the ways they are justified, how they are transmitted from one generation to the next and their consequences for society and for the individual. More generally, the questions raised by the concepts of equality and inequality are inextricably part of the whole of the intellectual tradition of Western thought.

The three dominant ideologies that make up our political culture — conservatism, liberalism and socialism — are, in large part, different ways of thinking about the inevitability, the nature and the justice of social inequality. Conservatives, because of their emphasis on and concern with order and stability, have typically defended traditional systems of hierarchy on the grounds that they give people a sense of "place," limits to their aspirations and continuity of culture. Liberals, on the other hand, have been mainly concerned with the basis of inequality; their answer is not to do away with inequality but to ensure that inequalities that do exist are based not on socially created differences but natural differences, those that allegedly derive from individual differences in ability and

416

talent. Finally, socialists have challenged both conservative and liberal views by questioning why there should be social inequality at all. For socialists, the problem of social inequality cannot be resolved through changing its basis but only by doing away with it altogether.

These are rather pure and clearly over-simplified depictions of these three positions. In practice, and as in many debates, the issues are often lost or confused because terms like equality, equality of opportunity, equality of condition are used too loosely and often interchangeably. Take for example the structural-functionalist's position on inequality in society. The classic statement is by Kingsley Davis and Wilbert Moore (1945). They argue that all societies have been stratified (that is, divided into unequal layers) and that such stratification is functional for the survival of societies. Inequality is necessary, they would argue, because one must reward those with the necessary skills and training to ensure that they perform the important jobs in society. But even if we were to accept the functions of inequality in these terms, this is not the same thing as accepting the inevitability and necessity of structured inequality, what sociologists call *social stratification.*

Social stratification implies continuity of inequality from generation to generation; one's place in the stratification system is to a large extent determined by the position of one's parents. In other words, even if Davis and Moore were right, once we move from inequality to social stratification, we must recognize that those at the top of the hierarchy will be able, to some extent at least, to pass on their positions of privilege to their children, whether or not they are the best-trained or best-skilled among us. And they are likely to have greatest access to the kind of training Davis and Moore were considering.

So we must distinguish between inequality and stratification. For example, by now we are all aware of the dramatic inequalities that women in most societies have had to endure. Certain occupations have been virtually closed to them, particularly those occupations at the very top. They have had to endure lower wages for the same work that men do. They have often been discouraged from work and when they did work, usually because of economic need, they were expected, at the same time, to perform the traditional "female" obligations of housework and childrearing. Women have experienced discrimination in occupation, education and the legal system, a fact which has persisted for generations. But we hesitate to describe this as a stratification system because women's inferior position is not passed down through the family. Rather, women, like men, are born into families that provide them with differential life chances. Sexual inequality, then, cuts across lines of social stratification.

In any case, Davis and Moore are also talking about two kinds of inequality. On the one hand they assume that *inequality of condition* is necessary; that is, people will always have different amounts of the scarce and desirable resources. On the other hand, their model implies *equality of opportunity;* that is, the rewards, ultimately, are distributed unevenly but everyone starts with an equal chance of obtaining these rewards. Indeed, when North Americans talk about equality, they usually mean equality of opportunity. This, since at least the eighteenth century, has been the liberal ideal: a *meritocracy,* where the people at the top got there because of their merit and ability. Liberals have criticized Davis and Moore for assuming that America had already achieved this, that ethnicity, family background and other ascribed factors did not matter. Radicals have criticized them because, they argue, equality of opportunity is impossible given inequality of condition. And it is a rather humble aspiration when one ought to be seeking full equality — equality of condition.

Why should we want equality of condition? The most influential answer remains that provided by Karl Marx. Marx saw the consequences of inequality of condition as dehumanizing and alienating to some extent for those at the top as well as at the bottom. While all societies were characterized by some form of inequality, for Marx capitalism represented the most vicious form of stratification. As we have seen, the particular feature of capitalism is that if capitalists are to survive they must make a profit; they must, in effect, exploit workers and never give them full value for their labour. Predictably, Marx was most concerned about the consequences of capitalism on the workers. What he saw in industrializing England encouraged him to believe that workers would experience increasing misery of toil and pauperization, that the gap between the owners, the *bourgeoisie*, and the workers, the *proletariat*, would widen and that, inevitably, overt conflict would ensue. Only through a revolution that would overthrow the bourgeoisie and end private ownership could people reach their full potential. The revolution would mean an end to people's alienation from one another, from their work and from themselves.

Marx's argument raises a further distinction that must be maintained in discussions of inequality and stratification: the distinction between objective and subjective social class. Bourgeoisie and proletariat are objective social classes defined not in terms of people's subjective perceptions, but in terms of their relationship to the means of production. Marx believed that people's subjective perceptions, their attitude and their consciousness could be predicted if one knew their objective social class. Certainly he was well aware and in fact insisted upon the role of *ideology* in masking the proletariat's real interests and in producing what he called a *false consciousness*, but he was also confident that people would inevitably realize their true interests, and that objective class would become subjective class.

Here he was mistaken, at least for most Western industrial societies. In Canada, for example, many of his insights and predictions still seem to be sound. The gap between the "haves" and "have nots" does seem to be widening. According to John Porter (1965) and, more dramatically, Wallace Clement (1975), more and more of our lives seem to be shaped by a corporate or economic elite. And liberal attempts to change this through trying to reduce the impact of racial and ethnic discrimination and through the promotion of universal education have not managed to change the picture very much. But Canada has not spawned a revolutionary class. Surely the N.D.P. would not be a third party if all Canadian workers recognized themselves as members of the proletariat.

Perhaps Marx underestimated the flexibility of capitalism, its ability to contain dissent and forestall revolutionary class consciousness. Perhaps, too, he could not have been expected to predict the powerful role of ideology, as expressed through the media, the pulpit and educational institutions, in promoting a benign acceptance of inequality. Credit cards, term payments, unemployment insurance and welfare cheques all serve to quiet dissent and even to give the appearance of more widespread affluence. And finally, Marx underestimated how much real affluence (even if not power) capitalism could engender for its workers.

CLASS, STATUS AND POWER

It is perhaps for these reasons that many American sociologists have found a greater affinity with the work of Max Weber than with Karl Marx. Weber, too, emphasized the importance of economic class, which he believed determined one's life chances, but he gave room to other dimensions of inequality, namely status and power. Status allows for the subjective dimension, recognizing that people's perceptions of various positions in society may vary to some extent independent of the economic benefits attached to those positions. For example, a member of the clergy with little income may still be seen as having high status. This means two things: first, the individual gains non-material rewards for his or her position, namely prestige; and second, he or she gains a type of power with this position, namely influence, at least in his or her immediate community. Indeed, most Canadians probably think of class in such status terms.

Power is the trickiest dimension to deal with, in part because Weber meant so many things by it. There is the power, for example, that comes with particular positions in society; that is authority, legitimated power. The power of your professor, your parents, politicians and so on, in part derives from your acceptance of their authority. In part, too their power is objective in that they control resources: grades, goods, money, practices and so on. The power of the economic or corporate elite is of a different kind. It is often invisible to us. We may not know who these people are. But decisions taken by a fairly small number of board directors may well shape much of our society and, therefore, our everyday lives.

EDUCATIONAL INEQUALITY

Any discussion of social inequality and social stratification leads, inevitably, to a consideration of the role of educational systems in sifting and sorting people into various positions in the class structure of industrial societies and, more important perhaps, socializing people to accept as just and proper their position in that structure. Of course, this is not the only role education plays in society. Education may be about jobs, job training and social mobility, but it is also about knowledge, about values, about shaping and developing human nature. It is for this reason, certainly, that utopian thinkers and social reformers have seen in education a panacea for the social and economic ills of society. It has long been argued that to create a better society we must first find a way to produce "better" people; and schooling, if done properly, has the potential to put right what parents often do so badly. And underlying many of the recent criticisms of education is the belief that it should not only be a means to an end, a place where we acquire the skills, values and credentials necessary for a good job, but an end in itself, a place where nonconventional ideas can be entertained, where people can develop and learn critical perspectives about their society, where people can learn to think. In short, whatever else may be discussed, there remains an implicit and often explicit commitment to the "ideal" of education and knowledge as essentially liberating and humanizing.

This ideal, however, is being overshadowed, as most people — educators, parents, students — increasingly come to view education primarily as a means to an end, specifically a good job, a better job than one's parents. Educators feel compelled to make their courses and programs relevant not in political but in occupational terms. Students demand that courses be justified in terms of their employment potential as they are increasingly called upon to play the credentials game. Parents worry about the educational choices their children make as they come more and more to believe that their children's life chances are determined by their educational achievement. It is, therefore, understandable that sociologists have generally focused on the relationship between education, social stratification and social mobility and have, in effect, equated education and equality.

Until the 1970s the most pervasive influence on the sociology of education came from the liberal-functional perspective (structural functionalism). This is a view of education that is both optimistic and familiar to most Canadians. Essentially, education is seen as a good thing for the individual and for society. On the one hand, it is the key to success and opportunity and, on the other, it is the way to bring about a more just and efficient society. For the most part, the task of sociologists working within this perspective is to document, understand and eventually eliminate the barriers — family background, ethnicity, poverty, sex — standing in the way of equality of educational opportunity. In sum, from a functionalist perspective, the educational system serves two related functions. It is functional for society because it helps to ensure that the skilled and specialized occupational roles of industrial society are filled more adequately and performed more efficiently. At the same time, the individual benefits because he or she has a better likelihood of turning talents and ability into upward mobility.

However, in recent years Marxist theorists have challenged many of the assumptions and conclusions of these functionalists. They have, for example, pointed out that although we have spent a great deal of money on educational expansion and reform, not much has actually changed. The basic patterns of inequality of condition and opportunity do not seem to be much affected by changes in the educational system. Rather, when viewed from a conflict perspective, it makes more sense to think about education as reproducing and legitimating class relations and class inequality. You cannot change society, say these theorists, by changing education because the structure and content of educational systems are shaped by capitalism and not the other way round. No matter how much the educational system is expanded not everyone can be upwardly mobile or made equal. Simply, in an unequal and stratified society some will end up at the top, but most will eventually be slotted into the less favoured positions in the hierarchy. Like other institutions, education does not exist in a cultural, economic and historical vacuum as structural functionalists have more or less implied. Like other institutions, it must, therefore, be viewed in the context of power and inequality and must be seen as the outcome of people's actions and decisions.

Finally, the approach and method of the symbolic interactionist perspective have forced our attention back to what goes on inside the school. One aspect of this has been a concern with the "hidden curriculum." It is a hidden curriculum because its content — the values, the uncritical acceptance of and compliance with existing structures, the conformity it teaches — is largely unintended and, until pointed out by sociologists, unrecognized. And others, by focusing on the social relationships within the school and on the very way schooling is organized, have shown how education in often very subtle ways accustoms children to the constraints and indignities they will later encounter in the wider capitalist and bureaucratic society.

There is, then, a good deal of rethinking and re-evaluation of the role and function of education in capitalist societies. And, compared to the rather benevolent and optimistic picture created by liberal, functionalist theorists, the general result is pessimism and gloom about the potential of educational change to bring about meaningful social change. At the same time, you should recall that one of the insights of the interaction perspective is that as people interact and try to make sense of their social world, social structures are often affected and altered in unexpected and unpredictable ways. To repeat, people are both products of social structure and producers of social structure, so that the outcomes of even the most repressive and constraining systems are always somewhat uncertain and are often novel. So, even those theorists most concerned with the repressive and ideological consequences of educational systems have, at the same time, remained confident that education, perhaps more than other institutions in capitalist society, has the potential to be a source of liberation rather than alienation.

ETHNIC INEQUALITY

In Canada, in particular, it is impossible to talk about inequality without some consideration of ethnic inequality. While it may be comforting to think of Canada as a rich, ethnic mosaic, to use Porter's (1965) terms, the mosaic is vertical. Canadians often seem to take pride in the assertion that Canada has no "race" problem. Perhaps we are simply "polite racists" (Hughes and Kallen, 1974: 214). Perhaps, too, our history of racist immigration policies has until recently kept "visible immigrants" to relatively small numbers. And, like poverty, perhaps our "visible ethnic groups" are hidden from us in inner city ghettos and isolated rural communities just as our race problem is hidden, largely in reserves. And finally, the reports by blacks and Asians would suggest that our racism is losing its polite veneer.

In the absence of evidence that skin colour can tell us anything about a person other than his race, it is significant that we nevertheless continue to make distinctions among people according to their race. For the most part sociologists prefer the term "ethnic group" because it emphasizes the social rather than the biological. Very often, of course, members of ethnic groups will have a colour and other features in common, but this is not inevitable. Rather, ethnic groups involve at least three crucial elements: (1) reference to common origins; (2) a conception of distinctiveness; and (3) the necessity that ethnicity is relevant only when two or more categories of people are involved in the same society.

As we suggested, in Canada, as in most multi-ethnic societies, one's ethnic background has been an important determinant of one's social and economic position. While it appears that many ethnic groups have achieved a degree of equality, it remains the case that if we were to draw a pyramid of the Canadian stratification system we would, predictably, find white Anglo Saxons at the top and aboriginal peoples at the very bottom. And for many ethnic groups, rising in the stratification system has meant giving up, even disowning, one's ethnic commitments.

It is in this context of ethnic inequality that we prefer to think of ethnicity as a *resource*. On the one hand, dominant groups, what Porter (1967) called *charter groups*, were able to use ethnicity to assure their privilege and exclude others through discrimination and ethnic nepotism. They were, in other words, able to impose an *entrance status* on some groups of immigrants. Further, the resurgence of ethnicity — the renewed concern with our roots — can be seen as an effective mechanism for defusing class consciousness, for creating divisiveness and competitiveness within the working class.

Ethnicity may also be seen as a resource used by subordinate groups to protect themselves against the dominance of others and as a rallying point for concerted collective action. In some cases ethnic consciousness, the awareness of ethnic inequality, may lead to class consciousness.

Finally, ethnicity may also be a resource we all use in our everyday lives as a way of presenting ourselves in some situations, as a way of identifying ourselves to others and as a way of establishing bonds with some. In this sense ethnicity is not a hard social fact but a matter of social definition, one of our many symbolic resources. Ethnicity, then, serves as a good illustration of the paradox: people are producers of society and products of society. In our everyday lives we use ethnicity to typify, to classify, ourselves and others. We may accept or reject, long for or detest ethnic designations. We may say that it is everything or that it matters not at all. But insofar as these designations have become real, structured and incorporated into the common stock of knowledge, they act back upon us, affecting our life chances, our range of choices and even our consciousness.

chapter

11

Social Inequality

As you will have discovered in reading through earlier chapters of this book, the issue of social inequality is, as we have also pointed out, a central concern to most sociologists. While in recent years much of the attention has been directed to gender and, perhaps ethnic, dimensions of social inequality, the selections in this chapter focus more explicitly on class and status inequality but, for the most part, also show how class, gender and ethnicity are interrelated ways that power is maintained in capitalist societies. The first two selections are largely theoretical discussions of the nature of class in modern capitalist societies while the latter shows you something of the personal and social consequences of class inequality for those with power and those without.

The brief excerpt from Frank Parkin's book *Class, Inequality and Political Order* goes a considerable way towards explaining why, despite Marx's prediction, capitalism has not been transformed through revolution. Parkin, a British sociologist, takes as his starting point that no system of inequality and oppression can be maintained for very long by force alone: the ruling group will always try to find ways to legitimate its privileged position. According to Parkin, if Marx went wrong in his analysis it was in underestimating the resources available to the ruling class (the dominant group) to help it justify its position: to make its values, its definitions of situations become *the* values, *the* definition of reality. As he suggests, it is able to do so because, as well as controlling the means of production, the ruling class also controls the main agencies of socialization: the media, education and religion. In addition, those in the subordinate group who nevertheless remain dissatisfied with their condition are likely to be encouraged to strive for individual advancement rather than for collective improvement.

The second selection, by Wallace Clement of Carleton University, is the lecture he gave in 1988 when he was selected as the Sorokin Lecturer at the University of Saskatchewan. Clement is a former student of the late John Porter and as a result of his earlier writing, particularly *The Canadian Corporate Elite* and *Continental Corporate Power*, his name is almost synonymous with a class analysis of Canadian society. In this selection, he draws upon that earlier work as well as his subsequent studies of hard rock mining and the fisheries to argue for the continuing importance of class analysis as a way to understand much of what is occurring in Canadian society. Here, he does not view class inequality in isolation or in abstract terms but as something that affects us in our everyday lives and intersects in complex ways with gender, ethnicity and regionalism. In reading this selection, you may want to think back to what was presented in Chapter 10, "Economic Perspectives" and in Chapter 9 "Canadian Sociological Perspectives" since all of the selections in those chapters also take for granted that "class matters."

The final selection is an excerpt from Peter Newman's *The Canadian Establishment*. He portrays Canada's ruling class in human rather than analytical terms and, at the same time, illustrates the processes by which power is maintained and passed on to the next generation. It is evident that whether "new" or "old" money, the position of the Canadian ruling class comes, as Marx was fully aware, ultimately from its control of the means of production, from the fruits of capitalism and private prop-

erty. But, in describing the subtle distinctions between "establishment" and "newcomers" to the ruling class, Newman also illustrates Max Weber's insights into how other resources besides economic ones enter into the attempts of groups to maintain and enhance their position and exclude others. Finally, however envious we may be of the lifestyle of the Establishment, Newman also captures the constraints and anxieties, perhaps alienation, that the extreme inequality of capitalism generates even for those supposedly benefitting from it.

RELATED READINGS

C. Wright Mills: "The Promise" (Chapter 1)
Robert Brym: "The Classic Questions of European Sociology" (Chapter 1)
Rhonda Lenton: "Homicide in Canada and the USA: A Critique of the Hagan Thesis" (Chapter 7)
Margrit Eichler: "And the Work Never Ends: Feminist Contributions" (Chapter 9)
Robert Brym: "The Great Canadian Identity Trap: Implications for the Comparative Study of Class and Power" (Chapter 9)
Susan Russell: "The Hidden Curriculum of School: Reproducing Gender and Class Hierarchies" (Chapter 12)

CLASS, INEQUALITY AND POLITICAL ORDER
Frank Parkin

Inequality in the distribution of rewards is always a potential source of political and social instability. Because upper, relatively advantaged strata are generally fewer in number than disadvantaged lower strata, the former are faced with crucial problems

From *Class, Inequality and Political Order* by Frank Parkin. Published by Granada Publishing Limited. Reprinted by permission.

of social control over the latter. One way of approaching this issue is to ask not why the disprivileged often rebel against the privileged but why they do not rebel more often than they do. In this way we can examine some of the social mechanisms which stabilize the stratification order and help to maintain the system of inequalities intact. A few industrial societies have solved this problem in a fairly crude and straightforward way: by the use or threat of physical coercion. The Soviet Union under Stalin, or South Africa at the present time, are examples of societies which have relied heavily on repressive means to maintain the distribution of privileges. This situation, though, is fairly uncommon among modern industrial societies. Even in social systems founded on the use of force, attempts are always made to win the hearts and minds of the populace. Thus, one of the central aims of any dominant class is to make the rules governing the distribution of rewards seem legitimate in the eyes of all, including those who stand to gain least from such rules. The greater the extent to which this is achieved, the more stable the political order is likely to be, and the less need for recourse to coercive means.

Elements of consensus and coercion are, of course, present in the control system of every society, although the actual balance between the two elements varies from one society to another. It is useful to bear in mind that even in the most apparently benevolent societies the state has important functions of coercion and control, as well as of welfare. Direct internal threats to the institutions supporting inequality often bring into play the physical forces which, ultimately, are designed to protect these institutions. Inside the velvet glove of any state is always an iron fist. The complexities of modern class-stratified societies cannot properly be understood unless the existence of both glove and fist are acknowledged.

For the most part, as we have said, the use of physical coercion is not commonly necessary to control members of the underclass. There are a variety of less drastic social mechanisms, mostly not deliberately created by the dominant class, which have a safety-valve effect on the stratification order. One of the more important of these safety-valves, and one having a number of political implications, is the process of social mobility.

The concept of a dominant value system derives from Marx's celebrated statement that "the ideas of the ruling class are, in every age, the ruling ideas." This proposition rests on the plausible assumption that those groups in society which occupy positions of the greatest power and privilege will also tend to have the greatest access to the means of legitimation. That is to say, the social and political definitions of those in dominant positions tend to become objectified and enshrined in the major institutional orders, so providing the moral framework of the entire social system. It is not of course necessary to posit any monolithic social or normative unity to the groups which cluster at the apex of the dominant class. Undoubtedly they display variations in political and social outlook — as, for example, between aristocratic or traditional *élites* on the one hand and managerial or entrepreneurial *élites* on the other. However, these differences are not likely to be fundamental with regard to the values underlying class inequality and its institutional supports. With the partial exception of that group or stratum loosely defined as the intellectuals, almost all groups within the dominant class tend to define the reward system as morally just and desirable. Dominant values are in a sense a representation of the perceptions and interests of the relatively privileged; yet by virtue of the institutional backing they receive, such values often form the basis of moral judgements of underprivileged groups. In a way, dominant values tend to set the standards for what is considered to be objectively "right." This holds not only for the rules governing the distribution of rewards but also for many other aspects of social life. In the sphere of culture, for example, the musical, literary and artistic tastes of the dominant class are accorded positive evaluation, while the typical cultural tastes and pursuits of the subordinate class are negatively evaluated. Thus in the allocation of national resources to the arts, or of honours to their practitioners, the claims of "*élite*" culture will tend to have precedence over the claims of "mass" culture. To take a somewhat similar example, the characteristic speech-patterns and linguistic usages of the dominant class are generally regarded as "correct," or what counts as the grammar of the language; the usages of the subordinate class are often said to be "incorrect" or ungrammatical where they differ from the former, even though such usages may represent the statistical norm. These examples serve to illustrate that what is essentially an *evaluative* matter can be transformed into an apparently *factual* one by virtue of the legitimating powers of the dominant class. And what applies to the evaluation of linguistic forms, or of artistic tastes, applies equally to evaluations of the reward structure. Thus, to accept Marx's proposition regarding the genesis of "ruling ideas" is not to subscribe to a conspiracy theory of society; it is rather to acknowledge that moral and political rules hold sway not because they are self-evidently "right," but because they are made to seem so by those who wield institutional power.

Now the more completely the subordinate class comes to endorse and internalize the dominant value system, the less serious will be the conflicts over existing inequalities. There is of course a good deal of variation in the extent to which lower strata come to accept the version of social reality held by upper strata. The caste system of traditional India provides an extreme case of a stratified order permeated throughout by values legitimizing the power and privilege of dominant groups. The subordinate class in industrial society does not generally subscribe so completely to a meaning-system which confirms its own inferiority. Nevertheless, certain tendencies in this direction are observable. Studies by McKenzie and Silver, and Eric Nordlinger have demonstrated that large segments of the British working class express moral commitment to many of the dominant class symbols and institutions which sanction inequality. Furthermore, there appears to be fairly widespread disapproval among the subordinate class for bodies such as trade unions which attempt to redress the balance of advantages in their favour.

This phenomenon of a class, or at least a large segment of it, endorsing a moral order which legitimizes its own political, material, and social subordination is open to somewhat different assessments. On the one hand, it can be taken as evidence of a socially desirable political consensus — a social order free from disruptive class conflicts. Or, on the other hand, it can be understood as an example of a society in which the dominant class has been especially successful in imposing its own definitions of reality on less privileged groups. Thus, to equate political and social consensus with the good society, as so many contemporary writers do, is really to state a concealed preference for a system in which the dominant class has effectively translated its own values into a factual moral order binding on all. From this point of view, societies such as France or Italy, where the dominant class has been less successful in shaping the workers' perceptions, are regarded as somewhat inferior political species. Unlike the "stable democracies" or the "civic cultures," the subordinate class in France and Italy is prone to *incivisme*; that is, it puts a different interpretation upon inequality, and its own place in the social order, from that provided by the meaning-system of the dominant class. Thus, from the consensualist standpoint, a class-conscious proletariat is regarded as dysfunctional for the political system, in so far as it is less amenable to normative control by the dominant class than is a deferential proletariat.

Deferential interpretations of the reward and status hierarchy stem from acceptance of the dominant value system by members of the subordinate class. It should be emphasized here that deference as a general mode of understanding and responding to the facts of low status does not necessarily entail a sense of self-abnegation. Rather, it tends to be bound up with a view of the social order as an organic entity in which each individual has a proper part to play, however humble. Inequality is seen as inevitable as well as just, some men being inherently fitted for positions of power and privilege. To acknowledge the superiority of such people is not to demean or belittle oneself, since all must benefit from their stewardship of society. . . .

Acceptance of the dominant value system by members of the subordinate class does not necessarily promote deferential orientations. Equally consistent with such acceptance is a view of the reward structure which emphasizes the opportunities for self-advancement and social promotion. This aspirational model of reality endorses the class and status system as it stands, but also represents it as a relatively open order in which men of talent and ability can, with effort, rise above their present station. Thus, whereas the deferential version of the social world accepts the class system as a fixed, unchanging order, the aspirational version allows for the social exchange of personnel between classes, while accepting the necessity for classes as such.

Aspirational interpretations of the reward structure appear to flourish among those in a quite different social situation. We should, perhaps, expect such an out-

look to be found most commonly among members of the working class who are downwardly mobile. Those who have had some experience of white-collar styles of life have access to a window on the social world which is closed to most of their class peers. Hence, their symbolic meaning-system is likely to incorporate many of the elements common to the dominant class, while also differing sharply from the deferential view, which draws essentially upon the experience of *inherited* subordinate status. In addition to the downwardly mobile, it could be expected that those whose occupations make them somewhat marginal to the working class would also be prone to visualize the reward system as a fairly open opportunity structure. Those in positions such as foreman, policeman, supervisor, etc., are in the anomalous situation of exercising authority over members of the subordinate class without actually being part of the dominant class. There is not much reliable evidence concerning the general outlook and attitudes of those who are "in" but not altogether "of" the subordinate class; but we might speculate that working-class authority figures would, by virtue of their position, be committed to dominant values, but not to a deferential interpretation of them. . . . [T]here are some indications that marginal members of the subordinate class are relatively successful in encouraging educational ambition and performances in their children. And this might be taken as one index of a general aspirational outlook similar to that held by the downwardly mobile. However, given the absence of information on this score, we cannot get much beyond plausible hunches. Even less appears to be known about the extent to which Western societies vary among themselves in the distribution of deferential and aspirational norms. British society, for example, is said to be especially productive of deference, while in the United States aspirational values are said to be far more entrenched. If this is in fact so, then it is clear that the interpretation of any given society's dominant value system is not simply a function of variations in the social location and attributes of different groups. Obviously, if American or Australian workers who are in face-to-face relations with their employers, or who live in small communities, do *not* tend towards a deferential outlook, then we cannot posit a general connection between images of society and structural factors. The stock of class symbols "available" in a society must to some extent be influenced by specific historical and cultural factors; consequently, we should expect to find variations in the dominant value systems of different societies, and therefore certain variations in the meanings given to inequality, structural similarities notwithstanding.

DOES CLASS MATTER? ACCOUNTING FOR THE DIRECTION OF CANADIAN SOCIETY

Wallace Clement

What is "class"? Gerhard Lenski (1966) defined virtually everything as "class," *including* racial, ethnic and religious groups, gender and age. R.M. MacIver's (1965) usage is even more diverse, including "intelligence-test classes, shape-of-head classes, color-of-hair classes." Lasswell and Kaplan's (1950) definition — "a *class* is a major aggregate of persons engaging in practices giving them a similar relation to the shaping and distribution (and enjoyment) of one or more specific values — is equally indiscriminate. They go on to say

From "Does Class Matter? Accounting for the Direction of Canadian Society" in Wallace Clement *The Challenge of Class Analysis* 1988. Reprinted by permission of Carleton University Press.

that "there are as many kinds of classes as there are values." These definitions are not particularly insightful.

Canadians were recently treated to a rare insight by the *Maclean's* Poll, conducted by Decima Research, which asked respondents to categorize themselves according to class. *Maclean's* reported that egalitarianism predominates; an overwhelming 89 per cent of respondents placed themselves in the middle class, while only 2 per cent described themselves as "upper class." But significantly, 9 per cent thought of themselves as "lower class." A closer look at the question asked reveals how they got these peculiar results. They were obtained by elmininating the working class. Respondents were forced into answering to either some type of "middle" class or "lower" class. Social scientists have known for the past thirty or more years that the self-identification of class requires inclusion of a working-class option; "lower class" is a derogatory and virtually meaningless category. In a recent national survey in connection with the International Class Structure Project, a similar question that included the category of working class was asked, and 36 per cent replied that they identified themselves as working class, 55 per cent as middle class and 9 per cent as upper middle class. The obvious lesson here is that the question asked respondents makes a considerable difference, especially for complex concepts such as class. For those who may be interested, the International Class Structure Project found that between 60 and 62 per cent of Canada's labour force can be specified as working class using structural and relational criteria. *Maclean's* slight of hand did not eliminate the working class forever.

Before addressing the question "Does Class Matter?" more systematically, it is worth briefly recalling the two principal traditions of class analysis as inspired by Weber and Marx. For Max Weber, classes are sets of people who experience the same status positions vis-à-vis a series of markets. Classes are specified in terms of control (or its absence) over goods and services; individuals are the unit of analysis. Both objective and subjective aspects are involved, but Weber argued that there tend to be overall constellations of positions, such as the relation to property ownership, the ability to acquire goods and services, marketable capacities and social status, which may collectivize and act together. The amount of unity exhibited by any such collectivity was considered variable. Weber divided everyone (that is, distributively) into "postively" and "negatively" privileged property classes and the "middle class." The criterion that seems to run consistently between each of these three major classes is the ability to acquire sufficient revenue to command a certain style or quality of life (which Weber terms "class situation").

The Weberian tradition of class inspired what are known as gradational class schemes. These are descriptions of different characteristics, such as occupation, educational attainment or social status, which can be used as evaluative tools measuring inequalities such as income distribution.

Contrasted to the Weberian tradition has been the Marxist one, which has stressed *relational* classes. Karl Marx was not attempting a scheme of ranks, but a theory of social change. As Z.A. Jordan has pointed out, Marx

concentrated on the differentiation of social classes and ignored the stratification based on income, education or occupation. . . . He used the term "class" in the collective sense, that is, he spoke either of the class as a whole or of a certain class property which only a class as a whole, and not each and every member of this class, may have. For instance, when Marx described the proletariat as a revolutionary class, he did not wish to say that each and

every proletarian was a revolutionary, but that the proletariat as a whole had this characteristic (1971: 23).

Whereas distributive properties of individuals can be ranked for all members of society, such is not the case for Marx's collective notion of class, which includes not only social roles, but social action and people with varying awareness of themselves as class actors.

It has been argued within the Marxist tradition that specific "economic interests" are a "necessary" but not a "sufficient" condition for defining social classes. Marx would seem to have confirmed this interpretation with his famous "sack of potatoes" remark in *The 18th Brumaire of Louis Bonaparte* when he said:

In so far as millions of families live under economic conditions of existence that separate their mode of life, their interests and their culture from those of the other classes, and put them in hostile opposition to the latter, they form a class. In so far as there is merely a local interconnection among these small-holding peasants, and the identity of their interests begets no community, no national bond and no political organization among them, they do not form a class (1963: 124).

For the purposes of this discussion, I will adopt the convention of defining classes in terms of property rights to the means of production and control over the labour power of others. The key in the following definition is that the classes are not merely categories, but relationships that are undergoing processes of change. The capitalist class controls property rights and commands the labour power of others. The working class is excluded from control over property and is obliged to sell its labour power. Estrangement from the *means* of labour and the *rights* of property are the key criteria for identifying the working class. This distinguishes them from the traditional petite bourgeoisie who control their own property (that is, access to the ability to labour). The modern petite bourgeoisie (or new middle class) performs the tasks of capital (which include surveillance and discipline along with coordination and direction) and the tasks of labour, thus exercising both the rights of property and the obligations of labour, even though, like the working class, it must sell its labour power.

The fundamental direct *contradiction* in this formulation is between the capitalist class and the working class, yet there are key *tensions* involving especially the trajectories of the new middle class and the traditional petite bourgeoisie. Relationally defined classes are always in tension: they are only in contradiction at particular historical moments. Tensions can promote social changes, whereas contradictions can transform entire epochs. Both are antagonisms, but of a different order.

The tradition of class studies in Canada has been influenced by both the Weberian and Marxist formulations. Currently class analysis is at a crossroads. It is under attack for being too limited and narrow, particularly with respect to gender, ethnicity and region, and overly rigid with respect to economic determination. I wish to make an argument for coaxing class analysis along a more nuanced, powerful path.

The academic exercise is not to *simplify*, but to *clarify* — to provide conceptual tools for richer understanding. Class, I contend, is one such clarifying concept, but one which has suffered greatly from simplification. I undertake to resurrect class from its contemporary abuse as a simplifying concept and attempt to raise it again to a clarifying one.

Part of the complexity of class is the fact that its analysis proceeds at several levels of abstraction. Mino Carchedi, for example, has identified four such levels: the "pure capitalist economic structure," which primarily involves the logic of surplus value production; the "capitalist socio-economic system," which includes political and ideological dimensions along with the economic; the "concrete society," which is composed of several co-existing modes of production; and the "conjunctural level," which is a specific junction of a concrete society and the level at which political action occurs (Carchedi, 1977: 18). A similar, yet less complex, set of levels has been identified by Ira Katznelson in his insightful book *City Trenches*. Most abstract is the level of capital accumulation and the mode of production. This is followed by the level of the labour market and workplace patterns. Finally, there is a class as "a happening" rather than "a thing" whereby classes act as an historical collective. Analysis can proceed at any of these levels of abstraction and should be able, at least theoretically, to move between levels while retaining its integrity.

Increasingly there have been demands, particularly led by social historians, that class be understood and analyzed at the most concrete level of class action. In part this is a response to the limitations of abstractions that tend to be economistic, thus failing to capture the political, cultural and ideological richness of the totality of class not only as a structure but as an experience. Moreover, the dimensions of class as economic/reproductive, political/legal and cultural/ideological are, at the most, moments of one another. Class cannot be only any one of these; class can only exist in their combination. To quote Michael Burawoy's most recent formulation of this issue in *The Politics of Production*, "Any work context involves an economic dimension (production of things), a political dimension (production of social relations), and an ideological dimension (production of an experience of those relations)" (1985: 39). Class in this sense is the combined "effect" of all these dimensions. At the conjunctural level of analysis, class is manifest through each of these dimensions, as my recent research on the emergence of resistance among Canadian fishers attests (Clement, 1986). Such "effects" are transparent among unionized fishers who sell to capitalist enterprises or even the state, but it is also the case for the more translucent co-operatives. Co-ops are class-based institutions. During their formative periods of struggle they were typically directed against large capital, yet as they began to operate, their principal struggle became against labour. Anti-capitalist ideologies and practices were tranformed into anti-labour ideologies and practices, both of which were comprehensible given the material conditions of co-op members and the market situation of co-ops as institutions. The Prince Rupert Fishermen's Co-operative, for example, has had its most bitterly fought struggles with unionized labour on the West Coast, including both the shore workers who process the fish and the crew on co-op member boats catching the fish. . . . [L]abour has been the Achilles heel of the co-op movement and has dramatically affected the ideology and politics of class experience within that movement.

. . . [C]lass relations are everywhere, but they never exist in "pure" form; that is, they always combine with other social relations (except at the very highest level of abstraction). These other social relations include gender, ethnicity, age and region. These combined social relations have significant effects on one another. Class-blind analysts, like gender-blind ones, fail to grasp essential facts of social life. A social scientist without a refined class tool is one ill-prepared to comprehend social relations. But class is more than an analytical tool. It is also an ideology and a practice. It involves not simply categories, but dynamic relationships.

Classes, I contend, never enter the political arena in "pure" economic form; that is, the political expression of class is always in combination with other forces whether they be over issues of nation, ethnicity, gender, region or even political party. Parties are not classes. Even in Sweden, where class has its clearest political expression, the Social Democratic Party is not identical with labour centrals, nor are either identical with the working class. Political parties, by their very nature, combine popular forces with class forces. To put the point even more forcefully, class forces can never exist alone in pure form at the concrete level; they must express themselves in other than strictly economic forms.

The primary contention of this discussion is that if one wishes to gain an understanding of Canadian society, class in isolation is not sufficient. Analysis requires gender, region, ethnicity, etc. Having said that, however, in order to grasp the essence of Canadian society, class is essential. Most enriching is the "chemistry" of class and other factors. The processes of class formation may be universal, but worthy of note are the specific configurations. While class "conditions" non-class social cleavages (gender, region, ethnicity, etc.), it is also conditioned by them. I am not arguing that class is an independent variable and all others are dependent variables. Instead, these factors are relational and interactive, not determined but dialectic.

The most significant challenge to traditional class analysis in recent times has come from the women's movement. Transformations in the household and the labour force, broadly speaking the social division of labour, were the material bases for the women's movement. That movement, it has often been observed, has an internal class character in a similar sense that class is also "gendered." The challenge is to bridge the gap between the workplace, home and community. This connection has been brought to the fore by women's greater labour force participation and the ensuing demands that have been articulated by the women's movement. Analytically these include issues of domestic labour and its impact on both paid labour and gender relations; politically it has involved struggles for day care, community services and family law reforms. Class issues have been affected in significant ways. I am obviously not referring to problems of dealing with domestics (an upper-class problem of servants), but the impact of domestic labour, including child rearing, on single parents or families. There are differences between the middle class, which can afford to commodify (that is, hire someone to perform) a good deal of this labour, as opposed to working-class families that have to struggle through their unions or community groups for basic affordable services.

Ironically, the domestic labour debate has been overly economistic, focusing upon the production of value and productive/unproductive labour, exchange in the context of the reproduction of labourers, and labour power — all of which are class issues, but at the highest level of abstraction. Patriarchy, for example, is a concept germane to gender relations, yet it does not operate at that purely abstract level. Patriarchy is a power relationship between genders wherein men dominate women; men expand their freedom at the expense of women, including the economic, political and ideological manifestations of that domination. What I find most important is the "chemistry" of class and patriarchy. Patriarchy is *not* confined to the family or domestic labour, but is practised in the "public" work world as well; that is, there are gendered patterns of labour force segmentation and patterns of workplace domination. There are no separate public and private worlds since each strongly shapes the other; each affects what is possible in the other through wages brought into the family or the availability for wage labour, depending upon the domestic situation. These issues are ignored at our peril, as Jane Barker and Hazel Downing's study of

gender and the office illustrates. They call for "a recognition that where, when and under what conditions women work is governed by the mechanisms of the family and patriarchy . . . patriarchal relations [are] increasingly firmly rooted in, and defined by the relations and needs of capital" (1980: 65).

A further challenge has come from race and ethnicity. Some of the most exciting recent work in this field has placed class at the centre of such discussions. An excellent example is Ron Bourgeault's (1983) work on class and native people, particularly noteworthy since gender is so integral to his analysis.

Calling upon my own research in the fisheries, . . . the Native Brotherhood of British Columbia is a solid example of the intersection of class and race. Historically racial conflicts in the B.C. fishery included Japanese, native and white fishers in bitter rivalries where class was the terrain of struggle. The Native Brotherhood incorporates within itself class relations that bring it at times in alliance with the United Fishermen and Allied Workers Union and at times in conflict. Within the Native Brotherhood there are both seine captains who employ crew and the crew members themselves, whereas the union excludes seine captains who own their boats. This rivalry is also gendered since native women tend to work in the fish processing plants, where the union is strongest, whereas the Native Brotherhood represents native men on the fishing vessels. It is impossible to comprehend adequately the West Coast fisheries without a firm grasp of gender, race *and* class.

A further feature too seldom examined with respect to class is age. Particularly noteworthy is the high unemployment among young people, but also the nature of the work they do experience. Increasingly they are being marginalized into part-time, non-union, low-skilled jobs. These jobs are expanding rapidly with the increasing use of franchises in areas of fast-food, retail stores, gas stations, etc. The responsibility of franchise holders is to supervise labour and direct operations according to the specified (and contractual) rules set by large-scale capital. This reduces large-scale capital's risk and its need to spend on the supervision and recruitment of labour. The class experience of young people who are the bulk of the labour force in franchise operations is being moulded. These jobs are uniform in every sense: clothing, procedures and practices. There is no room for innovation or initiative, and it is dead-end work. They do not even have to add — only be able to identify a "Big Mac."

This type of work is not developing talents, initiative or solid class traditions. In today's labour market, many young people find that when they are out of school this type of work is all that is available, often stringing together several part-time jobs to make ends meet. Recently, Ester Reiter (1986) published her study of "Life in a Fast-Food Factory." She shows that Canadians now spend a third of their food dollar outside the home and much of that in franchise establishments that maximize the use of minimum-wage, part-time labour. She identifies "the emerging market importance of the young worker" as fast-food franchises reach industrial proportions wherein "young workers become ideal commodities; they are cheap, energetic, and in plentiful supply." It is worth quoting her findings:

Making up about 75 per cent of the Burger King workforce, the youngsters who worked after school, on weekends, and on holidays were called "part-timers". . . . The daytime workers — the remaining 25 per cent of the workforce were primarily married women of mixed economic backgrounds. . . .

The women and teenagers at Burger King are under the sway of a labour process that eliminates almost completely the possibility of forming a workplace culture independent of, and in opposition to, management — there are indications that the teenagers and women who work in this type of job represent not an anomalous but an increasingly typical kind of work, in the one area of the economy that continues to grow — the service sector (Reiter, 1986: 321, 324).

The character of the working class is being transformed by such developments and is impacting disproportionately on young people and women who are structured out of the traditional industrial working class, which is unionized and male (not to mention central Canadian). Marginalization is not confined to franchises. Increasingly the central firms and employers (such as municipalities) are using subcontracting of non-union firms for cleaners, garbage collection and a multitude of services (airlines, for example, contract out as much work as possible). Alongside these practices is the increasing use of part-time workers in clerical and sales jobs. Again these disproportionately affect women and young people.

The drawing upon reserve labour pools is an issue that involves women and young people, but in Canada it is also a regional issue. . . . Region itself is relationship; that is, regions can only be a region in relation to something else. Regions are not simply areas of unequal power. They are areas in relation to one another and connected in such a way that one is enhanced at the expense of the other. I would argue that regionalism is a consequence (rather than cause) of uneven economic development. Uneven development is historical, spatial and, most crucially, relational; that is, it represents the unfolding of unequal power relations with regional manifestations. The basis of these unequal power relations is class. Class in this case is manifest both at the level of control over capital accumulation and making pools of surplus labour available.

Class and region are bound together in numerous ways. A rather bold example is the so-called resettlement program in Newfoundland. It involved the transformation of the outport household as both a production and consumption unit. Families were relocated from outports to "centres" such as Arnold's Cove. Once moved, there was a commodification of their consumption patterns, involving food preparation, child care, clothing and shelter, which forced families to seek greater wage income. The Arnold's Cove resettlement was tied, not coincidentally, to the Come by Chance oil refinery project. Its failure left the people detached from their new jobs and from their previous means of realizing their labour power. Eventually they readopted fishing in Placentia Bay (although many had moved on to Ontario in search of jobs). To practise fishing, the men must return to their old berths in the abandoned outports during the week while the women work for wages in the new National Sea fish plant. The plant is supplied by two collector boats that make daily rounds to the fish camps. An available labour force was created by detaching people from their subsistence and means of realizing their labour power and drawing them into a situation where wages were required. These workers are "free" to remain unemployed should the fish plant follow the path of Come by Chance. Once again, it is evident that the class relations of this situation are not only regional, but gendered: men become *dependent* commodity producers and women industrial workers, both detached from earlier domestic commodity production which they shared. The major actors in this drama are the large-scale capitalists who control the oil refineries and the fish plants.

Not all social relations are class relations, but class affects all social relations; that is, gender, region, ethnicity, and so on are all *relational* concepts that are affected by class (although class does not *deter-*

mine these relations). This does not mean that gender, regional or ethnic groups are "classes." A key corollary of this argument is that classes *never* exist in isolation — "pure" classes only exist in abstraction. Conversely, classes are *always* conditioned by other social relations.

What needs to be stressed are relations and processes. At its highest level of abstraction, class struggle hinges on the contradiction between the development of the forces of production in capitalism and the limitations imposed by the relations of production inherent in that system. It is this contradiction that provides class with its dynamic, its motor force. At the socio-economic level the politics of class struggle include a history, culture and ideology that give life to basic economic situations. As Marx noted in the *Grundrisse*, "Society does not consist of individuals, but expresses the sum of interrelations, the relations within which those individuals stand." Classes are not "things." They are relations and processes. Since these relations and processes are experienced through people, they never manifest themselves in "pure" form, but take on and are affected by the characteristics of people — that is, their gender, race, region, etc., all of which are themselves social characteristics. Similarly, objective positions in the labour process are not *identical* with class, nor is class reducible to such positions; yet these positions have social, political and ideological effects that contribute to the experience of class.

Having discussed some factors that interact with and impact on class, I will now briefly turn to some of the processes under way within class relations in order to reflect upon current changes.

A key process in the transformation of class relations is that of proletarianization. People enter the labour market because they are separated from the means to realize their labour power and must provide for their basic needs. The means of production are also their means of realizing their labour; that is, these are opposite sides of the same process whereby capital accumulates. Just as it is necessary for capital to accumulate or die, so is it equally necessary for labour to seek a place to utilize its labour power or perish. In the terms introduced earlier, when the traditional petite bourgeoisie experiences the effects of proletarianization, they increasingly come to resemble the working class or, if the process is completed, actually become members of the working class. There is also another side to the proletarianization process, which involves the differentiation of aspects of capitalist rights into the new middle class. As that new middle class declines in performance of the rights of capital and increases in performing the obligations of labour, it too experiences proletarianization. Proletarianization is a *process*; to be proletarian is a condition. They are part of a relationship between the rights of capital and the obligations of labour, on one side expressed in processes involving the traditional petite bourgeoisie and labour, while on the other side, the relation between capital and labour.

The new middle class arises out of the division of capitalist rights concerning surveillance and discipline, but also out of productive activities necessary for the working class which involve co-ordination and direction of the labour process. Surveillance and discipline involve the realization of surplus value (unproductive labour), while co-ordination and direction involve creation of surplus value (productive labour), to use a language appropriate to the highest level of abstraction. Whereas the traditional middle class was "independent" in the sense of not employing the labour power of others (aside from its family where patriarchy acts as a key relationship), the new middle class truly stands between capital and labour exercising both co-ordination and surveillance aspects of the labour process.

A central feature of the new middle class is its supervisory activity. I will take one piece of evidence from the International Class Structure Project concerning supervisors and work through some implications for types of control structures. In Sweden 8 per cent of the men and 6 per cent of the women are supervisors, while in Finland 5 per cent of each are supervisors. In the United States these proportions rise to 15 per cent for men and 12 per cent for women, while in Canada a similar 11 per cent of men and 9 per cent of women are supervisors. Don Black and John Myles (1986) have done some detailed analysis of similar patterns. Notable are the significant differences in the proportions of supervisors, but also in their types of activities. They report that "virtually all Canadian and American supervisors have sanctioning authority," which I have been calling surveillance and discipline, while "only a minority of the Swedish supervisors have such authority. For the most part, Swedish supervisors merely coordinate the labour of others." This is what I have been calling co-ordination and direction. Black and Myles make an interesting observation: "What is most remarkable is the enormous amount of "administrative overhead" that goes into the work of control and surveillance in Canada and the United States. In the United States, almost 29% of all employees are engaged in disciplining other employees as compared to less than 12% in Sweden. For Canada as a whole the figure is 23% but rises to 28% in the extractive/transformative industries." The Swedes and Finns have much lower expenditure on supervision and adhere much more to administrative or bureaucratic forms of control. They also have a fearless approach to technology (which is made possible by labour market policies that ensure employment at decent minimum standards).

The introduction of technology is often a key point of struggle in relations between capital and labour in North America. Labour often resists because of the way technology is implemented (that is, to maximize capital accumulation rather than to improve the quality of work life), which in turn is determined by the industrial relations context of its implementation. Although both operate within capitalist economies, it is evident the Scandinavians have created a much more productive and less conflict-ridden system of industrial relations than in North America, where unproductive supervision flourishes. The Scandinavians have a system that provides much more autonomy for workers and has less need to spend on coercive control structures.

Bureaucratic control structures that operate in place of direct supervision are not without their problems. It is through bureaucratic structures that unions are often drawn into management's system of control. In order to protect the interests of present members, unions have often neglected part-time workers, who are often excluded from the advantages of concessions gained through bureaucratic arrangements such as grievance procedures, bidding for jobs, pensions, etc. Such arrangements often operate to the disadvantage of women and young people, as does the way technology is introduced into the office through automation.

Automation is not uniform in its impact on the working class because the working class itself is not homogeneous by skill, industrial sector or gender. . . . The point is that class and automation are not simple processes. They are uneven within the working class and have different effects on various fractions of the working class which correspond to variously skilled and gendered jobs. Assessing the impact of automation requires a textured understanding of class and class fractions.

Another aspect of class demanding careful attention is its so-called "subjective" side. This means more than "class consciousness" as traditionally understood by that term. It means class *experiences* and class *struggle*, which are actual manifestations of class. More important "consciousness" per se is ideology, which provides an account or explanation for people's practices. The leading voice in this tradition has been E. P. Thompson who, in his classic *The Making of the English Working Class*, tells us that "class experience is largely determined by the productive relations into which men [and we should add women] are born — or enter involuntarily. Class-consciousness is the way in which these experiences are handled in cultural terms; embodied in traditions, value systems, ideas, and institutional forms. If the experience appears as determined, class-consciousness does not."

I have tried to apply some of these principles in two case studies of class formation and experience. In *Hardrock Mining* I focused on managerial strategies and workers' resistance as manifestations of class struggle. In the fisheries study, *The Struggle to Organize*, the focus was on differences in the politics and organization of capitalist, petty bourgeois and proletarian "characters" of unions, co-operatives and associations. The purpose was not only to distinguish organizational types, but to explain the behaviour of each. I used class analysis, for example, to explain differences in the ideology and behaviour between the two largest unions, the United Fishermen and Allied Workers Union, which excludes skippers who regularly employ three or more crew, and the Newfoundland Fishermen, Food and Allied Workers Union, which includes skippers. The class content within these unions explains their tendencies and concrete practices.

To this point attention has been focused on the working and middle classes, but some brief comments on the upper class are appropriate. Using my earlier studies on corporate power as a baseline, the theme here is continuity rather than change. Three brief illustrations will make the point. The first is almost a caricature of Canadian capitalism. After leaving the post as Ontario premier from 1971 to 1985, William Davis moved into the very top continental financial circles. His crowning glory has been his appointment to the board of the U.S. financial giant First Boston, adding to his directorships on the Canadian Imperial Bank of Commerce, Ford Motor Company of Canada, Inter-City Gas, Power Corporation and Seagram Company. Some practices die slowly, if at all.

The second illustrates media concentration. In 1984 there were five private broadcasting companies in Saskatchewan, but that has changed over the past year as Baton Broadcasting (a joint holding of the powerful Bassett and Eaton families) bought Yorkton Television's five stations and then gained 90 per cent control of the CTV affiliate CKCK-TV in return for a 10 per cent interest to Harvard Developments of Regina in CFQC, a subsidiary of Baton. The only remaining private broadcaster is CJFB, Swift Current's privately held CBC affiliate.

Now to really serious matters. It is inappropriate to gaze at the upper class in isolation. The Davis example looked only at the interconnections of the elite and the Baton example the concentration of corporate power. This final illustration demonstrates that the actions of the ruling class make a difference for the lives of ordinary people. The St. Lawrence, Newfoundland fluorspar mines, formerly operated by the Aluminium Company of Canada, were reopened recently under the control of Minworth Limited, a British company. The Peckford government induced the company with exclusive rights to the rich fluorspar deposits and a forgivable grant for $6.8 million plus equity financing of $1.5 million. Transport Canada kicked in another $1.5 million to repair the docks. Why such concessions? Only 15 per cent of the town's labour force is currently employed, a situation that has persisted since Alcan withdrew in 1978. The town's council is so desperate for work that they struck a three-year agreement with Minworth that sets the following conditions: (1) wages will be set at $9 to $10 per hour (nearly half the rate for hardrock miners elsewhere in Canada); (2) employees will not join a national or international union, but may form a local association; and (3) no strikes. These are demeaning conditions, but the people are desperate and all three levels of the Canadian state are scurrying to satisfy the wishes of capital with all too little protection for the workers. Yet these are precisely the workers most in need of the ability to protect themselves: St. Lawrence has a lung cancer death rate twenty-nine times the Newfoundland average; radioactivity in the mines has been from two and a half to ten times maximum standards (in some sections 193 times recommended levels). A provincial Royal Commission in 1969 identified 150 miners who had already died from these conditions, with another 100 permanently disabled. It took five years after the first medical studies before miners were finally told of the medical dangers. Should capital really be trusted again with the lives of St. Lawrence's workers?

It would be difficult to exaggrate the disparities of power between the ruling class and working class. The Canadian state is most accommodating to capital and both are highly integrated. The implications of this highly concentrated power are enormous for Canadians as consumers and as employees. The actions of the ruling class have consequences for everyone. They do not exist in isolation, but in relation to the working class as employers and to everyone as controllers of valuable goods, resources and information. To study class relations should also mean to investigate the consequences of class power.

The implications one chooses to draw from class analysis are just that, implications. How they guide the actions of the analyst or which actions the analyst follows are related but independent phenomena. The analyst engaging in education is involved in a form of action. How and to whom the results are disseminated are political acts (although we are not always conscious of them as such). Why should one care about class theories? Theories are intended to lend insight into building explanations, which in turn guide the way individuals think about and act toward their society. It is the contention of this discussion that class can and should be an integral part of such an understanding. Class, however, cannot be narrowly understood if it is to fulfil its analytical promise. Class does matter, but not isolated from gender, region, politics, ideology, culture and classes in relation to one another. Indeed, without these various social relations class is a static, economistic category. With them it is a dynamic explanatory concept central to the social sciences and fundamental to everyday life.

THE EL DORADO CROWD

Peter C. Newman

No matter how often the politicians may proclaim that Canada's economic system spreads abundance among the many, in reality, it creates wealth for the few.

Their skin belongs to the afternoon sun. They hold common assumptions so deeply that they communicate through raised eyebrows and shared silences. They view Pierre Trudeau as a dangerous socialist, worship John Turner, and refer to Quebec separatism as "René Lévesque's show." They breed horses and mid-Atlantic accents, having mastered the trick of looking down their noses and talking through them at the same time.

From *The Canadian Establishment* by Peter C. Newman. Used by permission of the Canadian Publishers, McClelland and Stewart Limited, Toronto.

They live in graceful ante-bellum mansions with white fluted pillars, twilit, book-lined studies, fastidious gardens, and drawing rooms awash with fragile antiques, Adam sideboards, Sheraton tables, the warming lustre of burnished bronze. They are surrounded by hangers-on — surrogate offspring with small lives, fusty bachelors and ladies-always-in-waiting, pretenders all, distinguished by their pettiness, an odd mixture of admiration, envy, and malice.

Most of their decisions evolve from the style in which they allow things to happen. Their lives are lived as a series of throw-away gestures, so that all the pleasures and all the splendour are made to seem effortless rather than planned, ordinary instead of ostentatious. They spend little time in self-evaluation and keep few records of their inward transactions.

They are the Canadian rich. The men and women who realize that no matter how often the politicians may proclaim that Canada's economic system spreads abundance among the many, in reality, it creates wealth for the few.

As a group, the Establishment rich are among the most envied of Canadians, with the climbers and the reachers constantly scouting their habits and their habitats, trying to define their essence, to grab a little of their magic for themselves. But like moths banging softly against a Coleman lamp in the moonlight, the upstarts are attracted to and kept away from the heart of the flame. Few newcomers make it into the magic circle. They don't know the rules and are too easily dismissed. ("Tell them we're busy, Peg. They're not our kind of people.")

The very rich enjoy a surprisingly stylized if highly sybaritic existence, one that touches only tangentially the mainstream of Canadian life. They are insulated from the economic jolts that can shake the merely prosperous, and their idea of hunger is being served a slightly rancid *filet de sole meunière* at a declining French restaurant. Most of their conversations spin around two topics: politicians and their perfidies, servants and their idiosyncrasies. They feel entirely at home only in each other's company, where everyone has money — vast sums, otherwise they're considered vaguely quaint. Connections are paraded, but discreetly. Nearly everybody is somebody's cousin. They all know each other's children, now in their bursting thirties and taking over family firms. The eldest offspring is often described as "a decent chap," meaning that he may be none too bright but at least he hasn't turned out to be a rebel or anything unfortunate like that. "He's done his homework" is the ultimate accolade, "he's blotted his copybook" the ultimate insult.

They still drink Madeira after dinner. They live in very English houses — very low key with lots of old chintz, not much colour sense, nervous maids, walls decorated with endless variations on bloodless hunting scenes, and dinners consisting of oyster soup, raw roast beef, and frozen strawberries on meringue, preceded by hors d'oeuvre of Triscuits and canned pâté. They're intensely interested in all things British and have usually met various minor baronets at the Marquess of Blandford's or somebody else's country house. London, not New York, is their spiritual home.

> "Where do you get your cigars now?"
> "Well, Fortnum and Mason has a good tobacco selection."
> "I'm certain they do. What about Dunhill's?" Are they still in business?"
> "Oh yes, but owned by Rothmans now."
> "I used to go to a place on Jermyn Street. Haven't seen it lately. Hmm," puff, puff, "yes. Excellent. Fortnum's. I'll remember."

Money can be a great comfort. In large quantities, there is nothing transitory about it, as there is about power. Yet even wealth doesn't put a wall between the individual and his fear of hurt and death, doesn't provide any automatic inner confirmation of one's existence. Unlike their corporate cousins who deal in power plays and can look themselves up in the *Canadian Who's Who* to check on their current standing and past achievements, the merely rich have no ready tally of accomplishments. They have little sense of irony to deal with life's mysteries.

The rich have a strange image of themselves. Senator Norman McLeod Paterson, the Fort William grain merchant who owned 109 elevators and one of the largest fleets on the Great Lakes, once had his picture taken in front of the Senate with his foot on the running board of his tug-sized Rolls-Royce, bellowing at the camera: "What do you mean, we're rich old men?"

The fear of giving away the source or sum of their fortune, of committing themselves to offers of friendship, gradually fills their minds with smoky, ill-defined resentments. They begin to feel alienated and suspicious, spying on themselves, becoming everybody's mercenary and no one's intimate. And so, furtively and without really meaning to do so, they withdraw into themselves even further and begin to desire not just wealth but limitless riches. Instead of being appreciated for what it can buy, money becomes despised for all the problems it didn't resolve, the magical expectations it didn't fulfil.

At the point where money ceases to have real meaning — and the limits of personal consumption are reached astonishingly quickly — the compounding of further wealth becomes a game. The objective of the game is not more money but the playing of the game itself, which takes on something close to sexual connotations. Roy Thomson, the late press lord, became one of the game's most successful players: "I mean, hell, I eat three meals a day (and I should probably eat two), and I'm not very particular about my dress anyway. I can spend only a small fraction of what I make. So what the hell am I doing? I'm not doing it for the money. *It's a game and I enjoy myself.* I like to look at another paper and think, 'Jesus, if only that was mine. Let's see the balance sheet.'"

What really separates the very rich from everyone else is the time frame in which they live. They seldom need to defer desires. Their money gives them the authority to purchase the time and services of others — in bed, at the office, around the house. Because time is a more precious (and much more exhaustible) commodity than money, they place great emphasis on its expenditure. This leads the very rich to worship efficiency in all things, whether it's a new computer that will streamline their personal accounting systems or a gadget that will heat their swimming pools a little faster.

It's because they hate to see anything wasted that the very rich are so stingy. One of Eric Harvie's accountants recalls that the Calgary millionaire once objected to being charged $3.00 instead of the previous $2.50 for his weekly car wash and that when an elderly couple who had spent twenty years as caretakers at his ranch left his employ, Harvie deducted five dollars from their final pay for some groceries they had taken with them. E. P. Taylor successfully sued the British government in the late sixties after the Board of Inland Revenue disallowed his claimed deduction for eight thousand pounds in transatlantic business trips. When John David Eaton's private plane was forced down near Winnipeg during a storm, he walked four miles through the snow with his pilot, Ralph Spadbrow, to send a telegram from the nearest railway station. Spadbrow remembered that they had to retrace their steps for several hundred yards when the station agent shouted after them that he had overcharged Eaton by fifteen cents.

These strange paladins of wealth obviously don't enjoy simple lives. One problem is that having exceptional fortunes no longer guarantees much personal distinction. That's why the rich are so zealously class conscious. No other class has the time or money to uphold such rigid common standards; at no level are class distinctions so minutely observed. Established money is obsessed with the notion of keeping the parvenus at bay — those cigar chompers and haunch grabbers in their silk suits and pomaded haircuts, whose status lust hangs out like a dirty shirt tail.

The difference that counts is between being Old Rich and New Rich. Adherents of both groups give themselves away in all sorts of subtle ways — where they summer or winter, how they decorate their houses and offices, what they wear, drive, and eat, whom they marry and sleep with. What the New Rich can never quite grasp is that the surest way of being excluded is to compare possessions. By specifying the exact length of their Chris-Craft, boasting about their latest car, gadget, mistress, or French Impressionist painting, they betray a gauche insecurity the true Establishmentarian never feels.

It all depends on what makes the blood pump. New Money likes Cadillacs with elk-grained cabriolet tops and regency custom grilles; Old Money prefers Rolls-Royces. Old Money follows the supermarket ads and knows when cans of B.C. salmon are on special. New Money tips lavishly. Old Money prefers subdued shades of brown; New Money loves primary colours, offices with red walls, and cigar lighters shaped like Model Ts. (You twist the spare tire and it belches forth a xylophone version of "The Impossible Dream.") Old Money goes with affected shabbiness, sailing trophies, lost duckhunting hats, and grandfather's walking stick. New Money has stuffed fish mounted on its recreation room walls. The New Rich buy a house, call in a professional, and order him to "decorate it." They talk about drapes, chesterfields, and homes. The Old Rich will employ decorators only to find specific pieces and talk about curtains, sofas, and houses. Old Money purchases the seagoing family pet a life preserver; New Money outfits him in a yachting jacket.

New Money buys his wife a necklace made of rubies and gold to wear over a brocade dress with sable cuffs. Old Money cultivates lapel orchids in the colours of his hunt. New Money builds an indoor snorkelling tank and keeps pogo sticks at poolside for additional exercise. Old Money turns to public service if it gets really exercised or really bored. Old Money in Europe seeks out neighbourhood left-bank hotels, enduring draughts and inferior foods as an annual adventure. New Money flies to the Paris Hilton and orders two cheeseburgers-with-the-works. Old Money knows not to wear diamonds before lunch, not to carry unfinished cocktails to the dinner table, that Thursday is maid's night out. Old Money's chauffeurs never slam doors or walk around the *front* of a car.

Old Money gets the children to help groom the horses, wearing worn T-shirts, jeans, and very expensive riding boots. New Money keeps careful profit-and-loss tallies on each animal and sells off the yearlings that aren't likely to make back their investments. Old Money plays tennis and squash and skies hard; New Money hires a masseuse to call at the house every morning. New Money gets the best tickets to the Super Bowl, the Indianapolis 500, and the Army-Navy Game. Old Money rents boxes at the Kentucky Derby and arranges foursomes at Burning Tree. New Money uses caterers and invites a few business associates so that it can write off its cocktail parties. Old Money engages a combo and refers to them as "the music"; New Money boasts, "We've got the Short Circuits!" Old Money buys expensive winter topcoats that endow their wearers with a faintly conspiratorial air. New Money buys leather or suede jackets.

New Money buys paintings by their dominant colours and pretends to understand modern art; Old Money collects "pictures" and hangs them in dark rooms with little dinky lights over them. Old Money will produce the occasional jeroboam of Château Mouton-Rothschild 1929 without drawing attention to the fact that it costs $8,000 a bottle; New Money boasts about his T'ang Dynasty vase — the dealer wanted $30,000 for it, but he got it for $25,000.

Old Money treats waiters as slightly retarded errand boys; New Money tries to impress them by speaking broken French with the intimacy of a Resistance fighter explaining the locaton of an arms drop. Old Money makes elaborate (and unsuccessful) attempts to treat servants benignly, knows exactly what happened to poor Emma's first cousin, and sends her a Christmas food parcel from Eaton's. New Money haggles with the maid about overtime. Old Money marries the right girl (and ogles cocktail waitresses); New Money marries the wrong girl, starves her to perfection, and sends her to Holt Renfrew with a charge account. Old Money refers to an errant partner's affair with his secretary as "Jimmy is having a little thing with Gloria." New Money trades in his wife.

The rich have a difficult time separating their money from their manliness. In the proving ground of their souls the two are indivisible. Money is God; the man makes the money; therefore the man is in charge. (There's almost always trouble if the money comes by inheritance from the woman's side of the family.) Most wives are relegated to being baubles. In this kind of partnership even pretty women seem flesh without magic. Attempting to fulfil their decorative function, they do the rounds of slimming classes, Maine Chance, beauty studios, skin specialists, face-lift surgeons. (But age remains the final conqueror, and, having been cheated so long, is seldom kind in victory.)

Wives try hard to keep up with whatever conversation is going and give glad little cries of interest at nearly everything mentioned. ("Kuwait — oh, fascinating! How primitive those Arabs must be!") They complain about trying to keep servants happy, their daughter's Italian fiancé (they fear he isn't "stable"), the new rug being woven in Portugal that hasn't been delivered yet — all the time glancing around the room to see how they're doing. Gradually they become non-persons, no longer decorative, no longer needed as mothers, no longer anything much but burdens their husbands uneasily bear.

Much of their excitement comes from the rumours and facts of endogamy — the who-married-whom-and-merged-with-what game. The rich are constantly inter-marrying, replanting the forests of family trees. The list is endless.

The "family" is a kind of sacred institution in these circles, not as the result of any unusual filial feelings but because it is the vessel that passes on the money. Most of the families that might have become great financial dynasties have petered out. They failed to establish systems of succession that would force the incapable to make way for those who could maintain and expand family investments. Family fortunes, no matter how great, were dispersed, the families left headless, without cohesion or thrust. When George Gooderham, a sixth-generation descendant of what was once a dominant Canadian family, was married, Lady Gooderham, his great-aunt, gave a shower for his bride. The more than a hundred women relatives who turned up had to be identified with name cards. Mrs. Jules Timmins has twenty-nine grandchildren.

An exception to this kind of scattering of resources is the Southam family. Before any member is given an executive job he must clearly establish his credentials. "We're fortunate that the family is so loyal to the company," says St. Clair Balfour, current head of the clan. "We wouldn't hesitate to ask a family member to leave if he wasn't working out, though we would remove him in as nice a way as possible."

"Inherited wealth," complained William K. Vanderbilt in 1905, "is a big handicap to happiness. It is as certain a death to ambition as cocaine is to morality." Many sons simply take over the desks of their fathers, uncles, or fathers-in-law. Charles L. Gundy, chairman of Wood Gundy, the Toronto investment house, inherited most of the twenty directorships in the companies financed by his father, including Canada Cement Lafarge, Massey-Ferguson, and Dominion Steel and Coal Corporation. Their family position did not save other sons from dreary years spent learning the business. G. Blair Gordon, who became president of Dominion Textile, worked as a fitter's helper in one of his father's mills, in spite of his preference for playing polo. He still has a scar on his brow from an inkwell hurled at him by a striker at Montmorency Falls in 1938. John David Eaton spent twelve years selling men's underwear and being moved through other departments before he was named to head Canada's largest retailing chain in 1942.

Johnny F. Bassett, son of the former *Telegram* publisher, who has inherited his father's nerve and bluntness, spoke for the new generation of rich men's sons when he told a journalist: "It's not a handicap being John Bassett's boy. I've had an excellent relationship with dad. He's a hell of a sounding board and he's a bright, bright son of a bitch. He's a great family guy; he'll back you. You can make a terrible mistake, and still he'll back you up. I don't remember ever feeling the pressure from being John Bassett's son. We're two different people. I mean there are two John Bassetts in Toronto now. . . . I suppose everybody in Toronto regards the Bassetts as Establishment. I don't. I regard the Establishment as being people who founded here in the 1880s, third and fourth generation. In 1952 my old man didn't have a pot to piss in when he bought a newspaper — thanks to Mr. Eaton —that was losing a million dollars a year."

chapter

12

Educational Inequality

The selections in this chapter touch very directly on concerns of immediate interest to you. Now, more than at any other time in your life, you may be asking what is the purpose and meaning of education. Two or three decades ago, liberal-functional sociologists would have answered these questions largely in terms of the educational system's contribution to economic efficiency and equality of opportunity. The emphasis in research was on demonstrating how far we were from reaching the goal of equal opportunity and equal access; but no one questioned whether this was a realistic and attainable goal. In the 1970s radical or conflict sociologists sought to demonstrate the inadequacies of the liberal-functional model and provided a much more pessimistic and critical view of educa-

tion. They argued that educational systems are essentially ideological: the main function of education is to reproduce, not alter, the class structure and to produce people accepting of the values of the dominant groups in capitalist society.

As a result of these critical analyses, one of your authors, in the late 1970s, wrote that the sociology of education was at something of a watershed and would, in future, have a very different research agenda (Richardson, 1977). That prediction has not been fully borne out during the 1980s, and here we present you with an array of images of education rather than a coherent and systematic introduction to the sociology of education. Clearly underlying all of the selections in this chapter is the view that education can be more than simply a means to an end (a good job, perhaps, or social control) but an end in itself — a liberating and humanistic experience.

In the first selection, Susan Russell explicitly draws upon both feminist and radical critiques of education as she explores, in one research setting, how gender and class are reinforced through what came to be known in the 1970s, as "the hidden curriculum" of the educational system. In our view she provides an excellent example of the use of a qualitative and essentially symbolic interactionist approach and does so without losing touch with social structure, the layers of social inequality created by class and patriarchy and how these structures shape the everyday lives of boys and girls in school.

The second selection comes from Janice Newson's and Howard Buchbinder's influential and controversial book *The University Means Business.* Their concern is how university teaching and research have been shaped by the needs of corporate capitalism for knowledge and teaching of skills that improve productivity and, ultimately, profit. In the excerpts included here, the authors are describing the competing visions of what should be the proper place of universities in society and are setting out what they view as the dangers of a too close relationship between capitalism and our educational systems.

The final selection, by Neil Guppy and his colleagues at the University of British Columbia, essentially describes the findings from research designed to test the controversy as to whether changes in educational policy have had impact on reducing inequality of educational opportunity, John Porter's hope in writing *The Vertical Mosaic.* As you will discover in reading this selection, they are rather cautious in concluding that the influences of family and class background have become less important over time. It seems that, for both men and women, these influences have weak-

ened in terms of the likelihood of Canadians completing high school but remain relatively important with respect to their likelihood of attending a university or community college. In short, it is quite possible that as a result of educational inflation the need in modern society for more and more credentials to "buy" the same occupational status, equality of educational opportunity may have improved with very little change in equality of opportunity, generally. And, while the authors do analayze men and women separately, of necessity, they are comparing their cohorts not with Mothers but with Fathers.

RELATED READINGS

Stephen Baron: "The Canadian West-Coast Punk Subculture: A Field Study" (Chapter 3)
Anthony Synnott: "Little Angels, Little Devils: A Sociology of Children" (Chapter 5)
Esther Greenglass: "Socialization of Boys and Girls: How Roles are Acquired" (Chapter 5)

THE HIDDEN CURRICULUM OF SCHOOL: REPRODUCING GENDER AND CLASS HIERARCHIES

Susan Russell

The school is a pivotal social institution mediating between ascriptive factors given at birth, namely social class and gender, and ultimate position in society. It is through schooling, mainstream functionalist sociologists posit, that all mem-

"The Hidden Curriculum of School: Reproducing Gender and Class Hierarchies" by Susan Russell in *Feminism and Political Economy: Women's Work, Women's Struggles* edited by Heather Jon Maroney and Meg Luxton, 1987. By permission of the publisher.

bers of society are offered equal life chances, based on their own ability and achievement. This "rosy" view of an egalitarian and just society cannot be taken seriously by feminist and marxist sociologists, keenly aware of gender and class inequalities in the labour force and the gender hierarchy in the family. For them, the task of a sociology of education is to reveal both the ways in which students in schools are encouraged to consent to these social inequalities, and signs of their resistance to them.

Girls in school, it is revealed through an analysis of the eduation process, are the focus of pressures to encourage them to accept subordinate positions in both the labour force and the family. They are encouraged to believe that their exclusive role is or ought to be childbearing and rearing, and that work that they take on in the labour force is secondary to their role in the family. School personnel exert these pressures through job counselling and through undermining the academic ability of girls while focusing on their domestic futures. It is under these pressures that the vast majority of girls sail through school and assume their subordinate roles in the domestic sphere and in the labour force.

It is not that schools "invent" these social hierarchies. They exist in male-dominated, capitalist society. Students, because of prior pressures from the home and media, enter school with a predisposition to accept these class and gender hierarchies and their place in them. Studies in the sociology of education reveal the ways in which these categories are also accepted in schools and students are encouraged to consent to them and not to consider alternatives. Thus schools contribute to the social reproduction of class and gender inequalities. The signs of resistance on the part of girls to these pressures can also be seen, but these are little, if at all, recognized as valid in schools.

In this [article] a brief discussion of the functionalist perspective in the sociology of education will be presented first, in Section I, since this is the analysis to which all subsequent ones respond. The contradictions inherent in that analysis led to other, more sophisticated, research questions and methods. The issues which generated debate are the impact of social class and gender in the school and classroom. Thus Section II concerns findings of research by marxist and feminist sociologists of education. It will be divided into three sections, each representing deeper levels of analysis of education: (1) the social organization of schools and how these are established formally to channel students to reproduce class and gender hierarchies; (2) the culture of working- and middle-class girls, both the elements which they share due to gender and those on which they diverge largely because of class differences; and (3) phenomenological research in the school, divided into three sections: (a) the advice of guidance personnel, (b) teacher-student interaction in the classroom, and (c) the content of classroom interaction, including "lessons" in the gender hierarchy and signs of resistance to them.

Although section 2, noted above, is not strictly speaking part of the sociology of education, since uncovering the world views and aspirations of students does not necessarily implicate schools, it is included here as an important transition to the subsequent section. What is revealed by this research is that school personnel accept and reinforce the "motherhood," "marriage," and "anti-school" aspects of girls' culture, while ignoring any others.

The primary data presented in this paper were collected in an academically oriented high school in Ottawa, Ontario, and offer insights into the process of schooling (Russell, 1978, 1979–80). The research was indepth, employing several modes of data collection: classroom observation in twenty-seven classes in the senior grade; interviews with a random sample of forty senior students, twenty-five of whom are girls; twenty-five teachers of the senior grade; and the five guidance counsellors in the school. Grades achieved by the entire Grade 12 class in Grades 8 and 11 were also analyzed. The initial purpose of the research was to study gender socialization in the school, but this was quickly seen to be impossible without also considering issues of social class. This realization that gender and class are intricately interrelated and must both be explored in analyzing students' behaviour and aspirations and school personnel's channelling of students highlights the importance of using both feminist and marxist perspectives. The experience of students in school varies enormously by both gender and class, and it is the goal of this [paper] to explore some of the ways in which this is true.

I. The Functionalist Perspective: Mainstream Sociology of Education

According to functionalist theory, which provides an ideological snapshot of how liberal democratic society is supposed to achieve its goals (O'Brien calls it "high-class daydreaming" (1981: 2)), schooling exists to provide equal opportunity for all children, regardless of ascriptive factors of birth (Parsons, 1959). As long as schools are open, and access to them is available, indeed required, at least to a certain age, schools are seen to be providing equality of opportunity. So-called "critical functionalists" such as Bourdieu, who writes about the social reproduction of social class in society (Murphy, 1979), and Porter, who shows through large-scale survey research in Ontario that girls and working-class students have lower aspirations to attend university than their middle-class

and male peers (Porter, Porter, and Blishen, 1982), question whether education is in fact offering equal educational opportunity. This they do without doubting that schools should and might offer equal opportunity, regardless of a society built on class and gender inequalities.

What draws together these three functionalists, who are on the surface very different, is their insistence that inequalities which do exist among students stem exclusively from the home and peer background, which either prepares a student successfully to take advantage of what school offers, or leaves him/her inadequately prepared to cope and compete in that milieu. Thus underpinning the work of Parsons and Porter is the "culture of poverty," while central to Bourdieu's work is the concept of "cultural capital," which bourgeois children possess in abundance from family ("correct" language, knowledge of the "arts," and information about and familiarity with the education system), and which working-class children lack. These related theories undervalue working-class culture and methods of negotiating in capitalist society, and by extension help to maintain and justify social class boundaries. As critical functionalists, both Bourdieu and Porter argue for compensatory education classes or financial assistance for futher education. Thus the process of schooling itself is not criticized by functionalist researchers. They just want more of it.

II. Marxist and Feminist Analyses of Schools

In opposition to the functionalist approach, marxist and feminist researchers of education turn their attention to the ways in which schools contribute independently to the perpetuation of male-dominated, capitalist society. Having rejected the dominant ideology that schools, by their simple existence, offer equal opportunity, or potentially might do so, educational researchers with a marxist or feminist perspective are free to examine the ways in which schools actively process student behaviour and activity to perpetuate social class and gender divisions.

1. SOCIAL ORGANIZATION OF SCHOOLS

The main contribution of schooling, as seen by marxist sociologists, is to legitimate the existing social hierarchy of jobs and rewards in capitalist society. The work by Bowles and Gintis (1976) develops a theory of "correspondence" between social class, classroom relationships, and work in the labour force. They argue that "ability" tests (IQ tests) used to separate children into the categories of "fast" or "slow" learners do not test the children's own potential as students, but, rather, their family backgrounds. Children, streamed by social class, are exposed to different types of education, both in terms of content (academic or vocational), and social relations with teachers and peers in the classroom. These different forms prepare them for different academic futures and, in turn, feed into different types of jobs — working-class, bourgeois, or petty bourgeois. A sensitive and personalized account of the marxist theoretical framework is to be found in "Downtown Kids Aren't Dumb," a brief presented by Toronto parents concerned with their children's welfare (Park School Community Council, 1974). It shows how ability testing and high school programs in Canadian schools process working-class children to maintain them in vocational streams which lead into poorly rewarded jobs. On the basis of this evidence, the marxist argument that schools reproduce the social class division of labour is well established.

Using a similar perspective, some feminist researchers focus on the ways in which schools are formally organized to ensure that girls and boys receive different educational experiences. Gaskell (1981) studied girls in Vancouver high school programs, showing how they moved directly into the sex-segregated labour force. She demonstrates that there are short-term advantages to both the girls and their employers, but that there are long-term detrimental effects for the girls with limited skill training and jobs without opportunities for advancement.

This type of analysis has prompted some feminist researchers to reexamine the contentious issue of the effects of single-sex verus co-educational schools. In many ways this remains a British and Australian issue. Canadians have tended to follow the American lead into comprehensive and co-educational schools as the ones which, it is argued, offer greater equality (by class, race, and sex). Arnot (1983) contends that both options should remain open for parents choosing a school for daughters and sons, and urges feminists to continue to study this issue. Shaw (1980) argues that although they may provide better facilities for science labs, co-educational schools may in fact contribute to greater sex role typing. Even if the move to single sex schools is perceived as a retrogressive step, perhaps students — especially girls in the thirteen-to-fifteen-year-old group, whose academic achievement typically falls — might benefit from the segregation. However, as Arnot has pointed out, in a society marked strongly by a sex-segregated labour force, a minimal separation in school would make little difference. Similarly, Canadian data substantiates Wolpe's (1978) point that even when girls achieve appropriate credentials in school, they are not likely to obtain positions in the labour force commensurate with their qualifications.

Thus, despite strategic differences, feminist researchers concur that the school system, from sex-typed courses through to its larger organizational structure, reproduces gender, like class, hierarchies.

2. STUDENT CULTURE

The work by McRobbie, Llewellyn, Sharp, and Willis on the culture of working-class girls and boys, as this is played out in schools, indicates the futility of the functionalist theory of equality of opportunity offered through education, and expands a marxist structural paradigm. McRobbie (1978) finds that working-class girls enter school with a predisposition to marry and have children, and so to ignore other kinds of work which they might also do. The anti-school culture of femininity and the short-term goal of romance take priority, in McRobbie's research, for working-class girls. Llewellyn's participant observation study of the culture of girls and girls' friendship groups offers interesting comparative findings to McRobbie's study, while at the same time adding to the underlying finding that school merely provides a setting for the playing out of an anti-school female culture deemed legitimate for young women in a male-dominated social environment (Llewellyn, 1980). The research by Sharp and her colleagues on the transition of working-class girls from school to work offers added insight into this process which depends on girls' perceiving family and motherhood as their central goals (Sharp and Roberts, 1983). Similarly, it is found that working-class boys develop an anti-school culture based on a disparagement of academic work, combined with an overvaluation of heavy labour and masculine superiority (Willis, 1977).

Anyon's recent work on the accommodation and resistance by working-class and upper-middle-class girls to the contradictory expectations of future work and motherhood provides valuable insight into forms of female culture (1983). After ex-

ploring both public and private forms of resistance and accommodation to the contradictory expectations of the female sex role, Anyon concludes that overall "their accommodation and resistance does not seek to remove the structural causes of the contradiction" (1983). Their resistance and accommodation represent creative and individually liberating forms of managing, but ultimately only assist women to survive in a male-dominated milieu where roles which are actually open to them are circumscribed.

The Ottawa study provides support for several of the ideas put forth by Anyon. Of the twenty-five girls interviewed, sixteen were middle or upper middle class from professional or managerial families, while nine were working class from unskilled or semi-skilled families. For the middle-class group, going to university was an accepted course of action, taken for granted. However, only three of them integrated plans for postsecondary education with a commitment to subsequent careers. For the majority university was seen as a time "to get my head together" or to fulfill parental dreams. For one it was something to do in case she was "late" in getting married. As she said, "when you get to be twenty-five or twenty-six everyone starts looking at you and wondering when you are going to get married."

For these girls, going to university or art college (a popular choice among the highest status) is mainly a route to motherhood. This, they were quite clear, would put an end to other activities:

I wouldn't want to work, after I had kids.

If I had kids I'd definitely stop working.

If I had kids I'd want to stay home and help them.

My career would be working with children and having my own kids would be my career.

Thus these middle-class girls for the most part foresaw a truncated future. Their way of solving the contradictions of being a middle-class woman was a two-stage program: some further education followed by full-time motherhood. The three who seemed committed to pursuing a career were clearly aware that this might prove problematic. One said she would be expected to do all the housework *and* have a job, while another said "anyone I had an interest in would just have to realize that my career was important to me."

All but one of the working-class girls were bemused by questions about education after high school. Some mentioned it as an ideal but one quickly dismissed it:

Sometimes my mother asks me if I'm thinking of going to college, and I say "I don't know, I think I might get a job first." And she says, "Oh, that's okay." She's pretty reasonable.

Another said, "I want to do something, but if I don't I won't be upset. . . . I always wanted to be a housewife." Another said that she didn't think she could do university work even though she wanted to be a teacher and had high grades. For the most part they anticipated getting a job at the end of high school. That was what parents wanted: "they just don't want me to be a slob. They want me to earn a decent living, like being a secretary." For others the motivation was to be financially independent: "My boyfriend always said he'd support me, but I don't want that. I can't stand that." Although university is not in the minds of working-class girls, they share the motherhood ideology with their middle-class sisters: "If you're going to go on with work and be married at the same time, I don't think you should have children."

The range of desires and expectations reveals how class differences arise within the structurally prescribed limits of femininity. While middle-class girls may be able to live out both of their typical future plans — full-time motherhood and a cyclical career — this is likely to be at some cost both to their work lives and earning capacities, and to their experience in childcare. . . . Given the levels of female and male working-class wages, it is highly unlikely that the working-class girls will be able to be financially independent or to not work to help support a household.

This research on the future plans of female high school students adds further support to the critique of functionalist theory and moves beyond organizational analyses where sex and class are all too often rigidly separated. Because functionalism assumes a high degree of consensus on middle-class values of achievement, it cannot see student cultures which develop partly in retaliation to socially imposed gender and class constraints. Given student resistance to what middle-class schooling has to offer in a capitalist, male-dominated society, there is little wonder that the functionalist aspiration that schools provide equal opportunity has failed. Functionalist and critical organizational analyses share a methodological assumption: they separate the formal organizational aspects of the school from the culture of the student population. Phenomenological research which focuses on what happens in schools in a largely informal way shows how the relationship between school personnel and students in the school and classroom contribute to the persistence of the status quo.

3. PHENOMENOLOGICAL RESEARCH ON INTERACTION BETWEEN STUDENTS AND SCHOOL PERSONNEL

Overall, it becomes evident in this research that at least two processes are operating in the classroom and school to lead students to accept and reproduce society based on class and gender hierarchical divisions. First, it becomes clear that sex and class are recognized by school personnel usually implicitly, as social categories to consider in guiding students in making "appropriate" future occupational and educational plans. They do not consider it to be appropriate for individuals to cross the gender division of labour or part ways with their own social class background, despite academic achievement which would allow them to do so. Middle-class girls are encouraged to go to university to achieve some professional or semi-professional skills *before* settling down to childbearing and domesticity, while working-class girls are expected to work, at least part-time, while investing their main attentions in family. Both are actively encouraged to put family first. These decisions are made with little or no consideration of actual school achievement or for individual interests.

The second factor which becomes apparent concerns the implicit devaluation of subordinate (non-middle-class male) cultures. This is most usually expressed by refusing to recognize or deriding resistant or opposing cultures. Girls' interests — or what Rosenberg calls feminine culture — are particularly subject to derision in the school. In writing about the successful hegemony of bourgeois culture in the school, Dale states

. . . what seems to be involved is the prevention of rejection, opposition or alternatives to the status quo through denying the use of the school for such purposes. (Dale, 1982)

Although Dale rejects seeing the school as "active" in the maintenance of this hegemony, choosing rather to see the status quo as being maintained by the "normal process" of the relatively autonomous school, it is a matter for research to investigate how much the "prevention of rejection, opposition or alternatives" is the passive stance of the school, and how much it is actively accomplished. Delamont (1983)

argues that the school is active in promoting the preservation of the hierarchical gender status quo and in fact is regressive in ignoring social change which has taken place.

Research presented here supports Delamont's view of the school, while at the same time showing how, simply by avoiding issues, the school takes stands supporting existing gender and class hierarchies. The following is broken down into three components for in-depth analysis: (a) the advice of guidance personnel, (b) teacher-student interaction in the classroom, and (c) the content of classroom interaction.

a) The Advice of Guidance Personnel

The evidence from this research indicates that students are not led to consider future work which would be inconsistent with their social class background or gender, regardless of personal academic achievement. Although survey research has found that scores on mental ability do not correlate very highly with educational aspirations, particularly for working-class students (Porter, Porter, and Blishen 1982), it is useful to examine how this is accomplished in the school. The statement holds true for girls and boys, but with the added twist that girls, no matter what their social class or academic achievement, are rarely urged to think of work as anything but secondary, with family responsibilities as primary. Thus the surplus labour force of largely unskilled or semi-skilled women who can be pulled into the labour force as required and pushed out again, back to the family, during times of economic recession, is also reproduced.

The names of the forty students interviewed were given to the guidance counsellors, who were asked what they knew of these students' future plans. The counsellors knew nineteen of the students well enough to discuss their plans, and, in a few cases, students were discussed by more than one counsellor. The counsellors assumed that none of the students aspired to break with their social class backgrounds. They were unaware of the one working-class girl who did aspire to go to university and study science. Instead, two counsellors claimed that this student was planning to be a legal secretary; and both thought that this was a good choice. On the other hand, the student herself stressed several times in her interview that she did not want to be a secretary. She realized that the counsellors knew of this "plan" because her mother had spoken with them about it. This was the only student interviewed who was consciously trying to overcome both social class background and stereotyped gender roles, and she obviously received no support from counsellors.

In some cases, counsellors discussed students whose academic achievement was inconsistent with what might be anticipated for their future work — that is, where it was "too high" for a working-class job, or "too low" for a middle-class or professional job. The working-class girl with the highest achievement of all forty in the sample had wanted to be a doctor but now planned to become a hospital technician. Her lowered goal met with approval from a counsellor:

She's always been an A student. . . . She is someone who is independent and doesn't have any financial backing behind her, so it's a case of economic necessity that she take on a job.

Another counsellor positively accepted a high-achieving working-class boy's decision to go directly into the army:

[A]s a counsellor I'm not going to say to someone who is unfamiliar, let us say, with the university career situation, perhaps not monetarily too well off, they have no aspirations in that line for that sort of thing, it's no use my saying "you should go to university". . . . My idea of guidance is to present to the student what opportunities

there are for them to take that suits them, what they feel comfortable with. And a lot of that comfort and advice and discussion goes on in the family.

These examples of working-class experience show that not only do most students seem predisposed to train for jobs that will maintain their social class background, but also that there is little positive encouragement and sometimes active discouragement from the school to alter these patterns.

Upper-middle-class students also seemed likely to maintain their class position, regardless of low academic achievement. Of the two boys in this situation, one intended to go to an American college and eventually to enter the marine business owned by his uncle. Doing this, he would probably be able to maintain his social class position. The second would also go to college, much as he preferred not to. In the meantime one had football, the other a jazz group to deflect attention from poor achievement. In both cases, family resources and direction, not advice from school, were instrumental in assuring their futures. In fact, the counsellors chose not to offer any comment or information on these two students, thereby showing the school's passivity in allowing the reproduction of class relations.

One upper-middle-class girl who was managing the academic program with great difficulty wished to move into the technical stream of another high school. Her parents forbade such a move and thus forestalled her chance of acquiring a skilled manual job. The guidance counsellors were unaware of her desire to go to the technical school and merely viewed her as a problem student.

Gender was a category used more explicitly than class in advising students, particularly girls. Several middle-class girls also had aspirations for working-class jobs. However, this was not seen as problematic, as long as the jobs were in the female segregated segment of the labour force. In four of five interviews, counsellors explicitly stated that girls had to realize that being future wives and mothers was of primary importance to their future plans. As one said:

I have certain feelings about home, etc. . . . Can a surrogate or substitute mother . . . replace the mother? There's no way. The bond is simply not there.

Another felt that a woman could do neither properly if she tried to have both a family and a job. A third said:

I think that the girl who is interested in marriage and children . . . might look for a career that she can leave for a few years and then go back to . . . where the knowledge of the job takes second place to the personality of the job.

He then proceeded to list several jobs in the predominantly women's branch of the labour force: social worker, teacher, saleswoman, secretary.

Overall, maintaining social class background was seen as appropriate by the counsellors. For the most part this implied also maintaining the sexual division of labour, but in several cases gender took precedence over social class. This meant that some of the sixteen girls from the middle class were heading for working-class jobs which were conspicuously open to women and would be compatible with their jobs as mothers, since they could be dropped and perhaps resumed. It would be incumbent upon these girls to maintain their social class position through marriage.

An important way in which counsellors sidestep issues of class is by "converting social hierarchies into academic hierarchies" (P. Bourdieu, quoted in Wexler, 1982: 278): upper middle class translates perniciously into "bright," working class into "dull." According to Keddie (1971),

teachers talk about the "dull" students in the lower stream (mostly working-class students) and the "bright" students in the higher stream (mostly middle-class students). It is through doing this that school personnel are able to maintain the myth of being "class-blind." Thus the words themselves may be neatly avoided, and a great step may be made in the social reproduction of class.

Student class origins affect the interpretation of falling grades by school personnel. Low-achieving middle-class children were labelled by guidance counsellors as "bright" but not well enough motivated. One middle-class girl whose grades had declined was "probably very bright. Her father's in the diplomatic corps." Another was "extremely bright, as are her brothers, . . . but there's no effort there whatever." On the other hand, working-class students whose grades declined were not seen as presenting problems. They were achieving according to what was expected of them. A girl from a divided family was a "very, very average student." A working-class boy whose grades dropped was a "solid 60 per-center. . . . It may be that there isn't the drive, the motivation in the family."

Social class and gender played closely connected roles in the advice of the high school counsellors. A content analysis of comments made about students indicated that counsellors knew as much about student family background as they did about academic achievement. Thus, school personnel actively contributed to homeostasis in the class and sex divisions of labour.

b) Teacher-Student Interaction

The observation of classroom activity confirmed previous findings that boys dominate in the classroom and that teachers contribute to this male dominance by focusing greater attention on the boys (Sarah, 1980; Spender, 1980; Sears and Feldman, 1974). Furthermore, teachers' interviews clearly revealed that they evaluated female and male academic abilities differently. Together, these teacher practices devalued girls and rendered them invisible in the classroom.

In the observation sessions in twenty-seven Grade 12 classes (eleven English literature, twelve math, two chemistry, two world religion), girls were found to dominate verbal interaction with the teacher in only 7 percent of the classes, while boys dominated in 63 percent. There were only minor discrepancies by sex in the remainder. On the one hand, in the English and math classes it was found that teachers directed between one and a half to five times as many questions to boys as to girls. On the other, in two exceptional classes (the woman teacher in the chemistry class and the man teacher in the numerically female-dominated world religion class), teachers directed equal numbers of questions to girls and boys. In all class periods boys independently asked more questions and made more comments than girls. Thus it was clear that both teachers and students were responsible for the dominance of boys in the classroom. Why teachers directed more attention to boys in their classes is illustrated by their comments on the behaviour of girls and boys in class. Although the typically non-disruptive behaviour of girls and their relative silence is often a relief to teachers, this does not lead teachers to appreciate them as students (Scott, 1980). Girls do not fit the "ideal client" image which Becker (1952) found was the student who responded to and appeared to learn as a result of the teacher's efforts. Several comments made by the women in their interviews revealed that they preferred boys as students; the men indicated that they thought boys were brighter. Teachers responded to girls' quietness in class and their decline in achievement over the years in school in ways which turned quietness into invis-

ibility. Ultimately teachers' attitudes fostered girls' further rejection of the school.

Eight of the ten women in the school who taught academic courses at the Grade 12 level confirmed that they preferred the classroom behaviour of boys. As one said:

The boys are very pointed in their questions. They want very specific information. The girls have a tendency to be vague, whereas the boys will be very specific. And I appreciate that, because then I can help more.

Boys were also seen as more fun than girls, as evident from this statement from another teacher, which opens with a clearly stated preference for male students:

The fellows I prefer to teach, more than the girls, because they don't get as up-tight about little things. Like I find in my Grade 10s they don't hold grudges and they're fun, while the girls are taking themselves far more seriously.

The issue of holding grudges and the duplicity of the girls was taken up by two other teachers. One talked with great admiration about how easy the boys made it for her, a petite young woman, to discipline them:

You know I even scold some of them, those tall guys. But the next day it's "good morning miss" and "good-bye miss" and that's it.

Girls, she said, were less forgiving. Another said:

I think in general that the boys are a bit more forthright. You're not as inclined to see somebody and say "now I wonder what he's thinking" as "I wonder what she's thinking." You feel that the boys are pretty much more open about things.

The women teachers spent much more time during the interview discussing the behaviour of the boys than that of the girls. One spoke extensively about the boys, comparing the dedicated student with the "he-men" whom she "tamed" in her classes. When prompted to discuss the girls, she said briefly:

Girls haven't caused me any trouble in years and years. They tend to talk a bit much, but it's never been any problem for me for years to stop the girls.

Boys were the subject of other "plugs" from the women, but the girls never were. A chemistry teacher noted that boys liked to put on airs about doing well even though they did no work. "But mind you," she said, "whenever you look at their homework it's done, and you only assigned three questions but they've got twenty-three done."

The sexual dynamic is a clear underpinning to the attraction between women teachers and the young adult males in their classes. It is only half perceived and unspoken, but it clearly led to admiration and respect. The mirror attraction, on the other hand, which must have existed (and had led to one marriage in the recent history of the school), did not generate a parallel respect of men teachers for female students. On the contrary, twelve of the fifteen men clearly denigrated the academic abilities of the girls. They were more aware than the women that the early high achievement of girls declined in the later years of high school. They called the girls in the junior grades "overachievers"; they did not see them as "underachievers" in later years. Rather, girls' decline in achievement over the years was felt to be due to the fact that in the upper grades "ability starts to take over." Another, who said that most overachievers were girls, defined the term:

By an overachiever I mean somebody who's getting marks above and beyond their innate ability level. Which can be done very easily at the 9 and 10 level by doing two hours of homework a night.

Implicit in this statement is a judgment that achievement is more a sign of ability in the upper grades since it is impossible to exceed ability at this level. The same teacher remarked that as he looked back, more

boys stood out in his mind as "really bright students."

The "overachievement" of girls in the lower grades is, according to several teachers, a result of their docility and conscientiousness. Girls gave the "party line," as one teacher said, and as a result were more successful than boys. They noted that girls passed through puberty and "settled down" before boys, and so they were initially able to do better. It took boys a bit longer to settle down and achieve according to their ability. One teacher said that girls did well in the early grades because at that stage they were still keen to learn things "by rote," and that "they could cope with this."

Girls did continue to excel in senior English classes. The male English teachers recognized this but attempted to explain away the success. Girls did well because "their work habits were so good" and "they read more." One painted a scenario of a girl spending the evening babysitting, since she had to wait for an invitation out, and this would provide a lot of quiet time to read. One noted that the pattern of girls excelling in English ended at the university level.

Two corollaries followed from the overachievement thesis. First, girls who declined in achievement and were doing relatively poorly by the end of high school were seen as achieving according to their ability. Boys, on the other hand, who did *not* do well by the end of high school were underachieving. The teacher of the "slow" senior math class said:

Girls are there pretty well because they should be there. I don't find too many underachievers amongst the females. You're going to get the boys in there who are capable of doing well but don't do well. They have decided not to achieve the way they should. (my emphasis)

Thus for boys there was seen to be an aspect of low achievement not strictly related to ability; but this possibility was not suggested for girls.

As a second corollary, girls who did manage to achieve high grades in the upper years were seen not as clever, but as plodders. In other words, they merely continued in the pattern of overachievement. As a teacher of chemistry said about the girls in his class:

... they tend to be very good workers. Maybe not the brightest, maybe not the cleverest, but they have plugged and done all their work to get there. ... Some of the boys have gotten there completely on their cleverness. But the girls who are there tend to be the ones who have worked.

Although it is not a disparaging comment to say that the girls worked hard, it was unnecessary to say that they were not really bright. The message was clear that these male teachers felt that the low achievement of the girls but not the high achievement was related to ability.

Thus there is an important, although largely hidden, way in which teachers in school undervalue female students and encourage their withdrawal from the educational field. Certainly the emphasis in the wider society on marriage and children is a source of their limited future aspirations, but the undervaluation of their behaviour and achievement in school is an important contribution to this outcome. It is probable that teachers themselves are also influenced by what they "know" about the future expectations of girls. It is not a finding particular to this research that teachers perceive boys as the better students. However, this merely serves to add support to the thesis that this is one way in which girls are rendered invisible in the school and are undervalued as students.

These assessments of the unequal relation of achievement to ability in boys and girls echoes those made about class and achievement. In both cases the dominant group — male and middle-class students — were assumed to be capable but unmotivated, whereas the subordinate group — female and working-class students — were judged to be simply intellectually unable. The conversion of preexisting social hierarchies of class and gender external to the school into achievement hierarchies in and by the school serves to reproduce them in the educational system and for the whole society.

c) The Content of Classroom Interaction

Ideology of male-superior, female-subordinate arises frequently in classroom conversation and discussion, and is accepted uncritically as natural. Previous research has shown that the acceptance of a gendered status quo has profound implications for girls' classroom experience and ability to learn. Spender cites the example of a male history teacher who encountered problems in getting girls to participate in a class discussion on war. When one girl did speak, she was ridiculed by boys in the class. Since most topics covered in classes do traditionally have a male orientation and since girls are discouraged from speaking to these topics, they withdraw and learn silence and passivity — a lesson well learned, judging from the classroom observation sessions.

One example from classroom observations in the Ottawa study shows how patriarchal culture is reproduced. In the world religions class, the teacher asked who in the Christian religion might be a good role model. When no-one answered, he suggested St. Paul, but then added that Paul would not be a good model for a woman, because he did not like women. Then he went on to note that few religious leaders had liked women. He also stated that woman had been created from a rib from Adam's side, to help and please him. At this stage I heard a girl in the class whispering that women and men had the same number of ribs. The misogyny inherent in the great religions of the world is an important topic, but it was never critically discussed or presented as in any way problematic. Instead misogyny was presented as "objective" classroom knowledge.

In another class, an English teacher criticized a play written by a student because in it the daughter did not cry or show enough emotion in pleading for the family car. A mathematics teacher merely smiled and nodded when a girl in his class said she wouldn't have to learn how to complete an income tax form because her "husband" would do it.

In each of these classroom episodes, the status quo is accepted as normal and natural. In the first, gender stereotypes are actively offered as legitimated knowledge; in the second they are used to judge student work; while in the third, the student is silently rewarded for conforming to gender stereotypes. None of them led to any critical discussions. Nor did any of the teachers challenge gender typing. Consequently, gender hierarchies are removed from the purview of education and given a status as fact of life.

In contrast is the example provided by a discussion in an English literature class which was remarkable because of the overwhelming participation of the girls. The content of this discussion is worth exploring. In this class, the teacher raised questions for discussion on Hardy's novel *Tess of the d'Urbervilles*. Did Tess know she was being seduced (it is often difficult to tell in Victorian novels!)? Did she love her baby as she said, or was she secretly relieved when the baby died? The girls participated fully in this class, not because the teacher altered his usual pattern of calling more often on the boys, but because the girls were eager to discuss these questions and independently raised issues elaborating on them. In fact, the teacher was overwhelmed by the flood of discussion he had started,

and actually appeared withdrawn and even embarrassed by it.

The fact that the teacher and the boys withdrew from the discussion suggests that the cultures of the girls and boys are kept very separate in the school. Male culture dominates in the school, as elsewhere, and the alternate culture, the feminine voice, is silenced, by being either ignored or undervalued when it does surface. The discussion about *Tess* obviously did strike a very responsive note among the girls. Since they are not even encouraged to discuss the issues which are of immediate concern to them, they learn to be silent generally in class, and the process of learning, of pursuing important questions, is stunted. Teachers encourage passivity on the part of girls and then criticize them for being silent and not participating in class. Conforming to female standards of passivity in patriarchal culture undermines the intellectual growth of girls, and teachers judge them as being less capable students.

The class discussion which I heard on *Tess* was in all probability rare, given that most topics covered in classes are from a masculine orientation. If the girls had been encouraged and respected for their participation in that discussion, they would feel more free to pursue their own orientation to issues in others.

Conclusion

A great deal transpires within the school and classroom to encourage students to accept the sex and class divisions of labour, at both a societal and a personal level. In part, alternatives are seen as unacceptable, in part the status quo is assumed to be just and appropriate.

As a result the school is characterized by these two related patterns which contribute to the social reproduction of society marked by economic and sex inequality. One way of accomplishing this is by ignoring the fact that inequalities do exist in male-dominated, capitalist society. The dominant culture is accepted as the only reality. The experience of students whose background or sex indicates that they are living another face of this reality is not recognized in the school. Consequently, students from subordinate cultures tend to reject schooling and all it represents.

A related way in which the school contributes to the hegemony of the dominant culture is by accepting that students' choices concerning their educational and occupational futures be consistent with the sex-segregated labour force and their social class background. Very often students who have not rejected schooling (usually because of parental pressure, or because they are very bright and curious) are encouraged because of their own financial limitations, or because of their future "plans," to become wives, mothers, and low-status workers; in other words, to make sex- and class-appropriate future choices. In these cases, actual academic achievement is placed second to factors of sex and class.

Thus these two components of schooling interact to contribute to the persistence of the dominant culture: at one level subordinate cultures are undervalued and most students make their own choices to reject schooling; at another, students are not encouraged to make "inappropriate" choices, given their sex and social class. They are, on the other hand, lauded for making "appropriate" choices. In this way, schools do in fact contribute to the inequalities inherent in male-dominated, capitalist society.

The enthusiasm that the girls showed in their discussion of *Tess* indicates that schools might be forced to change if girls generally assert themselves and do not rest with whispering, "Women and men have the same number of ribs." However, the subordinate position of women in society is clearly reflected and promoted in schools as they exist now.

ALTERNATIVE VISIONS OF THE UNIVERSITY

*Janice Newson and
Howard Buchbinder*

As the shift towards fiscal restraint and contraction took hold during the 1970s, the university was often represented as being in a state of crisis. Like a ship without a rudder, it was seen to be paralysed in the face of fiscal problems it was ill equipped to manage and to be lacking a sense of purpose in a rapidly changing society (Neilson and Gaffield, 1986; Watson, 1985). Perceptions of the nature of this ongoing crisis and diagnoses of its causes have varied widely. Nonetheless, the sense of crisis has provoked serious thought. How can the crisis be resolved? How can the university regain its stability and purpose?

The search for an answer to these questions leads to our second analytical theme: alternative visions of the university and of its relation to society.... [T]he liberal vision of the university ... incorporated a broadly based public consensus on expansion and guided university growth during the late 1950s and the 1960s. In the face of fiscal constraint and contraction, however, the liberal vision began to be dismantled as a guide for university development. Some continued to advocate the model of a liberal university and the principles related to it: broad accessibility, diversity, and inter-disciplinary and multidisciplinary scholarship. However, the public consensus began to erode, and lack of funds encouraged policy-makers and academics alike to think about the role of the university in other terms.

This rethinking did not happen overnight or lead in only one direction. Never-

From Janice Newson and Howard Buchbinder *The University Means Business*, Garamond Press, Toronto, 1988. Reprinted with permission of Garamond Press and the authors.

theless, new visions of the university began to surface, often piecemeal, in editorial columns, at conferences, and in discussions in university hallways. Some of these formulations were not new but old ones revived and reshaped to address current problems. However, before discussing these substitute visions, we need to explain what we mean by "visions" and how we intend to use this idea as an analytical device.

The Idea of "Visions"

First, we want to distinguish our idea of "visions" from popular and philosophical conceptions that might easily be confused with it. We are not referring to an imaginary ideal of what a university might be or ought to be or could be if all constraints were removed. Nor are we referring to a Weberian "ideal type" in which the properties of the university would be grouped together to represent a mental construct against which real universities could be measured. We are not using this term in the way some scholars understand "ideology" — a complex collection of mental fabrications that functions to prevent members of society from seeing the real source of their social oppression. Although "visions" of the university can serve such purposes, we are interested in understanding how the content of these visions relates to changes taking place in universities. We are focusing not on the way they mystify "real" underlying social conditions in order to maintain these conditions, but on how particular interests use them to shape social conditions.

Our use of "visions" assumes that social process is rooted in material (rather than abstract) political and economic forces and that these forces are brought into play through human agency. The liberal vision, for example, is a way of summarizing the real practices, policies, and economic and political resources put into place in univer-

sities largely during the period of expansion. These practices, policies, and resources created the material basis that encouraged a particular view of the desirable role for universities in society. In this way, the liberal vision served as the blue-print for guiding expansion; it provided a rationale for using resources in particular ways. The later dismantling of the liberal vision meant that it no longer served as the agreed-upon blue-print for university development and that many concrete aspects of university functioning associated with the liberal vision were eliminated or under threat of being eliminated. The "vision" is both the blue-print and the effects of using the blue-print; visions are shaped by political and economic forces in their formulations and in the ways they are implemented in concrete social institutions.

The active thrust in our concept of visions does not necessarily imply that people developing or implementing a particular vision are self-consciously pursuing it. Even though their actions point in a particular direction, they may be based on pragmatic reasons rather than deliberate design. Pragmatic reasons are those that "work" within the prevailing economic and political context. They are "practical" responses rather than actions guided by well-formulated strategies. Yet these responses represent and add up to a guiding vision, since the totality of responses is shaped by the political-economic context. These guiding visions have the potential for mobilizing and bringing into play the human agents and the necessary political and economic resources that can and do control events. To the extent that they do this, these visions contribute to the present process of change in universities.

First, they shape debate over university policy within governments and various quasi-governmental bodies, as well as within universities themselves. For example, they provide hooks on which to hang funding formulae, new curricular designs, and new criteria for hiring, tenuring, and promoting academic staff. In this sense, the struggle to control the academic work process described in the previous chapter can be seen as a struggle to implement different visions of the university. Second, they provide a basis for justifying the use of resources in the service of their related objectives. Through appeals to a particular vision of the university, public monies can be diverted to support some institutions of higher learning more than others, or some programmes more than others, or some students more than others. Third, they lead to the creation of committees, agencies, offices, positions, and organizational structures designed or used to bring a particular vision into existence. Visions have real sponsors who have specific institutional, socio-political, and economic locations. They can be used by various people and groups to justify patterns of change already under way and, therefore, can help to build the capacity to carry them further. By the same token, alternative visions of the university can also help to build the capacity to resist trends under way and to move in a different direction entirely.

In the following sections, we will illustrate the points we have made through a discussion and comparison of three replacement visions put forward over the past decade, as the effectiveness of the liberal vision began to wane. These three visions see the university as:

- an academic haven;
- a tool for economic growth; and
- a means for social transformation.

Although these visions have shown their faces in a variety of contexts, we have chosen to focus on three recent publications that use them as a basis for arguments for reform and change in universities.

The University as Haven for Scholars

The vision of the university as a haven for scholars is well represented in *The Western University on Trial*, Chapman (1983). Chapman challenges the academic community to reinstate the university as *the* institution of modern liberal civilization, with "a primary allegiance to cognitive rationality, to disciplined search for truths." Over the past two decades, the academic and moral integrity of the Western university has been eroded, and brought into disrepute, by the politicization of knowledge, by efforts to democratize the university as though it were a microcosm of society at large, and by the pursuit of utilitarian aims. Restoring it to its rightful place requires the moral fortitude to resist these pressures.

Raymond Polin expresses the position well:

Any university worthy of its name has to resist cultural, ideological, and political pressures that would bend it to requirements irrelevant to the life of the mind and loyalty to truth. A host of pressure groups . . . seek to subvert academic ideals and corrupt the university and their methods include propaganda, dogma, indoctrination, and cultural, even physical, terrorism. In response, the academic community must exercise autonomy in the shape of intellectual virtue . . . The will for autonomy takes the form of a will for intellectual honesty and loyalty to truth (Chapman, 1983: 48).

This undermining of the university's purpose is attributed to the radical student movement of the 1960s and the ascendancy in some disciplines of Marxist "ideology" as an intellectual paradigm. The New Left is viewed as having displaced "cognitive objectives with political ones" and thereby as having promoted the "concept of the university as an organization that can and should be used to transform society." Many other types of harm have flowed from this, for example, the acceptance of political criteria in hiring and tenure decisions, the lowering of academic standards in student selection, the adoption of equalizing mechanisms such as affirmative action programmes, and the introduction of adversarialism into university governance.

The recent decline in public support for universities, and the threat to university autonomy posed by increasing government intervention, are seen to be effects, rather than causes, of the university's own weaknesses. In other words, grade inflation, the granting of tenure to too many individuals without the benefit of national competition, the adoption of "practical" courses and programmes, and faculty unionization all have led to a decline in public confidence and have invited outside interference. Only by raising standards, limiting the numbers of tenured positions, eliminating vocationally oriented programmes, and reasserting authority through strong capable administrative leadership can universities reverse the process.

Up to this point, then, *The Western University on Trial* is an uncompromising argument in support of the vision of the university as a haven for scholars, uniquely engaged in the disciplined search for truth. The recent crisis is rooted not in external political and economic pressures but in failure to maintain the highest standards of intellectual and moral integrity. Even as the recent problems arise from within, so too is the solution to be found within. The university must withdraw from its over-involvement in the community around it and return to its primary commitment to cognitive rationality.

The book appears to be arguing for reinstating the university as it is presumed to have existed in an earlier era, before the "corrupting" influences of the expansionist period. But a harder look reveals the influ-

ence of more recent trends. The section called "The Pursuit of Truth" is devoted almost exclusively to the importance of research and what needs to be done to promote more support for it. There is virtually no mention of teaching as an important component of the pursuit of truth. Although most of the contributors agree that "present trends" are exacerbating the longer-term pattern of separating research from teaching, most of them comment on it with resigned acceptance — in glaring contrast to the forcefulness and passion directed at the corrupting influences of the student radicalism, left-wing intellectualism, and social liberalism of the 1960s.

Further, except for Walter Ruegg's essay on research in the humanities, the emphasis of this section is on large-scale, quantitatively based projects, even though the contributors acknowledge that such studies drain the university's fiscal resources, disrupt its collegial structures, and almost inevitably require large donations from external sponsors who have an interest in their findings. This focus on one type of research, and one that threatens the university's autonomy, is surprising in a book that, elsewhere, argues that the university should be the servant of no creed or party and should rid itself of outside pressures that might shape its priorities and purposes.

Most important, *The Western University on Trial* argues that research is important to the university's mission primarily because of its contribution to economic growth and technical innovation. This is a striking contradiction to one of the premises of the lead section of the book, where one writer argues that utilitarian considerations "do little to validate the mission of the university as a total institution." In fact, the idea of the university as a means for pursuing social equality and emancipation is unequivocally resisted throughout the book, on the basis that such distractions have undermined the university's primary purpose. Yet the book clearly endorses the idea of the university as a tool for achieving economic progress and technical superiority. Strangely enough, the advocates of this version of "the university as academic haven" appear unconcerned that the high standards of moral and intellectual integrity to be expected of the academic sanctuary can be undermined by economic and technological agendas. We will comment further on this contradiction, after we have outlined the other substitute visions.

The University as Tool for Economic Growth

Our second vision is represented in *Partnership for Growth* by Judith Maxwell and Stephanie Currie (1984). . . . [T]he Corporate Higher Education Forum [is an] organization established in Montreal in May 1983. [It] is made up of the presidents of most of Canada's universities and the chief executives of many major Canadian corporations, such as Xerox, Shell, the Royal Bank, and Northern Telecom. The purpose of the Forum is to "promote dialogue between the corporate and academic communities [by] bringing together the country's leading entrepreneurial forces and its primary intellectual resources" (Maxwell and Currie, 1984, p. 101).

The main premise of *Partnership for Growth* is that university research and curricula need to be tuned more closely to the needs of the marketplace, in order to facilitate economic recovery and successful transition into the emerging "high-tech" society. During the expansion of the university system in the 1950s and 1960s, governments provided most if not all the funds to support university activity. However, with the decline of "baby boom" enrolments, and the fiscal pressures of the 1970s, governments became less willing and able to support this expanded system. Universities will continue to be affected by lack of funds, and to experience all the resulting effects, such as declining programme quality, deterioration of buildings and facilities, and cuts in vital services, unless they can sell their wares more effectively. This hypothesis sets the scene for greater collaboration between universities and the business community.

Until recently, neither universities nor corporations in Canada had the motivation to seek more interaction, because universities were securely funded through government grants. Universities valued academic freedom and institutional autonomy, and corporations had little interest in research. But, argue Maxwell and Currie, present economic forces "will draw corporations and universities together." These forces include vigorous international competition, which is forcing the development of high-tech production. The resulting new processes and products will require new styles of management and employee skills.

By implication, the nature and standards of research and education at Canadian universities will become increasingly important to the corporate sector (Maxwell and Currie, 1984, p. 1).

Corporations' need for technological know-how, coupled with underfunding of universities, provides ideal conditions for forging partnerships between the academic and business communities. Such partnerships should be allowed to evolve naturally, through free-market forces. In this way, over time, universities will become more specialized as they tailor programmes and research to the needs of corporate clients.

According to Maxwell and Currie, increased funding from corporations for programmes and research that interest them is the way out of the current crisis for universities. But there is a cost. Universities must be willing to give up, or modify, "cherished traditions" such as academic freedom and institutional autonomy. These traditions are "cultural obstacles" to collaboration, because corporate environments stress profit and commercialization, production deadlines, proprietary rights on new ideas, and a competitive edge in the marketplace.

So, although the new collaboration is presented as a "partnership," it is not one of equals. Corporations will define the needs, and universities will compete with each other to meet them. As well, universities will have to change some of their principles of work. They must be willing to surrender at least some control over research priorities, curriculum design, student admission standards, and rules governing research publications:

Universities must confront the financial squeeze head on with a strategic plan for the 1990's. The strategic plan should define the university's mission, select areas of specialization, identify ways to build managerial flexibility and to open up collaboration with key corporations and with local industry (Maxwell and Currie, 1984, p. 4).

Partnership for Growth contains a detailed blue-print for altering the institutional arrangements of universities to conform to this vision of the university as a tool for economic growth and technological innovation. It provides an interesting perspective on *The Western University on Trial.* The latter book presents an older, more élitist and cloistered vision of the university. But its almost singular emphasis on research and its importance to economic growth and technological development fits well with the vision in *Partnership.* Both arguments play on the concern felt by many academics over the declining quality of university programmes, facilities, and equipment that has accompanied fiscal restraint and contraction.

The Western University blames this decline on a "failure of nerve on the part of academics in the face of difficult times" and calls for more stringent standards (Chapman, 1983, p. x). *Partnership* offers a solution: namely, restoring quality through the use of corporate funds in exchange for universities' contributing to corporate needs. Perhaps for this reason, the contributors to *The Western University* do not acknowledge the threat to autonomy posed by increased corporate funding.

The University as a Social Transformer

In our third book, *Education for the Future*, Stephen Castles and Wiebcke Wüstenberg (1979) offer a vision of the university helping to tranform society. Although this task belongs to society as a whole, educational institutions are to transform the consciousness associated with all social, economic, and political relationships, in order to make possible long-term changes in social structures. They locate this vision in the aims and accomplishments of polytechnic education as originally formulated by Karl Marx. Polytechnic education is intended to eliminate the gulf between mental and manual work and, thereby, the stratified social relations that derive from the division of labour; integrate theoretical and practical knowledge; make students subjects, rather than objects, of the learning process, so they will be active, creative citizens as well as good workers; and stress comprehensive understanding of the relations between the forces of production and the social, political, and cultural spheres of society.

Some efforts have been undertaken in the past to implement this vision, mainly in societies engaged in the transition towards full socialism. However, Castles and Wüstenberg argue that in recent years educational policy in advanced capitalist and some socialist societies such as Russia, China, and the German Democratic Republic (GDR) has been following the same direction. The emphasis has been on narrow specialization for the majority of students and broader, more flexible programmes for a smaller "élite" of students, most of whom are educated in universities. As well, education for the élite cohort increasingly stresses abstract, theoretical knowledge over practical knowledge; the mass cohort acquires vocational skills rather than comprehensive knowledge of the production process or of the social and economic relations in which production is embedded.

Capitalist societies have followed these directions for some time, even though they represent a significant departure from the more liberal versions of capitalist education. For socialist societies, they are diametrically opposed to the principles of polytechnic education and differ from the transformational vision. Castles and Wüstenberg account for the shift in terms of the transitions to high-tech production.

These societies have adopted high-tech production techniques in order to increase their competitive edge internationally. Educational policy increasingly is designed for an information-based society, which requires a small cadre of supervisory, system-oriented, managerial personnel with flexible skills and comprehensive knowledge and a large pool of lower-level workers with narrowly specialized job skills. The research capabilities of universities are seen as sources of innovation, especially in scientific and technological areas that feed high-tech productivity. These changes are designed to create adaptable individuals who will obediently and enthusiastically perform whatever functions are required of them. They are also designed to prevent the education of individuals to control production and so-

ciety. Of recent educational policy in capitalist Britain, Castles and Wüstenberg say:

Future workers are to be trained in schools and further education institutions not only to be disciplined and submissive at work, but also to accept the necessity of mobility and down-grading in response to "technological necessity" and to cope with unemployment without posing a threat to law and order (Castles and Wüstenberg, 1979, p. 145).

But also, they say of socialist China in recent years:

The Chinese education system inculcates its pupils with moral values designed to make them willing and competent workers, eager to use all their abilities to achieve economic and political aims set not by themselves, but by an all powerful bureaucracy (ibid, p. 138).

Having shown similarities in policy in advanced capitalist and some socialist societies, Castles and Wüstenberg point out that the recent educational crisis in the West originates only in part from adjustment to new technologies. Educational policy is controlled largely by those who own the means of production, whose interests are antipathetic to the majority of the workforce. The crisis therefore assumes particular dimensions under capitalism.

[Educational change] originates from the changing nature of the labour process and the new problems of maintaining social and political stability in a crisis situation (ibid., p. 147).

The rapid expansion of educational opportunity in the 1950s and 1960s, followed by its abrupt reversal in the 1970s, has created a serious problem of legitimacy. Transition into a high-tech phase of capitalism exacerbates this problem. Educational policy designed to meet the demands of high-tech production anticipates a protracted, indefinite period of declining social mobility for ever larger segments of the labour force. The crisis of educational institutions in capitalism results from the struggle to confront this problem of legitimacy:

The debates and changes of the mid 1970s have had a new quality: they have been concerned with the content and form of teaching at all levels of education, and the way it prepares young people for working and social life. More efficient ways of inculcating formal knowledge are no longer the main issue. It is a question of purveying the ideologies, attitudes and behaviour patterns necessary for providing loyal and disciplined wage workers during a period of crisis and restructuring of capitalist social and economic relations (ibid., p. 144).

The vision of the university contained in *Education for the Future* is based on the view that educational systems express and sustain the essence of the societies that contain them. The route to "free" education is through transforming all social, political, and economic relations in directions that support truly "free" individuals. Because universities have a part to play in this transformation, they must be deeply connected to their societal context to enable them to respond to the pressures that otherwise might threaten them. However, because some socialist régimes and advanced capitalist societies have both succumbed in recent years to the power of new forces of production, higher-education policy in both types of societies has been affected in similar ways. Rather than being a force for transformation, the university as seen by Castles and Wüstenberg is instead serving the demands of these new forces of production.

Replacement Visions and the Political-Economic Context

The previous arguments have all been published over the last decade, during the period of fiscal restraint and contraction. Each provides its own analysis of the crisis that has affected universities during this period. Each also proposes its own solution, based on a vision that prescribes the role of the university and its relationship to society as a whole. Although they differ in these regards, the views converge on the political and economic pressures bearing on universities to assist in the economic transition to a high-tech society. The visions they put forward relate in different ways to these pressures.

The advocates of the university as economic tool exhort the university to "sell out" to these pressures. They argue that universities have a responsibility to assist in economic recovery and expansion, even though to do so they may have to alter their practices and abandon some "cherished traditions," such as institutional autonomy and the protection of academic freedom.

Supporters of the university as haven benignly accede to the pressures. They reject the idea that the university has a responsibility to serve a wide range of social priorities, and they view attempts to do so as corrupting of its primary purpose. Yet they assume that the university ought to fulfill an economic and technological agenda, and they are blind to its dangers. In fact, their proposals for protecting the university against invasive social pressures aid the aims of those who see the university as economic tool. For example, more restricted access will help to create the anticipated work-force of high-tech production: a well-informed élite cadre and a larger, less educated pool of narrowly skilled workers. As well, support for strong and effective administrations and denunciation of the adversarialism brought about by collective bargaining can help make university workplaces more compatible with corporate environments. The professional management now so prevalent in universities will have the flexibility to encourage corporate-university collaboration, without resistance from strong faculty unions.

Those who see the university as social transformer present their vision as a basis for resisting political and economic pressures. However, the priority already given to economic growth and technological innovation has undermined resistance to these pressures. Within capitalist societies such as our own, some academics who hold to a transformational vision are less able to subvert prevailing trends because they have become marginalized, in ways described earlier. Effective resistance begins with a strategy for resisting marginalization. In other words, if universities are to play a role in social transformation, academic workers must be able to control their own work process. *Education for the Future* clearly points in this direction:

One of the major tasks of transitional society is to create the conditions necessary for overcoming the distinction between mental and manual work. Obviously, education has a major role to play in this. It must help to make all citizens capable not only of doing productive work, but also of planning and organizing this work — not individually, but collectively with their workmates. *They can only control production in their own interest and in the interest of society in general, if they all have a full grasp of the technological, economic and political relationships between their own workplace and the whole system of social production (Castles and Wüstenberg, 1979, pp. 5–6, emphasis ours).*

Conclusion

In the recent debates over how to resolve the crisis in Canadian universities, the visions of the university as academic haven and as tool for economic growth have acquired more prominence than that of the university as transformer. They have gained currency for two related reasons. First, in different ways, each one supports changes in the university that are compatible with external political and economic pressures. Second, each posits a (different) model of the university compatible with the patterns of change already under way, such as the changes in the academic work process we have outlined.

Those who advocate the university as haven do not entirely concur with those who favour the university as economic tool. In many ways, their views are opposed. Yet, in the present political and economic climate, these two visions exist symbiotically; each one feeds off the changes proposed by the other. Aspects of both are intermingled in attempts to mobilize support for the new objectives that members of the university community are being enjoined to embrace. The "pursuit of excellence" — a slogan recently imported from business — is a good illustration of this intermingling. University presidents have been calling on faculty to support "quality" and "academic excellence" by increasing research and raising standards for student enrolment and performance. At the same time they have been making deals with corporate clients to pay for new research facilities and equipment in the interest of promoting technological transfer and economic productivity.

Neither the academic haven or the university as economic tool has attracted sufficient support to generate the kind of public consensus attached earlier to the liberal vision. However, a new term coined by the Science Council of Canada — the "service university" — brings together the central thrusts of these two visions of the university: promoter and guardian of academic achievement at the highest level and instrument of high-tech corporate development.

The idea of the "service university" is deceptively compelling; it implies that the university exists to serve the needs of society as a whole. Proponents may see it as the basis for forging a broad consensus on the direction for university development in the 1980s and beyond. . . .

We began this book with a question: Is there a danger in a continuing link between business and academe? We have provided a basis for an answer by describing some emerging consequences of such links. However, there is a more present danger: this question is rarely being asked, and even more rarely being answered, even though corporate-university connections develop apace. Faculty members, administrators, politicians, and editorial writers have begun to take it for granted that corporate links are an essential feature of the new blue-print for higher education. We have attempted to show how the apparent acceptance of this blue-print is based not on public debate and critical evaluation but on the changes of the past two decades.

Universities were made vulnerable to this new corporate agenda in the years of contraction following expansion. To accommodate budgetary shortfalls, academic work was reorganized in ways that now facilitate implementation of the service university model. Changes in administrative structures and the shift of control to full-time managers to deal with the fiscal crisis are being consolidated in order to develop relations with corporate clients and to exercise strong leadership in the new "indusversity" marketplace. Demoralized by more than a decade of underfunding and its impact on quality, members of the university community are welcoming the new sources of funding and the renewed value being placed on their work in exchange for applying their energy and talents to the needs of the corporate sector.

But if the implementation of the service university vision has had and will continue to have the effect on academic work described in this book, why is there so little critical response from academics themselves? After all, it was not long ago that university campuses were the focus of demonstrations protesting involvement with the "military-industrial complex." Even ac-

ademics who did not support the radical tactics of the demonstrators were unshakeable in their support of university autonomy, especially in relation to the special interests of big business. Could their commitment to the old liberal vision have been bought off so easily with the promise of financial rescue?

We think there are several reasons for the apparent silence. First, many academics will not recognize the university as the work-place and themselves as the academic workers we have described in this book. Although they recognize teaching, research, and service as functions of their role as faculty members, they tend not to acknowledge the place of the institution in shaping the way they carry out these functions. Instead, they believe that, as professionals, the way they allocate their time and energy results from their own choices — the university is the base from which they carry out their own priorities. Consequently, many academics have not noticed the institutional ground shifting beneath them, as their careers have moved through good time into bad. They have been preoccupied instead with increasing teaching loads, ill-equipped students, rejected grant proposals, and more and more committee work, with less and less power to determine the outcomes. They have searched for a place of retreat — space to "do their own work" because the institution seems to be demanding something that isn't "their own." If successful at finding this space, they have narrowed their vision and concentrated their efforts on work they "have chosen" to do. They have been content to leave the rancour and confusion of the institution for full-time managers to sort out with a few militant unionists.

Second, even though they see themselves as continuing to choose their own work priorities, many academics believe that they have no choice in resolving the financial crisis of the past decade. Although corporate funding may exact a price that would be better not paid, it is seen to be the "only game in town." The "economic situation" is taken as a given, and its political consequences for universities are seen to be unchangeable. The fact that government funding policy has manoeuvred the university into this position through creating and encouraging dependence on the private sector has not been recognized, or, if it has, is not seen to be challengeable. To not co-operate with the forces at hand will further jeopardize the university: programmes will continue to decline, research will suffer, buildings will deteriorate, and the institution will lose public respect.

Third, some academics enthusiastically welcome increasing links between universities and business, either as a good in themselves or because they believe no harm will result from them. They believe that the university can serve the interests of business without compromising or precluding many of its traditional functions.

We have written this book to challenge the silence and the reasons for it. We have attempted to show how the changes that have given rise to the corporate agenda, as well as the changes that flow from it, have the potential for fundamentally altering the nature of academic work and, therefore, the role of the university in society. So significant a change to publicly funded institutions should not be allowed to proceed without serious reflection and debate.

We urge academics who cherish the discretion they have exercised in carrying out their faculty roles to consider the implications of our analysis: the continuation of current trends will increasingly limit their range of choice over priorities and methods of work. Whether or not such limits would serve the public interest needs to be argued in a public forum and should not be left to the accommodations of individual academics. Those who believe that they are powerless to resist the pressures on univer-

sities to conform to the corporate agenda should understand that the fragmentation of academic work and the resulting divisions have created their sense of powerlessness. A collective response to the new policy direction being promoted by third-party bodies, government officials, and administrative leaders is still possible. If, as those who advocate the corporate agenda claim, academic workers are a valuable asset to Canadian economic development, then it follows that the collective academic voice could exert considerable leverage in pressing for thorough public debate and evaluation of this policy direction before it is further implemented.

Finally, those who believe that the benefits of corporate-university collaboration will far outweigh any harm done to the university must seriously assess the likelihood of the anticipated pay-off. Historically, the Canadian business community has not had sufficient resources to support the university system. Even advocates of the current trend have warned that universities should not anticipate a level of donations that will solve their financial problems. What if, indeed, universities make structural and functional changes to facilitate corporate links, but the financial support is not forthcoming? Will the university be better, then, with its expensive administrative apparatus and office of technology transfer, powerful senior executive officers, high student-faculty ratios, stratified system of academic workers, and programmes aimed to the marketplace? To answer this question, we need to answer another: what kind of university do we want?

. . . [T]he unionization of academic workers during the years of contraction was a defensive strategy and was not based on a guiding vision of the university. The need for a guiding vision at this time is essential, if an offensive is to be mounted against the pressures towards the service university. We have suggested that the corporate agenda represents a renewed expansion of the role of capital in universities. We do not envision the disappearance of North American capital within the next few months. Likewise, we do not expect the processes we have described in this book to fade away if we spend enough concentrated time cloistered in our offices, studies, or libraries. Also, we do not expect to challenge these processes without a struggle. We have already outlined the organizational axes of struggle and the divisions in attitudes affecting the way academics engage in the struggle. These divisions run deep and affect many.

A guiding vision of the university on which to base an offensive stance must be strategically related to possibilities inherent in the present situation. We see two such possibilities. The first strategy would build on the vision of the service university. Although this term is now being advanced as a euphemism for the corporate agenda, nothing prevents the appropriation of the idea of a service university by those who define very differently the community to be served. Although the idea of "service to society" is included in both the university as haven and the liberal visions, neither of these adequately incorporates the idea that the university should exist for the society that contains it. Even though the emphasis on social consciousness during the expansion period provided room for extending university services to Canadian society in a broad sense, little progress was made in building institutional links between the university and external groups — links that would ensure that the needs and interests of these groups would flow back to the university itself. The emphasis on university autonomy and professional control — supported by advocates of both the liberal and academic haven visions — prevented such a development. However, in light of the current inroads by business into university autonomy and professional control,

an effective counter-strategy might be to broaden the definition of "service" to advance other interests, such as those of community groups, the unemployed, unions, minority-group organizations, etc. The "service" university model could be used to challenge those who have long prevented the university from being truly accessible and responsive to the most broadly defined interests of Canadian society.

The second strategy is specifically directed to those who, as we do, see themselves as critics of contemporary capitalist society and, particularly, to those who locate themselves on the political left. For us, the present situation in the university poses a dilemma. Socialists have long argued that universities in capitalist societies are engaged primarily in the spread of capitalist ideology and the reproduction of capitalist labour — i.e. universities are predominantly bourgeois institutions. Yet many of us who have made this argument have shaped our own working lives in universities as if we accepted the liberal vision. After all, the liberal model provides space for socialist intellectual work and counter-ideological reflection. At the same time, we have speculated on more desirable roles for universities in a socialist society but have rarely explored or spoken publicly about another vision for universities now, in the present social order.

We believe that an alternative vision to the liberal model must be developed. . . . we put this idea forward as follows: "If specific formulations can be used to support patterns of change that are already under way, they help to build the material capacity to carry further these patterns of change. In a similar vein, alternative formulations can help to build the capacity to resist the trends that are under way." Our inclination is to the polytechnic vision, since it accords most closely with our view of society and the university. In concrete terms, adopting this strategy for the long run could mean, in the short run, appropriating the socially oriented version of the service university vision just described. Even in the socialist societies studied by Castles and Wüstenberg, high-tech needs for a new type of student over-ruled the polytechnic vision that appeared to be in place.

The path ahead is not simple; but without an alternative vision to guide us, there will be no basis for resisting the corporate agenda, and no foundation on which to build.

CHANGING PATTERNS OF EDUCATIONAL INEQUALITY IN CANADA

Neil Guppy
Paulina D. Mikicich
Ravi Pendakur

In this paper we address the question of historical changes in Canadian educational inequalities. In particular, we focus on the influence of social origin upon educational attainment (see Cuneo and Curtis, 1975; Porter, et al., 1982). There has been no systematic assessment of whether the relationship between origin and attainment has altered over the course of this century. To address this issue, we present cohort data on the extent to which students from differing social backgrounds, as measured by father's occupation and parental education, have unequal probabilities of school attainment.

Sociologists focusing on inequality in Canada present very different views concerning possible *changes* in the relationship between social origin and school-

From "Changing Patterns of Educational Inequality in Canada" by Neil Guppy, Paulina D. Mikicich and Ravi Pendakur. *The Canadian Journal of Sociology*, Volume 9: 3, 1984. By permission of *The Canadian Journal of Sociology*.

ing. On the one hand, certain writers perceive a reduction in levels of educational inequality in Canada. Hunter (1981: 74–75) notes that "a general upgrading in the educational qualifications of the Canadian population" has been accompanied by "a progressive reduction in the level of educational inequality" (see also Harp, 1980: 231; Harvey, 1977: 10–11). On the other hand, several analysts have concluded that inequalities in schooling continue — that "ascriptive factors . . . have not diminished in importance and indeed seem to be persistent and patterned obstacles which . . . limit actual [educational] achievement" (Himelfarb and Richardson, 1982: 305; see also Marchak, 1981: 27–28). The latter view is stated even more emphatically by Forcese (1980: 95), who contends that "formal education is a cause of persistent and *increasingly* rigid stratification" (our emphasis).

One of the striking features of this disagreement is the lack of any systematic empirical investigation that would support or undermine either view. Any solid conclusions about trends in educational inequality should be based on data which cover extended time periods; however, to date, trend studies have been rare, have not always employed national data and have been restricted to short time-spans of less than a single decade (e.g., Hunter, 1981; Harvey, 1977).

Methodological differences among studies and diverging claims about what is happening over time to educational inequalities can also be found in the comparative international literature. Boudon (1974: 53), for example, concluded that "Western societies are characterized by a steady and slow decline of inequalities in educational opportunities." Conversely, Halsey, Heath, and Ridge (1980: 205) maintained that in the United Kingdom "school inequalities of opportunity have been remarkably stable over the forty years which

[the] study covers." These divergent conclusions probably reflect, among other things, differences inherent in the countries studied and in the methodologies used.

The purpose of this paper is to conduct a systematic analysis of the historical changes in Canadian educational inequalities. Using a national survey, we determine the extent to which students from differing social origins have unequal probabilities of school success. More importantly, we consider the ways in which this relationship has changed in Canada since early in this century. Our interest centres, then, on the three-way interaction between origin, cohort, and schooling — does the relationship between social origin and educational attainment vary systematically for different cohorts?

As we have shown, the Canadian literature contains two differing hypotheses with respect to this question. Some writers (Himelfarb and Richardson, 1982; Marchak, 1981; Forcese, 1980) maintain that educational inequalities have persisted so that the impact of social background on educational attainment has continued — a "constant effects" hypothesis. Others (Hunter, 1981; Harp, 1980; Harvey, 1977) suggest that across time the strength of the relationship between origin and attainment has weakened — a "diminishing effects" hypothesis.

Data and Methods

In order to assess these two hypotheses, we chart the educational attainments of Canadians from different social origins grouped into *birth* cohorts spanning a forty-year period (1913–1952).

The data for the analyses are drawn from the 1973 Canadian Mobility Study conducted by Boyd et al. (1977). The study focused on males and females over the age of 17 who were not full-time students (a constraint which we discuss below). The final sample consisted of 44,868 respondents. We restrict our attention to a subset of this larger sample by focusing on birth cohorts composed of respondents between the ages of twenty and sixty and eliminating anyone receiving part of their education outside of Canada.

We employ the following strategy to operationalize our variables. Our first measure of social origin is based on father's occupation (when the respondent was 16), which we have collapsed into four categories: farmers, blue collar, white collar and professional/managerial (prof/man) workers. Parental education, our second indicator of social origin, is a three-valued measure based on whether neither parent, one parent, or both parents completed high school. We assess historical trends by examining the educational attainments of people from four birth cohorts: 1913–22, 1923–32, 1933–42 and 1943–52. Toward the end of the analysis we further subdivide the cohorts to provide greater detail.

There are four caveats we should note before proceeding. First, our use of birth cohorts with cross-sectional data is subject to the usual problems of such studies: respondent recall, cohort mortality, etc. . . . Second, we do not assess types of educational attainment falling outside the typical elementary, secondary, and post-secondary spheres (e.g., continuing or adult education, manpower or other job training programs, etc.). Third, we examine only general patterns and trends so that much of the detailed quality and precise nature of schooling (e.g., educational streaming within schools) is not captured by our analysis streams. Fourth, we investigate neither ethnic differences . . . nor regional differences. . . . These limitations, while important, do not undermine the general utility of our analysis which appears to be the first of its kind in Canada.

In our initial analysis we use high school completion rates as our measure of educational attainment. However, because the three-way interaction of origin, cohort, and schooling varies for different measures of educational attainment, we also employ other indicators of school survival and achievement. It is important to consider, for example, whether over time socioeconomic inequalities have diminished at the high school level while remaining constant at post-secondary levels.

Data Analysis

Table 1 shows the bivariate relationship, controlling for sex, between father's occupation and high school completion. For respondents with prof/man backgrounds the rate of high school completion is 78.9 percent. In contrast, for respondents from farming backgrounds, the completion rate is only 36.2 percent. The relationship between origin and high school completion is similar for males and females, although for all categories of social origin a greater percentage of women complete high school.

While Table 1 examines the association of origin and attainment, our primary interest centres on whether this relationship changes over time. Therefore, Table 2 presents findings on the percentage of respondents completing high school by social background and birth cohort. As shown in this table, high school completion rates have risen across the four cohorts from 37.1 percent to 67.5 percent. Futhermore, high school completion rates have increased for each socioeconomoic category. Completion rates have remained the highest for the prof/man strata, increasing from 71.6 percent to 84.9 percent. For those from farming backgrounds the rates have changed from 24.0 percent in the first cohort to 58.8 percent in the last cohort; the largest percentage increase over time for any occupational category.

However, a direct comparison of the percentage differences creates potential problems of "floor" and "ceiling" effects because of the relative magnitudes of the

Table 1.
THE RELATIONSHIP BETWEEN SOCIAL ORIGIN (FATHER'S OCCUPATION) AND EDUCATIONAL ATTAINMENT (HIGH SCHOOL COMPLETION) CONTROLLING FOR RESPONDENT'S SEX (IN PERCENTAGES).

RESPONDENT'S HIGH SCHOOL COMPLETION	FATHER'S OCCUPATION				
	PROFESSIONAL MANAGERIAL	WHITE COLLAR	BLUE COLLAR	FARM	ROW TOTALS
Yes Male	78.1	65.8	49.0	31.4	24.8
Female	79.6	67.1	49.8	41.1	27.2
Total	78.9	66.5	49.4	36.2	52.0
					(N = 12,528)
No Male	21.9	34.2	51.0	68.6	24.6
Female	20.4	32.9	50.2	58.9	23.4
Total	21.1	33.5	50.6	63.8	48.0
					(N = 12,202)
Column percent	13.7	10.8	50.3	25.1	100.0
Column N's	(3,399)	(2,680)	(12,440)	(6,211)	(24,730)

Table 2.
PERCENTAGE OF RESPONDENTS WHO HAVE COMPLETED HIGH SCHOOL BY
FATHER'S OCCUPATION AND BIRTH COHORT.

FATHER'S OCCUPATION	BIRTH COHORT				
	1913–22	1923–32	1933–42	1943–52	ROW TOTALS
Professional	71.6	70.6	79.8	84.9	79.0
managerial	(385)	(445)	(615)	(1,230)	(2,675)
	1.09	.94	.65	.37	
White collar	57.9	61.3	64.9	73.4	66.6
	(256)	(294)	(412)	(811)	(1,773)
	.88	.80	.44	.22	
Blue collar	35.4	37.8	47.8	63.2	49.5
	(746)	(990)	(1,390)	(3,003)	(6,129)
	.39	.32	.14	.07	
Farm	24.0	27.5	41.7	58.8	36.2
	(442)	(465)	(556)	(772)	(2,235)
	0	0	0	0	
Column totals	37.1	40.5	52.6	67.5	
	(1,829)	(2,194)	(2,973)	(5,816)	(12,813)

percentages involved. For example, from a base of 71.6 percent, the completion rate within the prof/man category could have increased a maximum of 28.4 percent, a magnitude smaller than the actual increase in the farm category (34.8 percent). We have, therefore, also calculated "log distances" which will allow us to make direct comparisons between socioeconomic strata.

The log distance between prof/man respondents and farm respondents decreases from 1.09 in the first birth cohort to 0.37 in the last cohort (a difference of 0.72 log units). While completion rates for both blue- and white-collar respondents have risen over time, the log distances between strata have continually fallen. This implies that the disparity in high school completion rates by social origin which occurred earlier in this century has diminished, although it has by no means vanished. Controlling for sex does not alter the general pattern of results here.

It could be argued that our measure of

social origin is inadequate. For this reason parental education is used as an alternative gauge to assess the influence of social origin upon high school completion (see Table 3). For the three categories of parental education, high school completion, in all but one case, increases over the four cohorts. As anticipated, the likelihood of a respondent completing secondary school is higher when both parents are also high school graduates. Consistent with the results in Table 2, the log distance between the first and third parental education categories drops over the four cohorts, from 1.02 to 0.45. Thus, using two different measures of social origin we find that the general relationship between family background and educational attainment has weakened over time.

Both Tables 2 and 3 suggest that egalitarian influences have increased for socioeconomic disparities between high school completion rates. However, we need to assess whether this pattern holds for higher levels of schooling. In order to do so, we replicated the analyses presented in Tables 2 and 3 for respondents who reported some attendance at university. . . .

Table 4 shows the percentages of respondents with some university experience by origin and cohort. On the whole, the percentage of respondents reporting some university attendance steadily increases over the four cohorts. It is nevertheless important to note that the disparities are far stronger at this level of education than was the case for high school completion (note the different sizes of the log distances). However there is some evidence that log distances have decreased over time although not as dramatically as was shown in Table 2. For example, the log distance between the prof/man strata and the farm category has declined by 0.41 log units (1.48 − 1.07). This decrease is more modest than the decrease of 0.72 log units found in Table 2 for high school completion (1.09 − 0.37). In short, comparing Tables 2 and 4 suggests that socioeconomic disparities are greater at the university level, and show only a modest reduction over time.

We have reason to believe, in fact, that the decline of 0.41 log units shown in Table 4 exaggerates the decrease. Because our sample includes only those respondents who have completed their education, the 1943–52 birth cohort underrepresents the actual number of university-educated respondents. While it is probable that some potential respondents from farm backgrounds were still at university at the time of the survey (1973), it is likely that many more possible respondents from prof/man backgrounds were attending higher levels of education, and, therefore, were excluded from the sample. One would have expected a higher percentage of prof/man respondents reporting some university experience, and, as a result, a more modest reduction in the log distance between the farm and prof/man categories. We present data below which suggest that this interpretation is probably correct.

In contrast to employing differing levels of educational experience, Table 5 presents results using completed years of education as the dependent variable. Furthermore, in order to provide a finer breakdown of re-

Table 3.
PERCENTAGE OF RESPONDENTS WHO HAVE COMPLETED HIGH SCHOOL BY
PARENTAL EDUCATION AND BIRTH COHORT.

	BIRTH COHORT				
PARENTAL EDUCATION	1913–22	1923–32	1933–42	1943–52	ROW TOTALS
Both parents completed	80.4	78.8	88.8	88.9	86.0
high school	(344)	(380)	(545)	(1,299)	(2,567)
	1.02	.89	.75	.45	
One parent completed	59.6	61.0	70.9	81.1	72.0
high school	(364)	(489)	(749)	(1,564)	(3,166)
	.72	.64	.53	.35	
Neither parent completed	29.0	32.3	41.9	56.9	41.4
high school	(1,157)	(1,327)	(1,699)	(3,100)	(7,283)
	0	0	0	0	
Column totals	37.1	40.7	52.3	67.5	
	(1,865)	(2,196)	(2,993)	(5,963)	(13,017)

Table 4.
PERCENTAGE OF RESPONDENTS WITH SOME UNIVERSITY EXPERIENCE BY SOCIAL
ORIGIN (FATHER'S OCCUPATION) AND BIRTH COHORT.

FATHER'S CLASS	BIRTH COHORT				
	1913–22	1923–32	1933–42	1943–52	ROW TOTALS
Professional	25.5	27.3	38.1	35.1	32.8
managerial	(137)	(172)	(294)	(508)	(1,112)
	1.48	1.42	1.37	1.07	
White collar	12.0	16.9	18.6	19.1	17.4
	(53)	(81)	(118)	(211)	(463)
	.73	.94	.65	.46	
Blue collar	7.3	6.3	11.6	12.1	9.9
	(154)	(166)	(337)	(574)	(1,231)
	.20	-.05	.18	.01	
Farm	5.8	6.6	9.7	12.0	8.1
	(106)	(111)	(129)	(157)	(502)
	0	0	0	0	
Column totals	9.1	9.8	15.4	16.8	
	(450)	(530)	(878)	(1,450)	(3,308)

sults, the birth cohort variable has been divided into eight rather than four intervals.

This table shows that, for all strata, average years of education have increased over the 1913 to 1947 period. In addition, disparities continue to exist across the cohorts. Up until 1937 there appears to have been a slight increase in the difference between the mean years of schooling for the prof/man and farm categories (see the bottom row of Table 5). This contrasts with the results for the last three cohorts where this difference is declining. However, the figure of 1.62 for the 1948–52 cohort appears suspiciously low. Consider, that for the other seven cohorts the figure for average years of education increases for the prof/man category (as expected), yet drops for the last cohort. This is probably due to the sampling underrepresentation mentioned above.

If we use the mean number of years of schooling for the first seven cohorts to predict the level for the eighth cohort, a value of 14.81 years results for the prof/man cate-

gory (as opposed to 13.60 years, as reported in Table 5). Using the same strategy to predict the average years of schooling completed for respondents in the farm category generates a figure of 11.75, suggesting that the actual completion rate for those with farm backgrounds (11.98 in Table 5) is reasonably accurate. The difference in years of schooling for the prof/man-farm comparison, based on the predicted figures, is likely to be in the neighbourhood of 2.5 years. We take this to mean that the reduction found in Table 5 may be exaggerated for the last cohort, *but* there is nevertheless a decline in socioeconomic disparities for years of schooling completed. . . .

Discussion and Conclusions

Our results indicate that the relationship between social origin and educational attainment has weakened over time. We hasten to stress that social origin continues to exert a strong influence on levels of

Table 5.
AVERAGE YEARS OF SCHOOLING COMPLETED BY SOCIAL ORIGIN (FATHER'S OCCUPATION) AND BIRTH COHORT (FIVE-YEAR INTERVALS).

FATHER'S CLASS	BIRTH COHORTS								ROW TOTALS
	1913–17	1918–22	1923–37	1928–32	1933–37	1938–42	1943–47	1948–52	
Professional managerial	12.17 (255)	12.31 (262)	12.31 (291)	13.22 (326)	13.86 (316)	13.98 (447)	14.37 (620)	13.60 (790)	13.46 (3,307)
White collar	11.42 (202)	11.29 (208)	11.99 (220)	11.94 (239)	11.70 (248)	12.61 (290)	12.84 (401)	12.86 (582)	12.30 (2,596)
Blue collar	9.52 (933)	9.78 (986)	9.96 (1,115)	10.24 (1,336)	10.70 (1,261)	11.17 (1,522)	12.15 (2,122)	12.05 (2,494)	11.02 (11,769)
Farm	8.73 (819)	8.85 (824)	8.90 (826)	9.62 (747)	10.15 (621)	10.83 (645)	11.61 (639)	11.98 (626)	9.95 (5,746)
Column totals	9.71 (2,209)	9.87 (2,280)	10.07 (2,465)	10.59 (2,655)	11.08 (2,471)	11.69 (2,961)	12.51 (3,904)	12.42 (4,471)	11.24 (23,417)
Mean difference (Prof./man.-farm)	3.44	3.46	3.41	3.60	3.71	3.15	2.76	1.62	

* The top figure is the average number of years of schooling and the bottom figure is the number of people whose years of schooling were averaged.

schooling, although the impact has declined through this century. However, even here we must be cautious because, while origin plays a decreasingly important role in high school completion, this decline is far less apparent with respect to post-secondary education. When we measure educational achievement as the probability of attaining some university experience, we find the effect of social origin has, at best, diminished only moderately over time (see Guppy, 1983; cf. Goyder, 1980). Furthermore, as noted above, our results do not take into account ethnic, regional, or other differences where educational inequalities could have remained constant, increased, or decreased.

The general patterns of our findings are inconsistent with the results of Halsey, Heath, and Ridge (1980) for males in the United Kingdom, where they found remarkable stability in school inequalities. Their results suggested that educational reforms had done little to equalize educational opportunities, possibly because of the influence of the strong "private" school sector in the British system.

In following Halsey, Heath, and Ridge (1980) our analysis has focused upon the cumulative impact of social advantage or disadvantage. As such, we have provided an overall portrait of disparities but we have not endeavoured to pinpoint the effects of social origin on each of the many transitions embedded in the educational system. That is, we have noted that large socioeconomic disparities exist at the post-secondary level but we have not examined exactly how this has come about. For example, students from blue-collar backgrounds may be underrepresented at university as a consequence of their failure to complete high school, their enrollment in high school programs which prevent immediate transition to university, their decision not to pursue a university education even

though eligible, or some combination of these and other factors.

Two final questions must be raised. First, is the gradual reduction, but not elimination, of educational inequality a trend or merely an historical anomaly soon to disappear? Second, while the influence of origin on years of schooling may have waned in recent years, is it also the case that the impact of social background on the acquisition of academic credentials has diminished?

With respect to the first question, our results do no suggest a gradual, uniform reduction in educational inequalities. In fact, it appears that no reduction whatsoever occurs in the socioeconomic differences in years of schooling attained until the cohort of 1938–42 is considered: a cohort that entered high school after World War II. The reduction in inequality *may* thus be interpreted as a consequence of educational reforms introduced in the 1950s and 1960s. Many of these reforms, such as student aid and open learning environments . . . were beneficial to working-class children. However, many of the reforms are now being withdrawn or sharply curtailed as governments react to the social and economic climate of the early 1980s. Should this process continue, the long term result of such retrenchment could be a return to the levels of educational inequality witnessed earlier in this century — a process which may enhance the importance of cultural capital as a vehicle of social reproduction (Bourdieu, 1977).

With respect to the question of academic credentials, we must stress that our work suggests that inequalities have reduced in terms of both general level of schooling attained and years of schooling completed. We do not, however, demonstrate that the importance of social background on the acquisition of scholastic credentials has diminished. For example, it is quite conceivble that although individuals from farm or blue-collar backgrounds are attaining ever higher levels of education, they may still be disproportionately underrepresented in selected educational streams which yield more valuable sets of credentials (e.g., professional schools, graduate schools, etc.). Furthermore, if general college and university degrees become increasingly ineffective tickets for occupational and income attainment . . ., then these professional or graduate degrees will likely prove to be of increasing importance as channels of intergenerational mobility for those from less privileged backgrounds.

In conclusion, our results suggest that as educational levels have increased for the Canadian population there has been a modest reduction in socioeconomic disparities in educational attainment. This claim must be cautiously made however, as we have noted several important caveats.

Ethnic Inequality

As with the sociology of education, we are unable to provide you with a coherent set of selections that neatly summarize the current state of the sociology of ethnic relations. In earlier editions we were able to offer you selections that reflected the way in which ethnicity is, at various levels, a resource, and how this fact explains the continuing importance of ethnicity in Canadian society. It is evident that, in recent years, the focus has shifted somewhat. On the one hand there is considerably less certainty that ethnicity inevitably means ethnic inequality. But on the other hand there seems to be less celebration of the mosaic ideology, the view that Canada is a nation consisting of ethnic communities, which somehow, and at crucial points, come together as the Canadian community. The failure of the Meech Lake Accord, the ugly confrontation at Oka and the growing concern about the social implications of new, and much more visible, groups entering into the Canadian mosaic have perhaps undermined the rather optimistic views about the future of ethnic diversity which characterized sociology at the beginning of the 1980s.

In the decade after publication of *The Vertical Mosaic*, John Porter maintained a consistent critique of the mosaic ideology on the grounds that to perpetuate ethnic differences is also to perpetuate ethnic stratification and discrimination. This view, about the inevitability of ethnic inequality and ethnic conflict is re-examined by Stephen Steinberg, an American sociologist. In these brief excerpts from his book *The Ethnic Myth*, Steinberg argues that ethnicity shapes our thinking and behaviour but is also shaped by social and economic factors and that ethnic conflict may often have a material base. We should not, in other words, assume that, even if ethnic groups are given equal access to good jobs and to political power, racial and ethnic conflict is inevitable within a society.

Some insights into how ethnic relations may, in the context of more general patterns of inequality become structured into ethnic conflict and segregation can be found in the second selection. David Stymeist, an anthropologist, set out to study relationships between Indians and Whites in a Northern Ontario town, which he gives the fictional name of "Crow Lake." In this excerpt from his book he provides us with a vivid ethnographic account of the subjective and situational nature of ethnicity and ethnic identity. His approach owes much to the work of Fredrik Barth who, in his book *Ethnic Groups and Ethnic Boundaries*, has shown that one's objective cultural or ethnic background is not always crucial in how, ethnically, we choose to present ourselves. While the people of Crow Lake did at times make use of ethnic labels and stereotypes, Stymeist shows that in their relationship to Indians in the community people downplayed and ignored their ethnic identities, even to the extent of regarding Chinese and blacks as "white." In the process of excluding and segregating Indians from the social and economic life of the community, the people of Crow Lake adopted a simplified set of ethnic distinctions and boundaries. Segregation emerges, then, as a process — a vicious circle — in which initial ethnic stereotypes structure and limit interaction between "whites" and "Indians." Once set in motion, these patterns oF interaction reinforce the stereotypes and, in effect, make them self-fulfilling prophecies.

In the late 1970s empirical evidence emerged which reflected Steinberg's argu-

ment that rather than a blanket allegiance to the notion of a vertical mosaic, we should be looking at the historical and structural factors that have resulted in the success of some ethnic groups and the failure of others to achieve structural assimilation. On the whole, it appeared that for most ethnic groups in Canada ethnic segregation and inequality was not as pronounced as John Porter's work in the 1950s and 1960s had implied and that, perhaps, multiculturalism is a policy out of tune with social reality. It is in the context of this optimism that Hugh Lautard of the University of New Brunswick and Neil Guppy of the University of British Columbia, attempt in the final selection to assess the extent that optimism is justified. Their rather cautious conclusion is that while there has been some decrease in the saliency of ethnicity in Canada, it is still too early to abandon the concept of the vertical mosaic.

RELATED READINGS

S.M. Lipset: "Historical Traditions and National Characteristics: A Comparative Analysis of Canada and the United States" (Chapter 3)

Gary Caldwell and Daniel Fournier: "The Quebec Question: A Matter of Population" (Chapter 8)

Hira Singh: "The Political Economy of Immigrant Farm Labour: A Study of East Indian Farm Workers in British Columbia" (Chapter 11)

Michael Asch: "Aboriginal Rights: The View of the Aboriginal Peoples" (Chapter 14)

George Mathews: "Quiet Resolution: Quebec's Challenge to Canada" (Chapter 14)

Reginald W. Bibby: "Mosaic Madness" (Chapter 14)

THE ETHNIC MYTH

Stephen Steinberg

The Demystification of Ethnicity

It is commonplace to think of ethnicity as a phenomenon that belongs to the cultural domain. By its very nature, ethnicity involves ways of thinking, feeling, and acting that constitute the essence of culture. That ethnic groups have unique cultural character can hardly be denied. The problem, however, is that culture does not exist in a vacuum; nor is it fixed or unchanging. On the contrary, culture is in constant flux and is integrally a part of a larger social process. The mandate for social inquiry, therefore, is that ethnic patterns should not be taken at face value, but must be related to the larger social matrix in which they are embedded. Though this principle itself is anything but controversial, its scrupulous application challenges many cherished ideas concerning ethnic phenomena.

The theoretical perspective that governs this study insists on establishing the social origins of ethnic values and trends. There is nothing in this approach that denies that ethnicity can be a determinant in its own right. Without doubt, ethnicity informs consciousness and influences behaviour. But what informs ethnicity and influences *its* character? The tendency in modern social thought has been to treat ethnicity as a given and to explore its consequences. The present study does not deny that ethnic factors can have causal significance, but its main purpose is to explore their historical and structural foundations.

Thus, the title is not meant to convey that ethnicity itself is mythical. Issue arises only when ethnicity is taken out of historical context and assumed to have independent explanatory power. The problem is fundamentally one involving the reification of culture. Reification occurs whenever culture is treated as though it is a thing unto itself, independent of other spheres of life. The reification of ethnic values has made a mystique of ethnicity, creating the illusion that there is something ineffable about ethnic phenomena that does not lend itself to rational explanation. This is especially the case when ethnic groups are assumed to be endowed with a given set of cultural values, and no attempt is made to understand these values in terms of their material sources. Thus, to demystify ethnicity requires an exploration of how social forces influence the form and content of ethnicity; and an examination of the specific relationships between ethnic factors on the one hand, and a broad array of historical, economic, political, and social factors on the other.

The "Iron Law of Ethnicity" Revised

Both the conventional wisdom and a considerable body of social theory adhere to what might be called "the iron law of ethnicity." According to this "law," where there is ethnic difference there will be ethnic conflict. The internal dynamics of group existence, if not human nature itself, are presumed to make ethnic conflict inevitable. According to one widely held view, since a sense of "we" presupposes a sense of "they," it follows that ethnocentrism, prejudice, and conflict are natural by-products of group identity and belonging (Allport, 1958). Admittedly, there is a great deal of superficial evidence to give credence to such a theory. In a wide range of nations — those in the East as well as the West, traditional as well as modern, socialist as well as capitalist — ethnic pluralism has been associated with dissension and instability and, not infrequently, such societies have been torn apart at their ethnic seams. Undeniably, the ideal of a plural society, where ethnic groups live in cooperation, harmony, and mutual respect, has proved a most elusive one.

Nonetheless, it is doubtful that the connection between ethnic difference and conflict is as automatic or as inevitable as is commonly supposed. What often appears to be an eruption of "traditional hatreds" on closer examination turns out to involve political and economic issues that are real and immediate. Perhaps the never-ending conflict in Northern Ireland provides the best illustration of this point. That there are "traditional hatreds" between Protestants and Catholics is obvious. The question, however, is whether these animosities would have endured, and would today be carried to such violent extremes, if not for the structural inequalities between the Protestant majority and the Catholic minority in terms of class, status, and power. In other instances — South Africa, for example — it is the minority that has enjoyed material advantages over a resentful and sometimes rebellious majority. Whether conflict occurs between a privileged minority and a disadvantaged majority, or vice versa, almost invariably institutionalized inequalities are at or near the center of the conflict. Indeed, whenever ethnic divisions occur along class lines, there is the likelihood, or at least the potential, that ordinary class conflict will manifest itself as ethnic conflict, in reality as well as appearance.

If there is an iron law of ethnicity, it is that when ethnic groups are found in a hierarchy of power, wealth, and status, then conflict is inescapable. However, where there is social, economic, and political parity among the constituent groups, ethnic conflict, when it occurs, tends to be at a low level and rarely spills over into violence.

Conditions in Switzerland help exemplify both sides of this "law." Amongst the German, French, and Italian minorities, there is a reasonable distribution of power and wealth, and though ethnic tensions exist, they have been successfully contained within institutionalized channels of conflict resolution. Yet, as portrayed in the Italian-made film *Bread and Chocolate*, migrant workers from Italy and other countries who have been imported to do the undesirable labor that native Swiss workers refuse to do not only exist as an underclass, but also experience intense prejudice and discrimination.

The lesson to be drawn from the Swiss case is that the fact of class difference is far more important than the fact of ethnic difference, and that ethnic conflict is often only a surface manifestation of a deeper conflict of an essentially social class character.

To emphasize the class character of ethnic conflict, however, is not to deny the operational significance of ethnic factors. Clearly, racial and ethnic stigma, even when rooted in patterns of class exploitation, assume a life of their own and have a capacity to inflict great harm, a notion Lorraine Hansberry expresses in her play *Les Blancs*. Against the backdrop of an anticolonial war in a mythical African colony, Tshembe, an African revolutionary educated in Europe, and Charlie, a liberal white journalist from the United States, debate the limits of race and class as explanations for colonial domination:

TSHEMBE: *Race — racism — is a device.*
No more. Nor less. It explains
nothing at all.

CHARLIE: *Now what the hell is that*
supposed to mean?

TSHEMBE: (Closing his eyes, wearily): *I said racism is a device that, of itself, explains nothing. It is simply a means. An invention to justify the rule of some men over others.*

CHARLIE: *But I agree with you entirely! Race hasn't a thing to do with it actually.*

TSHEMBE: *At — but it has!*

CHARLIE: (Throwing up his hands): *Oh, come on, Matoseh. Stop playing games!*

TSHEMBE: *I am not playing games.* (He sighs and now, drawn out of himself at last, proceeds with the maximum precision and clarity he can muster) *I am simply saying that a device is a device, but that it also has consequences: once invented it takes on a life, a reality of its own. So in one century, men invoke the device of religion to cloak their conquests. In another, race. Now, in both cases you and I may recognize the fraudulence of the device, but the fact remains that a man who has a sword run through him because he refuses to become a Moslem or a Christian — or who is shot in Zatembe or Mississippi because he is black — is suffering the utter* reality *of the device. And it is pointless to pretend that it doesn't* exist *— merely because it is a lie!* (Hansberry, 1973)

ETHNICS AND INDIANS
David H. Stymeist

Crow Lake as a Complex Society

Crow Lake is divided and stratified in various ways. The social life of the town does not have a uniform pattern or texture, but is greatly varied. There are those who cling tenaciously to the teachings of an established religion, others who attend church regularly more for social than religious reasons, and some who are generally unconcerned with religion or religious activity. There are Roman and Greek Orthodox Catholics, Anglicans, Moslems, Baptists, members of the United Church, and Jehovah's Witnesses. Some people are closely associated with the bush, their major interests being fishing, hunting, and camping. Others pursue these activities to some extent, and still others are totally uninterested in the surrounding forests and lakes. In another area, there are those who eagerly accept the ideologies of capitalism and progress and work persistently for individual maximization. Others work simply to survive and regard their jobs as nothing more than a necessary evil, while a few float through life living from hand to mouth. All of these people live in the same community, interact with each other and pursue their aims independently, but in concert with others who do not necessarily share their aims. There is, then, no single pattern of life, no archetypal member of the community, no real unity in terms of aspirations, needs, standard of living, or cultural orientation. There are instead individuals and small knots of people who structure or attempt to structure a definite and at times consciously different pattern for their lives. However, they do not do this in a vacuum. They do not exist as isolates. All their desires to do what they want to do, have to do, or feel that they somehow should do exist within the framework of constraints and incentives set by the local and larger society.

Non-Native Ethnicity in Crow Lake

Ethnicity is one of the factors adding depth and variety to the existing social spectrum. It is one complex of ideas and relationships — real or assumed — that appears to be significant in the daily conduct of the community's life.

Evidences of ethnicity and indications of the apparent importance of ethnicity are not difficult to discover. On the walls of one of the town's hotels, for example, hangs a framed poem stitched on white linen:

Take a little bit of Welsh
Now just a little bit
Mix well with Irish Pluck
And some Scottish Grit.
Blend in England's sons
From town and village sweet.
And call the mixture Britain
For it's dashed hard stuff to beat!

Walking down the main street one passes a Chinese restaurant in which several related families are gathered in the back talking in their native language and reading letters from relatives in China. In the pooll hall Mike G. sits and reads an Italian-Canadian newspaper. From time to time he stands up and shouts advice to one of the players. Other Italians drop in to visit. On the street corners retired men stand talking to each other in Ukrainian or Finnish or Icelandic.

The local chapter of the Canadian Legion holds a "Scotch Night" and an "Irish Night." The Catholic Women's League sponsors a "Pakistani Tea" and the Knights of Columbus a "Traditional Italian Spaghetti Supper." In a pub one man shouts to the barkeep: "What did this damn Frenchman order? Ex? Give me a Black Label. I'm not drinking any beer that these Frenchmen drink." He nudges the man next to him and his companions break into laughter.

From such observations one might assume that not only do discrete ethnic groups exist in Crow Lake, but that ethnicity itself is an important social parameter. It is slightly disconcerting to find upon closer examination, however, that the appearance of ethnicity is often no more than that: an appearance. The traditional view of the ethnic group assumes that members are regarded as "full-time ethnics"; that ethnicity, wherever it exists, canalizes social life; that, as Barth has said, ethnicity is "imperative in that it can not be discarded and temporarily set aside by other definitions of the situation" (1969: 17). But in Crow Lake one finds that ethnic distinctions once made are not permanent; that certain people can make announced shifts in ethnic identity from time to time. Moreover, the ethnic dimension becomes a structuring principle only in some contexts and on certain occasions. Within the non-Indian segment of Crow Lake's population one does not find the existence of permanent, stable ethnic groups in which "ethnicity identity is superordinate to most other statuses, and defines the permissible constellations of statuses, or social personalities, which an individual with that identity may assume" (Barth, 1969: 17). What one does find is a series of ethnic categories out of which, from time to time and place to place, "ethnic groups," quasi-groups, or assemblages are formed.

The Ethnic Dimension as a Conceptual Structure

The ethnic dimension in Crow Lake begins most properly in the minds of the people of the community. Ethnicity, if it refers directly or indirectly to origin (as it does in Crow Lake), begins with the perception of differences in origin. The actual words "ethnicity" or "ethnic group" are not often used in the community. Instead, people refer to "nationalities." One's "nationality," used in this special sense, is seen as an integral part of his identity. In addition, it is assumed that every person has this dimension, an ethnic affiliation. This is perhaps the first and most significant general "law" of ethnicity in Crow Lake. The ethnic dimension is understood as a total system of identities within which each person has a place. And his place, or "nationality," is determined by his name or parentage, by his ultimate biological origin.

Ethnicity, as thus defined, is inescapable. From time to time someone will attempt to state that he is simply Canadian and not Italian-Canadian or Icelandic-Canadian. But even if he is of third or fourth generation immigrant stock, such claims are generally ignored. He is pressed about his ultimate "ethnic" origins, and will, in this position, usually acquiesce.

Categories Inside Categories

As might be imagined, such a system of total ethnic membership is not left circulating in people's heads as an inexhaustible list of place names. It is instead codified and presented as a series of related social categories. Such a system, however, is not all-inclusive. It does not include the exact origin status of every individual in the community, but is instead a simplified list of geographical or political areas which serve as origin reference points. Thus, although certain families distinguish between Sicilians and Neopolitians, such a distinction is not current in the general social consciousness; to most people in the community the category that "fits" in this case is "Italian."

This system of social categories is not one-dimensional and linear, but layered. It reflects both different degrees of specificity, and current folk ideas of geographical and cultural connection which in a sense parallel the now dated culture-area approach in cultural anthropology.

Briefly, certain ethnic categories are nested inside other ethnic categories, the different levels corresponding to more or less specific identification of one's origin. The major, central categories are thus often expanded and diluted of specific meaning. For example, the central category "English" breaks down into several categories.

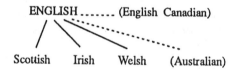

This system is interesting in various ways. The word "English" can be used to refer to an immigrant from London, a Canadian of English parentage, to the people of Britain as a whole, or to "English-speaking" people. Used this way, the term "English" subsumes the somewhat more precise categories that fall within its domain; it refers to and can imply a range of specific ethnic identities each of which can at other times and in other circumstances, stand alone. The term "Irish," therefore, is a highly precise term in the lexicon of ethnic conceptualizations in Crow Lake. To be categorized as "Irish" does not mean that one cannot be classified as "English" in other situations. But when "Irish" is used, it is meant in an exact sense which differentiates it from English, Welsh, and Scottish memberships. While related to the category "English" it exists at a different level of conceptualization.

Existing Possibilities of Multiple Affiliations

None of this in itself is surprising. However, in Crow Lake the nesting of ethnic categories is a central feature of the entire system. It operates at all levels and in all directions, and may take some surprising turns. The major non-Native ethnic categories current in the community are English, Finlander, Ukrainian, Chinese, Italian, Pakistani, German, and French. Each of these contains sub-categories which may sometimes operate as separate categories. A few of these subordinate categories exist only as conceptual categories, relating to memberships that were represented in the past or perhaps will be represented in the future. Thus:

The way this nesting system works is less a case of people agreeing that a "Pole" is in many ways similar to a "Ukrainian" than a kind of loose identification with the category "Ukrainian" of an individual whose ancestors were Poles.

An example of such a situation occurred one night in a local pub. J., an "Englishman," exclaimed: "What! Am I supposed to buy this worthless Uke a drink?" Somewhat later I purposely broke the rules of this interaction situation by asking D., the "Ukrainian," if he was actually Ukrainian. The answer was yes. "Well," I asked innocently, "what part of the Ukraine did your family come from?"

"They didn't. They came from Poland. I'm a Polack." D. in this situation was not really confused about this ethnicity. He was a second generation "ethnic"; his parents were both of the same ethnic category. Yet in this and in other interaction settings he chose to present himself as a Ukrainian and his companions chose to accept this definition of the situation.

The group at our table that night was well mixed: there were two "Englishmen" (both of whose great-grandparents were born in Canada), a "Frenchman" (a French-Canadian who spoke little French and whose parents had lived in Ontario all their lives), two "Ukrainians" (a third generation Ukrainian and a second generation Pole), and a "Finlander" (a second generation Norwegian). Under these circumstances, ethnic jokes and insults were rather broad in scope. They pertained to the larger, more visible social categories of ethnicity. Individual memberships were subsumed under the appropriate major category and people would defend "their" ethnic category, making jokes about the assumed specific ethnicity of others.

Somewhat later, however, C., a second-generation Ukrainian from Manitoba, referred to B., in a moment of minor irritation, as "that God damn Polack." While B., him-

self, would make disparaging comments from time to time as to the level of intelligence of those "Ukrainians." He distributed a photocopied drawing of what was identified as a "Ukrainian Target Pistol" — a Smithinski-Wesonovitch 32 caliber.

This was by no means an isolated occurrence. It was part of a general pattern that was often repeated and elaborated. It could, furthermore, reach levels bordering on the absurd. As in the case of one person of ultimate Scottish ancestry who claimed from time to time that he was a North American Indian, that "Indians are people that you whites will never understand." This man had lived with Indian people for many years and was well acquainted with the North. His periodic identification with Native people was neither completely accepted by the majority of the townspeople, nor completely denied. Similarly, it seemed that various Native people regarded him in a somewhat different light than other white men.

And yet, on occasion, this man would claim that he was Scottish or rather "really" Scottish. He was born and grew up in a rather isolated part of Scotland and came to Canada and the North as a young man. Periodically he maintained that he was more Scottish than the Anglo-Saxons of Edinburgh or Glasgow. Often he would make announced shifts in identity in the course of an evening. These shifts might occasionally be questioned, but no more seriously than in many less ambiguous cases.

The Attributing of Culture and Identity to Persons

The fact that the system allowed such announced shifts in identity is important. It indicates, first of all, that ethnicity in Crow Lake was a domain of identity relating to culture and to folk ideas of culture. Ethnic comments, labels and stereotypes usually centred on certain cultural traits or customs: food, dress, personal habits, and proclivities. Secondly, ethnicity was something that was often more attributed than "real." The Scot/Indian mentioned above was obviously neither a "full" Indian nor a "full" Scot. His attitudes, activities, and orientations were all very much the same as those of the town's "Ukrainians," "Italians," "Finlanders," and "Chinese." In Crow Lake specific ethnicity was thus often attributed without being the source of a total, unchangeable identity or status.

Instead, certain "ethnic" cultural traits were continually being expanded into stereotypes and used indiscriminately in social interaction. A person was not simply regarded as an "Italian" or a "Finlander," but a whole range of supposedly specific phenomena were related to him because of his alleged ethnicity. These phenomena were either "really" ethnic or they were not, but they were often regarded as being ethnic in specific interaction situations.

For example, one day G. and B. were drinking coffee together and G. happened to make a gesture with his hands, upsetting his cup slightly. B. jokingly said, "Christ, G., do all of you Frenchmen have to talk with your hands and spill things?" Earlier, however, the question of G.'s "nationality" had arisen. It had been stated that at one time G.'s family was French, but that he was not "really" French or even French-Canadian. Objectively, it was this earlier statement that was perhaps the more accurate.

Italians were supposed to like spaghetti and to make their own wine. When they did eat spaghetti or drink homemade wine, they were regarded by others as engaging in activities that were part of their cultural heritage. Similarly, since Ukrainians were alleged to prefer vodka over all other alcoholic beverages, when they drank vodka their ethnic membership was noticed and often commented upon. When they drank beer or rye, however, it was not. When Finnish people ate fish or enjoyed a sauna, their "ethnicity" was occasionally pointed out. However, many people other than Finns took saunas in Crow Lake, and many ate spaghetti and drank vodka even though they were neither Ukrainian nor Italian. The indication was that ethnicity was not simply perceived cultural difference or perceived differences of origin. It was instead an identity system, a structural system, with a certain existence and importance of its own.

Indians in Crow Lake

What I have said so far does not necessarily apply to Crow Lake's Indian population. Although Native people are an obvious part of the community's social spectrum, few have jobs or houses in town and rarely do they participate in friendship cliques with whites. Individuals and groups appear daily on the streets, in the theatre, in certain pubs and restaurants, in the schools, jails and courts, and in the hospital. At present the Native population is relatively low: there are approximately sixty to seventy resident adult Native people in Crow Lake. This figure, however, is somewhat misleading — only half of these people are residents with steady, secure jobs and housing. The other half, although they have jobs in Crow Lake and may have lived there for six months or a year, are not firmly established, and it is likely that many of them will leave town after a short time. This has been a common pattern in Crow Lake's history.

In the past, however, the resident Native population of Crow Lake was much smaller than it is today. For many years it was non-existent. The census of Canada lists no resident Native people for the years 1911, 1921, 1931, and 1941. In 1961 forty Indian people were reported living in the community. Yet during all these years Native people were in fact present in the town in appreciable numbers as transients. This pattern continues today, with the transient population usually outnumbering the residents. Indians visit the town to trade, to have a holiday, to work for short periods of time in bush camps or fire-fighting camps outside the town limits, or to be educated, hospitalized, or tried in court. Their presence is quickly apparent in the streets.

In the early days, Indians came to Crow Lake for a variety of specific purposes. They came first of all to trade and in certain instances to be treated by the town's doctors. One non-Native resident of the community recalled this period in these terms:

The store did a fair amount of business with the Indians who were encamped on an island on the west side of Pelican Lake towards the Sioux mountain. A half dozen or more Indians would enter the store, sit down on anything available, and begin to trade. As they purchased a side of bacon, or perhaps a quantity of tea, they paid for each article separately, as they were unable to add up the amount of their purchases. All this meant that they occupied the store most of the day.

An Indian boarding school was established outside the town in 1925, and the children would often be visited by their parents and relatives. They would gather outside the fence that surrounded the school's playground and were allowed to talk to their children and perhaps touch them through the wire fence.

The period of early contact between Indians and whites in Crow Lake is generally regarded by older residents as a romantic interlude. Indians were considered a separate people who occasioned no threat to the ideological or economic security of the community. They were interesting and colourful; they were people about whom non-Natives could write their friends and relatives in other parts of Canada. As such, their presence was not actively resented. During the thirties, moreover, Native people from immediately surrounding areas sold fish and wild meat from door to door in town. A large barrel of fish was reportedly sold for twenty-five cents while a hind-quarter of moose went for fifty cents. The productive efforts of Native people were, during this period, important for the non-Natives in town.

At the same time, the town had no use for the Indians' intelligence or labour on a larger basis. As the labour camps established for the construction of the railroad were intended to be stable, the contractors were interested in obtaining a steady work force. The main source of supply for these camps was immigrant labour. It is clear from conversations with men who worked in these early camps that Indians were strictly excluded as a labour source: they were considered to be unreliable. One railroader stated:

No, they didn't hire many Indians on the railroad in those days either. I think that they had one crew out east somewhere, and of course it didn't work out too well. Indians will work hard it's true. But they won't work hard for very long, and back then the railroad could hire people in the cities — your Italians, Ukrainians, Swedes and so forth — who had no family ties and nowhere else to go.

The resident Native population of the town, therefore, was low or non-existent for many years simply because there were no real opportunities for work available other than trading. Crow Lake, unlike certain industrial northern towns, did not develop a pattern of Indian settlement outside the town limits. Some families did move close to the town, but such settlement was minimal.

The small increase in Native resident population in recent years has resulted from the changes in the town's economic orientation. The early economy was based on the transportation and extractive industries and the direction of interaction with the rest of the country was toward the east, west and south. But with the establishment of an administrative and bureaucratic economy, interest has increasingly been directed toward the north. These changes have brought about an increase in Native population, both resident and transient, in the town.

However, the economic and social position of Native people in Crow Lake has not changed significantly over the years. Although greater numbers have settled in town, secured jobs there and intermarried, for most Indians Crow Lake is still just a place to trade, to buy automobiles, outboard motors, guns, axes, boats, or clothing; it is a place where they come to receive medical care or attend school. Changes have taken place in these areas: the system of education for Indian people in town is no longer as obviously brutal as it once was, and the medical services available are better and more specialized. But in Crow Lake Indians are still regarded as outsiders, as people who have no real place in the community.

Indians and whites meet most often, most typically and most informally in the town's three central beer parlours. These situations provide the greatest opportunity for contact and are the settings for most conflict and tension between Indians and whites. While there is a tendency to assume the existence of "an Indian drinking problem," it would be misleading to consider the patterns of drinking as they exist among certain Native people without talking about similar patterns among the town's whites. In Crow Lake it is obvious that if differences exist between the two categories with regard to the use of alcohol, they lie primarily in the fact that whites drink considerably more and more steadily than do Native people. Members of both categories get drunk occasionally and some habitually, but on the whole it seems that whites drink more per capita than Indians, perhaps simply because they can afford to. Drinking in a pub or in a private home is the major form of recreation in the region, and it is so regarded by Native and non-Native alike.

But since alcohol is not readily available on most reserves in the immediate area, the pubs in town become centres of social activity for many Native people.

Potentialities for Conflict in the Pub Situation

In the pub situation both categories maintain a certain social distance. Native people occupy the rear section of a beer parlour while whites tend to sit closer to the front. This is a customary spatial segregation; it is not explicitly enforced in any way, although from time to time it will be commented upon. The rear of the beer parlour is often poorly lighted and many Native people may prefer to sit where they will be less noticeable.

Fights between individual Native people and individual whites do occasionally occur. These individual encounters, however, can quickly escalate into a serious altercation. The Indian in this situation is virtually helpless. No white will help him (or occasionally her) against the onslaught of other whites, and if an Indian is successful in defending himself, friends and relatives of the defeated white will seek retribution.

Furthermore, it is regarded by many Indians and most whites as a mistake for an Indian to seek help from the police or law in such a situation. Whites who are guilty of assault against a Native person will be tried if apprehended and almost always will be found guilty. Yet the Native person who places a charge against a white is in more serious trouble than if he had not pursued the matter. The very fact than an Indian can place a charge against a white is regarded by many as an insult against all whites, an insult that must be repaid. One case may be illustrative. Some nights following the arrest and trial of the white man involved in the previously mentioned assault against an Indian, the victim and the perpetrator met in the beverage room of one of the town's hotels. The Indian was called over to the table where the white youth was sitting and forced to relate an account of the extent of his injuries to a chorus of laughter. The white then said:

I don't want to see you around here again. It's bad enough that I have to pay $50 for a bloody savage; I don't have to look at your ugly face. From now on, keep looking over your shoulder because if I see you around, in some dark alley maybe, this time I'm going to kill you for sure. . . .

Although to this date the threat has never been carried out, it was clear to both the victim and to various onlookers that the threat was at least partly serious. The Indian in question had gained a number of dangerous enemies.

The significant point that emerges is that the Native person is ultimately helpless against the violence of the whites. Differences in physical strength matter little in such encounters; in a real sense the Native person enters a strange and hostile territory when he or she comes into town, and in such an environment he cannot rely upon friends and relatives for support. Even if friends are present in conflict situations, they will attempt as far as possible to avoid open conflict, knowing they have little chance of winning either temporarily or on a long-term basis against the combined force of the whites. Virtually all whites in town are united in their opposition to Indians. Differences which pertain in other circumstances are forgotten in the face of a confrontation between whites and Native people; in this case whites bond together to "protect" themselves.

Defensive Strategies of Native People

If the Native person is helpless against the whites' physical violence, he or she is at even more of a disadvantage against their insults. Social tradition in Crow Lake demands that insults made in earnest be repaid by further insult or by physical aggression. For the Native person, however, such reaction could easily lead to arrest or hospitalization. Insults range in degree from the crude and obvious to the subtle, and Native people adopt various strategies according to time and circumstance in order to deal with them.

One strategy is simply to ignore the insults gratuitously offered and walk away. Such a strategy is effective if allowed. However, as a Native person becomes known to the whites of the town and is seen more often on the streets, it becomes less likely that this reaction will be allowed. Another strategy is less passive, but perhaps more personally destructive. It involves clowning, joking, and self-humiliation. This strategy becomes increasingly necessary for an Indian who visits the town often or remains there long. Those non-resident Native people who attract the most attention, are seen and heard most often, become targets for greater and greater abuse.

One form of joking strategy is shown in the case of an obviously inebriated Indian who successfully purchased a case of beer by making a clerk laugh. As the man came through the door, the clerk's face assumed an expression of cold disapproval. But then the Indian asked in a loud and aggressive voice, "What colour are Indians?" For a moment the clerk was taken aback and seemed somewhat confused. The Indian,

however, continued, "They're black, ain't they? Well, you had better give a case of Black [Black Label beer] then." The clerk was relieved and went to bring out the beer.

In a somewhat different form this strategy involves promises that both parties — Indian and white — know will not be fulfilled. The owner of one of the town's beer parlours stated:

I get a lot of them coming in here asking to borrow money or telling me that they will bring me some wild rice if I would only give them five dollars. Well, of course I don't believe them, but sometimes I will give them a beer just for the fun of listening to all of that bullshit.

Both of these forms have been discussed in the anthropological literature, by Carstens (1971) with reference to "joking relationships" and by Braroe (1963) in what he calls "reciprocal exploitation." However, Braroe does not emphasize the ultimate defensive nature of his "reciprocal exploitation." All present strategies adopted by Native people in Crow Lake are passive and defensive, and act as continual confirmations of white prejudice, yet they are regarded by many Native people as necessary if they are to survive even temporarily in the hostile environment of the town.

The Position of Indians in Non-Native Conceptual Systems of Ethnicity

The question arises at this point: What are the causes of the structural dichotomy operating in Crow Lake? This question may be approached from two directions. I will examine first the conceptual system of the community as it pertains to Native people; then the informal methods of exclusion that operate in the town to prevent Indian people from becoming a full part of the community.

Indian people as a whole are not a part of that complex system of ethnic categories that so characterizes non-Native ethnicity in Crow Lake. Although there is a category "Indian and although the people of the community use that category in daily conversation, it is of a different order than are the categories "English," "French," "Italian," or "Finn." It occupies a position outside the community's regular system of ethnicity. It pertains not primarily to distinctions of culture, but to folk ideologies of race. As a category, "Indian" is compared, juxtaposed, and contrasted to "white." All non-Natives are referred to or are considered to be "white men," including Chinese, Pakistanis and West Indians. Both Indians and whites are fully conscious of the differences in ultimate origin between an Englishman and a Chinese person, yet these two categories will be lumped together and seen as a whole when compared to Native people.

Self-Differentiation of Native People: Residence and Culture

The definition of the situation in virtually all Indian/non-Indian encounters is precisely that: Indian encounters non-Indian and the boundaries between the two categories are very precise and rigidly drawn. Indians in Crow Lake may be "good" or "bad" but are Indians nonetheless. Among Native people themselves distinctions are established between different bands and different reserves, between, as many Native people put it, different "countries." Beaver House is contrasted to Fort James, Big Otter Lake is distinguished from Sagito. These distinctions are in many ways similar to the ethnic distinctions operating among the non-Native population of the town. The many different reserves in the area surrounding Crow Lake are divided up

and classified according to certain principles.

Crow Lake acts as the main service centre for several major Indian communities to the north and as a secondary administrative centre for certain others. The various bureaucratic orders in town divide up their territory somewhat differently. One Native community that is served by the community's Zone Hospital may not be under the jurisdiction of the town's local office of Indian Affairs, and similarly a community that is under the jurisdiction of the local Indian Affairs office may not be directly served by the zone office of the Department of National Health and Welfare. In any case, there is a certain degree of overlap and Crow Lake serves a significant number of northern Indian communities. In addition, each of the larger settlements has a number of smaller satellite settlements joined to it by geographical proximity, ties of kinship, and ultimate origin. Thus Big Otter Lake possesses the satellites Sagito, Deerskin, Washinee Lake, and others, while Mud Lake has the satellite North Star Lake.

This means that the Indian population of the area is not one undifferentiated whole. The differences are noted by the Indian people themselves and by some whites who have jobs in the various bureaucratic organizations involved with Indian people. Secondly, there is a certain nesting of the categories of residence that is similar in many ways to the nesting of white ethnic categories within the town. Thus a person from Deerskin will sometimes identify with that community, and at other times with the larger community, Big Otter Lake. In addition, and of central importance, Native people will often distinguish themselves culturally. A difference will be noted between "true Indians" and "white Indians," a distinction that parallels in some sense Dunning's (1964) distinction between "Indian" and "Indian-status" persons. As one Indian man stated:

*I know some of the people of X but I don't
know them too well. Most of those people
there don't trap or fish or hunt anymore. They
aren't like the people here. We are still in the
bush.*

There is presently emerging something
akin to a system of ethnic stereotypes.
Native people are able to make generalized
statements about the characteristics of the
various reserves and Native communities
in the area. Poplar Lake is regarded by both
Indians and whites as a reserve in which
people tenaciously maintain aboriginal traditions; Rat Rapids as a reserve that is presently faced with a great deal of social tension; Mud Lake as an area in which there
are strong political leaders; and Big Otter
Lake as a reserve that has many visitors
and commands a good deal of attention
from outside government.

Conceptual Opposition Between the Categories Indian and White

The Native population of the area thus divides itself up according to certain principles just as does the white population of the
town. Indian is clearly differentiated from
white and the two major categories subsume a series of lesser, although significant, subordinate categories. The two systems do not mesh or interpenetrate, but
rather touch and relate to, or against, each
other.

Within this system, then, it becomes relatively meaningless to talk about Indian-Chi-
nese relations or Indian-Italian relations
for as such they cannot be said to exist.
When a Native person has dealings with a
Ukrainian, the latter's ethnicity is of little
importance in terms of the relationship that
exists or may be established between them.

The categories "white" and "Indian" reflect the rigidly adhered to social distance

between the two. The man mentioned in the
previous chapter who claimed to be both
Indian and Scottish was, in the year and a
half that I spent in Crow Lake, the only
white of the community to claim to share
identity in the category "Indian." Many
other whites fiercely denied the humanity
of Native people. They expressed this in
various ways. Some acted through the violence of physical assault or insult. Many
others were more covert in the expression
of their feelings. Their attitude was largely
one of contempt caution. They indicated
that their sensibilities would be offended
by less formal and less occasional contact
with Native people. This contempt was not
often openly expressed; their fears were
expressed more often when they would informally state the "facts" of their case.

Non-Native Attitudes to Natives in Crow Lake

Much of the talk about Indians occurred
when they were not present. These discussions had a ritualistic quality. A group of
white men would be talking and the subject
of Indians would arise. The definition of the
situation then changed subtly: it became
"us against them." What usually followed
was a list of stock complaints made in a
serious or half-serious tone: Indians are
dirty; they smell bad, they are lazy; they
won't work; they are all drunks; they live off
welfare; they are given too much, and so on.
This recital was often made in a very theatrical manner. The statements were rarely
challenged; instead they were repeated
and elaborated.

These discussions usually concluded
with a summary: a philosophical position
was taken or a conglomerate of opinion
presented as "fact." It might be concluded
that the existing situation was impervious
to change or solution:

I don't care what they do for or to the Indians. Nothing that they do will do any good, and it's a waste of time and money to think that anything around here will ever change.

Or the position might be taken that the whites were the ultimate victims:

Throughout all of history it's been the case that the conqueror took all. We conquered the Indian, but look what's happened, look who gets all today . . . who gets everything for nothing . . . the Indian, that's who.

Or, rarely, a statement was made which openly acknowledged racism:

They are simply not equal . . . not physically, morally, intellectually, or spiritually. They are not equal and they just can't compete, but this socialistic type of government in Ottawa just keeps on giving and giving and taking and taking from us to give to them.

The Existing Conceptual Structure as Cause or Result

It might be argued that this entire edifice of prejudice and discrimination is in fact caused by the position of Native people in the conceptual order of the community's social consciousness. The symbolic opposition between Indian and white is of a higher order than that existing between any two categories at the lower level in the respective systems. The tension and hostility generated is also greater.

In some ways, however, this is a "magical" argument: it does not explain the tension nor the kind of structuring that has occurred in Crow Lake's ethnic system. I suggest that the present structural position of Native people in Crow Lake is reflected in both their position in the conceptual order and in the prejudice and discrimination acted out against them. This structural position can be seen as the result of certain historical and contemporary economic factors.

Mechanisms of Informal Exclusion

Indian people are part of the town and yet they are not. Very few Indian families are able to live and work in Crow Lake; they are prevented from doing so not by any law or statute, but by a subtle process of informal exclusion.

Briefly, what happens is that valuable items of information concerning "town opportunities" are not published openly but are passed by word of mouth through various information networks. One hears about jobs and apartments not through the newspaper or notices on bulletin boards, but through friends and acquaintances.

R was working as a clerk for the railroad. Over his desk one day an announcement was passed that in three days the CNR would be hiring additional brakemen. The next day he submitted his application for the job. He was the first to do so, but by the end of the day twelve others had applied. R had informed some of these people himself; they were friends. Others found out about the job competition through equally informal channels. All were white, all had lived in the town for most of their lives, and many had relatives working for the CNR. Accordingly, there was no public announcement of the intention of the railroad to hire additional brakemen.

Similarly, P, who worked at the General Hospital with D, discovered one morning that D had just bought another house which he planned to rent. P immediately rented the house himself as he was planning to be married soon. The fact of the rental, however, was kept secret because, as P said, "I don't want the whole town to know my plans yet." Meanwhile R, an Indian from

Smoke Lake, had several weeks previously obtained a job working for the town's Indian Hospital. He was married, but his wife and three children remained in Smoke Lake because he could not find a place to rent. "It's pretty tough," he said, "there just doesn't seem to be anything available." He later suggested that if he couldn't find a place for his family to live he would return to Smoke Lake where there were houses, but few jobs.

None of the white people involved in these incidents acted out of conscious desire to exclude Indian people from either jobs or rental accommodation. Rather, they acted in familiar patterns of individual or familial maximization. However, during the time I lived and worked in Crow Lake these scenes were, with variations, repeated again and again. The ultimate effect was to rigidly exclude most Indians as job-holders or residents: Indian people were simply not part of the "right" information networks. It was a classic vicious circle in that it was difficult if not impossible for an Indian person to become part of an information network unless he was already part of that network, to get a job unless he already had a job, or to find a place to live unless he already had a place to live. Such informal patterns of exclusion operate in virtually every area of Indian-white encounter.

Violence further acts to exclude Native people from the town. A person who has suffered violence tends to avoid situations in which the experience may be repeated. The violence that occurs in the pubs also occurs among Indian and white students in the town's schools. Essays written by children attending school on the reserves tend to bear this out:

I am not going to High School when I finish grade 8. I am going to have lots of things to do at home. I hate to go to High School because I heard about it, what happens because of White people. The ones that go to the High School get drunk and try and beat people up. That is why I hate High School. I think work will help people better than High School. White boys try to beat up Indians. Why?

Maybe I will hate cities because of the big traffic and the pollution of the cities. If we ever go to High School and live in White people's houses. I guess all they need is money and get paid nearly a hundred dollars a month while we don't get more than fifty dollars probably 25 bucks from the government. I think I hate White kids because they really like to fight. I am scared of going away because in the city there are rapists, killers and high school students get drunk and beat up people and probably get kicked out of High School. I'd rather quit school.

What I am going to do when I finish grade 8 is quit school because I have lots of things to do at home when I finish grade 8. I hate to go to High School because I hate to get into trouble and they'll send me home. I like to stay at home. That is more better than trouble. Some of the High School students had lots of trouble. That's why they were sent back home. They said that the White people tried to beat them up by fighting the Indians. That's why I get scared to go to high school.

(From essays collected for the Zone Hospital, Summer 1972.)

The courts also act to exclude Native people both formally, through jail sentences, and less formally, through prejudicial treatment. In one case, for example, an Indian man and his wife were involved in an argument or fight outside one of the town's hotels. The man pleaded guilty and assumed all blame, for he feared and was advised by the crown attorney that if he didn't both he and his wife would likely be found guilty and sentenced to jail. During the proceedings, however, the judge snarled, "What were you people doing in town anyway? Did you have a job here?" The defendant answered, "No." The judge continued, "Well, if you would stay out of places that you don't belong none of this would happen to you. Fifty dollars or thirty days."

Drinking in a pub can also lead to arrest and ultimate exclusion. Most arrests of Native people in Crow Lake are for public intoxication. Ontario Provincial police cars park outside of the entrance to the Crow Lake Hotel, the town's largest central pub, for an hour or so before and after the pub closes. The waiters will ask a drunk white man, who is perhaps a relative, friend, or steady customer, if he wants them to call a cab. The cab will arrive at the back door of the hotel and the man in question will leave unseen. Many Indians, however, are arrested as they leave the pub, and some have been arrested for public drunkenness as they were climbing the stairs to their rooms in the hotel. The hotel is so structured that one cannot walk directly from the pub in the basement to the rooms upstairs; one must actually step outside where the police are waiting. It is significant that waiters will not ask an Indian if he wants them to call a cab. Such service seems to be generally reserved for well-known white customers.

An Indian arrested in these circumstances will be locked up overnight and released in the morning with instructions to return on a specified date for his trial. Many do not bother to return to Crow Lake for trial. Surprisingly, warrants are not often issued for their arrest. Instead, they are summarily found guilty and sentenced to the night that they have already spent in jail. Their case is thus closed. According to several officers this is done to avoid the expense and trouble of tracking them down on such a petty charge. Occasionally, however, if a person has had a series of arrests and summary convictions, or if the judge remembers him, a warrant will be issued for his arrest. What is important is that a Native person who fails to appear for his trial after being arrested may not know for a considerable length of time whether or not a warrant has been issued. In the meantime he may stay away from town.

Avoidance of Informal Exclusion

When they are in Crow Lake for any reason Indian people often inquire about jobs as well, with an eye toward settling or working in town if the opportunity arises. These attempts are usually unsuccessful. Seasonal or part-time work as guides or bush workers is sometimes available, but permanent jobs are rare.

Those who have managed somehow to find permanent work and living accommodation in town are of diverse backgrounds. Most are from the immediate area, but some, significantly, are not. One is an Iroquois of the Six Nations reserve in southern Ontario who traps and works on various odd jobs, but has worked in factories in Toronto and Port Hope. Another describes himself as a "French Indian from Quebec," and a third is from Alberta. All three have spent some time in urban areas. Several others have worked in mining communities. The backgrounds of these people are complex, but there is in all of them a history of being or working in communities larger than Crow Lake. Many have acquired skills through this experience that have been useful in finding jobs here. In any case, they have partially escaped the situation in which most Native people of the immediate area are enclosed, and have thus been able to avoid as well some of the existing barriers of informal exclusion. Others, particularly women, have avoided many of these barriers by marrying resident whites, but such unions are rare.

Potential Similarities Between Native and Non-Native Ethnics

Many people in town insist that relatively few whites are actively and openly prejudiced against Native people, and objectively this seems to be true. Contact between Indians and whites is limited to a number of special contexts in which many whites are rarely involved. The quasi-ritualistic exchanges of insults and jokes about Indians usually occur when whites are alone and thus do not directly affect Native people. Nor does the town directly exploit Native people either economically or in terms of their labour. Indians pay the same prices for goods as whites do and, although of brief duration, seasonal jobs they can get pay an acceptable wage.

Moreover, despite their generally poor image among whites in Crow Lake, Indians are respected for certain qualities. Their knowledge of the bush and its animal life and their ability to survive in that environment are regarded as superior to most white men's. When they are praised either collectively or individually, for their prowess at hunting, fishing, or handling a canoe, most whites will accept such judgements. Significantly, this knowledge of the natural environment is highly prized in Crow Lake.

The Lack of Mediation

The differences between Indians and other "ethnic groups" in Crow Lake are not perceived consistently. Indians, like white ethnic categories, have in the consciousness of the community a series of both "strong" and "weak" points. But as far as Native people are concerned the "weak points" are exaggerated and projected to virtually all-encompassing proportions. The "strong points" are recognized comparatively rarely and briefly. Between Indian and white, in effect, there is rarely established that equivalence that eases relations between the non-Native ethnic categories in town.

This mediation does not occur primarily because there are few Indians in Crow Lake who are in a position to make it occur. Native people cannot obtain jobs or houses

in town because the community won't accept them, but also because the community does not need them. The residents of the community are busy protecting their own economic and social interests. This involves helping their friends, relatives and neighbours — people who are in a position to help them in return. It does not generally involve helping strangers and especially Native strangers.

The town exists in a precarious economic environment, and opportunities in Crow Lake are limited indeed. Both jobs and housing are in short supply. The local social system is therefore regarded by the residents as a means to economic survival which secures for them as many jobs and houses as necessary. Under present economic conditions Indians are simply not needed or wanted in the community, partially because they are Indians, but also because they are outsiders.

THE VERTICAL MOSAIC REVISITED: OCCUPATIONAL DIFFERENTIALS AMONG CANADIAN ETHNIC GROUPS

*Hugh Lautard and
Neil Guppy*

John Porter's portrayal of Canadian society as a vertical mosaic is a powerful metaphor in contemporary social science research (Porter, 1965). Porter's image of the mosaic depicts Canada as a composite of enduring social groups defined principally by class and ethnicity, but also by language and religion. As well as delineating group boundaries, Porter demonstrated the vertical

---

ranking of these communities on a series of inequality dimensions. In the context of ethnicity, the distinctive communities of the mosaic capture the potent force of ethnic identity, whereas the vertical alignment accentuates the hierarchy of ethnic inequality. It is an argument first of social differentiation, and second of social stratification.

The composition of the Canadian population has changed since Porter first wrote, but social cleavages based on ethnicity remain important. In the 1980s the imagery of a vertical mosaic has been reinterpreted in government circles (Abella, 1984; Boyer, 1985), where the subordinate positions of women, the disabled, Native Indians, and visible minorities have been highlighted. Responding to a growing human rights movement, new policies (e.g., the 1986 Employment Equity Act) have been enacted to facilitate equality and erode the vertical mosaic.

Ironically, at a time when governments are reacting to appeals concerning human rights, some sociologists have begun questioning the durability of ethnicity as an organizing principle in the vertical mosaic. Indeed, two decades after publication of *The Vertical Mosaic*, Porter himself co-authored a paper proclaiming "the collapse of the vertical mosaic" (Pineo and Porter, 1985: 390; see also Pineo, 1976; Darroch, 1979; Denis 1986). This view is at odds with new government policy as well as with other sociological research demonstrating the continuance of intense ethnic antagonism and discriminatory behaviour (Henry and Ginsberg, 1985; Robson and Breems, 1986).

Sorting out the reasons for this divergence of opinion in the current literature is our starting point (see also Reitz, 1988). In reviewing that literature, we pay particular attention to research findings concerned with historical trends in the salience of ethnicity as a central component of the vertical

mosaic. We then present new data, affording the longest historical perspective yet available on the association between ethnicity and occupation, using fifty-five years of census data, from 1931 to 1986. As did Porter before us, we stress both social differentiation and social stratification, although clearly the latter is the key to debates about the *vertical* mosaic.

The Declining Significance of Ethnicity?

In *The Vertical Mosaic* Porter offered three distinct observations about ethnic inequality. First, he argued that "charter status" groups, the French and English, commanded greater power and privilege than did "entrance status" groups (i.e., other immigrants) arriving later. Second, he noted an asymmetry of power favouring the English over the French. Third, he claimed that among non-charter immigrant groups too, ethnic inequality persisted. These three aspects of inequality he saw as core features in the distribution of power and privilege in Canada.

Porter's most renowned evidence highlighted the economic elite, where he found that "economic power belong[ed] almost exclusively to those of British origin" (Porter, 1965: 286). While the French were significantly under-represented, members of non-charter minority groups were virtually absent among economic power-brokers. Clement's more recent (1975) sketch of the economic elite suggested a waning of British dominance, although of 775 elite members 86.2 per cent still were English Canadian, 8.4 per cent were French Canadian, and only 5.4 per cent were of other ethnic origins.

Porter (1965) also presented data from the 1931, 1951, and 1961 censuses. Cross-classifying ethnic origin and occupation, he determined the extent to which various groups were over- and under-represented in different job categories. In the 1931 census he found British and Jewish groups ranked high (i.e., over-represented in professional and financial occupations, and under-represented in low-level, unskilled, and primary jobs); and, as he continued, the "French, German, and Dutch would probably rank next, followed by Scandinavian, Eastern European, Italian, Japanese, 'Other Central European', Chinese, and Native Indian." He concluded that by 1961 and "except for the French [who had slipped], the rough rank order [had] persisted over time."

Porter offered two complementary, although independent, explanations for the differential representation of ethnic groups by occupation level. First, immigrants compose a significant portion of the Canadian labour force (more than one in five as late as 1971), and traditionally Canada has attracted a polarized population of both the well educated and the poorly educated, with relatively few people in between. New entrants to Canada reinforce traditional patterns of occupational inequality, since one difference between ethnic groups is the occupation level of their immigrants. For instance, new British immigrants acquire professional and financial jobs more often then do recent "Central European" immigrants, who disproportionately take up unskilled, lower-level positions.

Second, Porter also suggested that once in Canada ethnic groups differed in the extent to which they aspired to upward occupational mobility. Some ethnic groups valued achievement less than others, either because of cultural differences (e.g., less emphasis on material reward) or because of perceived or experienced discriminatory barriers (for a recent statement see Pineo and Porter, 1985: 360–1). However, to the extent that ethnic assimilation occurred, Porter reasoned that ethnic origin exerted less impact on individual occupational mobility. Conversely, in the face of continued ethnic affiliations, mobility was limited — a thesis of "ethnically blocked mobility."

Darroch (1979) has undertaken an ambitious revision of Porter's original interpretation. He suggests that Porter paid too much attention to the persistence of a "rough rank order" over the three censuses, and failed to note the diminishing strength of the association between ethnicity and occupation level. Quite simply, Porter was not sensitive enough to the fact that the occupational over- and under-representation of ethnic groups was much less in 1961 than had been the case in 1931. Darroch reviewed other evidence, including data from the 1971 census, to show that the salience of ethnicity for occupational allocation had diminished over time. He concluded that the idea of blocked ethnic mobility had no foundation in fact and that we should be "skeptical of the idea that ethnic affiliations are a basic factor in generally limiting mobility opportunities in Canada."

These sentiments were echoed by Winn (1985) in the context of government policy debates. He was sharply critical of the Abella Commission's (1984: 4) call for the introduction of affirmative-action programs to augment mobility prospects for those groups whose progress had remained "unjustifiably in perpetual slow motion." Winn reviewed data from the 1971 and 1981 censuses, concluding that his evidence provided "no empirical support for the premise that Canadian society is immobile and that visible or low prestige groups cannot make economic progress." Affirmative action was unnecessary, he said, because the ethnic inequality implied by the vertical mosaic was exaggerated.

A more pessimistic conclusion concerning the continuing salience of ethnicity as a basis for inequality appears in Lautard and Loree (1984). Using more detailed occupation data, they agreed with Darroch's finding that occupational inequality among ethnic groups had declined over time. But whereas Darroch was willing to conclude that ethnicity was no longer a fundamental source of inequality, Lautard and Loree maintained that "occupational inequality is still substantial enough to justify the use of the concept 'vertical mosaic' to characterize this aspect of ethnic relations in Canada."

Porter (1985: 44–51) repeated his earlier analysis with the 1971 census and, agreeing with Lautard and Loree, claimed that "ethnic stratification has persisted through to 1971." Here he offers no hints about a "collapse" of the vertical mosaic. The census, however, contains data for both the foreign-born and the native-born, and so it confounds the two explanations that Porter offered for the association between ethnicity and occupation.

Working with Pineo (Pineo and Porter, 1985), Porter demonstrated that the strength of the association between ethnic origin and occupational status had attenuated in recent decades (up to 1973), at least for males from the major European ethnic groups. They also showed that for native-born Canadian men, ethnic origin had no significant influence on individual occupational mobility. This latter finding suggests that the thesis of 'blocked ethnic mobility' does not persist for second- and third-generation Canadian men (from the major European ethnic groups).

If, as these data show, occupational mobility is not limited by ethnic origin for many groups, then of Porter's two explanations for the ethnicity-occupation link, immigration would seem now to be the remaining factor. Boyd's (1985) research on the influence that birthplace exerts on occupational attainment supports this interpretation. For foreign-born men and women, she showed that ethnic origin had a definite effect on occupational attainment, even after controlling for differences

in the average age, education, social origin, and place of residence of ethnic groups. For women she found evidence of a double negative for being female and foreign-born. Indeed, she concluded by noting the "importance of birthplace and sex as factors underlying the Canadian mosaic" (Boyd, 1985: 441).

A small part of the dispute over whether an ethnic component to the vertical mosaic has persisted in Canada is captured by the proverbial "is the glass half-full or half-empty?" Exactly how much inequality is enough to attribute it "fundamental" status? However, a far larger part of the dispute turns on matters of both theoretical definition and methodological procedure. For example, both Winn and Porter (in his early work) relied mainly on rank-ordered data, and Darroch was surely correct in contending that the size of the gap between ranks is crucial. But further, as Lautard and Loree insisted, the gap's size depends on the number of occupations considered, and so they improved the quality of evidence by looking at a wider range of occupational levels. In addition, the use of differing ethnic categories (especially notable in survey-based as oppposed to census data), makes comparison and definitive conclusion precarious.

Key issues of theoretical and methodological dispute revolve around three aspects: the ethnic groups studied, the occupation levels considered, and the purity of historical comparability. These are reviewed in turn.

ETHNIC GROUPS

The definition of ethnicity remains contentious in social-science literature, and this debate touches directly on ethnic inequality and the vertical mosaic. Census data have been among the principal sources of evidence in evaluating the association between ethnic origin and occupation level. However, until 1981 the census definition of ethnicity relied on tracing ancestral male lineage, often a difficult task after several generations, especially given inter-ethnic marriages and historical changes around the world in national boundaries.

In addition, Statistics Canada is reticent about releasing detailed information for relatively small groups, and so ethnic categories have frequently been combined to form groups of mixed origin (e.g., Asian, Scandinavian). Typically the following ethnic categories have been used in the census: British (English, Irish, Scottish), French, German, Italian, Jewish, Dutch, Scandinavian, Eastern European (Polish, Ukrainian), Other European, Asian, and Native Indian.

OCCUPATIONS

Porter (1965) relied on five broad occupation groups and a residual category for his 1931 to 1961 census analysis: professional and financial, clerical, personal service, primary and unskilled, agriculture, and all others. By 1961 the residual category (all others) had swollen to 58 per cent of the total. Darroch's (1979) reanalysis was forced to employ these crude groupings, but Lautard and Loree (1984) began afresh and used more refined occupation distinctions, amounting to hundreds of separate job categories for each census.

Also at issue here is how occupations are seen to be related. Attention can centre on whether or not ethnic groups tend to be concentrated in different occupations (a focus on the ethnic division of labour — i.e., social differentiation). Alternatively, if ethnic groups tend to congregate in different occupations, then there is a concern with the degree of status inequality between ethnic groups (a focus on the occupational prestige hierarchy — i.e., social stratification).

HISTORICAL COMPARABILITY

Changes in the occupation structure and in the countries of origin of immigrants have meant that census procedures have had to be revised over the years. For occupation this has meant both the addition and deletion of job titles (e.g., computer programmer). For ethnicity one crucial change is in reporting procedures; for instance, in the early years when European groups dominated, little detail was made available for such visible minorities as Blacks or Indo-Pakistanis (even though both groups have a long history in Canada). Also, in 1981 the census questions for ethnicity changed (Kralt, 1980).

Since census definitions of occupations have changed over time there are advantages and disadvantages in the use of both broad and narrow occupation groups. The broad groups maximize comparability over time because most specific jobs are still classified in the same broad categories from one census to the next. However, the broad categories obscure crucial status gradations and are thus more useful in distinguishing social differentiation than social stratification, and the latter is the more important component in the current debate. Using more occupations gives a more refined calibration of inequality at any one point in time, although it does so by sacrificing comparability over time.

Methods

We begin by reviewing the results reported by Lautard and Loree (1984) for 1931–71. We then present results for 1971, 1981, and 1986, based on unpublished census data, permitting an examination of seventeen ethnic groups. To enhance comparability for the latter census years, we employ the 1971 occupational classification in both 1981 and 1986.

Although all of the nearly 500 detailed occupations of the 1971 classification are used in our full analysis of differentiation and stratification among ethnic groups, the broad occupational groups [examined] . . . enable us to see persisting aspects of the vertical mosaic. For example, British males and Jewish males and females are over-represented in managerial and administrative occupations, whereas Italians, Portuguese, Greeks, Yugoslavs, Chinese, Blacks, Native Indians and Métis, as well as South Asian (Indo-Pakistani) females are under-represented in this same occupational niche. Conversely, the British and the Jews are under-represented in service occupations, where there is an over-representation of Portuguese, Greeks, Chinese, and Blacks, as well as Yugoslav and Native Indian and Métis females.

Although we could continue to [identify] . . . such differences, it is unlikely that doing so would give us a coherent sense of the overall differentials among the ethnic groups shown — there are simply too many possible comparisons. However, if we calculate the total of either the positive or the negative percentage differences between the occupational distribution of an ethnic group and the total labour force, we obtain a figure indicating the percentage of the members of the group who would have to have different occupations for that group's occupational distribution to be the same as that of the total labour force. Called the index of dissimilarity, this measure allows us to compare occupational differentiation among groups.

For example, . . . the index of dissimilarity for Black males is approximately 20, indicating that roughly one out of five Black men in the labour force would have to be in a different occupational category for there to be no difference between their occupational distribution and that of the total male labour force. The equivalent proportion for Native Indian and Métis men is

approximately 28 per cent, indicating even greater differentiation.

Again, however, the broad occupational categories [used in our analysis] . . . result in lower measures of dissimilarity than do the hundreds of more detailed occupations used for the results presented below. For example, although [the overall analysis] . . . shows the percentage of British males in transport-equipment operating occupations is no different than that of the total male labour force, detailed occupational data indicate that British males are over-represented among air pilots and under-represented among taxi drivers.

Finally, measures such as the index of dissimilarity are most appropriately calculated for a group in comparison with the total labour force minus that group, to correct for the presence of the group itself in the total (Duncan and Duncan, 1955: 494). Accordingly, the results presented in the next section indicate the differentials between each ethnic group and the rest of the labour force, rather than between groups and the total labour force (as in the examples given above).

Dissimilarity, however, does not necessarily mean disadvantage. For example, the highest index of dissimilarity that can be calculated from the data . . . is for Jewish males, at 43; this is the result of their over-representation in most of the categories in the upper half of the table and their corresponding under-representation in the remaining occupational categories. There is another measure, however — the index of net difference — that may be calculated with occupational data ranked according to socio-economic scales such as those prepared by Blishen (1958) for 1951; Blishen (1967) for 1961; Blishen and McRoberts (1976) and Blishen and Carroll (1978) for males and females, respectively, for 1971; and Blishen et al., 1987) for 1981. Related to the index of dissimilarity but more complicated in its calculation, the index of net difference provides a measure of the overall occupational ranking of a group in relation to the rest of the labour force. Indexes of net difference may be negative as well as positive, with a minus sign indicating comparatively lower occupational status, and a positive sign comparatively higher status; zero would indicate overall equality of occupational status.

We now turn to the results of the analysis of ethnic occupational differentiation and stratification in Canada, using the indexes of dissimilarity and net difference.

Results

Table 8.1 contains Lautard and Loree's (1984) indexes of occupational dissimilarity for the ethnic groups examined by Porter (1965) and Darroch (1979) for the census years 1931 through 1971. These indexes show the decline in occupational differentiation found by Darroch, although the levels of dissimilarity are considerably higher. The indexes for men in 1961, for example, include no values lower than 15 per cent, and the mean (29) is more than double that yielded by Darroch's analysis (14). By 1971 there is one value for men lower than 15 per cent, but again the mean (24) is nearly double that calculated by Darroch (14) for both sexes combined. After 1931, when the average dissimilarity for females is the same as that for males (37 per cent), ethnic differentiation among women in the paid labour force is less than

Table 8.1
OCCUPATIONAL DISSIMILARITY BETWEEN SELECTED ETHNIC GROUPS AND THE REST OF THE LABOUR FORCE, BY SEX: 1931, 1951, 1961, and 1971

ETHNIC GROUP	MALE				FEMALE			
	1931	1951	1961	1971	1931	1951	1961	1971
British	22	20	19	15	27	23	22	16
French	15	17	16	14	26	23	17	17
German[a]	24	23	17	15	20	14	13	11
Italian	48	34	40	35	39	24	45	38
Jewish	65	63	59	51	51	40	34	32
Dutch	21	20	17	17	14	17	15	15
Scandinavian	29	23	18	17	25	13	10	12
Polish	34[b]	23	18	15	45[b]	21	17	14
Ukrainian		28	21	15		22	21	16
Other European[c]	43	21	19	21	49	18	20	23
Asian[d]	61	46	45	36	50	25	20	25
Native Indian[e]	49	57	57	41	59	53	48	31
Mean ($\bar{X}$)	37	31	29	24	37	24	24	21
Std. Dev. (s)	17	16	17	13	15	11	12	9
V (s/$\bar{X}$)	.46	.52	.59	.54	.41	.46	.50	.43
Number of occupations	(388)	(278)	(332)	(496)	(265)	(226)	(277)	(412)

Sources: 1931 (Dominion Bureau of Statistics, 1936: Table 49); 1951 (Dominion Bureau of Statistics, 1953: Table 12); 1961 (Dominion Bureau of Statistics, 1964: Tabel 21); 1971 (Statistics Canada, 1975: Table 4).

[a] Includes Austrian in 1931.
[b] Eastern European (Polish and Ukrainian combined).
[c] Other central European in 1931.
[d] Weighted average of Chinese and Japanese in 1931.
[e] Includes Eskimos in 1951.

Reproduced with permission from Lautard and Loree (1984: 338).

that among men, but even by 1971 only four groups (German, Dutch, Scandinavian, and Polish) have indexes of 15 per cent or less, and all these are above 10 per cent; the mean for women in 1971 is 21 per cent. Thus, on average, in 1971 a quarter of the male labour force and a fifth of the female labour force would have to have had different occupations in order for there to have been no occupational dissimilarity among ethnic groups. It is also evident from Table 8.1 that while the standard deviations, like the means, decline between 1931 and 1971, relative variation (V) undergoes a net increase for both sexes. The rankings of ethnic groups by degree of dissimilarity, moreover, remain remarkably stable, with the Italian, Jewish, Asian, and Native Indian groups tending to be more dissimilar from the rest of the labour force than other groups.

As noted in the previous section, occupational dissimilarity does not necessarily involve inequality of occupational status. Table 8.2 presents Lautard and Loree's (1984) indexes of net difference in occupational status between each ethnic group and the total labour force for 1951 through 1971. The few positive indexes reflect the relatively high occupational rank of the British, Jewish, and, by 1971, Asian groups, as well as a slight advantage in 1951 and 1961 for Scandinavian females. The negative values indicate the relatively low status of the other groups. With one exception (women of Italian origin in 1971), the largest negative indexes are those for Native Indians, for whom even the 1971 indexes exceed −.30 for males and −.20 for females. Between 1951 and 1971, mean ethnic inequality declined, as did the standard deviations and the relative variation (V),

Table 8.2

NET DIFFERENCE IN OCCUPATIONAL STATUS BETWEEN ETHNIC GROUPS AND THE TOTAL LABOUR FORCE, BY SEX: 1951, 1961, and 1971

ETHNIC GROUP	MALE			FEMALE		
	1951	1961	1971	1951	1961	1971
British	.09	.11	.07	.11	.12	.07
French	−.11	−.10	−.04	−.11	−.07	−.01
German	−.03	−.06	−.07	−.13	−.11	−.09
Italian	−.15	−.28	−.21	−.08	−.37	−.34
Jewish	.41	.42	.35	.20	.21	.24
Dutch	−.10	−.09	−.09	−.15	−.12	−.10
Scandinavian	−.04	−.05	−.08	−.01	−.03	−.01
Polish	−.14	−.07	−.07	−.20	−.16	−.12
Ukrainian	−.11	−.10	−.09	−.20	−.19	−.12
Other European	−.12	−.11	−.11	−.17	−.19	−.20
Asian	−.14	−.03	−.10	−.06	−.05	−.01
Native Indian[a]	−.68	−.63	−.34	−.55	−.47	−.23
Mean ($|\bar{X}|$)	.18	.17	.14	.16	.17	.13
Std. Dev. (s)	.19	.18	.11	.14	.13	.10
V ($s/|\bar{X}|$)	1.06	1.06	.79	.88	.76	.77
Number of occupational ranks	(208)	(298)	(496)	(178)	(252)	(412)

Sources: 1951 (Dominion Bureau of Statistics, 1953: Table 12); 1961 (Dominion Bureau of Statistics, 1964: Table 21); 1971 (Statistics Canada, 1975: Table 4).

[a] Includes Eskimo in 1951.

Reproduced with permission from Lautard and Loree (1984: 338).

but the latter remains very high for both sexes. The most pronounced shifts in the rank-order of the ethnic groups by relative occupational status include the Asian and Polish men, rising from a tie at third-lowest in 1951 to second- and sixth-highest respectively in 1971; and Italian females dropping from fifth-highest in 1951 to lowest in 1971. Otherwise, the ranking of ethnic groups by relative occupational status is about as stable as that by occupational dissimilarity.

Table 8.3 contains indexes of dissimilarity for sixteen ethnic groups as of 1971, and seventeen as of 1981 and 1986. With the exception of the indexes for German, Dutch, and Polish males and Jewish females (which are slightly higher in 1986 than in 1971), and those for French males and Polish females (which are the same in 1986 as in 1971), the figures in Table 8.3 indicate continuing declines in ethnic occupational differentiation. However, the replacement of "Other European" with Hungarian, Portuguese, Greek, and Yugoslav, and "Asian" with Chinese and South Asian, results in higher average dissimilarity for 1971 than in Table 8.1: 30 and 27 per cent, for males and females respectively, compared to 24 and 21 per cent. As of 1986, a quarter of the males and a fifth of the females would

Table 8.3
OCCUPATIONAL DISSIMILARITY[a] BETWEEN SELECTED ETHNIC GROUPS AND THE REST OF THE LABOUR FORCE, BY SEX: CANADA, 1971, 1981, and 1986

ETHNIC GROUP	MALE			FEMALE		
	1971	1981	1986	1971	1981	1986
British	15	10	10	16	9	8
French	14	14	14	18	14	14
German	15	15	17	11	9	10
Dutch	16	17	18	15	13	14
Scandinavian	17	18	13	12	12	11
Ukrainian	15	13	14	16	9	11
Polish	15	14	16	14	10	14
Hungarian	21	19	19	20	15	16
Italian	35	26	24	38	25	22
Portuguese	46	42	39	57	48	40
Greek	48	45	42	51	42	37
Yugoslav	33	31	25	35	29	21
Jewish	51	49	49	32	33	34
Chinese	52	44	42	34	30	30
South Asian	46	34	30	31	27	25
Indian and Métis	41	37	38	32	29	30
Black	NI	32	28	NI	30	27
Mean ($\overline{X}$)	30	27	26	27	23	21
Std. Dev. (s)	15	13	12	14	12	10
V ($s/\overline{X}$)	.50	.48	.46	.52	.52	.48
Number of occupational ranks	(498)	(496)	(496)	(464)	(495)	(495)

Source: Special tabulations of census data.

[a] Each figure in the table indicates the percentage of the ethnic group that would have to have a different occupation in order for there to be no difference between the occupational distribution of that group and the rest of the labour force.

NI: not included.

have to have a different occupation in order for there to be no occupational differentiation among these ethnic groups. As well, relative variation remains around 50 per cent, with the British, French, Germans, Dutch, Scandinavians, Ukrainians, Polish, and Hungarians below the means, and — except for Italian males and Yugoslavs of both sexes, in 1986 — the Italians, Portuguese, Greeks, Yugoslavs, Jews, Chinese, South Asians, Indians, and Métis, and Blacks above the means, for each year under consideration.

Table 8.4 presents indexes of net difference in occupational status between each of the ethnic groups and the rest of the labour force. The results for 1971 are consistent with those in Table 8.2. With the exception of the indexes for the British, the Jews, and the South Asians of both sexes, all values for 1971 are negative. As well, in 1971, the Italians, Portuguese, Greeks, Yugoslavs, and Native Indians and Métis have lower overall occupational status than the rest of the groups examined. In 1981 and 1986, the pattern is somewhat different, particularly for males. In addition to British and Jewish males, Scandinavian, Ukrainian, Polish, Hungarian, and South Asian males have positive indexes for both 1981

Table 8.4
NET DIFFERENCE IN OCCUPATIONAL STATUS BETWEEN SELECTED ETHNIC GROUPS AND THE REST OF THE LABOUR FORCE, BY SEX: CANADA, 1971, 1981, and 1986

ETHNIC GROUP	MALE			FEMALE		
	1971	1981	1986	1971	1981	1986
British	.13	.06	.05	.14	.06	.04
French	−.06	−.04	−.01	−.02	.00	.01
German	−.08	−.02	−.03	−.09	−.04	−.05
Dutch	−.09	−.06	−.05	−.10	−.06	−.05
Scandinavian	−.08	.01	.01	−.01	.03	.06
Ukrainian	−.09	.01	.02	−.13	.00	.01
Polish	−.08	.03	.05	−.12	−.01	−.02
Hungarian	−.06	.03	.04	−.13	−.03	−.02
Italian	−.22	−.12	−.09	−.35	−.19	−.14
Portuguese	−.38	−.33	−.30	−.62	−.40	−.34
Greek	−.27	−.31	−.28	−.48	−.36	−.31
Yugoslav	−.12	−.05	−.03	−.29	−.18	−.11
Jewish	.36	.30	.34	.24	.27	.29
Chinese	−.04	−.08	−.05	−.20	−.14	−.13
South Asian	.26	.09	.03	.19	−.09	−.11
Indian and Métis	−.35	−.25	−.24	−.23	−.18	−.16
Black	NI	−.02	−.11	NI	−.02	−.05
Mean ($|\bar{X}|$)	.17	.11	.10	.21	.12	.11
Std. Dev. (s)	.12	.11	.11	.16	.13	.11
V ($s/|\bar{X}|$)	.71	1.00	1.10	.76	1.08	1.00
(Number of occupational ranks)	(498)	(468)	(468)	(464)	(467)	(468)

Source: Special tabulations of census data.

[a] A negative figure indicates relatively lower overall occupational status, a positive figure relatively higher status. Zero indicates overall equality of occupational status. The greater the absolute size of the index, the greater the inequality.

[b] May not equal the number of occupations in Table 8.3 because of tied ranks.

NI: not included.

and 1986. The relative occupational status of Black males is comparable to that of German males in 1981, while the overall rank of Chinese males is similar to that of the Dutch in 1981. Finally, Yugoslav males are positioned between French and Dutch males in 1981 and tied with German males in 1986. Otherwise the basic pattern holds.

Among women, the British and the Jews have positive indexes for both 1981 and 1986, as do the Scandinavians. Overall equality of occupational status vis-à-vis the rest of the labour force in 1981 is indicated for both the French and Ukrainian groups, which are tied at +.01 in 1986. The overall status of Black females falls between that of Polish and Hungarian women in 1981 and is tied with that of both German and Dutch women in 1986. Otherwise, the pattern prevails: Italian, Portuguese, Greek, Yugoslav, Chinese, South Asian, and Indian and Métis women have lower relative occupational status than do women of the other groups under consideration, in both 1981 and 1986. For both sexes, moreover, the Portuguese have the lowest occupational status, and (except for males in 1971) Greeks the second-lowest status, in all three census years. On average, although occupational inequality among ethnic groups appears to have continued to decline between 1971 and 1986, relative variation in occupational status remains very high.

The results considered above are for the country as a whole, and they could merely reflect regional differences in both ethnic composition and economic structures. Analysis of occupational differentiation as of 1986 among ethnic groups by region, however, indicates that occupational dissimilarity among ethnic groups is generally greater than that observed at the national level. Average ethnic occupational dissimilarity in both the male and female labour forces, as of 1986, is higher in the Atlantic region, in Quebec, on the Prairies, and in British Columbia than in the country as a whole, while the means for Ontario are the same as the national averages. Moreover, the rankings of ethnic groups by degree of occupational dissimilarity in most regions are similar to those observed for the country as a whole.

Finally, occupational differentials among ethnic groups could result from educational differences among groups. We do not have educational data for 1986, but we do have such data for 1981 for the British, French, German, Dutch, Scandinavian, Ukrainian, Polish, Italian, Portuguese, Jewish, Chinese, and Native Indian and Métis groups. Average ethnic dissimilarity for men with a high-school education or the equivalent and men with post-secondary education is two points lower than that among all men, while it is four points higher for men with less than high school. Among women, only these with a high-school education or the equivalent show lower mean occupational dissimilarity among ethnic groups (by 3 points) than do all women, while those with post-secondary education have the same average ethnic dissimilarity as all women. Among women with less than high school, mean ethnic occupational dissimilarity is 5 points higher than that for all women. Moreover, at all educational levels and for both sexes, the general ordering of ethnic groups according to degree of occupational dissimilarity follows the now-familiar pattern.

Average ethnic occupational inequality for men with less than high school or the equivalent and men with a post-secondary education is only one point less than that for all men, and only two points less than for those with high school or the equivalent. Among women with less than a high-school education, average ethnic occupational inequality is one point higher than for all women. Only for women with high school or the equivalent and women with post-secondary education is ethnic occupation inequality substantially reduced, by about one-half and nearly two-fifths, respectively. Nevertheless, for both men and women in each educational category, relative variation remains extremely high, and the ranking of ethnic groups by relative occupational status is generally the same as that previously observed. The vertical mosaic, therefore, is based on more than either regional or educational differences.

Discussion

The historical comparison of ethnic inequality, as measured by occupational differences, suggests that between 1931 and 1986 a decline in the significance of ethnicity has occurred. The decline has been moderate, however, and ethnic origin continues to influence occupational destination.

The trend in occupational dissimilarity indicates a reduction in the ethnic division of labour of roughly 50 per cent in 55 years. Social differentiation based on ethnicity is slowly eroding. The comparable results in ethnic occupational stratification reveal a similar degree of reduction, although over a shorter time span (from 1951 to 1986). These historical comparisons are admittedly crude, and we caution that precise calculations are impossible.

Do these results imply a "collapse" in the vertical mosaic? Using 1971 census data, Porter himself felt that "ethnic stratification" had persisted. For males Tables 8.3 and 8.4 both reveal very small declines in differentiation and stratification between 1971 and 1986, affording no firm grounds for repudiating Porter's claim. For females the 1971 to 1986 changes have been larger, but by 1986 levels of differentiation and stratification among women of various ethnic groups are still similar to those for men.

An alternative method of illustrating how large or how small the reported differences are is to compare the differentiation and stratification among ethnic groups with

similar differences between women and men. Using a comparable classification of occupations for the 1981 census, Fox and Fox (1987) report an index of dissimilarity for the occupational distributions of women and men of 61 per cent. This figure is greater than the 1981 averages we report (27 per cent for men; 23 per cent for women) and indeed is greater than the index figure for any single ethnic group. Still, certain ethnic groups, notably the Jewish, Greek, Chinese, and Portuguese among men, and the Portuguese and Greek among women, have dissimilarity scores approaching the figure for gender.

Using socio-economic status as the dimension that best illustrates the issue of vertical mosaic, the ethnic distribution can once more be compared with differences between women and men. In this case, ethnic inequality is greater than is gender inequality (see e.g., Darroch, 1979: 13). This comparison obscures much of the known inequality between women and men (SES scores combine education and income, and typically women in the labour force are paid less but have higher levels of schooling than men). The index of net difference value for women compared with men is very close to zero in 1986, whereas the average value for ethnicity is .10 among men and .11 among women.

What these two comparisons suggest is that the gendered division of labour is more marked than is the ethnic division of labour. That is, men and women tend to be clustered in "sex-typed" jobs more often than members of specific ethnic groups are concentrated in "ethnic-linked" jobs. However, when the comparison is made on the dimension of socio-economic status, inequality is more marked among ethnic groups than it is between the genders (granting, however, the limitations of SES comparisons between women and men).

Porter's "vertical mosaic" interpretation of Canadian society rested upon far more than ethnic occupational differentiation. As we noted above, the penetration of ethnic members into elite groups, a key element of the vertical mosaic, has remained limited. Nevertheless, some progress has been made here too, as the new "entrepreneurial" immigration category suggests, and certainly visible minorities have done well in selected occupational niches — among professionals, for example (Lambert, Ledoux, and Pendakur, 1989).

The research design that we have employed prohibits us from investigating which of Porter's two dynamics best explains the continuing level of ethnic inequality: differential immigration or blocked mobility. Our reading of the research literature suggests that immigration continues as the more important factor, especially in terms of visible minorities (McDade, 1988). But even here, the bimodal character of Canadian immigration, to which Porter initially drew attention, continues.

PART

5

CONCLUSION

PROCESSES OF SOCIAL CHANGE

Although we end the book with a chapter on change, social change is implicit throughout the readings that you have already seen. We focus on change *per se* in this chapter because it is so integral to the sociological perspective. But this chapter is probably not presented in the usual way. We do not, for example, discuss or present articles on general theories of social change. You will not find in this part much consideration of whether change is evolutionary or cyclical. More than anything else, this part might be seen as a conclusion to the book.

Two themes dominate: our concern is to present material that illustrates people's active attempts to change their world and shape their futures while appreciating the structural constraints that limit such attempts. In short, people produce social structure often through concerted collective action directed toward achieving a better future, but frequently what they will produce will have unintended and perhaps unanticipated results. And, while many changes may seem to be beyond anybody's control, they are not simply social forces, or things that happen to us; we must also interpret and decide how to respond to these changes.

COLLECTIVE BEHAVIOUR

Historically, collective behaviour, such as mob violence, race wars and mass protests, has presented a problem to conservative thinkers. On a personal level they have found such activities abhorrent, senseless and, because of their apparent irrationality, dangerous to the fabric of society. And, as with the case of deviants and criminals, they had to ask: If our society works so well, why are these people doing these things? Often they looked for the answers in *"types of people" explanations.* So we read in the literature references to the "criminal classes," "riff raff," "losers and misfits" as the mainspring of collective action. Other theorists have accounted for such apparently inexplicable behaviour by reference to such notions as *contagion* or circular reaction, which implies that something mystical happens to people when they are in large crowds: they supposedly lose their critical faculties and become suggestible to the influence of others, particularly leaders (often outside agitators) who wish to incite them to violence. And a variety of theorists, *mass society* theorists, have argued that this is most likely to happen in a society where large numbers of people are alienated from its institutions, from kinship, community and associational ties. And so we return to the beginning: collective behaviour is the action of the alienated, the outcasts.

George Rudé's (1964; 1970) historical studies have done the most to explode these myths, to challenge the notion that these crowds are irrational, violent and made up of the alienated and the powerless. Indeed, he argues quite the contrary. Such work has forced us to re-examine our approaches to and definition of collective behaviour. Collective behaviour was a term meant to capture not only the obvious political actions described in the readings, but also other apparently spontaneous and unstructured activities involving large numbers of people: fads, crazes and panics as well as protest. By lumping all of these together, however, we de-legitimize the protest and make such activities seem pointless; we turn dissent into deviance or even trivia.

None of this tells us very much about protest, about people's sometimes violent attempts to express their dissatisfaction with the order and to ask for or create change. Conflict theorists remind us that such behaviour is predictable, a natural outcome of the kinds of structured inequalities discussed throughout the readings. It is as important, they argue, to account for the lack of protest as to account for protest. In this they focus on ideology and coercion, on deceit and force.

From a conflict perspective, the study of protest is a natural part of sociology. By adopting a historical approach these theorists show us that such behaviour cannot be spontaneous and irrational, but rather the result of a long process whereby people come to recognize and share their grievances. Of course the fact that large numbers of people share political or economic dissatisfaction does not mean that this will result automatically in collective action.

Whether this dissatisfaction is acted upon and the kind of expression it receives will depend on a number of structural factors. Is effective leadership available and willing to articulate an ideology and organize activities? Do there exist effective channels of communication and communal or associational links between members of the collectivity? Anthony Oberschall (1973) sums up these issues rather well. He argues that to predict whether collective action will occur at all we must look first at social segmentation: what are the major splits in society and how closely are the segments tied together? In particular, we must look at the links between the dominant and the dominated: how much access do the dominated have to the powerful, how much protection and how many benefits do they receive? If the segmentation is sharp rather than integrated, collective behaviour is very likely.

To understand the form that this collective action takes, we must then look to the links within the collectivity: do there exist effective channels of communication and ties between the members, or are they atomized, unable to communicate and organize effectively? In the latter case, collective action, when it does occur, is likely to be sporadic, inarticulate and primitive. If the links in the collectivity are strong, however, more sustained protest, such as that which is necessary for social movements and even revolution, is more likely.

But as Marx pointed out, even primitive collective action may be an important stage to more sustained and ideologically grounded political activity. That is, in the very act of conflict, as one interacts with others who share the same interests and confront the power of the state as represented, for example, by the police, one's political consciousness may be transformed. Indeed, in order to understand collective action and its absence one must look at the role of the state in controlling, often forcefully, incipient protest and emerging social movements.

•
•
•

chapter

14

Dimensions of Social Change

This chapter is in some ways a summary of the book. Almost all the chapters deal in one way or another with change. In this chapter, however, we focus on people's concerted and deliberate attempts to change their worlds.

The first three selections are all about some aspect of Canada after the failure of the Meech Lake Accord. The excerpt from George Mathews, "Quiet Resolution," offers a scenario for Quebec's future that many Canadians will find discomfiting. Nevertheless, Mathews, a Quebec economist, does offer some intriguing insights about what kind of society Quebeckers may shape for themselves, and something of a challenge for the rest of Canada to develop a collective vision of the future.

Reginald Bibby, a sociologist from the University of Lethbridge, offers a very dif-

ferent perspective in this excerpt from his *Mosaic Madness*. While Mathews and Bibby define the problem, the issue, quite differently, both ask the same question: Do Canadians have a shared vision of the future and the will to create it? Despite the title of his book, Bibby is clearly concerned with more than issues of ethnicity. Rather, he is concerned with the implications of maintaining Canadian culture and of developing Canadian symbols of excessive individualism and relativism, and the resulting values of pluralism.

Clearly official and unofficial policies promoting multiculturalism are but one, though a particularly vivid, illustration of the extent to which pluralistic values are dominant characteristics of the Canadian culture. More generally, as we are seeing in the National Unity Debate, what seems to make Canadian culture unique from that of many other societies, most notably the United States, is our unwillingness to subsume regional, ethnic and religious differences to some set of national symbols and overriding cultural identity. It remains to be seen whether this uniqueness will ultimately be our strength or our downfall as a nation.

The excerpt from Michael Asch's *Home and Native Land*, offers yet a different challenge for the future. Asch, an anthropologist at the University of Alberta, describes aboriginal perceptions of their rights. He does so in the context of section 35 of the *Constitution Act*, which for the first time (1982) explicitly acknowledged the existence of aboriginal peoples and aboriginal rights. Although written some years before the traumatic events at Oka in the summer of 1990, the description Asch gives you here of the view from the aboriginal peoples side may offer some context in which to understand this conflict and the many others — some in the form of legal battles and others in the form of face-to-face confrontations that presently characterize relationships between government and aboriginal peoples in Canada. Still, Asch reaches the rather hopeful conclusion that the aspirations of aboriginal peoples must and can be accommodated within the framework of Canadian federalism.

In 1986, Pat Marchak of the University of British Columbia, received the John Porter Award for her book *Green Gold*, a study of the B.C. forest industry. In the following year she therefore gave the John Porter Lecture at the annual meetings of the Canadian Sociology and Anthroplogy Association. The final selection is a slightly abridged version of that lecture. It is, of course, explicitly directed to an audience of sociologists. In thinking over her own work and the new directions her more recent work is moving, she also presents a challenge for sociologists to find their appropriate role in this time of rapid change and uncertainty.

RELATED READINGS

Alexander Himelfarb: "Public Opinion and Public Policy" (Chapter 2)
Margrit Eichler: " 'The Family' as a Political Issue" (Chapter 6)
C. James Richardson: "Family Law Research in a Decade of Change" (Chapter 6)
Roderic Beaujot: "The Family in Crisis?" (Chapter 8)
Robert J. Brym: "The Great Canadian Identity Trap" (Chapter 9)
John Myles: "The Expanding Middle: Some Evidence on the Deskilling Debate" (Chapter 10)
Wallace Clement: "Does Class Matter? Accounting for the Direction of Canadian Society" (Chapter 11)

QUIET RESOLUTION: QUEBEC'S CHALLENGE TO CANADA
Georges Mathews

Internal divisions are nothing new in Canada. The country has had its share of existential crises since 1867. They always concerned relations between the two nations. What is new, at the beginning of 1990, is the profound division within English Canada, where a minority is willing to take a modest step towards Quebec while the majority considers Quebec just another province, no more, no less. Once again, Quebec is dividing the country. It is not Brian Mulroney, as Pierre Trudeau feigns to believe. Seeking to soothe the wounds Trudeau inflicted on Quebec in 1981, Mulroney

From *Quiet Resolution: Quebec's Challenge to Canada* by Georges Mathews, 1990. By permission of Summerhill Press Ltd.,Toronto.

has involuntarily allowed Canadian atavism to rise once more to the surface.

Quebec is at the heart of the Canadian problem. It must therefore be at the heart of the solution.

The Rules of the Game

President Lyndon Johnson campaigned in 1964 on the theme of peace, while his Republican opponent, Barry Goldwater, focused on halting the spread of communism in Indochina. Johnson scored a crushing victory. In January 1965, he began applying Goldwater's policy in Indochina. In every respect it was an American disaster, but no one challenged the legitimacy of the president.

During the election campaign of 1968, Pierre Trudeau failed to describe the real contours of his policy on bilingualism. In 1969, there appeared the Law on Official Languages. In the 1974 campaign, Trudeau ridiculed the commitment of his opponent, Conservative leader Robert Stanfield, to implement wage and price controls to suppress inflationary pressures. He scored an easy victory. By the fall of 1975, he was bringing in — wage and price controls. In 1980, he said nothing about the patriation of the Canadian constitution. And as for his solemn commitment during the referendum campaign, we now know what that was all about.

Yet no one even remotely suggested that he call a referendum or that he resign because his initiative was illegitimate.

Brian Mulroney, campaigning for the Conservative leadership in the spring of 1983, flatly turned down the idea of a free trade deal with the United States. It was a proposal endorsed by his main adversary, John Crosbie. During the 1984 federal election campaign, Mulroney said nothing about free trade and did not repudiate his earlier position. But, in the spring of 1986, he approached Ronald Reagan with the idea of opening negotiations on a free trade agreement. No one asked for a referendum.

All these politicians acted with the strictest legality. Such are the rules of the game: an elected government is an elected government. It governs the country according to its own conception of the national interest. There is always a next election. But these rules are to be accepted only if they apply equally to all. Isn't this the meaning of the legendary British fair play?

It is also possible to conclude from this brief list that no political party can be asked to describe its future strategy during an election campaign, since it has no knowledge of the problems that might surface once it is in power.

With this description of the rules of politics, we can now look at the post-Meech period.

No doubt the formal failure of the Meech Lake Accord will trigger feverish activity in Quebec and growing anxiety, tinged with resignation, in English Canada. After the verbal fireworks typical of the Quebec discourse in the preceding months, everyone will be expecting a dramatic gesture from the Quebec government. It would be unthinkable not to mark the occasion. There must be a reaction, and a rather swift one. But what?

Raising the ante? One can hear the laughter from English Canada: "We refused them a quarter and now they ask for four of them. That's a good one! Ha ha!" Raising the ante while threatening to cut federal ties? That was played out early in 1990. Taking it up again would destroy Quebec's credibility and perpetuate the unhealthy climate with which the new decade has begun, and which is slowly destroying Canadian political life.

Only one gesture is possible, and the Liberal rank and file will have understood what it is.

They will likely meet together sooner than anticipated. That day, the premier of

Quebec will be able to alter the momentum of Canadian politics by addressing the people of Quebec.

The Premier's Speech

My dear fellow citizens,

Quebec has reached a turning point in its history. As you certainly know, the efforts of your government to ensure the minimum required for the development of Quebec within Confederation have failed because of the opposition of two provinces. In reality, these provinces were able to maintain their opposition to the end simply because they had support in most of the other provinces. Unfortunately, they have been able to thwart the prime minister of Canada and his government, who have long supported this project of national reconciliation. National reconciliation was the basis of the Meech Lake Accord, so poorly understood by those who preferred a simplistic and outworn concept of Canada.

Some will say we have been wasting our time. That is not my opinion, and that is not the analysis carried out by your government. First of all, the Meech Lake Accord was signed in June 1987 by the eleven heads of government in Canada, a resolution few people thought possible at the time. Unfortunately, time has undone this superb unanimity that gave us such hopes. In this respect, I want to point out that the clause, inserted in the constitution of 1982, giving the provinces three years to ratify a new agreement, introduces an element of extreme rigidity in the procedure for amending the fundamental law of the land.

In this sense, those who repatriated the constitution locked it up tightly, despite the injustice it did Quebec. It not only reduced Quebec's jurisdiction immediately without its consent but also left Quebec open to further raids because the amending formula rendered it defenseless before a coalition of seven other provinces. This explains

why Canada had to be brought back on a course more respectful of Quebec. No, we have not been wasting our time.

However, we must take note of the new situation and draw the proper conclusions. The world today moves with unbelievable speed. One only has to look at Europe, particularly at the Eastern European countries, which have decided, belatedly it is true, to adapt to the world of today. This world, which is ours as well, is one of international economic competition, accelerated technological development, and ever larger enterprises whose component parts must be ever more efficient. The state can't take the place of entrepreneurs, but it must provide the broad context that will encourage them on the road to excellence, the only one that can ensure a high level of social solidarity.

The government of Quebec, the only one exclusively concerned with the supreme interests of the province, does not currently have all the powers necessary to map out the economic future of Quebec. These powers, let me remind you, have been claimed by all the governments of Quebec, since Jean Lesage, the greatest Liberal in Quebec history, set the Quiet Revolution in motion.

The Meech Lake Accord was only the first step towards an overhaul of the Canadian system and included only the most urgent items on the agenda. Quebec's insistence on limitations to the federal government's spending power, written into the accord, shows that the present government of Quebec has never lost sight of the problem of the division of powers. Quebec also obtained the consolidation of its authority in matters of immigration, crucial for the future, as everyone knows. Unfortunately, we have been forced back to the starting point . . . and nothing suggests the possibility of a breakthrough for many years.

Can we afford to wait that long without any guarantee of success? If nothing is achieved by a combination of moderate demands from Quebec and a prime minister's tireless struggle for national reconciliation, isn't it illusory to expect that we will ever be in more favourable circumstances? To ask the question is to answer it. However, Quebec cannot afford to be a simple observer in the global village.

For several years, Quebec has been penalized by the fiscal and monetary policies of the federal government.

I have already indicated that there were limits to Quebec's patience. On many occasions, I have told representatives of other provinces that Quebec would have to respond should they fail to ratify the accord, which only awards the bare minimum. The conditions set out by Quebec in 1986 remained in effect, as long as there was an agreement, until June 23, 1990. There was no question of putting Quebec on stand-by after that date.

In spite of our goodwill, we of Quebec were unable to act in concert with our Canadian partners. We must therefore act quickly to seek a solution consistent with the superior interests of Quebec and the integrity of the common Canadian home. Our interests are often similar to those of other regions in Canada. We hope to preserve these links and enhance them. However, as regards the fundamental area of domestic policy — culture, communications, social affairs, and, naturally, the general framework of our domestic economic activity — the present organization of Canada is not the best suited to the goals and needs of the people of Quebec.

Conscious of my responsibilities as premier of the only French-speaking state in North America, tomorrow, in the name of the government of Quebec, I will be asking the Liberal Party convention to accept a resolution, supported by many constituencies, dealing with the creation of a new Canadian Economic Community, founded on the mutual respect of the two founding nations.

There are two fundamental points about the new Community. First, all direct and indirect taxes paid by Quebec residents and corporations will accrue to the government of Quebec, which will renounce any fiscal claims on the rest of Canada. Your government will thereby acquire the same latitude in social and economic matters that it now enjoys in education. Second, the Canadian economic entity, with all of its freedoms, will be preserved and consolidated, once there is an agreement for dividing the assets and liabilities of the government of Canada.

The maintenance of a common currency, and hence of a single central bank, is in the interest of both nations. Its management could be assigned to a board whose members would be appointed by each government in proportion to their population. As regards defense and foreign policy, which are now in flux because of upheavals in Europe, Quebec could remain associated with Canada, except for relations with the rest of the French-speaking world.

Links within the Canadian Community would still be closer than they will be within the European Economic Community, even after 1992. The Europe of 1993 will still be lacking a common currency, foreign policy and defense.

If the resolution is accepted by the Liberal Party, it will be submitted to the National Assembly as early as next week with the conviction that it will receive widespread support. Quebec will then be ready to start negotiations with its Canadian partners as soon as possible. With goodwill on each side, the talks could proceed rapidly to minimize concern and ensure the stability of the community. Quebec undertakes to submit the results of the negotiations to the population by way of referendum.

This marks a new start for Quebec and Canada. I have no doubt that the solidarity of Quebec and the intelligence and friendship of our Canadian friends will be present on this occasion when History beckons.

My fellow citizens, good night. *A bientôt.*

The Wild Fortnight

One can be sure that few people, particularly on the right bank of the Ottawa River, expected such a quick move. It destabilized the patchwork coalition opposing any modification of the status quo. The news went round the world, with a tremendous impact on money markets. The Canadian dollar took a dive until more realistic views prevailed in money markets and business, helped on by the developing political situation.

Uncertainty breeds instability. The premier's statement came as a shock. However, expecting as much, he remained calm. He held jokers that would ensure progress on three fronts simultaneously.

All the shots fired by Canadian and Anglo-Quebec opponents were aimed at a single spot: the presumed lack of mandate. For the first few days, Canada talked of nothing else but the fall of the dollar and the absence of a mandate. In Quebec, things were different, a re-enactment of November 15, 1976. Praise was lavished on the premier. The first polls, coming out a few days after the televised statement, showed he had the support of 65 percent of the population. Protests on the absence of a mandate faded away somewhat, and old slogans from 1980 were heard again: "Canada will not negotiate" or "There is nothing to negotiate."

Someone from Bay Street or Rue St-Jacques might tell them that, although they are riding the same horse, the racetrack has changed. A pencil and a sheet of paper explains it all with a few simple figures. The federal debt is twelve times higher than that of the Quebec government. Because of its composition (more short- than long-term loans) it is very vulnerable to momentary interest rate fluctuations. A rise of one percentage point can impose on Quebec an additional yearly outlay of about $70 million, while the corresponding burden for Ottawa is in excess of *$1.5 billion*. Not *noblesse* but *déficit oblige*.

Uncertainty affected the economy of Canada as well as that of Quebec. There is only one money market, and it would be surprising if, in such a situation, portfolio managers would trade Quebec and Ontario bonds for Canadian ones! Should they give in to panic, they would choose the American dollar. Canadian bonds would feel the blow. The Bank of Canada would have its hands full defending the Canadian dollar, by raising interest rates to arrest the flight of capital . . .

The government of Quebec wouldn't be in such a bad situation. If need be, it could count on the Caisse de dépôt et placement. But the whole point of "Operation Instability" lies elsewhere. The extra costs amount to a net loss for Ottawa. Things are very different with Quebec, which can expect a net gain of *at least* $1 billion a year by bringing its marbles home from Ottawa. This fact will help to cushion a few weeks of rocky weather and face the storm unleashed by stock exchanges and money markets. In addition, Quebec manufacturers find the Canadian dollar to be overvalued. So this is not David facing Goliath, or Lithuania against the Soviet Union.

Industrial and financial circles in Canada would soon voice the opinion that the marriage of the Maple Leaf with the Fleur-de-Lis isn't worth this whirlwind (particularly when most economic indicators are already sliding), and that the two governments might do well to sit down at the same table. They will say that this premier of Quebec is preferable to the leader of the Parti Québécois. "The devil we know is better than the one we don't."

And then the National Assembly had just passed with a very big majority the resolution proposing a New Canadian Community. Only anglophone members voted against it. Others swallowed hard . . . since the premier made the whole issue a matter of confidence. A large number of Canadians told themselves how embarassing it was to go against such a clear expression of the popular will, particularly as Canada had no alternative to offer.

Finally, the premier's proposal didn't seem so extravagant after all. He started circulating a little chart comparing his New Canadian Community (NCC) with the advancement of the European Economic Community at the beginning of 1991. One saw that, with respect to integration and

cooperation, that the NCC was way ahead of the EEC. The argument about going against the current of history was in trouble.

The Canadian government had lost its bearings. Contradictory signals were coming from the media and from all parts of the country. To negotiate or not to negotiate? Conservatives from Quebec were pressing the prime minister to opt for the first solution, but without making a fuss. It was a very delicate situation. How could a Canadian prime minister from Quebec possibly negotiate in Canada's name the "secession" of his home province? A tricky proposition. And shouldn't there be one last battle to

COMPARISON OF THE NEW CANADIAN COMMUNITY AND THE EUROPEAN ECONOMIC COMMUNITY JANUARY 1, 1991

	NCC	EEC
Free movement of persons	Yes	Minimal customs controls for nationals Customs controls for foreigners
Free movement of internal capital	Yes	Beginning July 1, 1990
Free movement of workers	Yes with exceptions	More or less for nationals None for foreign workers
Immigration policy	Two	Twelve
Citizenship	One, accessible	Twelve, difficult
Monetary policy	One	Quite a few, although subject to constraints
Fiscal policy	Two with constraints	Twelve
Income gap between rich and poor areas	1.5 to 1.0	5 to 1
Defence policy	Two armies one common policy	Twelve armies several policies
Foreign policy	Important common thread	Several common points Many discordant policies
Charter of minority language rights	Yes	No

prevent the breakup of the country? It was obvious, however, that he couldn't do anything without the support of the Quebec caucus, which sided more or less with Quebec.

Meanwhile, the Canadian finance minister was seeing red. Every attempt to deal with the deficit, causing the ruling party's popularity to sink, would come to nothing if this basic problem was not resolved very soon. But few of his cabinet colleagues were eager to get their feet wet, fearing the political consequences of being soft on Canada. No one wanted to be called the Canadian Chamberlain.

The premier of Quebec went around repeating that his plan safeguarded the essential point, the integrity of economic links with Canada, and that the new political arrangement did not put in doubt the friendship of Quebecers for Canadians. He had even committed himself to enshrining the rights of Quebec anglophones in a charter of minority rights to be annexed to the founding treaty of the New Canadian Community. But to bring the period of instability to an end, it was urgent to agree on a general draft. Accountants would have plenty of time later to assess the value of railway lines, highways, and buildings belonging to the federal government, and to split in a fair way the federal public debt.

No doubt English Canada would have accepted the proposition in the end. The positive aspects of Quebec's gesture were beginning to emerge: no more constitutional quarrels or language conflicts. Some people saw the prospect of a stronger Canadian government, while political parties calculated their own chances in the new Canada. Others claimed that the refusal to take Quebec's extended hand risked a real breakup of this two-headed country.

The idea of holding a referendum at the *end* rather than at the beginning of the whole process seemed to be the winning one. It had two objectives: to place the burden of instability on the country as a whole and to force the Canadian government to play its hand *before* an electoral consultation in Quebec. How can one ask the population to give its opinion of some initiative whose institutional ramifications are largely unknown?

No one was thinking about the new leader of the Opposition in the House of Commons and his confederates in the wings.

Finesse Royal

There was nothing surprising in his intervention. The Liberal Party of Canada had long believed itself the legitimate depository of power: it had ruled the country almost without interruption from 1921 to 1984. But without Quebec, it had little chance of regaining its former position. It had to strike a powerful blow. Since it had lost power in 1984, the party still had a master card, which it had used on two occasions. It would serve once again.

It was with a great pomp that the new leader of the Liberal Party announced that he would never allow the prime minister to destroy the country, claiming that neither Canada nor Quebec had any mandate for this sinister job, and promised he would use the Senate's veto if necessary to block any legislation authorizing Canada-Quebec negotiations. The new leader's occasional "godfather" applauded openly, hoping his prestige would tip the scales. Apparently, the people of Quebec would never be free of him. The duo put forward a very simple solution to end the deadlock, a referendum in Quebec asking voters "Are you in favour of Quebec independence?"

A short digression is in order at this point.

The Canadian Senate has a poor media image in Quebec. In fact, it is an intriguing problem for any democrat. If the criterion of democracy is the rule of law, in so far as laws are voted democratically, then the Senate can legitimately make use of the powers conferred under the constitution, including the refusal to ratify laws passed by the House of Commons. Democracy is sometimes incongruous, but the Senate and its powers survived in the constitution of 1982, adopted by the House of Commons by a wide majority.

The example shows that accepting the rules of the game does not always come easy. The paradox becomes more complicated when the Senate supports what we all consider the foundation of democracy, the right of citizens to pass judgement on particularly important pieces of legislation. This was the case when the Senate, at the request of John Turner, forced the Conservative government to go before the voters with the Free Trade Agreement before ratifying it. Unfortunately, few commentators seem to have understood that, if one happened to believe in democracy, it was possible to support both John Turner's decision *and* the Free Trade Agreement. End of digression.

But one can always be outsmarted. The Liberal opposition's decision to block the beginning of a dialogue between Quebec and Ottawa was the straw that broke the camel's back in Quebec; it also drew the reprobation of the English Canada, which thought it was an incendiary gesture. The premier of Quebec saw an opening allowing him to use his fourth joker — and to alter once again the dynamics of the situation to his advantage.

The quick succession of events took everyone by surprise. The ball started rolling when the Conservative minister from Lac St-Jean, head of the Quebec wing of the caucus, rose in the House of Commons to read in French a statement prepared by the government at a special all-night meeting. It was also read in English by the deputy prime minister, who still enjoyed modest credibility in English Canada. The state-

ment announced a three-point plan to end the stalemate.

First of all, a draft treaty would immediately be signed with Quebec to guarantee, whatever happened, the maintenance of the Canadian economic union and of the Canadian currency. The plumbing was safe.

Secondly, a referendum would be held on the same day in Quebec and in English Canada, at the earliest possible moment. The question would be identical, except for two words. In Quebec, responsibility for the referendum would fall on the provincial government which, after consultation, had agreed to the wording of the question:

The Government of Quebec wishes to repatriate all taxes paid by Quebecers to the Canadian Government and exempt Quebec from Canadian laws, while preserving the Canadian common market and the Canadian currency, the foundations of the New Canadian Community. Are you ready to give the Government of Quebec a mandate to negotiate these points speedily and in good faith with the Government of Canada?

In the question addressed to English Canada, where the referendum was to be held under federal authority, the words Quebec and Canada were interchanged in the last sentence.

The law making the referendum possible would be introduced as quickly as possible in Parliament.

The move did not necessarily thwart possible obstruction by the Senate. Hence, the third paragraph in the statement, which reasserted the government's intention to obtain amicably or otherwise the Senate's assent to the referendum bill. End of statement.

The opposition was obviously stunned, particularly the Liberals. Their threat of obstruction had boomeranged. Some New Democrats, nimble with figures, were already assessing their chances of becoming the official Opposition in the new Canada.

A great many people were surprised at the absence of the prime minister on this historic day. They did not have to wait long for an answer. A terse communiqué from the Prime Minister's Office, that very evening, disclosed that he had resigned his political functions. The failure of the Canada he had known and loved was also his own, and he had drawn the proper conclusions.

Stockbrokers and money traders worked as hard that day as they had on preceding ones, but the atmosphere was certainly more relaxed. Investors were bargain-hunting, and there was no lack of opportunities. People had lost their heads for a while, but in the end the New Canadian Community was still the land of the future, whatever its name, wasn't it?

The United States and France quickly dispatched telegrams of congratulation to the deputy prime minister, who was acting as caretaker until the Conservative Party chose a temporary successor for the former prime minister.

The premier of Quebec knew that evening that he had won the game of a lifetime. The rest was just a series of formalities.

The Great Clarification

Political reporters managed to piece together the events leading to this dramatic dénouement. The reconstituted story was as follows.

Anger was running high in the Quebec Conservative caucus, ever since the Liberal leader of the opposition had put his cards on the table. Many MPs, remembering the days of May 1980 and November 1981, felt it was now or never.

A few of them worked out a strategy supported by a majority in the caucus. The situation required a common front, complete solidarity. From the very beginning of the crisis, ministers had been in constant contact with Quebec. The background of

the historic statement was coming into view. The idea of a national referendum had taken most people by surprise. Many thought it was a trap, but finally understood that it was the logical outcome of the course chosen by Quebec.

The policy of the outstretched hand to English Canada required some mechanism allowing English-Canadian groups, who were eager to reciprocate but unwilling to go public about their feelings, to express their views. It was a checkered coalition, if ever there was one. It included friends of Quebec, people who were fed up with bilingualism (half the population), and the diehards who wanted Quebec out. It comprised a large number of people. The idea of the referendum also signaled that a page had been turned and that the time had come to think of the future. In this context, common sense was on the Yes side.

English Canada's Yes would not necessarily be enthusiastic. However, that English-Canadians were getting a chance to decide on a historic change directly concerning them gave the Yes campaign an important psychological advantage, which helped Quebec's cause. Moreover, public opinion polls could be expected to create a strong movement in English Canada in favour of the Yes side, particularly because of its very strong and early lead in Quebec.

Post-referendum negotiations would therefore proceed much more smoothly, with troublemakers out of the way.

But how could this simple and elegant solution be imposed on the Canadian government? The minister from Lac St-Jean was given the mission, requiring all the diplomacy of which he was capable. He also had plenty of ammunition and had the support of almost all of the other ministers from Quebec, who had put aside their disagreements for the occasion.

He could also count on the support of the Bloc Québécois, which gathered behind the charismatic figure of a former ambassador to France quite a few ex-Conservatives, and even some ex-Liberals.

The message was a simple one. The government could accept the three conditions (to be made public the next day), continue in power after the referendum, and enter into negotiations with Quebec. It would thus become the first government of the new Canada and earn the public's gratitude for having skilfully steered the ship through the storm and avoided the worst. Or it could reject the three conditions, in which case it forfeited the support of the Quebec caucus. Ministers from English Canada winced, being aware of the latest poll results. An election at this moment would be disastrous for the country, and would certainly bring about the destruction of their party in English Canada.

The prime minister violently objected to the proposal of his Quebec minister. But he was alone. The alternative he proposed was a constitutional conference of eleven heads of government, which seemed ridiculous in the context. Someone made the remark that this possibility had been closed since June 23, 1990.

All members of the government were aware of the choice before them: a showdown with Quebec, whose outcome and consequences no one could predict, or a new kind of political community. Canadians were basically reasonable people who wanted only one thing: get this Quebec business over with once and for all. But now the choice was between the prime minister and a more serene future. Politics is not an easy game. Many of them were holding back tears as the prime minister shook their hands one last time before disappearing into the night.

End of the reconstitution.

Announcement of the national referendum took everyone by surprise. The Liberal opposition was completely non-plussed when the government took its suggestion literally, deciding to consult the population. It had little credibility in Quebec, home of its leader. It could hardly campaign for the No west of Quebec without risking serious accusations. Wasn't this the party that had ruthlessly tried to build an impossible Canada, which had misled English Canada about the true feelings of Quebec? And it continued to fan the flames?

Voters were eager to get it over with. A single cry emerged from English Canada: *Referendum now!*— Members of the Senate made themselves scarce. The referendum bill was given three readings in quick succession in the House of Commons; just enough senators turned up for speedy approval by the Senate.

A number of developments during the referendum campaign came as no surprise to attentive observers of the Canadian scene. First, few groups in English Canada openly supported the No, except in the Maritime provinces, whose geographic situation was now thought very unfavourable. The Maritimes insisted on comparing themselves with the Pakistan of old, while others suggested that Alaska might be more appropriate. French minorities across Canada were in mourning, in spite of various proposals for a charter of minority language rights, and even though a few had come to the conclusion that the future, with or without Quebec, was not bright. The anglophone minority in Quebec waged a lonely campaign for the No. It was a far cry from the heady days of 1980.

Everyone else had reasons for voting Yes. Ontario was eager to preserve close economic ties with Quebec. The western provinces saw Quebec's departure as an opportunity to play an expanded role in the new Canadian federation, whose centre of gravity would necessarily be shifting westward. The Reform Party, the rising star of

Canadian politics, was campaigning enthusiastically for the Yes.

Finally, the campaign allowed national parties, who were feeling their way carefully (except for the Reform Party) in the new political configuration, a kind of dress rehearsal.

Canadian Liberals finally grasped what a disastrous choice they had made on June 23, 1990, when the leadership was taken over by a Quebecer who had once been highly popular in English Canada. Events had moved incredibly fast. The new leader was now resigned to the inevitable. He was the wrong man at the wrong place at the wrong time. The party had gone downhill and a new "salesman" was necessary. The choice quickly focused on a woman who had made a good impression during the long leadership campaign in the first half of 1990.

The referendum campaign constituted a period of reflection on the future of the new Canada. Topics of discussion were not lacking: should certain provinces be merged for better use of available human resources? Was a new constitution necessary? The west was highly impatient over the Senate, which would certainly be reformed. On the other hand, the possibility of joining the United States was hardly mentioned. The omission confirmed the views of a renowned American sociologist who concluded, at the end of the eighties, that Canada and the United States were like two trains that, after traveling along parallel lines for quite a long distance, found themselves after two hundred years as far from each other as ever.

Many observers thought the campaign in English Canada was the more interesting, the Quebec one becoming repetitive for lack of serious opposition.

The outcome of the double vote soon became self-evident.

The premier of Quebec thus enjoyed a strategic success worthy of George Patton, one of the celebrated generals of this century. Quick to spot openings and take advantage of them, Patton could not resist being sarcastic about his rival, General Montgomery, whose wait-and-see tactics proved to be extremely costly for the Anglo-American Allies in 1944 and 1945. The premier, with the support of public opinion, had masterfully played the card of instability. He had never been a peddler of dreams. He was content to be the man of common sense.

His happiness was marred only by one vexing little cloud. Some friendships had been lost, probably forever. But hadn't politics always been his first love?

D-Day

The treaty defining the legal framework and the institutions of the New Canadian Community was negotiated quickly and in good faith. Many passages were borrowed from the Canada–U.S. Free Trade Agreement and from the regulations of the European Economic Community. More contentious questions, such as sharing the assets of Crown corporations, were to be submitted to the newly created Court of the Community.

On D-Day, all assets of the federal government in Quebec became the property of the Quebec government, which renounced all property claims on the rest of Canada. Quebec's estimated share of the federal public debt was added to its own. All federal civil servants working in Quebec kept the same offices and the same bosses. Quebecers working for the federal government in Ottawa were relocated for the most part to Hull in comparable jobs. A few years would be needed to rationalize all this.

All federally chartered companies obtained charters from Quebec.

Obviously, there would be another anglophone exodus from Montreal, which would be partly offset this time by an influx of former federal civil servants and francophones from other parts of Canada who were finally deciding to live as members of a majority.

Some companies were hesitant about investing in Quebec. However, the government planned to make use of its greater budgetary leeway to support basic research, the restructuring of Quebec firms, and their participation in international trade. The government also planned to fully use for marketing purposes Quebec's social and cultural distinctiveness. Furthermore, many mandarins, who had made the jump from Ottawa to Quebec, were eager to get down to work.

Many analysts were beginning to take bets on the chances of the former province and of the New Canadian Community. In the year 2000, would they be speaking about the economic miracle of Quebec, or of its economic demise?

The answer to this question rested with about seven million people. There could be no scapegoats now.

This will be another story altogether. We know for sure that it will have its share of surprises.

Epilogue

Two nations, who do not dislike each other (too much), are about to set their public affairs in order and draw the line on half a century of conflicts and recriminations. They will exchange a difficult and costly cohabitation for a cooperative relationship, which has every chance of being simple and fruitful. What France and Germany have achieved, in spite of the very painful events of the past — would that be out of reach for Quebec and Canada?

There are some who believe that the balkanization of Canada, followed by [annexation] to the United States, will be inevitable after Quebec's political exit. In other words, Quebec has been simultaneously the most discordant unit of Confederation and its cement! This is a paradox for students of philosophy. We tend to forget that people in the rest of Canada will recover *their* homeland and that their desire for independence is just as keen as Quebec's.

These two nations might have understood each other if merchants of illusion had not been so long in power. With a great deal of arrogance, they proposed unattainable goals. They had self-confidence and believed they were in tune with the thrust of History, when in fact they perched on one of the accidental peaks of the century. History is following its course, and these utopians from another age will disappear from its rearview mirror.

The failure of the Meech Lake Accord, the irrationality of Canadian federalism and its attending costs, will inspire Quebec to cut the Gordian knot. Who knows if the project for a new Canadian community will not become a model for European countries trying to come to grips with the inextricable problem of nationalities?

Time will pass and, some day, people will wonder about these Byzantine discussions on the pertinence of a solution wholly in line with contemporary developments.

And others will come to join us, participating with us in the growth of Quebec, this French land in America.

MOSAIC MADNESS
Reginald W. Bibby

On an ordinary September night in 1988, a far from ordinary event took place. A man from Canada did something no other human had previously done. He blazed

From *Mosaic Madness: The Poverty and Potential of Life in Canada* by Reginald W. Bibby, 1990. By permission of Stoddart Publishing Co. Limited.

down a track in Korea in the fastest time ever, and a nation enjoyed a rare moment of collective ecstasy as he leaned over and accepted the gold. The fact that he was assisted by a banned drug soon transformed jubilant celebration into painful disappointment and anger. Millions who had passionately cheered now passionately chided. Some reminded the critics that any young man might well have broken under the pressure of such gigantic national expectations. In the end, Ben Johnson seems to have done what was best for Ben Johnson. And a nation walked away. Did Ben Johnson have any obligation to Canada? Did Canada have any obligation to Ben Johnson? Was it wrong for him to break the rules? Was it wrong to have any rules? Was it wrong only because he got caught?

In Victoria just a few weeks earlier, Canada's largest Protestant denomination acknowledged that sexual orientation should not be a barrier to full participation in the Church. Practicing homosexuals could be ordained as Christian ministers. While some applauded the United Church decision as prophetic, large numbers of members and adherents felt betrayed, and some threatened to leave. The controversy continues into the 1990s. If individual faith is tied to religious community, what happens when one's group does not represent one's views? Is the individual led by God? Is the group led by God? Is no one led by God? Is truth just an outdated illusion, replaced in our time by personal preference?

Canadians were no better prepared to respond to an international controversy that erupted in early 1989 after an author attacked a major religion and found himself condemned to die. It was an unlikely matchup — Salman Rushdie v. Ayatollah Khomeini — with a worldwide audience looking on. Is ultimate good found in being open to unlimited expression, or are there times when such expression is purchased at the price of others' pain, and therefore

must be denied? Does freedom of expression include the freedom to assail what some cherish or, in turn, to assail the assailer . . . and then to assail the assailer of the assailer? Is there no limit to such a regression of individual rights, some boundary that preserves what is socially important?

Then there was the turban controversy. In 1989, the federal Solicitor General announced that the face of the RCMP would be altered to better reflect the changing nature of Canadian society. Variations to the uniform would be considered; Sikhs might be allowed to wear turbans. A great outcry was heard, particularly from western Canada. Some people, including the Prime Minister, saw the protest as blatant racism. Others maintained that the changes represented the dismantling of one of the cherished symbols of Canadian life. In a pluralistic society, is it possible to have *any* collective symbols that do not offend the cultural inclinations of some? Is it possible to have consensus on anything at a national level? Does the invitation to come to Canada carry an expectation that accommodations will be made to our culture? Are we expecting more of ourselves than other people would expect of us in their countries?

The June 1990 failure to ratify the Meech Lake Accord renewed speculation that Quebec would abandon its traditional place in Canada. After three years of doomsday proclamations and mounting anxiety, Canadians were left, not with a positive outcome, but with more uncertainty than ever about the country's future. Is such ongoing strain really necessary? Can Quebec and the rest of Canada not decide what is best for each other? When will Quebec decide what it wants from Canada? When will the rest of Canada respect Quebec's wishes and get on with life? How long must we live in such political limbo, giving our resources and energies to such debilitating "nation-building"?

Incidents and issues such as these are a reflection of a crisis in social life that Canadians are experiencing from coast to coast. It's more than Meech Lake; together or apart, Canada and Quebec will continue to experience the crisis. It's more than Free Trade or the GST. It's more than federalism or regionalism, racism or sexism. It's almost Canadian sacrilege to say it, but still it needs to be said: the crisis stems from the unintended consequences of the policy that is our pride and joy — *pluralism.*

The Heralded Mosaic

Faced with the problem of creating a society in which people of varied linguistic and cultural backgrounds can live together, Canadians have decided to convert a demographic reality into a national virtue. We have decreed that what is descriptively obvious should be prescriptively valued. Canada, we have concluded, will be a multinational society, a multicultural mosaic of people from varied backgrounds who will have the freedom to live as they see fit.

FREEDOM FOR EVERYONE

In this country, there will be no pressure, as there is in some other countries — notably the United States — to discard one's cultural past, and conform to the dominant culture. The name of the Canadian cultural game is not *melting* but *mosaic.* Our premier spokesman for a multinational Canada, Pierre Elliott Trudeau, eloquently expressed things this way: "Canada . . . is a human place, a sanctuary of sanity in an increasingly troubled world. We need not search further for our identity. These traits of tolerance and courtesy and respect for our environment and one another provide it. I suggest that a superior form of identity would be difficult to find." The central goal of Canadian life has become harmonious coexistence, the central means equality

and justice. We aspire to accept and respect the ideas and lifestyles of one another, to be equitable and fair. Beyond mere platitudes, Canada has enshrined good intentions in bilingual and multicultural policies, along with a Charter of Rights and Freedoms.

In Canada, we decry any signs of racism or bigotry, exploitation or abuse. We have written laws into our criminal code that prohibit the willful promotion of hatred against any identifiable group. Our social scientists — going back at least to Carleton University's John Porter and his *Vertical Mosaic* of 1965 — have given preeminent attention to issues of equality and justice as they affect minorities, women, the poor, and others. The media instill in us the primacy of such issues by consistently treating charges of racism or unfair treatment as front-page news.

Few events have more dramatically disclosed the importance that Canada officially gives to equality than the national soul-searching that followed the tragic slaying of fourteen young women at the University of Montreal in November 1989. As Canadians, we have aspired to coexistence; there is no place here for disrespect, let alone hatred. The charges of rampant sexism and misogyny in the aftermath of Montreal left the nation dazed. What was being attacked was not our Achilles heel but our heart. Peaceful coexistence has been our national dream. In Montreal, that dream was interrupted by a nightmare.

Canada might not be among the world's elite nations, especially when we compare ourselves with our giant cousin to the south. But we like to believe that we have one special thing going for us — our mosaic. Joe Clark's oft-cited phrase sums up our self-image: "We are a community of communities." Such an endorsement of pluralism, we have believed, gives us a social system and a social outlook that is right for the day. As two York University sociologists, Linda Hunter and Judith Posner, put it "Canada as a whole presents a neutral, affable face that distinguishes the country, for example, from its more exuberant and aggressive neighbor. . . . Canada's gentler cultural presence may be ahead of its time."

There we have it: a country comprised of diversified groups that together comprise a mosaic — except there's more. Our emphasis on *individual* freedom means that beyond the cultural groups that comprise the national mosaic, we also have individual mosaic pieces within each group. If the prophet Ezekiel saw "wheels within wheels" as he looked toward the heavens, those looking toward Canada today see "mosaics within mosaics."

Our mosaics have not stopped with the sphere of intergroup relations. Pluralism at the group and individual levels has become part of the Canadian psyche. Some time ago it left its cultural cradle. The pluralism infant has been growing up in the past three decades. It has been traveling across the country, visiting our moral, religious, family, educational, and political spheres. We now have not only a cultural mosaic but also a moral mosaic, a meaning system mosaic, a family structure mosaic, a sexual mosaic. And that's just the shortlist. Pluralism has come to pervade Canadian minds and Canadian institutions.

Everywhere it has traveled, pluralism has left behind its familiar emphases — tolerance, respect, appreciation for diversity, the insistence that individuals must be free to think and to behave according to their consciences. The result is that ours has become a society in which everything seems possible.

IMPROVING ON TRUTH

Pluralism translates into emancipated groups and emancipated individuals. Indispensable to such a posture is the accompanying declaration that all viewpoints are equally valid and that all pursuits are equally noble.

Such legitimization of diverse choice has been provided by the widespread acceptance of *relativism*. Absolutists assert that truth transcends cultures and individuals. In contrast, relativists assert that viewpoints reflect the social and intellectual settings from which people come. "Truth" is socially constructed. Consequently, the origin of ideas is not mysterious; ideas can be traced back to social locations.

The emphasis on relativism grew out of the laudable desire of nineteenth-century social scientists to described foreign cultures in the cultures' own terms. Marriage and sexual practices in Polynesia, for instance, should be described in Polynesian terms, rather than in terms that flow from Western assumptions and practices. Many philosophers made similar efforts. Ethical relativism, for example, recognizes that fundamental differences in ethical views and practices fall along cultural lines, with no one position necessarily transcending all cultures.

In Canada, pluralism articulates the pathway to group and individual freedom. But relativism plays the important role of providing the rationale for freedom of thought and behavior. If pluralism is the pitcher, relativism is the center-fielder. Relativism pronounces that it is appropriate and ideal that a culture encourage a wide variety of views and lifestyles. Pluralism establishes choices; relativism declares the choices valid.

It all sounds reasonable and logical, maybe even a shade ingenious. The picture that emerges, according to sociologist Carol Agòcs, is one of Canadian culture as an intricate tapestry of many hues, woven from the strands of many cultures. At its best, Canada stands as a model to the world, a nation that can be a home to people of all nations and cultures, a microcosm of the harmony and peace that are possible when cultural diversity is tolerated and respected.

But then again, not a few times in history the unsound has been mistaken for the profound.

Too Much of a Good Thing

Social life has always required a balance between the individual and the group. It also has required a balance between encouraging choice and insisting on the careful evaluation of choices in order to determine which positions are better, best, and true.

Since the 1960s, Canada has been encouraging the freedom of groups and individuals without simultaneously laying down cultural expectations. Canada has also been encouraging the expression of viewpoints without simultaneously insisting on the importance of evaluating the merits of those viewpoints. During the past thirty years, colorful collages of mosaics have been forming throughout Canadian life. Our expectation has been that fragments of the mosaic will somehow add up to a healthy and cohesive society. It is not at all clear why we should expect such an outcome.

To encourage individual mosaic fragments may well result in the production of individual mosaic fragments — and not much more. The multiculturalism assumption — that a positive sense of one's group will lead to tolerance and respect of other groups — has not received strong support, notes McGill University sociologist Morton Weinfeld. The evidence, he says, "suggests a kind of ethnocentric effect, so that greater preoccupation with one's own group makes one more distant from and antipathetic to others."

The evaluation research, however, has just begun. The official enshrinement of pluralism is a fairly recent development, dating back only to 1969 in the case of bilingualism, 1971 for multiculturalism, and 1982 for the Charter of Rights and Freedoms. The truth of the matter is that we know very little about the effects of pluralism on our culture as a whole. We also don't have the luxury of being able to look to other countries to get some sneak previews of how things will turn out. While other societies may be pluralistic in the sense that they are culturally diverse, virtually no other country actually declares itself "multicultural." England, for example, is culturally varied, but people are expected to be "English" — however culturally inflated that concept may be. Similarly, the United States is culturally diverse, but there has been a historical sense that people who come to America become Americans, regardless of how much they may value the cultures of their homelands. Demographer Myron Weiner comments that societies are rarely open to the arrival of persons with racial or ethnic characteristics different from their own. Consequently it is no exaggeration to say that Canada is a world leader in enshrining multinationalism and multiculturalism. "In a sense," says sociologist Roderic Beaujot of the University of Western Ontario, "Canada is trying something unique and needs to ensure that this continues to be a successful experiment."

The early returns for pluralism's impact on life in this country are just now starting to come in. The preliminary results indicate that pluralism is having some significant, unanticipated consequences. For starters, our rights are outdistancing our rules. Armed with our new Charter, groups and individuals are insisting that they are entitled to the right to equal expression, participation, and prosperity. Racial minorities, women, the elderly, and the disabled are working hard to combat inequities. Individuals are invoking the Charter as they square off on every topic imaginable — abortion, homosexuality, knowingly transmitting AIDS, euthanasia, blood transfusions, the spreading of hatred, crosses in Remembrance Day celebrations, Sunday shopping, religion in the schools, female participation in sports, the wearing of turbans, membership in private clubs, age- and gender-based insurance rates, mandatory breathalyzer tests, mandatory wearing of seat belts, displaying excessive tattoos, being drunk in a public place, gun controls, opposition to all-White male regiments, and on and on.

As George Bain put it, in his nationally syndicated column of June 16, 1990: "... Canadians have a lamentably limited capacity to see a national interest broader than the membership list of the occupational, economic, cultural, ethnic, gender, environmental, or other groups with which they identify in spirit if not formally."

Given our emphasis on equality and justice, it's fair enough that we Canadians insist on our rights. However, when our own rights conflict with another person's rights — as is increasingly the case —we obviously have a problem. Something has to give. Unfortunately, pluralism Canadian-style is showing a limited ability to provide a way out.

RESOLVING CONFLICTING RIGHTS

One possibility is for both of us to give a little and seek a solution where we both win, where we both get as much as is socially possible of what we want. In popular parlance, the goal is a win-win outcome. But the current Canadian obsession with group and individual rights doesn't seem to include the inclination to give up much of anything. People seem to want a total victory, "a blow out." Many Canadians come precariously close to equating "win-win" with the forfeiting of integrity, "win-lose" with the triumph of right.

The abortion debate is a case in point. Both sides have shown little sign of being willing to settle for anything less than a shutout of the opposition. Nothing short of a win-lose situation will do. For politicians, the abortion debate is a no-win issue because everyone wants a win-lose outcome, including many politicians themselves. Following the May 1990 Commons' passing of the new abortion legislation, Justice Minister Kim Campbell told reporters, "We have found some common ground." But anti-abortionist Liberal Don Boudria said, "If the government thinks this issue is going to go away, it is mistaken." Pro-abortionist Dawn Black of the NDP predicted that women would "continue to struggle" until they are "fully equal, participating citizens in this country."

Future historians will note with interest that we applauded a Charter of Rights and

CRISIS? WHAT CRISIS?

	% AGREEING					
	NAT	BC	PR	ONT	QUE	ATL
In general, the Charter is a good thing for Canada.	81	76	79	82	89	80
The Charter of Rights will strengthen Canadian national identity.	63	58	62	59	66	71
The idea that everyone has a right to their own opinion is being carried too far these days.	38	34	35	32	48	40

Source: *Charter Survey*, YorkXdays.

Freedoms but had no counterbalancing Charter of Social Responsibility. As long as we ourselves won, we frequently were content to blank our opponents.

If win-win is out of the question, a second logical way to resolve conflicting rights might be to introduce an outside standard to determine which position is the more correct or appropriate. The problem here however is that relativism has decreed that all viewpoints have equal value.

No one viewpoint is superior to or more accurate than others; no one lifestyle is more valid than others. To live by the sword of relativisim, which sanctioned collective and individual pluralism, may also be to die by it.

In Canada, truth has become little more than personal opinion. "It's all relative," declare Canadians from British Columbia to Newfoundland. Consequently, we aren't sure how to respond to Ben Johnson, to homosexuals who want to be ordained, to writers whose works upset others, to the desire to preserve valued cultural symbols. Relativism has slain moral consensus. It has stripped us of our ethical and moral guidelines, leaving us with no authoritative instruments with which to measure social life. Our standards for evaluating ideas and behavior have been restricted to our local cultural and religious domains. Those same historians who never found our charter of social responsibility will further note that we were a country that was a champion of choice, that we triumphantly discarded the idea that there are better and best choices in favour of worshipping choice as an end in itself.

A CAUSE FOR PAUSE

If we don't resolve our difficulties by pursuing a win-win solution or by using an outside ethical standard, the remaining recourse is the courthouse. And, in case no one has noticed, that's where we are in-

creasingly ending up. As we approach the new century, we find ourselves playing a disorganized social game. We are stressing individual rights over social rules and hiring legal technicians as our referees. Our team spirit — our social spirit — is frequently nonexistent. The Canadian social game is also bogging down because we are cheering for all plays instead of the best plays. In declaring everything equal, we are ceasing to explore what is better and best, personally and socially. The attention given to the individual's rights and potential has been extremely important in this century, but it has become increasingly detached from what is socially beneficial, resulting in excessive *individualism.*

Together, individualism and relativism make social life difficult indeed, in the long run perhaps impossible. Individualism focuses on the individual to the detriment of the group. Relativism, taken to an extreme, erases agreement on the norms that are essential to social life.

Unbridled individualism and relativism are obviously not new problems. But conditions do not have to be new in order to be destructive. Moreover, conditions that don't go away may well be more threatening to societies at some points in history rather than at others. In our time, excessive individualism and relativism may well be two of the most serious threats to social life in Canada. With the movement of many of the world's nations toward greater freedom and individualism and toward pluralism and relativism, there is good reason to believe that the threat to social life will become increasingly global as well.

In its zeal to promote coexistence, Canada may find itself a world leader in promoting the breakdown of group life and the abandonment of the pursuit of the best. Individually, we have been emancipated; socially, we are in disarray. Despite a generally high level of affluence, Canadians these days seem frustrated, restless, and nervous. Author Pierre Berton recently said, "I haven't seen the country as mean-spirited since the Depression." In April 1990, Montreal *La Presse* columnist Ly-sianne Gagnon wrote, "Obviously the mood of the country is terrible." In the same month, *Winnipeg Free Press* editor John Dafoe described the nation as "fract-ious," saying that the most disturbing thing is "a certain lack of community. People seem to be very wrapped up in their own problems." *Maclean's* editor Kevin Doyle summed things up this way: "At a time when the world seems to be on the brink of a new era of hope and change and freedom, symbolized by the events in Eastern Europe and the Soviet Union, Canadians [seem] to be blocked in a time warp, iso-lated and anxious about the future."

Such is the madness characterizing the country today. . . .

I'm a fairly typical Canadian. My grand-parents on my father's side were Amer-icans from Pennsylvania and Missouri, a generation removed from England. My mother's parents were from small Welsh villages. The Welsh link has been dominant — with some regularity I venture back to Cardiff and wander around rural Wales, imagining what the past may have been like. I also feel at home in the United States. I have lived there for two stretches of three years each, and frequently visit.

But while I cherish my national heritages, I am a Canadian, which for me means much more than being a Welsh-American hybrid who attends Welsh song festivals and watches American sports on TV. Living in Canada means more than merely sharing common geographical turf with an assort-ment of other cultural hybrids and pure-breds who are all encouraged to give pre-eminence to the national cultures of their origins.

Why? For one thing, I have only a slight grasp of my Welsh past, and my American heritage was never really cultivated. More-over, what I know of both leaves me with an appreciation for the aspects of each that are positive, but with no desire to perpetuate the features that need improvement.

So where does that leave me, and thou-sands — no millions — of other Canadians, in a country that tells us that our national end is to live out our cultural heritages? The answer lies in taking a closer look at our ancestral past.

The Dream That Created Diversity

The vast majority of our parents, grand-parents, and great-grandparents came to Canada not to live out the old life here, but to find a new life, one much better than what they had known in the countries of their birth.

In May 1990, as I drove up the winding narrow road that leads to the village of Nasareth in northern Wales and again looked at the rolling, sheep-dotted hill-sides, I thought of the risk that my grand-father — then only a young man in his early twenties — had taken embarking on that long voyage to Canada, never to return. As I walked down the narrow little main street of Corris in central Wales, where my grand-mother had walked as a child, I was moved to think of the risk she had taken as a young woman heading off to the distant and un-known land of Canada. She too, would never see her homeland again.

They and so many other hundreds of thousands of immigrants came to Canada because they had a dream of a better life. Historically, there is perhaps no single characteristic more common among those varied new arrivals than that dream. Our relatives who preceded us from Britain and France, from the rest of Europe and Asia and Africa and the Americas, came because they saw hope of better things. It is not an exaggeration to say that the dream of a better life is the very source of our cultural diversity.

That dream needs to be reemphasized in our time. We, like they, want to stay alive and live well. That's why it's so important that we resolve the issue of coexistence, so that we who have come to Canada and those who were here when we arrived together can give our energies to pursuing the best existence possible in this land.

Our cultural diversity is one of our richest assets. Our dream of well-being — along with a willingness to work for it — is a goal that brings cohesion to that diversity. Social sanity lies in refocusing on the dream that created a multinational Canada.

What It Will Take

A question of motivation emerges from this analysis: What will it take for Canadians to move on to better things? What will lead people to become more concerned about a balance between individualism and the group, more concerned about pursuing the best of available choices? What will lead institutions to encourage such emphases, when they have thought it to be in their best interests to stress individualism and relativism?

One can appeal to altruism, urging Canadians to have a greater concern for the social good. I would like to believe that there are large numbers of people from Newfoundland to British Columbia who would respond to such a plea. While individualism is rampant, there is, I believe, a growing recognition of some of its destructive results. Many of us feel a certain revulsion when individuals and organizations experience success at the expense of others. We certainly applaud winning; but little affirmation is given to those who win with callous disregard for those who lose. Many, I think, are attracted to the idea of a Canada that is committed to the goal of social and personal well-being, that values individuality while emphasizing themes like problem-solving and communication as means to better group life.

Similarly, the importance of pursuing the best of available possibilities is not "a hard sell." To call Canadians to be discerning is to ask them to think more, not less.

Many of these "reflective altruists" are, of course, already well aware of the need for balance and pursuit of the best. The hope is that they will be joined by other people who have aspired to good personal and group life, but just now are beginning to catch a glimpse of what it is going to take to make it happen.

The appeal to altruistic concern for the well-being of the entire society of course has definite limits. Philosophers provide the arguments and sociologists and psychologists the data that make the conclusion clear: significant numbers of Canadians are guided by self-interest, plain and simple. Egoism is alive and well in this country. That leaves us with the tough question: What will it take to bring these people around?

Fortunately, there is an answer: their very self-interest! As Freda Paltiel, a senior policy adviser to Health and Welfare Canada recently put it, when people who have power are asked to share it, they tend to have three typical responses. The first is, "Gee, ma, do I have to?" The second is, "Are you going to make me?" And, if the first two fail, the third is, "What happens to me if I don't?" We now are at the "what happens to me" stage. It would be preferable for Canadians to opt for balance and pursuit of the best out of concern for the society as a whole; however, the truth of the matter is that, in the long run, no one has much choice.

If we continue to insist on individualism at the expense of society as a whole, at best we are simply going to coexist and subsist, nationally, institutionally, relationally. At worst, we are going to experience ever-increasing social disintegration. Large chunks of the nation are going to be snapped off; the possible secession of Quebec, rather than being the end of a problem, will only be the beginning of many more. Other parts — the Atlantic region, the West, the Territories — could just as readily follow suit. Organizationally and interpersonally, excessive individualism and relativism will make group life and personal relationships all the more difficult.

Where does it all end? That's hard to say. Where does sanity begin? That's easy to say: it begins with Canadians, whether motivated by concern for others or concern for self, finding a balance between the individual and the group, and together pursuing the best kind of life possible. The alternatives lie before us like a divided highway that is coming up fast. One side is marked with a "proceed" arrow, the other with a circled X. I hope we will opt for sanity.

The Moral of the Canadian Story

And so we return to where we began. A world that is intent on freedom and increasingly open to individualism, pluralism, and relativism would do well to watch the drama being produced in Canada. Former British Columbia Supreme Court justice Thomas Berger goes so far as to say that "the idea of two linguistic communities living and working together is something that *has* to succeed. If we can't do it in this country," he says, "what hope do they have in countries like Israel, Ireland or Pakistan? We have an educated population, a tolerant population and we have a high standard of living. If we can't make it work, who can?"

We may well see not only Canada but our *world* slip increasingly into social chaos. Still, that's the worst scenario. Many times in our history and world history, when compassion and reason have failed, a re-

sidual resource has surfaced: necessity. It's almost as if the gods let us "mess things up" close to the point of self-annihilation, and then say, "Enough's enough, the game is over; it's time to get serious and tidy up."

In Canada and elsewhere, the altruist and egoist alike may soon have little choice but to give up the luxury of their differences and give increased attention to balance and best. The alternative is not attractive. The times call for people to make social life work, to embark on problem-solving and the conscious pursuit of the best kind of existence possible. Whether born of virtue or expediency, there is still much hope. Nationally and globally, madness can yet give way to sanity. But it's time to make our move.

ABORIGINAL RIGHTS: THE VIEW OF THE ABORIGINAL PEOPLES
Michael Asch

Aboriginal peoples have long maintained that they have "special" rights that differentiate them from other Canadians. These rights, which include property rights (such as title to unceded lands), rights to hunt, fish and trap on traditional lands and political rights (such as the right to self-government), are presently called "aboriginal rights." . . . I shall describe the current position of aboriginal organizations with respect to political rights, only. Although there are different ways to conceptualize the basis of the legitimacy of special property and use rights . . ., it is apparent that, ultimately, aboriginal peoples would perceive these as flowing from the same source as their political rights. In this sense, then, while focussing on political rights, the discussion will bear some relationship to the position taken by aboriginal peoples on the issue of aboriginal rights as a whole.

Two preliminary questions must be posed at the outset of this task. The first is whether it is possible for a non-native person to understand the meaning of "aboriginal rights" well enough to express it accurately. The second is whether a consensus view of the meaning of aboriginal rights can be discovered for there is no single official body from which one can elicit the "official" position of the aboriginal nations as a whole. The first concern will be dealt with during the course of the chapter. The second I shall address now.

The central difficulty with respect to this question is the large number of groups that have an independent standing to speak on behalf of a legitimate aboriginal constituency. Since the constitution defines aboriginal peoples as consisting of three distinct groups (Indian, Inuit and Metis), they are represented by at least four national organizations: the Assembly of First Nations (AFN), which represents status Indians; the Native Council of Canada (NCC), which speaks for non-status Indians and Metis, the Metis National Council (MNC), which also speaks for Metis; and the Inuit Committee on National Issues (ICNI), which represents the Canadian Inuit. Further, each of these national organizations is a coalition of smaller ones. The AFN, for instance, includes the provincial organizations that represent status Indians in each of the ten provinces and two territories. Each of these, in turn, is composed of sub-regional and local groupings such as tribes and bands. Each unit within the AFN, from the individual band to the national organization itself, has a legitimate right to put forward a stance on aboriginal rights independent of any other body. When the situation within the AFN is multiplied by the same situation within the Metis and

Inuit organizations, the scope of the difficulty in deciding which group is representative becomes obvious. To further complicate matters, there is a second national Indian organization. Called the Coalition of First Nations, it has taken positions on the resolution of specific issues of self-government that are at variance with the stand taken by the Assembly of First Nations.

What is difficult to do under the circumstances, then, is to decide which group(s) is representative. Fortunately, this does not have to be done here, for although the various aboriginal peoples speak with different voices, my analysis of the documentation on aboriginal rights indicates virtual unanimity concerning the meaning of the principle, and, despite some exceptions (such as the position of the Coalition of First Nations . . .), a high degree of consensus with respect to how the principle is to be carried out in practice. It is, furthermore, a point of view that has been maintained for over fifty years.

The current position of aboriginal nations on their rights was stated by the AFN, NCC, MNC and ICNI at the March 1983 First Ministers' Conference on Aboriginal Rights. It is this meeting that will be the focus of attention below. Although I shall concentrate on the words of the spokespersons for the four national organizations, what they state is consistent with virtually every other statement to which the reader might wish to refer.

The Definition of Aboriginal Rights

The nature of the consensus view of aboriginal rights is not hard to identify. For the Inuit, according to John Amagoalik, co-chairperson of the Inuit Committee on National Issues:

Our position is that aboriginal rights, aboriginal title to land, water and sea ice flows

from aboriginal rights and all rights to practise our customs and traditions, to retain and develop our languages and cultures, and the rights to self-government, all these things flow from the fact that we have aboriginal rights. . . . In our view, aboriginal rights can also be seen as human rights, because these are the things that we need to continue to survive as a distinct peoples in Canada. (Canada, 1983a: 130)

For the Metis, Clem Chartier of the Metis National Council, asserted:

What we feel is that aboriginal title or aboriginal right is the right to collective ownership of land, water, resources, both renewable and non-renewable. It is a right to self-government, a right to govern yourselves with your own institutions, whichever way you want your institutions to run; the right to language, to culture, the right to basically practice your own religion and customs, the right to hunt, trap and fish and gather are certainly part of that, but it is not all of it. (Canada 1983a: 134)

These views are replicated, as well, in the draft proposal to amend the constitution presented by National Chief David Ahenakew on behalf of the Assembly of First Nations. Included within this draft are specific provisions that would guarantee autonomous cultural and economic status for aboriginal peoples, protect historically acquired lands and, most crucially, entrench the following political rights:

1. The right of the First Nations to their own self-identity, including the right to determine their own citizenship and forms of government.
2. The right to determine their own institutions.
3. The right of their governments to make laws and to govern their members and the affairs of their people . . .
4. . . . Their right to exemption from any direct or indirect taxation levied by other governments.

5. The right to move freely within their traditional lands regardless of territorial, provincial, or international boundaries. (Assembly of First Nations 1983: 5.5)

An examination of the content of these and other statements presented at the conference indicates that the most significant concepts in the minds of the spokespersons pertain to a political jurisdiction that includes a land base. For example, David Ahenakew argues that central to the position of the AFN is the notion of some measure of Indian "sovereignty" and "jurisdiction" (1983: 8). He states: "we are . . . asserting that Indian governments have jurisdiction over Indians, Indian lands and resources" (*ibid.*: 9). Echoing this sentiment, Mr. Clem Chartier asserts that "the purpose of our participation in this conference is to entrench in the Constitution the right of the Metis people to a land base and self-government" (Canada, 1983a: 30). The same view recurs in statements made by every native organization that has put forward a position on aboriginal rights, from the band to the national levels.

A consensus view is also expressed with respect to the conceptual basis upon which these assertions are justified. Singularly important are two firmly held convictions. The first is that aboriginal rights is founded on the fact of "original" sovereignty. That is, as Georges Erasmus, president of the Dene Nation, put it at the Constitutional Conference (Canada, 1983b: 43): "We are talking about the title that our people had prior to contact with the European people and obviously . . . the rights we also had at the first contact was full sovereignty." The second is the notion that the continuing existence of those rights that are founded on this original sovereignty have not been extinguished through the subsequent occupation of Canada by settlers from Europe and other parts of the world. It is a proposition explained in contrasting but equally relevant manners by two aboriginal spokespersons from British Columbia. For James Gosnell, chief of the British Columbia region of the AFN, the position derives from an ontological premise based on the principle of the "gift from God," which is reminiscent of the traditional basis for the assertion of sovereignty under a European feudal polity. He says (Canada, 1983a: 114 f):

It has always been our belief, Mr. Chairman, that when God created this whole world he gave pieces of land to all races of people throughout this world, the Chinese people, Germans and you name them, including Indians. So at one time our land was this whole continent right from the tip of South America to the North Pole . . .

It has always been our belief that God gave us the land . . . and we say that no one can take our title away except He who gave it to us to begin with.

For Bill Wilson of the Native Council of Canada, the principle of original sovereignty is linked to the principle of liberation that motivated Canadian involvement in the Second World War. As he states (Canada, 1983a: 122):

When the German forces occupied France, did the French people believe they didn't own the country? I sincerely doubt that there was one French person in France during the war that ever had the belief that France belonged to Germany, which is why, of course, they struggled with our assistance to liberate their country and once again take it back for themselves.

Later, he adds (p. 124):

So what we say is we have title and that is why we are talking to you about aboriginal rights, but we are not talking English Common Law definitions . . . international law definitions that have been interpreted and re-interpreted and sometimes extinguished by conquest and ceding treaties and other agreements like that. We are talking about the feeling that is inside . . . all of us as Metis, Indian and Inuit people that this country belongs to us.

In sum, then, aboriginal rights can be described as encompassing a broad range of economic, social, cultural and political rights. Of these, it appears that the notion of a land base within a separate political jurisdiction is fundamental. These rights flow, first of all, from the fact that the aboriginal peoples were in sovereign occupation of Canada at the time of contact, and secondly from the assertion that their legitimacy and continued existence has not been extinguished by the subsequent occupation of Canada by immigrants.

That this is the consensus view, there can be no doubt. The question is, whether such a notion is comprehensible within, and compatible with, a non-native conceptual framework?

At first blush, it would appear that it may not even be possible to discover the answer. The concern pertains to an ability to communicate cross-culturally the understanding of the meaning of this term as it is conceptualized by native peoples within their cultures. It is a concern which was put most forcefully by Bill Wilson when he stated (Canada, 1983a: 128): "My whole point [is] that we stop viewing [aboriginal rights] from the point of view of the dominant society if we are ever going to understand what the Indian people, the Inuit people and the Metis want." The first issue, then, is whether there is a means of understanding this concept from the native point of view.

At some level, this is a problem that cannot be completely resolved, at least not without in-depth training and detailed study of a particular culture. The reason for this is simple. Concepts do not exist in a vacuum, but rather are understood in relation to other concepts. Therefore, in order to know the meaning of "aboriginal rights" as it is understood within a particular native society, it is necessary to know how it relates to other notions within that society. This matter is complicated further by the fact that the term itself may be merely an English gloss that is used for convenience' sake, but at the same time encapsulates a bundle of notions that cannot be readily translated from a native language into English. Thus, without knowing a native culture and understanding the logical structure of meaning of a particular native language in some depth and breadth, one can only hypothesize in general terms about the viewpoint held by any grouping of aboriginal peoples. That is, the best one can do is provide an interpretation that comes close to capturing the general meaning as it is understood within a native culture and language.

Such a task is made much easier if one can find an analogue from the conceptual schema used in one's own society. As the above indicates, such an orientation cannot do justice to the full sense of the concept as it is understood by native societies, but it can, I believe, provide a framework for cross-cultural understanding. The question, then, is whether there is a concept within our intellectual framework that is analogous to the notion of a peoples' right to a land base and self-government that derives from original sovereignty and remains unextinguished, even in the face of the acquisition of sovereignty by a new political authority.

At first, the answer would seem to be "no" — for a logical reason. World history has seen so much population movement and conflict over land that were a concept of ongoing rights based on original habitation to be accepted as valid, a general state of confusion in world affairs would result. This is an argument that was put most forcefully by Prime Minister Trudeau when, in a retort to Mr. Wilson and Chief Gosnell, he said (Canada, 1983a: 127):

Going back to the Creator doesn't really help very much. So He gave you title, but you know, did He draw on the land where your mountains stopped and somebody else's began . . .? God never said that the frontier of France runs along the Rhine or somewhere

west of Alsace-Lorraine where the German-speaking people of France live. . . . I don't know any part of the world where history isn't constantly rewritten by migrations and immigrants and fights between countries changing frontiers and I don't think you can expect North America or the whole of the Western Hemisphere to settle things differently than they have been settled everywhere else, hopefully peacefully here.

This is a persuasive argument, and, speaking in general terms, it is this point of view and not that of the aboriginal peoples that has become adopted in the conceptual schema of the world community.

There are, however, circumstances in which the world community appears to recognize, in principle, an exception to this general proposition. One situation, alluded to by Mr. Wilson in his comment about the French under German rule in World War II, is when the inhabitants of a previously recognized country fall under the occupation of what is perceived by the world community to be a foreign power. This principle is encapsulated in the proposition respecting the territorial integrity of nation-states (United Nations, 1961). A second and perhaps more appropriate circumstance pertains to the situation of colonialism, in particular that aspect of colonialism in which peoples of non-European origin came under European rule. In both kinds of circumstances, the consensus view of nation-states acknowledges that, despite the self-evident emergence of a new sovereign and even immigration, the rights of the indigenous people (be they French or African), and in particular their sovereign rights, may not be completely extinguished or eliminated — at least in principle — even by the overt act of the new sovereign. It is, I believe, to these circumstances that one must turn if one is to comprehend, through analogy, the basis of the declarations made by aboriginal spokespersons.

The general concepts within which the expression of these sentiments legitimized within the world community's intellectual schema are "self-determination," or the "recognition of the right of all people to rule themselves" (Cranston, 1966: 92), and especially that right as it is perceived to exist under the condition of "colonialism," or "the aggregate of various economic, political and social policies by which an imperial power maintains or extends its control over other areas of peoples" (*ibid.*: 17). Although these terms are not precise or obvious with regard to meaning (see, for instance, the question of the definition of "self" in self-determination), it is my view that these general notions describe well the position implied in the expression "aboriginal rights."

Further evidence that this is the case can be derived by comparing the words of the aboriginal leaders cited above with the wording of a number of international accords, such as the Charter of the United Nations (Chapter XI), the Covenant of the League of Nations (Article 26) and, in particular, resolution 1514 (XV) of the United Nations General Assembly. Entitled the Declaration on the Granting of Independence to Colonial Countries and Peoples, this resolution passed without a dissenting vote in 1961. In part, the words say:

Mindful *of the determination proclaimed by the peoples of the world in the Charter of the United Nations to reaffirm faith in fundamental human rights, in the dignity and worth of the human person, in the equal rights of men and women and of nations large and small and to promote social progress and better standards of life in larger freedom.*

Recognizing *the passionate yearning for freedom in all dependent peoples and the decisive role of such people in the enforcement of this independence.*

Recognizing *that the peoples of the world ardently desire the end of colonialism in all its manifestations.*

Convinced *that all peoples have an inalienable right to complete freedom, the exercise of this*

sovereignty and the integrity of this national territory.

Solemnly proclaims *the necessity of bringing to a speedy and unconditional end colonialism in all its forms and manifestations;*

And to this end

Declares *that:*

1. *The subjugation of peoples to alien subjugation, domination and exploitation constitutes a denial of fundamental human rights, as contrary to the Charter of the United Nations and is an impediment to the promotion of world peace and cooperation.*

   (and)

2. *All peoples have the right to self-determination; by virtue of that right they freely determine their political status and freely pursue this economic, social and cultural development.*

Compare this to the Dene Declaration that was passed unanimously by the Dene chiefs at a meeting in Fort Simpson in 1975:

We the Dene of the Northwest Territories insist on the right to be regarded by ourselves and the world as a nation.

Our struggle is for the recognition of the Dene Nation by the Government and people of Canada and the peoples and governments of the world . . .

The New World like other parts of the world has suffered the experience of colonialism and imperialism. Other peoples have occupied the land — often with force — and foreign governments have imposed themselves on our people. Ancient civilizations and ways of life have been destroyed.

Colonialism and imperialism is now dead or dying. Recent years have witnessed the birth of new nations or the rebirth of old nations out of the ashes of colonialism . . .

The Dene find themselves as part of a country. That country is Canada. But the Government of Canada is not the government of the Dene. These governments were not the choice of the Dene, they were imposed upon the Dene.

Although it is not clear that the United Nations had the situation of the aboriginal peoples of Canada in mind when it passed resolution 1514 (XV) and other resolutions, there is evidence to suggest that, in principle, its point of view parallelled the sentiments expressed by aboriginal peoples. As well, the sentiments expressed in these documents appear to concur with the perceptions of aboriginal peoples. Hence, I would argue that an appropriate analogy exists between the two points of view.

In sum, I would assert that the notion of aboriginal rights in the perceptions of the native leaders is analogous to the right to self-determination acknowledged by the world community as applicable to peoples living under colonial regimes. Here, then, is the counter-argument to the prime minister's position. Canada in this view is not a "normal" nation-state to which "normal" legal processes such as those cited by the prime minister apply. Rather, Canada is seen as a colonial manifestation, that, in principle, has no more right to assert permanent sovereignty over the land mass of Canada and over its original inhabitants than did, say, the British in Kenya or the French in Indo-China.

What, then, is the implication of making such an assertion? Although the resolution of the rights of an indigenous population under colonial rule to self-determination has taken many forms, in the classical scenario it is accomplished through the establishment or reestablishment of a nation-state founded on an indigenous sovereignty. Is this what is being asserted by the aboriginal peoples in Canada? Are they, in other words, calling for the breakup of Canada?

In principle, one must accept that, according to the logic of their position, they would be justified in demanding such an action. What is abundantly clear, however, is that their proposals eschew such a solution. That is, no proposition from the four national organizations calls for the sever-ance of the aboriginal population from the Canadian state or for the formation of an independent, autonomous nation-state or nation-states based on an indigenous sovereignty. Rather, the solution is always seen as realizable within the context of Confederation. Thus, the Metis National Council states (1983a: 1):

The purpose of our participation in this Conference is to entrench in the Constitution the rights of the Metis people to a land base and self-government. We believe the realization of these rights is essential to the preservation and development of our aboriginal nationality within the Canadian federation.

And Chief Ahenakew of the AFN states (1983: 5):

I ask . . . that no one misinterpret our positions, strongly held, or our words, no matter how strongly spoken to mean that we are separatists — seeking to divide Canada and assert the status of foreign nations. . . . We are committed to strengthening and building Canada — not to dismantling it.

That this is a consensus view of long standing can perhaps best be seen by referring to the conclusion of the strongly worded Dene Declaration cited above: "What we seek . . . is independence and self-determination within the country of Canada."

How, then, do the aboriginal peoples propose to resolve their right to self-determination? Here, native organizations differ significantly, especially with respect to specifics. . . . Nonetheless, they agree on two fundamental points. First, all assert that the objective is limited to insuring that the aboriginal peoples continue to survive and develop as distinct nations; and second, that this necessitates a restructuring of the Canadian political system in a manner that will guarantee aboriginal people the exclusive legislative authority deemed "necessary for (our) survival and development as a distinct people (or peoples)" (Metis National Council, 1983a: 1).

In general, all native organizations agree that to achieve this end requires jurisdiction over aboriginal lands and over those aspects of the lifestyle of aboriginal peoples that influence directly economic, linguistic, cultural, educational and other related matters. They specifically exclude aspects that are of less direct consequences; for example, the AFN suggests that their demands do not include the establishment of "our own armies and our own foreign relations" (Ahenakew, 1983: 9).

The national native organizations propose that the creation of new institutions of responsible self-government is the key solution. However, there is a wide divergence in viewpoint concerning the shape these institutions should take. Two positions tabled at the conference serve as examples. The AFN envisages the replacement of the present binary division of powers between the federal and provincial levels with one based on a tripartite set of jurisdictions. These would incorporate the present federal and provincial areas with a new one that would be known as "Indian Governments." The latter would have responsibility over matters of direct concern to the survival and development of the aboriginal nations. They would consist of band governments with an overarching jurisdiction responsible for issues common to the various nations. It appears to envisage no alteration to the current jurisdiction or composition of the federal and provincial jurisdictions.

The result of this proposal would be the creation of three equal governments, each with sovereignty within its own jurisdiction; that is, as the AFN proposal suggests (Ahenakew, 1983: 10):

Indian governments will have exclusive sovereignty and jurisdiction over matters coming within our powers; the Federal Government will continue to have exclusive sovereignty and jurisdiction over matters coming within its powers; and the Provincial Governments will continue to have sovereignty and jurisdiction over matters coming within their domain. Relations between our Governments and other orders of government in Canada will be altered only by mutual agreement, as is the case today between the Provinces and the Federal Government.

The second proposal was put forward jointly by the Native Council of Canada and the Metis National Council in separate position papers. It advocates both the establishment of new institutions of native self-government and changes in the present federal Parliament and provincial legislatures. With respect to this latter aspect, the proposal calls for the replacement of the present system of membership in these bodies with one that, in addition to the present system, would add a guaranteed number of seats reserved exclusively for the descendants of the aboriginal peoples. The proposal is unclear as to the nature of the new native jurisdictions. Whereas it calls for the establishment of new institutions of self-government, it does not make explicit whether these jurisdictions would be co-equal to that of the federal and provincial governments, as is advocated in the AFN proposal, or whether they would have a level of authority junior to the present structures. There is evidence to support both views. For example, the latter position holds first of all because the interpretation was not firmly rejected by the representatives of the Metis and non-status Indians at the Constitutional Conference, and second because this is the most probable justification for the insistence on guaranteed seats in the federal and provincial legislatures (that is, special seats should have special responsibilities). However, other evidence, such as the statement made by the Manitoba Metis Association, asserts (Manitoba Metis Rights Assembly, 1983: 11): "We do not want token seats (in Parliament and the Manitoba legislature) as an alternative to real self-government," and as such lends weight to the former interpretation.

Regardless which interpretation proves correct, it seems clear that the position held jointly by the MNC and the NCC does not differ in fundamental philosophy from that proposed by the AFN. In effect, both propositions call for an identical kind of transformation of the Canadian political system from its present form to one that explicitly recognizes, within its political structure, the existence of an autonomous aboriginal entity. The difference really is only in emphasis and in the degree to which this recognition is to be acknowledged within the political structure of the Canadian nation-state. Thus, it follows that from the point of view of the native organizations, although the assertion of aboriginal rights does not call for the breakup of Canada, it does demand changes to its present institutional structure.

Summary and Conclusion

In my understanding, the nub of the position of the native organizations is that aboriginal peoples have the right to maintain ways of life that are distinct from those of recent immigrants to Canada. These ways of life are not to be interpreted as ethnic in the sense of a Canadian mosaic, but rather as a composite of autonomous systems that integrates languages, economies, social organizations, political organizations, religions and other values into a total culture. Central to the ongoing viability of these is a land base and self-government.

The right to preserve and develop such autonomous systems in Canada is perceived to derive, in part, from the manifest failure of the current programs designed to establish viable lifeways for the majority of the aboriginal population. However, at the core, it arises from a vision of Canada as a colonial manifestation and from the perception of aboriginal peoples as "colonized" nations that, like those indigenous populations on other continents, have an inherent right to assert their self-determination and control over their own affairs. It is a goal that is perceived to be attainable within the context of Confederation.

In this view, then, the inclusion of a clause on aboriginal rights in the constitution symbolizes the recognition of a legitimate claim to political rights analogous to those found in colonial situations. Seen in this light, the proposals for self-government must be considered moderate indeed, for they call for a resolution without disrupting the continuity of the Canadian state. Short of denying any right to political self-determination, the proposals represent the least possible position from the point of view of aboriginal peoples.

Nevertheless, such a view of aboriginal rights is not widely shared by Canadians, or even by representatives of government. Thus I am certain that no matter how moderate the solutions appear to be, there will be some who would continue to object to the principle itself. Still, ... the Canadian state has recently advanced positions that are more favourable to the aboriginal peoples' position on political rights. Indeed, ... objections raised to the entrenchment of these rights today, as a general rule, rely much more on practical concerns or considerations of a possible negative impact on liberal-democratic institutions, ... than they do on simple rejections of the stand itself. The key to this change is a shift in the manner in which aboriginal peoples are conceptualized at the time of first contact. It is a change that receives its first important acknowledgement by the Canadian state in court decisions concerning the legitimacy of the claims to aboriginal title to lands as yet unceded to the Crown. ...

THE UNCERTAINTY PRINCIPLE

M. Patricia Marchak

I can think of no honour that I could more cherish than the Porter award, both because I admired John Porter and because I have always felt that the CSAA is my scholarly community. It provides the congenial and tolerant environment for experiments, and trusting yet again to its tolerance I propose to try an experiment today.

You may have expected me to talk about shakes, shingles, and chips, since this award is for a book on the forest industry. The problem is that I have a lisp and three "sh" sounds in a row would do me in. I can't even talk about for whom the tree falls, because what is happening in B.C. is that the whoms I have enjoyed denouncing in the past are moving out of Canada. Among the reasons are eucalyptus trees, grown on plantations in hot climates in seven year cycles. These can now be transformed into high grade pulp, a technological development that may save our environment though perhaps the problem will be merely displaced. In any event, Canada's softwood forests are losing a fair portion of their market, so we may have trees in future, even if we cannot afford to live among them.

Such events incline one to be more philosophical. Besides, I am obliged to follow David MacGregor's fine address on Hegel last year, and if his Owl of Minerva cares to listen, I will offer some musings on an uncertain world by way of response. MacGregor welcomed us to the age of Hegel by way of departing from the age of Marx. My concern is with the need to depart from

both, as we consider the implications of Heisenberg's version of a universe that is far too complex for either approach to its social mechanisms.

Natural and Social Laws

Physicists are concerned with natural laws, and very much concerned in our time with the dynamic quality of nature, which turns out to be less easily comprehended than was anticipated only a half-century ago. They are discovering that they cannot separate the parts from the whole, the stationary from the dynamic, or the definition from the reality.

Social scientists are less clear about whether they are dealing with natural laws, social laws, or some hybrid. As Polanyi pointed out in the mid-1940s, many versions of capitalist economies have elevated economic tendencies to the status of natural laws, and though Marx repudiated nature's intervention in human history, he nonetheless gave humans precious little opportunity to alter the process. Even today, while inclined to adopt the notion that humans carve out their own destinies, we have generally felt much kinship with social philosophers who have presumed an order of natural rights for individual humans. This is, however, a mild contradiction that we manage to live with, much as many humans live with the contradictions of an apparently tragic world governed by a beneficent god: without the notion of god, they say, they could not tolerate the tragic world he invented — and the "he" is deliberate in that sentence because in our particular time and space, nature is not perceived as a loving mother.

It is difficult enough to be a physical scientist confronted with the proposition that mind cannot be separated from matter; that is, that human brains impose order on reality, and what we can understand of nature

From "The Uncertainty Principle" by M. Patricia Marchak which appeared in *The 1987 John Porter Memorial Lecture* issue published by *The Canadian Review of Sociology and Anthropology*. Edited by James Curtis and C. James Richardson, 1988.

necessarily filters through that imposed order. The very definition of nature as an object to be studied, controlled, and altered by human action is itself a manifestation of human ordering. This definition can even be historically dated, so historians inform us. It made sporadic appearances in Arabic and Greco-Roman civilizations, then disappeared under the shield of Christianity, reappearing in Europe from the 13th century onwards. Socially, nature has changed for us; and with sometimes terrifying impacts on nature.

It becomes even more difficult to be a social scientist simultaneously imposing order and attempting to identify how we impose order. We may assume, with Berger and Luckman, that social reality is a human construction, but how social reality so constructed interacts with natural reality is unclear. Nature may have an ontological status of a different order but for humans, it is, nonetheless, apprehended through socially constructed definitions. Further, we are a component of nature, and our brains, sustained within a social context, must, like the rest of nature, have their own dynamic; certainly our biological clocks have their own, often infuriating, momentum.

We may learn from the physicists a particularly important understanding: that individual particles are discrete only when we choose to visualize them that way. They are simultaneously particles and waves, and we may choose to visualize the waves rather than the particles. In both forms, the physical world is an organic whole, conceptualized now as energy in constant flux. If we concentrate on the parts, we cannot understand the relationships or the dynamic of their changing appearance; if we concentrate on the relationships, we may miss understanding the variable properties of the parts. Our intellectual construction is thus inevitably partial, and we are obliged to recognize uncertainty as its operating principle. Our predictions must be probabilistic rather than deterministic.

By analogy, we are dealing with human individuals as particles, their relationships and institutionalized patterns of interaction as waves, but the organic whole is not society, which is what makes it even more complicated for us; the whole is a number of quite different social arrangements plus the rest of the natural universe, both as these may exist objectively and as our own brains organize them for our senses.

It is true, of course, that the complications in the physical sciences are still largely intellectual; there is sufficient known order to build bridges and alter genes. A mechanistic version of physical reality still has utility, and the practical problems arising from random variation at the core of things are not likely to upset the engineering profession. But there is also a growing awareness that the universe needs to be perceived as a gestalt, in which, to use Heisenberg's words, "the world thus appears as a complicated tissue of events, in which connections of *different* kinds alternate *or* overlap *or* combine and thereby determine the texture of the whole."

Survival Strategies and Different Levels of Organization

Now suppose we were to try to think in similar terms about human society, and at least metaphorically employ the more organic version of natural processes for social reality. If we resist the temptation to force humans into the slots we now have, we have difficulty discerning any obvious laws about either individuals or societies, except the most basic, which seems to be more in the form of a natural than a social law: that both as particles and waves, as individuals and species subdivided into organized groups, there is an apparent inclination to seek ways of surviving. That seems pretty mundane, but in fact it may offer a novel way of considering our problem, for the reason that if it is true, then we should assume that social relations are always infused with the unavoidable tension of diverse survival strategies employed at different levels of organization.

The species, much like others, survives through diversity of form; in the human case the form is social and cultural organization. Variations in these organizations, societies, may be greater than individual variation, but there is also diversity in individuals, and the survival patterns of individuals may well be contrary to those of the society. As well, large societies normally have numerous subdivisions, any of which may develop independent survival strategies contrary to the interests of others. Societies as a whole, internally dominated by any of these subgroups, may threaten the survival of other societies and even the species by developing strategies with reference only to their own survival. Further, and in this respect apparently unlike other natural forms, human actors identify, believe, reconstruct, reflect, and formulate ideas about how and why they act; and the same individuals in different phases may conceptualize the behaviour in contradictory ways. Thus the whole enterprise seems to operate in accordance with a mixture of socially constructed realities and natural laws. The trick for the social scientist is to keep in mind that the same particles are involved in the different levels, and that societies and cultures are variable ways by which human animals organize subsistence within a natural world.

The tension infusing human systems thus appears inevitable, and it would be surprising indeed if very much stayed stable for any prolonged period. By definition, societies bear the seeds of their own destruction; this is not a peculiarity of capitalism, it is a condition of existence.

While the potential variations may be infinite, there do seem to be repetitive patterns in human experience, for which we should be truly grateful since our profession would be in grave trouble were it not so. Under specific conditions — to which, as social scientists, we need pay more attention — social organizations tend to behave in particular ways, and individuals at different positions in a social hierarchy tend to respond in fairly predictable ways. The conditions include the known food resources, utilizable energy resources, and perceptions of the limits of these; thus our relationship to nature and our versions of nature are crucial. They also include population densities and demographic dispersion: societies with large dependent populations apparently have rather different internal dynamics than those with a bell-shaped distribution; large populations have different options than smaller ones inhabiting similar territories. Within these limiting conditions, we may be able to discern not so much laws as patterns sufficiently repetitive that we might predict their probable development when the conditions are in force.

Among the repetitive patterns in societies with a certain but to the best of my knowledge, as yet undiscovered density is the development of social hierarchy. I think we do not really know why this is the case, though similar hierarchies apparently occur amongst other animals with group lives, so perhaps this, too, is attributable to nature. It may be that a large number of human animals cannot organize their subsistence if all are equal in power; the density equation may mean that at some point group and individual survival begin to diverge because redistribution rituals become unmanageable. Perhaps there is some sort of jungle law about the strong subjugating the weak, or it may be that the fundamental cause lies in the human psyche, in some impluse requiring order. Any of these hypotheses — all have been advanced by someone or other, I'm sure — could still be entertained. None can be absolutely refuted. It would be consistent with the understanding that tension is inevitable in diverse strategies for survival, to argue that social hierarchy is recurrent as an always temporary outcome of struggles. There is nothing in that deduction which imputes positive functions to any particular form of order: societies may construct hierarchies that destroy them.

Certainly the bases of hierarchies differ both through history and in our own time. Possession of land or industrial property obviously provides the basis over the last several centuries in Europe and European offspring societies, but even among these we discover instances — Argentina for example — where a military caste has developed such power that its behavior can not be linked in any simple way to the interests of a propertied class. In Argentina, the regimes of the Peronistas and the generals were expensive, unpredictable, self-serving, and destructive of commerce and industry. A country that, in the 1920s, was hailed as an emerging industrial giant has since devolved into a midget, its incipient civil war won not by capital but by a military junta. Only military defeat in the Malvinas has weakened their grip on power. This is not to argue that no military regimes are unsupported by international or domestic capital; nor even to say that no propertied interests supported the military in Argentina. My argument is rather that the tragedy of the Argentine has to be understood in terms that acknowledge the existence of a class whose power does not derive from industrial property.

So far we have two possible facts to work with: that individuals and social groups strive to survive, and that populations with sufficient density tend to create hierarchies, though the hierarchies are not necessarily based on the same nexus. There may be tendencies for people to organize similar systems in similar conditions, but there is nothing in this process which suggests that only one way of solving existential dilemmas would be possible. Further, though different societies may carve out similar hierarchies and orders in response to similar developments, they may also carve out quite divergent exits from these orders as time passes. Within capitalism, and restricting ourselves to societies with similar economic bases in say, 1880, the differences by 1980 between Sweden and France, or Canada and Argentina, are considerably more interesting than the similarities.

If we proceed in this fashion, we cannot lean on any version of historical laws, whether of a material or an ideational nature. Similar historical experiences would tend to give rise to similar contemporary solutions, and some societies may superimpose their histories and solutions on others, but these observations are quite dissimilar from the notion of laws of history. The problem with the historical laws thesis is that it is too narrow; it is not history which is regulated, but rather history is the multifaceted consequence of more fundamental natural laws interacting with diverse social constructions.

History as Tableaux: Feudalism

In place of historical laws, suppose we imagined history as a range of social alternatives, a series of tableaux offering variations on persistent themes. Our task is to understand the internal dynamics of a tableau, the similarities between it and other social arrangements in like climatic and demographic conditions, and possibly the nature of its transformation.

European feudal society offers a series of related tableaux. With all its defects, it apparently provided sustenance to an agrarian population for several centuries. But by the 14th century, its values and the custodial order for them were disintegrating. There seem to have been two different sources of the deterioration: one in the marketplace and the other at the margins.

In the marketplace, pushing camels through needle eyes was not a preoccupation, and while monks contemplated an eternal truth on the mountain-tops, merchants in the valleys were discovering the joys of temporal profits. They created their own universities to overcome the monopoly on knowledge held by the priests. The industrial revolution and the mechanistic version of the universe were the outcomes, not the origins, of this development, it seems, but the transformation took fully five centuries if we begin dating with the first wave of the Inquisition.

At the margins were growing numbers of dislocated people for whom the system offered no subsistence; some organized as bands of roaming brigands, others as religious sects, and ultimately the two were indistinguishable. Umberto Eco, in *The Name of the Rose*, creates a character who describes his participation in one of the sects. This has a familiar sound in the world of the 20th century:

And we burned and looted because we had proclaimed poverty the universal law, and we had the right to appropriate the illegitimate riches of others, and we wanted to strike at the heart of the network of greed that extended from parish to parish, but we never looted in order to possess, or killed in order to loot: we killed to punish, to purify the impure through blood.

The precise causes of the transition from feudalism are, of course, still under debate, with varying emphases placed by different historians on the growth of urban centres and international markets, the steady increases in landless peasants moving into these centres, the successful resistance of the peasantry to landlord's rents and taxation, and the gradual development of new ideas about both nature and human life. What most strikingly emerges in the debates between Anderson, Brenner, Dobb, Sweezy, Hilton, and Wallerstein, is that the outcomes of struggles, whether between serfs and lords or between bourgeois merchants and the whole feudal order, led to an extensive landed petty-bourgeoisie on small farms in some parts of Europe, while it led to large scale capitalist farming in others. Western and Eastern Europe diverged considerably in their outcomes to similar struggles, and within western Europe, Britain and France came out of the frays in different ways, ultimately altering their modes of entry into industrial capitalism.

History as Tableaux: Industrial Capitalism

The bourgeois society that emerged in the European marketplace is another tableau. Like its predecessor, this society had its classes, but it was not the gaining of control over the labour of others that distinguished the bourgeoisie from the monastery and the aristocracy of the fading medieval period. Control of labour was central to the earlier society, some of it even paid by a wage or something very much like it, and some of it being regularly bought and sold in labour markets according to Fernand Braudel. The bourgeoisie continued and enlarged on the practice. What made the difference between these two societies were the full development of a market for exchange of goods and sale of labour; the growth in potential goods available by virtue of the applications of science; and an entirely different mental set about nature, human intervention, and the future.

Science, growing with and intricately embodied in the industrial society, provided material means for controlling nature and expanding the universe of survival options. But it would be as inaccurate to attribute capitalism to science as to attribute the feudal order to medieval Christianity; values are not disembodied, are neither causes nor epiphenomena. They are dynamic and integral forces within every social context, and in this context scientific values together with technologies based on scientific research led to a shrinking population producing primarily its own use values, an expanding population surviving through the extraction and processing of non-renewable natural resources.

A society living on limited resources necessarily constructs a moral reality recognizing the finite range of behaviour appropriate to survival. But moral limitations on greed in an ever expanding world have declining force on individual aspirations. Moreover, if it can be demonstrated that individual greed results in expansion of the options, there seems little to be gained by social limitation. Thus as European society secularized knowledge, it also secularized the moral order, infusing it with the market analogy. Demystified, god could no longer convey strictures against greed. Indeed, a separate, secular body of social knowledge became established which explicitly justified individualism in pursuit of profit. The English language gradually desexed much of the material world. Things and nature were neutered as befits manipulable objects. Likewise, the familiar forms of address and many other linguistic signals of differences between child and adult, lovers and strangers, disappeared from the language that pioneered the industrial society.

By the time Karl Marx entered the discourse, a market was already well established for industrial products, a bourgeoisie was firmly in place, the university had dislodged the monastery, and the industrial mode of production as well as capitalist control of it were all features of the social world. Not surprisingly, he conceived of science as did his contemporaries: as a mode of actively intervening in natural processes for purposes of changing human conditions. The world for him was a machine, set in motion by laws of history, ultimately predictable, and subject to manipulation.

What is the mode of production if not a mode of thinking about the natural world? What is the industrial mode of production if not a mode of thinking that justifies, and then provides the means for, intervening in that world? To call this the capitalist mode of production is to add a dimension of power: it is the industrial mode of production under the direction and control of a particular group. Marx did not question whether humans should control nature; he assumed as much. His concern was not with the propriety, it was with the property rights, of industrial modes of production. And as it turns out, the same industrial mode of production under the control of a state bureaucracy is but a variation on a theme; dispensing with a class which has formal property rights does not dispense with the central dilemma, and the social relations of production turn out to be similar whether the surplus is destined for private profit or public investment.

Thus both capitalism and socialism as ideologies, as ways of organizing reality and dealing in an evaluative way with its contradictions, have shared a mental universe divorcing humanity from nature, and treating nature as something to be consumed or transformed in production.

Yet Marx was not wholly a product of the industrial revolution. What he wrote was a Judaeo-Christian condemnation of property rights, his anti-market polemics demanding that societal survival take precedence over individual greed. It is the moral linkages that remain so electrifying in Marxist theory. We, the readers, strive to provide the empirical content and frequently the logical links as well, to correspond to the moral relations. We do this because we share the belief that where morality is but a market exchange, the disenfranchised at the margins increase, and even at the centre, the society corrodes. Here, the contradictions are believed to be peculiar to a particular arrangement, not endemic to the human or social condition.

Ironically, where industrial society was instituted without a market nexus, Marx was elevated to godhood. Congealed into a state doctrine in Eastern Europe, Marxism became a strait jacket, a religion as dogmatic, as unforgiving as Christianity under the Inquisition. In the western capitalist countries, paradoxically, it grew and changed through interaction with non-Marxist ideas, and what today is called Marxism in capitalist universities has little more at its core than agreement that material conditions circumscribe political and spiritual social constructions; and the moral concern with vast inequalities, untenable inequities between the propertied and the unpropertied. Virtually every element of the Marxist theory has been persuasively countered not solely by neo-classical economists and historians, nor even primarily by them, but by those who are sympathetic to the moral concerns of the paradigm. Even the fundamental labour law of value no longer holds the paradigm together, as is so painfully evident in contemporary theories of the capitalist crisis.

Gradually we recognize that in focusing on the subjugation of labour and the unequal distribution of surplus, we have forgotten about the central and distinguishable feature of industrialism: control of nature; and about the distinguishing feature of capitalism: the market place.

How much do we know about the market? Neo-classical economists have disappointed us because they divorced the market from social relations; in consequence

their explanations of market forces are frequently static, divorced from reality, and sterile. To say that the labour theory of value fails to yield an explanation for contemporary social existence is not to say that social relations within the capitalist system are irrelevant, and that is, it seems, the conclusion embedded in much of neo-classical theory. That, indeed, is why so many sociologists turned to Marxist economics: their sense of the society informed them that the market could not be understood in a social vacuum. The problem for sociology, however, is that it then reversed the error: it forgot about the market in its zeal to comprehend the social relations.

Perhaps because we take the market for granted (even while condemning it) we cannot fully recognize the range of influence it exerts in capitalist society. Perhaps the societies now introducing markets under controlled conditions, China and the U.S.S.R., will produce the superior theories of their operations. The same cannot be said of our relationship to nature since non-market industrial societies have objectified and consumed it as thoroughly as the market societies have commoditized it.

History as Tableaux: The Development of Democratic Politics

One of the effects of capitalist markets is the development of democratic politics. In the core industrial and capitalist countries, a central puzzle is posed by the nature of the democratic state embodying a unique notion of the rule of law. Democracy is not at all like military regimes, and the naming of civil rights is not at all like the invocation of natural rights. What, then, is the relationship between the market and these institutions?

On one side we have the "new right" damning democracy because it fails to support the free market and unfettered accumulation. On the other, there are still some neo-Marxists damning democracy because it only supports accumulation. One might mention that Marx himself, at least in *Class Struggles in France*, specifically noted the contradiction between universal suffrage and private property, and pointed out that the political realm provided a new arena for struggle against the rights of property. But that single phrase about the executive of the bourgeoisie in the *Communist Manifesto* is more easily recalled.

The reactionaries have launched a frontal attack on democracy, and the left is scarcely capable of defending what for so long it dismissed as a bourgeois front. For a tradition that has so strongly argued in favor of historical analysis, many neo-Marxist theories pose surprisingly static versions of the relations between democracy and capitalism, ignoring an evolution that has occurred in some, and not all, capitalist countries.

Parliamentary government, the forerunner to democratic government, is unlikely to have originated as a response to the demands of workers, since in its origins and for a considerable period following its introduction in Europe the franchise was limited by property rights. A proposition more in keeping with the composition of these governments is that they were introduced by way of containing intra-ruling class conflict. European parliaments were inhabited largely by landlords until well past the middle of the 19th century, and only toward the last quarter of that century were merchants and industrialists politically involved. Hannah Arendt argues that the bourgeoisie's disinclination to concern itself with political governance prior to that was the very reason for the full development of nation states with their claims to be above all classes.

Representative democracy is a late 19th,

early 20th century phenomenon which emerged with the second industrial revolution, mechanization, mass production, the creation of mass markets, and the growth of global markets and imperialist expansion. In this process, family firms gave way to publicly traded companies. Gradually, inheritance rights ceased to automatically include controlling positions in companies, and companies rather than individuals and separate families became the dominant economic units of industrial society. Government of properties thus required an expansion of the recruitment base and of legislative powers respecting inheritance, trade, taxes, corporate rights, and publicly traded properties. Governments increased their roles as allocation agencies between competing capitals, and became actively involved in imperialist ventures. At the same time, labour now had to be educated, urban centres had to be provided with facilities, transportation and communication links had to be constructed. These required an expansion of the public taxation base, and that, in turn, required an expansion of voting rights. We might note in passing the similarity in patterns, though of course not in substance, to events preceding the great peasant uprisings of the medieval period, and the French Revolution. When governments need to extract wealth from the governed, something is demanded in return.

During the early period of parliamentary rule and industrial capitalism, class struggle occurred, and for the most part failed, in the workplace. With the extension of the franchise, a new arena was opened up for struggles. Gradually workers won the right to engage in collective bargaining, a modest gain, but much too significant to be dismissed as a legitimation exercise.

The startling fact about liberal democratic states in the last few decades is that they have actually distributed some portion of the wealth gained in the enormous post-war expansion. The proportions of national income going to the rich and poor did not change, as you will be quick to tell me; but the level of subsistence for the bulk of the population did change, upwards. This came about through labour legislation, public education, welfare provisions, and employment in the state sector: the social wage. In very recent history, the democratic state has provided some essential conditions for the emancipation of women and decreased the capacity of capital to profit from racial divisions within the working class. The concept of a rule of law, Gide notwithstanding, has grown to include civil rights. These actions have substance, they have had significant bearing on the outcomes for capital over the past thirty years. Indeed, it is for this reason that, by the 1980s, we are witnessing the reactionary politics of the new right.

Democracy may not be compatible with capitalism when either is theorized as pure and unencumbered by the other; but, even so, they have co-existed precisely because neither fits their theories. The same, amoral marketplace within which profit is the guideline of behavior, and labour as well as goods are sold, is the nexus for the development of political life; the same individualism that motivates economic behavior gives rise to the notion of civil rights; the same imperialism that provided wealth and law to populations in the northern hemisphere at the expense of those in the southern, now creates a new global order that paradoxically may release the same forces in the south at the expense of the north. The transformation of feudalism took five centuries; our own transformation is only started and at this stage no one can predict the eventual outcome.

Uncertainty as a Principle for Social Science

In this infinitely complex global society, with all its tensions and with no version of immutable laws of history to guide us, how might we engage in our vocation as social scientists? It seems to me that our task is precisely to examine the complexity, the variations, the tensions, the costs of alternative arrangements. Markets are neither evil nor good, they are among the survival strategies human societies have constructed, and like all survival strategies they benefit some at the expense of others; like all, they create and destroy at the same time; like all, they bear the seeds of their own demise. More problematic for the earth is the conquest of nature, and that supports industrialism whatever the hierarchical form it takes, whatever the mode of distribution. This, I believe, deserves attention from the social as well as physical sciences.

This is not the age of Marx. It is not the age of Hegel. It is not, if Arthur Kroker is listening, the age of Nietzsche. It is not even the age of Heisenberg. It is but another age of uncertainty. It has Nietzschean tragedy to be sure, but it also has visions that go beyond its current confines; among them, the still evolving sciences which may, eventually, help humans to socially construct a more harmonious relationship with the rest of our natural world.

BIBLIOGRAPHY

Abella, Rosalie
1984 *Equality in Employment: A Royal Commission Report.* Ottawa: Ministry of Supply and Services.

Abercrombie, Nicholas, and John Urry
1983 *Capital, Labour and the Middle Classes.* London: George Allen and Unwin.

Abplanalp, Judith
1983 "Pre-menstrual Syndrome: A Selective Review." In *Lifting the Curse of Menstruation*, edited by Sharon Golub. New York: The Haworth Press.

Abrams, Philip
1982 *Historical Sociology.* Somerset: Open Books.

1988 "The Difficulty of Studying the State." *Journal of Historical Sociology* 1(1): 31–43.

Acker, Joan
1973 "Women and Social Stratification: A Case of Intellectual Sexism." *American Journal of Sociology* 78: 936–45.

Addelson, Katherine Pyne
1983 "The Man of Professional Wisdom." In Harding and Hintikka. (1983).

AFL-CIO Committee on the Evolution of Work
1985 *The Changing Situation of Workers and Their Unions.* Washington, D.C.: American Federation of Labour and Confederation of Industrial Organizations.

Ahenakew, David
1983 "Opening Remarks to the Constitutional Conference of First Ministers' on the Rights of Aboriginal Peoples." Ottawa.

Albas, D., and C. Albas
1984 *Student Life and Exams: Stresses and Coping Strategies.* Dubuque: Kendal/Hunt.

Alford, Robert R.
1963 *Party Society: The Anglo-American Democracies.* Chicago: Rand McNally.

Allen, Robert
1986 "The Impact of Technical Change on Employment Wages and the Distribution of Skills." In *Adapting to Change:*

Labour Market Adjustment in Canada, edited by W. Craig Riddel. Toronto: University of Toronto Press.

Allport, Gordon
1958 *The Nature of Prejudice.* New York: Holt, Rinehart and Winston.

Ambert, Anne-Marie
1976 "Swinging: A Study of Decision Making in Marriage." In *The Canadian Family in Comparative Perspective*, edited by Lyle Larson. Toronto: Prentice-Hall Canada.

1980 *Divorce in Canada.* Toronto: Academic Press.

Anderson, John
1982 "The Structure of Collective Bargaining." In *Union Management Relations in Canada*, edited by John Anderson and Morley Gunderson. Toronto: Holt, Rinehart and Winston.

Anderson, M.
1975 "Family, Household and the Industrial Revolution." In *Sociology of the Family*, edited by Michael Anderson. Harmondsworth: Penguin.

1980 *Approaches to the History of the Western Family, 1500–1914.* New York: Macmillan.

Anderson, R., ed.
1979 *North Atlantic Maritime Cultures.* The Hague: Moulton.

Anderson, R., and C. Wadel
1972 *North Atlantic Fishermen.* St. John's, Nfld.: The Institute for Social and Economic Research.

Anthony, P. D.
1977 *The Ideology of Work.* London: Tavistock.

Antler, E.
1976 "Women's Work in Newfoundland Fishery Families." Unpublished Paper, Newfoundland Centre.

Anyon, J.
1980 "Social Class and the Hidden Curriculum." *Journal of Education* 16: 2.

1982   "Ideology and United States History Textbooks." In Apple (1982).

1983   "Intersections of Gender and Class: Accommodation and Resistance by Working-Class and Affluent Families to Contrary Sex-Role Ideologies." In Walker and Barton (1983).

Apple, M.
1982   *Cultural and Economic Reproduction in Education.* London: Routledge and Kegan Paul.

Appleby, Joyce Oldham
1978   *Economic Thought and Ideology in Seventeenth-Century England.* Princeton: Princeton University Press.

Ariès, Philippe
1962   *Centuries of Childhood.* New York: Random House.

Armstrong, D., *et al.*
1977   "The Measurement of Income Distribution in Canada: Some Problems and Some Tentative Data." *Canadian Public Policy* 3: 479–88.

Armstrong, Pat
1984   *Labour Pains: Women's Work in Crisis.* Toronto: The Women's Press.

Armstrong, Pat, and Hugh Armstrong
1984   *The Double Ghetto.* Toronto: McClelland and Stewart.

1983   "Beyond Sexless Class and Classless Sex: Towards Feminist Marxism." *Studies in Political Economy* 10: 7–43.

Arnold, Stephen, and James G. Barnes
1979   "Canadian and American Character as a Basis for Market Segmentation." In *Research in Marketing*, edited by J. Sheth. Greenwich, Conn.: JAI Press.

Arnold, Stephen, and Douglas J. Tigert
1974   "Canadians and Americans: A Comparative Perspective." *International Journal of Comparative Sociology* 15: 68–83.

Arnot, M.
1983   "A Cloud Over Co-education: An Analysis of the Forms of Transmission of Class and Gender Relations." In Walker and Barton (1983).

Assembly of First Nations
1983   *Proposals for Amendments and Additions to the Constitution Act, 1982.* Unpublished Manuscript.

Astell, Mary
1701   *A Serious Proposal to the Ladies for the Advancement of Their True and Greatest Interest.* London: Wilken.

Atwood, Margaret
1972   *Survival: A Thematic Guide to Canadian Literature.* Toronto: Anansi Press.

1984   *Second Words: Selected Critical Prose.* Boston: Beacon Press.

Babbie, Earl
1979   *The Practice of Social Research.* Belmont, Calif.: Wadsworth.

Bacon, Francis
n.d.   *Essays.* London: Chandos Classics.

1964   *The Philosophy of Francis Bacon.* Liverpool: Liverpool University Press.

Baer, Doug, Edward Grabb, and William Johnston
1989   "The Values of Canadians and Americans: A Critical Analysis and Reassessment." *Social Forces.*

Bailey, Kenneth D.
1987   *Methods of Social Research.* New York: Free Press.

Bailey, Martha
1990   "Unpacking the 'Rational Alternative': A Critical Review of Family Mediation Movement Claims." *Canadian Journal of Family Law* 8: 61–94.

Bain, George S., and Robert Price
1980   *Profiles of Union Growth: A Comparative Statistical Portrait of Eight Countries.* Oxford: Basil Blackwell.

Baker, Maureen, and May-Anne Robeson
1981   "Trade Union Reactions to Women Workers and Their Concerns." In *Work in the Canadian Context: Continuity Despite Change*, edited by K.L. Lundy and B.D. Warme. Toronto: Butterworths.

Baldwin, E.
1977   "On Methodological and Theoretical
        Muddles in Clement's Media Study."
        The Canadian Journal of Sociology 2
        (2): 215–22.

Bane, Mary Jo
1976   *Here to Stay: American Families in the
        Twentieth Century*. New York: Basic
        Books.

Baran, Paul A.
1957   *The Political Economy of Growth*. New
        York: Monthly Review Press.

Barker, Jane, and Hazel Downing
1980   "Word Processing and the Transforma-
        tion of the Patriarchal Relations of
        Control in the Office." *Capital and Class*
        10: 65.

Barret, Michele, and Mary McIntosh
1980   "The Family Wage: Some Problems for
        Socialists and Feminists." *Capital and
        Class* 1: 51–72.

1982   *The Anti-Social Family*. London: Verso

Barth, Frederick
1969   *Ethnic Groups and Ethnic Boundaries*.
        Boston: Little Brown.

Barthes, Roland
1957   *Mythologies*. Paris: Editions du Seuil.

Bashevkin, Sylvia
1985   *Toeing the Lines: Women and Party
        Politics in English Canada*. Toronto:
        University of Toronto Press.

Baumrind, Diana
1980   "New Directions in Socialization Re-
        search." *American Psychologist* 35(7):
        639–52.

Baxandall, Rosalyn
1976   "Women in American Trade Unions: An
        Historical Analysis." In *The Rights and
        Wrongs of Women*, edited by A. Oakley
        and J. Mitchell. Harmondsworth:
        Penguin.

Beaujot, Roderic
1988   The Family in Crisis?" *Canadian Journal
        of Sociology* 13(3).

Beaujot, Roderic, and Kevin McQuillan
1982   *Growth and Dualism: The Demographic

Development of Canadian Society*.
        Toronto: Gage.

Becker, Howard
1952   "Social Class Variations in the Teacher-
        Pupil Relationship." *Journal of Educa-
        tional Psychology* 25(4).

1963   *The Outsiders*. New York: Free Press.

Beekman, Daniel
1977   *The Mechanical Baby*. New York: New
        American Library.

Beer, Samuel
1973   "The Modernization of American
        Federalism." *Publius: The Journal of
        Federalism* 3: 49–95.

Bell, Daniel
1973   *The Coming of Post-Industrial Society*.
        New York: Basic Books.

1981   "A Reply to Weizenbaum" In *The Mi-
        croelectronic Revolution*, edited by
        T. Forester. Cambridge: MIT Press.

Bell, D., and Lorne Tepperman
1979   *The Roots of Disunity: A Look at
        Canadian Political Culture*. Toronto:
        McClelland and Stewart.

Bendix, Reinhard
1971   *Scholarship and Partisanship: Essays
        on Max Weber*. Berkeley: University of
        California Press.

Benston, Margaret
1982   "Feminism and the Critique of Scientific
        Method." In *Feminism in Canada: From
        Politics to Pressure*, edited by
        Geraldine Finn and Angela Myles.
        Montreal: Black Rose Books.

Bercovitch, Sacvan
1981   "The Rites of Assent: Rhetoric, Ritual
        and the Ideology of American Consen-
        sus." In *The American Self: Myth, Ide-
        ology and Popular Culture*, edited by
        Sam B. Girgus. Albuquerque: University
        of Mexico Press.

Berger, Bennet
1963   "On the Youthfulness of Youth
        Cultures." *Social Research* 30(2):
        319–42.

Berger, Brigitte, and Peter Berger
1983   *The War Over the Family: The Search

for a Middle Ground. New York: Basic Books.

Berger, Carl
1976 *The Writing of Canadian History.* Toronto: Oxford University Press.

Berger, Peter, and Hansfried Kellner
1970 "Marriage and the Construction of Reality." In *Recent Sociology*, edited by Hans Peter Drietzel. New York: Macmillan.

Berger, Peter, and Thomas Luckmann
1967 *The Social Construction of Reality.* New York: Anchor Books.

Bernard, Jessie
1972 *The Future of Marriage.* New York: Bantam Books.

1973 "My Four Revolutions: An Autobiographical History of the ASA." *American Journal of Sociology* 78(4): 11–29.

1981 *The Female World.* New York: Free Press.

Bettelheim, Bruno
1982 *Freud and Man's Soul.* New York: Alfred A. Knopf.

Bissel, Claude
1979 "The Place of Learning and the Arts in Canadian Life." In *Perspectives on Revolution and Evolution*, edited by Richard A. Preston. Durham, N.C.: Duke University Press.

Black, Don, and John Myles
1986 "Dependent Industrialization and the Canadian Class Structure: A Comparative Analysis of Canada, the United States and Sweden." *The Canadian Review of Sociology and Anthropology* 23(2): 157–81.

Blishen, Bernard
1958 "The Construction and Use of an Occupational Class Scale." *Canadian Journal of Economics and Political Science* 24: 519–31.

1967 "A Socio-economic Index for Occupations in Canada." *The Canadian Review of Sociology and Anthropology* 4(1): 41–53.

Blishen, Bernard, and William Carroll
1978 "Sex Differences in a Socio-economic Index for Occupations in Canada." *The Canadian Review of Sociology and Anthropology* 15: 352–71.

Blishen, Bernard, William Carroll, and Catherine Moore
1987 "The 1981 Socio-economic Index for Occupations in Canada." *The Canadian Review of Sociology and Anthropology* 24(4): 465–88.

Blishen, Bernard, and Hugh A. McRoberts
1976 "A Revised Socio-economic Index for Occupations in Canada." *The Canadian Review of Sociology and Anthropology* 13(1): 71–79.

Bloch, Marc
1966 *French Rural Society.* Berkeley: University of California Press.

Block, J. H.
1976 "Issues, Problems, and Pitfalls in Assessing Sex Differences: A Critical Review of the Psychology of Sex Differences." *Merrill-Palmer Quarterly* 22: 283–308.

1978 "Another Look at Sex Differentiation in the Socialization Behaviours of Mothers and Fathers." In *The Psychology of Women: Future Directions in Research*, edited by J.A. Sherman and F.L. Denmark. New York: Psychological Dimensions.

Bluestone, Barry, and Bennett Harrison
1982 *The Deindustrialization of America.* New York: Basic Books.

Blumer, Herbert
1969 *Symbolic Interactionism.* Englewood Cliffs, N.J.: Prentice-Hall.

Bordo, Susan
1986 "The Cartesian Masculinization of Thought." *Signs* 11(3).

Bornat, Joanna
1978 "Home and Work: A New Context for Trade Union History." *Radical America* 12(5).

Boston Women's Health Collective
1976 *Our Bodies, Ourselves.* New York: Simon and Schuster.

1984 *The New Our Bodies, Ourselves.* New York: Anchor Books.

Bottomley, Ann
1985   "What is Happening to Family Law? A Feminist Critique of Conciliation." In *Women in Law*, edited by Julia Brophy and Carol Smart. London: Routledge and Kegan Paul.

Boudon, R.
1974   *Education, Opportunity and Social Inequality*. New York: John Wiley.

Bourdieu, P.
1977   "Cultural Reproduction and Social Reproduction." In *Power and Ideology in Education*, edited by J. H. Karabel and A. H. Halsey. New York: Oxford University Press.

Bourgeault, Ron
1983   "The Indians, the Metis and the Fur Trade: Class, Sexism and Racism in the Transition from Communism to Capitalism." *Studies in Political Economy* 12.

Bowles, Samuel, and Herbert Gintis
1976   *Schooling in Capitalist America*. London: Routledge and Kegan Paul.

Bowles, Samuel, David Gordon, and Thomas Weisskopf
1983   *Beyond the Wasteland; A Democratic Alternative to Economic Decline*. Garden City: Doubleday.

Boyd, Monica
1985   "Immigration and Occupational Attainment." In Boyd, *et al.* (1985).

Boyd, Monica, *et al.*
1977   "The Canadian National Mobility Study." *Canadian Studies in Population* 4: 94–96.

1982   "Sex Differences in the Canadian Occupational Attainment Process." *The Canadian Review of Sociology and Anthropology* 19(1): 1–28.

1985   *Ascription and Achievement: Studies in Mobility and Status Attainment in Canada*. Ottawa: Carleton University Press.

Boyd, Susan
1987   "Child Custody and Working Mothers." In *Equality and Judicial Neutrality*, edited by S. Mahoney and K. E. Mahoney. Toronto: Carswell.

Boyer, J. Patrick
1985   *Equality for All*. Ottawa: Supply and Services.

Bradbrook, P.
1980   "The Telegraph and Femal Telegraphists in Newfoundland." Unpublished Paper, Newfoundland Centre.

Brake, Mike
1980   *The Sociology of Youth Culture and Youth Subcultures*. London: Routledge and Kegan Paul.

1985   *Comparative Youth Culture*. London: Routledge and Kegan Paul.

Branthwaite, Alan, and Tony Lunn
1985   "Projective Techniques in Social Market Research." In *Applied Qualitative Research*, edited by Robert Walker. London: Gower Publishing.

Braroe, Niels
1963   "Reciprocal Exploitation in an Indian-White Community." *Southwestern Journal of Anthropology* 21: 166–78.

Braverman, Harry
1974   *Labor and Monopoly Capital: The Degradation of Work in The Twentieth Century*. New York: Monthly Review Press.

Brenner, Robert
1986   "Agrarian Class Structure and Economic Development in Pre-Industrial Europe." In *The Brenner Debate: Agrarian Class Structure and Economic Development in Pre-Industrial Europe*, edited by T. H. Aston and C. Philipin. Cambridge: Cambridge University Press.

Bronfenbrenner, Urie
1972   *Two Worlds of Childhood*. New York: Simon and Schuster.

Brown, Penelope, and L. J. Jordanov
1981   "Oppressive Dichotomies: The Nature/Culture Debate." In *Women in Society*, edited by The Cambridge Women's Studies Group. London: Virago Press.

Brown, Russell M.
n.d.   "Telemachus and Oedipus: Images of Tradition and Authority in Canadian

and American Fiction." Department of English, University of Toronto.

Brownmiller, Susan
1975   *Against Our Will: Men, Women and Rape.* New York: Simon and Schuster.

1984   *Femininity.* New York: Simon and Schuster.

Brox, O.
1969   *The Maintenance of Economic Dualism in Newfoundland.* St. John's, Nfld.: The Institute for Social and Economic Research.

Brunvand, Jan H.
1983   *The Vanishing Hitchhiker: Urban Legends and Their Meaning.* London: Picador.

Brym, Robert J.
1979   "New Directions in Anglo-Canadian Historical Sociology." *The Canadian Journal of Sociology* 4(3): vii–xi.

1986   "Incorporation Versus Power Models of Working-Class Radicalism: With Special Reference to North America." *The Canadian Journal of Sociology* 11(3): 227–51.

1989   "Canada." In *The Capitalist Class: An International Study*, edited by Tom Bottomore and Robert J. Brym, 177–206. New York: New York University Press.

Brym, Robert J., Michael W. Gillespie, and Rhonda L. Lenton
1989   "Class Power, Class Mobilization and Class Voting: The Canadian Case." *The Canadian Journal of Sociology* 14(1): 25–44.

Burawoy, Michael
1978   "The Functions and Reproduction of Migrant Labour: Comparative Material from Southern Africa and the United States." *American Journal of Sociology* 81(5).

1985   *The Politics of Production.* London: Verso.

Burstyn, Varda
1983   "Masculine Dominance and the State." *The Socialist Register.* 45–49.

Caldwell, Gary
1983   *Les études ethniques au Québec: bilan et perspectives.* Quebec: Institut québécois de recherche sur la culture.

1986   "English Farmers in Quebec." Research Report. Quebec: Institut québécois de recherche sur la culture.

Callard, E. D.
1964   *Achievement Motive in the Four Year Old and Its Relationship to Achievement Expectancies of the Mother.* Ph.D. Dissertation, University of Michigan.

Campbell, C., and G. Szablowski
1979   *The Superbureaucrats: Structure and Behaviour in Central Agencies.* Toronto: Macmillan of Canada.

Canada
1983a   First Ministers' Conference on Aboriginal Rights. Unofficial and Unverified Transcripts, March 15.

1983b   First Ministers' Conference on Aboriginal Rights. Unofficial and Unverified Transcripts, March 16.

Canada, Government of
1984   *Sexual Offences Against Children* (Vol. 2) Ottawa: Ministry of Supply and Services.

1985a   *Royal Commission on the Economic Union and Development Prospects for Canada.* Ottawa: Ministry of Supply and Services.

1985b   *Pornography and Prostitution in Canada.* Ottawa: Canadian Government Publishing Centre.

Caplan, P., and J. Bujra
1978   *Women United: Women Divided.* London: Tavistock.

Caplow, Theodor, *et al.*
1983   *Middletown Families: Fifty Years of Change and Continuity.* Minneapolis: University of Minnesota Press.

Carchedi, Mino
1977   *On the Economic Identification of Social Classes.* London: Routledge and Kegan Paul.

Careless, J. M. S.
1963   *Canada: A Story of Challenge.*
Cambridge: Cambridge University
Press.

Carroll, William K.
1986   *Corporate Power and Canadian Capitalism.* Vancouver: University of British
Columbia Press.

Carstens, Peter
1971   "Coercion and Change." In *Canadian
Society: Pluralism, Change and Conflict,*
edited by R. Ossenberg. Toronto: Prentice-Hall Canada.

Cashmore, E. Ellis
1984   *No Future.* Guildford: Biddles Ltd.

Castles, S., and G. Kossak
1972   *Immigrant Workers and Class Struggle
in Western Europe.* London: Routledge
and Kegan Paul.

Castles, S., and W. Wüstenberg
1979   *Education for the Future.* London: Pluto
Press.

Castonguay, Charles
1980   "Sur quelques indices de propension a
l'exogamie et au transfert linquitique."
Cahier québécois de démographie 9(3):
53–70.

1985   "Transferts et semi-transfers linguist-
ique au Québec d'après les recense-
ments de 1981." *Cahiers québecois de
démographie.* 14(1): 59–85.

Center for Applied Research in the Apostolate
1983   *Values Study of Canada.* Code Book.
Washington, D.C. May.

Chaison, Gary N., and P. Andippan
1982   "Characteristics of Female Union Officers." *Relations Industrielles* 37(4).

Chandler, Marsha A.
1983   "The Politics of Public Enterprise." In
Crown Corporations in Canada, edited
by Robert J. Pritchard. Toronto:
Butterworths.

Chapman, J., ed.
1983   *The Western University on Trial.*
Berkeley: University of California Press.

Charbonneau, Hubert, *et al.*
1971   "Le recensement nominatif du Canada
en 1681." *Histoire Sociale* 7: 77–98.

Charles, Lindsey, and Lorna Duffin, eds.
1985   *Women and Work in Pre-Industrial England.* London: Croom Helm.

Cheal, D.
1978   "Religion and the Social Order." *The
Canadian Journal of Sociology* 3(1):
61–69.

Chiaramonte, L. J.
1970   *Craftsman-Client Contracts: Interper-
sonal Relations in A Newfoundland
Fishing Community.* St. John's, Nfld.:
Institute of Social and Economic
Research.

Chodorow, Nancy
1978   *The Reproduction of Mothering: Psychoanalysis and the Sociology of Gender.* Berkeley: University of California
Press.

Christian, William, and Colin Campbell
1983   *Political Parties and Ideologies in Canada.* Toronto: McGraw-Hill Ryerson.

Clare, Anthony
1983   "The Relationship Between Psychopathology and the Menstrual Cycle." In
Lifting the Curse of Menstruation, edited by Sharon Golub. New York: The
Haworth Press.

Clark, Alice
1982   *Working Life of Women in the Seventeenth Century.* (1919) London: Routledge and Kegan Paul.

Clark, Lorenne M. G., and Debra J. Lewis
1977   *Rape: The Price of Coercive Sexuality.*
Toronto: Women's Press.

Clark, S. D.
1938   *Canada and Her Great Neighbor: Sociological Surveys of Opinions and Attitudes in Canada Concerning the
United States.* Toronto: Ryerson Press.

1948   *Church and Sect in Canada.* Toronto:
University of Toronto Press.

1950   "The Canadian Community." In *Canada,*
edited by George W. Brown. Berkeley:
University of California Press.

1962   *The Developing Canadian Community.* Toronto: University of Toronto Press.

1976   *Canada Society in Historical Perspective.* Toronto: McGraw-Hill Ryerson.

Clarke, Michael
1974   "On the Concept of Subculture." *British Journal of Sociology* 25: 428–41.

Clement, Wallace
1975   *The Canadian Corporate Elite: An Analysis of Economic Power.* Toronto: McClelland and Stewart.

1977   *Continental Corporate Power.* Toronto: McClelland and Stewart.

1981   *Hardrock Mining: Industrial Relations and Technological Change at Inco.* Toronto: McClelland and Stewart.

1983   *Class, Power and Property: Essays on Canadian Society.* Toronto: Methuen.

1986   *The Struggle to Organize: Resistance in Canada's Fisheries.* Toronto: McClelland and Stewart.

Clinard, M. B., and R. E. Meier
1985   *Sociology of Deviant Behaviour.* Toronto: Holt, Rinehart and Winston.

Cloward, Richard A., and Lloyd Ohlin
1960   *Delinquency and Opportunity.* Glencoe, Ill.: The Free Press.

Cohen, Albert K.
1955   *Delinquent Boys.* Glencoe, Ill.: The Free Press.

Cohen, Ronald
1985   "Childsaving and Progressivism, 1885–1915." In *American Childhood*, edited by Joseph Hawes and Ray Hiner. Connecticut: Greenwood Press.

Cohen, Stanley
1980   *Folk Devils and Moral Panics.* London: MacGibbon and Kee.

1985   *Visions of Social Control.* London: Basil Blackwell.

Condry, J., and S. Condry
1976   "Sex Differences: A Study of the Eye of the Beholder." *Child Development* 47: 812–19.

Conrad, Peter
1975   "The Discovery of Hyperkinesis: Note on the Medicalization of Deviant Behaviour." *Social Problems* 23(1): 12–21.

Conrad, Peter, and Joseph Schneider
1980   *Deviance and Medicalization.* St. Louis: Mosby

Copp, Terry
1974   "The Conditions of the Working Class in Montreal, 1897–1920. In *Studies in Canadian History*, edited by Michael Horn and Ronald Sabourin. Toronto: Oxford University Press.

Corbin, Alain
1986   *The Foul and the Fragrant.* Cambridge, Mass.: Harvard University Press.

Cowan, Ruth Schwartz
1983   *More Work for Mother: The Ironies of Household Technology From the Open Hearth to the Microwave.* New York: Basic Books.

Crabtree, Adam
1985   *Multiple Man: Explorations in Possession and Multiple Personality.* Toronto: Praeger.

Craig, C., *et al.*
1983   "Women's Pay in Informal Payment Systems." *Employment Gazette* 91(4).

Cranston, Maurice, ed.
1966   *A Glossary of Political Terms.* London: Bodley Head.

Crean, Susan
1988   *In the Name of the Fathers: The Story Behind Child Custody.* Toronto: Amanita Enterprises.

Creighton, Donald
1957   *Harold Adam Innis: Portrait of a Scholar.* Toronto: University of Toronto Press.

1970   *The Commercial Empire of the St. Lawrence, 1760–1850.* Toronto: Macmillan (1937).

Croll, E.
1978   *Feminism and Socialism in China.* London: Routledge and Kegan Paul.

Cross, D. D.
        "The Neglected Majority: The Changing Role of Women in the Nineteenth Century." In Trofimenkoff and Prentice (1977).

Cuneo, Carl
1979   "State, Class and Reserve Labour: The
       Case of the 1941 Canadian Unemploy-
       ment Insurance Act." *The Canadian
       Review of Sociology and Anthropology*
       16(2): 147–70.

1980   "Class, Stratification and Mobility." In
       Sociology, edited by R. Hagedorn.
       Toronto: Holt, Rinehart and Winston.

Cuneo, C., and J. Curtis
1975   "Social Ascription in the Educational
       and Occupational Status Attainment of
       Urban Canadians." *The Canadian Re-
       view of Sociology and Anthropology*
       12(1): 6–24.

Curtis, Jim, Ed Grabb, Neil Guppy, and Sid
Gilbert
1988   *Social Inequality in Canada: Patterns
       and Policies.* Scarborough: Prentice-
       Hall Canada.

Dale, R.
1982   "Education and the Capitalist State:
       Contributions and Contradictions." In
       Apple (1982).

Dalton, Katharina
1978   *Once a Month.* Glasgow: Fontana
       Books.

Daly, Mary
1978   *Gyn/Ecology: The Meta-Ethics of Radi-
       cal Feminism.* New York: The Modern
       Library.

Dancis, Bruce
1978   "Safety Pins and Class Struggle: Punk
       Rock and the Left." *Socialist Review*
       8(3): 58–83.

D'Andrade, R. G.
1966   "Sex Differences and Cultural Institu-
       tions." In *The Development of Sex
       Differences*, edited by E. E. Maccoby.
       Stanford: Stanford University Press.

Darling, M.
1925   *The Punjab Peasant in Prosperity and
       Debt.* London: Allen and Unwin.

Darroch, Gordon
1979   "Another Look at Ethnicity, Stratifica-
       tion and Social Mobility in Canada."

The Canadian Journal of Sociology 4(1):
1–26.

Darwin, Charles
1955   *The Expression of the Emotions of Man
       and Animals.* New York: Philosophical
       Library.

Davis, Arthur K.
1971   "Canadian Society and History as Hin-
       terland Versus Metropolis." In *Cana-
       dian Society: Pluralism, Change and
       Conflict*, edited by Richard J. Ossen-
       berg. Scarborough: Prentice-Hall
       Canada.

Davis, D.
1979   "Social Structure, Sex Roles and Female
       Associations in a Newfoundland Fish-
       ing Village." Unpublished Paper, New-
       foundland Centre.

1980   "Women's Experiences of the Men-
       opause in a Newfoundland Fishing Vil-
       lage." Ph.D. Thesis, University of North
       Carolina.

Davis, Kingsley
1972   "The American Family in Relation to
       Economic Change." In *Demographic
       and Social Aspects of Population
       Growth*, edited by Charles Westoff and
       Robert Parke. Washington: U.S. Govern-
       ment Printing Offices.

Davis, Kingsley, and Wilbert E. Moore
1945   "Some Principles of Stratification."
       American Sociological Review 21(2):
       242–49.

Davis, Murray
1983   *Smut: Erotic Reality/Obscene Ideology.*
       Chicago: University of Chicago Press.

Davis, Ralph
1973   *The Rise of the Atlantic Economies.*
       London: Weidenfeld and Nicholson.

de Beauvoir, Simone
1972   *The Second Sex.* Harmondsworth:
       Penguin Books.

Degler, Carl
1980   *At Odds: Women and the Family in
       America from the Revolution to the
       Present.* New York: Oxford University
       Press.

Delamont, S.
1983   "The Conservative School? Sex Roles at
        Home, at Work and at School." In
        Walker and Barton (1983).

Delaney, Janice, *et al.*
1976   *The Curse.* New York: E.P. Dutton.

Delaney, Janice, M. J. Lupton, and Emily Toth
1976   *The Curse: A Cultural History of Men-
        struation.* New York: E.P. Dutton.

Delphy, Christine
1977   *The Main Enemy.* London: Women's
        Research and Resources Centre.

de Mause, Lloyd, ed.
1975   *The History of Childhood.* New York:
        Harper and Row.

Demos, John
1978   "Infancy and Childhood in Plymouth
        Colony." In Gordon (1978).

Denis, Ann
1986   "Adaptation to Multiple Subordination?
        Women in the Vertical Mosaic." *Cana-
        dian Ethnic Studies.* 18(3): 61–74.

Denton, Frank, Christine M. Feaver, and Byrin
G. Spencer
1980   *The Future Population and Labour
        Force of Canada: Projections to the
        Year 2051.* Ottawa: Ministry of Supply
        and Services.

Devereux, Edward C., *et al.*
1976   "Child Rearing in England and the
        United States: A Cross-national Com-
        parison." In *The Canadian Family in
        Comparative Perspective*, edited by L.
        Larson. Scarborough: Prentice-Hall
        Canada.

Dinnerstein, Dorothy
1976   *The Mermaid and the Minotaur: Sexual
        Arrangements and Human Malaise.*
        New York: Harper and Row.

Dobb, Maurice
1963   *Studies in the Development of Cap-
        italism.* New York: International
        Publishers.

Donzelot, Jacques
1979   *The Policing of Families.* New York:
        Pantheon Press.

Douglas, Ernest, and Bruce Quarrington
1952   "Differentiation of Interiorized and Ex-
        teriorized Secondary Stuttering." *Jour-
        nal of Speech and Hearing Disorders* 17:
        377–85.

Douglas, Mary
1966   *Purity and Danger: An Analysis of Con-
        cepts of Pollution and Taboo.*
        Harmondsworth: Penguin.

Downes, D.
1966   *The Delinquent Solution.* London:
        Routledge and Kegan Paul.

Downes, D., and P. Rock
1982   *Understanding Deviance.* Oxford: Clar-
        endon Press.

Drache, Daniel
1970   "The Canadian Bourgeoisie and its Na-
        tional Consciousness." In *Close the
        49th Parallel etc.: The Americanization
        of Canada*, edited by Ian Lumsden.
        Toronto: University of Toronto Press.

1977   "Staple-ization: A Theory of Canadian
        Capitalist Development." In *Imperi-
        alism, Nationalism and Canada*, edited
        by Craig Heron. Toronto: New Hogtown
        Press.

1978   "Rediscovering Canadian Political
        Economy." In *A Practical Guide to
        Canadian Political Economy*, edited by
        W. Clement and Daniel Drache.
        Toronto: Lorimer.

Dubinsky, Karen
1984   "Lament for a 'Patriarchy Lost' — Anti-
        feminism, Anti-abortion and R.E.A.L.
        Women in Canada." Ottawa: Canadian
        Research Institute for the Advancement
        of Women.

Duffy, Ann
1986   "Reformulating Power for Women." *The
        Canadian Review of Sociology and An-
        thropology* 23(1): 22–46.

Duncan, Otis Dudley, and Beverly Duncan
1955   "Residential Distribution and Occupa-
        tional Stratification." *American Journal
        of Sociology* 60: 493–503.

Durkheim, Emile
1950   *The Rules of the Sociological Method.*
        Glencoe, Ill.: The Free Press (1895).

1951   *Suicide: A Study in Sociology.* New York: Free Press (1897).

Economic Council of Canada
1987   *Making Technology Work: Innovation and Jobs in Canada.* Ottawa: Ministry of Supply and Services.

Edwards, P. K., and G. S. Bain
1988   "Why Are Trade Unions Becoming More Popular? Unions and Public Opinion in Britain." *British Journal of Industrial Relations* 26(3).

Ehrlich, Carol
1977   *Socialism, Anarchism and Feminism.* Baltimore: Research Group One Report No. 26.

Eichler, Margrit
1973   "Personal Dependents: A Critique of Theories of the Stratification of the Sexes and an Alternative Approach." In *Women in Canada,* edited by Marylee Stephenson. Don Mills: General Publishing Co.

1985   "And the Work Never Ends: Feminist Contributions." *The Canadian Review of Sociology and Anthropology* 22(5): 619–44.

1985   "The Pro-Family Movement: Are They For or Against Families?" Ottawa: Canadian Research Institute for the Advancement of Women.

1988   *Canadian Families Today.* Toronto: Gage (1983).

Eisenberg, Leon, and Arthur Kleinman
1981   *The Relevance of Social Science for Medicine.* Boston: D. Reidel Publishing.

Eisenstein, Zillah
1981   *The Radical Future of Liberal Feminism.* Boston: Northwestern University Press.

1984   *Feminism and Sexual Equality.* New York: Monthly Review Press.

Elias, Norbert
1978   *The History of Manners.* Oxford: Basil Blackwell (1939).

1982   *Power and Civility.* New York: Pantheon Books (1939).

Elkin, Fredrick
1968   *The Family in Canada.* Ottawa: The Vanier Institute.

Engels, Friedrich
1942   "Engels to Sorge." (1890) In *Selected Correspondence,* edited by Karl Marx and Friedrich Engels. New York: International Publishers.

1953   "Engels to Sorge." (1888) In *Letters to Americans,* edited by Karl Marx and Friedrich Engels. New York: International Publishers.

Enzensberger, Christian
1972   *Smut: An Anatomy of Dirt.* New York: Seabury Press.

Esping-Anderson, Gosta
1987   *Post-industrial Employment Trajectories: Germany, Sweden and the United States.* Florence: European University.

Everhart, R.
1982   *The In Between Years.* London: Routledge and Kegan Paul.

Fagot, B. I.
1977   "How Parents Reinforce Feminine Role Behaviours in Toddler Girls." *Association for Women in Psychology.* St. Louis, Miss.

Fanon, Franz
1965   *The Wretched of the Earth.* New York: Grove Press.

Faris, J.
1972   *Cat Harbour.* St. John's Nfld.: The Institute for Social and Economic Research.

Fee, Elizabeth
1981   "Is Feminism a Threat to Scientific Objectivity?" *International Journal of Women's Studies* 4(4).

1983   "Women's Nature and Scientific Objectivity." In *Women's Nature: Rationalizations of Inequality,* edited by Marian Lowe and Ruth Hubbard. New York: Pergamon Press.

Festinger, Leon
1954   "A Theory of Social Comparison Processes." *Human Relations* 7: 117–40.

Fine, Gary, and Sherryl Kleinman
1979   "Rethinking Subculture: An Interactionist Analysis." *American Journal of Sociology* 85(1): 1–20.

1983   "Network and Meaning: An Interactionist Approach to Structure." *Symbolic Interaction* 6(1): 97-110.

Finkelstein, Barbara
1985   "Casting Networks of Good Influence: The Reconstruction of Childhood in the United States, 1790–1870." In *American Childhood*, edited by M. Hawes and R. Hiner. Connecticut: Greenwood Press.

Finlayson, Ann
1987   "A New Emphasis on the Family." *Maclean's* January 5.

Firestone, M.
1967   *Brothers and Rivals*. St. John's, Nfld.: The Institute for Social and Economic Research.

Firestone, Shulamith
1970   *The Dialectic of Sex*. New York: Morrow.

Fling, S., and M. Manosevitz
1972   "Sex Typing in Nursery School Children's Play Interests." *Developmental Psychology* 7: 146–52.

Flynn, Charles P.
1977   *Insult and Society*. Port Washington: Kennikat Press.

Flynn, John
1920   *The Influence of Puritanism*. Port Washington: Kennikat Press.

Foot, David, and Noah Meltz
1985   "The Economic Determinants of Changes in Occupational Structure in Canada, 1961–1981. "Paper presented at the Annual Meetings of the Canadian Economics Association.

Forcese, Dennis
1980   *The Canadian Class Structure*. Toronto: McGraw-Hill Ryerson.

Form, William
1987   "On the Degradation of Skills." *Annual Review of Sociology* 13: 29–47.

Fortune, W. F.
1939   "Arapesh Warfare." *American Anthropologist*. 41: 22–41.

Foucault, Michel
1965   *Madness and Civilization*. New York: Random House.

1975   *The Birth of the Clinic: An Archaeology of Medical Perception*. New York: Random House.

1979   *Discipline and Punish: The Birth of the Prison*. New York: Vintage Books Edition.

Fox, Bonnie, ed.
1980   *Hidden in the Household*. Toronto: The Women's Press.

Fox, Bonnie, and John Fox
1987   "Occupational Gender Segregation in the Canadian Labour Force, 1931–1981." *The Canadian Review of Sociology and Anthropology* 24(3): 374–97.

Fox Keller, Evelyn
1981   "Women and Science: Two Cultures or One?" *International Journal of Women's Studies* 4(4).

1983   "Gender and Science." In Harding and Hintikka (1983).

Fraiberrg, Selma
1977   *Every Child's Birthright: In Defense of Mothering*. New York: Basic Books.

Frank, Andre Gunder
1966   "The Development of Underdevelopment." *Monthly Review* 18(4): 17–31.

Frazer, J.
1958   *The Golden Bough: A Study in Magic and Religion*. New York: Macmillan.

Freidson, Eliot
1970   *Professional Dominance*. New York: Atherton Press.

Freud, Sigmund
1961   *Civilization and Its Discontents*. New York: W.W. Norton.

1977   *New Introductory Lectures on Psychoanalysis*. Harmondsworth: Penguin.

Frith, Simon
1978a *The Sociology of Rock*. London: Constable.

1978b "The Punk Bohemians." *New Society* 43: 535–36.

1983   *Sound Effects: Youth, Leisure and the Politics of Rock*. London: Constable.

1985   "The Sociology of Youth." In *Sociology: New Directions*, edited by Michael Harabos. Ormkirsk: Causeway Press.

Frye, Northrop
1953   "Letters in Canada: 1952. Part I: Publications in English." *The University of Toronto Quarterly* 22: 269–80.

Fuchs, Victor
1983   *How We Live.* Cambridge: Harvard University Press.

Galtung, Johan
1971   "A Structural Theory of Imperialism." *Journal of Peace Research* 8(2): 81–117.

Garai, J. E., and A. Scheinfeld
1968   "Sex Differences in Mental and Behavioural Traits." *Genetic Psychology Monographs* 77: 169–299.

Gaskell, Jane
1981   "Sex Inequalities in Education for Work: The Case of Business Education." *Canadian Journal of Education* 6(2).

Gaylin, Willard
1983   *The Killing of Bonnie Garland: A Question of Justice.* New York: Penguin.

Geoffroy, Renée, and Paule Sainte Marie
1971   *Attitude of Union Workers to Women in Industry.* Ottawa: Information Canada.

George, C. E.
1971   "The Making of the English Bourgeoisie, 1500–1750," *Science and Society* 35: 385–414.

Gerth, Hans, and C. Wright Mills
1946   "The Man and His Work." In *From Max Weber: Essays in Sociology*, edited by H. H. Gerth and C. W. Mills. New York: Oxford University Press.

Gibbins, Roger
1982   *Regionalism: Territorial Politics in Canada and the United States.* Toronto: Butterworths.

Gibbons, D. C.
1981   *Delinquent Behaviour.* Englewood Cliffs, N.J.: Prentice-Hall.

Giddens, Anthony
1981   *A Contemporary Critique of Historical Materialism.* London: MacMillan.

Gilligan, Carol
1979   "Women's Place in Men's Life Cycle." *Harvard Educational Review* 49(4): 431–46.

1982   *In a Different Voice.* Cambridge: Harvard University Press.

Glaser, Barney, and Anselm Strauss
1967   *The Discovery of Grounded Theory: Strategies for Qualitative Research.* New York: Aldine.

Glazer, Nathan, and Daniel P. Moynihan
1975   "Introduction." In *Ethnicity: Theory and Experience*, edited by N. Glazer and D. Moynihan. Cambridge: Harvard University Press.

Glazier, Kenneth M.
1972   "Canadian Investment in the United States: Putting Your Money Where Your Mouth Is." *Journal of Contemporary Business* 1: 61–66.

Gmelch, G.
1971   "Baseball Magic." *Society* 8(8): 39–41.

Godelier, M.
1980   "Work and Its Representation: A Research Proposal." *History Workshop Journal:* 158–69.

Goffman, Erving
1959   *The Presentation of Self in Everyday Life.* New York: Doubleday.

1963   *Stigma.* Englewood Cliffs, N.J.: Prentice-Hall.

1967   *Interaction Ritual.* Garden City, N.Y.: Doubleday.

Goldberg, S., and M. Lewis
1969   "Play Behaviour in the Year-Old Infant: Early Sex Differences." *Child Development* 40: 21–31.

Goldenberg, Sheldon
1987   *Thinking Sociologically.* Belmont, Calif.: Wadsworth Publishing.

Good, Byron, and Mary-Jo Delvecchio Good
1981   "The Meaning of Symptoms: A Cultural Hermeneutic Model for Clinical Practice." In L. Eisenberg and A. Kleinman (1981).

Goode, William J.
1970   *World Revolution and Family Patterns.*

New York: Free Press.

Goodenough, E. W.
1957   "Interest in Persons As an Aspect of Sex Differences in the Early Years." *Genetic Psychology Monographs* 55: 287–323.

Gordon, Linda, and Ellen Dubois
1984   "Seeking Ecstasy on the Battlefield: Danger and Pleasure in Nineteenth Century Feminist Sexual Thought." In *Pleasure and Danger: Exploring Female Sexuality*, edited by Carole S. Vance. London: Routledge and Kegan Paul.

Gordon, Michael, ed.
1978   *The American Family: Past Present and Future.* New York: Random House.

Gordon, Milton M.
1947   "The Concept of Subculture and Its Application." *Social Forces* 26: 40–42.

Goubert, Pierre
1973   *The Ancient Regime.* New York: Harper and Row.

Goyder, John
1980   "Trends in the Socio-economic Achievement of the University Educated: A Status Attainment Model Interpretation." *Canadian Journal of Higher Education* 10(2): 21–38.

Goyder, John, and James Curtis
1979   "Occupational Mobility in Canada Over Four Generations." In *Social Stratification: Canada*, edited by J. Curtis and W. Scott. Toronto: Prentice-Hall Canada.

Grant, John Webster
1973   "At Least You Knew Where You Stood with Them: Reflections on Religious Pluralism in Canada and the United States." *Studies in Religion* 2: 340–51.

Grant, George
1965   *Lament for a Nation.* Toronto: McClelland and Stewart.

Gray, T. S.
1984   "Herbert Spencer on Women: A Study in Personal and Political Disillusion." *International Journal of Women's Studies* 7(3).

Grayson, J. P., and L. Grayson
1979   "The Canadian Literary Elite: A Socio-

Historical Perspective." *The Canadian Journal of Sociology* 3(3): 291–308.

Greenfield, Sidney M.
1973   "Industrialization and the Family in Sociological Theory." In *Readings on the Changing Family*, edited by David A. Schulz and Robert A. Wilson. Englewood Cliffs, N.J.: Prentice-Hall.

Griffin, Larry, *et al.*
1986   "Methodological Innovations in the Analysis of Welfare-State Development." In *The Futures for the Welfare State*, edited by Norman Furniss. Bloomington: Indiana University Press.

1989   "National Variation in the Context of Struggle: Postwar Class Conflict and Market Distribution in the Capitalist Democracies." *The Canadian Review of Sociology and Anthropology* 26(1): 37–68.

Griffiths, Curt T., *et al.*
1980   *Criminal Justice in Canada.* Toronto: Butterworths.

Griffiths, Naomi
1976   *Penelope's Web: Some Perceptions of Women in European and Canadian Society.* Toronto: University of Toronto Press.

Grindstaff, Carl
1985   "The Baby Bust Revisited: Canada's Continuing Pattern of Low Fertility." *Canadian Studies in Population* 12(1): 103–10.

1984   "Catching Up: The Fertility of Women Over 30 Years of Age, Canada in the 1970's and 1980's." *Canadian Studies in Population* 2: 15–22.

Gross, Beatrice, and Ronald Gross
1977   *The Children's Rights Movement.* New York: Doubleday.

Grumet, Madeleine
1981   "Pedagogy for Patriarchy." *Interchange* 12(2–3): 165–84.

Guppy, N.
1983   "Social Change and Access to Higher Education in Canada." Unpublished paper. Vancouver: University of British Columbia.

Gustavson, Carl
1944   "A Talisman and a Convalescence."
        Quarterly Journal of Speech 30(1):
        465–71.

Hacker, Helen
1951   "Women as a Minority Group." *Social
        Forces* 30(1): 60–69.

Hagan, John
1984   *The Disreputable Pleasures: Crime and
        Deviance in Canada*. Toronto: McGraw-
        Hill Ryerson.

Hagan, John, and Jeffrey Leon
1978   "Philosophy and Sociology of Crime
        Control." In *Social System and Legal
        Process*, edited by Harry M. Johnson.
        San Francisco: Jossey-Bass.

Hagedorn, R., and S. Labovitz
1973   *An Introduction to Sociological Orienta-
        tions*. Toronto: Wiley and Sons.

Halfpenny, Peter
1982   *Positivism and Sociology: Explaining
        Social Life*. London: Allen and Unwin.

Hale, Sylvia
1988   "Male Culture and Purdah for Women:
        The Social Construction of What
        Women Think." *The Canadian Review
        of Sociology and Anthropology* 25(2):
        276–98.

Halsey, A., A. Heath, and J. Ridge
1980   *Origins and Destinations: Family, Class
        and Education in Modern Britain*.
        Oxford: Clarendon Press.

Hamilton, Richard, and M. Pinard
1977   "Poverty in Canada: Illusion and Real-
        ity." *The Canadian Review of Sociology
        and Anthropology* 14(2): 247–52.

Hamilton, Roberta
1978   *The Liberation of Women*. London:
        Allen and Unwin.

1986   "The Collusion with Patriarchy: A Psy-
        choanalytic Account." In Hamilton and
        Barrett (1986).

1987   "Does Misogyny Matter?" *Studies in
        Political Economy* 23: 123–39.

Hamilton, Roberta, and Michele Barrett, eds.
1986   *The Politics of Diversity: Feminism,*

Marxism and Nationalism. London:
Verso.

Hardin, Herschel
1974   *A Nation Unaware: The Canadian Eco-
        nomic Culture*. Vancouver: J.J. Douglas.

Harding, Sandra, and Merrill Hintikka, eds.
1983   *Discovering Reality: Feminist Perspec-
        tives on Epistemology, Metaphysics,
        Methodology and the Philosophy of
        Science*. Derdrecht, Holland: D. Reidal.

Hareven, Tamara, ed.
1978   *Transitions: The Family and the Life
        Course in Historical Perspective*. New
        York: Academic Press.

Harp, J.
1980   "Social Inequalities and the Transmis-
        sion of Knowledge: The Case Against
        the Schools." In *Structured Inequality
        in Canada*, edited by J. Harp and J.
        Hofley. Toronto: Prentice-Hall Canada.

Harris, Marvin
1979   *Cultural Materialism: The Struggle for a
        Science of Culture*. New York: Random
        House.

Harris, R. C., and J. Warkenton
1974   *Canada Before Confederation: A Study
        of Historical Geography*. Toronto:
        Oxford University Press.

Hartmann, Heidi
1976   "Capitalism, Patriarchy and Job Segre-
        gation by Sex." *Signs* 1(3): 137–70.

Hartz, Louis
1955   *The Liberal Tradition in America*. New
        York: Harcourt Brace.

1964   *The Founding of New Societies*. New
        York: Harcourt Brace and World.

Harvey, E.
1977   "Accessibility to Post-Secondary Educa-
        tion." *University Affairs* October: 10–11.

Hatfield, Elaine, and Susan Sprecher
1986   *Mirror, Mirror: The Importance of
        Looks in Everyday Life*. Albany, N.Y.:
        SUNY Press.

Hawkins, Darnell F.
1986   "Black and White Homicide Differen-
        tials: Alternatives to an Inadequate The-
        ory." In *Homicide Among Black
        Americans*, edited by D. Hawkins. New

York: University Press of America.

Hayden, Dolores
1981   *The Grand Domestic Revolution: A History of Feminist Designs for American Homes*. Cambridge: Harvard University Press.

Hein, Hilde
1981   "Women and Science: Fitting Men to Think About Nature." *International Journal of Women's Studies* 4(4).

Henley, Nancy M.
1977   *Body Politics: Power, Sex and Non-Verbal Communication*. New York: Simon and Schuster.

Henry, Frances, and Effie Ginsberg
1985   *Who Gets the Work?* Toronto: Urban Alliance on Relations and the Social Planning Council of Toronto.

Henshel, Anne-Marie
1973   *Sex Structure*. Don Mills: Longman, Canada.

Henslin, J.
1967   "Craps and Magic." *The American Journal of Sociology* 73: 316–30.

Heron, Craig
1980   "The Crisis of the Craftsman: Hamilton's Metalworkers in the Early Twentieth Century." *Labour/Le Travailleur* 6 Autumn.

Heron, Craig, and Robert Storey, ed.
1986   *On the Job*. Kingston: McGill-Queen's University Press.

Higgins, Paul C.
1980   "Social Reaction and the Physically Disabled: Bringing the Impairment Back In." *Symbolic Interaction* 3: 139–56.

Hilbert, Richard A.
1984   "The Acculturation Dimension of Chronic Pain: Flawed Reality Construction and the Problem of Meaning." *Social Problems* 31(4): 365–78.

Hill, Christopher
1969   *Reformation to Industrial Revolution*. Harmondsworth: Penguin Books.

Hilton, Rodney
1976   *The Transition from Feudalism to Capitalism*. London: New Left Books.

1986   "A Crisis of Feudalism" In *The Brenner Debate: Agrarian Class Structure and Economic Development in Pre-Industrial Europe*, edited by T. H. Ashton and C. H. E. Philpin. Cambridge: Cambridge University Press.

Himelfarb, Alexander, and C. James Richardson
1979   *People, Power and Process: Sociology for Canadians*. Toronto: McGraw-Hill Ryerson.

1982   *Sociology for Canadians: Images of Society*. Toronto: McGraw-Hill Ryerson.

Hirschorn, L.
1978   "The Political Economy of Social Service Rationalization: A Developmental View." *Contemporary Crisis* 2: 63–81.

Hoffman, L. W.
1977   "Changes in Family Roles, Socialization and Sex Differences." *American Psychologist* 32: 644–57.

Homans, George
1941   "Anxiety and Magic." *American Anthropologist* 43: 164–72.

Hopsen, Janet, and Anne Rosenfeld
1984   "Puzzling Monthly Symptoms." *Psychology Today* August: 30–35.

Hornell, J.
1980   *Fishing in Many Waters*. Cambridge: Cambridge University Press.

Horowitz, Gad
1977   *Repression: Basic and Surplus Repression in Psychoanalytic Theory*. Toronto: University of Toronto Press.

Horowitz, Irving L.
1973   "The Hemispheric Connection: A Critique and Corrective to the Entrepreneurial Thesis of Development with Special Emphasis on the Canadian Case." *Queen's Quarterly* 80: 336–37.

Hubbard, Ruth
1983   "Have Only Men Evolved?" In Harding and Hintikka (1983).

1983   "Social Effects on Some Contemporary Myths About Women." In *Women's Nature: Rationalizations of Inequality*, edited by Marian Lowe and Ruth Hubbard. New York: Pergamon Press.

Hueglin, Thomas O.
1984   "The End of Institutional Tidiness?
        Trends of Late Federalism in the United
        States and Canada." *Queen's Quarterly*
        80: 327–59.

Hughes, D., and E. Kallen
1974   *The Anatomy of Racism: Canadian Di-
        mensions*. Toronto: Harvest House.

Hughes, Patricia
1985   "Pornography: Alternatives to Cen-
        sorship." *Canadian Journal of Political
        and Social Theory* 9(1–2): 96–126.

Hunt, David
1970   *Parents and Children in History: The
        Psychology of Family Life in Early
        Modern France*. New York: Basic
        Books.

Hunt, James
1863   *Stammering and Stuttering: Their
        Nature and Treatment*. London: Long-
        mans and Green.

Hunter, Alfred
1976   "Class and Status in Canada." In *Intro-
        duction to Canadian Society*, edited by
        G. N. Ramu and S. Johnson. Toronto:
        MacMillan of Canada.

1986   *Class Tells: On Social Inequality in
        Canada*. Toronto: Butterworths (1981).

Illick, Joseph E.
1974   "Child Rearing in Seventeenth Century
        England and America." In de Mause
        (1975).

Innis, Harold
1956   *Essays in Canadian History*. Toronto:
        University of Toronto Press.

1973   *Essays in Canadian Economic History*.
        Toronto: University of Toronto Press.

1970   *The Fur Trade in Canada*. Toronto:
        University of Toronto Press.

Irigaray, Luce
1974   *Speculum de l'autre femme*. Paris: Edi-
        tions de Minuit.

Irving, Howard
1972   *The Family Myth*. Toronto: Copp Clark.

Irving, Howard, *et al.*
1984   "Shared Parenting: An Empirical Study
        Using a Large Data Base." *Family Pro-
        cess* 23: 561–69.

Ishwaran, K., ed.
1971   *The Canadian Family*. Toronto: Holt,
        Rinehart and Winston.

Jahoda, G.
1969   *The Psychology of Superstition*. Har-
        mondsworth: Penguin.

James, Selma
1974   "Sex, Race and Working Class Strug-
        gle." *Race Today* January.

Jenkins, C.
1982   "Push-Pull in Recent Mexican Migration
        to the U.S.A." *New Left Review*.

Johnson, Wendell
1944a   "The Indian has No Word for It: Part 1,
        Stuttering in Children." *Quarterly Jour-
        nal of Speech* 30 (October): 330–37.

1944b   "The Indian has No Word for It: Part 2
        Stuttering in Adults." *Quarterly Journal
        of Speech* 30 (December): 456–65.

Jordan, Z. A.
1971   *Karl Marx: Economy, Class and Social
        Revolution*. London: Michael Joseph.

Kaestle, Carl, and Maris A. Vinovskis
1978   "From Fireside to Factory: School Entry
        and School Leaving in Nineteenth Cen-
        tury Massachusetts." In Hareven
        (1978).

Katz, Michael
1972a   "The People of a Canadian City: 1851–
        52." *Canadian Historical Review* 53:
        249–301.

1972b   "Who Went to School?" *History of
        Education Quarterly* 12: 432–54.

1975   *The People of Hamilton West: Family
        and Class in a Mid-Nineteenth Century
        City*. Cambridge: Harvard University
        Press.

Katznelson, Ira
1981   *City Trenches: Urban Politics and the
        Patterning of Class in the United States*.

Chicago: University of Chicago Press.

Kaufman, Michael, ed.
1987 *Beyond Patriarchy: Essays by Men on Pleasure*. Toronto: Oxford University Press.

Kealey, Gregory, and Peter Warrian, eds.
1976 *Essays in Canadian Working Class History*. Toronto: McClelland and Stewart.

Kealey, Greg
1976 "The Honest Workingman and Workers Control: The Experiences of Toronto Skilled Workers, 1860–1892." *Labour/Le Travailleur* Spring.

Keat, Russell, and John Urry
1982 *Social Theory as Science*. London: Routledge and Kegan Paul.

Keddie, N.
1971 "Classroom Knowledge." In *Knowledge and Control*, edited by Michael Young. London: Collier-Macmillan.

Kelly, Joan
1984 *Women, History and Theory: The Essays of Joan Kelly*. Chicago: University of Chicago Press.

Kelner, M.
1970 "Ethnic Penetration into Toronto's Elite Structure." *The Canadian Review of Sociology and Anthropology* 7(2): 128–37.

Kendal, Denise B.
1978 "On Variations in Adolescent Subculture." *Youth and Society* 19(4): 372–84.

Killian, Crawford
1985 *School Wars: The Assault on B.C. Education*. Vancouver: Star Books.

Kira, Alexander
1976 *The Bath Room*. New York: Viking Press.

Klein, Alice, and Wayne Roberts
1974 "Besieged Innocence: The Problem and Problems of Working Women — Toronto, 1896–1914." In *Women at Work*, edited by J. Acton *et al.* Toronto: The Canadian Women's Educational Press.

Kleinman, Arthur
1980 *Patients and Healers in the Context of Culture*. London: University of California Press.

Kochanm, Thomas A.
1979 "How American Workers View Labour Unions." *Monthly Labour Review* April: 23–31.

Kotarba, Joseph K.
1977 "The Chronic Pain Experience." In *Existential Sociology*, edited by Jack Douglas and J. M. Johnson. Cambridge: Cambridge University Press.

Krahn, Harvey, Timothy F. Hartnagel, and John W. Gartrell
1986 "Income Inequality and Homicide Rates: Cross-National Data and Criminological Theories." *Criminology* 24: 269–95.

Krahn, Harvey, and Graham S. Lowe
1984a "Public Attitudes Towards Unions: Some Canadian Evidence." *Journal of Labour Research* 5(2): 149–64.

1984b "Community Influences on Attitudes Towards Unions." *Relations Industrielles* 39(1): 93–112.

Kralt, John
1980 "Ethnic Origin in the Canadian Census: 1871–1981." In *Changing Realities: Social Trends Among Ukrainian Canadians*, edited by Roman Petryshin. Edmonton: Canadian Institute of Ukrainian Studies.

Kressel, Kenneth
1985 *The Process of Divorce*. New York: Basic Books.

Kruger, Arthur M.
1971 "The Direction of Unionism in Canada." In *Canadian Labour in Transition*, edited by Richard Miller and Fraser Isbester. Scarborough: Prentice-Hall Canada.

Kudrie, Robert T., and Theodor R. Marmor
1981 "The Developments of Welfare States in North America." In *The Development of Welfare States in Europe and America*, edited by Peter Flora and Arnold J. Hedehemmer. New Brunswick: Transaction Books.

Kuhn, Thomas S.
1970 *The Structure of Scientific Revolutions*. Chicago: University of Chicago Press.

Kuttner, Bob
1983   "The Declining Middle." *The Atlantic Monthly* (July): 60–72.

1985   "The Poverty of Economics." *The Atlantic Monthly* February.

LaBelle, Beverly
1980   "Snuff: The Ultimate in Woman-Hating." In *Take Back the Night*, edited by Laura Lederer. New York: Bantam Books.

Labovitz, Sanford
1974   "Some Evidence of Canadian Ethnic Racial and Sexual Antagonism." *The Canadian Review of Sociology and Anthropology* 11(3): 247–54.

Ladurie, Emmanuel Le Roy
1980   *Monaillou*. Harmondsworth: Penguin.

1974   *The Peasants of Languedoc*. Chicago: University of Illinois Press.

Lakoff, Robin, and Raquel Scherr
1984   *Face Value: The Politics of Beauty*. London: Routledge and Kegan Paul.

Lambert, M., M. Ledoux, and R. Pendakur
1989   "Visible Minorities in Canada 1986: A Graphic Overview." Ottawa: Policy and Research Unit, Multiculturalism and Citizenship.

Lambert, R., et al.
1986   "Canadians' Beliefs about Differences Between Social Classes." *The Canadian Journal of Sociology* 11(4): 379–99.

Lamoreux, Josée
1981   "The Women's Struggle and Socialism." In *In Struggle!* Speech for Women's International Day.

Lansky, L. M.
1967   "The Family Structure Also Affects the Model: Sex-Role Attitudes in Parents of Pre-School Children." *Merrill Palmer Quarterly* 13: 139–50.

Lapidus, Philip
1981   "The Knotted Skein." *The Journal: National Council of Adult Stutterers* (Winter): 10–12.

Larson, Lyle
1976   *The Canadian Family in Comparative Perspective*. Scarborough: Prentice-Hall Canada.

Lasch, Christopher
1977   *Haven in a Heartless World: The Family Besieged*. New York: Basic Books.

1979   *The Culture of Narcissism*. New York: Norton.

Laslett, Peter
1965   *The World We Have Lost*. London: Methuen.

1972   *Household and Family in Past Time*. Cambridge: Cambridge University Press.

Lasswell, H. D., and A. Kaplan
1950   *Power and Society*. New Haven: Yale University Press.

Laudan, L.
1977   *Progress and Its Problems: Towards a Theory of Scientific Growth*. Berkeley: University of California Press.

Lautard, Hugh, and Donald Loree
1984   "Ethnic Stratification in Canada, 1931–1971." *The Canadian Journal of Sociology* 9(3): 333–44.

Laxer, Gordon
1985   "Foreign Ownership and Myths About Canadian Development." *The Canadian Review of Sociology and Anthropology* 22(3): 17–35.

1989a   *Open for Business: The Roots of Foreign Ownership in Canada*. Toronto: Oxford University Press.

1989b   "The Schizophrenic Character of Canadian Political Economy." *The Canadian Review of Sociology and Anthropology* 26(1): 178–92.

Laxer, Robert, ed.
1973   *Canada Ltd.: The Political Economy of Dependency*. Toronto: McClelland and Stewart.

Laurin-Frenette, Nicole
1989   "The Sociology of Social Classes." *The Canadian Review of Sociology and Anthropology* 26(3): 457–84.

Lazarsfeld, Paul F.
1982   "An Episode in the History of Social Research: A Memoir." In *The Varied Sociology of Paul Lazarsfeld*, edited by Patricia L. Kendall. New York: Columbia University Press.

Leach, Edmund
1973 "Levels of Communication and Problems of Taboo in the Appreciation of Primitive Art." In *Primitive Art and Society*, edited by Anthony Forge. London: Oxford University Press.

Légacé, Michael D.
1968 "Educational Attainment in Canada." Ottawa: Queen's Printer.

Lemert, Edwin
1967 *Human Deviance, Social Problems and Social Control*. Englewood Cliffs, N.J.: Prentice-Hall.

1987 "Roast Pig Revisted: The Social Construction of Crime." Paper presented to the annual meeting of the American Society of Criminology, Montreal.

Lenin, Vladimir
1939 *Imperialism, The Highest Stage of Capitalism*. New York: International Publishers.

Lenski, Gerhard
1966 *Power and Privilege*. New York: McGraw-Hill.

Levitt, Kari
1970 *Silent Surrender: The Multinational Corporation in Canada*. Toronto: Macmillan.

Lewin, H. M., and R. W. Rumberger
1983 *The Educational Implications of High Technology*. Palo Alto, Calif.: Institute for Research on Educational Finance and Governance, Stanford University.

Lewis, M.
1972 "State as an Infant-Environmental Interaction: An Analysis of Mother-Infant Behaviour as a Function of Sex." *Merrill Palmer Quarterly* 18: 95–121.

Lieberson, Stanley
1975 "Rank-sum Comparisons between Groups." In *Sociological Methodology*, edited by David Heise. San Francisco: Jossey-Bass.

Lipman-Blumen, Jean
1984 *Gender Roles and Power*. Englewood Cliffs, N.J.: Prentice-Hall.

Lipset, Seymour Martin
1954 "Democracy in Alberta." *The Canadian Forum* 34: 175–77.

1963 "The Value Patterns in Democracy: A Case Study in Comparative Analysis." *American Sociological Review* 28: 515–31.

1964 "Canada and the United States: A Comparative View." *The Canadian Review of Sociology and Anthropology* 1: 173–85.

1970 *Revolution and Counterrevolution: Change and Persistence in Social Structures*. Garden City, N.J.: Doubleday.

1976 "Radicalism in North America: a Comparative View of the Party Systems in Canada and the United States." *Transactions of the Royal Society of Canada* 14: 19–55.

1977 "Why no Socialism in the United States?" In *Sources of Contemporary Radicalism*, edited by S. Bialer and S. Sluzar. Boulder, Colorado: Westview Press.

1979 *The First New Nation: The United States in Historical and Comparative Perspective* (3rd ed.). New York: Norton Library Edition.

1983 "Socialism in America." In *Sidney Hook: Philosopher of Democracy and Humanism*, edited by P. Kurtzed. New York: Prometheus Books.

1985 "Canada and the United States: The Cultural Dimension." In *Canada and the United States*, edited by C. F. Doran and J. H. Sigler. Englewood Cliffs, N.J.: Prentice-Hall.

1986a "Labour Unions in the Public Mind." In *Unions in Transition*, edited by S. M. Lipset. San Francisco: ICS Press.

1986b "North American Labour Movements: A Comparative Perspective." In *Unions in Transition*, edited by S. M. Lipset. San Francisco: ICS Press.

1986c "Historical Traditions and National Characteristics: A Comparative Analysis of Canada and the United States." *The Canadian Journal of Sociology* 11: 113–55.

Lipset, Seymour Martin, and William Schneider
1983 *The Confidence Gap: Business, Labour and Government in the Public Mind*. New York: Free Press.

Liska, A. E.
1987   *Perspectives on Deviance.* Englewood Cliffs, N.J.: Prentice-Hall.

Locke, John
1690   *Essay on Human Understanding.*

1693   *Some Thoughts Upon Education.*

Lofland, John, and Lyn Lofland
1984   *Analyzing Social Settings.* Belmont, Calif.: Wadsworth.

Lofland, Lyn
1975   "The Thereness of Women: A Selected Review of Urban Sociology." In *Another Voice: Feminist Perspectives on Social Life and Social Science*, edited by M. Millman and R. M. Kanter. New York: Anchor Books.

Loudon, J. B.
1977   "On Body Products." In *The Anthropology of the Body*, edited by John Blacking. London: Academic Press.

Lower, Arthur
1958   *Canadians in the Making.* Toronto: Longman Canada.

Lumpkin, Katherine, and Dorothy Douglas
1937   *Child Workers in America.* New York: International Publishers.

Lupri, Eugene, and James Frideres
1981   "The Quality of Marriage and the Passage of Time: Marital Satisfaction Over the Life Cycle." *The Canadian Journal of Sociology* 6(3): 283–305.

Luxton, Meg
1980   *More Than a Labour of Love.* Toronto: The Women's Press.

Lynn, D. B.
1974   *The Father: His Role in Child Development.* Monterey, Calif.: Wadsworth.

Maccoby, E., and C. N. Jacklin
1974   *The Psychology of Sex Differences.* Stanford: Stanford California Press.

MacIver, R. M.
1965   *The Web of Government.* New York: Free Press.

Mackie, Marlene
1983   *Exploring Gender Relations: A Canadian Perspective.* Toronto: Butterworths.

Mahon, Rianne
1977   "Canadian Public Policy: The Unequal Structure of Representation." In Panitch (1977).

Malinowski, Bronislaw
1913   *The Family Among the Australian Aborigines.* London: University of London Press.

Manitoba Metis Rights Assembly
1983   "Manitoba Metis Rights Position Paper." Manitoba Metis Federation. Unpublished Manuscript.

Manning, Brian
1978   *The English People and the English Revolution.* Harmondsworth: Penguin.

Manning, Peter, and Horacio Fabrega
1973   "The Experience of Self and Body: Health and Illness in the Chiapas Highlands." In *Phenomenological Sociology: Issues and Applications*, edited by George Psathas. Toronto: John Wiley and Sons.

Mantoux, Paul
1961   *The Industrial Revolution in the Eighteenth Century.* London: Jonathan Cape

Manzer, R.
1974   *Canada: A Socio-Political Report.* Toronto: McGraw-Hill Ryerson.

Marchak, M. Patricia
1973   "Women Workers and White Collar Unions." *The Canadian Review of Sociology and Anthropology* 10(2)

1979   *In Whose Interests?* Toronto: McClelland and Stewart.

1981   *Ideological Perspectives on Canada.* Toronto: McGraw-Hill Ryerson.

1985   "Canadian Political Economy." *The Canadian Review of Sociology and Anthropology* 22(5): 673–709.

Maroney, Heather
1986   "Embracing Motherhood: New Feminist Theory." In Hamilton and Barrett (1986).

Marsden, Lorna
1975   "Population Issues in the Immigration Debate." *Canadian Ethnic Studies* VII (5): 22–29.

1980   "Review of *The Superbureaucrats.*" The *Canadian Review of Sociology and Anthropology* 5(4): 449–50.

1984   "Culture and the State." *Canadian Public Policy — Analyse de Politiques* 10(3): 267–77.

Marx, Karl
1904   *A Contribution to the Critique of Political Economy.* Chicago: Charles H. Kerr (1859).

1963   *The 18th Brumaire of Louis Bonaparte.* New York: International Publishers.

1967   *Capital: A Critical Analysis of Capitalist Production.* Vol. 1 New York: International Publishers (1887).

1972   "The German Ideology." In *The Marx-Engels Reader*, edited by Robert Tucker. New York: Norton (1932).

1973   *The Grundrisse.* Harmondsworth: Penguin.

Marx, Karl, and Friedrich Engels
1972   "Manifesto of the Communist Party." In *The Marx-Engels Reader.* edited by Robert Tucker. New York: Norton (1848).

Mathews, Georges
1984   *Le choc démographique: le déclin du Québec est-il inevitable?* Montreal: Boreal Express.

Matza, D., and G. M. Sykes
1961   "Juvenile Delinquency and Subterranean Values." *American Sociological Review.* 26: 712–19.

Maxwell, Judith, and S. Currie
1984   *Partnershp for Growth.* Montreal: The Corporate-Higher Education Forum.

Mayhew, Henry
1968   *London Labour and the London Poor.* New York: Dover Publications.

McClelland, David C., *et al.*
1953   *The Achievement Motive.* New York: Appleton Century Crofts.

McCormack, Thelma
1975   "Towards a Non-Sexist Perspective on Social and Political Change." In *Another Voice: Feminist Perspectives on*

Social Life and Social Science, edited by M. Millman and R. Moss Kanter. Garden City, N.Y.: Anchor Books.

1981a   "The New Criticism and the Sick Role." *The Canadian Review of Sociology and Anthropology* 18(1): 30–47.

1981b   "Good Theory or Just Theory? Toward a Feminist Philosophy of Social Science." *Women's Studies International Quarterly* 4(1): 1–12.

1984   "Culture and the State." *Canadian Public Policy* 10(3): 267–77.

1987   "Feminism and the New Crisis in Methodology." Paper presented at Conference on the Effects of Feminist Approaches on Research Methodologies." Calgary, Alberta.

McDade, Kathryn
1988   "Barriers to Recognition of the Credentials of Immigrants in Canada." Ottawa: Institute for Research on Public Policy

McDougall, Robert L.
1963   "The Dodo and the Cruising Auk." *Canadian Literature.* 18: 6–20.

McGraw, Onalee
1980   *The Family, Feminism and the Therapeutic State.* Washington: The Heritage Foundation.

McInnis, Edgar W.
1942   *The Unguarded Frontier.* Garden City, N.Y.: Doubleday.

McLaren, P.
1980   *Cries from the Corridor: The New Suburban Ghetto.* Toronto: Methuen.

McMillan, Charles J.
1978   "The Changing Competitive Environment of Canadian Business." *Journal of Canadian Studies.* 13: 38–48.

McMullan, John
1984   *The Canting Crew: London's Criminal Underworld, 1550–1700.* New Brunswick: Rutgers University Press.

McRae, Frances
1983   "The Politics of Menopause: The 'Discovery' of a Deficiency Disease." *Social Problems* 3(1): 111–23.

McRobbie, A.
1978   "Working Class Girls and the Culture of Femininity." In *Women Take Issue*, edited by A. McRobbie. London: Hutchinson.

Mead, Margaret
1935   *Sex and Temperament in Three Primitive Societies*. New York: William Morrow.

Meigs, Anna S.
1978   "A Papuan Perspective on Pollution." *Man* 13: 304–18.

Meisner, Martin, *et al.*
1975   "No Exit for Wives: Sexual Division of Labour." *The Canadian Review of Sociology and Anthropology* 12: 4(1): 424–39.

Meltz, Noah M.
1985   "Labour Movements in Canada and the United States." In *Challenges and Choices Facing American Labour*, edited by Thomas A. Kochan. Cambridge: MIT Press.

Merton, Robert K.
1957   *Social Theory and Social Structure*. Glencoe, Ill.: The Free Press.

Messner, Steven M.
1982   "Societal Development, Social Equality and Homicide: A Cross-National Test of a Durkheimian Model." *Social Forces* 61: 225–40.

Métis National Council
1983a   "Opening Statement to the Constitutional Conference of First Ministers' on the Rights of Aboriginal Peoples." Ottawa.

1983b   *The Rights of the Métis Peoples to be Entrenched into the Canada Act, 1982.* Ottawa.

Michaud, Marshale, and Claude Riberg
1982   *Sexisme et science humaine*. Lille, France: Presses Universitaires de France.

Middleton, Chris
1983   "Patriarchal Exploitation and the Rise of English Capitalism." In *Gender, Class and Work*, edited by E. Garmanikov.

London: Heinemann.

Miliband, R.
1969   *The State in Capitalist Society*. New York: Basic Books.

Miller, W. B.
1958   "Lower Class Culture as a Generating Milieu of Gang Delinquency." *Journal of Social Issues* 14: 5–19.

Mills, C. Wright
1956   *The Power Elite*. New York: Oxford University Press.

1959   *The Sociological Imagination*. New York: Oxford University Press.

Miles, Angela
1978   "Feminism and Class Analysis." *Atlantis* 11(2).

1982   "Ideological Hegemony in Political Discourse: Women's Specificity and Equality." In Miles and Finn (1982).

1983   *Feminist Radicalism in the 1980's*. Montreal: Black Rose Books.

Miles, Angela, and Geraldine Finn, eds.
1982   *Feminism in Canada: From Pressure to Politics*. Montreal: Black Rose Books (2d ed. 1989).

Minton, C., *et al.*
1971   "Maternal Control and Obedience in the Two-Year Old." *Child Development* 42.

Minuchin, Salvador, *et al.*
1978   *Psychosomatic Families: Anorexia Nervosa in Context*. Cambridge: Harvard University Press.

"Miss Manners" (Judith Martin)
1984   *Common Courtesy*. Toronto: Collier Macmillan.

Mitchell, Juliet
1966   "The Longest Revolution." *New Left Review*.

Mnookin, R., and L. Kornhauser
1979   "Bargaining in the Shadow of the Law." *Yale Law Journal*.

Moodie, Susanna
1962   *Roughing It in the Bush*. Toronto: McClelland and Stewart.

Montagu, Ashley
1981   *Growing Young*. New York: McGraw-Hill.

Montaigne, Michel de
1979   *Essays*. Harmondsworth: Penguin.

Montessori, Maria
1965   *Dr. Montessori's Own Handbook*. New York: Schocken Books.

1975   *Childhood Education*. New York: New American Library.

Morris, Celise
1988   "The Politics and Experience of Co-Parenting: An Exploratory Study of Shared Custody in Canada." *The Criaw Papers* No. 20.

Morris, Eileen
1979   "A Child's Bill of Rights." *Homemakers Magazine*

Mossman, Mary Jane
1986   "Family Law and Social Welfare in Canada." In *Family Law and Social Welfare Legislation in Canada*, edited by I. Bernier and A. Lajoie. Toronto: University of Toronto Press.

Muir, Frank, and Simon Brett
1980   *On Children*. London: Heinemann.

Mumford, Emily
1983   *Medical Sociology: Patients, Providers and Policies*. New York: Random House.

Murdock, G. P., and C. Proust
1973   *Social Structure*. New York: Macmillan.

1973   "Factors in the Divison of Labour by Sex: A Cross-cultural Analysis.' *Ethnology* xii 2: 203–25.

Murdock, Graham, and Robin Mccron
1973   "Scoobies, Skins and Contemporary Pop." *New Society* 26: 690–92.

Murphy, Ray
1979   *Sociological Theories of Education*. Toronto: McGraw-Hill Ryerson.

Myles, John
1984   *Old Age in the Welfare State: The Political Economy of Public Pensions*. Boston: Little Brown.

1988   "Decline or Impasse? The Current State of the Welfare State." *Studies in Political Economy* 26: 73–107.

Myrdal, Gunnar
1944   "Appendix 5. A Parallel to the Negro Problem." In *An American Dilemma* by G. Myrdal. New York: Harper and Row.

National Citizens' Coalition
1986   "Pay Discrimination: A Blueprint for the Radical Restructuring of Our Society — How it Will Demean Women, Help Break Down the Traditional Family and the Free Market System." Ottawa: Consultation Panel on Pay Equity.

National Council of Welfare
1985   *Opportunity for Reform: A Response to the Consultation Paper on Child and Early Benefits*. Ottawa: Minister of Supply and Services.

1986   *1986 Poverty Lines*. Ottawa: Minister of Supply and Services.

Naylor, R.T.
1972   "The Rise and Fall of the Third Commercial Empire of the St. Lawrence." In *Capitalism and the National Question in Canada*, edited by Gary Teeple. Toronto: University of Toronto Press.

1975   *The History of Canadian Business, 1867–1914*. Toronto: Lorimer.

Neeson, J. M.
1984   "The Opponents of Enclosure in Eighteenth Century Northhamptonshire," *Past and Present* 105: 114–39.

Neilson, W., and C. Gaffield, eds.
1986   *Universities in Crisis: A Medieval Institution in the Twenty-First Century*. Montreal: The Institute for Research on Public Policy.

Newson, John, and Elizabeth Newson
1965   *Patterns of Infant Care in an Urban Community*. Harmondsworth: Penguin.

Oakley, Ann
1981   "Interviewing Women: A Contradiction

in Terms." In *Doing Feminist Research*, edited by Helen Roberts. London: Routledge and Kegan Paul.

Oberschall, Anthony, ed.
1983   *The Establishment of Empirical Sociology: Studies in Continuity, Discontinuity and Institutionalization.* New York: Harper and Row.

O'Brien, Mary
1981   *The Politics of Reproduction.* London: Routledge and Kegan Paul.

1982   "Feminist Praxis." In Miles and Finn (1982 & 1989).

1983   "Feminism and Education: A Critical Review Essay." *Resources for Feminist Research* 12(3): 3–16.

O'Connor, James
1973   *The Fiscal Crisis of the State.* New York: St. Martin's Press.

O'Connor, Julia, and Robert J. Brym
1988   "Public Welfare Expenditure in OECD Countries: Towards a Reconciliation of Inconsistent Findings." *British Journal of Sociology* 39(1): 47–68.

Ogmundson, R.
1976   "The Sociology of Power and Politics." In *Introduction to Canadian Society*, edited by G. N. Ramu and S. Johnson. Toronto: Macmillan of Canada.

1977   "A Social Profile of Members of the Manitoba Legislature: 1950, 1960, 1970." *Journal of Canadian Studies* 12(4): 79–84.

1981   "Social Inequality." In *Essentials of Sociology*, edited by R. Hagedorn. Toronto: Holt Rinehart and Winston.

Olsen, D.
1977   "The State Elites." In Panitch (1977).

Olsen, Gregg
1990   *The Limits of Social Democratic Reform: The Case of the Swedish Meidner.* Ph.D. Thesis, Toronto: University of Toronto.

Ornstein, Michael D.
1983   "Class, Gender and Job Income in Canada." *Research in Social Stratification and Mobility* 2: 41–75.

1989   "The Social Organization of the Canadian Capitalist Class in Comparative Perspective." *The Canadian Review of Sociology and Anthropology* 26(1): 151–77.

Ossowski, Stanislav
1963   *Class Structure in the Social Consciousness.* London: Routledge and Kegan Paul.

O'Toole, Roger
1982   "Some Good Purpose: Notes on Religion and Political Culture in Canada." *Annual Review of the Social Sciences of Religion* 6: 177–217.

Palma, Gabriel
1981   "Dependency and Development: A Critical Overview." In *Dependency Theory: A Critical Reassessment*, edited by D. Seers. London: Frances Pinter.

Palmer, Brian
1983   *Working-Class Experience: The Rise and Reconstitution of Canadian Labour, 1800–1980.* Toronto: Butterworths.

Panitch, Leo
1981   "Dependency and Class in a Canadian Political Power." *Studies in Political Economy* 6 (Autumn).

Panitch, Leo, ed.
1977a   *The Canadian State: Political Economy and Political Power.* Toronto: University of Toronto Press.

1977b   "The Role and Nature of the Canadian State." In Panitch (1977).

1978   "Comment on Burawoy" *Alternate Routes* 2: 15–22.

Parr, Joy, ed.
1982   *Childhood and Family in Canadian History.* Toronto: McClelland and Stewart.

Parsons, Talcott
1951   *The Social System.* Glencoe, Ill.: The Free Press.

1959a "The School as a Social System." *Harvard Educational Review.*

1959b "The Social Structure of the Family." In *The Family: Its Function and Destiny,* edited by R. N. Ashen. New York: Harper & Row.

Parsons, Talcott, and Renee C. Fox
1968 "Illness, Therapy and the Modern Urban American Society." In *A Modern Introduction to the Family,* edited by Norman Bell. New York: The Free Press.

Patnisky, Ben
1976 "Writer has speech p-p-problem." *The Montreal Star.* August 18, D8.

Pentland, H. C.
1959 "The Development of a Capitalistic Labour Market in Canada." *Canadian Journal of Economics and Political Science* 25: 450–61.

Peterson, M. Jeanne
1972 "The Victorian Governess: Status Congruence in Family and Society." In *Suffer and Be Still,* edited by M. Vicinus. Bloomington: Indiana University Press.

Petrunik, Michael
1974 "The Quest for Fluency: Fluency Variations and the Identity Problems and Management Strategies of Stutterers." In *Decency and Deviance,* edited by J. Haas and W. Shaffir. Toronto: McClelland and Stewart.

1977 *The Quest for Fluency: A Study of the Identity Problems and Management Strategies of Adult Stutterers and Some Suggestions for an Approach to Deviance Management.* Ph.D. Dissertation, Department of Sociology, University of Toronto.

1982 "Telephone Troubles: Interactional Breakdown and Its Management by Stutterers and their Listeners." *Symbolic Interaction* 5: 299–310.

Petrunik, Michael, and Clifford Shearing
1983 "Fragile Facades: Stuttering and the Strategic Manipulation of Awareness." *Social Problems* 31(2): 125–38.

Phillips, Roderick
1988 *Putting Asunder: A History of Divorce in Western Society.* Cambridge: Cambridge University Press.

Pineo, Peter
1976 "Social Mobility in Canada: The Current Picture." *Sociological Focus* 9(2): 109–23.

Pineo, Peter, and John Porter
1985 "Ethnic Origin and Occupational Attainment." In Boyd *et al.* (1985).

Pogrebin, Letty
1981 *Growing Up Free: Raising Your Children in the Eighties.* New York: Bantam Books.

Polanyi, Karl
1944 *The Great Transformation.* Boston: Beacon Press.

Porter, John
1965 *The Vertical Mosaic: An Analysis of Social Class and Power in Canada.* Toronto: University of Toronto Press.

1979 *The Measure of Canadian Society.* Toronto: Gage.

1985 "Canada: The Social Context of Occupational Allocation." In Boyd *et al.* (1985).

Porter, John, Marion Porter, and Bernard Blishen
1982 *Stations and Callings: Making it Through Ontario Schools.* Toronto: Methuen.

Porter, Marilyn
1983 "The Tangly Bunch: The Political Culture of Outport Women." Unpublished Paper.

Poulantzas, Nicos
1977 "The New Middle Class." In *Class and Class Structure,* edited by Ian Hunt. London: Lawrence and Wishart.

Power, Eileen
1965 "The Position of Women." In *The Legacy of the Middle Ages,* edited by G. G. Crump. Oxford: Clarendon Press.

Prebisch, R.
1950 *The Economic Development of Latin America and Its Principal Problems.*

Lake Success: N.Y.: U.N. Department of Economic Affairs.

Prentice, Alison, and Susan Houston, eds.
1975   *Family, School and Society in Nineteenth-Century Canada*. Toronto: Oxford University Press.

Presthus, Robert
1973   *Elite Accommodation in Canadian Politics*. Cambridge: Cambridge University Press.

1974   *Elites in the Policy Process*. Toronto: Macmillan of Canada.

1977   "Aspects of Political Culture and Legislative Behaviour: United States and Canada." In *Cross-National Perspectives: United States and Canada*, edited by Robert Presthus. Leiden: Brill.

Presthus, Robert, and William V. Monopoli
1977   "Bureaucracy in the United States and Canada: Social, Attitudinal and Behavioural Variables." In *Cross-National Perspectives: United States and Canada*, edited by Robert Presthus. Leiden: Brill.

Rausch, Jeffrey L., and David S. Janowsky
1983   "Premenstrual Tension: Etiology." In *Behaviour and the Menstrual Cycle*, edited by Richard C. Friedman. New York: Marcel Dekker Inc.

Reeves Sanday, Peggy
1981   *Female Power and Male Dominance: On the Origins of Sexual Inequality*. Cambridge: Cambridge University Press.

Reiter, Ester
1986   "Life in a Fast-Food Factory." In Heron and Storey (1986).

Reiter, Ranya
1975   *Toward an Anthropology of Women*. New York: Monthly Review Press.

Reitz, Jeffrey
1988   "Less Racial Discrimination in Canada or Simply Less Racial Conflict? Implications of Comparisons with Britian." *Canadian Public Policy* 14(4): 424–41.

Reuther, Rosemary
1973   "The Cult of True Womanhood." *Commonwealth* 9: 127–32.

Reynaud, Emmanuel
1983   *Holy Virility: The Social Construction of Masculinity*. London: Pluto Press.

Rheingold, H. L., and K. V. Cook
1975   "The Contents of Boys and Girls Rooms as an Index of Parents' Behaviour." *Child Development* 46: 459–63.

Rich, Adrienne
1980   "Compulsory Heterosexuality and Lesbian Experience." *Signs* 5(4): 631–60.

Rich, Harvey
1976   "The Vertical Mosaic Revisited." *Journal of Canadian Studies* 11: 14–31.

Richardson, C. James
1983   *Attempting to Restructure Family Law: Unified Family Court Experiments in Canada*. Ottawa: Department of Justice, Canada.

1986   *Evaluation of the Divorce Act, 1985: Baseline Study*. Ottawa: Department of Justice, Canada.

1987   "Children of Divorce." In *Family Matters*, by K. Anderson *et al*. Toronto: Methuen.

1988   *Divorce and Family Mediation Research Study in Three Canadian Cities*. Ottawa: Department of Justice, Canada.

1989a   *Court-Based Divorce Mediation in Four Canadian Cities: An Overview of Research Findings*. Ottawa: Ministry of Supply and Services.

1989b   *Research Initiatives in the Area of Divorce Mediation*. Ottawa: Department of Justice, Canada.

1990   *Evaluation of the Divorce Act, 1985: Implementation and Monitoring*. Ottawa: Department of Justice, Canada.

Roberts, K., *et al*.
1977   *The Fragmentary Class Structure*. London: Heinemann.

Roberts, Wayne
1976   *Honest Womanhood: Feminism, Femi-*

ninity and Class Consciousness Among Toronto Working Women, 1893–1914. Toronto: New Hogtown Press.

Robertson, Priscilla
1975 "Home as a Nest: Middle-Class Childhood in Nineteenth Century Europe." In de Mause (1975).

Robson, Reginald, and Brad Breems
1986 *Ethnic Conflict in Vancouver.* Vancouver: British Columbia Civil Liberties Association.

Rocher, Guy
1970 "Research on Occupations and Social Stratification." In *French Canadian Society*, edited by M. Rioux and Y. Martin. Toronto: McClelland and Stewart.

Rock, Paul
1980 "Has Deviance a Future?" In *Sociological Theory and Research*, edited by Hubert Blalock. New York: The Free Press.

Rogers, Katherine
1966 *The Troublesome Helpmate, A History of Misogyny in Literature.* Seattle: Washington Paperbacks.

Rogerson, Carol
1989 *Review of Support Factors and Objectives in Case Law Decided Under the Divorce Act, 1985.* Ottawa: Department of Justice, Canada.

Rose, Joseph B., and Gary N. Chiason
1985 "The State of the Unions: United States and Canada." *Journal of Labour Research*, 6 (Winter): 97–111.

Rossi, Alice S.
1977 "A Biosocial Perspective on Parenting." *Daedalus* 106, Spring: 2.

Rousseau, Jean-Jacques
1969 *Emile.* London: Dent.

Rowbotham, S.
1972 *Women, Resistance and Revolution.* London: Allen Lane.

Rowland, Robyn
1984 *Women Who Do and Women Who Don't Join the Women's Movement.* London: Routledge and Kegan Paul.

Rubin, J., *et al.*
1974 "The Eye of the Beholder: Parents' Views on Sex of Newborns." *American Journal of Orthopsychiatry* 44: 512–19.

Rubin, Lillian
1975 *Worlds of Pain.* New York: Basic Books.

1979 *Women of a Certain Age.* New York: Harper & Row.

1981 "Sociological Research: The Subjective Dimension." *Symbolic Interaction* 4(1): 97–112.

Rudé, George
1964 *The Crowd in History.* London: Wiley.

1970 *Paris and London and the Eighteenth Century: Studies in Protest.* London: Fontana Books.

Russell, Diana
1982 *Rape in Marriage.* New York: Collier Books.

Russell, Susan
1978 *Sex Role Socialization in the High School.* Ph.D. Thesis, University of Toronto.

1979–
1980 "Learning Sex Roles in the High School." *Interchange* 10(2).

Ryerson, Stanley
1976 "Who's Looking After Business?" *This Magazine.* 9: 41–46.

1973 *Unequal Union.* Toronto: Progress Books.

Sacks, Oliver
1983 *Awakenings.* New York: Dutton.

1984 *A Leg to Stand On.* New York: Summit Books.

1985 *The Man Who Mistook His Wife for a Hat.* London: Duckworth.

Safarian, A. E.
1969 *The Performance of Foreign-Owned Firms in Canada.* Washington, D.C.: National Planning Association.

Safilios-Rothschild, Constantina
1969 "Family Sociology or Wives' Family Sociology? A Cross Cultural Examina-

tion of Decision Making." *Journal of Marriage and the Family* 290–301.

Sampson, Robert J.
1987   "Urban Black Violence: The Effect of Male Joblessness and Family Disruption." *American Journal of Sociology* 3: 348–82.

Sarah, E.
1980   "Teachers and Students in the Classroom: An Examination of Classroom Interaction." In Spender and Sarah (1980).

Sarsby, Jacqueline
1983   *Romantic Love and Society.* Harmondsworth: Penguin.

Satir, Virginia
1964   *Conjoint Family Therapy: A Guide to Theory and Technique.* Palo Alto: Science and Behaviour Books.

Scase, R., and R. Goffee
1980   *The Real World of the Small Business Owner.* London: Croom Helm.

Schactel, E.
1962   "On Alienated Concepts of Identity." In *Man Alone: Alienation in Modern Society*, edited by E. Josephson and M. Josephson. New York: Dell.

Scheff, Thomas
1966   *Being Mentally Ill: A Sociological Theory.* Chicago: Aldine.

Schneider, J., and P. Conrad
1980   "In the Closet with Illness: Epilepsy, Stigma Potential and Information Control." *Social Problems* 28: 32–44.

Schoenfeld, Stuart
1978   "The Jewish Religion in North America: Canadian and American Comparisons." *The Canadian Journal of Sociology* 3(2): 209–31.

Schur, Edwin M.
1984   *Labelling Women Deviant: Gender, Stigma and Social Control.* Philadelphia: Temple University Press.

Schwartz, M., and G. Carter
1986   *Stop Stuttering.* Markham: Fitzenhry and Whiteside.

Science Council of Canada
1972   "Innovation in a Cold Climate: Impediments to Innovation." In *The Canadian Challenge*, edited by Abraham Rotstein and Gary Lax. Toronto: The Committee for an Independent Canada.

Scott, M.
1980   "Teach Her a Lesson: Sexism Curriculum in Patriarchal Education." In Spender and Sarah (1980).

Scott, Robert
1968   *The Making of Blind Men.* New York: Russel Sage.

Sears, P., and D. Feldman
1974   "Teacher Interaction with Boys and Girls." In *And Jill Came Tumbling After: Sexism in American Education*, edited by J. Stacey. New York: Academic Press.

Secombe, Wally
1980   "Domestic Labour and the Working-Class Household." In Fox (1980).

1986   "Patriarchy Stabilized: The Construction of the Male-Breadwinner Wage Norm in Nineteenth-Century Britain." *Social History* 11(2): 53–76.

Seve, Lucien
1975   *Marxism and the Theory of Human Personality.* London: Lawrence and Wishart.

Shanin, Teodor
1983   *Late Marx and the Russian Road: Marx and the Peripheries of Capitalism.* London: Routledge and Kegan Paul.

Sharma, H. P.
1982   "Asian Struggles in British Columbia." *South Asia Bulletin* Spring.

Sharp, M., and H. Roberts
1983   "Boys Will Be Boys — But What Happens to the Girls?" *Educational Research* 25(2).

Shaw, J.
1980   "Education and the Individual: Schooling for Girls or Mixed Schooling — A Mixed Blessing." In *Schooling for Women's Work*, edited by R. Deem.

London: Routledge and Kegan Paul.

Shifrin, Len
1986   "Middle Class Threatened by Shift in Occupations." *The Ottawa Citizen* March 13.

Shkilnyk, Anastasia
1985   *A Poison Stronger Than Love: The Destruction of an Ojibwa Community.* New Haven: Yale University Press.

Shorter, Edward
1975   *The Making of the Modern Family.* New York: Basic Books.

Shragge, E.
1982   "The Left in the 80's" *Our Generation* 15(2): 5–12.

Shuttle, Penelope, and Peter Redgrove
1980   *The Wise Wound: Menstruation and Everywoman.* Harmondsworth: Penguin.

Sider, Gerald M.
1986   *Culture and Class in Anthropology and History.* Cambridge: Cambridge University Press.

Siegler, M., and H. Osmond
1974   *Models of Madness; Models of Medicine.* New York: MacMillan.

Simoons, Frederick J.
1961   *Eat Not This Flesh.* Madison: University of Wisconsin Press.

Skolnick, Arlene
1973   *The Intimate Environment: Exploring Marriage and the Family.* Boston: Little Brown, pp. 125–135.

Skopcol, Theda
1980   "Political Response to Capitalist Crisis: Neo-Marxist Theories of the State and the Case of the New Deal." *Politics and Society* 10(2): 75–87.

Skopcol, Theda, Peter Evans, and Dietrich Ruesmeyer, eds.
1985   *Bringing the State Back In.* New York: Academic Press.

Sloan, R., and W. Greenaway
1988   *Divorce and Family Mediation Study: Winnipeg.* Ottawa: Department of Justice, Canada.

Sloss, Elizabeth, ed.
1985   *Family Law in Canada: New Directions.* Ottawa: Canadian Advisory Council on the Status of Women.

Smelser, Neil
1964   "Toward a Theory of Modernization." In *Social Change,* edited by Anita and Eva Etzioni. New York: Basic Books.

Smiley, Donald V.
1984   "Public Sector Politics, Modernization and Federalism: The Canadian and American Experiences." *Publicus: The Journal of Federalism* 14: 52–59.

Smith, A. J. M.
1979   "Evolution and Revolution as Aspects of English-Canadian and American Literature." In *Perspectives on Evolution and Revolution,* edited by Richard A. Preston. Durham, N.C.: Duke University Press.

Smith, Charles W.
1979   *A Critique of Sociological Reasoning.* Ottawa: Littlefield.

Smith, Dorothy
1973   "Women, the Family and Corporate Capitalism." In *Women in Canada,* edited by Marylee Stephenson. Toronto: New Press.

1975   "An Analysis of the Ideological Structures and How Women are Excluded." *The Canadian Review of Sociology and Anthropology* 12(4).

1977   "Some Implications of a Sociology for Women." In *Woman in a Man-made World,* edited by N. Glazer and H. Youngelson. Chicago: Rand McNally.

1978   "A Peculiar Eclipsing: Women's Exclusion from Man's Culture." *Women's Studies International Quarterly* 1(4): 281–96.

1979   "A Sociology for Women." In *The Prism of Sex,* edited by J. Sherman and E. Beck. Madison: The University of Wisconsin Press.

1984   "The Renaissance of Women." In *CRIAW, Knowledge Reconsidered: A Feminist Overview.* Ottawa: Canadian

Research Institute for the Advancement of Women.

Smith, Michael R.
1978   "The Effects of Strikes on Workers: A Critical Analysis." *The Canadian Journal of Sociology* 3(4): 457–72.

Smith, R. M.
1979   "Kin and Neighbours in a Thirteenth Century Suffolk Community." *Journal of Family History* 4(3): 219–56.

Sontag, L. W., *et al.*
1969   "The Fetal and Maternal Cardiac Response to Environmental Stress." *Human Development* 12: 1–9.

Spender, D.
1980   "Talking in Class." In Spender and Sarah (1980).

1980   *Man Made Language.* London: Routledge and Kegan Paul.

Spender, D., and E. Sarah
1980   *Learning to Lose: Sexism and Education.* London: Women's Press.

Spenner, Kenneth
1983   "Deciphering Prometheus: Temporal Change in the Skill Level of Work." *American Sociological Review* 48: 824–37.

Spock, Benjamin
1958   *Baby and Child Care.* London: The Bodley Head.

Stack, S.
1980   "The Political Economy of Income Inequality: A Comparative Analysis." *Canadian Journal of Political Science* 13: 273–86.

Stanley, Liz, and Sue Wise
1985   *Breaking Out: Feminist Consciousness and Feminist Research.* London: Routledge and Kegan Paul.

Statistics Canada
1984   *Current Demographic Analysis, Fertility in Canada From Baby Boom to Baby Bust.* Ottawa: Minister of Supply and Services.

Steed, Judy
1986   "The Middle Class is Under Pressure

and Losing Ground as the Rich Get Richer and the Poor Get More Numerous." *The Globe and Mail.* October 4.

Steele, Freda M.
1985   "The Ideal Marital Property Regime." In Sloss (1985).

Stephenson, Bette
1983   "Statement of the Hon. Bette Stephenson, M.D., Minister of Education, Minister of Colleges and Universities in the Legislature (Ontario)." Toronto: Ministry of Education, Ministry of Colleges and Universities.

Stephenson, Marylee, ed.
1973   *Women in Canada.* Don Mills: General Publishing.

Stinchcombe, Arthur
1978   *Theoretical Methods in Social History.* New York: Academic Press.

Stone, Lawrence
1974   "The Massacre of the Innocents." *New York Review of Books* 14.

1977   *The Family, Sex and Marriage in England, 1500–1800.* London: Weidenfeld & Nicholson.

Stone, Philip J.
1978   "Women's Time Patterns in Eleven Countries." In *Public Policy in Temporal Perspective*, edited by William Michelson. The Hague: Moulton.

Stouffer, S., *et al.*
1949   *Studies in Social Psychology in World War II: The American Soldier, Combat and Its Aftermath.* Princeton: Princeton University Press.

Strauss, Anselm
1959   *Mirrors and Masks: The Search for Identity.* Glencoe, Ill.: The Free Press.

Sutherland, Ronald
1977   *The New Hero: Essays in Comparative Quebec/Canadian Literature.* Toronto: Macmillan of Canada.

1982   "A Literary Perspective: The Development of a National Consciousness." In *Understanding Canada*, edited by William Metcalfe. New York: New York

University Press.

Swartz, Donald
1977   "The Politics of Reform: Conflict and Accommodation in Canadian Health Policy." In Panitch (1977).

Swinton, Katherine
1979   "Judicial Policy Making: American and Canadian Perspectives." *The Canadian Review of American Studies* 10: 89–94.

Symons, D.
1979   *The Evolution of Human Sexuality*. New York: Oxford University Press.

Szala, K. V.
1952   "Clean Women and Quiet Men: Marriage in Shepherd's Harbour." Unpublished Paper, Newfoundland Centre.

Szasz, Thomas
1974   *The Myth of Mental Illness*. New York: Harper and Row.

Tanner, Julian
1978a   "New Directions for Subcultural Theory: An Analysis of British Working-Class Youth Culture." *Youth and Society* 19(4): 343–73.

1978b   "Youth Culture and the Canadian High School: An Empirical Analysis." *The Canadian Journal of Sociology* 3(1): 89–102.

Taylor, Charles L., and David A. Jodice
1983   *World Handbook of Political and Social Indicators* (Vol. 2). New Haven: Yale University Press.

Taylor, Ian
1983   "Some Reflections on Homicide and Violence in Canada." In *Crime, Capitalism and Community*, edited by Ian Taylor. Toronto: Butterworths.

Tepperman, Lorne
1975   *Social Mobility in Canada*. Toronto: McGraw-Hill Ryerson.

1977   *Crime Control: The Urge Toward Authority*. Toronto: McGraw-Hill Ryerson.

1978   "Sociology in English-Speaking Canada." *Canadian Historical Review* 59: 453–56.

Terry, J.
1983   "The Political Economy of Migrant Farm Labour." *Insurgent Sociologist* II (4).

Thomas, Ted. E.
1983   "The Gun Control Issue: A Sociological Analysis of United States and Canadian Attitudes and Policies." Oakland, Calif.: Department of Sociology, Mills College.

Thompson, Dorothy
1984   *The Chartists: Popular Politics in the Industrial Revolution*. London: Temple Smith.

Thompson, E. P.
1967   "Time, Work-Discipline and Industrial Capitalism." *Past and Present* December.

1968   *The Making of the English Working Class*. Harmondsworth: Penguin.

1978   *The Poverty of Theory and Other Essays*. London: Merlin Press.

Tilly, Louise, and Joan Scott
1978   *Women, Work and Family*. New York: Holt, Rinehart and Winston.

Tilly, Louise, and Charles Tilly, eds.
1981   *Class Conflict and Collective Action*. London: Routledge and Kegan Paul.

Tocqueville, Alexis de
1945   *Democracy in America*. Vol. 1. New York: Vintage Books.

Toffler, Alvin
1970   *Future Shock*. New York: Bantam Books.

1981   *The Third Wave*. New York: William Morrow.

Trofimenkoff, Susan Mann, and Alison Prentice, eds.
1977   *The Neglected Majority: Essays in Canadian Women's History*. Toronto: McClelland and Stewart.

Truman, Tom
1971   "A Critique of Seymour M. Lipset's Article." *Canadian Journal of Political Science* 4: 513–25.

Trypuc, Joann
1984   *Gender Differences in Hospitalization: A Study of Ontario Acute Care Hospital*

Usage. Doctoral Dissertation, York University.

Tucker, M. J.
1975   "The Child as Beginning and End: Fifteenth and Sixteenth Century English Childhood." In de Mause (1975).

Tunstall, J.
1962   *The Fishermen.* London: MacGibbon and Kee.

Tyree, A.
1979   "Gaps and Glissandos: Inequality, Economic Development and Social Mobility." *American Sociological Review* 44 (3): 410–24.

Underhill, Frank
1960   *In Search of Canadian Liberalism.* Toronto: Macmillan of Canada.

United Nations General Assembly
1961   *Declarations on the Granting of Independence to Colonial Countries and Peoples.* New York: United Nations.

Ure, A.
1835   *The Philosophy of Manufacturers.* London: Charles Knight.

Valentine, Charles A.
1968   *Culture and Poverty: Critique and Counterproposals.* Chicago: University of Chicago Press.

Valentine, Charles A., and Betty Lou Valentine
1975   "Brain Damage and the Intellectual Defense of Inequality." *Current Anthropology* 16: 117–49.

Van Gelder, L., and C. Carmichael
1975   "But What About Our Sons?" *Ms* 4: 52–56.

Van Riper, Charles
1946   "Speech Defects Among the Kalabash." *Marquett County Historical Society* 8 (December): 308–22.

1971   *The Nature of Stuttering.* Englewood Cliffs, N.J.: Prentice-Hall.

Vaz, E. W.
1969   "Delinquency and Youth Culture in Upper and Middle-Class Boys." *Journal of Criminal Law* 60(1): 33–46.

Vedel, Morgall, and Gitte Vedel
1985   "Office Automation: The Case of Gender and Power." *Economic and Industrial Democracy* 6: 93.

Verbrugge, Lois M.
1985   "Gender and Health: An Update on Hypotheses and Evidence." *Journal of Health and Social Behaviour* 26: 156–82.

Vogel, Ezra, and Norman Bell
1968   "The Emotionally Disturbed Child as a Family Scapegoat." In *A Modern Introduction to the Family.* Edited by N. Norman Bell. New York: The Free Press.

Wadel, C.
1973   *Now Whose Fault is That?* St. John's, Nfld.: The Institute for Social and Economic Research.

Walker, S., and L. Barton, eds.
1983   *Gender, Class and Education.* London: Falmer Press.

Wallerstein, Immanuel
1974   *The Modern World System: Capitalist Agriculture and the Origins of the European World Economy in the Sixteenth Century.* New York: Academic Press.

Wallerstein, Judith, and Joan Kelly
1980   *Surviving the Breakup.* New York: Basic Books.

Wallman, S., *et al.*
1982   *Living in South London.* London: Gower Press.

Watkins, Mel
1977   "The State in a Staples Economy." Paper presented to the Conference on the American Empire and Dependent States, Toronto.

Watson, C., ed.
1985   *The Professoriate: Occupation in Crisis.* Toronto: OISE and Higher Education Group.

Wax, Rosalie H.
1971   *Doing Fieldwork: Warnings and Advice.* Chicago: University of Chicago Press.

Weaver, John Charles
1973   *Imperilled Dreams: Canadian Opposition to the American Empire, 1918–1930.* Ph.D. Dissertation, Department of History, Duke University.

Weber, Max
1947   *The Theory of Social and Economic Organization.* New York: Free Press (1922).

1949   "Objectivity in Social Science and Social Policy." In *The Methodology of the Social Sciences*, edited by Max Weber. New York: The Free Press (1904).

1958   *The Protestant Ethic and the Spirit of Capitalism.* New York: Charles Scribner's Sons (1904–5).

Weeks, Jeffrey
1981   *Sex, Politics and Society: The Regulation of Sexuality Since 1800.* London: Longman.

Weideger, Paula
1982   *Female Cycles.* New York: Alfred A. Knopf.

Weitz, Rose, and Deborah Sullivan
1985   "The Politics of Childbirth: The Re-emergence of Midwifery in Arizona." *Social Problems* 33(3): 163–73.

Weitzman, Lenore
1985   *The Divorce Revolution: The Unexpected Consequences for Women and Children in America.* New York: The Free Press.

Weizenbaum, J.
1981   "Once More, the Computer Revolution." In *The Microelectronic Revolution*, edited by T. Forester. Cambridge: MIT Press.

Weller, Geoffrey
1984   "Common Problems, Alternative Solutions: A Comparison of the Canadian and American Health Systems." Thunder Bay: Department of Political Science, Lakehead University.

Westhues, Kenneth
1978   "Stars and Stripes, the Maple Leaf and the Papal Coat of Arms." *The Canadian Journal of Sociology* 3(1): 245–61.

Wexler, P.
1982   "Structure, Text and Subject: A Critical Sociology of School Knowledge." In Apple (1982).

Whitaker, Reginald
1977   "Images of the State in Canada." In Panitch (1977).

Whyte, John D.
1976   "Civil Liberties and the Courts." *Queen's Quarterly* 83: 655–63.

Wiley, Norbert F.
1967   "Marriage and the Construction of Reality: Then and Now." In *The Psychosocial Interior of the Family*, edited by Gerald F. Handel. New York: Aldine.

Williams, Glen
1988   "On Determining Canada's Location Within the International Political Economy." *Studies in Political Economy* 25 (Spring): 47–63.

Williams, Kirk R.
1984   "Economic Sources of Homicide: Re-estimating the Effects of Poverty and Inequality." *American Sociological Review* 49: 283–89.

Williams, Raymond
1977   *Marxism and Literature.* Oxford: Oxford University Press.

1972   *Women Unite!* Toronto: Women's Education Press.

Willis, P.
1977   *Learning to Labour: How Working Class Kids Get Working Class Jobs.* Westmead: Saxon House.

Wilson, H. T.
1977   *The American Ideology: Science, Technology and Organization as Modes of Rationality in Advanced Societies.* London: Routledge and Kegan Paul.

Wilson, Peter J.
1974   *Oscar: An Inquiry Into the Nature of Sanity.* New York: Random House.

Wilson, Robert A.
1966   *Feminine Forever.* New York: M. Evans.

Wilson, W.
1942   "Miners' Superstitions." *Life and Letters Today.*

Winn, Conrad
1985 "Affirmative Action and Visible Minorities: Eight Premises in Quest of Evidence." *Canadian Public Policy* 11(4): 684–700.

Winn, Marie
1981 "What Became of Childhood Innocence?" *New York Times*, 29 January.

Wolf, Eric
1966 *Peasants*. Englewood Cliffs, N.J.: Prentice-Hall.

Wolff, Edward, and David Howell
1986 "Direct Measures of Labour Productivity in the U.S." Paper presented at Eighth International Conference on Input-Output Techniques, Sapporo, Japan.

Wolfgang, Marvin, and Franco Ferracuti
1967 *The Subculture of Violence: Towards an Integrated Theory in Criminology*. London: Tavistock.

Wollstonecraft, Mary
1792 *A Vindication of the Rights of Women*. London: Printed for J. Johnson.

Wolpe, Annmarie
1978 "Education and the Sexual Division of Labour." In *Feminism and Materialism*, edited by A. Kuhn and A. Wolpe. London: Routledge and Kegan Paul.

Wood, John
1978 "East Indians and Canada's New Immigration Policy." *Canadian Public Policy* Autumn.

Wood, Louis
1975 *A History of Farmers' Movements in Canada*. Toronto: The Ryerson Press.

Woolf, Virginia
1929 *A Room of One's Own*. London: Hogarth.

1977 *Three Guineas*. Harmondsworth: Penguin.

Wright, Erik Olin, and Bill Martin
1987 "The Transformation of the American Class Structure." *American Journal of Sociology* 87(2): 1–29.

Wuthnow, Robert
1985 "State Structures and Ideological Outcomes." *American Sociological Review* 50: 799-821.

Yolles, Louise
1986 "Subjectivity: The Road to Objectivity." Paper presented at The Learned Societies Meetings.

Yorburg, Betty
1973 *The Changing Family*. New York: Columbia University Press.

Young, Jock
1971 *The Drugtakers*. London: Macgibbon and Kee.

Zaretsky, Eli
1976 *Capitalism, Family and Personal Life*. New York: Harper & Row.

Zola, Irving K.
1971 "Medicine as an Institution of Social Control." In *The Sociology of Health and Illness: Critical Perspectives*, edited by Peter Conrad and Rochelle Kern. New York: St. Martin's Press.

Zuker, Marvin A., and June Callwood
1971 *The Law is Not for Women*. Toronto: Copp Clark Pitman.

STUDENT REPLY CARD

In order to improve future editions, we are seeking your comments on this text, SOCIOLOGY FOR CANADIANS: A READER, second edition, by Himelfarb/Richardson.

After you have used the book, please answer the following questions and return this form via Business Reply Mail. *Thanks in advance for your feedback!*

1. Name of your college or university: ————————————————

2. Major program of study: ————————————————————

3. Your instructor for this course: ————————————————

4. Are there any sections of this text which were not assigned as course reading?————
   If so, please specify those chapters or portions:

5. How would you rate the overall accessibility of the content? Please feel free to comment on reading level, writing style, terminology, layout and design features, and such learning aids as chapter objectives, summaries, and appendices.

6. What did you like *best* about this book?

7. What did you like *least?*

If you would like to say more, we'd love to hear from you. Please write to us at the address shown on the reverse of this card.